D0953248

The New York Public Library WRITER'S GUIDE TO STYLE AND USAGE

The New York Public Library WRITER'S GUIDE TO STYLE AND USAGE

A STONESONG PRESS BOOK

HarperCollins*Publishers*

Grateful acknowledgment is made for permission to reprint the following:

The Chinese romanization table, appearing on page 529, is adapted from *Collier's Encyclopedia*, volume 6, copyright © 1987 by Macmillan Publishing Co. It is reprinted by permission of P.F. Collier, L. P.

The Hebrew alphabet chart, appearing on page 533, is adapted from a chart from *The First Hebrew Primer for Adults*, by Ethelyn Simon et al., copyright © 1983 by EKS Publishing Co. It is reprinted by permission of the publisher.

"Restrictive or Nonrestrictive: An Easy Way to Tell," appearing on page 141, is excerpted from "That vs. Which: Is the Distinction Useful?" by Mary Jackson Scroggins, copyright © 1989. It is reprinted by permission of the author.

The comparison of editing and proofmarks, appearing on pages 753–756, is excerpted from *Mark My Words: Instruction and Practice in Proofreading*, second edition, copyright © 1993 by Margherita S. Smith. It is reprinted by permission of the author.

A STONESONG PRESS BOOK

FIRST EDITION

Designed by Abigail Sturges

Library of Congress Cataloging-in-Publication Data

The New York Public Library writer's guide to style and usage. — 1st ed.

p. cm.

"A Stonesong Press book."

Includes bibliographical references and index.

ISBN 0-06-270064-2

1. English language—Style. 2. English language—Usage. I. New York Public Library.

PE1421.N46 1994

808'.027—dc20 93-33255

96 97 98 PS/RRD 10 9 8 7 6 5 4 3

CONTENTS

Part Four: Preparing the Text 537

Part Five: Production and Printing 685

PREFACE

Today's writers and editors work in a variety of settings, not only at traditional book and periodical publishers, but also at corporations, research centers, institutions, associations, and government agencies around the world, producing a continual stream of books, reports, newsletters, magazines, and business and technical documents of all kinds. These are the people who helped create the information explosion, a phenomenon brought about in part by the personal computer. Word processing, graphics, and desktop publishing programs (not to mention multimedia and hypertext software) are changing the world of writing and editing and bringing more and more people into the business of writing and publishing. To help those who are new to the field, as well as to guide experienced writers and editors through the many changes taking place, we were commissioned by The New York Public Library and The Stonesong Press to develop this book to provide commonly needed information and as an addition to a group of Library-sponsored one-volume reference works.

The scope of this book goes beyond ordinary style and usage manuals in several ways. Recognizing that the massive and ever-changing English lexicon brings with it many opportunities for confusion, we have provided an easy-to-find section explaining the nuances in the meaning of more than 1,000 frequently misused words. The chapters on editorial style stress the need for consistency and consideration of the audience; they then offer guidance on all types of publications, from business and technical to scholarly. Grammar, although taught less thoroughly today than ever before, is still an important concern, and our chapters on grammar focus on common problem areas and controversial issues.

Because writers and editors are increasingly being drawn into the layout and production phases of publishing, we have included information throughout that reflects the changes brought about by the computer, from a discussion of the pitfalls of hyphenation programs in word processing software to chapters on charts, graphs, maps, and tables. Other chapters on photographs, illustrations, typography, design, production, and printing give basic principles and offer advice to writers and editors who find themselves dealing with these aspects of publication. In short, this book was conceived to provide answers to the many questions that arise on the way to publication, from writing the first draft to delivering camera-ready pages or computer disks to the printer. Here's a brief summary of the contents.

Part One, Usage, begins with an overview of current thinking about English usage. It offers practical advice on dealing with the many problems associated with avoiding bias in language. This discussion is followed by explanations of the most frequently encountered misused and confused words.

Part Two, Grammar, is organized to help writers find quick, clear answers to common (and a few not-so-common) questions in a way that avoids the standard grammar textbook approach and terminology. All sides are presented when the authorities disagree so that readers can make informed decisions based on their own needs. Many of the example sentences come from published writing, to give readers a look at real-life problems.

Part Three, Style, covers topics that include punctuation, capitalization, use of numbers, formatting of lists, mathematical expressions, abbreviations (including up-to-date lists of common abbreviations in several subject areas), and hyphenation and compound words. The purpose of an editorial style is to impose order and consistency on a language that has boundless possibilities; for example, should "president" be capitalized or lowercased? (The answer is, It depends.) Although the style points themselves may be arbitrary and mechanical, the goal of an editorial style—consistent treatment within a document—is important. A book or article that has been edited for style as well as spelling and grammar is more credible and authoritative than one in which inconsistencies and errors convey a subtle message of careless preparation.

Part Four, Preparing the Manuscript, describes the various aspects of assembling and checking the parts of a manuscript for publication. Chapters discuss what an editor does to help the author achieve the goal of good writing; copyright law as it applies to the printed word; the parts of a book, with information on page numbering and organization; how to develop and evaluate tables, charts, graphs, and maps; how to obtain and prepare photos and illustrations; and how to create a professional index.

Part Five, Production and Printing, explains the role of personal computers in the publishing process and points out capabilities as well as limitations. The basic principles of design and typography are described, followed by a chapter on the steps involved in managing the production process. The section closes with a comprehensive chapter on offset printing.

The *annotated bibliography* is arranged by general topic areas and lists the many sources referred to in writing this book; it also includes books recommended for further reading.

This book was written by a team of 18 writers and editors who work for EEI (formerly Editorial Experts, Inc.), an editorial and production services company in Alexandria, Virginia. Special thanks are due the EEI editors who were the primary chapter authors; their names are listed on the frontispiece. We also wish to thank our other contributors and reviewers, including EEI editors Mia Cunningham, Carol Edwards, Jane Burson, Mark Stoughton, Keith Ivey, Doreen Jones, and Betsy Chesky; writers Joan Holleman and Bruce Boston; indexer Susan Lohmeyer; librarian Peter de la Garza; copyright attorney Ellen Kozak; printer's representatives Henriette Warfield and Mark Schwartz; and bookstore owner Richard Farkas. We also appreciated the review, advice, and cooperation of The New York Public Library.

Finally, we wish to thank Claire Kincaid, EEI president, for her enthusiasm and support throughout the many months of this project; Maron Waxman, former editorial director of HarperReference, for her ideas, guidance, and sound editorial advice every step of the way; Helen Moore, managing editor of HarperReference, who completed the work begun by Ms. Waxman; and Paul Fargis, president of The Stonesong Press, Inc., for giving us this wonderful opportunity.

Andrea J. Sutcliffe
Editor

PART ONE

USAGE

1

USAGE

USAGE

Usage means, simply, the words we use and how we use them. Defining *good* usage has always been more difficult; it has traditionally meant how educated people speak and write English. But over the years, the way educated people write and speak has changed—slowly in some areas, more radically in others—largely reflecting changes in society as a whole. In addition, English, throughout its 1,600-year history, has always been remarkably flexible and open to change. Today, with 350 million native speakers adding new words and new usages at the rate of 15,000 a year—spread at amazing speed by satellites and computers—English continues to evolve.

Many of us find such change disconcerting, evidence of a recent and deplorable decline in standards. But it may help to know that our concerns are almost as old as English itself. Maintaining the purity of the language has been an issue since the 1500s, when the first protectors of English voiced their outrage at the introduction of hundreds of words borrowed from Latin, words that are basic to our vocabulary today. Every century since has seen proposals to standardize English. Throughout the 1700s, writers and scholars called for government-sponsored academies to fix the language, and although their specific efforts may have failed, their larger goal was eventually achieved: Publishers of dictionaries and grammar books began to flourish, and "grammar" schools did the rest.

By the early 1800s, most of the rules of grammar we take for granted today, really the preferences and interpretations of the educated elite, had been laid down. Almost 200 years later, we accept most of these rules as being basic and immutable, as if they had been carved in stone from the beginning of time. But as more and more people speak English and as their needs and ways of communicating change, some usages will fall away and others will take their place. The challenge facing careful writers, therefore, is knowing which "rules" are holding fast and which are in transition. This chapter and this book as a whole attempt to explain how English is used by good writers today.

WHAT IS GOOD USAGE?

Good usage means using the right words at the right time for the right reasons. Usage today covers two broad areas: In addition to the traditional topics of word choice, grammar, spelling, and pronunciation, writers must be alert to the ways language can reflect and perhaps reinforce biases. This chapter provides an overview of both aspects, with cross-references to more detailed discussions in other chapters.

Good usage adds force, precision, and credibility to all writing, from business letters to published books. Good usage is important because it offers evidence that the writer has ideas and thoughts that are worth reading. Put another way, writing that is marked by grammar and spelling errors may raise questions about a writer's qualifications.

Good usage also means selecting just the right words to convey specific thoughts or emotions; the treasure of English is its amazing wealth of nouns and verbs, each with its own shades of tone and meaning. The right word in the right place adds clarity, strength, and vitality to any kind of writing; for example, many writing teachers suggest favoring shorter, more descriptive Anglo-Saxon words over those derived from Latin: *light* instead of *illuminate, rain* instead of *precipitation, steer* instead of *navigate, steep* instead of *precipitous.*

All of this sounds easier than it really is, however. Writers who seek advice often find that language experts disagree and that standards vary widely. In many cases, the best a writer can do is step back and look at the broader issues, perhaps learn about the origins of a particular usage, compare the thoughts of respected authorities, and then make an informed decision. Throughout this book, sidebars and text offer background and guidelines on many usage hot spots; this chapter summarizes the broader issues.

Basic to the discussion that follows is acknowledging the first consideration of good usage: A writer must select the level of language appropriate to the reader and the material. Although usage experts may differ in how they describe these levels, in general there are four: formal, standard, informal, and substandard.

- *Formal language* is used in government, legal, scholarly, and other similarly "official" contexts; it often uses technical terms and stylized forms of expression.

- *Standard language* is written language that is characteristic of educated people; Kenneth Wilson, in *The Columbia Guide to Standard English,* calls this semiformal or "edited English."
- *Informal or familiar language* is the language used in more relaxed, usually conversational, contexts. This level covers a broad range of usage that includes everything from coined words and phrases to jargon, dialect, slang, and shoptalk.
- *Substandard* means language that is generally deemed unacceptable by the literate community but is nevertheless commonly understood. It can also include archaic or obsolete language.

Careful writers may not be consciously aware of these levels, but they should understand the distinctions. By determining the needs and expectations of the intended audience, the writer can decide on tone, word choice (for example, whether slang or jargon has a place), spelling (to some degree), and even such points of grammar as the use of contractions and the use of first or second person. An example of how the needs of readers dictate style is shown on the next two pages. The selections illustrate how different writers described the same topic—the physical characteristics of baseball's curveball—for very different audiences.

THE TRADITIONAL CONCERNS: WORD CHOICE, GRAMMAR, AND SPELLING

Word Choice

After establishing the level of language, careful writers must work to convey their thoughts clearly, without distracting or losing the reader. Helped by a solid grasp of proper spelling, grammar, and word choice, writers should also care enough to learn about the fine points of language; one example is understanding the distinctions between words like *further* and *farther, latter* and *last, continual* and *continuous, shall* and *will, comprise* and *compose, whether* and *if, while* and *although,* and *less than* and *fewer.* These and several hundred other similar words and terms are explained in Chapter 2, Misused and Easily Confused Words.

Wordiness, jargon, clichés, and euphemisms are also marks of poor usage. Wordiness can take many forms—for example, using more words than necessary to express the meaning (*at the present time* instead of *now, due to the fact that* instead of *because*); using repetitious words (*each and every, one and the same, in this day and age*); and using adjectives or adverbs that duplicate parts of the nouns they modify (*old adage, might possibly*).

Jargon may be appropriate in specialized or technical writing, where it is

THE CURVEBALL, FROM SIX VIEWPOINTS

Scientists and sportswriters alike have used the language of physics to describe the scientific sides of golf, bowling, boxing, tennis, and skiing. But no subject has been more thoroughly analyzed in this way than baseball. The variety and range of observations on the physics of baseball can demonstrate how writers on the same topic adjust the level of language for an intended audience. Notice how these writers vary their style, approach, and choice of words, especially their use of jargon, slang, and contractions.

Scholarly

Audience: professional scientists

. . . a curve thrown with a velocity slightly higher than the onset of the drag crisis might slow down along its path, and experience a sudden increase of force as the drag coefficient changes from about 0.1 to 0.5. . . . Since presumably the lift forces associated with spinning also change significantly during the drag crisis, the ball's trajectory would be changed by the increases in both the drag and lift forces.

—CLIFF FROHLICH. Aerodynamic drag crisis and its possible effect on the flight of baseballs. *American Journal of Physics* 52:330, 1984.

Technical

Audience: well-informed laypeople

Balls curve as a consequence of asymmetries in the resistance of the air through which they pass. . . . Aside from generating curved paths, this resistance affects the flight of the pitched ball by reducing the velocity of a ball thrown . . . at a speed of 100 mph to a velocity of 90 mph as it crosses the plate about 0.40 seconds after it leaves the pitcher's hand. If the ball is not spinning very fast, during the time of flight it will fall almost three feet below the original flight line.

—ROBERT K. ADAIR. *The Physics of Baseball.*

General

Audience: readers who want more detail than the sports page

Unlike a fastball, which has a natural backward rotation, a curveball is given an unnatural spin by twisting the arm or wrist or both. (A curveball is harder on the arm than a fastball because the pitcher spins the ball while generating high arm speed.) . . . "You don't see the big curveball like you used to with Erskine, Podres, Koufax. . . . But Hershiser has the big curve." . . . [Hershiser's] curve is really several pitches because he can "tighten" the break. "If the hitter is the kind who reacts early to the ball when it leaves your hand, I'll throw more of a sweeping large curveball. If it's a good disciplined hitter who reads that pitch very well, . . . I shorten the break to get the ball to look like it's really going to be a strike the whole way and then quickly break at the end." Because Hershiser changes the trajectory and velocity, "there might be ten different curveballs in my arm."

—GEORGE F. WILL. *Men at Work: The Craft of Baseball.*

Instructional
Audience: fellow professionals, well-informed readers

To throw a curveball, all you have to do is set your forearm, wrist, and fingers in a karate-chop-type position and rotate your fingertips over the top of the seams to get the ball to break. Your middle finger is placed next to the seam, the index finger provides support while the thumb is placed underneath to get the most rotation at release point. Your arm speed is the same as when throwing a fastball; the difference is that you're putting rotation over the top of the baseball instead of applying force through the center of the baseball.

—NOLAN RYAN. *Nolan Ryan's Pitcher's Bible.*

Journalistic
Audience: general readers who want a report of a game

Blyleven has traditionally been an Orioles nemesis. He entered tonight's game with 20 career victories against them, more than any other active pitcher. His knee-buckling, jaw-dropping curveball always was a more-than-formidable foe for the Orioles' relatively free-swinging clubs of years past. . . .

He breezed through the Orioles' lineup in the early going, spotting his fastball effectively to get ahead on the count, then getting batters to swing at curves thrown in the dirt.

—*Washington Post,* April 11, 1990

Fiction
Audience: general reader

Kid Scissions throws two balls to Shoeless Joe.

"Throw a curve," says Eddie. "Throw a curve, dammit. . . ."

Kid Scissons does throw the curve, and it hangs over the plate as big as a cantaloupe, and Joe swats it over the third baseman's head. It lands soft as a balloon along the foul line, and lies there while the third baseman races back and the left fielder charges in. When the dust settles, Joe stands on second.

—W.P. KINSELLA. *Shoeless Joe.*

useful in conveying specific shared meanings, but rarely in writing published for more general audiences. For example, computer jargon (*input, interface*) is best reserved for computer manuals. When writing for people outside their field, experts who use jargon, whether out of carelessness or a desire to impress, will fail to communicate and lose their readers.

Clichés, expressions that were once fresh but have become trite through overuse, are sometimes unavoidable because they convey meaning more precisely than any detours around them. More often, though, they amount to verbal tics and should be avoided—for example, *each and every, foregone conclusion, moment of truth, it goes without saying.*

Euphemisms, indirect language used to avoid terms that are unpleasant or possibly offensive, range from *pass away* for *die* to what William Lutz calls "doublespeak," which covers terms used to inflate as well. He cites examples of cab drivers being called urban transportation specialists, potholes known as pavement deficiencies, and poor people referred to as fiscal underachievers.

Other fine points of word choice involve the application of logic. A list introduced by *include,* for example, suggests that the items that follow are a partial listing of a larger set. "The panel members include Smith, Johnson, and Jones" implies that other members exist but are not mentioned. Similar logic problems are contained in such redundancies as *consensus of opinion, free gift, join together, present incumbent,* and *circle around.* In more recent times, terms like *HIV virus* come to mind; because the *V* in *HIV* stands for *virus,* the term *HIV virus* is redundant. The correct term is *HIV* or the *AIDS virus.* Careful writers must think about the content of the words they use.

Finally, knowing which words are standard English and which are not is basic to good writing. Words like *irregardless, ain't,* and *flied* (except in baseball) are never acceptable in good writing, with the possible exception of dialogue in fiction. Slang is also best avoided in all but fiction and the most informal writing; a good current dictionary can help writers decide whether a word that was once slang has been accepted into standard usage. *The American Heritage Dictionary,* third edition, is especially helpful, specifying three types: slang, offensive slang, and vulgar slang.

Grammar

Not until the 18th century did English finally begin to be pinned down to a formal system of grammar. Before then, it was largely a spoken language, its Germanic base greatly simplified and expanded by Britain's many conquerors and invaders. One of the language's first grammarians, Samuel Johnson, set forth only four syntactic rules in his *Dictionary of the English Language* in 1755: the verb must agree with its subject, adjectives and pronouns do not vary in form, the possessive noun is the genitive case, and transitive verbs and prepositions take objects in the "oblique" case. In the years that followed, grammar books proliferated and the number of rules increased, usually based on Latin grammar.

By the late 1700s the idea that grammar should follow usage—as spoken by the educated few or by the masses—was rejected in favor of fixed rules that could be easily taught to generations of unenthusiastic students. The introduction to Part Two, Grammar, gives a brief history of the evolution of English grammar.

In recent years, grammar as a traditional, distinct school subject has been tucked into a broader category called language arts and often is not taught at all. Nevertheless, most people still view grammatical errors as evidence of ignorance or poor education, and today's careful writers must keep up to date on the do's and don'ts. For example, usage has finally prevailed over rigid 1800s rules against all split infinitives, sentences that end with prepositions, and sentences that begin with *and, but,* or *however.* In fact, many people are surprised to learn that good writers break these "rules" daily, with the blessing of most language authorities. Because all living languages change over time, some of the rules set forth a century or two ago no longer reflect the way even educated people speak and write today. The following paragraphs offer a sampling of a few other perpetually thorny issues of grammar that are discussed in more detail in other chapters of this book.

Is It "Data Is" or "Data Are"? The words *data* and *media* are examples of words that until recently had maintained their Latin singular and plural forms but that now are so commonplace that the distinction is being abandoned; the singular verb has become widely acceptable with *data* and *media* when used in the collective sense (for example, "the media has ignored indications that . . ."). Collective nouns like *couple* and *none* also plague writers. For advice on these and similar problems, see Chapter 6, Subject-Verb Agreement.

"Winston Tastes Good—Like [As?] a Cigarette Should." The use of *like* as a conjunction goes back about 600 years, although many authorities have argued against its use since the 1800s. Careful writers, to be safe, reserve *like* for pointing out resemblances in sentences when it precedes a noun not followed by a verb or a verb that is only weakly implied: "She talks like a sailor." That sentence could be rephrased to bring out the implied verb—"She talks as if she were a sailor"—but it would be incorrect to simply substitute *as* for *like* and say, "She talks as a sailor." Note that a verb must follow in constructions that contain *as, as if,* and *as though.* Writers should also be careful not to use *like* to compare things that logically cannot be compared: "Like baseball, hand-eye coordination is important in golf and

tennis." "Hand-eye coordination" and "baseball" are not being compared; here, *as* is correct: "As in baseball, hand-eye coordination is important in golf and tennis."

"Hopefully, You Won't Feel Badly About the Outcome." The public debate over the use of adverbs like *hopefully* and *badly* has been around for many years. A few language authorities, including William Safire and Kenneth G. Wilson, have come to accept the use of *hopefully* as a sentence adverb—that is, an adverb that can introduce a sentence or an independent clause ("Hopefully, she will not forget her gloves")—but careful writers will still substitute *it is hoped that* or *I hope* in such cases ("I hope she will not forget her gloves"). *Hopefully* is always correct when used as an adverb to mean "full of hope ": "She began her dance career hopefully."

The confusion in the use of *bad* and *badly* usually results from the speaker's or writer's attempts to appear grammatically correct. But the fine point to remember is that the adjective *bad* is correct when used with the verb *to be* and the verb *feel* and with words that express the human senses, including *smell* and *taste.* Chapter 7, Modifiers, explains this distinction.

"Whom May I Say Is Calling?" The misuse of *whom* similarly results from a misguided effort to be grammatically correct. In general, the ear rebels more against the use of *whom* when *who* is called for—as in this sentence, in which *who* is the subject of *is calling*—than vice versa. Chapter 4, Pronouns, offers tips to help writers make the correct choice. Also discussed are the distinctions between *that* and *which* and *who* and *that.*

"Contact Me by Tuesday If You Can Chair the Committee." Turning nouns into verbs, although decried by many purists, has in fact been going on for hundreds of years; examples are words like *deluge* (1593), *debut* (1830), and *demarcate* (1816). In most cases, the passage of time determines a noun's true usefulness as a verb. *Contact* as a verb, for example, was rejected by almost two-thirds of the usage panel of *The Harper Dictionary of Contemporary Usage* in the mid-1970s; by 1993, however, 69 percent of the usage panel of *The American Heritage Dictionary,* third edition, accepted that usage. In 1980, usage expert Roy Copperud had considered the use of *chair* as a verb to be journalese, and the year before *New York Times* editor Theodore Bernstein had called it a fad word, but by the 1990s *chair* as a verb had gained acceptance by most authorities. There is less controversy over *chair* as a verb than over *chair* as an alternative to *chairman, chairwoman,* or *chairperson.*

Turning nouns and adjectives into verbs by adding the suffix *-ize* has also been an English tradition for centuries; *scandalize,* for example, was first seen in writing in 1566. Today the practice is especially popular in business and government writing. Some of these words—for example, *final-*

ize and *prioritize*—were considered shameless bureaucratic jargon when they first appeared but have become slightly less jarring over time; however, many authorities still oppose their use. Of course, many others are being coined almost daily—*incentivize, gerundize, customerize*—and careful writers should avoid such words until dictionaries show them gaining standard acceptance.

Proper Prepositions. Use of the proper preposition with certain words is another aspect of usage. For example, *different from* and *different than* have been debated for 400 years, with *different from* almost always the safe choice. *Compare with* is used when the similarities or differences of things are being examined, whereas *compare to* is appropriate when two things are being likened or put in the same category; *compare with* is much more common. *Capacity of* is used with volume, and *capacity for* is used when speaking of ability. These points and others are discussed in Chapter 2, Misused and Easily Confused Words.

Spelling

Spelling becomes a usage issue when dictionaries differ or offer more than one way to spell a word. Because spelling in English is influenced by frequency of occurrence as well as historical precedence, decisions made by lexicographers are sure to vary.

With the explosion of printing in the 1700s, readers began to demand consistent spellings; before then, spelling was a relatively trivial concern, varying wildly from writer to writer and printer to printer. Although a few English dictionaries were published in the 1600s, their emphasis was on "hard" or unfamiliar words and technical terms. The first comprehensive English dictionaries began appearing in the 1700s, and the first American English dictionary was published by Noah Webster in 1829. Webster is credited with setting down certain distinctly American spellings, such as *honor* instead of *honour, traveler* instead of *traveller,* and *theater* instead of *theatre.*

Understanding how dictionaries can differ in their approach is the first step in learning how to decide on proper spelling. Dictionaries come in two varieties: prescriptive, in which the editors take a stand on the spellings that *should* be used, often backing up their decisions with usage notes; and descriptive, in which the editors simply report spellings and usages with little or no comment. For example, a descriptive dictionary might list both *momento* and *memento,* noting the former spelling as a variant; a prescriptive dictionary might list only *memento.* Examples of prescriptive dictionaries are *Webster's New World Dictionary,* second college edition, *Random House Dictionary,* second edition (unabridged), and *The American Heritage Dictionary,* third edition. Examples of descriptive dictionaries are *Webster's*

Third New International Dictionary, Merriam-Webster's Collegiate Dictionary, 10th edition, and *Random House Webster's College Dictionary.*

Next, careful writers should understand how dictionaries treat words that have more than one spelling. A dictionary's explanatory notes will define words used in definitions, such as *or* and *also.* For example, *or* in *Merriam-Webster's 10th* means that either spelling listed may be used, but if the spellings are not in alphabetical order, they are equal variants and the first one listed is slightly more common. The word *also* means that the second spelling is acceptable but seen less frequently than the first. In either case, the reader is left to decide which spelling to use. In the case of *also* spellings, careful writers are safe in using the first spelling listed. In the case of *or* spellings, writers and editors must consider prevalent usage, not always an easy feat. Here are a few general but not always foolproof guidelines to consider when writing for an American audience.

In some cases the second choice is really a British spelling, even though the dictionary may not note it as such. Words like *judgment/judgement, acknowledgment/acknowledgement, gray/grey, driveling/drivelling,* and *offense/offence* are examples. In general, it may help to remember that the British tend to prefer *e* after *dg; -ise,* not *-ize; -our,* not *-or; -re,* not *-er; -nce,* not *-nse;* and *ae* and *oe,* not *e.* Other British spellings, such as *tyre* for *tire* and *cheque* for *check,* are more obvious and less easily confused. And, except for *glamour,* words ending in *-our,* like *labour, saviour,* and *splendour,* can be assumed to be British spellings.

For certain words, the best approach is to decide whether the simpler form—as in *catalog/catalogue* and *esthetics/aesthetics*—is more appropriate for the intended readership. Popular publications tend to use the simpler spellings, whereas formal or scholarly writing favors more traditional spellings.

Finally, in the case of changing spellings, it is almost always safer to go with the traditional spelling. Like *momento* and *miniscule,* some misspellings finally become so commonplace that they make it into dictionaries. In fact, it seems likely that many more such spellings will gain legitimacy now that computers are used to sift through electronic files of newspapers and periodicals to count how words are used and spelled. Spelling, like other aspects of usage, is subject to the same forces of change that affect language as a whole. (Chapter 15, Spelling, covers many other aspects of the topic, including the formation of plurals.)

BIAS-FREE USAGE

Probably the most talked-about aspect of usage today is what is commonly called *politically correct* language. In recent years, we have become more aware of the narrow point of view of some writers and the possible discriminatory effects—conscious or unconscious—that language can have when used to describe characteristics such as race, sex, sexual orientation, ethnic origin, physical attributes, and even age. We seem to be in a period of continual reexamination and updating of such descriptive terminology in an attempt to avoid offending individual or group sensitivities; as a result, the need for guidelines has never been greater. A few general thoughts follow.

First, the adjectives used to describe a person or group in terms of racial, sexual, ethnic, or physical characteristics should be examined: Is the description essential to the story being told? Most writers do not intend to show bias, but they sometimes need to take a second look at what they say. If the word or words are not an integral part of the story, they could be viewed as biased and probably should be cut. For example, a newspaper feature about a horse breeder might describe the woman as a heavyset spinster. The fact that the woman is overweight probably has no bearing on the story and should be left out. The fact that she is unmarried may or may not be relevant, but *spinster* certainly has negative connotations; *unmarried* or *never married* is preferable, if the information is necessary at all.

Second, the writer should ask whether the term being used is the most currently acceptable. It is important to keep abreast of changes in preferred terminology as reflected in published writing. Like it or not, these terms can and do change, and a writer who uses *Negro* instead of *African American* or *black* will be viewed as either hopelessly outdated or, more likely, racist. In the area of physical attributes, references to *the handicapped* and even *the disabled* are giving way to terms that include the word *people,* for example, *people with disabilities.* On a political level, *developing countries* is preferred to *less-developed countries.*

The problem of biased language has no simple answers; many new terms have relatively short lives as groups continue to devise alternatives. Writers, then, face the tough task of trying not to offend while also trying to avoid euphemistic language that may itself reveal bias for one group over another or even invite ridicule (for example, *differently abled*). The safest approach is to use a term only when it seems to have become widely accepted, as evidenced in respected national publications. The next sections offer some specific advice.

Nonsexist Language

Inclusive Usage. "Exclusive" language means words that by their form or meaning discriminate on the basis of gender—*craftsman, weatherman, forefather, gentlemen's agreement.* These usages are now being abandoned, and "inclusive" language that incorporates both sexes—*artisan, meteorologist, ancestor, unwritten agreement*—is being substituted. The idea that "women are included" in such terms as *mankind, freshman,* and *middleman* has also been questioned, and gender-neutral usages like *people, first-year student,* and *negotiator* are being substituted with no great loss to the language. A few words, however, still contain *-man* simply because gender-free alternatives seem so farfetched; these include *baseman, foreman, midshipman,* and *ombudsman.*

The desire to avoid sexist language is widespread, affecting even conservative religious institutions. Many church leaders have been revising hymnals and prayer books in recent years, rewriting phrases that used masculine nouns and eliminating the masculine pronoun in reference to God. The United Church of Christ, for example, revised its hymnal to replace *God* with words like *Creator, Savior, Love, Spirit, Wisdom,* and *Shepherd. Men* and *brethren* have been replaced by *people* and *all.*

The Problem of Man. In Anglo-Saxon English, the word *man* meant simply "human being," as it still does in German, where the undeclinable pronoun *man* means simply the indefinite "one, people in general." In the eighth century A.D. a male human being in Old English was *wer,* a female *wyf* (whence *wife*). *Wer* eventually dropped out of English—except in the two terms *wergild* and *wer[e]wolf*—and *man* acquired its current meaning, adding the sense of "male" to the original sense of "human being." Thus the word *mankind* may not be inherently sexist in its linguistic origins, although some people now perceive it as such. In usage the perception becomes the reality, and the word *man* creates problems in contemporary writing and speaking, although *humankind* seems widely accepted in place of *mankind.* Note that a number of English words containing the word *man* derive from the Latin word *manus,* which means "hand"—*mandate, manual, manufacture, manifestation, manipulate.* These are not regarded as sexist terms.

One form of the *man* problem is its presence in words and phrases like *man and wife, manmade, man in the street.* The recommended approach here is to search for an acceptable substitute—*husband and wife, manufactured, average person.* Another aspect of the problem arises from the tendency of English to add *-man* to functional verbs to name the person performing the action—*salesman, spokesman.* A common strategy to rid such usages of bias is to substitute *-person* for *-man.* Although some of these usages have caught on, such as *spokesperson* (best used when the sex of the person involved is unknown), this strategy has led to usages that many people find awkward (*congressperson, foreperson*) and to some that are downright silly (*personhole cover*). For these and other reasons, the suffix *-person* is falling out of favor as a remedy, and gender-neutral substitutes, such as *representative, supervisor,* and *maintenance hatch,* are becoming commonplace. Other solutions include *personnel, workers, employees,* or *workforce* instead of *manpower; work hours* or *staff hours* instead of *man hours;* and *chair* instead of *chairman, chairwoman,* or *chairperson.*

The Problem of Assumed Gender. Gender-biased usage often arises when writers and speakers assume a gender when referring to specific occupations or walks of life. When speaking of a pilot, secretary, doctor, nurse, or professor whose sex is unknown, it is unnecessary to assume that the person is either male or female; for example, a sentence like "After the pilot landed the plane, he headed straight for the hangar" should be replaced by "After landing the plane, the pilot headed straight for the hangar."

The Problem of Which Gender to Use in Pronouns. The warning flag of possible gender bias should also go up when writers and speakers are forced to choose a gender for a needed pronoun. Prior practice dictated the choice of masculine pronouns, but fewer women permit this choice to be made on their behalf.

Several gender-neutral substitutes, such as *s/he, co, cos, ter, sher, shim, herm, tey, tem, ve,* and *ver,* have been proposed; not surprisingly, these words have failed to catch on. With a little thought, the problem can usually be solved by revising the sentence. In most cases, the change is simple. Here are some strategies for avoiding pronoun gender problems.

- Recast the noun and pronoun in the plural.

  Not: Although a CEO is busy, *he* should always take time to listen.
  But: Although CEOs are busy, *they* should always take time to listen.

- Delete the pronoun altogether.

  Not: A good engineer relies on *his* common sense.
  But: A good engineer relies on common sense.

- Replace the masculine pronoun with an article.

  Not: Every trainee should bring *his* manual to class.
  But: Every trainee should bring the manual to class.

- Use first or second person instead of third person.

  Not: A careful writer checks *his* prose for gender bias.
  But: As a careful writer, *you* should check your prose for gender bias.

- Recast the sentence to change the subject.

  Not: A good secretary makes sure *she* completes *her* assignments on time.
  But: *Completing assignments on time* is part of being a good secretary.

- Use *he or she* (not *s/he* or *he/she*), but only sparingly.

  Not: A lawyer's success depends on whether he argues well.
  But: A lawyer's success depends on whether he or she argues well.

Although most careful writers frown on the practice because it violates a basic rule of grammar, using the plural pronoun *their* with singular, indefinite pronouns such as *everybody, everyone, anybody,* and *anyone* is becoming increasingly acceptable as a way to avoid sexist language and cumbersome rewrites ("Does everybody have to bring *their* [avoiding *his or her*] own food?"). Part of the reason for the increasing acceptance of *their* is that the usage is common in everyday speech. Some of the finest writers of English, from Jane Austen to Ernest Hemingway, have used this construction. However much some may regret it, the usage seems on its way to becoming standard. (See Chapter 4, Pronouns, for a full discussion.)

Another strategy often seen is an alternation between genders in reference, say, to various children in the course of a discussion or chapter. It is important to avoid mixing pronouns in reference to the same person, however, as in this example: "A professor who leads a seminar should take his time explaining the semester's requirements. Otherwise her students won't know what to expect."

The Problem of the Feminine Suffix. Feminine suffixes such as *-ette, -ess,* and *-trix* have been passing out of use for some time. Feminine suffixes come, in part, from the fact that English has borrowed so many terms from inflected languages that have masculine and feminine forms—*alumnus[i]* and *alumna[e], blond* and *blonde.* Because gender differentiation is called for by Latin and French but not by English, two words spring up where only one is needed. If there is no question about the gender of the person referred to, either gender-neutral words—*graduate* instead of *alumna, flight attendant* instead of *stewardess,* or the more common form (*heir* and *waiter* instead of *heiress* and *waitress*)—should be used. Even a long-time holdout, *comedienne,* is now giving way to *comedian,* and *actor* has supplanted *actress.*

The Problem of Courtesy Titles. Most newspapers and other periodicals no longer use the courtesy titles of *Mr., Mrs., Miss,* or *Ms.* People are introduced by their first and last names, and second references are to the last name alone for women as well as for men, a practice that can be confusing when both a husband and wife are referred to more than once in a passage. Some styles, however, retain courtesy titles in the case of dignitaries and high-level government officials—for example, *Mr. Roosevelt, Mrs. Thatcher.* Whenever *Ms., Miss,* or *Mrs.* is used, for whatever reason, it is important to determine which title the woman being referred to prefers, if her preference is known.

If a married woman has retained her own name, connecting it to her husband's name with a hyphen (for example, *Jane Hodges-Brown*), both names are used as her last name. If the woman uses no hyphen (*Jane Hodges Brown*), the last name alone is used on second reference: *Brown.* Note, by the way, that the term *maiden name* is now considered sexist by many; some wedding announcements in newspapers simply state, "Ms. Blandings is keeping her name."

The Problem of Occupational or Social Titles. In some contexts, to say "John Smith and his wife, Mary" may seem to place the woman in a subservient position; "John and Mary Smith" is preferred. Common sense must prevail, however. If the story is primarily about John Smith, it is certainly acceptable to describe Mary as being his wife: "John and his wife, Mary, have two children."

Terms like *woman lawyer* or *male nurse* are almost always considered sexist; unless the description is integral to the context, a person's occupation should stand on its own, without the need for a gender qualifier.

Words like *grandmother, housewife, homemaker, widow,* and *divorcée* can also have sexist overtones. Stating that a *grandmother* or *housewife* runs a business or was elected to public office tends to denigrate the woman's professional experience and abilities. One way to check the necessity of such labels is to ask whether a similar term would be used if the person being described were a man.

Racial and Ethnic Bias

Members of racial and ethnic groups rightly refuse to tolerate stereotypical descriptions. Whether a term is meant to be derogatory is not the issue; how it is perceived, is. The first question to ask before using any racial or ethnic term is whether the term is relevant to the story being told; sometimes it is, but usually it isn't.

Writers must be aware that the terms groups prefer can and do change, and usage also varies from region to region and country to country. In the United States, *Negro* gave way to *colored,* which gave way to *black,* which gave way to *Afro-American,* which has given way to *African American;* nevertheless, *black* is still preferred by many and is used correctly to refer to Caribbean- and African-born persons of that race. The term *coloured* (sometimes capitalized) is still used in South Africa, where it refers to people of mixed European and African descent.

People of European descent first called the indigenous peoples of the Western Hemisphere *Indians,* then *Amerindians* by some, and now *American Indians* or *Native Americans.* This last term is out of favor among some North American Indian groups because its scope is so broad; many groups prefer to be referred to by their specific tribal name. Writers should also be aware that some groups find the term *native* to be condescending; an exception is *Alaskan natives,* which is used with pride by the Aleuts, Indians, and Eskimos of Alaska.

Some terms are acceptable among their own groups but considered derogatory when used elsewhere. For example, *Canuck* is viewed as neutral as a term for *Canadian* within Canada but is used pejoratively in the northeastern United States. And although *Eskimo* is the proper term for certain tribes living in the northernmost parts of North America, it should not be used to refer to all peoples of those lands.

Americans who are of Mexican, South American, Central American, or Spanish-speaking Caribbean descent are generally best referred to as *Hispanics;* the terms *Latino/Latina* and *Chicano/Chicana* (the masculine plurals are *Latinos* and *Chicanos;* feminine plurals are *Latinas* and *Chicanas*) are favored by some and not by others. Puerto Ricans prefer to be known as Puerto Ricans unless they are being grouped with other Hispanics.

Keeping up with changes on an international level is often more difficult, requiring writers to be alert to current events. For example, although residents of the former Soviet Union used to be called Soviets, under the Commonwealth of Independent States there is no one descriptive term for the people of that nation; instead, they should be referred to as citizens of their particular state: citizens of Russia are Russians, citizens of Ukraine are Ukrainians, and so on.

Citizens of China are Chinese, never Chinamen or Orientals. *Asian* may be used as a general adjective to describe peoples from that world region, but it is preferable to use the specific nationality whenever possible.

Finally, certain ethnic slurs have been a part of the language for so long that they may not be obvious at first glance. Terms like *welshing on a bet, coolie wages,* and *hot-blooded Latin* should almost always be avoided.

Biases That Reflect Social Differences

Sexual Orientation. The word *homosexual* is the general term; *gay* has become standard for describing homosexual men and *lesbian* for describing homosexual women. The term *sexual orientation* is now preferred over *sexual preference* because the word *preference* implies choice, and some research seems to point to a biological basis for homosexuality. The preferred term to describe a person in a homosexual relationship is *companion,* not *lover* or *partner,* both of which have other connotations.

Family Relationships. Many people with adopted children do not care for the label *adopted child* because it stresses a distinction that they do not see as relevant—the child is as much theirs as a biological child.

The term *illegitimate child* can also be viewed as value-laden. If the distinction is important, the term *child of unmarried parents* is preferred.

Biases Based on Physical Attributes

People who used to be called *handicapped,* which in turn was a replacement for terms like *crippled,* now usually prefer to be called *people with disabilities.* They wish to avoid the implication that their physical condition prevents them from functioning productively in society. *Disabled* and *physically challenged* also are used; preferences vary among groups and across time. Even the terms used to describe the activities of such people can carry negative connotations; for example, it is better to say that a person *uses* a wheelchair rather than he or she is *confined* to one. *The American Heritage Dictionary,* third edition, suggests reserving *handicapped* for describing "a disabled person who is unable to function owing to some property of the environment. Thus people with a physical disability requiring a wheelchair may or may not be *handicapped,* depending on whether wheelchair ramps are made available to them" (page 819).

Some—but certainly not all—groups and individuals prefer to use *visually impaired* for *blind* and *hearing impaired* for *deaf.* The problem with these newer terms is that they allow for the possibility of degrees of blindness or deafness and therefore are not precise. Writers should take special care to determine personal or group preference; usage in this area is in flux.

Age is another area of sensitivity. Female human beings over the age of 18 are *women,* not *girls;* similarly, male humans age 18 and over are *men,* not *boys. Middle-aged* is a term to be used with care by younger writers, particularly as the ever-youthful baby boomers enter into that category. *Senior citizen,* once an obvious euphemism, has become widely accepted, preferable to *elderly, oldster, old person,* or *aged. Senior,* the shortened form, is also used as a noun: *a discount plan for seniors.*

Biases That Reveal a Local Point of View

One last area of bias involves what might be called seeing the world from a local point of view. As communication satellites and ease of travel have helped to shrink our world, we need to resist the natural inclination to put ourselves at the center of the universe. For example, consider the word *American.* Although citizens of the United States are certainly Americans in their own country, as well as to much of the world, it is important to remember that there are other "Americans" on two continents. Canadians are certainly residents of the Americas, but if the general term is used, they prefer to be called North Americans, not Americans. To confuse matters, residents of Mexico usually refer to a U.S. citizen as being a North American, *un norteamericano.* Similarly, writers should take care when using the pronouns *we* and *our.* For a community newsletter, this usage may be fine; for a publication with a national or international audience, however, these pronouns are inappropriate.

Other terms reflect value judgments on the part of the writer and should not be used: for example, *Red China* and *Communist China.*

Writers should also be aware of their geographic location—thus, the preference is for specific designations like *Asia* rather than *Far East* or *the Orient,* which describe the writer's location in relation to these areas rather than the areas themselves.

Names of countries are constantly changing, and writers and editors should keep an up-to-date almanac at hand. *Merriam-Webster's Collegiate Dictionary,* 10th edition, published in 1993, contains an excellent comprehensive geographic listing.

Conclusion

What, then, should writers and editors do when faced with terminology that is changing and disputed even among members of the groups in question? They should first determine whether a particular description is important to the story being told. If it is, they should then try to determine the currently preferred term for the person or group being described. In the process, they should not forget that even if the words are correct, politically or otherwise, tone is just as important.

Unless a writer is consciously writing an inflammatory piece or speech—or fiction that attempts to reproduce a milieu—he or she is responsible for using bias-free language. Clarity does not suffer and neither does the language as a whole. Terms that are found useful will stay and pass into common use, and those that are not will disappear.

2

MISUSED AND EASILY CONFUSED WORDS

MISUSED AND EASILY CONFUSED WORDS

Where do you turn for help when the correct choice of words is not entirely clear? English is a language of enormous size, choice, and complexity. Hundreds of words sound like other words that don't mean the same thing; many others look like words that have completely different meanings or are close in meaning but have slightly or even significantly different connotations. And the way we use words to express certain meanings is undergoing constant change. Once-questionable words and usages are now acceptable and holding firm. Sometimes these words are referred to as *confusables* (or *confusibles*), a term first coined by British lexicographer Adrian Room in the late 1970s.

Looking up misused or easily confused words in a desk dictionary, especially one with usage notes, is a good start, but strict definitions don't always tell the whole story. It can still be hard to know which word best fits the context of a sentence. Dictionaries devoted solely to confusables are, of course, helpful but so comprehensive that finding a quick answer is difficult. Our list is different. Here are more than 1,000 of the spelling, meaning, and usage confusables that editors and writers most frequently encounter or feel hesitant about, explained in context and in most cases with example sentences.

Unlike other dictionaries, this list assembles closely related sets of two, three, or more words that, as comprehensive entries, help clarify puzzling relationships. Entries have been written not to enlighten grammarians or etymologists, but to serve the practical needs of those who wrestle with these distinctions in their daily work. For example, the semantically close words *ability* and *capacity* can be found in many other sources, but the additional discussion of a third, related word, *capability*, is original to this list—though it's just as likely to cause trouble for writers and editors.

Our list includes

- Words that sound virtually the same but have different spellings and meanings (*discreet, discrete*)
- Words that look similar but have different meanings (*militate, mitigate; forward, foreword*)
- Words that look similar and share closely related meanings (*emigrate, immigrate; effect, affect; subconscious, unconscious*)
- Words that, though different in meaning, have displaced one another because of close association over time (*prejudice, bias; peruse, skim*)
- Words mistaken for phrases and vice versa (*a while, awhile*)
- Words with connotations that have *bemused,* if not *amused,* generations of writers (*flounder, founder*)
- Overly formal or outmoded constructions (*comprise*) that are better replaced with simpler ones (*are composed of, are made of*)
- Noteworthy transitional but still not formally correct usages (*hopefully; snuck, sneaked; farther, further*)
- Distinctions that impinge on grammar (*lie, lay; try and, try to*)

The approach of this list reflects widely observed contemporary American usage, with the goal of including benign changes while preserving valuable distinctions. Without being overly prescriptive, the advice in these entries should give writers and editors enough information to save them from appearing careless or foolish in print. In some cases, the correct choice depends on the situation, and we have used certain words in the entries to denote acceptable contexts: For a professional, scholarly, or otherwise informed audience, *formal* or standard usage is safe and expected (we often use the term *careful writer* to describe this choice); for a less demanding audience, *informal* usage may be appropriate and is sometimes preferable; *idiomatic* usage or *regionalisms* are best avoided in all writing but fiction and the most informal situations; and *substandard* usage is not considered correct in any case.

Sources for this list were Theodore M. Bernstein's *The Careful Writer,* Roy H. Copperud's *American Usage and Style: The Consensus,* Wilson Follett's *Modern American Usage, The American Heritage Dictionary of the English Language,* third edition, William and Mary Morris' *Harper Dictionary of Contemporary Usage,* Marjorie Skillin's *Words Into Type,* Laurence Urdang's *The Dictionary of Confusable Words, Random House Webster's College Dictionary, Webster's Dictionary of English Usage, Webster's Ninth New Collegiate Dictionary,* and *Merriam-Webster's Collegiate Dictionary,* 10th edition.

A

abbreviation, acronym. *Abbreviation* is the general term for a shortened form of a name or word, such as "FL" or "Fla." for "Florida." An *acronym* is composed of the opening letters of a group of words that can be pronounced as a word. Over time, an acronym may completely supplant the original words, as in the case of *radar* (*ra*dio *d*etecting *a*nd *r*anging) and *modem* (*mod*ulator *dem*odulator). Some use the word *initialism* to mean an abbreviation composed of the initial letters (or syllables) of the words in a name or term that cannot be pronounced; this word is not yet commonplace, although *Merriam-Webster's Collegiate Dictionary*, 10th edition, includes it. The wide range of initialisms and acronyms represent organizations (Care, UNICEF, NATO, UL-approved), medical and scientific terms (mph, MMPI, AIDS), computer systems and processes (DOS, WYSIWYG, ASCII), and conversational shorthand (gone AWOL, a COB deadline, do it ASAP). See Chapter 14, Abbreviations, for a full discussion and guidelines on treatment.

ability, capacity, capability. *Ability* may be either innate or acquired and thus is used when referring to people rather than things: "With such natural ability the skater needed little coaching." "After hours of practice the skater acquired the ability to perform a triple axel." *Capacity* means inherent potential and thus cannot be acquired: "A child's capacity for learning a foreign language diminishes with age." *Capacity* can also indicate volume, as in "a capacity of two quarts." It is pompous to use *capacity* to mean "job," as in "serving in the capacity of director." A generally efficient person may be described as "able" or "capable," but a person or thing with the attributes necessary to perform a task or function is said to have the *capability* to do the job.

about. See *around, about, nearly.*

abridge, abstract, excerpt. To *abridge* a piece of writing is to physically shorten or condense it by omitting words without sacrificing sense or original purpose. To make an *abstract* of a piece of writing is to write a summary that distills the main points, as a prelude to publication or a guide for researchers. To *excerpt* material from a piece of writing is to select a representative passage for citation or to publish an extract in a context separate from the original work, as in an anthology.

abrogate, arrogate. Both words describe the exercise of power over others by an authority. To *abrogate* means "to do away with lawfully," but to *arrogate* is "to make unwarranted claims or seizures." *Arrogate* can also connote ascribing something to ourselves presumptuously or making a claim on another's behalf.

absence. See *lack, deficiency, absence.*

abstract. See *abridge, abstract, excerpt.*

abstruse, obtuse. *Abstruse* describes an argument or concept that is difficult for people without specialized knowledge to understand. Someone who lacks mental sharpness or sensitivity is said to be *obtuse* and would have trouble understanding even something simple.

abuse, maltreatment, misuse. *Abuse* (n.) indicates a corrupt practice or improper treatment of a general kind, as well as *maltreatment*—that is, cruel or rough physical treatment. *Misuse* connotes incorrect or mistaken treatment. (The prefixes *mal-*, from the 15th century, and *mis-*, from the 18th century, both derive from the Old French for "bad.") *Misusage* is also given by dictionaries as a synonym for abuse—or faulty practice—of the language.

academic. See *moot, academic.*

accept, except (from). This is a spelling confusable. To *accept* an assignment is to agree to undertake it; to *except* someone from a duty or an activity is to make an exemption for that person or to excuse him or her from it.

accessible, assessable. If something is *accessible,* it can be reached or gained. Something whose value can be estimated is *assessable.* These words are usually confused because of a pronunciation error; the first syllable of *accessible* is pronounced with a hard *c.*

accused. See *alleged, accused, suspected.*

acronym. See *abbreviation, acronym.*

acute. See *chronic, acute.*

adapt, adopt, adept. *Adapt* means to make a change to meet some demanding circumstance; *adopt* means to accept or, as with a child, to take in by choice; *adept* means skilled. *Adapted* should not be used as a synonym for *suitable* because to *adapt* implies change, not merely appropriate action or behavior.

admission, admittance. Both denote the possibility of gaining entry, but *admittance* means allowing or permitting physical entry into a place, while *admission* carries the meaning of access to privileges or opportunities. This distinction is blurred by such common phrases as "the price of admission," which seems to include both the privilege of getting to attend an event and the fact of getting through the door.

admit, confess. Although these verbs are often used synonymously, careful writers acknowledge a distinction regarding the degree to which guilt is disclosed. To *admit* means to concede the factual truth of events that may or may not prove culpability; to *confess* is reserved for a legal or religious context in which all facts necessary for proving guilt are voluntarily provided.

admittance. See *admission, admittance.*

adopt. See *adapt, adopt, adept.*

advanced. See *sophisticated, advanced.*

adverse, averse (to). Circumstances or things may seem to be *adverse*—difficult or unpleasant to endure—but the person who is reluctant to endure hardship or suffering is said to be *averse* to it. "Despite the adverse weather, the teacher was not averse to staying late to coach the debate team." *Adverse to* is incorrect in statements like this: "The weather was adverse to her plan of driving home late."

advise (to), inform (of). Journalists and politicians routinely use *advise* to mean say, tell, write, or *inform:* "The senator advised his staff that he would not run for reelection." To *advise,* however, means "to give advice."

affect, effect. Copperud says that confusion of these two words is perhaps the most common error in the English language, but these simple mnemonics may help. To *affect* is "to have influence on": "Audience reaction *a*ffects a speaker's confidence." To *effect* is "to cause something to happen": "*E*ffect a solution to the problem by making the *e*ffort." *Effect* is also a noun that means "result." *Affect,* a noun used in psychology, means "emotion."

aggravate, exacerbate. Once the bane of English teachers who taught that it should not be used to mean "irritate or exasperate," *aggravate* is now allowed in that sense: "Your whistling aggravates me." Formally, *aggravate* means "to make something worse." *Exacerbate* is a stronger verb because it denotes an intensification of something that is already unpleasant, violent, bitter, or severe.

aid, aide. An *aide* is the helpful person who gives *aid.* Although the two are used interchangeably to mean "assistant," *aide* is often seen in job titles in military, government, and medical settings.

alibi, excuse. *Alibi* has a technical meaning in law. It is a defense against a charge that shows the accused person was somewhere else when the crime occurred. Popular use of *alibi* to mean an *excuse*—justification for an action or an attempt to remove blame—is generally approved.

alleged, accused, suspected. All three adjectives are used, especially by journalists and lawyers, to refer to someone who may have committed a crime. Because proper syntax allows only a thing or condition, not a person, to be *alleged* to be true, the phrase "an alleged thief" is incorrect. "Police allege that he stole the car" is correct. Also, by definition, *thief* means "someone proved guilty of theft" and contradicts the equivocal nature of an allegation, accusation, or suspicion that may well prove unfounded. Such constructions as "suspected spy" are intended to deflect the impression that a direct accusation of guilt is being made and so to avoid libel. In law, however, to *allege* is to make a charge of liability for which the proof will be forthcoming. More generally, neither to *accuse* nor to *suspect* necessarily implies that proof can or will be provided: "The accused felon was released when the only witness recanted."

allegory. See *analogy, allegory.*

allergic, allergenic. The material or agent (an *allergen*) that causes a medically *allergic* reaction is said to be *allergenic.* Popularly, to be "allergic" to something is to have an unfavorable or adverse reaction; this is accepted informal usage.

all ready. See *already, all ready.*

all right. See *alright, all right.*

all together. See *altogether, all together.*

allusion, illusion, elusion. An *allusion* (from the verb *to allude*) makes reference to something, as in a literary allusion. For example, "Lunch at our house when the children were small resembled the Mad Hatter's tea party" alludes to an episode in Lewis Carroll's *Alice's Adventures in Wonderland.* To understand the *allusion,* one must be familiar with the source. An *illusion* is a false conception or impression, as in "Her carefully assembled though inexpensive wardrobe gave the illusion she shopped in the best stores." An *elusion* (rarely found used as a noun; more often, as "to elude") is an escape from something, as "Your *allusion* to John Stuart Mill may give others the *illusion* your point is well taken, but the point of your story *eludes* me." The adjective forms *elusive* and *illusive* are spelling confusables; a reader may wonder at the cynicism of a writer who mistakenly describes as "illusive" the bright "elusive" butterfly of love.

almost never, seldom ever. Both are examples of what Copperud calls "fuzzy writing and muddy thinking." They are contradictions in terms better replaced with "seldom if ever" or "rarely."

already, all ready. *Already* as one word means before now or by this time, as in "You should have finished that assignment already." When *already* is used with an adjective, as in "an already finished assignment," no hyphen is needed because *already* is an adverb. The adjective phrase *all ready* means completely prepared: "I am all ready to tackle the next assignment." *All ready* does not mean "everyone is ready" unless "all" is used as a pronoun to refer to every member of a group: "Are the children washed and all ready for bed?"

alright, all right. Currently, the one-word form is less commonly accepted, though it is increasingly seen in business and fiction writing for *all right* and could eventually become standard.

altar, alter. This is a spelling confusable: to *alter* is to change, while an *altar* is a place or structure designed to be a focus of reverence or worship; *altar* is used cynically in a phrase such as "altar of commerce" to mean an object of inappropriate devotion.

alternative, choice, option, alternate. The Latin prefix *alter-* means "the other of two." Some writers and editors prefer a strict meaning for *alternative,* but most agree that, as a noun, *alternative* is acceptable to mean "a choice among several [not just two] possibilities." Expanding the original definition made possible the vogue term *alternative lifestyles.*

However, deciding on an *alternative* is not the same as a making a *choice* (for example, what, if anything, to have for dessert). *Choice* encompasses the additional possibilities of making no choice at all or choosing something that was not among the *options* offered, whereas *alternative* signals that a decision of some kind needs to be made (ask for a raise, apply for a promotion, look for another job—but not passive sulking). *Option* is somewhat overworked; the common expression "That's not an option" is really a contradiction in terms: "That's not an alternative" is what's meant because *options* exist freely rather than as a delimited set.

The verb *alternate* means "to move regularly back and forth between two acts, places, or conditions": "She alternated between hope and cynicism." As a noun, *alternate* means "a substitute": "We have an alternate lined up in case the key speaker is detained." Not a true synonym for *alternative,* the adjective *alternate* is sometimes misused to mean "optional" when more properly it means either "happening in successive turns" (alternate seasons) or "serving in place of another": "The alternate route was just as bumpy as the one under construction."

although, though, while. *Although* and *though* are synonymous and may be used interchangeably in informal and formal writing, although many editors still prefer the longer form. Some authorities advise reserving *while* to denote concurrent events because using it as a synonym for "although" to indicate contrast can result in ambiguity. For example, "While I write quickly under deadline, I tend to grind my teeth" could be understood to mean either "Whenever I write quickly . . . I grind my teeth" or "Despite the fact that I write quickly . . . I grind my teeth." The teeth-grinding is either habitual and the most significant fact or incidental and a by-product of writing well under pressure.

altogether, all together. The adverb *altogether* means wholly or totally and often modifies adjectives as well as verbs: "I do not altogether agree with you, but I may not be altogether informed." *All together* means everybody taken together or all at the same time, as in "The horses huddled all together in the middle of the field, nose against flank, creating a barricade of steam against the icy spring shower."

alumnae, alumni. The plural *alumnae* refers to female graduates of a school, college, or university; the singular is *alumna.* The plural *alumni* refers to male graduates (singular, *alumnus*), but it is usually used to describe a group of mixed sexes; the careful writer who prefers nonsexist usage can use *graduates* instead.

amateur, novice, tyro. An *amateur* is someone who does not pursue a skill or activity professionally. A *novice* is someone who is generally inexperienced or, in a religious context, on probationary status before becoming a nun. *Amateur* is also frequently used as an adjective with a noun describing a specific pursuit, as in "amateur photographer." Journalists use *tyro* as both noun and adjective to describe a beginner in a sport.

ambiguous, ambivalent. *Ambiguous* describes a thing or an action that can be interpreted as having several conflicting meanings or aspects in a given context. *Ambivalent* describes the state of mind of a person who has two contradictory attitudes: "fight or flight," "love or hate." *Ambivalent* is popularly misused to mean "having two sides," as in "the ambivalent issue of abortion." The effect of the misuse is to substitute the idea of simple duality for the sense of tension and conflict present in *ambiguous.* In general, only people are ambivalent.

amiable, amicable. Friendly, pleasant people whose manner shows warmth and cordiality are characterized as *amiable;* relationships, events, and negotiations of a contractual nature that are conducted with goodwill and a desire not to quarrel are referred to as *amicable.* "The amiable divorcing couple maintained an amicable relationship while they negotiated a property settlement."

amid, among. *Amid* refers to things that are not usually or cannot be counted: "digging amid the gravel for the lost car keys." *Among* is used for countable things: "walking among the flowerbeds." *Amidst* has an archaic or British flavor.

among, between. Strict usage calls for *among* to be used for a relationship that includes three or more objects or persons and reserves *between* for only two things or persons. But *between* is often used when expressing the close relationship of any number of individual things, where *among* would be weaker: "Between school, sports, and volunteer work, many students lack time for restorative daydreaming."

amoral, immoral, unmoral. *Amoral* applies to a person who is "without morals," one who does not recognize morals as relevant to behavior. *Immoral* describes the behavior of someone "not moral," one whose behavior is deliberately contrary to prevailing standards. *Unmoral* is synonymous with *amoral.*

amount, number. *Amount* should be used for indeterminate quantities, not for countable numbers. "Given the large amount of zucchini we harvested, the number we gave away to neighbors was in the dozens."

amuse, bemuse. *Amuse* means to entertain. *Bemuse* means to confuse or bewilder and is not a more elegant version of *amuse.*

a myriad of. See *myriad, a myriad of, myriads.*

anachronism, anomaly. An *anachronism* occurs when a writer refers to an activity or object that did not exist during the particular time period in which it is placed or that is described in historically inappropriate terms, for example, the appearance in a Victorian novel of a woman carrying a flashlight while taking a nighttime walk. An *anomaly* is something inconsistent, inappropriate, or paradoxical (other than chronological), such as ascribing to a hermit a gift for conversation.

analogy, allegory. In literature, an *analogy* is a comparison of things that resemble each other but are different in nature: "My heart was pounding like a jackhammer." An *allegory* is a story told in symbolic terms—for example, *The Pilgrim's Progress*—using fictional characters to express truths about human existence.

anarchism, anarchy. *Anarchism* is the political theory and practice that asserts all forms of governmental authority are unnecessary and should be replaced with voluntary cooperation among citizens and factions. *Anarchy,* the older term, means a condition of social and political disorder resulting from the lack of governmental authority, as well as the ideal of a utopian society of completely free individuals.

and/or. Although widely used in law and business to mean "A or B or both," this construction is misleading when the number of possibilities is more than two, as in, "A, B, and/or C." That can mean "A, B, and C" or "A + (either B or C)" or "Either (A + B) or C." *And/or* is not considered careful usage in most formal writing.

and, to. Such constructions as "try and stop me," "be sure and," and "stop and think" have traditionally been considered inelegant and more characteristic of informal speech than of formal usage, which requires the infinitive form: "try to stop me," "be sure to come." But support for both these usages is well documented.

annihilate. See *decimate, annihilate.*

annoyed at, by, with. The correct preposition to use with *annoy* depends on whether someone "feels annoyed at" or "is annoyed by" and whether the offender is a person, event, or thing. "The teenager is annoyed by an early curfew; his parents became annoyed at him for resisting the curfew; the family annoyed the neighbors with their loud arguments."

anomaly. See *anachronism, anomaly.*

ante-, anti-. With some exceptions, *ante-* is a prefix meaning "prior to, in front of, or earlier than": *Antediluvian* means the biblical time before the flood or something antiquated. *Anti-* is a prefix meaning either "of the same kind but moving in an opposite direction" or "opposite in kind to": An *antihero* is a rebel—someone, like Marlon Brando or Bart Simpson, admired for reasons contrary to the traditional attributes of nobility.

anticipate, expect. In addition to the sense of to *expect* or simply look forward to something, to *anticipate* can mean "already being prepared for what has not yet happened," a much more restricted meaning that is seldom called for. "Alicia expected George to arrive by noon; she had anticipated his hunger and prepared fat sandwiches." As nouns, *anticipation* and *expectancy* convey a slightly different sense of hopeful or pleasant eagerness: "As George seated himself at Alicia's dining table, expectancy lit his face." Where the simpler *expect* fits, it should be used, but using *anticipate* and *expect* as synonyms is no longer frowned on but may be inappropriate in formal writing.

anxious (about), eager (to). These words are not synonymous. *Eager* means earnestly desiring something; *anxious* means uneasy, apprehensive. "We are anxious about the weather because we are eager to go skiing." Thus, despite its frequency, the phrase "I am anxious to hear from you" that often closes letters is not correct usage.

anybody . . . their. See *anyone . . . their, anybody . . . their.*

anymore, any more. *Anymore* is an adverb meaning "does no longer," as in "Alice doesn't live here anymore." *Any more* is used when the *any* could be deleted and *more* would make sense alone: "Please do not give me any more brussels sprouts." Use of *anymore* in the following way is colloquial: "All I do anymore is work and sleep."

anyone . . . their, anybody . . . their. As pronouns, both *anyone* and *anybody* are one-word forms. Although grammatically singular as antecedents, they are sometimes followed by plural references: "Anyone who makes a reservation is shown to their table immediately." Strict grammarians are usually on the traditional side of this issue, insisting on the singular pronoun, but the plural use is sanctioned by those who resist the awkwardness of "his or her, him or her" and favor the utility of "their" or "them" at conveying gender-free inclusiveness. The latter authorities include Val Dumond in *Elements of Nonsexist Usage* and *Webster's Dictionary of English Usage,* which cites Copperud, Flesch, and *American Heritage.* Bernstein is characteristically pragmatic in suggesting that the best solution is often "to recognize the imperfections of the language and modify the wording." In addition, for the past 400 years, *they, their,* and *them* have been used to refer to *everyone* and *everybody.* See Chapter 4, Pronouns, for a full discussion.

THE TWO MEANINGS OF *ANTI-*

Most people don't make the connection between the prefix *anti-* and two interesting words, *antipasto* and *antimacassar. Antipasto* does not mean "against the pasta" but is the first course of a meal (*pasto* means meal in Italian) composed of typically Italian hors d'oeuvres. In this case, *anti-* is a variant form of the prefix *ante-* meaning "before, first, or in front of." An *antimacassar* is a doily or cloth, often delicately crocheted or embroidered, that was once commonly placed on the back and arms of an easy chair or sofa. *Anti-* here indicates a covering that protects the furniture literally "against the hair oil" once commonly applied by the well-groomed man. This oil, originally derived from the seeds of a tree grown in the Macassar area of an Indonesian island, ended up on the upholstery when the greasy head of the household leaned back to rest after a long day's work—perhaps with a plate of prosciutto and provolone in hand.

apiary, aviary. *Apiary* is where a collection of hived bees is kept for making honey; *aviary* is a large but confined place where selected birds are kept, for example, in a zoo.

appose. See *oppose, appose.*

appraise, apprise. To *appraise* means "to set a value on something," but it is often confused with to *apprise (of),* "to notify or inform."

apropos. See *germane, relevant, apropos.*

apt, likely, liable, prone. Much confusion reigns here. Both *apt* and *likely,* when followed by an infinitive, may be used to indicate "probability of" or "tendency toward" an activity or quality. *Apt* may also be used as an adjective to mean "having an inherent inclination toward": "She is apt/likely to succeed as a novelist because she is an apt observer of human foibles." *Likely* may also be used as an adjective to suggest degrees of probable truth or value ranging from the credible ("a likely story") to the promising ("a likely candidate"). In contrast, *liable* and *prone,* when correctly used, tend to point to failure or difficulty—the likelihood of a negative outcome. *Liable* is often informally used to mean "likely," but it has a legal connotation of "subject to" (followed by a noun): "The database is liable to corruption in a storm," but the database is not "liable to be corrupted," nor is the storm "liable to corrupt" the database. *Prone* implies an unfortunate predisposition: "The book reviewer was prone to judge authors against the bias of his own pet thesis."

arbitrate, mediate. To *arbitrate* means to hear and judge evidence and make an award. To *mediate* is to help opposing sides reach an agreement through compromise. Arbitrators must not become involved in prehearing negotiations; mediators have no power to enforce a final decision. Thus these nouns are not interchangeable.

aren't I? Dictionaries give the meaning "am not" for *aren't,* and although technically ungrammatical, this construction is used by those who wish to avoid either the stilted sound of "am I not?" or the disapproved "ain't I?" *Aren't* is on the way to respectability since the compromise form "a'n't" (which became "ain't") never caught on.

aroma, scent, odor, smell. An *aroma* or a *scent* is a pleasant smell, whereas an *odor* or a *smell* can be generically pleasant or unpleasant but is normally reserved for the latter. Some use *aroma* in a humorous way when commenting on a bad smell, but this usage borders on euphemism.

around, about, nearly. Many authorities agree that *around* and *about* are standard synonyms for *nearly* to mean "approximately." But *around,* particularly, still carries an informal connotation and detracts from the authority of formal writing.

arrogate. See *abrogate, arrogate.*

as. See *because, since, as* and *like, such as, as.*

as bad or worse than. This common usage is an example of what Bernstein calls "incomplete alternative comparison." In the sentence, "My headache is as bad or worse than yours," "is . . . worse than yours" makes grammatical sense, but "is as bad . . . than yours" does not. One way to avoid this problem is to say "as bad as yours" and add "or worse" at the end. Another is to rewrite: "My headache is at least as bad as yours."

ascribe, subscribe. To *ascribe* (to) means "to give a person or agency the credit for being the cause, source, or author of something." To *subscribe* (to) means "to feel favorably disposed toward, agree with" and can be remembered by its association with the choice to "subscribe" to a newspaper whose political or editorial stance resembles one's own.

as if, as though, like. *As if* and *as though* can be used interchangeably to mean "as something or someone would be, do, look, and so forth, if different conditions were true." *Like* was used in old English in the form "like as," with *like* meaning "in the same manner" and *as* serving as a conjunction. It became shortened to *like,* but grammarians still reject this usage despite its widespread use in speech. As Bernstein says, "There is no logical reason why *like* should not be regarded as a conjunction; on the contrary, there are sound logical and historical reasons why it should be." Dictionaries define *like* as a conjunction but warn that it is still debatable in place of either *as if* or *as though* when used as a conjunction before a clause. For example, "The production manager acted like she was about to quit" should read "The production manager acted as if she was about to quit." (This construction leads to another question, Should the subjunctive mood always be used with "as if" and "as though" clauses? See Chapter 5, Verbs, for a complete explanation.) In formal writing, reserve *like* for cases when the phrase "similar to" or "such as" could be substituted: "She looks like my sister." In other words, when *like* is followed by a noun (but not a verb), it serves without debate as a preposition.

assay, essay. To *assay* is "to analyze the value of"; to *essay* is "to try." "The diamond merchant's discerning eye essayed to tell the difference between stones assayed as perfect and those deemed flawed." Both verbs should carry a warning label for all but the most formal writing: "Danger! Inflated language can lead to glazed eyes."

assert. See *claim, assert.*

assessable. See *accessible, assessable.*

assume. See *presume, assume.*

assure, ensure, insure. To *assure* means to make (someone else) confident about something when the element of doubt is present. Both to *ensure* and to *insure* also mean to make certain of something. Despite the journalistic trend away from the traditional use of to *insure,* most careful writers still prefer *ensure* except to denote the reduction of financial risk.

asterisk. The last syllable of this word is often misspelled and mispronounced "ick" by those who find the sibilance hard to handle.

as though. See *as if, as though, like.*

Attic, Hellenic, Hellenistic. *Attic* is the adjective that refers to the area, people, language, and so forth in the part of Greece surrounding Athens. *Hellenic* (the ancient Greeks called themselves *Hellenes* and their land *Hellas,* as Greeks continue to do today) refers to the history, language, and culture of ancient Greece, specifically from about the time of Homer to the death of Alexander the Great. *Hellenistic* refers to the areas, history, language, and culture of the ancient world influenced by the Greeks in the wake of Alexander's conquests.

attorney, lawyer, counsel, counselor. The phrase "power of attorney" is the key to what *attorney* means: one, not necessarily a lawyer, authorized to act on behalf of another. A *lawyer* is a person licensed to practice law, but *attorney* sounds more dignified to the many lawyers who prefer it. *Counsel* designates one who advises, in this case a lawyer who gives legal advice, so *counselor* is a term of address for a lawyer acting as *counsel.*

attribute. See *credit, attribute.*

audience, spectators. A group of listeners is an *audience,* but the word is also used to describe groups that are both looking and listening, such as the audience in a theater. *Spectators* is the term for those who are onlookers at an event, such as sports fans and those who gather at the scene of an accident.

authoritative, authoritarian. An *authoritative* person is someone who speaks or acts as one who knows—an expert—and is therefore likely to inspire voluntary respect or deference. An *authoritarian* personality or agency is dominating and favors strict submission to rules; the word also connotes inflexibility and unfairness.

average, mean, median. Used informally as interchangeable to mean "about the midpoint," these terms are distinctly different in mathematical or statistical contexts, and these distinctions should be recognized in formal prose. The *average* of a set of quantities is their sum divided by the number of items in the group. The *median* is the midpoint above which half of a set of quantities will occur and below which the other half will occur. The *mean*—the midpoint between the two extremes of a set of numbers—will normally be the same as the *average* for the same set.

averse. See *adverse, averse (to).*

avert. See *avoid, evade, avert, prevent.*

aviary. See *apiary, aviary.*

avocation. See *vocation, avocation.*

avoid, evade, avert, prevent. To *avoid* implies "to keep away from something by sidestepping it"; *evade,* "to avoid something by escaping from it." To *avert* and to *prevent* both mean "to keep something, usually dangerous or unpleasant, from happening."

awhile, a while. *Awhile,* an adverb, is properly written as one word and cannot be modified. " 'Stay awhile and visit,' our tireless host demanded." The phrase *a while* should be introduced by a preposition, usually *for,* which is the signal that the two-word form is required. *A while,* because it is a noun phrase, may be modified. " 'Stay for a short while at least,' our host begged."

B

bad, badly. Traditionally, statements such as "I feel badly about your accident" have been considered incorrect because *badly,* an adverb, technically cannot modify a noun or pronouns; here, "feel" is a linking, or intransitive, verb, and *bad* functions as an adjective modifying the subject. In such constructions, *badly* literally modifies *feel,* so that "I feel badly" means "my sense of touch is faulty." This is the chief source of confusion; in speech, however, *badly* is standard after the verbs *want* and *need* (in the sense of severely) and *do* (in the sense of poorly). However, according to

❧

BIOGRAPHY, AUTOBIOGRAPHY

There's an easy way to remember that an *autobiography* is an account of a person's life as told by that person: The prefix *auto-* means "self," so it's a "self-biography." A *biography* is the life story, written by another, of a person who dictionaries say is the *biographee.* (That's a good example of a word with a dictionary life—since 1841—although most people wouldn't think of using it.) *Memoir* is a term for a more idiosyncratic version of both kinds of life stories. An autobiographical account, usually referred to in the plural as one's *memoirs,* is a loose report of events based on the writer's personal experience or observation, such as *The Life It Brings: One Physicist's Beginnings* by Jeremy Bernstein or May Sarton's *Encore: A Journal of the Eightieth Year.* A *biographical memoir* is an evocative sketch of the life of someone noteworthy or significant to the author, such as Susan Cheever's *Home Before Dark.*

There are two interesting modern offshoots of the memoir. One is the *fictionalized biography,* a form that evokes the context of a life by weaving imaginative elements with real events and relationships. An example is Bruce Duffy's fictional life of Ludwig Wittgenstein, *The World As I Found It.* Another variation is the *psychobiography,* a study that stresses the childhood traumas and unconscious motivations of a subject. In both this form and the fictionalized biography, the biographer is no longer a reporter and is more than an interpreter; the biographer has invested in a thesis about someone else's life, as Joe McGinnis did in *The Last Brother.*

Copperud, the current American consensus is divided evenly between those who support the strict distinction and those who accept as standard the interchangeable use of *bad* and *badly* for both mental and physical conditions. When usage is truly transitional, as here, a careful writer continues to observe the distinction.

barbarian, barbaric, barbarous. *Barbarian,* usually used as a noun, can be an adjective but is used less often than either *barbaric* or *barbarous* to mean "relating to barbarians," primitive people whose culture is believed to be inferior. All three words are used to describe "a lack of refinement, a state between savagery and civilization." *Barbaric* can be used in a nondisparaging way for "wild, uncultivated" (the barbaric energy of the cast of *Hair*) but also to mean "harsh, cruel." *Barbarous* is used primarily when speaking of words and expressions ("barbarisms") that are illiterate, coined, obsolete, or jarringly inappropriate.

based on. See *predicated on, based on.*

bathos, pathos. *Bathos* is a literary term used to describe the interjection of droning, hackneyed, or trite language into an otherwise lofty or elegant context, reducing the sublime to the laughable; a writer doesn't indulge in *bathos* intentionally. "A tinge of bathos marred the wedding ceremony when the justice of the peace said, 'I now pronounce you lovebirds.' " *Pathos,* though it sounds enough like *bathos* to be mistaken for it, means something entirely different: "causing or feeling sympathetic pity," usually found in adjective form as "pathetic."

because. See *for, because.*

because of. See *due to, because of.*

because, since, as. When the causal conjunctions *because* and *since* are used to mean "for the reason that," they are grammatically interchangeable. Careful writers, however, avoid using *since* when it may logically mean both "because of" and "from the time of." For example, "Since the acquisitions librarian left the collection has become a shambles" can mean either that the trouble began when the librarian left or that the loss of the librarian caused the problem. The best writing avoids *as* in the sense of "because" to prevent the reader from stumbling, for example, in the sentence "He couldn't hear the ambulance siren as he was listening to the car radio." The *as* phrase could mean "because" he was listening or "during the time" he was listening, depending on the context. In addition to being confusing, *as* can sound stilted when used to mean "because."

before. See *prior to, before.*

belie, evince. *Belie,* which means "to misrepresent or contradict the truth" of something, is increasingly used when *evince*—"to show or indicate the truth" of something—is the actual meaning. Follett, in *Modern American Usage,* attributes the dilution of the word *belie* to a tendency to equate it with "betray," which in turn has been made ambiguous by its use to mean "to give evidence of, show." It may be helpful to think of *belie* as meaning "to give the lie to," as in the example, "Your bitter smile belies your apology."

bellicose, belligerent. *Bellicose* implies a predisposition to start a war or a fight and is a synonym for "pugnacious." *Belligerent* means being actively engaged in warlike hostilities, but it can also mean "having a quarrelsome nature."

bemuse. See *amuse, bemuse.*

beneficent, benevolent. *Beneficent* describes a person who is "kind and charitable." In addition to denoting kindness, *benevolent* also may describe something organized for a good cause or conducted with goodwill. Both adjectives and their noun forms (*beneficence* and *benevolence,* respectively) imply generosity.

beside, besides. The distinction between these once overlapping words was first outlined in 1858 by Edward S. Gould: *Beside* is obsolete as a synonym for *besides* either as an adverb meaning "as well, moreover" ("Besides, you never know when you'll need a can of creamed corn") or as a preposition meaning "in addition to" ("Besides my dislike of seeing caged animals, I'm too agoraphobic to visit the zoo"). *Beside,* correctly, is a preposition meaning "by the side of" or "compared with": "The pain of writing pales beside the joy of being published." Finally, although using *beside* to mean "except, other than, together with" is, says *Webster's Dictionary of English Usage,* "not wrong, nor rare, nor nonstandard, *besides* is the word most people use." "Who besides me wants lemon pie tonight?"

between. See *among, between.*

between you and I. Because the preposition *between* takes the objective case of a pronoun as its object, *I,* which is nominative case, is ungrammatical, despite the well-meaning but misguided speakers and writers who think *I* sounds more formal than *me. Between you and me* is correct; so is *between him and me.*

biannual, semiannual, biennial. Dictionaries define *biannual* as "occurring twice a year; sometimes: biennial." *Semiannual* means "occurring every six months or twice a year" because *semi-* means "precisely half of." *Biennial* means "occurring every two years" but also "continuing or lasting for two years." Several sources advise replacing the ambiguous and potentially misleading prefixes *bi-* and *semi-* with a clear statement—for example, "The directory is published every two years" rather than "The directory is published biennially."

bias, discrimination, prejudice, bigotry, predilection. The use of different prepositions with these words substantially changes the meaning from positive to negative; all except *predilection* are now most often used in a negative sense. A *bias* is a mental or emotional state that can, in principle, predispose a person to be and act either in favor of or against something. In practice, however, *bias* (like *discrimination* and *prejudice*) has increasingly acquired the negative connotation of unfairness to others. That is, to act on one's "*bias* against" hiring older people is to practice "*discrimination* against" them. To be "*biased* against" is also to be "*prejudiced* against or toward"; *prejudice* is by definition a preconceived idea (a prejudgment) that is almost always negative—"a *discrimination* against." *Bigotry* is the intolerant adherence to one's beliefs, whatever they may be. To be "*biased* or *prejudiced* in favor of" means to have a strong "*predilection* for or in favor of" something based on one's experience or temperament—for example, a predilection for classical music. (*Penchant, propensity,* and *proclivity* are synonyms that also indicate a liking for something, someone, or some course of action.)

biennial. See *biannual, semiannual, biennial.*

bigotry. See *bias, discrimination, prejudice, bigotry, predilection.*

bisect, intersect. To *bisect* is to cross something at the midpoint, dividing it into equal halves. To *intersect* is to cross or divide so that two things meet at some point, not necessarily at the midpoint.

blatant, flagrant. Although popularly used as synonyms conveying the sense of being "conspicuously offensive," these adjectives differ in their emphasis. *Flagrant* is the stronger term, indicating something that is "evil, reprehensible, or a willful flouting of law or morality not to be condoned," as a *flagrant* human rights violation. The emphasis is on "despicably offensive." *Blatant* means "loudly obnoxious, glaringly obvious, shamelessly contrived," as a *blatant* lie. The emphasis is on "conspicuously offensive."

born, borne. *Born* is misused for *borne* when the past participle of the verb "to bear" meaning "to carry" is meant (airborne viruses; the insult borne with dignity). *Born* refers to birth, with the exception of the usage "she has borne twins" (she bore twins; twins were born).

bring, take. This perennial confusable is easily solved with a mnemonic: "At an elegant dinner, a server *brings in* new courses and *takes away* dirty plates to be scraped." That is, when to *bring* denotes action, it is action toward someone or something; to *take* describes action away from a speaker, writer, actor, or event. Whether an activity is toward or away from shifts as the speaker, writer, or actor shifts. Remember where the activity is being directed and who is doing the acting in each case. "Bring a dictionary with you to class and take your essays home for revision; remember to take your dictionaries home and bring your revised essays back to class tomorrow."

burglary. See *robbery, larceny, theft, burglary.*

buses, busses. This is a spelling confusable. *Buses* is the plural form for *bus,* the public transportation vehicle; *busses* is the third person singular form for to *buss,* to kiss, and the plural of the noun *buss*, also meaning *kiss*.

byzantine. Do not capitalize this adjective when using it figuratively to mean "devious and complicated in manner of operation" or "labyrinthine."

C

calculate, suppose. *Calculate* is dialect for to *suppose,* meaning "to assume," and should be used informally if at all.

callus, callous, calloused. These words all carry the idea of "hardening or thickening." The noun *callus* means a buildup of hardened tissue on the skin: "Guitar players get calluses on their fingertips." *Callus* can also be a verb: "Playing guitar callused his fingers." However, the adjective that means "having calluses" is spelled *calloused:* "the calloused hands of the farmer." The adjective *callous* means "insensitive": "The supervisor's public scolding showed a callous disregard of the employee's feelings." Strange but true, *callous*—without the *-ed*—is the only correct form for this meaning, not "Our hearts became calloused." *Callous,* as well as *calloused,* can also be used as a verb: "An unfair performance review calloused the employee's sense of loyalty."

can but. See *cannot help, can but, cannot help but.*

can, may. As each new generation tries to learn these confusables, parents at dinner tables and teachers everywhere can be heard retorting, "I can excuse you if you can say 'May I.' " *Can* strictly means the ability of one to perform or the possibility of something being performed. *May* asks or gives permission to act. In informal usage they are interchangeable, and the use of *can* for permission is growing, although *may* remains preferred for permission.

cannot, can not, can not only. *Cannot* is the preferred form except for the rare instance when a writer wishes to emphasize the *not,* for example, in juxtaposition to *can* statements: "You can run and you can hide, but you can not escape me." When *can not only* is used, the trick is to remember that *not* is working with *only* as a conjunction; *can* is an auxiliary that must be parallel with the rest of the statement: "The restaurant can not only serve a delectable lasagna, but also [can] bake [not bakes] a sinful chocolate cake."

cannot help, can but, cannot help but. These phrases are all commonly used as a shorter way of saying "to be unable to do otherwise than." *Can but* has an affected literary ring; *cannot help but* has been criticized by traditionalists. *Cannot help* is the expression safest from criticism, but Copperud says "the weight of authority overwhelmingly favors the legitimacy" of *cannot help but* both informally and in highly regarded contemporary writing.

can't seem. Surprisingly, even though it sounds ungrammatical, *can't seem* is accepted as a standard idiom that is no less awkward than saying "seems to be unable," according to Copperud, who refers to the approval of six other commentators.

canvas, canvass. *Canvas* is a kind of heavy cloth; to *canvass* is to go from door to door soliciting (*canvassing*).

capability. See *ability, capacity, capability.*

capacity. See *ability, capacity, capability.*

capital, capitol. This is a common spelling confusable. A *capitol* is a

THE DIFFERENCE BETWEEN BRITAIN AND ENGLAND

There's no quicker way to alienate a British reader than to ignore the distinctions among *England, Britain, Great Britain, the United Kingdom, the British Isles, English,* and *British*—but most Americans don't know the difference. Courtesy demands that Americans try to keep these geographic and national terms straight.

Great Britain, or *Britain,* describes the island that contains the countries of England, Wales, and Scotland. When Northern Ireland is added to the group, the official name for these countries as a national entity is "The United Kingdom of Great Britain and Northern Ireland"—or simply, the *United Kingdom* (or U.K., for short). The *British Isles* refers to the United Kingdom and Ireland (which is neither English nor British but an independent country) and several offshore islands.

English as an adjective refers to someone or something from *England. Britain* and *British* are used to describe things related to the people of *Britain.* Otherwise, the Scots, Welsh, or Northern Irish should be referred to specifically. People who live in Northern Ireland tend to call themselves *British* unless they are ethnically *Irish.* Here are some examples: Britain (not England) votes in the United Nations. British (not English) troops were defeated in the American Revolution; the individual soldiers might have been English, but they fought under the British flag. However, the language we Americans share is *English,* and the nationality of writers, musicians, or others who are natives of England may be referred to by Americans as either *English* or *British.*

By the way, never refer to someone from Scotland as being *Scotch;* the proper terms are *Scottish* or *Scots. Scotch* is an English contraction that most *Scottish* people frown on.

---

building or group of buildings where government functions are performed; the city where these buildings and operations are located is a *capital.* A mnemonic worth trying is to think of the *o* in *capitol* as standing for the *o* in *dome* or the *o* in *office* building.

carat, karat, caret. A *carat,* also spelled *karat,* is the unit of weight for precious stones and metals ("There are 200 milligrams in a carat"). A *caret* is the mark (^) that editors and proofreaders use to insert material in copy.

careen, career. To *careen* is to lean over or sway, like a boat in the current. To *career* is to move erratically at high speed. *Careen* seems to be replacing *career* as an all-purpose verb for both these meanings and is most frequently used by journalists; however, many careful writers preserve the distinction between the careening of a boat between buoys and the careering of race cars around a slippery track.

caret. See *carat, karat, caret.*

category, class, division. Other than in a scientific context, *category* is a somewhat pretentious term, despite its usage as quiz show jargon for "type of [*class* of] questions." *Category* means a *division* in a scheme of classification. See also *character, kind, sort.*

Celsius, centigrade, Fahrenheit. *Celsius,* which has been the preferred designation since 1948, and *centigrade* are two names for the same temperature scale (abbreviated C), on which the freezing point of water is zero degrees and the boiling point is 100 degrees. On the Fahrenheit scale (abbreviated F), used mainly in the United States, the freezing point of water is 32 degrees and the boiling point is 212 degrees. Both *Celsius* and *Fahrenheit* scales were named for their inventors, which explains why these names are capitalized.

censor, censure. To *censor* is to prohibit or prevent some form of expression (writing, film) or to examine with the intention of exercising censorship. To *censure* is to sharply criticize a person for some behavior.

center around. These words create a logical contradiction, but the idiom is common nonetheless to express the idea of concentration. *Centered in, centered on,* and *centered at* are the terms that careful writers prefer.

centigrade. See *Celsius, centigrade, Fahrenheit.*

centrifugal, centripetal. *Centrifugal* refers to a force that tends to move objects away from the center. *Centripetal* refers to a force that tends to pull objects toward the center. A spinning merry-go-round creates *centrifugal* force; the sun's gravitational force creates the *centripetal* force that causes the Earth's rotation.

ceremonial, ceremonious. *Webster's 10th* considers these words to be synonymous, but usage experts maintain a distinction. *Ceremonial* refers to aspects of a ceremony (things); *ceremonious* describes a person acting "in an ostentatiously grave manner." However, *ceremonious* can also mean "in a deliberate, ceremonial manner," without the connotation of pomp.

certainty, certitude. Both carry the meaning "lack of doubt," but the distinction is that *certainty* resides in objective proof, whereas *certitude* implies faith in something for which there may be no proof.

character, kind, sort. *Character,* which can be used to refer to both people and things, means "distinctive qualities": "The character of the wine was enhanced by chilling." *Character* is sometimes wrongly used where *kind* or *sort* is correct: "I can tell a liar by the kind of eye contact he makes."

childish, childlike. *Childlike* connotes "simple and innocent" and is a positive term that describes seemingly unsophisticated adult behavior: "She showed a childlike sense of wonder as she toured the natural history museum." *Childish* is a derogatory term whether used to describe adults or children (though only a childish adult could fault a child for being childish) who are "selfish, irresponsible, and heedless": "Their childish refusal to compromise infuriated us."

choice. See *alternative, choice, option, alternate.*

chorus. See *verse, stanza, chorus.*

chronic, acute. A *chronic* (habitual) complaint is one that continues for a long time, from weeks to years. An *acute* (severe) illness usually lasts only a few days, although it may become *chronic* if it persists. "An acute ear infection is painful while it lasts, but a chronic ear infection can cause permanent hearing damage."

cite. To *cite* a fact or a truth about something means that it must exist; *cite* is misused when making an unproven allegation: "The lawyer cited her client's cooperative behavior as grounds for a lenient sentence," but not "The lawyer cited her client's generous attitude toward her friends." To *cite* also means "to quote by way of example" or "to refer to or quote an authoritative source." *Cite* should be followed with a noun or noun phrase—"He cited Joan's patience as her chief virtue"—not with a noun clause: "He cited that Joan was innocent." See also *site, sight, cite.*

claim, assert. Journalists treat these verbs as synonymous, but there is a distinction. To *claim* the fact or truth of something implies that some evidence exists; *claim* should be reserved by careful writers for asserting a provable title to something: "Philip claimed he was his father's legitimate heir." To *assert* means simply to say or declare without necessarily having either the evidence or the right to do so: "Amanda asserted that she was entitled to go to the front of the line."

class. See *category, class, division.*

classic, classical. Careful writers reserve *classical* for things pertaining specifically to Roman or Greek culture (often capitalized: "a Classicist") or to established methods or systems ("a classical education"). *Classic* is commonly used as both a noun and an adjective to denote an outstanding performance or something that has enduring value: "Leonard Bernstein's classic recording of Beethoven's Ninth Symphony is a joy for classical music lovers."

cliché, truism. *Cliché's* original French meaning was "stereotype or pattern," something presented repeatedly in the same form. The word has come to mean an overworked term or phrase. The danger in using clichés is that a reader or an audience will groan, but there is still room for the occasional cliché in conversation. After all, many clichés began as apt metaphorical expressions and were reduced to hackneyed status only through their popularity. A *truism* is a self-evident platitude that is too obvious or trivial to bear repeating ("To get ahead in life takes hard work") and is thus not a candidate for ever becoming a *cliché,* which at least originally was worth its salt and may still kick up its heels once in a blue moon.

climatic, climactic. *Climatic* refers to the weather, or climate. *Climactic* describes a situation in which a climax, or high point, occurs. "The climatic phenomenon of global warming may have climactic consequences in the next century."

climax, crescendo, culminate. *Climax* technically means a process of gradual ascent, not the apex or culmination, but it is correctly accepted in the latter sense. Similarly, a *crescendo* is a gradual rising in loudness or intensity, but it is sometimes carelessly used to mean "a culmination": Thus, "The music rose to a crescendo" is incorrect; instead, "The crescendo of a Sousa march always includes a rousing chorus." *To culminate* does not mean "to finish" but to rise through a series of steps to the highest point.

cohort. Careful writers reserve *cohort* to mean "a band, members of a large group engaged in a common endeavor," or a group of individuals having a statistical factor in common (for example, age) in a demographic study. *Cohort* is also widely accepted for "colleague, associate, collaborator." In an informal context, *cohort* has a slight connotation of "partner in crime."

collide, collision. A moving object may be said to *collide* with either another moving object or a stationary one: "The drunken driver collided with the utility pole"; "The car thieves collided with a police car in a high-speed chase." But a *collision* involves only the meeting of two objects that are both in motion, as in "Two speeding cars were destroyed in a head-on collision." So, technically, the phrase "rear-end collision" is not correct unless both cars were moving at the time of impact.

colloquial. When this term is used in dictionaries and by writers on language, it is not intended to be disparaging; its original meaning was "conversational." But *colloquial* has acquired a derogatory association with inferior "everyday, ordinary speech" versus "formal, correct speech," when in fact many colloquial forms are acceptable in "serious" writing. *Webster's Dictionary of English Usage* says that this misunderstanding is so commonplace that many dictionaries have stopped using the term and have adopted "informal" in its place.

common. See *mutual, reciprocal, common.*

company, firm, concern. A *company* is a corporation or *concern* engaged in business or manufacturing; *firm* is used to refer to a business partnership, usually involving the practice of a profession: "a plumbing *concern,*" but "a law *firm.*" A *firm* is legally recognized as an entity apart from the members forming it, unlike a corporation, and thus technically is not a synonym for the latter. However, most dictionaries define *firm* as "any business or company, whether or not incorporated," and allow "company" as a synonym.

compare with, compare to. *Compare with,* the more everyday term, is used when things or concepts are placed side by side to examine their differences and similarities: "Compared with a one-eyed alley cat in Bangkok, my tabby leads a royal life." *Compare to* puts like things in the same category to create an analogy: "My contented cat's purring could be compared to the hum of a full refrigerator."

complement, compliment. A favorite of advertising copywriters, *complement* is a candidate for one of the most misspelled words in everyday use. A *complement* is something that accompanies, strengthens, or enhances something else. A *compliment* is praise. "He received many compliments about the way the fluorescent chartreuse tie complemented his khaki suit."

complete. See *replete, complete.*

compose. See *comprise, compose.*

compound. See *confound, compound.*

comprise, compose. For centuries, writers have used *comprised of* and *composed of* interchangeably for "to be made up of" despite a difference that springs from the literal meaning of *comprise,* which is "to contain, to be made up of": "My teenaged son's library comprises an astounding number of science fiction titles." *Comprised of* is therefore redundant because it repeats the meaning of *comprise. Comprise* is also frequently seen instead of *compose*—with a plural subject—meaning "to make up": "Her tactful remarks comprised a painless rebuke." *Webster's 10th* and other dictionaries list *compose* as a synonym for *comprise.* However, careful writers keep in mind the traditional dictum that "The whole *comprises* the parts; the parts *compose* the whole." Substituting "is composed of" will avoid controversy. Too, *comprise* often sounds stilted.

compulsion, compunction. These two words are miles apart in meaning but are sometimes confused because of the sense of urgency that both convey. A *compulsion* (from the Latin for "to compel") is an irresistible impulse to perform an irrational act. *Compunction* is the sense of misgiving, reluctance, distress, or anxiety of someone who feels guilty. The Latin root for *compunction* means "to prick," as one's conscience.

concept, idea. *Concept* is not a more formal term for *idea,* although it is commonly found misused that way. A *concept* is a generalization derived from a set of particular facts or theories, such as "the concept of universal entropy." An *idea* means a notion, thought, mental image, or pure abstraction. It is also used to refer to plans for action or programs: "The employees' idea [not concept] for an in-house daycare center was approved by management because it would reduce absenteeism."

concern. See *company, firm, concern.*

condign, consign. *Condign* is an adjective meaning "deserved, worthy, or appropriate": "The judge strove to mete punishment condign with each offense." To *consign* is "to give into another's care or commit to a final destination": "I consign to the flames of hell whoever ate the last of the ice cream and put the empty container back in the freezer."

condole, condone. To *condole* is to express sympathy with another's sorrow. To *condone* is to pardon or view as harmless another's behavior.

confess. See *admit, confess.*

confidant, confident. A *confidant* (n.) is someone who is trusted with secrets; some dictionaries give the spelling *confidante* as the form for a female, but American usage does not make that distinction. One who is *confident* (adj.) is assured.

confound, compound. To *confound* is to puzzle, frustrate, or refute; to *compound* is to add to or increase. "Our hopes for a pleasant trip were confounded by the flight's late arrival, and our dismay was compounded when the hotel announced it had lost our reservation."

connive, conspire. *Connive* comes from Latin and French (*conniver*) meaning "to shut one's eyes" or wink. It means to ignore something evil or disagreeable, although it is often used to mean to *conspire*—"to engage in intrigue, to scheme or plot." Such common phrases as "conniving thief" are actually incorrect; in fact, a guard who pretended not to observe prisoners escape would be the "conniving" one. Writers who are unsure about the correct usage of *conniving* sometimes replace it with "winking at," its original meaning: "The guard winked at the prisoners' escape."

connote, denote. This pair can give even the most loyal word-lover pause when trying to digest the meaning and usage of an expression. A dictionary definition of a word *denotes* its literal, explicit meaning. The nuances, overtones, and implicit meanings of a word used in context are aspects of what it *connotes.* The word "hearth" *denotes* the physical area around a fireplace, but it *connotes* warmth, security, and welcome.

consign. See *condign, consign.*

consist in, consist of. To *consist in* means "to lie or reside in"; *consist of* means "to be composed of." *Consist in* is considered slightly more formal and is sometimes used where *consist of* is called for. The following sentence illustrates correct usage of both: "The only solution *consists in* asking for arbitration when the arguments *consist of* irreconcilable demands."

conspire. See *connive, conspire.*

consul. See *council, consul, counsel.*

contact. Follett said almost 30 years ago that people who hate the verb *contact* to mean "get in touch with" had better get used to it because "there is no way to arrest or reverse the tide of its popularity." He was right.

contagious, infectious. *Contagious* means having an *infection* that is easily and quickly spread to others. All contagious diseases are *infectious* (caused by an infectious agent), but not all infections are *contagious.* Laughter and other pleasant things such as goodwill are said to be both *contagious* and *infectious,* but *contagious* is usually used for unpleasant things while *infectious* has positive connotations.

contemporary, contemporaneous. These adjectives are predominantly considered synonyms, but *contemporaneous* usually means "existing at the same time (either now or in the past)," and *contemporary* often refers to something or someone "present-day or modern." The noun *contemporary,* however, describes a generational peer, though it implies *contemporaneous* (both past and present) sharing of experience.

contemptible, contemptuous. In general, *contemptible* means "worthy of contempt" and *contemptuous* means "showing contempt." In constructions such as "The crowd grew contemptuous of the candidate's patently empty promises," *contemptuous* takes the preposition *of.*

continual, continuous. The differences between these words are so subtle that most dictionaries consider them to be synonyms. *Continual* means starting and stopping in steady succession; *continuous* means occurring without stopping. "An airplane's running lights blink continually; a river flows continuously." As Copperud noted: "Writers who want to be sure their readers perceive the difference would be better off using *intermittent* for *continual* and *incessant* or *uninterrupted* for *continuous.*"

converse, contrary, opposite, reverse. Definitions and a paradigm are the clearest ways to show the distinctions among these terms. All relate to an argument with an original statement. *Converse* means the reversal in order and relation of important elements. Altering Bernstein's example in *The Careful Writer,* if "All editors are crackpots," the *converse* is "All crackpots are editors." *Contrary* means a fact or condition that, if true, is incompatible with the first statement because both cannot be true. The *contrary* to our original statement is "Not all editors are crackpots." *Opposite* means the extreme *contrary* form, or the antithesis. The *opposite* of the original statement is "No editors are crackpots." *Reverse* denotes oppositeness in the most general way, and it includes all the meanings of the other three terms. Bernstein says that "reverse is the word to use unless the writer has a special purpose in mind and a precise knowledge of the meaning of the alternative word . . . selected." In that case, if "All editors are crackpots," the *reverse*—"All crackpots are editors"—is certainly false.

convince. See *persuade, convince, satisfy.*

copious. See *fulsome, copious.*

copyright, patent, trademark. A *copyright* is the exclusive right to prohibit unauthorized publication, production, or sale of a literary, dramatic, musical, or other artistic work. It is granted for a specific period, usually from the date of creation until 50 years after the author's death. A *trademark* is a symbol, design, logo, word, letter, motto, slogan, or the like used by a business to distinguish itself or its products from its competitors. A *patent* in the broadest meaning is simply the granting of some right or privilege; specifically, a *patent* describes a monopoly to produce, sell, or otherwise profit from some invention or process. The most common error in the use of these terms is to say that someone has a *copyright* for a design or logo for a business. Such designs are *trademarked.* (See Chapter 18, Signs and Symbols, and Chapter 23, Copyright, for fuller discussions.)

corespondent, correspondent. A *corespondent* is the third party in an adulterous triangle, the "other" man or woman. *Correspondent* refers to a newspaper, radio, or television reporter, often one who sends in stories from distant locations.

corporal, corporeal. *Corporal* means physical in nature, as in "corporal punishment"; *corporeal* distinguishes the bodily and material realms from the spiritual.

correspondent. See *corespondent, correspondent.*

cost, price, value, worth. *Cost* and *price* both mean the amount paid for something; they can also connote the expenditure of effort or suffering. Although *value* and *worth* often refer to monetary importance, they also ascribe esteem, merit, or excellence to someone or something.

could of. See *should of, would of, could of.*

council, consul, counsel. A *council* is a governing or deliberative body; a *consul* is the representative of a foreign country's interests, an emissary. To *counsel* is to give advice or guidance. See also *attorney, lawyer, counsel, counselor.*

counselor. See *attorney, lawyer, counsel, counselor.*

couple, couple of. One of the confusing collective nouns, *couple* ("a pair of people") traditionally takes a plural verb and, generally, a plural pronoun because it means "more than one person": "The couple are on their way to their honeymoon in Rome." *Couple* is singular when it refers to the couple as a unit: "The couple owns a sumptuous condo." *A couple* meaning two things takes the preposition "of": "May I borrow a couple of eggs?"

create. See *invent, create, discover, develop.*

credible, creditable, credulous. *Credible* means "believable." *Creditable* means "worthy of esteem or praise." *Credulous* describes someone who "believes too easily without proof." A criminal defense lawyer may present *creditable* witnesses, but their testimony may not be *credible* if the jury is a *credulous* one convinced by circumstantial evidence that the charges are true.

credit, attribute. To *credit* (with) has a positive connotation but is often used when "to blame" is actually meant. In this sense, the verb *attribute* (to) is called for. "Police *credit* international terrorists with the bombing of the taxi" is certainly an odd statement, implying as it does that the terrorists deserve credit rather than blame. "Police attribute the bombing of the taxi to international terrorists" is better.

creditable. See *credible, creditable, credulous.*

credulous. See *credible, creditable, credulous.*

crescendo. See *climax, crescendo, culminate.*

crevice, crevasse. A *crevice* (the first syllable is stressed) is a narrow opening or fissure resulting from a split or a crack, as a toehold in rock; a *crevasse* (the second syllable is stressed) is a deep crevice or fissure.

cruelty. See *sadism, cruelty.*

culminate. See *climax, crescendo, culminate.*

curricula, curriculums. Both are correct plural forms in English of "curriculum," but *curricula,* the correct Latin plural, is still more widely used.

cynical, pessimistic, skeptical. Americans have a surprising abundance of words for describing the distrustful disposition or cheerless point of view. They describe a person with a negative attitude toward life. *Cynical* means having a sneering or contemptuous attitude about others' actions or motives: "The electorate has become *cynical* about all politicians' promises." *Pessimistic* implies a pervasively gloomy outlook on life's possibilities: " 'What can go wrong will go wrong' is the *pessimistic* premise known as 'Murphy's Law.' " *Skeptical* means habitually doubtful or unbelieving about things most people accept: "Melanie took Rhett's offer of help at face value, but Scarlett was more *skeptical* because of how he had tricked her before."

D

daily, mundane. *Daily* means "happening every day," not "occurring in the daytime." *Mundane* means "commonplace, ordinary," in the sense of being "characterized by the practical, daily concerns of the world." *Mun-*

dane has a more negative connotation of "boring," whereas *daily* is neutrally descriptive.

damage, injury. *Damage* is the loss or harm that results from injury and, in the plural, can mean the money given to compensate for that loss. *Injury* is damage done to someone physically or morally, as when rights or reputations are violated. "The hurricane caused much property *damage,* but few people suffered *injury.*"

data. The plural verb is always appropriate with the word *data,* which is the plural of *datum.* This usage is in transition, however, and technical writers increasingly use a singular verb with *data* to indicate a body of statistics. "The data proves" may be correct someday, but careful writers have not yet adopted it.

deadly, deathly. *Deadly* means something "lethal, leading to death," but it is often used in a humorous way to mean "drastic" or "serious." *Deathly* means "acting in a deathlike way, resembling the state of death." "A *deathly* silence fell over the press conference when the senator made the *deadly* mistake of telling an ethnic joke."

decimate, annihilate. To *decimate* means "to destroy a large part" of something, literally a tenth of it. To *decimate* is not a synonym for to *annihilate,* which means "to destroy completely." Neither verb makes sense when used with the adverb *nearly* or *completely: decimate* means "largely" and so precludes either, while *annihilate* already includes "completely" and precludes "nearly."

deductive, inductive. These are very different forms of reasoning. A *deductive* argument moves from an established general principle to a specific conclusion. The classic example is "All men are mortal; Socrates is a man; therefore, Socrates is mortal." Note that in the *deductive* argument the conclusion is derived only from information included in the premises. *Deductive* reasoning is best for subjects such as algebra. The danger is that, precisely because information is circumscribed, a false premise will lead to a false conclusion: "If all writers are temperamental, and you are a writer, you are temperamental."

An *inductive* argument moves from specific instances to a general principle: "All the parents I know who are working parents have trouble arranging daycare for their children; therefore, all parents who work have trouble arranging daycare." In the *inductive* argument, the conclusion reaches beyond the information available. *Inductive* reasoning is best for a context such as geometry, where tendencies to the distortion of error, prejudice, and solipsism (the theory that the self is the only thing that can be truly known and one's perceptions are the basis for reality) can be controlled. The truth of the original premise, whether a generalization or an instance, is critically important to the validity of the conclusion.

deficiency. See *lack, deficiency, absence.*

DEBUT AS A VERB

Webster's Dictionary of English Usage and *Merriam-Webster's Collegiate Dictionary,* 10th edition, are among those that accept the widespread journalistic use of *to debut* for "to make (intransitive) or to give (transitive) a first appearance." *To premiere* (or *premier*) has also been used this way since 1933; both seem to be well established as verbs and are fast becoming standard. Interestingly, dictionaries give the past tense form for *premiere* but not for *debut.* If a ballet *premiered* at the Kennedy Center, why shouldn't a reporter write that a new prima ballerina *debuted* in it? Perhaps because adding *ed* to what is, after all, a French cognate ending in a silent *t* creates a word that looks odd, whereas adding a *d* to *premiere* does not seem to be asking English to bend its normal rules for making past participles.

Debut and *premiere* are examples of the "verbing" of nouns, a practice that saves journalists space and provides active wording for headlines but offends and dismays many traditional writers, editors, and lexicographers. Those who consider such usage colloquial at best may use "make a debut," "start," "go into effect," "appear," or "be introduced," but the gauntlet has been tossed: *Debut* appears regularly in such respected newspapers as the *Washington Post* and the *New York Times.*

definitely, definitively. *Definitely* means "assuredly, free from equivocation": "We are definitely planning to attend." *Definitively* means something that is "conclusive, authoritative, or precisely documented." "The study definitively showed a correlation between stress and susceptibility to disease."

deist, theist, religious. A *deist* is one who subscribes to the philosophy of "natural religion" that says the existence of God can be demonstrated by reason alone, without divine revelation. A *theist* simply believes in a god or, more usually, in one God who transcends the world but acts on it as a creator and ruler, known to believers by self-revelation. A *religious* person is devoted to belief in some deity and directs his or her life accordingly, usually but not necessarily observing reverent practices. Both *deists* and *theists* are *religious.*

delay, postpone. Both verbs stall for time: to *delay* connotes the idea of some hindrance preventing something from happening; to *postpone* means "to formally delay until a later time." "The referees will delay the announcement that the game has been postponed until all players arrive."

delegate. See *relegate, delegate.*

delimit. See *limit, delimit.*

demure, demur. These words are spelling and pronunciation confusables. The second syllable is stressed in both, but pronounced "myoor" and "merr," respectively. A *demure* person is "reserved, modest," whereas *to demur* is "to object to something"—something a *demure* person would seldom do, and then only in a polite, low voice.

demurral, demurrer. A polite objection is a *demurral,* except when it's a *demurrer,* the response in a court proceeding by a defendant who agrees that an allegation is true but disputes it as grounds for legal action.

denote. See *connote, denote.*

deprecate, depreciate. To *deprecate* means "to disapprove of," as "A teacher deprecates habitual tardiness." However, *deprecate* is often used to mean to *depreciate,* or "to belittle, disparage, or diminish in value," as "The lawyer's summation deprecated the prosecution's case." This use of *deprecate* for *depreciate* is accepted by dictionaries and some authorities, but careful writers should note that the opposite of *depreciate* is *appreciate* and the opposite of *deprecate* is *approve.* Using these words interchangeably leads to a loss of the distinction between a critical attitude and antagonistic behavior.

deserving of, worthy of. These synonyms carry different connotations. Although each may be followed by nouns of either a positive or negative nature, preferred usage reserves *worthy of* for expressing excellent or meritorious consequences: an action may be both *deserving of* and *worthy of* a bonus, but an evil deed is *deserving of,* not *worthy of,* blame.

deter. Because to *deter* means "to prevent or discourage behavior from happening" and implies intimidation, it is used to refer to animals or people but not directly to things. "The prospect of a $50 ticket deters drivers from speeding"; it does not "deter speeding."

determinism, fatalism, predestination. *Determinism* is the doctrine that all human choices and natural or social phenomena are ruled by cause and effect, meaning that there is no real freedom of will: events govern personal choices. *Fatalism* is the philosophical theory that every detail of our lives is controlled by some external force that has decreed the outcome; we are powerless to avoid or change outcomes or events, especially death. *Fatalism* also connotes personal resignation in the face of inexorable forces. *Predestination* is a technical theological term for the Calvinist doctrine that the salvation of some individuals has been foreordained in accordance with God's knowledge of what their free choices will be; it is not a synonym for either *determinism* or *fatalism.*

deterrent, detriment. A *deterrent* is something that prevents behavior; a *detriment* is an injury or damage.

"The execution of an innocent person is a detriment to the tenet that capital punishment serves as a deterrent to crime."

detract, distract. To *detract* is to take away from something. To *distract* is to draw or direct attention toward a different object or in different directions at the same time.

detriment. See *deterrent, detriment.*

develop. See *invent, create, discover, develop.*

diagnose. A doctor *diagnoses* a patient's condition, not the patient: *not* "Has the doctor diagnosed him as a hypoglycemic?" *but* "Has the doctor diagnosed his dizziness as hypoglycemia?" *or* "Has the doctor made a diagnosis of hypoglycemia?"

dialect. See *vernacular, dialect.*

different. See *varied, various, different.*

different from, different than. *Different from* is the prevalent form, although most authorities agree that *different than* is standard when followed by a clause such as "different than we had heard it would be." The phrase following *different from* should be parallel in structure with the phrase preceding *different from.* For example, "Requirements for women applicants should be no different from men" should be rewritten "no different from those for men" or "no different from the requirements for men." Copperud agrees with Follett and *American Heritage* that *different than* is least acceptable in place of *different from* when making simple comparisons such as "Little boys are simply different than little girls."

differ from, differ with. To *differ from* is to be unlike; to *differ with* is to disagree. *Differ from* may also be used to show disagreement when the nature of the difference is made clear: "The Israelis differ from the Palestinians over the future of Jewish settlement on the West Bank."

diffident, indifferent. *Diffident* describes a person who lacks self-confidence or is shy or reserved. An *indifferent* person may either have a neutral attitude or be aloof, unfeeling, or apathetic. "The *diffident* student hid his eagerness for friendship by acting *indifferent* toward his schoolmates."

dilemma, predicament. A *dilemma* is a situation in which a person must choose between two (or more, according to *American Heritage*) equally undesirable choices. A *predicament* is simply any difficult or dangerous situation.

disapprove. See *disprove, disapprove.*

disassemble. See *dissemble, disassemble.*

disburse. See *dispense (with), disburse, disperse.*

disc, disk, diskette. *Disc* is used to refer to media that is read optically, such as audio compact *discs* (CDs), video *discs,* CD-ROM and WORM (write once, read many) *discs. Disk* refers to media that is read magnetically, such as fixed internal computer drives or removable *diskettes,* also called *disks.* Generally speaking a thin circular object is spelled *disk.*

discerning, discriminating. Someone who is *discerning* sees and understands differences; someone who has *discriminating* taste makes judicious choices among many alternatives.

discomfit, discomfort. These two words are frequently confused in print. To *discomfit* originally meant "to defeat" but has come to mean "to upset or to frustrate someone's plans or expectations." To *discomfort* is "to cause uneasiness or annoyance." "Discomfited by the long wait for a taxi, I was then discomforted by my driver's rapid lane changes."

discover. See *invent, create, discover, develop.*

discreet, discrete. A *discreet* person is cautious and prudent and exercises good judgment. *Discrete* means "separate and distinct," as the *discrete* patterns of the marbles in a collection or the *discrete* parts of a computer. Confusion may arise not only because these words are pronounced alike, but also because the noun form of *discreet* is *discretion,* and dictionaries give "to break down operations into *discrete* parts" as one definition of discretion.

discriminating. See *discerning, discriminating.*

discrimination. See *bias, discrimination, prejudice, bigotry, predilection.*

disingenuous. See *ingenuous, disingenuous, ingenious.*

disinterested, uninterested. *Disinterested* connotes a lack of bias or self-interest, impartiality. *Uninterested* indicates lack of emotional or mental involvement or someone who is bored; an *uninterested* party to a transaction means someone with no financial stake in the outcome. "A disinterested trustee was appointed to watch over the senile investor's funds; relatives were uninterested in taking him into their homes but interested in asking for loans."

disk. See *disc, disk, diskette.*

dispense (with), disburse, disperse. Similar meanings and pronunciations contribute to this set of confusables. To *dispense with* means to suspend or do without, while to *dispense* means to distribute. To *disburse* is to pay out from a fund; to *disperse* is to scatter or spread widely about. "Let us dispense with formalities; we must vote on a plan to dispense charity to our neighbors. If you'll authorize the treasurer to disburse funds for the local food bank, we can disperse hope among those who lack recent good fortune."

disprove, disapprove. To *disprove* an idea or contention is to show that it is false; to *disapprove* of something is to have an unfavorable opinion about it.

dissemble, disassemble. One who *dissembles* pretends or takes pains to present a picture of things as being other than they really are: "When his young nephew proposed an impromptu concert, Uncle Mort dissembled his distaste for the accordion with a rapt expression." To *disassemble* means to take apart.

distinctive, distinguished. A *distinctive* person or thing is "clearly different or recognizable," such as a *distinctive* accent. *Distinguished* means someone or something outstanding in the sense of being eminent, such as a *distinguished* professor or a *distinguished* career.

distract. See *detract, distract.*

distrust, mistrust. Both as verbs and nouns, these are synonyms for "lack of trust or confidence," but *mistrust* also connotes "to suspect or surmise that one is being taken advantage of." "Dogs do not forsake even the harshest owner until, abandoned and starving, they begin to distrust all humans." "She mistrusted his invitation to a private showing of his New Wave etchings."

division. See *category, class, division.*

dock, pier, quay, wharf. In a watery context, a *dock* is the space between two piers or a space designated in the shoreline where ships may anchor. Thus the *dock* is the waterway where the ship itself berths. A *pier, quay,* or *wharf* is the bridgelike physical structure for loading and disembarking passengers and cargo. However, these terms are used interchangeably by all but the saltiest sailors.

double, redouble. To *double* and to *redouble* both mean to make twice as great in size or volume, but *redouble* also connotes "to intensify," while *double* is limited to denoting twoness. "The house painter could double his income if he'd redouble his efforts to learn plastering."

doubtful, dubious. *Doubtful* and *dubious* may both mean "suspicious, unsettled in opinion, or unsettled as to outcome": "The bank is doubtful that I can [or dubious about my ability to] repay the loan I've applied for; I'm dubious about [or doubtful of] my prospects for getting the loan." But *dubious* tends to imply mistrust, whereas *doubtful* suggests simple lack of conviction.

dual, duel. This is chiefly a spelling confusable. *Dual* means "consisting of two parts or elements." A *duel* is formal combat between two people or an antagonistic encounter of ideas or forces.

dubious. See *doubtful, dubious.*

due to, because of. *Due to* is not yet completely accepted as a prepositional phrase equivalent to "because of" in formal writing, but it is well on its way to standard status because of widespread, long-established usage:

"Traffic was delayed due to an overturned oil tanker." But careful writers will still use *because of* for cases of clear cause and effect ("The trucker lost control on the slippery pavement because of [not due to] bald tires") and use *due to* only following forms of the verb *to be,* as in "His fall was due to the icy pavement."

E

each other. See *one another, each other.*

eager. See *anxious (about), eager (to).*

economic, economical. *Economic* refers to economics—the analysis of how goods and services are produced, distributed, consumed, and invested—and is more widely used than *economical,* which means thrifty: "A recession is a vicious economic cycle. Economical consumers try to increase savings but often deplete them on necessities; spenders are better for the economy as a whole but increased personal debt is the nail in a recession's coffin. Thus, neither economical nor spendthrift consumer activity alone can break through an economic recession." These variant forms, however, like other words with the *-ic* and *-ical* suffixes, share some crossover of meaning and therefore usage. See *-ic, -ical* for further discussion of how to make the distinction.

effect. See *affect, effect.*

effective. See *efficient, effective, effectual, efficacious.*

effectual. See *efficient, effective, effectual, efficacious.*

effete, effeminate, feminine. *Effete* means "exhausted, having lost virility or strength, decadent." *Effeminate* is a derogatory description of males who have qualities, tastes, habits, or mannerisms traditionally considered female—such as sensitivity and gentleness. *Feminine* means "appropriate to or characteristic of women." *Effete* is accepted as including an overall connotation of weakness, as is *effeminate.*

efficient, effective, effectual, efficacious. *Efficient* ("functioning properly and economically") is the least likely among these adjectives to be used incorrectly. *Effective,* which means "having or causing a desired result," is close in meaning to *effectual* ("successful at producing a desired result"), but the latter also can mean "binding, valid" in a legal context. *Efficacious* further means "having the power to find an effective solution or remedy." In general, *effective* adequately covers the meaning of both *effectual* and *efficacious,* which are slightly pretentious.

egoism, egotism. The basic distinction here is that an *egoist* is selfish and places self-interest first, while an *egotist* tends to be conceited and self-laudatory. Increasingly, however, au-

ECOLOGY VERSUS ENVIRONMENT

As Americans face the probability that decades of industrial neglect have caused irreversible damage to natural resources, a new vocabulary has emerged to discuss the issues. *Ecology,* technically a term for a branch of science, has been adopted into popular usage to mean both "the study, and the interrelationships themselves, of organisms and their environment": "Using ladybugs instead of poison to control an aphid infestation is ecologically sound." Thus, *ecology* refers to biological balance within the natural *environment,* or specific niches. But *the environment* is also now used as a general term for the resources and species involved in the *ecology* of an area or the country as a whole: "We must recycle waste products to prevent harm to the environment" is a way of saying "We must recycle to preserve overall ecological balance." Containers whose labels proclaim them "environmentally sound" can be recycled or are biodegradable, that is, they do not interfere with the healthy ecology of air, land, and water available to support living creatures. *Ecology* is more specific and is usually reserved for discussing niches or issues: "The ecology of wetland areas is threatened by the development of tract housing."

---

thorities are accepting them as interchangeable.

elder, older. There is no strong distinction. Both can be used for people and things, though *elder* is usually used for people.

elemental, elementary. *Elemental* refers to the forces of nature; *elementary,* to what is basic or introductory. As Sherlock Holmes might have said, "That creatures are governed by their elemental drives is elementary, my dear Dr. Watson."

eliminate. See *obviate, eliminate.*

elusion. See *allusion, illusion, elusion.*

emigrate, immigrate, migrate. People who *emigrate from* (leave) one country to enter another *immigrate into* the new country and settle there. *Migrate to* means to travel from one place, country, region, or climate to another. A mnemonic for the distinction is "*E*migrants *e*xit, *i*mmigrants come *i*n, and *m*igrants *m*ove around."

eminent, immanent, imminent. An *eminent* person is prominent or conspicuous; an *immanent* phenomenon is present or operating from within; an *imminent* event is one about to happen. "A new biography of the eminent poet Rilke, whose spirit is immanent in German romanticism, is imminent."

empty, vacant. *Vacant* means unoccupied by or lacking the customary inhabitant: "a vacant house." It can also refer to the appearance of lacking intelligence: "a vacant stare." *Empty* means completely deprived of contents: "an empty cupboard." When *empty* is used instead of *vacant* to mean "unoccupied," a shorter or more temporary period of absence is indicated: "The conference room is empty now."

enervate, energize. To *enervate* means to make tired; it is not a synonym for *energize,* despite the many times journalists say "The conference speaker enervated the audience."

enormity, enormousness. *Enormity* can connote large size (enormousness) but primarily means "outrageous or wicked behavior" ("the enormity of Nazi war crimes"). *Enormousness,* as *Webster's Ninth* says, "is simply not a popular word," but other synonyms for it can convey a sense of great size without the negative association of *enormity*—"immensity," "hugeness," "vastness"—and thus preserve a useful distinction endorsed by most authorities.

ensure. See *assure, ensure, insure.*

enthuse. *Enthuse* is still not an acceptable word to most authorities though its colloquial use as a verb meaning to "act in an enthusiastic manner" is rampant.

envisage, envision. *Envisage* means to imagine, while *envision,* which is less poetic and means to visualize, has a more realistic connotation.

envy, jealousy. Although often used synonymously, they are different. *Envy* means to covet someone else's possessions or advantages, while *jealousy* implies suspicion that a rival exists.

epigram, epigraph, epitaph. An *epigram* is a witty saying: "Advertising is the rattling of a stick inside a swill bucket" (George Orwell). An *epigraph* can be either an inscription on a building—"The past is prologue" appears on the National Archives Building in Washington, D.C.—or a short introductory statement, often a quotation or motto, placed at the beginning of a book or chapter. An *epitaph* can be either a short tribute to a dead person or an inscription on a tombstone: The writer John Jerome wrote that he was such an optimist that his headstone should read "The good thing about this is. . . ."

epithet. Though widely considered to be a pejorative term, an *epithet* is any term or phrase that describes a person or thing—"carpetbagger," "superman"—or that is used as an evocative substitute for a name, title, or phenomenon—"Wizard of Menlo Park" (Thomas Edison), "inside the Beltway" (the myopic self-absorption of federal bureaucrats working in Washington, D.C.). In theory, an *epithet* may be positive or negative; in practice, most examples are at least tinged with disparagement or disapproval. "Do-gooder" and "supermom" are interesting examples of such *epithets* that combine both good and bad aspects but result in pegging someone as being "naively idealistic" and "overachieving," respectively—undercutting the core of good. The use of catchy *epithets*—"glass ceiling," "Teflon politician"—by journalists may well be the modern replacement for the euphemism.

epitome. *Epitome* once meant a "summary or a part that is representative of the whole," but today it is more often used to mean the very essence of a thing: "She is the epitome of tact." It remains incorrect to use *epitome* for "the very best," "the acme or climax," as in "Winning the gold medal was the epitome of his track career."

equable, equitable. *Equable* means uniform or steady, lacking in extreme or unpleasant variations; it has the sense of "tranquil." "She manages the vagaries of production scheduling with an equable disposition." *Equitable* describes fair and equal dealings, as in "an equitable division of labor."

equally as. This is a redundant construction because *as* means "to the same degree, equally." "The Brontë sisters were equally talented."

equate. To *equate* does not mean "to equal" but "to make equal" and so must be followed by *with* or *to.* "Many people who equate social services programs with freeloading have earned their success the hard way, without help."

equitable. See *equable, equitable.*

equivalent, equivocal, equivocate. *Equivalent* means "equal"; to be *equivocal* is to be "ambiguous or evasive"; to *equivocate* is "to use ambiguous language in an attempt to avoid committing oneself."

error. See *fallacy, error.*

eruption, irruption. An *eruption* is a "surging or spewing forth"; an *irruption* is a "sudden upsurge or violent breaking in." Both nouns have verb forms—*erupt* and *irrupt.* "The audience erupted with applause at the irruption of the Marx Brothers onto the stage."

especially, specially. The former means "to an outstanding extent"; the latter, "for a particular purpose." *Special* is often superfluous when used to describe something obviously outstanding, as a "special commemorative award." "We are especially indebted to Thurlow, who handloomed these napkins specially for this dinner."

essay. See *assay, essay.*

etc. Commonly misspelled "ect." and best avoided in formal writing to mean "and other similar things."

eternity. See *infinity, eternity.*

euphemism. A *euphemism* is a less offensive word substituted for a more generally offensive one. While softening the shock of certain words for the sake of social discretion is legitimate, the danger exists that in moving so far away from the original meaning, euphemisms actually misrepresent reality. In fact, a euphemism itself can become unpleasant when it is too coy or insinuating. The trend is away from falsely genteel terms like "social disease" for syphilis and the rather devilish "therapeutic misadventure" for a patient's dying from a surgeon's error.

evade. See *avoid, evade, avert, prevent.*

everybody, everyone . . . their. The pronoun reference for both *everybody* and *everyone* should as a rule be singular *(his, her,* or *his or her)* except when that leads to obviously ridiculous syntax, as "Everyone has voted and it's a good thing he or she did," where "Everybody voted and it's a good thing they did" is better. (See Chapter 4, Pronouns, for a complete discussion of this practice.)

evince. See *belie, evince.*

evoke, invoke. To *evoke* is "to call forth" but also "to re-create imaginatively or remind"; to *invoke* is "to petition or appeal for help or support." "The president's speech evoked widespread voluntarism when he invoked 'the illumination of a thousand points of light.' "

exacerbate. See *aggravate, exacerbate.*

exalt, exult. To *exalt* means to glorify; to *exult* is to feel joy or triumph.

example, sample. An *example* is a pattern or model to be imitated (or not). A *sample* is one particular product that is meant to represent the quality of all similar products.

except. See *accept, except (from).*

excerpt. See *abridge, abstract, excerpt.*

excuse. See *alibi, excuse* and *extenuate, excuse.*

exercise, excise. To *exercise* is to put something potential into action: "Citizens may exercise the right to vote"; "The school board exercised its authority to cancel all field trips out of the county." *Exercise* also means to undertake actions intended to develop the mind or body or, as a noun, those actions. To *excise* is to remove or cut out something. "I hope this exercise will help excise a few inches from my thighs."

expatiate. See *expiate, expatiate.*

expect. See *anticipate, expect.*

expedient, expeditious. *Expedient* means "suitable or opportune" (adj.) or "a means to an end" (n.); *expeditious* means "undertaken speedily and efficiently." Garrison Keillor's paean to Powdermilk Biscuits—"Heavens they're tasty, and expeditious"—while amusing, doesn't make much sense.

expiate, expatiate. To *expiate* a sin is "to atone" for it; to *expatiate* on the virtues of walking a mile a day is "to expound in rambling detail" on many aspects and tangents of the topic.

explicit, implicit. *Explicit* means plainly or clearly stated. *Implicit* means understood (because clearly implied) but not stated.

extemporaneous, impromptu. *Extemporaneous* remarks may have been carefully prepared but are presented both unmemorized and without recourse to notes or text, as if spontaneously. *Impromptu* remarks are improvised on the spur of the moment.

extenuate, excuse. To *extenuate* is to lessen or mitigate the seriousness of something; the commonly used adjective is *extenuating*. To *excuse* is to forgive without diminishing the gravity of the offense, often because of *extenuating* circumstances.

exult. See *exalt, exult.*

F

face, face up to. Both are acceptable verbs. The former means "to confront" and the latter, "to stand one's ground" or "to admit or acknowledge the facts or truth" about something.

factitious, fictitious. *Factitious* means artificial or contrived but not necessarily intending to deceive; *fictitious* means invented.

Fahrenheit. See *Celsius, centigrade, Fahrenheit.*

fail. To *fail* means to fall short at something undertaken, but it is often misused to indicate something simply did not happen or occur: In the example, "We failed to awaken in time," waking up is not a true undertaking. When no deliberate attempt has been made, the appropriate word is *neglect:* "The committee proposing a new tax neglected [not failed] to take the strength of public opposition into account."

fallacious. See *specious, plausible, fallacious.*

fallacy, error. A *fallacy* is a plausible but erroneous or illogical argument that may be misleading; an *error* is simply a mistake, something wrong. "A mistake in calculation results in an erroneous [not fallacious] checkbook balance."

false. See *synthetic, false.*

famous. See *notorious, infamous, famous.*

farther, further. Careful writers still observe the differences: *Farther* indicates a physical distance (think "*far away*"); *further* means "in addition to." Most authorities have observed that this distinction has either disappeared or is about to. An informal survey of current writing supports their conclusion.

fatal, fateful. *Fatal* means causing death. *Fateful* describes important or prophetic consequences that may be good or evil; it is more often used for ominous or disastrous events, however.

fatalism. See *determinism, fatalism, predestination.*

feasible. See *practical, practicable, feasible, possible.*

feature. As a verb, *feature* got its start as a journalistic term for "to show or exhibit prominently." Although overused, this word is now generally accepted as both verb and noun.

feel, feel like, think. Although once widely criticized when used to indicate anything other than emotion or groping, to *feel* is now standard—except in strictly scientific writing—for the senses of "to *think,* believe, perceive, and be convinced of." Conversely, to *think* can imply belief and emotion: "I think you should apologize immediately." *Feel like* is incorrect in the sense of to *think.* When used as a substitute for *think* or *believe, feel* is considered incorrect by careful writers: "The city health department feels a need to change its AIDS notification policy."

feminine. See *effete, effeminate, feminine.*

fewer, less. The distinction that survives between these words strikes an impressive blow for preservation of the language. Little by little, it seems, grocery and other retail store managers across the nation have been persuaded by alert customers to correct the signs at quick check-out lanes to read "Fewer [not less] than 10 items." Here's the distinction. *Fewer* is used with plural nouns for things that can be counted one by one. *Less* modifies singular nouns denoting a quantity or a concept that does not have separately countable parts. "Fewer working parents spend time reading with their children because they have less free time [or fewer free hours] to spare."

fictitious. See *factitious, fictitious.*

figuratively. See *literally, figuratively.*

(to) figure, it figures (that). Meaning "to conclude, decide, think," to *figure* is standard but informal; *it figures* is slang for "it is to be expected."

fine. *Fine* is considered by some to be dialectal when used as an adverb, as in "The new spreadsheets are working out fine," but the sense of "very well" has long been established.

fire. When used to mean "to dismiss from employment," *fire* is considered a colloquial American expression. To *fire* seems refreshingly blunt when compared with today's prevalent corporate euphemisms, such as "to reduce in force" or "dehire."

firm. See *company, firm, concern.*

fix. This all-purpose verb is usually better replaced with a more precise one—repair, prepare, locate, determine.

flack. See *flak, flack.*

flagrant. See *blatant, flagrant.*

flail, flay. These words may sound similar, but they are quite different in meaning. To *flay* is to tear the skin off; a second meaning is to criticize sharply. To *flail* is to move in a whipping or swinging motion; it comes from the noun *flail,* a device used to thresh grain by hand.

flair, flare. This is a spelling confusable. *Flair* means an innate power of discernment, or a natural aptitude or bent. *Flair* originally meant an odor or sense of smell; it can be traced back to the Old French verb *flairer,* to give off an odor. A *flare* is a flame or a light used to signal or illuminate; it also means a widening, as "flared nostrils."

flak, flack. *Flak* means "antiaircraft fire and its shell fragments" but has also come to mean excessive criticism; *flack,* a variant spelling for both of those meanings, is also slang for a public relations person. Interestingly, *flak* was originally a German acronym for ***Fl**ieger**a**bwehr**k**anonen,* literally, "flyer defense cannon." More recently, *flak* has been used by journalists as a verb meaning "to promote or publicize"—in other words, to "run interference" for a third party with the press. This seems to be a mistaken variation on the noun *flack,* which is already a variant form. Dictionaries do not yet list *flak* in this verb sense; once again, popular ingenuity may be at work rearranging the linguist's neat patterns.

flammable, inflammable. Historically, these words have been interchangeable. They are derived from the same Latin root, *flammare,* "to set fire." If something can catch fire and burn, it is *flammable,* and a warning to that effect on a product should use this unambiguous word. The prefix in *inflammable* serves as an intensifier to mean "to set violently on fire." There's good reason to avoid using this word on a warning label: Some people may think the prefix is negative and believe that *inflammable* means "not flammable." The coinage *flameable* has been used by some manufacturers as way to show the meaning more clearly, but *flammable* is a safe choice.

flare. See *flair, flare.*

flaunt, flout. These two are frequently confused in both print and speech. To *flaunt* is to show off or proudly display something; to *flout* is to scorn or ignore a convention or rule. "Youth flaunts its belief in immortality by flouting the speed limit."

flay. See *flail, flay.*

flounder, founder. A person who *flounders* is struggling or flailing clumsily. A ship that *founders* fills with water and sinks; this word can also mean collapse or fail.

flout. See *flaunt, flout.*

fluid, liquid. Technically speaking, a *fluid* can mean either a liquid or a gas. A *liquid* is the form of matter that is neither gas nor solid.

for, because. Both words can be used as conjunctions, but the difference between them lies in the way they join additional material to a main clause. *For* is used more as a coordinating, not a subordinating, conjunction; it adds some explanatory information rather than establishing a cause-effect relationship with the main clause: "Clarence's application was unanimously approved, for his qualifications were superior." *Because* is a subordinating conjunction that builds a stronger cause-effect relationship between the main and subordinate clauses: "Clarence applied for the scholarship because his family's finances were stretched thin." The use of *for* as a subordinating conjunction is now considered somewhat oldfashioned in tone: "Clarence's prospects were brilliant, for he had a Harvard degree."

forceful, forcible. *Forceful* is the preferred of these two similar adjectives except when denoting purely physical or extraordinary use of force: "The rescue crew joined in a *forcible* lifting of the car's front end to free the trapped pedestrian."

forego, forgo. Although some dictionaries give these words as alternate spellings, careful writers distinguish between them. To *forego* means "to go before or precede"; to *forgo* means "to abstain from or do without" something. The adjective forms *foregone* and *forgone* carry similar meanings: "a foregone conclusion" is one that was made beforehand; a "forgone plan" is one that was not carried out.

foreword, forward. *Forward* is often seen instead of *foreword* in reference to the introductory pages of a book. Remembering that the *foreword* means "words that come in the front of the book, be*fore* the book itself begins" will help writers with this spelling confusable. By the way, *preface* and *foreword* are now accepted as synonyms, although traditionally the preface is written by the author and the foreword by someone else—the publisher, an editor, or a colleague.

for free, gratis, pro bono. These all convey the idea of "without cost," but each has a specific application. The idiom *for free* is well-established in general prose but is not appropriate in formal writing. *Gratis* conveys a slightly superior tone but is correct in a formal context; it adds the sense of "serving without fee or compensation." *Pro bono* means "for the public good" and usually indicates the reduction or waiving of fees for professional services to the indigent or for a worthy cause.

forgo. See *forego, forgo.*

form. See *formulate, form.*

formidable, impressive. *Formidable* should be reserved for contexts where a feeling of awe or apprehension or a level of great difficulty is being indicated; *impressive* conveys respect or admiration.

formulate, form. To *formulate* is pretentious except when used literally to mean "work out as a formula" as in math or science. To *form* is preferred in most cases to mean "to give shape or structure to something": "Two-year-old children can form simple sentences without knowing one rule of grammar."

forthright, forthcoming. A *forthright* person is one who is frank or candid. A person who is *forthcoming* is accessible, or responsive; information that is said to be *forthcoming* will be available soon.

fortuitous, fortunate. Although some dictionaries consider these words synonyms, there is a difference worth preserving. *Fortuitous* means "happening by accident or chance," whereas *fortunate* means "lucky."

forward. See *foreword, forward.*

founder. See *flounder, founder.*

fulsome, copious. Both words mean "abundant," but careful writers should be aware that *fulsome,* now as in the 17th century, is a mild, all-purpose term of abuse: To say that someone has offered his boss "fulsome praise" is to indicate bootlicking.

further. See *farther, further.*

G

gamut, gantlet, gauntlet. Originally a musical term for a series of notes, *gamut* is now widely used to express the idea of entire series, "a range that is run through," as in "a gamut of emotions." A *gantlet* is "a course of abuse that is run through" in the sense of being endured. A *gantlet* was a military punishment whereby the accused was forced to run through two files of peers while they flailed away at him. A *gauntlet* is a glove, "thrown down" to signify a challenge. Some dictionaries give *gauntlet* as a synonym for *gantlet.*

gather. See *glean, gather.*

gender, sex. *Gender* is, strictly speaking, a grammatical attribute of agreement between nouns and pronouns and adjectives in some languages. It does not always connect logically to *sex* in the sense of what we consider to be maleness or femaleness, as witnessed by the gender category "neuter." *Gender* is routinely misused for *sex,* especially in social science and medical parlance, but terms like "gender role" and "gender gap" have gained such acceptance that the distinction is fast disappearing. *Gender* is useful, however, in a context where *sex* might inadvertently connote "sexuality"; "gender politics" is an example.

germane, relevant, apropos. Something *germane* is not only relevant but appropriate—that is, fitting to a situation or occasion. *Relevant* implies that a logical, significant connection can be shown, and something *apropos* is both relevant and opportune—convenient and timely. "Not religious beliefs but relevant education and experience are germane to an employment application. It is apropos to bring an extra copy of one's résumé to an interview." *Apropos* can also mean "by the way," as a preface to adding a comment related to the context. "Apropos of your plans to move, I know a good real estate agent who covers that area."

get. This simple verb gets around; *The American Heritage Dictionary* defines more than 100 distinctive connotations. The use of the passive in phrasal verbs—"The train got delayed," "We just got by on one paycheck," and "He got promoted"—should be avoided in formal writing. In the last example, *got* serves to add emphasis to the role of the subject: It's implied that the promotion wasn't a matter of course ("As a result of his success, he was promoted") but was struggled for ("He finally got what he deserved"). Such constructions are obviously useful; that's why there are so many. In less formal writing, you can get away with them.

gibe, jibe. To *gibe* means "to taunt or jeer at." To *jibe* is "to correspond or be in agreement with." Because they are pronounced identically, and some dictionaries allow *jibe* as a synonym for *gibe,* care should be taken to make the context clear. A commonly heard mispronunciation of *jibe* is "jive."

glean, gather. To *glean* means to gather (collect) little by little, with great labor; *glean*'s original meaning was to gather grains left on the ground by reapers. In the sense of "to learn, understand, or discover," both *glean* and *gather* are standard.

good, well. Students were once taught that "I feel good" is incorrect as a statement of health and well-being. But James Brown sang it with impunity, and today most grammarians agree that both *good* and *well* are acceptable predicate adjectives after linking verbs. But a few distinctions are made by most speakers. Saying "You look well" or "I feel well" is more often used to express good health. "I feel good" adds the element of high spirits or happiness to health. "Blue looks good on you" or "Calling in sick wouldn't look good" refers to appearance or image rather than health. Otherwise, *well* is the correct choice for adverbial use with nonlinking verbs.

The use of *good* as an adverb—primarily in speech and journalistic writing, especially about sports—is less correct, though stubbornly widespread. *Good* is preferred even by many speakers who "know better" when they want to convey the sense that something has been performed admirably; it seems more vivid than the more neutral *well. Webster's Dictionary of English Usage* gives the example of a coach who said his team played *good* but went on to say that they shot and rebounded *well.* A standard adverbial use of *good* is to modify the adjective *many:* "A good many coaches have been heard to say their teams played good."

gourmet, gourmand. The original distinction—a *gourmet* is a connoisseur and a *gourmand* is a glutton—is increasingly being lost, as dictionaries show the two words to be synonyms.

graduated (from). The correct form of statement is "The seniors will graduate from college in May." Neither "They will be graduated from college" nor "They will graduate college" is correct.

gratis. See *for free, gratis, pro bono.*

grill, grille. A cooking grate or an informal restaurant is called a *grill;* other kinds of grates may be spelled either *grill* or *grille,* although the latter is considered pretentious. To *grill* is colloquial for "to interrogate," a usage derived from the idea of torturing victims by applying heat, literally "grilling" them.

grisly, grizzly. Perhaps because they are pronounced alike, *grisly,* meaning "gruesome," is often misspelled *grizzly,* meaning "gray" or "grizzled."

H

hail. See *haul, hale, hail.*

hale. See *haul, hale, hail.*

hanged, hung. *Hanged* is now used only in the sense of being executed by hanging. *Hung* is also heard informally to mean executed, but usually, "We hung the wreath on the front door" and "The judge dismissed the hung [stalemated] jury."

happen. See *transpire, happen.*

hardly. The adverbial form of *hard* is preferably also *hard,* not *hardly,* which may be misunderstood for "scarcely" when the opposite—"severely" or "strongly"—is intended. "The batter hit the baseball hard"; "The rain fell hard on the parched clay."

has got to, has to. These informal equivalents of the auxiliary *must* are transitional and are not completely acceptable in formal usage.

haul, hale, hail. To *haul* is "to carry"; to *hale* is "to bring into court" and derives from to *haul;* to *hail* is "to greet with enthusiasm."

healthy, healthful, wholesome. *Healthy* chiefly means the condition of being free from disease and therefore suggests vitality and strength: "To stay fit and healthy, exercise and eat a healthful diet." But it can also mean *healthful,* which describes something that promotes health: "Yelling can be a healthy way to express anger." The choice between *healthy* and *healthful* is a matter of emphasis—on a state of being or a conducive agent. *Wholesome* suggests attractive healthiness: "She showed a wholesome appetite for learning."

Hellenic. See *Attic, Hellenic, Hellenistic.*

hilarious. This adjective means "noisily boisterous" or "mirthful," so it is not merely synonymous with "wildly comical" unless the laughter involved is loud and long.

historic, historical. *Historic* means significant to history (a historic landmark or occasion). *Historical* means based on a particular period of history or events that happened in the past (a historical novel, historical records). Both adjectives take *a*, not *an*, which is now considered pretentious. Persistent use of *an* dates from a period of English pronunciation when the *h* in *history* was not pronounced and *an* provided elision.

hoard, horde. To *hoard* is to save in a miserly fashion; a *horde* is a teeming crowd.

Hobson's choice. This phrase means "no real choice at all, an ultimatum," as originally delivered by Thomas Hobson, a 16th-century stablekeeper who told his clients: "Take the horse closest to the door or take no horse at all." It does not mean a dilemma.

homogeneous, homogenous. *Homogeneous* means "uniform throughout in structure and composition" and is the more common term. The strict meaning of *homogenous* refers to a "correspondence between parts that share a common ancestral origin," but it appears frequently as a misspelling of *homogeneous.*

hopeful. See *optimistic, hopeful.*

hopefully. *Hopefully* means "in a hopeful manner," not "I hope (that)" or "it is hoped," but the misusage is so common that even some otherwise conservative editors and authorities have given up hope and are allowing it. The usage panel of *The American Heritage Dictionary,* however, did not accept this usage in 1992. *Hopefully* usually begins a sentence: "Hopefully [we hope that], voicemail will improve our ability to respond to the increased volume of callers." Rarely is *hopefully* correctly used: "Hopefully [with hope], the child lifted the cookie jar lid." Rewriting with a conditional expression is often the best way to convey a desired course of action: "Installing voicemail should improve our ability to respond."

horde. See *hoard, horde.*

human, humane, humanitarian, humanistic. *Human* means mortal, fallible, or related to generic mankind; *humane* means acting in a sympathetic, considerate way toward other people and animals. *Humanitarian* means acting to promote human welfare and social reform; *humanistic* means devoted to the humanities or describes an attitude that supports the dignity, worth, and potential of each individual. The *Washington Post* quoted a spokesman for a group of prison inmates who had collected $1,300 to help pay medical bills for a child injured by vicious dogs, as saying, "We have committed crimes. But we are human. And this is the humanitarian thing to do." These inmates are paid 53 cents an hour;

their generosity may be called *humane* as well.

hung. See *hanged, hung.*

hyperbola, hyperbole, hyperbolic. A *hyperbola* is a geometric shape formed by slicing off the side of a cone at the fat end; *hyperbole* is extravagant exaggeration or inflated language. The adjective *hyperbolic* may refer to either meaning.

hypocritical, hypercritical. *Hypocritical* describes people who pretend to have virtues or qualities that they do not in fact possess; *hypercritical* means overly or unduly censorious.

I

-ic, -ical. Some *-ic, -ical* pairs have clearly distinctive meanings when used as adjectives: a "music teacher"—who teaches music—is not the same as a "musical teacher"—who sings or plays an instrument or otherwise participates personally in the practice and enjoyment of music. Other such pairs, like *electric* and *electrical,* are, for all intents and purposes, interchangeable. There does not seem to be any clear rule, although in some cases the *-ic* form tends toward exclusive usage as a noun, as in the case of *fanatic.*

idea. See *concept, idea.*

identical to, identical with. Both prepositions are correct when describing sameness.

idle, idyll. To be *idle* is to be inactive; an *idyll* (also spelled *idyl*) is a romantic interlude or a simple, rustic, pastoral scene or mood.

if, whether. *Whether* and *if* are interchangeable as long as the meaning is clear and the construction sensible. *Whether* is considered the more formal word and is preferred at the beginning of a sentence to introduce a noun clause: "Whether any of us had won the office football pool was the topic of the morning." When the clause does not begin the sentence, either *if* or *whether* may be used after such verbs as *ask, doubt, hear, learn,* and *know:* "Did you ask if we must be present to win?"

A note of caution: *If* can be confusing in some cases when *whether* would be clear: "Tell me if I have spinach between my teeth" could be taken to mean "Tell me when and if I do" or "Tell me now whether or not I do." *Whether* implies "or not," so saying "whether or not" is usually unnecessary, though it has been considered as acceptable idiom for more than 300 years. The one case where adding "or not" is not optional is the use of *whether* to introduce a noun clause that functions in the sentence as an adverb: "Whether or not you agree with my politics, you must let me practice them."

ignorant. See *oblivious, ignorant.*

ilk, kind, kin. The use of *ilk* to mean *kind* or "class" should be avoided. Chiefly a Scottish idiom, *ilk* means "the same in name or place." *Kin* is always a collective and therefore plural reference to relatives.

illegal, illicit, illegitimate. What is *illegal* is against the law; something *illicit* is not permitted or not moral but may not be against the law. *Illegitimate* means something not sanctioned by law or custom or born of parents who were not married to each other.

illegible, unreadable. *Illegible* means undecipherable handwriting or type, and *unreadable* means writing that cannot be understood because of poor construction or phrasing. Now that machines can "read," *unreadable* is also used to refer to pages of type that text scanning devices cannot process.

illegitimate. See *illegal, illicit, illegitimate.*

illicit. See *illegal, illicit, illegitimate.*

illusion. See *allusion, illusion, elusion.*

immanent. See *eminent, immanent, imminent.*

immigrate. See *emigrate, immigrate, migrate.*

imminent. See *eminent, immanent, imminent.*

immoral. See *amoral, immoral, unmoral.*

immured, inured. These words sound somewhat alike but are quite different. To be *immured* is to be enclosed in or walled in; to be *inured* is to be accustomed to hardship or something disagreeable.

impact, influence. All but the most punctilious of grammarians have given up the fight over the use of *impact* as a verb synonymous with "to *influence* or have an effect on." However, a caveat: editors and readers who hate to see *impact* used this way really, really hate it. Some don't even like *impact* as a noun if *effect* can be used instead: "The president's open manner had a positive effect on the participants in the peace talks." All agree with this usage, however: "The earth's atmosphere diminishes a meteor's impact."

impassable, impassible, impassive. An *impassable* road is one that blocks travel; an *impassible* face shows no outward sign of pain or suffering; an *impassive* face is generally expressionless.

impasse. See *stalemate, impasse.*

implicit. See *explicit, implicit.*

imply, infer. To *imply* means to insinuate or express indirectly. To *infer* means to derive a general conclusion from specifics or by the use of inductive reasoning. "Listeners can *infer* from a speech a point of view contrary to what the speaker intended to *imply.*"

impressive. See *formidable, impressive.*

impromptu. See *extemporaneous, impromptu.*

inartistic, unartistic. Someone who is *inartistic* does not conform to or appreciate the principles of art. Someone who is *unartistic* has no artistic ability.

in behalf of, on behalf of. *Webster's Dictionary of English Usage* says that numerous commentators (especially the British) insist on preserving a distinction between these phrases, along these lines: Use *in behalf of* to mean "for the benefit of" and *on behalf of* to mean "serving as the representative or spokesman for." Copperud and others, however, agree with the predominantly American usage of either *in* or *on* for both senses. Including the word *the* before *behalf* is unnecessary.

inchoate. See *incoherent, inchoate.*

incipient, insipid. The former means "about to begin or soon to become apparent." The latter means "dull, flat, lacking in interesting qualities." When these words are confused, an association with the condition of boredom is the likely culprit: "incipient boredom" is on its way; something "insipidly boring" is flatly uninspired.

incoherent, inchoate. An *incoherent* speaker makes no sense because his or her thoughts are irrelevant or lack organization, although they may form complete sentences. *Inchoate* thoughts or ideas are only partly formed: "When Dan began to speak, his discussion of the categorical imperative was merely inchoate; by the time he finished, he was so incoherent that we cried out, 'We simply Kant take any more!' "

indifferent. See *diffident, indifferent.*

individual, person. Although as nouns the two words are recognized by dictionaries as synonyms, *person* is preferred except when single human beings are being contrasted with an organization or group: "To paraphrase Thoreau, a free and enlightened state must recognize the individual as a higher and independent power." See also *persons, people.*

inductive. See *deductive, inductive.*

in effect, in fact. *In effect* is not set off with commas when used to mean "for practical purposes." *In fact* is often set off with commas when it is used to mean "in addition to, moreover."

ineffective, inefficacious, ineffectual. These terms are synonymous; *inefficacious* is rarely used and is considered pretentious.

in fact. See *in effect, in fact.*

infamous. See *notorious, infamous, famous.*

infectious. See *contagious, infectious.*

infer. See *imply, infer.*

infinity, eternity. *Infinity* indicates an unlimited extent of both time and space, or an indefinitely great number or amount (with *of*). *Eternity* denotes limitless or immeasurable time only.

inflammable. See *flammable, inflammable.*

influence. See *impact, influence.*

inform. See *advise (to), inform (of).*

ingenuous, disingenuous, ingenious. *Ingenuous* means unguarded or naive; *disingenuous* means lacking in candor or pretending innocence. *Ingenious,* often confused with *ingenuous,* means clever or inventive.

in half. This is acceptable usage to mean divided into two equal parts or halves.

in, into. *In* means located inside an area or limits. *Into* means in the direction of the interior, or toward something. See Chapter 8, Articles, Prepositions, and Conjunctions, for further discussion.

injury. See *damage, injury.*

inquiry. See *query, inquiry.*

insert, inset. *Insert* means to put in or introduce something from outside into another body. An *inset* is the part, section, or thing that fits inside the outer whole. In other words, an inset is inserted, but not vice versa.

insipid. See *incipient, insipid.*

insistent. See *persistent, insistent.*

instinctive. See *intuitive, instinctive.*

insure. See *assure, ensure, insure.*

intense, intensive. *Intense* implies strong focus or concentration; *intensive* means a strong effort.

intercede, intervene. To *intercede* means to come between parties in order to reconcile differences. To *intervene* is to interrupt or to come between parties to directly influence the outcome of a dispute. "Once the fight started, the teacher realized she was too late to intercede, but she decided to intervene before anyone was seriously injured."

inter-, intra-. *Inter-* is a prefix meaning "between." *Intra-* is a prefix meaning "within." An *inter*state highway runs between states; an *intra*state road runs within the borders of one state.

internecine, internal. *Internecine* carries the sense of mutually destructive *internal* behavior: "The real estate agents' internecine competition drove clients away."

interrupt. See *intrude, interrupt.*

intersect. See *bisect, intersect.*

intervene. See *intercede, intervene.*

into. See *in, into.*

intra-. See *inter-, intra-.*

intrude, interrupt. *Intrude* connotes trespassing or entering a place uninvited; *interrupt,* to stop or hinder an activity or a conversation by breaking in.

intuitive, instinctive. These words represent different avenues or origins for unpremeditated acts, feelings, insights, or knowledge. *Intuition* is immediate or direct "knowing" without using reason or analysis. *Instinct* is inborn, unlearned behavior that leads creatures (including humans) to respond, without thinking or conscious intention, to certain stimuli. Good writers observe the distinction between an inferred mental process *(intuition)* and an internal process with demonstrable effects *(instinct).* "She instinctively blinked when the lights came on" is correct, but "She instinctively knew the car would swerve into her lane" is not. In the latter sentence, the realization is *intuitive*—that is, without conscious thought. Some feelings straddle the distinction between the two: In a statement like "He intuitively [or instinctively] distrusted the salesman," either may be correct.

inured. See *immured, inured.*

invent, create, discover, develop. To *invent* and to *create* are given by dictionaries as synonyms for bringing something into existence, but *invent* connotes "producing something useful for the first time after ingenious thinking and experimentation"; *create* implies evoking life where it did not exist or bringing something into being for its own sake. "The invention of the portable computer makes it easier for a writer to create a document while traveling." To *discover* is to gain knowledge, for the first time, about something that already exists. To *develop* means to advance or perfect something that exists. "The discovery of gold started a frantic rush to stake and develop claims."

inventor. See *progenitor, inventor.*

invoke. See *evoke, invoke.*

ironic, sarcastic, sardonic. Many Americans seem to like their humor on the tart side. The following terms describe tones of voice or kinds of posturing that convey a critical attitude. *Sarcastic* means marked by bitterness and the intent to hurt by making stinging remarks: " 'Would you like to borrow my toothbrush, too?' Ruby sarcastically remarked to her younger sister, who had just used her comb and hand mirror." *Ironic* implies "an attempt to be provocatively amusing by saying the opposite of what is meant: " 'It's in the newspaper so it must be true,' the reporter ironically asserted to his colleague." *Sardonic* connotes a scornful facial expression or mocking tone of voice: "The title clerk permitted herself a small sardonic smile as she pulled down the Go to the Next Window sign."

irregardless. This word is criticized as a redundancy and a barbarism for *regardless.*

irruption. See *eruption, irruption.*

iterate. See *repeat, iterate, reiterate, recur (reoccur), recapitulate.*

it figures. See *(to) figure, it figures (that).*

its, it's. *It's,* the contraction for "it is," is often mistakenly used for the possessive pronoun *its.*

-ize. This suffix had its start as a useful tool for creating new English verbs. It expresses submission to the idea or activity given in the root word (popular-ize, marginal-ize). Unfortunately, in the past 20 years the device has been sorely overworked, perhaps because those who use it think a longer word sounds more important. *Finalize,* for example, is merely an ostentatious way to say "decide" or "settle" or "finish."

J

jealousy. See *envy, jealousy.*

jibe. See *gibe, jibe.*

K

karat. See *carat, karat, caret.*

kin. See *ilk, kind, kin.*

kind. See *character, kind, sort* and *ilk, kind, kin.*

kind of (a), sort of (a). These expressions are inappropriate as adverbs in formal writing when used to mean "somewhat, in a sense," as in "I'm kind of [or sort of] confused about that," and also when used with the article *a* before a noun. They are standard usage to mean "an approximation of, characterized as": "Music can be a kind of tranquilizer," but not "Music can be kind of a tranquilizer." Problems of agreement arise because speakers routinely get away with using *kind of* and *sort of* in ways that formal writing does not permit. The following examples are incorrect: "What kind of a [omit the *a*] movie is it?" "Those kind of movies [movies of that kind] lead to aggressive behavior." "Those kinds of films [use film—singular is preferred for the generic class] are cathartic fun." "That kind of movies [movie] makes a fortune." As a rule, if the noun following *kind of* or *sort of* is abstract, make it singular, and don't preface it with an article.

kudos. Though it looks plural, *kudos* is a singular noun derived from a Greek word meaning acclaim or praise and thus takes a singular verb.

L

lack, deficiency, absence. A *lack* is a *deficiency* (shortage) of something that is essential or desirable. Mere *absence*—being away—implies neither a loss nor a shortage of something needed.

languid. See *limpid, languid.*

larceny. See *robbery, larceny, theft, burglary.*

last, latest, past. *Last* and *latest* are usually interchangeable and clearly understood in context, though *last* can mean "final" and *latest* can mean "most recent." Avoid using *last* when *past* is more accurate: "during the past decade" (meaning the decade immediately preceding this one), but "during the last decade of the 19th century" (meaning the 1890s).

later, latter. *Later* means after some point in time. *Latter* means the second of two things just previously mentioned. Avoid using *latter* when the series has more than two items; *last mentioned* is more accurate.

latest. See *last, latest, past.*

laudable, laudatory. Something that deserves praise is *laudable;* a person or speech that confers praise is the *laudatory* agent.

lawyer. See *attorney, lawyer, counsel, counselor.*

lay. See *lie, lay.*

lectern, podium. A *lectern* is a rack or reading desk on which a speaker places notes; a *podium* is the raised platform, or *dais* (pronounced either day-is or die-is), that a speaker or conductor stands on.

lend. See *loan, lend.*

less. See *fewer, less.*

liable. See *apt, likely, liable, prone.*

liaison, liaise. Often misspelled *liason, liaison* originally was reserved for "a linking up or connecting of two or more entities" or "an illicit love affair." Its use has expanded to encompass the person whose function it is to make and maintain a connection. To *liaise* is a British colloquialism for "establishing a liaison with" and should be avoided in formal language.

lie, lay. To *lie* is an intransitive verb; it means to recline (lie, lay, lain). To *lay* is a transitive verb; it means to put something down (lay, laid, laid).

lighted, lit. Either is acceptable as past tense and past participle of *light.* "George lit [or lighted] the fire."

like. See *as if, as though, like.*

like, such as, as. *Like* is used by careful writers when making a simile: "Commuting in bumper-to-bumper traffic to work is like a penance for polluting the air with exhaust." Copperud says that *like* is often preferable to *such as* when making a simple comparison, as, for example, "Poems are made by fools like me." *As* is reserved for creating a metaphor: "She is as lovely as a summer's day." *Like* and *as* are not interchangeable as conjunctions. It's hard to find agreement on the use of *such as;* many authorities do not even discuss it. Attempts by some to make a distinction by reserving *such as* to introduce examples and *like* to compare resemblances have been called nitpicking by Theodore Bernstein. *Webster's Dictionary of English Usage* says, "The fact that opinions vary so greatly on this matter is enough to suggest that standard usage itself varies a great deal." "Poems are made by fools like me" sounds simpler than the stilted "Poems are made by fools such as I," but the point is that in either case meaning is not ambiguous. See *as if, as though, like* for a history and further commentary.

likely. See *apt, likely, liable, prone.*

limit, delimit. *Limit* is "to enclose within a boundary" (verb) or is "the utmost extent" (noun). *Delimit* is used only as a verb and means "to fix or define the limits of." A *delimiter* is a character that marks the beginning or end of a unit of data on magnetic tape, for example.

limpid, languid. *Limpid,* from the Latin *limpa* for water, means clear and simple in style or serene and untroubled. *Languid* means weak, slow, drooping, or exhausted.

liquid. See *fluid, liquid.*

lit. See *lighted, lit.*

literally, figuratively. *Literal* means "true to the exact meaning of the words," but many writers use it misguidedly to "warn" readers that a description is *figurative*—meaning "so to speak, but not strictly true"—thereby defeating the very definition. The sportswriter who writes "The crowd greeted the umpire's call with a roar that literally woke the dead" does not mean that zombies filled the infield. He means "with a roar that would have awakened the dead if they could be awakened." The problem may be that using the word *figurative* is often redundant; no one would ever say "She figuratively bent over backwards with kindness." *Literally* is used more legitimately to emphasize the reality of facts or events that could be mistaken as figurative: "He literally fell on the floor laughing." In general, *literal* is overused both as a disclaimer and an enhancer; it should be reserved to mean "without exaggeration": "Kuwait was literally in flames when the Iraqis left."

livid, lurid. *Livid* means "black and blue," as discolored by bruises, or ashen; it also means "enraged." *Lurid* means "red or flaming" as well as gruesome, grisly, or hellish. Because *livid* can mean "angry," often it is thought incorrectly to mean "reddened."

loan, lend. *Loan* is a noun meaning "that which is borrowed"; *to lend* is the verb to use when meaning "to allow to borrow." *Loan* is widely accepted instead of *lend* in the context of money: "The bank loaned me the money to have the house repainted."

loath, loathe. To be *loath* (adj.) is to be reluctant; to *loathe* (verb) is to despise.

lurid. See *livid, lurid.*

luxuriant, luxurious. *Luxuriant* means abundant in growth, as "a luxuriant head of hair." *Luxurious* means something that offers great sensuous pleasure or comfort, usually at some cost: "The hotel was luxurious beyond our wildest imaginings."

M

maltreatment. See *abuse, maltreatment, misuse.*

mantel, mantle. The *mantel* is a shelf above a fireplace; some dictionaries give *mantle* as an alternative spelling. A *mantle* is a cloak or covering.

marginal, peripheral, minimal. *Marginal* had its start as an economics term meaning "barely enough to yield a profit." It is overused to mean *minimal*—"narrow or slight." *Marginal* is also confused with *peripheral*—"outside the boundary of something." "Because stock market activity was minimal [not marginal] over the holiday, the broker stood on the periphery of the trading floor and noted the marginal returns on two recent investments."

marine, maritime, naval, nautical. A *marine* (not capitalized) is a member of the U.S. Marine Corps, but *marine* is also an adjective that means related to the sea. *Maritime* more specifically means bordering on the sea, or relating to navigation or commerce on the sea. *Naval* means related to ships or shipping or to a navy, and *nautical,* the most inclusive of all these adjectives, covers anything associated with sailors, navigation, or ships.

marital, martial, marshal. *Marital* refers to marriage but is often misspelled *martial,* which means "warlike" or referring to a law invoked by a government in an emergency and carried out by the military. *Marshal* (not *marshall*) is pronounced like *martial* but means to place in proper rank or position or to lead ceremoniously (as a verb) or someone who arranges and directs a ceremony (as a noun). In some places, *marshal* is also a military rank above general, and it is used with "fire marshal," "police marshal," and "sheriff's marshal."

maritime. See *marine, maritime, naval, nautical.*

marshal. See *marital, martial, marshal.*

masterful, masterly. *Masterful* means "domineering," and *masterly,* "skillful or expert." The adverb form of *masterful,* "masterfully," which means "in an expert manner," leads to further confusion about the use of these words.

material, materiel. *Materiel* means military supplies and equipment and is not interchangeable with *material.*

may. See *can, may.*

maybe, may be. *Maybe* is an adverb indicating uncertainty about an outcome. *May be* is a conditional verb phrase meaning "it is possible that." "We may be asked to contribute to the cause, and maybe we will."

may, might. Sometimes *may* is used in error, especially followed by *well,* to describe conditional or past events; *might* is better in this context. "If we had known that the real estate tax was about to be doubled, we might [not *may* well] have moved."

mean. See *average, mean, median.*

meantime, meanwhile. *Meantime* may be either a noun ("in the meantime") or an adverb just like *meanwhile.*

media, medium, mediums. *Media* is the plural of *medium* and takes a plural verb, although some authorities recognize it as singular as well. *Media* are channels or systems of, usually, mass communications. *Mediums* is the standard plural for *medium* when it means a person through whom the spirits of the dead are alleged to contact the living.

median. See *average, mean, median.*

mediate. See *arbitrate, mediate.*

medium. See *media, medium, mediums.*

might. See *may, might.*

migrate. See *emigrate, immigrate, migrate.*

militate. See *mitigate, militate.*

minimal. See *marginal, peripheral, minimal.*

mistrust. See *distrust, mistrust.*

misuse. See *abuse, maltreatment, misuse.*

mitigate, militate. These two are frequently confused, no doubt because they contain so many of the same letters. To *mitigate* is to lessen the harsh effect of some circumstance or make it less severe. To *militate,* which must be used with *against,* means to contradict or weigh against the effect of some consequence. "Mitigating circumstances for a criminal act can militate against a long jail sentence."

model, paradigm, paragon. A *model* can serve as a pattern or represent something worth emulating—a high standard. A *paradigm* is a clearly laid out example or pattern, as in Latin, where "amo, amas, amat, amamus, amatis, amant" is the paradigm for all verbs of a certain kind—a guiding conjugation. A *paragon* is a model of excellence or perfection that cannot be improved upon or copied—an inspiration.

moot, academic. *Moot* originally meant "hypothetical, arguable, open to debate" but is almost universally now used to mean "irrelevant." The change may have come about because of its strict legal meaning: "without legal significance, although decided." A "*moot* court" is an unofficial trial, the findings of which will neither be enforced nor set formal judicial precedent. Some critics disagree with *moot* as a synonym for "meaningless," but 59 percent of *The American Heritage Dictionary* usage panel accepts that usage. *Academic* conforms to and seems to be a substitute for the original legal meaning of *moot:* "theoretical, without practical purpose, lacking reference to the outside world." But *academic,* unlike current usage for *moot,* is not equivalent to "meaningless." "What a professor sees as a hands-on exercise in professional research will be moot if students think it has purely academic value."

moral, morale. *Moral* (noun and adjective) means "ethical" in the sense of approved, professional behavior or otherwise having to do with right and wrong. *Morale*'s first dictionary meaning is "moral principles or teachings," but the word is usually used to indicate an individual's or a group's level of psychological well-being and attitude—confidence, enthusiasm, discipline, cooperation—with respect to a task at hand.

morbidity, mortality. *Morbidity* has to do with disease or lack of health; *mortality,* with either being mortal (human) or with death, particularly on a larger scale. The confusion may arise from an association of the word *morbid* (meaning gruesome or grisly) with the details of death itself.

more than, over. Despite a long and illustrious battle by grammarians to preserve the distinction between countable units *(more than)* and cumulative quantities *(over),* all dictionaries, most commentators, and many excellent writers make no distinction between the use of *more than* and *over.* To write "The patient waited over two hours for the results of the test" or "We've lived here for more than a year" is not incorrect. In cases where the distinction is logical and obvious, writers will, however, be perfectly correct to use *more than* with countable units and *over* with quantities, as in these examples: "I have waited *more than* three days for you to return my phone message" and "It's been *over* a year since I heard from my niece in Louisiana." See *fewer, less* for discussion of a related concern.

mortality. See *morbidity, mortality.*

mundane. See *daily, mundane.*

mutual, reciprocal, common. Copperud wryly notes that these words have been the cause of much hair-splitting by "precisians." However, *mutual* has come to be accepted as meaning "the reciprocal relationship—the give and take—of two or more people to one another": "mutual admiration." *Reciprocal,* aside from its strictly mathematical meaning, means "functioning as a return in kind, corresponding"—that is, not so much sharing as exchanging: "a reciprocal agreement among the board members." Because it includes the idea of reciprocity, *mutual* is thus considered by many dictionaries and commentators to be redundant when used with terms that imply close sharing—rather than exchanging—of interests or activities: cooperation, friendship, partnership, each other. Those terms express a *common* relationship: thus, "a common hobby," or "the hobby we have in common." However, others grudgingly allow *mutual* and *common* as synonyms: for example, "mutual friend" is correct but partly to distinguish "shared" from "ordinary" friend.

myriad, a myriad of, myriads. This example, taken from a newspaper, is a rare case of correct usage of this usually mangled term: "The developments were the latest in a case that has raised myriad questions about the proper bounds of psychotherapy. . . ." Because *myriad* means "a great number of persons or things," it is redundant to say either *a myriad of* or *myriads.*

N

nadir, zenith. The *nadir* is the lowest point; the *zenith,* the highest point.

nauseous, nauseated. *Nauseous* once meant "causing nausea" but has come to be widely used to mean "affected by nausea." "I become *nauseated* if I read in a moving car" is correct, but so is "Reading in a moving car makes me *nauseous.*" However, many careful writers still fervently observe the distinction; it functions much like a secret handshake between alumni of a certain school of grammar.

nautical. See *marine, maritime, naval, nautical.*

naval. See *marine, maritime, naval, nautical.*

nearly. See *around, about, nearly.*

neglectful, negligent. Both adjectives describe failure to take care or to be prudent. *Neglectful,* the more disapproving term, implies laziness or deliberate shirking of responsibility; *negligent* implies inattention to one's business.

none is, none are. Either may be correct, depending on the sentence. See Chapter 6, Subject-Verb Agreement, for a complete discussion.

not only . . . but (also). This construction has its origins in the stock Latin construction *non modo (solum) . . . sed etiam.* The most important thing to remember about this conjunctive pair is that the structure should be parallel: "The wind not only damaged branches but also lifted roofs." The *also* is necessary, as Bernstein writes, when *not only* is used in the sense of "partly," as it was in the example sentence above. In such constructions, *but also* has the meaning of "as well" or "in addition." *Also* can be dropped when *but* by itself is clearer: "Your behavior is not only an embarrassment to me but intolerable in any subordinate." One last word of warning: Some writers not only get hooked on *not only . . . but also* but also overuse it, leading to a loss of effectiveness, as this sentence itself shows.

notorious, infamous, famous. *Notorious* means well known for unfavorable reasons, as a "notorious liar"; its connotation is always negative, although it is often misused to refer to celebrity or fame; *infamous* is a synonym. *Famous* means notable for admirable qualities or actions. However, *notorious* can be used—when describing inanimate objects only—to mean "commonly known to have the property of," as in "the notorious tendency of time to go quickly when you are having fun."

nourish. See *wean, nourish.*

novice. See *amateur, novice, tyro.*

number. See *amount, number.*

O

obdurate, obstinate. *Obdurate* describes a person who stubbornly persists in wrongdoing, is inflexible to correction, or behaves in an unyielding manner. *Obstinate* describes a problem that resists remedy or a person who perversely adheres to an opinion or a course of action despite reasoning or persuasion. A person can be obstinate without implying wrongdoing so much as foolhardiness. "The obstinate leak under the sink finally reduced the usually obdurate Mr. Fix-it to calling a plumber."

oblige, obligate. These words are nearly synonymous, but to *oblige* is the more general word, meaning to make someone indebted or constrained in a physical, legal, or moral way. "I'm obliged to inform you that if you don't move your car it will be towed away." "To be obliged" also means to be grateful to someone for performing a service or a courtesy. "I'm obliged to you for reminding me to move my car." To *obligate,* the slightly more legalistic term for binding or compelling someone by a social, moral, or legal tie, has the added sense of "force" as well as duty. "In most religious orders, nuns are no longer obligated to wear formal habits." The use of to *oblige* in the sense of offering entertainment is too phonily formalistic: "Mary, would you oblige us with one of the folk songs you sing so beautifully?" (But if she sings, you'll be obliged to clap.)

oblivious, ignorant. Usage experts have debated over *oblivious* for years, but most agree that it means being either forgetful or unaware of something that a normal person should remember or take into account. When it means forgetful, *oblivious* takes the preposition *of;* when it means unaware of, it takes the preposition *of* or *to:* "Larry was oblivious to the cold as he bicycled home from his paper route." *Ignorant* means lacking in knowledge: "Larry was ignorant of the dangers of frostbite."

observance, observation. An *observance* is a customary practice or the act of following a custom or a rule. *Observation* is the act of noting or making a statement about a fact or occurrence; it is also the statement made on the basis of what one has observed.

obstinate. See *obdurate, obstinate.*

obtuse. See *abstruse, obtuse.*

obviate, eliminate. To *obviate* is to prevent something by anticipating it, making it unnecessary. *Obviate* is often misused for to *eliminate,* which is to discard, remove, or disqualify something. "When Sheriff Pat Garrett eliminated Billy the Kid, the need for a trial was obviated."

occur. See *take place, occur.*

odor. See *aroma, scent, odor, smell.*

older. See *elder, older.*

on behalf of. See *in behalf of, on behalf of.*

one another, each other. Although strict grammarians have always preferred *one another* to be reserved for "three or more" and *each other* for "only two," these terms are used interchangeably by many careful writers who do not observe that distinction; the possessive forms are *one another's* and *each other's.*

one of the . . . if not the. This construction can lead to a problem of parallel agreement, as in this example: "You are one of the few, if not the only, poets who make a decent living at the craft." The words *the only* do not agree with *poets* as *the few* does. Rewriting is necessary: "You are one of the few poets who make a decent living at the craft, if not the only one."

opaque, translucent, transparent. *Opaque* is used to describe an object that light cannot pass through. *Translucent* means that light can be diffused through an object, but nothing beyond the object can be seen clearly. *Transparent* describes an object that is clear and lets light through without scattering it; objects behind something *transparent* are easily seen.

opportunistic. See *pragmatic, opportunistic.*

oppose, appose. To *oppose* is to be against something; to *appose* is to be alongside it. The noun forms are *opposition* and *apposition.*

opposite. See *converse, contrary, opposite, reverse.*

optimal, optimum. *Optimal* is an adjective meaning the best possible or most desirable: "A greenhouse offers optimal conditions for growth." *Optimum* is a step down from *optimal* and means the most favorable or best under the circumstances: "For optimum results when scanning typeset material, use the original document instead of a photocopy."

optimistic, hopeful. *Optimistic* describes an attitude of looking at things in the best possible light. In many cases, however, *hopeful* is better, especially when referring to a particular event: "I am hopeful about our chances for winning." *Optimistic* is the wrong word to use when describing an estimate that proves to have been exaggerated: "Our projected earnings were overly optimistic" should be "We miscalculated our projected earnings."

optimum. See *optimal, optimum.*

option. See *alternative, choice, option, alternate.*

oral, verbal. What's the difference between an *oral* and a *verbal* agreement? None. Strictly speaking, *oral* means "spoken" as opposed to written. *Verbal* often means "having a facility in the use and comprehension of words," including writing, but most usage experts agree that *verbal* also means "spoken": Students may show *verbal* aptitude (facility with words, either in speech or writing) when they take either written or *oral* (spoken) exams; a *verbal* (specified orally, not written) contract may later be upheld by the court after *oral* (spoken) testimony. The distinction lies in the restriction of *oral* to mean simply "uttered," while *verbal* can mean either writing or speaking ability or, in a special case, an unwritten contract.

ordnance, ordinance. *Ordnance* is artillery or a full complement of military weapons, including ammunition. An *ordinance* is a law or statute.

ought to. See *should, would, ought to.*

over. See *more than, over.*

P

palpable. See *tactile, tangible, palpable.*

panacea, remedy. A *panacea* is a remedy for all ills; *a remedy* is a particular treatment or medicine that cures or counteracts a disease. "Penicillin at first seemed to be a panacea, but many bacteria have grown immune to the remedy it once provided."

paradigm. See *model, paradigm, paragon.*

paragon. See *model, paradigm, paragon.*

parameter, perimeter. Perhaps because both words denote a limiting or constraining factor, *parameter,* a mathematical term meaning an arbitrarily defined constant, has crept into general usage to mean a boundary that helps define something, that is, a characteristic element. *Perimeter* is the boundary of a body or a figure, or a line around the outer limits of an area. *Parameter* is misused in the sense of being within a proper range ("Getting coffee is not within the parameters of Beth's job") or in the sense of a requirement ("The parameters for entrance to the class were extensive").

past. See *last, latest, past.*

patent. See *copyright, patent, trademark.*

pathos. See *bathos, pathos.*

peaceful, peaceable. *Peaceful* means "untroubled, quiet, or tranquil"; dictionaries offer it as a synonym for *peaceable,* but careful writers will note that *peaceable* implies "not quarrelsome, quietly behaved." *Peaceable* is therefore best used to describe a person's characteristic demeanor, while *peaceful* is appropriate to describe a temporary condition or a setting: "The children played peacefully in the sandbox under the watchful eyes of their peaceable mother."

pending. *Pending* means as yet undecided or unconcluded; adding *now* or *still* creates a redundancy.

people. See *persons, people.*

percent, percentage. *Percent* and *percentage points* are used with a number (5 percent); when used without a number or the word *point, percentage* is preferred: "The percentage [not percent] of loss was estimated"; "We estimated a large percentage of loss." (When preceded by *the,* percentage takes a singular verb. After *a,* the verb is singular or plural depending on the number of the noun in the following prepositional phrase.) A word of warning: Editors should learn the difference between "a 5 percent difference" and "a 5 percentage point difference"; these are two completely different numbers. A difference that amounts to 5 percent of the total is "a 5 percent difference." But the difference between, say, 15 and 20 percent is expressed as "a 5 percentage point difference." Also, writers and editors should remember that a quantity can be increased by any percentage, but decreased by no more than 100 percent. To say "The number of defective part claims has been reduced by 150 percent" is to claim the impossible.

perimeter. See *parameter, perimeter.*

peripheral. See *marginal, peripheral, minimal.*

persecute, prosecute. To *persecute* is to harass or afflict someone; to *prosecute* is to carry out a legal charge.

persistent, insistent. *Persistent* means existing for a long time despite interference or an attempt to counteract, as "a persistent case of bronchitis." *Persistent* may also be used to describe doggedly continuing efforts or activities: "the dog's persistent efforts to dig under the fence." *Insistent* is to be resolute, firm, or emphatic about something: "insistent tone," "insistent manner."

person. See *individual, person.*

persons, people. Questions about the use of *people* to mean *persons* began in the mid-19th century. The traditional view was that *people* referred to a large group and *persons* should be reserved for referring to countable individuals—including "several" and "many"—but especially after a number. Several critics and dictionaries still hold to this preference for *persons* with an exact number, but *The American Heritage Dictionary* and *Webster's Dictionary of English Usage* consider the words interchangeable for all but the largest numbers, which require *people.* To others, the use of *persons* sounds pretentious in any case. Although usage is changing rapidly, the distinction is still encouraged by many sources.

persuade, convince, satisfy. All are correctly used to mean "bring about belief by means of argument." Follett, in *Modern American Usage,* says that *satisfy*'s other meaning, "taking pleasure," is unlikely to be misconstrued in this context. There is one hitch: *persuade*—not *convince*—is the correct choice when an infinitive follows as a complement. For example, a juror may be *convinced of* capital punishment's moral acceptability (or *satisfied about* it), but be *persuaded* by the evidence to vote for an acquittal. A summary of idiomatic usage with prepositions and infinitives follows: *convinced* takes of, about, that, as to (not to + infinitive); *satisfied* takes about, that, as to (not of); and *persuaded* takes to + infinitive, about, that, as to, of.

peruse, scan, skim. *Peruse* means "to read thoroughly," though it is often misused to mean "glance over or *skim.*" "I don't have time to peruse the ads for just the right opening" is correct, if stilted. Terms such as "a quick perusal" were unacceptable to 66 percent of *The American Heritage Dictionary* usage panel. *Scan* and *skim,* however, have become accepted as synonyms for "to look through quickly," though *scan* once meant solely "to examine in detail, scrutinize." *Skim* (literally "to touch lightly on the surface") is the better choice if *scan* could confuse a reader; for example, "Scan the help wanted ads" could be taken to mean either "Read through every ad" or "Look over all the ads quickly."

pessimistic. See *cynical, pessimistic, skeptical.*

pier. See *dock, pier, quay, wharf.*

pitiful, pitiable, piteous. *Pitiful,* once synonymous with *pitiable* to mean "deserving of pity," has come to imply a pejorative, almost scornful description, as in "poor pitiful me." *Piteous* means "expressing suffering," as "a piteous cry."

pivotal, vital. Something that is of crucial importance to the outcome of an issue is *pivotal.* In many cases, this word is used where the less dramatic *vital* ("important, essential, or critical") would be satisfactory.

plausible. See *specious, plausible, fallacious.*

podium. See *lectern, podium.*

pore, pour. These are most often confused in sentences like "John pored [not poured] over his books to find the answer." *Pore* means to read studiously, while *pour* means to flow or cause something to flow.

possible. See *practical, practicable, feasible, possible.*

postpone. See *delay, postpone.*

postulate. See *stipulate, postulate.*

pour. See *pore, pour.*

practical, practicable, feasible, possible. These similar adjectives define degrees of ability, capacity, or realization of potential in the "real world." *Practical* and *practicable* both indicate something that can be put to actual use or practiced, but *practical* implies tangible success: "A practical way to save money is to spend less." *Practical* also describes a person who meets concrete demands: "A practical person will save money." The other three adjectives are often used interchangeably in error. *Practicable* means something that sounds workable, although results may be uncertain: "Job-sharing is practicable for many administrative tasks." Something that is *feasible,* "capable of being done," is necessarily *possible,* "may occur under the right conditions." But the reverse is not always true. Some things that are *possible*—such as thunderstorms—are not properly said to be *feasible,* despite such commonly heard comments as "It's entirely feasible that the picnic will be rained out."

practically. See *virtually, practically.*

pragmatic, opportunistic. To be *pragmatic* is to be wise in the ways of the world, practical. Pragmatism, when taken to the extreme, can lead to becoming *opportunistic.* An *opportunistic* person grasps after and contrives to obtain advantages, often with little regard for principles or consequences.

precedence, precedents. These words sound alike, but *precedent* means something said or done that later serves to justify similar actions; *precedents* is the plural form. "To take *precedence* over" and "the *precedence* of" refer to something that takes priority.

precede, proceed. These words are confused for reasons of similar pronunciation and spelling. To *precede* means to go before or in front of; to *proceed* means to go forward or move ahead. Bernstein says that the commonest error is spelling *preceding* "preceeding."

preceding, previous, prior. These adjectives all carry the sense that something has happened before the present. *Preceding* denotes going before in time or place, *prior. Previous* and *prior* also imply that something existed or occurred earlier.

precipitous, precipitate. *Precipitous* means steep; *precipitate* means foolishly hasty.

predestination. See *determinism, fatalism, predestination.*

predicament. See *dilemma, predicament.*

predicated on, based on. Both phrases are universally regarded as standard and interchangeable, though *predicated on* is somewhat pretentious.

predict. See *presage, predict.*

predilection. See *bias, discrimination, prejudice, bigotry, predilection.*

predominant, predominate. Both are considered standard adjectives. Confusion of the adjective *predominant* with the verb *to predominate,* meaning to be superior, could occur and explains a slight preference for using *predominant. Predominately* is often used incorrectly for *predominantly,* which means mainly.

prefatory, preparatory, preliminary. *Prefatory,* except for referring in general to the material in the front of a book (more simply called *front matter*), is considered pretentious, like *preparatory* (to) and *preliminary.* It is simpler to use "before" or "in preparation for."

preferable. This is an absolute modifier; something cannot be said to be "more" or "less" *preferable* when some sense of "desirable" is meant. Either something is "preferred above all others" or it is not. "A is preferable to B."

prejudice. See *bias, discrimination, prejudice, bigotry, predilection.*

preliminary. See *prefatory, preparatory, preliminary.*

preparatory. See *prefatory, preparatory, preliminary.*

prepositions. Which preposition to use after certain verbs, adjectives, and nouns has been a problem for grammarians since the 18th century. The root of their concern has been the abundance of idiomatic combinations that defy logic. Meanwhile, speakers and writers have happily gone about the business of using these prepositions.

In fact, *Webster's Dictionary of English Usage* says an idiom is "generally used by usage experts for some construction or expression that they approve of but cannot analyze . . . for some reason *idiom* often refers in English to combinations involving prepositions and adverbs." Idiomatic prepositions often give sticklers the uneasy sense that some principle of grammar is being violated, but correct use is less at issue than familiar convention. Even native speakers, however, sometimes have trouble choosing the right preposition to express a relationship: of space, time, accompaniment, cause, or manner, and so on. The following list shows the prepositions that may be used with certain words in different contexts.

For a closer look at more troublesome combinations that have become usage thorns, see the discussion of each of these words at their entry in this chapter: accept, except (from); adverse, averse (to); advise (to), inform (of); and, to; annoyed by, with, at; center around; compare with, compare to; comprise, compose; consist in, consist of; couple, couple of; deserving of, worthy of; different from, different than; differ from, differ with; dispense (with); due to, because of; emigrate, immigrate, migrate; equally as; face, face up to; graduated (from); has got to, has to; identical to, identical with; in behalf of, on behalf of; question as to, question of whether; should, would, ought to; should of, would of, could of.

aberration. from, of
abhorrent. to
ability. at, with
absolve. from, of
abstain. from
abstract. from
abut. against (a wall), on (a line)
accommodate. to, with
accompanied. with (things), by (persons)
accordance. with
accountable. to (person), for (act)
acquiesce. in
acquit. of
adjacent. to
adopt. to, for, from
advantage. of, over
advocate. of, for
affinity. between, with

alien. from, to
ally. with, to
alternate. with
amenable. to
amused. at, by, with
analogous. to
angry. at (an action), with (a person)
annoyed. by (something), with (a person)
antecedent. to
anxious. about
append. to
apportion. to, among, between
approximation. of, to
assimilate. to
astonished. at, by
augmented. by, with

based. on, upon, in
basis. for, of
bereave. of
boast. of, about
border. on, upon

capable. of
capacity. for (ability), of (volume), to (possibility)
caution. against
chide. for
circumstances. in, under
clear. of
concur. in (a decision), with (a person)
conform. to, with
consent. to
contend. with, against, about
correspond. to, with

decide. on, upon
defend. against
despair. of
destined. to, for
detract. from
differ. with, on, from
disgusted. at, by, with
divide. between, among
dwell. in, at, on

eligible. to, for
enamored. of (a person), with (something)
encouraged. by, with
encroach. on, upon
end. with, in
enter. on, upon, into
estimated. at
excused. from, for
exonerate. from, of
experience. in, at
expert. in, at, with

faced. by, with
fascination. for
favorable. for, to, toward
feed. on, off
fondness. for
forbid. to
friend. of, to

grateful. to, for
grieve. at, for, after
guard. against, from

hanker. after, for
healed. of (disease), by (something)
honor. with, by, for
hope. for, of

identical. with, to
identify. with
impress. on, with, into, upon
impressed. by, with
improve. on, upon
incorporate. with, into
indulge. in, with
infer. from
inquire. for, about, after, into

inspire. by, with
instill. in
instruct. in
intent. on, upon
intervene. in (dispute), between (disputants)
intrude. on, upon, into
invest. in, with

justified. in

lament. for, over
laugh. at, over
lean. on, upon, against
liable. for (acts), to (prosecution)

made. from, out of, of
mix. with, into

necessary. to, for
necessity. of, for

occupied. by, with
opportunity. of, for
originate. in, with
overlain. by, with

parallel. to, with
part. from, with
partake. of, in
partial. to
persuaded. by, of, to
pleased. at, by, with
possessed. of, by, with
predestined. to, for
preface. of, to
preference. to, over, before, above
pregnant. with, by
preoccupied. with (something), by (a person)
prevail. on, upon, with, against, over
proficient. in, at
profit. by, from
provide. with, for, against
punish. by, with, for
purge. of, from

qualify. for, as

receptive. to, of
reconcile. to, with
rejoice. at, in
replete. with
rich. in

scared. at, by
solicitous. of, for, about
suffer. with, from
suitable. to, for
surprised. at, by

tendency. toward, to
tolerance. for, of, toward
tormented. by, with

unfavorable. for, to, toward
useful. in, for, to

variance. with
vary. from

worthy. of, to

zeal. for, in

prerequisite. See *requisite, prerequisite.*

presage, predict. To *presage* is to give an omen or warning of disaster and has the connotation of magical prescience (knowing something before it happens). Someone *predicts*, however, based on experience, observation, or expertise.

prescribe, proscribe. To *prescribe* is "to set down in writing" a plan for medical treatment or, in a broader sense, "to recommend a course of action." To *proscribe* means "to prohibit or rule against." "Physicians are proscribed from prescribing medicine for their own families."

presume, assume. The very thin distinction between these verbs may be expressed as the difference between "taking something for granted without any evidence"—to *assume*—and "believing something to be true based on the circumstances"—to *presume.* Thus, "Stanley was correct when he said, 'Dr. Livingstone, I presume.' "

prevent. See *avoid, evade, avert, prevent.*

preventive, preventative. *Preventive* is preferred as both an adjective and a noun. "We took the preventive measure of giving blood before our colleague's surgery."

previous. See *preceding, previous, prior.*

price. See *cost, price, value, worth.*

principal, principle. These may well be the most common spelling confusables of all. *Principal* is used as both a noun and an adjective. "The principal [head of a school] is the principal [main] authority in school-based administration." (Even today, some editors draw on the mnemonic learned in grade school: "The princi*pal* is your *pal.*") To add to the confusion, *principal* also refers to the sum of money (think "capit*al*") on which interest is paid or received. A *principal* is also a leading performer or someone who hires an agent. *Principle* is always used as a noun, meaning rule or precept ("A princip*le* is a ru*le*").

prior. See *preceding, previous, prior.*

prior to, before. If you plan simply to take a walk *before* dinner, why prolong your hunger with the extra time it takes to pretentiously perambulate *prior to* the roast beef?

problematic, troublesome. *Problematic* does not describe something that "causes problems," but instead something "difficult to settle, solve, or decide." "It's problematic whether the mechanic will be able to find out why the brake pads are wearing unevenly." *Troublesome* is used in constructions like "The uneven brake pad wear is a troublesome matter."

pro bono. See *for free, gratis, pro bono.*

proceed. See *precede, proceed.*

proclivity, propensity. A *proclivity* is a strong inherent inclination or a predisposition toward something, usually something objectionable. A *propensity* is a deeply ingrained and often intense or even irresistible preference or longing. "He had a proclivity for biting his nails"; "My propensity for eating chocolate has left its mark on my hips."

progenitor, inventor. A *progenitor* is an ancestor; an *inventor* is an originator of a thing or a process.

prone. See *apt, likely, liable, prone.*

prone, prostrate, supine. Although *prone* and *prostrate* both mean "lying face down," they are often used more generally as synonyms for "lying flat," regardless of position. This usage is acceptable except where precision is at stake: More carefully, a *prone* figure is one that is resting against a supportive surface, whereas a *prostrate* posture implies submission, defeat, or physical collapse. "Blondie sighed as she eyed Dagwood's prone figure on the sofa and Daisy on the floor, prostrate with wistfulness." *Supine* is the opposite of both words and always means "lying down on one's back, face up"—a position that could connote inertness or depression. "Supine on the bed, the child tracked the shapes made by the cracks in the ceiling." By the way, many people mistakenly refer to the male prostate gland as the "prostrate gland," presumably because *prostrate* is the more common word. (Careful writers don't take such errors lying down.)

propensity. See *proclivity, propensity.*

prophesy, prophecy. To *prophesy* (last syllable rhymes with *sigh*) is to make a *prophecy* (last syllable rhymes with *see*). "Prophesize" is sometimes heard, but it is not a word.

proscribe. See *prescribe, proscribe.*

prosecute. See *persecute, prosecute.*

prostrate. See *prone, prostrate, supine.*

purposefully, purposely. *Purposefully* describes behavior that is directed toward attaining a goal. *Purposely* means something done willfully or intentionally.

Q

quay. See *dock, pier, quay, wharf.*

query, inquiry. *Query* and *inquiry* may both mean "question," but *query* is not synonymous with "investigation or formal inquiry." "During their inquiry into the suspect's activities, the police queried his coworkers."

question as to, question of whether. The words *as to* and *of* should be left out in nearly every case: "We had a question as to whether he had received our message." "Can you resolve the question of whether the missing sock can be found?"

quite. See *very, rather, quite.*

quote, quotation, quotes. *Quote* used for *quotation* is generally accepted as standard ("Rupert liked to stalk in the woods intoning the 'lovely, dark, and deep/But I have miles to go before I sleep' quote [or quotation] from Robert Frost's poem"). *Quote marks* and *quotes,* although slightly informal, are widely used in printing and publishing to mean "quotation marks."

R

rack, wrack, wreak. A *rack* is a frame (noun); as a verb, it means to stretch or strain or to torment: "Rack your brains for the place where you hid the key." *Wrack* means a wreck: "His betting compulsion has driven him to wrack and ruin." To *wreak* (rhymes with *reek,* not a homonym for *wreck*) is to inflict a damaging blow, usually as in "wreaking havoc": "Flu is wreaking havoc with student attendance." All the examples here are clichés.

raise, rear. As Bernstein says, both pigs and children may now be said to be raised, though it is not always easy to tell the difference. Properly speaking, we *raise* cattle and *rear* children, but some think that if we did more *rearing* (nurturing) of the children the difference would be more obvious.

raise, rise. To *raise* is always a transitive verb ("Let's raise the hemline a bit"); to *rise* is intransitive ("We rise before dawn to do calisthenics"). As a noun, *raise* means an increase in pay, so "pay raise" is redundant. A *rise* is an elevated level, as in temperature.

rare, scarce. *Rare* means distinctive or unusual. *Scarce* means difficult to find or in limited quantity. These meanings may overlap when speaking, for example, of precious stones. The distinction becomes important in such examples as "a rare [not scarce] virus," which is likely to be unusual but perhaps also profuse.

rather. See *very, rather, quite.*

ravish, ravage. To *ravish* is to carry away with passionate emotion—including, at its extreme, the violent act of rape. To *ravage* means "to destroy or lay waste" and conveys only violence, not emotion. These verbs are not interchangeable.

rear. See *raise, rear.*

reason is because, reason . . . why, reason . . . that. Grammarians say *because* means "for the reason that," and therefore the construction *reason is because* is redundant. But *reason is because* has been used for more than four centuries in some of the best writing by those who say *because* can also mean "the fact that" when it introduces a noun clause. This construction, however, along with *reason why,* may bring criticism to students and writers. The careful writer will say "The reason I choose not to use the other idioms is that I fear being incorrect" (not "The reason I choose not to use the other idioms is because I fear being incorrect").

rebut. See *refute, repudiate, rebut.*

recapitulate. See *repeat, iterate, reiterate, recur (reoccur), recapitulate.*

reciprocal. See *mutual, reciprocal, common.*

recur. See *repeat, iterate, reiterate, recur (reoccur), recapitulate.*

redouble. See *double, redouble.*

refute, repudiate, rebut. To *refute* means to disprove, not simply to deny, contest, or *repudiate* (reject) the accuracy or truth of something. To *rebut* has a specific meaning in debating: to oppose—though not necessarily to refute—an opponent's position by offering a formal argument or contradictory proof.

regrettably, regretfully. *Regrettably* describes a condition that calls for or causes regret. *Regretfully* describes someone who feels full of regret; it should not be used for *regrettably* in any case. "We regretfully gave up on our dream of a new house. Regrettably, the interest rates decreased soon after."

reiterate. See *repeat, iterate, reiterate, recur (reoccur), recapitulate.*

relegate, delegate. To *relegate* is to consign or banish someone or something to a lower position. Although it can mean "to hand over something to another for decision or action," *relegate* has a negative connotation, as in "relegating to the tardy student the job of cleaning the boards." *Delegate* is the better choice for the act of assigning a task or responsibility to another.

relevant. See *germane, relevant, apropos.*

religious. See *deist, theist, religious.*

reluctant. See *reticent, reluctant.*

remedy. See *panacea, remedy.*

repeat, iterate, reiterate, recur (reoccur), recapitulate. The first four of these verbs and their adjective forms are loose synonyms. *Repeat,* the most general term, means "say, do, perform, or experience something or express oneself again in the same way or with the same words as before." *Repeat* can also mean "recite something from memory or tell it to another." *Iterate* is a more formal synonym; it can also refer to a computational process for arriving at a specific result by repeating the same set of instructions or operations through a series of increasingly close approximations. *Reiterate* is another formal term and borders on jargon because it usually means simply "say or do again": "In closing, I'd like to reiterate my position: No new taxes"; "Overwork at a computer keyboard can cause reiterative motion injuries." *Recur* means "happening or coming up again or returning to mind": "The recurring nightmares the child was having made him balk at going to bed"; "If the disease recurs, you'll have to resume medication." Note that *reoccur,* though often seen and heard, is not a word.

Recapitulate means "to repeat in a concise form or make a summary." The addition of brevity to the sense of repetition distinguishes it from the other verbs here; though heard in the context of someone offering a brief summary, a *recapitulation* is usually longer than the average audience wishes—and the word itself is longer and fancier than any context normally requires.

repellent. See *repulsive, repellent, repugnant.*

replace. See *substitute, replace.*

replete, complete. The distinction between these adjectives is between "an abundant supply of something"—for example, a telephone line that sags *replete* with mourning doves—and "something that has all the normally necessary components"—for example, a CD player that comes complete with speakers and earphones. As a related matter, *complete* was once considered an absolute construction—not open to qualification—but *The American Heritage Dictionary* usage panel considers it correct to say something is "more" or "less" *complete:* "Your collection of antique syrup bottles is the most complete I've seen."

replica, reproduction. A *replica* is a facsimile (almost an exact copy) or a copy made by the original artist; a *reproduction* is synonymous with "model, duplicate, copy" and is preferred for all but the special cases of virtual likeness to the original object.

repudiate. See *refute, repudiate, rebut.*

repulsive, repellent, repugnant. These words connote various degrees of the same general meaning. *Repulsive,* alien to one's ideas or tastes, is stronger than *repellent,* generally forbidding or unpleasant, when used to describe something that causes aversion. Something or someone *repugnant* evokes disgust but suggests a reaction less drastic than the emotion something *repulsive* causes.

requisite, prerequisite. *Requisite* means something essential or necessary for carrying out a function; *prerequisite* means a precondition to carrying out an activity. "The engineer has the requisite skills for the job but lacks the visa that is a prerequisite for working in France."

respective, respectively. Omit these words whenever the meaning of a sentence is clear without them, as in "The students returned to their respective classrooms." When some sorting out of what belongs to whom is necessary, use *respectively:* "The votes for Balder, Dash, and Smithereens were 101, 97, and 52, respectively."

reticent, reluctant. *Reticent* is often misused for *reluctant,* but the meanings are different. *Reticent* means quiet or restrained; *reluctant* means hesitant: "Jack was reluctant to jump over the candlestick, but he was too reticent to object when Mother Goose insisted."

reverse. See *converse, contrary, opposite, reverse* and *versus, reverse, vice versa.*

rigid. See *turgid, turbid, rigid.*

rise. See *raise, rise.*

rob, steal. A place or person is *robbed,* but the valuables themselves are not robbed; what is taken by a robber is *stolen.* "Their house was robbed while they were away; even their cat was stolen."

robbery, larceny, theft, burglary. *Robbery* involves the use of violence or threat in committing *larceny,* which is "wrongful taking of property." *Theft* is stealing property without violence or threat. *Burglary* means unlawful entry into a building for the purpose of stealing.

S

sadism, cruelty. Often used loosely as a synonym for *cruelty, sadism* is more specifically the sexual perversion of taking pleasure from inflicting mental or physical pain on another.

sample. See *example, sample.*

sarcastic. See *ironic, sarcastic, sardonic.*

sardonic. See *ironic, sarcastic, sardonic.*

satisfy. See *persuade, convince, satisfy.*

scan. See *peruse, scan, skim.*

scarce. See *rare, scarce.*

scenario. A *scenario* is the script or plot outline for a dramatic work, but its popular use since 1960 to mean "a projected sequence of events" has gained wide acceptance, despite some critics' dismay. "To play out a worst-case scenario" means to forecast a possible outcome. Perhaps what started out as a vogue word has been grafted onto the language, but like most new words, it should be used sparingly to avoid the charge of careless or clichéd writing.

scent. See *aroma, scent, odor, smell.*

Scots, Scottish, Scotch. *Scottish* people, or the *Scots* from Scotland, frown on *Scotch,* an English contraction. In general, certain things, such as broth and whiskey, may be *Scotch,* but people are always *Scots* or *Scottish.*

scrimp. See *skimp, scrimp.*

seasonable, seasonal. *Seasonable* events come at the appropriate time of year, such as mild spring temperatures in the spring or snow in February; *seasonal* events occur at a particular time of year, such as end-of-model-year car sales in September.

see. See *witness, see, watch, view.*

seldom ever. See *almost never, seldom ever.*

semiannual. See *biannual, semiannual, biennial.*

sensual, sensuous. The original distinction here is between a physical or even sexual appetite *(sensual)* and the more refined or intellectual enjoyment *(sensuous)* derived from the use of the senses, as when appreciating art, music, or poetry. However, these adjectives are frequently used and widely accepted as interchangeable.

separate (adj.). Aside from being frequently misspelled, *separate* is often misused to reinforce "quantity," as in "He offered ten separate excuses for being late," when "different" is meant.

service, serve. To *service* specifically means "to provide maintenance or repair." This verb is jargon to be avoided where *serve* is adequate, as in "The caterer will serve three parties this weekend."

set, sit. *Set* is a transitive verb (the subject acts upon an object—"I set my watch on the table") except when the sun "sets." *Sit* is intransitive, except when one "sits" a horse.

sewerage, sewage. *Sewage* is the waste that is disposed of by being passed through the *sewerage system.*

sex. See *gender, sex.*

shall, will. Americans have abandoned the distinction between these verb auxiliaries except when expressing mandatory actions, especially in legal or regulatory writing. *Shall* is viewed as old-fashioned or pretentious when used to lend an air of formality or gravity: "I shall be there at noon." Both *shall* and *will* can express both determination and futurity, contrary to what some of us were taught in school. See Chapter 5, Verbs.

should of, would of, could of. *Of* mistakenly replaces *have* in these constructions; the substitution is illiterate.

should, would, ought to. *Should,* the past tense of *shall,* is used as a synonym for *ought to:* "One should help where one can." *Would,* the past tense of *will,* is used to indicate the conditional (often with *if*): "I would be glad to help if you need volunteers." *Would* is also used to refer to ingrained habit or behavior, as in "You are the kind of friend who would never reveal a confidence."

sight. See *site, sight, cite.*

simplistic. *Simplistic* describes a fact or event that has been oversimplified, not something simple or uncomplicated. A "simplistic solution" is one that does not consider all aspects of a problem; a "simple solution" is one that is easy to carry out.

simultaneous. Some authorities say *simultaneous* is an adjective only, not an adverb, though *simultaneously* is often found in good writing for "happening at the same time." Most dictionaries say that the adverb form is legitimate, much as the analogous *contemporaneously* and *concurrently* are accepted.

since. See *because, since, as.*

sit. See *set, sit.*

site, sight, cite. These are spelling confusables. A *site* is a "location"; *sight* is "vision or the act of viewing"; and to *cite* is "to give an example" or "to make a legal charge against."

skeptical. See *cynical, pessimistic, skeptical.*

skim. See *peruse, scan, skim.*

skimp, scrimp. Both verbs imply penurious savings. To be inadequate in providing attention, effort, or funding is to *skimp,* for example, "skimping on the refreshments." To *scrimp* is to be stingy or excessively frugal to acquire savings: "We scrimped to be able to serve refreshments."

smell. See *aroma, scent, odor, smell.*

sneaked, snuck. Unbelievable as it may seem to those of us who had the verb *snuck* drummed out of us in elementary school, it has survived as a pure Americanism with the tenacity of beggar's lice. Although many writers and editors continue to resist *snuck* as the past tense for *sneak, The American Heritage Dictionary* usage panel says that "in recent years, *snuck* has been quietly establishing itself in formal writing," especially among younger speakers but also among the well educated. However, the panel found that *sneaked* is preferred 7 to 2 based on 10,000 citations. *Snuck* does sound more stealthy, but use it advisedly.

sometime, some time. The use of *sometime* as an adjective is archaic—"a sometime rival for." As an adverb, *sometime* means "eventually": "She will marry sometime." *Some time* written as two words is a phrase meaning "an interval" with *for* being understood: "We waited some time."

sophisticated, advanced. Formerly applied only to worldly wise people, *sophisticated* is now standard usage for characterizing highly developed methods, equipment, and processes; it is synonymous with *advanced* in the sense of "state of the art."

sort. See *character, kind, sort.*

sort of (a). See *kind of (a), sort of (a).*

specially. See *especially, specially.*

specialty, speciality. *Specialty* is the preferred American spelling; *speciality* is preferred in British English. This preference is similar to that of *judgment* (the preferred American spelling) and *judgement* (the preferred British spelling). American dictionaries give both spellings as acceptable, but most editors consider *specialty* and *judgment* to be the correct spellings for American audiences.

specious, plausible, fallacious. Despite a misconception that *specious* means simply "false," a *specious* argument is one that "has the ring of truth"—that is, seems *plausible*—but that, on closer inspection or as a result of testing, proves to be faulty. *Plausible* means "seemingly valid" and is a synonym. Thus, "Your reasoning is specious" does not mean "You are wrong" but "Your reasons are *plausible*, but they are flawed." *Fallacious* means wrong on the face of it, without deception. See also *credible, creditable, credulous.*

spectators. See *audience, spectators.*

spiral. *Spiral* means to move either up or down in a circular motion. Because it is accepted widely to mean "rapid and continuous rising," to specify "a downward spiral" is not redundant; *spiral* technically encompasses both possibilities.

stalactite, stalagmite. Both are calcium carbonate deposits formed in limestone caves. *Stalactites* hang down from the roof, and *stalagmites* build up from the floor. A mnemonic is "stalac*t*ites hang from the *t*op of the cave."

stalemate, impasse. A *stalemate* is a final outcome, with no possibility of any alternative action. An *impasse* is a predicament to which there is no obvious, immediate solution, but which may eventually be overcome.

stanza. See *verse, stanza, chorus.*

stationary, stationery. *Stationary* means staying in pl*a*ce, not moving; *stationery* is l*e*tter writing paper.

steal. See *rob, steal.*

stimulant, stimulus. Both nouns indicate something that rouses or excites, but there is a scientific distinction: a *stimulant* is an agent, such as caffeine, that increases an organism's active functioning. A *stimulus* is an environmental change, such as subzero temperature, that produces a reaction in living tissue; it is the more commonly used word. Otherwise, in most cases they are synonyms.

stipulate, postulate. To *stipulate* is to make a contractual agreement to do or not to do something or to specify something as a condition. To *postulate* is to demand, claim, or assume that something is true or necessary.

strategy, stratagem. *Strategy* is an overall plan of attack; a *stratagem* is a trick for deceiving the enemy. Notice that these related words have different vowels—*e* versus *a*—in the middle.

subconscious. See *unconscious, subconscious.*

subscribe. See *ascribe, subscribe.*

substitute, replace. *Substitute* is used with the preposition *for* as a transitive verb meaning "to put in the place of": "Vigilantes wish to substitute order for the rule of law." In the sense of *replace, substitute* is used with the preposition *by* or *with:* "Nations with internal revolution often substitute the rule of law with force."

succeed. See *supersede, succeed.*

such as. See *like, such as, as.*

suit, suite. A coordinated outfit of clothing is a *suit;* an organized grouping of furniture, rooms, or musical themes is a *suite.*

supersede, succeed. *Supersede* (often misspelled *supercede*) means "take the place of," often by rendering someone or something obsolete; it has the connotation of gaining superiority over another. *Succeed* also means "to replace," but in the sense of "coming after, following" in a natural or orderly sequence.

supine. See *prone, prostrate, supine.*

suppose. See *calculate, suppose.*

suspected. See *alleged, accused, suspected.*

syndrome. Originally a medical term for "a constellation of symptoms," *syndrome* is now in wide use as a figurative term to mean any recognizable and defining set of characteristics. This use is acceptable as long as it is not overdone; it carries a taint of jargon.

synthetic, false. A *synthetic* process or material brings together many different parts or elements to create a new whole, and in that sense *synthetic* is positive. But *synthetic* also can connote "fake or false" because what is created is artificial in that it did not occur naturally.

systemic, systemwide, systematic. These words are not interchangeable. *Systemic* means "acting commonly throughout an organic physical system." *Systemwide* means "influential across all the integrated parts of a system" other than the body. *Systematic* means "formulated as a methodical, efficient, or precise plan or arrangement." For example, "The landscape firm adopted a systemwide [in all offices] policy of using systemic [taken through the roots] pesticides systematically [in all cases] as a last resort."

T

tactile, tangible, palpable. These words describe degrees of perception of a thing or phenomenon. If something is *tactile,* it can be perceived through the physical sense of touch. *Tangible,* too, means capable of being perceived by touch, but it also means capable of being perceived as real or substantial. *Palpable* also describes something easily touched or felt but includes the aspect of being detectable.

take. See *bring, take.*

take place, occur. These verbs are synonymous. Although some writers prefer to use *take place* with events and actions that are planned and to reserve *occur* for use with things that happen by chance, these are not strict rules.

tangible. See *tactile, tangible, palpable.*

that, which. See Chapter 4, Pronouns, page 138.

theft. See *robbery, larceny, theft, burglary.*

their. See *everybody, everyone . . . their.*

theist. See *deist, theist, religious.*

the then. The consensus of usage experts is that a construction such as "the then President John Kennedy" is correct, and no hyphen with the noun is required to make this adjective form.

think. See *feel, feel like, think.*

though. See *although, though, while.*

till, until, 'til. *Until* is usually used in formal writing, but *till* is acceptable, even at the beginning of a sentence; *till* is in fact the older word and not an abbreviation of *until. 'Til* is a variant of *until* found in poetic writing and used for metric purposes, and many mistake it for a "more correct" short form of *till,* but it is not used in standard prose.

to. See *and, to.*

tortuous, torturous. *Tortuous* means "winding, twisted, complex, or roundabout." *Torturous* also can mean extremely complex but further connotes "torture or excruciating pain." *Torturous* is often used in an ambiguous way when either definition could be construed, as in "a torturous race course"—one that is possibly both painful and winding. The words can overlap but *tortuous* is reserved by careful writers for "winding path."

toward, towards. The former is the more common American choice, while the British prefer the latter, but the distinction is minor.

trademark. See *copyright, patent, trademark.*

transcendent, transcendental. The chief distinction between these adjectives is that *transcendent* is preferred simply to mean "surpassing," while *transcendental* has further philosophical and metaphysical connotations. To make things interesting, it is acceptable to say, for instance, that "in her naiveté she made transcendental errors in judgment," in the sense of "egregious or abysmal."

translucent. See *opaque, translucent, transparent.*

transparent. See *opaque, translucent, transparent.*

transpire, happen. As Bernstein explains, *transpire* originally meant "to be emitted as a vapor" or "become known or apparent," but several authorities currently accept its use as a synonym for "happen." In the past few years, it seems to have gained in popularity and is fast becoming overused. To say "It transpired" to mean "It happened" sounds a bit pretentious as well.

trooper, trouper. A *trooper* is a police or military officer. A *trouper* is someone game enough to keep trying despite hardships. For example, a *trooper* who stops to help a desperate traveler stranded on the shoulder of the interstate with a flat tire is a *trouper,* too, and is to be blessed.

troublesome. See *problematic, troublesome.*

trouper. See *trooper, trouper.*

truism. See *cliché, truism.*

try and, try to. See *and, to.*

turgid, turbid, rigid. *Turgid* means "a swollen state" or, in the case of language, "bombastic." *Turbid* means "muddy, disordered, or obscure," as flood waters. *Rigid* is "stiff and unyielding," as boar bristles.

tyro. See *amateur, novice, tyro.*

U

unartistic. See *inartistic, unartistic.*

unconscious, subconscious. *Unconscious,* the more general of these terms, means "not knowing or perceiving" in the various senses of "free from self-awareness," "having lost consciousness," or "not possessing mind at all." *Subconscious* refers to "mental activities or thoughts existing in the mind just below the level of awareness," and its connotations are more psychological.

under way, underway. Still spelled as two words, the adverb *under way* ("The project manager's ideas seemed to stall under way") is derived from the context of a ship that has lifted ("weighed") anchor and is moving through the water. *Underway* is an adjective used to describe something in motion: "The bombers could reach their targets only if underway refueling were possible."

unexceptional, unexceptionable. *Unexceptional*—using exception in the sense of "varying from the usual"—means "normal, not extraordinary." *Unexceptionable*—using exception in the sense of "an objection"—means "circumspect, not open to objection."

uninterested. See *disinterested, uninterested.*

unique. *Unique* means unequaled, one of a kind—not rare or unusual—so there are no degrees of uniqueness, such as "most unique."

unmoral. See *amoral, immoral, unmoral.*

unquestioned, unquestionable. If something is *unquestioned,* it has not yet been the subject of dispute but might be at some point. *Unquestionable* means something that cannot be questioned because it is indisputable.

unreadable. See *illegible, unreadable.*

until. See *till, until, 'til.*

usage, use, utilize. The noun *usage* refers to "a standard or traditional practice or customary manner of functioning," with a specialized meaning for the way language is assembled. *Use* has the sense of "employing or putting something into action or service." It would be pretentious to say, "Compact discs enjoy wide *usage*" and incorrect to say, "The *usage* of elliptical constructions should be parallel." (Such constructions are themselves an aspect of usage, however.) Similarly, the verb *utilize,* which strictly speaking means "to make the best practical, productive use of something obviously not intended for the job," is often used pretentiously to mean simply *to use.* "Desert farmers *utilize* every square inch of irrigated land," but "the method they *use* is drip irrigation." In most cases (noun or verb), when there is no particular sense of exigency, *use* is preferred.

V

v. See *vs., v.*

vacant. See *empty, vacant.*

value. See *cost, price, value, worth.*

varied, various, different. *Varied* (adj.) means "to be made different," "to become diversified," or "an indefinite number of, several of." Things that are *various* are "distinctly different from one another," "diverse." *Varied* emphasizes the intentional creation of selective differences; *various* emphasizes the existence or natural occurrence of individual differences: "New contact lens colors are wildly varied to suit the various tastes of style-conscious young professionals." *Different,* not a true synonym for either *varied* or *various,* is often used redundantly, as in "I'd like to see samples of at least three different cover designs." Copperud suggests that *different* should be omitted in a sentence if *unlike* cannot be substituted for it. *Various* is preferable to indicate diversity within a category: "Various [not *different*] grammarians object to the use of *different* as an incomplete comparison, especially in advertising." With respect to the latter issue, several dictionaries do, however, recognize the use of *different* to mean "unusual": "I like it. It's different."

vehement, violent, virulent. *Vehement* describes a manner that is marked by great force or strong feelings, as in "a vehement debate." *Violent* also means marked by extreme force or sudden, intense energy, but possibly to loss of self-control, as "a violent temper." *Virulent* means marked by a rapid and severe course, as "a virulent case of measles."

venal, venial. These are spelling and pronunciation confusables. *Venal* means capable of being bought off or mercenary; *venial* means forgivable or excusable.

verbal. See *oral, verbal.*

verbiage, verbosity. Both mean "wordiness." *Verbosity* is generally understood to be synonymous with long-winded speech, while *verbiage* indicates redundant written language. *Verbiage* is not correctly used to mean "speech in general" or "wording" because the sense is disparaging. Thus, "excess verbiage" is itself a redundancy. *Verbiage* is the more familiar noun; the adjective *verbose* is more common than *verbosity.*

vernacular, dialect. As a noun, *vernacular* means the language or dialect of a region or country that is used by its natives, as distinct from what is considered the standard formal usage; as an adjective, *vernacular* is descriptive of what is characteristic of a period, place, or group. "Idiomatic usage"—the *vernacular*—may eventually become accepted as standard. *Dialect* is any expression in the usage of a language that cannot be explained by syntactical elements or standard conventions and tends to persist as an identifiable part of the *vernacular* (especially regional) language.

verse, stanza, chorus. *Verse*, the broader term, can mean a line of poetry, a poem, a group of poems, or poetry as distinguished from prose. A *verse* is also a metrical division of a poem, hymn, or other musical composition, that is, a series of lines arranged in a repeating pattern of rhythm, rhyme, or both. Outside poetic scansion, the latter meaning of *verse* is synonymous with *stanza*. A popular song is generally divided into *verse*, or the lyrics, and *chorus*, or refrain, which repeats the opening statement. A *chorus* can also be a multipart composition written for many singers.

versus, reverse, vice versa. Although most readers will know that contradiction of some statement is implied by any of these terms, they can be confusing and are better avoided unless a true logical "opposite" is clearly at issue. For example, the statement "A fare increase will reduce subway ridership, and the reverse is also true" [or vice versa] could mean that reduced ridership increases fares or that reduced fares would increase ridership; in effect, the writer's point is lost. See also *converse, contrary, opposite, reverse*.

very, rather, quite. These qualifiers tend to weaken rather than to strengthen descriptions, and writers should be restrained in their use. Grammarians disagree on the past participles *very* may be used with; adding *much* can avoid awkwardness, as in "very much mistaken." *Had rather* and *would rather* are standard idioms in all but the most formal writing to mean "would prefer." *Quite* may mean "entirely" or "somewhat" and may be ambiguous; *quite a* is a standard construction, as in "quite a few," although its literal logic is loose.

vice versa. See *versus, reverse, vice versa*.

view. See *witness, see, watch, view*.

violent. See *vehement, violent, virulent*.

virtually, practically. *Virtually* means "in effect though not in fact" and not "nearly, almost." Experts disagree on the use of *practically* for any of the foregoing terms, so it is best avoided formally except to mean "in a practical manner." "Misuse of these confusables is virtually guaranteed because, practically speaking, we all routinely interchange them."

virulent. See *vehement, violent, virulent*.

vital. See *pivotal, vital*.

vocation, avocation. A *vocation* is a profession or calling; an *avocation* is a hobby or secondary interest.

vs., v. Though *versus* should usually be spelled out, *vs.* is the correct abbreviation in most cases; *v.* is used in citations of legal cases, where it is sometimes italicized.

W

watch. See *witness, see, watch, view.*

wean, nourish. To *wean* does not mean to bring up on or to *nourish* but to end dependence on. One is "weaned away from," so it is not correct to say "We were weaned on proper use of the subjunctive."

well. See *good, well.*

wharf. See *dock, pier, quay, wharf.*

whereas. See *while, whereas.*

whether or not. In cases where a clear alternative is not being proposed, *or not* should be omitted from this expression. "Whether you keep your appointment is up to you, but you will pay for an office visit whether or not you show up." See also *if, whether.*

which, that. See Chapter 4, Pronouns, page 138.

while. See *although, though, while.*

while, whereas. Since the early 20th century, grammarians have been divided on the advisability of using *while* in any other than a temporal sense ("during the time that," "as long as"). Other uses are "standard and established," according to *Webster's Dictionary of English Usage,* and some sources consider *while* less stilted than *whereas* to mean "despite the fact that," "while on the contrary." "I've had enough of this snow, whereas you revel in it" is correct but perhaps overly formal; "I hate snow, while you love it" is unambiguous. Such informal use of *while* is extremely common and does not impede meaning.

Copperud and others, however, advise against interchanging these conjunctions. In formal writing and where ambiguity could result, a careful writer will replace *while* with *whereas* to indicate contradiction. "I've been making soup while you were cross-country skiing" is correct in a temporal sense, but means something quite different if *whereas* is substituted: "I've been slaving away over a stove whereas you've been off having fun" becomes the implied message.

who, whom. See Chapter 4, Pronouns, page 136.

wholesome. See *healthy, healthful, wholesome.*

will. See *shall, will.*

witness, see, watch, view. *Witness* has a legalistic connotation that is inappropriate for ordinary contexts: not "witness a basketball game," but perhaps "witness a child steal a ball." To *see* is the most general of the other terms and can encompass all their meanings, but to be exact, to *watch* implies focused attention over time ("The parent should watch that light-fingered child more carefully") and to *view* implies to examine or look at in a particular light: "People who view the world as their oyster often discover pearls."

worth. See *cost, price, value, worth.*

worthy of. See *deserving of, worthy of.*

would. See *should, would, ought to.*

would of. See *should of, would of, could of.*

wrack. See *rack, wrack, wreak.*

wreak. See *rack, wrack, wreak.*

X

Xerox, photocopy. *Xerox* is a trademark and should be capitalized. *Photocopy* is the correct generic term. Other product names, such as *linoleum,* have fallen into general use and have lost their trademark status. Chapter 9, Capitalization, lists some frequently seen trademarks and their generic substitutes.

Z

zenith. See *nadir, zenith.*

PART TWO

GRAMMAR

INTRODUCTION

During its first 1,200 years the English language grew and changed, borrowing something of value from every tribe and nation that invaded the British Isles. Its many adopted speakers, particularly the Vikings and the Normans, simplified its grammar and expanded its vocabulary. Primarily a spoken language, English bent easily to suit the everyday needs of a small island's diverse population.

By the 1700s, however, the world was becoming increasingly literate, and written English began to rival Latin, Greek, and French as the language of choice for British and American scholarly works. The flexibility that had blessed English with its richness and strength was now seen by many as instability, a threat to the permanence of the written word. It was time for rules, satirist Jonathan Swift declared in 1712, and he proposed a royal academy to come up with a method for "ascertaining and fixing our language forever."

Swift's not-so-modest proposal ultimately failed; Samuel Johnson, the first great English lexicographer, was one of many language scholars who opposed the idea. They recognized that rules for any language are arbitrary and that the purpose of these rules is to set standards, not to restrict change.

The first English standard-setters were the printers of the 16th, 17th, and 18th centuries. In the absence of dictionaries, style manuals, and grammar books, these early printers set rules as they set type, and some of their decisions are with us today (see Chapter 15, Spelling). Because printers worked independently, however, the variations in grammar, punctuation, and spelling persisted. By the late 1700s, the door was open for someone to write a book on the subject, which three well-known nongrammarians did with some success: Joseph Priestley, the discoverer of oxygen; Robert Lowth, later the bishop of London; and Lindley Murray, an American

THE IMPORTANCE OF STUDYING GRAMMAR

In *A Grammar of the English Language* (1833), author William Cobbett addressed this advice to his 14-year-old son:

> In the immense field of [book] knowledge, innumerable are the paths, and GRAMMAR is the gate of entrance to them all. . . .
>
> The actions of men proceed from their *thoughts*. In order to obtain the co-operation, the concurrence, or the consent of others, we must communicate our thoughts to them. The means of communication are *words;* and grammar teaches us *how to make use of words*. Therefore, in all the ranks, degrees, and situations of life, a knowledge of the principles and rules of grammar must be useful; in some situations it must be necessary to the avoiding of really injurious errors; and in no situation, which calls on a man to place his thoughts upon paper, can the possession of it fail to be a source of self-gratulation, or the want of it a cause of mortification and sorrow.
>
> . . . Grammar, perfectly understood, enables us not only to express our meaning fully and clearly, but so to express it as to enable us to defy the ingenuity of man to give our words any other meaning than that which we ourselves intend to express. This, therefore, is a science of substantial utility.

lawyer. Murray's 1795 work, *English Grammar,* proved to be the most influential. It established a system and a set of rules that were adopted by many 19th-century grammarians and are familiar to us today. This book went through 50 editions in its original form and 150 editions in a revised, abridged form. By 1850, between 1.5 and 2 million copies had been sold.

Murray's work marked the beginning of grammar as a popular topic, both in schools and among the public at large. Between 1800 and 1865, some 265 books on English grammar were published in the United States alone. To provide a foundation for their rules, these early grammarians turned to a well-ordered and universally respected language that couldn't change—Latin. As a result, ways of writing that even Shakespeare had used became "wrong." Double negatives were wrong because they didn't exist in Latin. Split infinitives were wrong because they were impossible in Latin—the infinitive form is one word in Latin. Ending a sentence with a preposition was wrong because prepositions never fall at the end of a sentence in Latin. And although it may sound more natural to answer "It's me" to the question "Who's there?" the proper reply in Latin translates as "It is I."

Those early grammarians are also credited with keeping alive such common bugaboos as the *who/whom* and *shall/will* distinctions, the subjunctive mood, and strict adherence to the rule that a pronoun must agree with its antecedent in number (*not* "Each leaning on their elbows," as Shakespeare once wrote). Long forgotten was playwright Ben Jonson's premise, in his 1640 book *Grammar*, that "Custome is the most certaine Mistress of Language." Custom, unfortunately, is just too hard to nail down.

In the past 50 or 60 years, though, many of these rules have been chipped away at by a less pedantic group of language watchers, from H.W. Fowler in the 1920s to Theodore Bernstein in the 1960s to William Safire and Edwin Newman today. The six chapters on grammar that follow take a similar view. The approach is prescriptive in areas where most writers, editors, and grammarians agree and descriptive where answers are not as clear-cut; we try to offer a balanced view of the rules, both old and evolving, so that the reader can decide on the best solution for a particular situation. Finally, these chapters make no claim to be comprehensive; instead, we concentrate on common problems and pitfalls, avoiding grammatical terminology as much as possible.

As science and technology continue to spread English to all parts of the globe, the language will continue to change, slowly in some ways and quickly in others. We can be sure of only one thing: that the points of grammar made here will continue to be examined and debated in the decades to come, just as they have been over the past three centuries.

3

NOUNS

NOUNS

Nouns are the foundation of any language, the words that name the sources and objects of our actions. They can be concrete—people, animals, places, and objects—or abstract—invisible substances (helium, air), qualities (abundance, kindness, cruelty), actions (reading, skiing), and measures of time and quantity (month, ounce).

Concrete nouns: Lawrence bought her an old green *trailer* and moved it into the *yard* behind his *house,* next to the *garden.* (Garrison Keillor, *Leaving Home*)

Abstract nouns: The *feeling* among educated *society* was that it was everyone's moral *duty* to aid the *cause* of *revolution,* a sacred *obligation* to the exploited people of Russia. (Alexander Solzhenitsyn, *August 1914*)

This chapter concentrates on three common problems with nouns: agreement of all related nouns in a sentence, possessives (for simple punctuation of possessive nouns, see "Apostrophe" in Chapter 10, Punctuation), and nouns with phrases of apposition. Other chapters address related problems. For rules on forming plurals, see Chapter 15, Spelling. Collectives, probably the most troublesome nouns, use a singular form to name something that is plural in meaning. Deciding whether words like *couple* and *staff* take singular or plural verbs is not always easy; Chapter 6, Subject-Verb Agreement, page 169, explains.

AGREEMENT OF NOUNS IN A SENTENCE

Nouns that relate to one another in a sentence must agree in number.

Correct: Bench and Yastrzemski made their last road *trips* around their *leagues* in the *styles* that suited their *personalities*. . . . (Roger Angell, *Season Ticket*)

❧

NOUNS AS INSPIRATION

Although verbs are usually the words that give action and life to writing, nouns can also evoke powerful images. In his book *Zen in the Art of Writing,* Ray Bradbury describes how he used nouns to fuel his writing as a young man:

> I began to make lists of titles, to put down long lines of *nouns.* These lists were the provocations, finally, that caused my better stuff to surface. I was feeling my way toward something honest, hidden under the trapdoor on the top of my skull.
>
> The lists ran something like this: THE LAKE. THE NIGHT. THE CRICKETS. THE RAVINE. THE ATTIC. . . . THE CROWD. THE NIGHT TRAIN. THE FOG HORN. THE SCYTHE. THE CARNIVAL. THE CAROUSEL. THE DWARF. . . .
>
> I was beginning to see a pattern in the list, in these words that I had simply flung forth on paper, trusting my subconscious to give bread, as it were, to the birds.

Incorrect: One slept with his mouth open and snored outrageously, another slept on his back with his arms folded over the top of the covers, two slept on *their side* with *their back* to me, and one wanted to cuddle all night long. (*Lear's,* June 1991, "Lovers and Other Husbands")

The rule sounds simple, but applying it isn't always easy, as the next section explains.

PROBLEMS WITH POSSESSIVES

Singular Nouns with Plural Possessive Pronouns

In some sentences with plural possessive pronouns, certain kinds of nouns are often singular. This exception to the general rule of noun and pronoun agreement has three categories, set forth below. This is one of those areas of grammar where common sense and the sound to the ear must enter into the writer's or editor's decision.

1. Nouns that are used as abstractions

The nation mourned when the seven astronauts of the space shuttle *Challenger* met *their* tragic *death.*

Even though we know seven *deaths* occurred, using singular nouns to express certain abstract concepts is accepted as idiomatic in English. To use the plural in such sentences would be too literal.

2. Nouns that denote something abstract, rather than concrete, held in common

   Throughout the ordeal, all family members maintained *their dignity.*

3. Nouns that are used figuratively

   Constance and Marianne were waiting for *their* big *moment.* In *their mind's eye,* they could see their pumpkin in the place of honor. (Stan and Jan Berenstain, *The Berenstain Bears and the Prize Pumpkin*)

Possessives with Gerunds

A possessive noun is used with a gerund (an *-ing* word that functions as a noun) to indicate ownership. Grammarians refer to this construction as *genitive with gerund.* Understanding when to use the possessive before a gerund is important because the possessive can change the meaning, as the following sentences demonstrate:

> I love the *man* dancing on the table.
> I love the *man's* dancing on the table.

The first sentence says, "I love the man." The word *dancing* is a participle acting as an adjective to modify *man;* it indicates which man is loved. The second sentence says, "I love the dancing of the man." The man in this sentence could be a stranger; the writer loves the dancing, not the man. *Man* modifies the gerund *dancing* and must be in the possessive case. Here's another example:

> We disapprove of *his* [not *him*] marrying our daughter.

Even the *New York Times* is not immune to this kind of error, as this headline about a job loss shows: "Behind Frohnmayer Losing an Arts Post" (February 27, 1992). The headline writer should have added an *'s* to make it "Frohnmayer's."

There are some words that either cannot be formed in the possessive or seem awkward with apostrophes.

> At times, the editor despaired of *anything* going right.
> We couldn't bear *Joe and Kathy* staying with us for 2 months.

If there is any chance that the reader will misinterpret such a sentence or if it sounds awkward, it is best to rewrite:

> We couldn't bear to have Joe and Kathy stay with us for 2 months.

Possessives with Inanimate Objects

Some grammarians say that possessives of inanimate objects should not be expressed by adding *'s:* the book's owner, the car's radio. But according to

Theodore Bernstein, in *The Careful Writer,* this distinction was never an ironclad rule; the choice is up to the writer. The possessive is always appropriate with expressions of time and measurement, for certain idiomatic expressions, and for phrases that imply personification.

this evening's news
a dollar's worth
for heaven's sake
heart's desire

Certain expressions that end in *s* or the *s* sound traditionally add an apostrophe only: for conscience' sake. See Chapter 10, Punctuation, for further discussion.

Double Possessives

A double possessive, also called double genitive, occurs in phrases that contain both *of* and a possessive—a friend of the boy's, the neighbors of the Smiths'. Although these constructions seem to overdo the idea of possession, most authorities accept them, especially in informal writing, arguing that they are idiomatic. To demonstrate how ingrained this usage is, consider that most of us would say "I'm a friend of hers" before we would say "I'm a friend of her."

Here's another type of double possessive: her aunt's father's house. This usage is correct but awkward; see Chapter 10, Punctuation, page 274, for further discussion.

NOUNS WITH PHRASES OF APPOSITION

When a noun is defined by an appositive, the appositive must refer to the correct noun. Editors should be especially alert for problems when appositional phrases appear.

Incorrect: In 1986 Elie Wiesel was named the Nobel Peace Prize recipient, an honor established by Alfred Nobel.

In this sentence, *honor* modifies *recipient,* which is incorrect; *honor* refers to the prize, not to Mr. Wiesel. One way to check whether the phrase is correct is to mentally delete the word or phrase being explained—here, *the Nobel Peace Prize recipient*—and see whether the sentence still makes sense.

Try: Elie Wiesel was named an honor founded by Alfred Nobel.

This makes no sense, so the sentence should read as follows.

Correct: In 1986 Elie Wiesel was named the recipient of the Nobel Peace Prize, an honor established by Alfred Nobel.

4

PRONOUNS

PRONOUNS

As most of us remember from elementary school, a pronoun takes the place of a noun. Pronouns are used when the speaker or writer does not want to use or repeat the noun. The noun that the pronoun replaces is called its *antecedent*.

There are several types of pronouns: personal, possessive, intensive (or reflexive), relative, interrogative, demonstrative, indefinite, and reciprocal. Knowing these terms isn't as important as being able to recognize a word as a pronoun and use its forms correctly.

Problems with pronouns abound. Agreement of pronouns with their antecedents is probably the most common, followed by use of the wrong case (consider the confusion between *who* and *whom,* for example), ambiguous references, and the perennial question of *that* versus *which.*

AGREEMENT

The general rule of pronoun agreement is that a pronoun must agree with the word or idea it stands for (its antecedent) in number (singular or plural), person (first, second, or third), and gender (masculine, feminine, or neuter).

Number

In general, a pronoun must agree with its antecedent in number. In other words, if the pronoun's antecedent is singular, the pronoun must be singular; if the antecedent is plural, the pronoun must be plural.

> *Vincent* went down to *his* suite to change shirts, to get out of the one *he'd* worn two nights in a row. . . . (Elmore Leonard, *Glitz*)

❧

ME, MYSELF, OR I?

Intensive and reflexive pronouns—the *-self, -selves* forms of the personal pronouns—are used only to refer to or emphasize the nouns or pronouns they represent, not to take their place. Therefore, these pronouns should not be used as the subject or object of a sentence.

> Stuart and *I* [not *myself*] will present the results of the first part of the study.
> The advice was for my sister and *me* [not *myself*].

> The most sinister thing about the fall of the *Roman Empire* was that the *people* who conquered *it* never understood that *they* had done so. (Robert Pirsig, *Lila*)
> When *hitting the post with a stone* lost *its* challenge as she gained skill with the sling, she set more difficult targets for herself. (Jean Auel, *Clan of the Cave Bear*)

The use of *they* in the next sentence is clearly wrong, however.

> *The magazine* got so many letters, *they* wrote us saying it'd be nice to do a feature article. (Allan Gurganus, *Oldest Living Confederate Widow Tells All*)

Here, the plural pronoun *they* incorrectly refers to the singular noun *magazine.* Of course, what the author meant by *they* was someone on the magazine's staff.

A pronoun should be plural if it refers to more than one noun, a noun and one or more pronouns, or two or more pronouns joined by *and.*

> She retired without speaking, *Clara* and *Heidi* following, happy in *their* minds at knowing the kittens were lying in a comfortable bed. (Johanna Spyri, *Heidi*)
> In some ways *we* are more alike, *she* and *I,* than she sees. (Alice Adams, *After You've Gone*)

When a pronoun refers to two singular nouns joined by *or* or *nor,* the pronoun should be singular.

> Either *John or Frank* will present *his* findings at the staff meeting.
> Neither *John nor Jane* has given *his* or *her* opinion to the judge.

Although the second example is correct, it could be easily recast to avoid the awkward *his or her* construction: "Neither John nor Jane has given an opinion to the judge."

When a pronoun refers to one singular noun and one plural noun joined by *or* or *nor,* the pronoun should agree with the closer noun. The second sentence below is easier to read and makes more sense because the plural noun is closer to the plural pronoun.

> Neither his parents nor *John* would give *his* permission.
> Neither John nor *his parents* would give *their* permission.

When a pronoun refers to a singular indefinite pronoun—*another, anyone, anybody, anything, each, each one, everyone, everybody, everything, every, many a, someone, somebody, something, either, neither, no one, nobody, nothing, one*—the pronoun is usually singular, with a few exceptions.

> *Neither* of the recommendations works as well as we thought *it* [not *they*] would.
> *Everyone* brought *his* or *her* favorite dessert to the office holiday party.

The second example could be improved by casting it in the plural.

> *All the staff members* brought *their* favorite desserts to the office holiday party.

The exceptions sometimes made to this rule pertain to the plural pronouns *they* and *their.* First, to avoid awkward wording in sentences with indefinite pronouns that are singular in form but may be plural in sense—*everybody* and *anybody* are two examples—many respected writers and editors use *their:* "Everybody should vote *their* conscience." Second, to avoid sexist language in sentences where *he or she* would be awkward, many authorities approve the use of *their* or *they* to refer to a singular subject. Several good arguments can be made for this seemingly audacious breaking of the rules; see the sidebar "Language in Transition: Breaking the Indefinite Pronoun Agreement Rule" for a discussion.

When a pronoun refers to a plural indefinite pronoun—*many, few, several, others,* or *both*—the pronoun should be plural.

> A *few* took off *their* pants, too, but only the few who possessed long underwear. (Larry McMurtry, *Lonesome Dove*)

Some indefinite pronouns—*all, none, any, some, more, most*—can be singular or plural, depending on the nouns they refer to. When a pronoun refers to one of these indefinite pronouns, the writer must first decide whether the sense of the pronoun is singular or plural and then make the pronoun that refers to it agree in number. If the pronoun precedes a

❧

LANGUAGE IN TRANSITION: BREAKING THE INDEFINITE PRONOUN AGREEMENT RULE

When a rule of grammar conflicts with sense, almost everyone breaks the rule, don't they? Doesn't he? Doesn't he or she? The move to eliminate sexist language has given this question new currency. But what do conscientious writers and editors do with such indefinite pronouns as *everyone, anybody,* and *each*, which are singular in form and plural in sense?

The agreement problem posed by indefinite pronouns and common-sex pronouns such as *person* stems from the fact that English has no singular personal or possessive pronoun that means both *he* and *she* or *his* and *her* and that can be used with either a singular or a plural antecedent. The only common-sex, common-number pronouns are the plurals *they* and *their.* In spoken English, there is no problem. Speakers regularly use *they* and *their* with singular pronouns: "Everyone on the team wanted their picture on the poster."

But what the ear accepts, the eye dissects. Writers must proceed more cautiously. From the dawn of modern English, reputable writers have, on occasion, used *they* with a singular antecedent. *The Oxford English Dictionary* lists Shakespeare ("*Everyone* to rest *themselves* betake"), Samuel Johnson ("*Everyone* sacrifices a cow or more, according to *their* different degrees of wealth or devotion"), and Thackeray ("A *person* can't help *their* birth").

In short, the usage persists because there is need for it; the other tools at our disposal cannot always provide adequate substitutes. Writers and editors who wish to hold the line, however, should consider recasting a sentence in the plural or using *he and she* to solve problems of sexism and agreement; often a better approach is to do a little creative editing:

Original: When I got to the last mile of the marathon, *everybody* started clapping. I was grateful for *their* support.
Revised: When I got to the last mile of the marathon, *everybody* started clapping. I was grateful for *the* support.

Original: Whenever *anyone* was ill, she let *them* know she cared.
Revised: Whenever *anyone* was ill, she let *the person* know she cared.

Original: Either the senator or her *husband* will have to excuse *themselves* from the reception line to speak with the caterer.
Revised: Either the senator or her *husband* will have to *leave* the reception line to speak with the caterer.

prepositional phrase—"All of the cake is gone," "Some of the muffins were eaten"—it is usually correct to let the noun in the *of* clause determine whether the pronoun (and therefore the verb) is singular or plural.

Person

Person is the characteristic of a pronoun that indicates whether a person is speaking (first person), is being spoken to (second person), or is being spoken about (third person). Many fiction writers use the first person (*I, we, me,* and so on) to tell a story from the point of view of one of the characters.

> Will and *I* went to the movies and sat and held hands like any old well-adjusted bushy-tailed couple. (Diana O'Hehir, *I Wish This War Were Over*)

Other writers, usually nonfiction and business writers, use the second person (*you, your, yours*) to address the reader directly. Self-help books, user manuals, and training materials are often written in second person because advice, steps, and directions are naturally expressed in this way.

> You must have at least twenty chapters, each must end with a hook to draw you on into the next chapter, and you must end with a bang. (John Braine, *Writing a Novel*)

Sometimes the *you* is understood, that is, not stated.

> To fix a small hole in wallboard, insert a patch in the damaged area. (Reader's Digest, *Complete Do-It-Yourself Manual*)

Most professional writing—whether fiction, nonfiction, journalistic, or business—uses third person (*he she, it, they, them,* and so on). In this form, the writer serves as a recorder of facts and actions. On its surface, third person seems to be the most objective, but the author's opinions often show through, as this sentence illustrates.

> They sat at a table near the window, and were waited on by a tall, fat, pale Frenchman with a Bourbon nose who was pompous and superior to the point of bursting. (Jean Rhys, *After Leaving Mr. Mackenzie*)

Mixing person within a manuscript is usually considered bad form, although sometimes the switch is made so subtly the reader is unaware of it; for example, many instructional books written in third person occasionally slip into second person. In other instances, the shift is jarringly obvious.

A common error, especially in business writing, is mixing first and third person within a sentence or even a paragraph.

> *Incorrect:* In addition to introducing *our* new routes to Florida, Short-Hop Airlines has doubled *its* number of planes.

❧

FIRST PERSON: THE PERSONAL POINT OF VIEW

Many of the great stories of English literature are told in the first person.

> Whether *I* shall turn out to be the hero of my own life, or whether that station will be held by anybody else, these pages must show. (Charles Dickens, *David Copperfield*)
>
> In the late summer of that year *we* lived in a house in a village that looked across the river and the plain to the mountains. (Ernest Hemingway, *A Farewell to Arms*)

Correct: In addition to introducing *its* new routes to Florida, Short-Hop Airlines has doubled *its* number of planes.

Correct: We at Short-Hop Airlines have added new routes to Florida and doubled *our* number of planes.

Writers also make the mistake of mixing second person singular and third person singular within a sentence or throughout the text.

Incorrect: If *anyone* wants to be considered for the position, *you* should submit an application by Friday.

Correct: If *you* want to be considered for the position, *you* should submit an application by Friday.

Even better: Anyone who wants to be considered for the position should submit an application by Friday.

Another common error is mixing third person singular with third person plural.

Incorrect: If *someone* needs assistance, *they* should call the personnel department.

Correct: If *employees* need assistance, *they* should call the personnel department.

Even better: Anyone needing assistance should call the personnel department.

Gender

Pronouns have masculine (*he, him, his*), feminine (*she, her, hers*), and neuter (*it, its*) forms. Pronouns and their antecedents must agree in gender.

> On the other side of their host sat *Meg Dennison,* delicately but unfussily peeling *her* grapes with pink-tipped fingers. (P.D. James, *Devices and Desires*)

If the gender is unknown, is unspecified, or does not apply, the neuter form is used.

The *dog* waited nervously in the car for *its* master to return.
The *language* keeps talking about *itself,* cannot seem to have enough of *itself.* (Lewis Thomas, *Et Cetera, Et Cetera*)

The feminine pronouns are traditionally used to refer to certain inanimate objects such as ships and nations.

. . . And all I ask is a tall ship and a star to steer *her* by. . . . (John Masefield, "Sea Fever")

Problems can arise when both genders need to be acknowledged. Before the late 1970s, writers traditionally used masculine pronouns to refer in a neutral way to both sexes. But the equal rights movement has made both readers and writers sensitive to the political and psychological implications of this use. The easiest approach—the use of *he/she* or *he or she*—works in most cases but can distract the reader when overused. In some cases, the writer or editor can recast sentences into the plural; in others, a complete rewrite may be necessary. Chapter 1, Usage, offers several approaches for avoiding sexist language.

CASE

Case refers to the way a pronoun is used in a sentence. Many pronouns change their form from case to case—subjective, objective, and possessive. Case is the problem in these frequently heard errors: "between you and I" and "Whom shall I say is calling?"

Subjective Case

The subjective case (*I, you, she, he, it, we, they, who, whoever*) is used when the pronoun is the subject of the clause or follows a form of the verb *to be.*

She locked her car keys in the car.
It was usually *I who* woke him from his nightmares. (Jill Ker Conway, *The Road from Coorain*)
Give this letter to *whoever* answers the door.
My brother Jeremy is a thirty-eight-year-old bachelor *who* never did leave home. (Ann Tyler, *Celestial Navigation*)
She was the only woman *he* knew *who* didn't get disoriented at Bloomingdale's. (Eileen Goudge, *Garden of Lies*)
The winner of the contest is *she.*

To determine the correct pronoun in a sentence like the last one, when a pronoun follows a form of the verb *to be (be, am, are, is, was, were, been, being)*, mentally rearrange the sentence so that the pronoun falls in the subject position: *She is the winner of the contest.*

Objective Case

The pronoun is in the objective case (*me, you, him, her, it, us, them, whom, whomever*) when it is the object or indirect object of a verb or the object of a preposition.

> The house where she had taken a room was uncomfortable and cramped, and the other boarders, with *whom* she had her meals, were dull defeated widows and old maids. (Helen Hoover Santmeyer, "*. . . And the Ladies of the Club*")
>
> The old fellow—*whom* I heard Daphne address as "Jenkins"—came round with a big silver tray of champagne. (Len Deighton, *Spy Line*)

Here's an incorrect example.

> Maria has aged, and there's no one to help her carry on the well-meaning idea of serving cheap meals to those who can't afford more—a tradition started by *she* and her husband, Miguel, in 1949 after they left Spain. (*Seattle Times*, March 15, 1992)

The writer should have said "*her* and her husband" or, better, "her husband and her."

Probably the most common error is the use of *I* in the objective position.

Incorrect: Marilla wants to talk to you and *I*.
Correct: Marilla wants to talk to you and *me*.

Mentally dropping the first pronoun makes the correct choice apparent: "Marilla wants to talk to me." Deciding whether *who* or *whom* is correct is sometimes more difficult; see page 136.

Possessive Case

The possessive case of a pronoun (such as *his, hers, its, mine, ours, yours, theirs, whose*) shows ownership. Apostrophes are never used in the possessive forms of pronouns.

> Sherman lifted *his* Yale chin, spread *his* shoulders, straightened *his* back, raised himself to *his* full height, and assumed the Presence. . . . (Tom Wolfe, *The Bonfire of the Vanities*)
>
> Life is for each man a solitary cell *whose* walls are mirrors. (Eugene O'Neill, *Lazarus Laughed*)

The next sentence shows an incorrect use of the plural possessive.

> Stanley deposited his *wife* in *their* reserved seats. (John Jakes, *Heaven and Hell*)

Is Stanley's wife so large that she needs more than one seat? The sentence should read "in *her* reserved seat."

A possessive pronoun is used before an *-ing* word that functions as a noun (known as a gerund).

> *Incorrect:* The principal objects to *us* discussing the issue with the parents. (The principal is not objecting to *us*.)
> *Correct:* The principal objects to *our* discussing the issue with the parents.

When an *-ing* word serves as an adjective (known as a participle), however, the *-ing* word should not be preceded by a possessive pronoun.

> *Incorrect:* I saw *his* acting in the role of Julius Caesar.
> *Correct:* I saw *him* acting in the role of Julius Caesar.

These two sentences have two different meanings:

> I saw *you* painting.
> I saw *your* painting.

In the first sentence, the emphasis is on *you,* and the pronoun *you* is modified by the participle *painting.* In the second sentence, the emphasis is on the noun *painting,* and the noun *painting* is modified by the possessive pronoun *your.*

CAN AN EDITOR BE TOO CORRECT?

E.B. White wrote, in *The Second Tree from the Corner,*

> People are afraid of words, afraid of mistakes. One time a newspaper sent us to a morgue to get a story on a woman whose body was being held for identification. A man believed to be her husband was brought in. Somebody pulled the sheet back; the man took one agonizing look, and cried, "My God, it's her!" When we reported this grim incident, the editor diligently changed it to "My God, it's she!"

❧

MORE PROBLEMS WITH PRONOUNS

Strict grammarians would disagree with the following sentence because the possessive pronoun *his* is introduced before the noun *Dickens,* which is technically its antecedent.

> In his novel *Great Expectations,* Dickens recounts much of his tormented childhood.

It would also be incorrect to say the following:

> In Dickens' novel *Great Expectations,* he recounts much of his tormented childhood.

Once a noun becomes possessive, it no longer is a noun; it is an adjective and cannot function as an antecedent. Also, a question could be raised about the pronoun *he* in the sentence above. Does *he* refer to Dickens or to a character in the novel?

The writer's job is to word the sentence so clearly that the reader cannot possibly misunderstand its meaning.

AMBIGUOUS REFERENCE

Writers and editors should always be alert for ambiguous pronoun antecedents, especially with the pronouns *it, they, them, this, that, these,* and *those.* A pronoun must always have a clear reference, either to a specific word (a noun or another pronoun) or to a complete idea.

> Always do right. *This* will gratify some people and astonish the rest. (Mark Twain)

Notice the pronoun antecedent problems in these sentences.

> *Ambiguous:* Have children help prepare fresh vegetables for a snack by washing and cutting *them* with plastic knives.
>
> *Ambiguous:* Pets with claws should not be roaming loose when visitors come unless *they* are well behaved.

There are two ways to eliminate ambiguity. One is to introduce the pronoun and its reference before a second noun appears in the sentence. The second—and usually better—way is to rewrite the sentence.

> *Improved:* Unless they are well behaved, pets with claws should not be roaming loose when visitors come.

Another problem of ambiguity occurs when a sentence implies an antecedent rather than actually stating one.

> CFCs have been linked to the depletion of the ozone layer in the upper atmosphere. *This* allows more damaging ultraviolet rays to reach the earth.

In this example, the intended antecedent for *this* was *depletion of the ozone layer* in the previous sentence. Sometimes the context is so clear that the reader does not get confused. But in other cases, the meaning may not be clear to the reader, and the editor must step in to ensure clarity of meaning.

> *Ambiguous:* Because his grandfather had taught him much about carpentry, he wanted to become one.

The pronoun *one* has no antecedent; the word *carpenter* is implied but not actually stated.

> *Improved:* He wanted to become a carpenter because his grandfather had taught him much about the craft.

The word *it* is often left standing alone in a sentence, either with no reference or with a reference that is so far away that any number of nouns might be the antecedent. The rule is that a pronoun should be placed so that it refers to the closest preceding noun.

> If the dog leaves any food in the bowl, throw *it* out.

Grammatically, the pronoun *it* refers to the noun *bowl*—probably not what the writer meant. The reader sees three nouns to which *it* could refer: *bowl, food,* or *dog.* The sentence is clear when rewritten as follows.

> Throw out any food the dog leaves in the bowl.

The reference for *it* in the next sentence is not stated.

> If the furnace is patched, *it* will save us money in the long run.

DEL CANO'S NEAT TRICK

This sentence appeared in a film review in the San Juan (Puerto Rico) *Star* on January 19, 1992.

> The same Alcazar is used in the film to portray Juan Sebastian del Cano, the Basque navigator who brought the Magellan expedition to a successful conclusion after he was killed by natives in the Philippines.

As the sentence stands, *it* refers to the furnace. In fact, an unnamed noun in the sentence—the repair—is what will save money. The sentence should be rewritten:

> We will save money in the long run if we patch the furnace now.

Here's another example of an ambiguous referent for *it.*

> There was a drill for this sort of emergency, and he barked orders to implement it. *It* only made things worse. (Tom Clancy, *The Hunt for Red October*)

The first *it* clearly refers to *drill,* but the second *It* is not immediately clear; in this case, however, the reader can determine the meaning of *It* from the context of the sentence.

Generally speaking, the same pronoun should not be repeated in a sentence, and sometimes not even in a paragraph, when it refers to two different antecedents.

> *Unclear:* Business owners whose only concern is money may try to exploit their employees, not caring about whether *they* are earning a decent wage but only whether *they* are earning large profits.

Deleting the only *they* in the sentence that refers to employees and then rephrasing the sentence can help remove the ambiguity.

> *Improved:* Business owners whose only concern is money may try to exploit their employees, not caring about offering fair wages but only about earning large profits.

WHERE IS *THERE*?

The service directory of the newly refurbished Algonquin Hotel, long a gathering place for literary figures in New York City, had more than a few glaring errors in its introductory essay when the hotel reopened for business, according to a report by journalist Christopher Hitchens in *The Nation* magazine (August 12, 1991). In addition to scores of grammar and punctuation errors, the profile reported that the wife of a former owner "introduced Thorton [*sic*] Wilder to William Faulkner in the elevator, and James Dean used to eat there when he started out."

Hitchens wrote, "I did not try eating in the elevator, keen as I am to be mistaken for James Dean."

WHEN *IT* CAN MEAN ANYTHING—OR NOTHING

It is sometimes used in English where an antecedent is vague or nonexistent—for example, in impersonal statements about the weather and events in general. This construction is not unique to English; the French also say, *"Il pleut"*—literally, "*It* rains" or "*It* is raining."

Often a sentence that begins with *it is* or *it was* (in such cases, *it* is known as an anticipatory subject) is wordy and weak because a rather blank phrase is placed in the strongest part of the sentence.

> *It was* not until four o'clock that I decided to start painting the bedroom.

By deleting the phrase *it was* and the word *that* and rearranging the remaining words, the sentence becomes stronger.

> I decided at four o'clock to start painting the bedroom.

Sometimes, however, *it* may be useful at the beginning of a sentence for stylistic reasons or when the antecedent would not read smoothly in the subject position.

> *It* was a romance over the years at least as persistent as Sylvester and Tweety's. (Thomas Pynchon, *Vineland*)

It may also receive the action of the verb, serving as the object.

> She made *it* a habit to gather as much information as possible before making a decision.

Finally, *it* is often used in idiomatic expressions.

> Let's make a night of *it*.
> If *it* hadn't been for your help, we wouldn't have made *it*.

Sentences like this one often have a few other problems as well, and a complete rewrite is usually the best solution.

> *Even better:* Business owners whose only concern is earning large profits may exploit their employees by paying unfair wages.

THE MOST COMMON PRONOUN PROBLEMS

Using certain pronouns correctly—especially *who* and *whom, that* and *which,* and *who* and *that*—is a challenge for even experienced writers and editors. Problems with possessive pronouns and their similar sounding contractions—*it's* and *its* and *who's* and *whose*—are seen every day, even in the most respected newspapers and magazines. Here are some tips for remembering which pronoun to use.

Who *and* Whom

To decide whether to use *who* or *whom* in a sentence, follow these steps:

1. Isolate the *who/whom* clause from the rest of the sentence.
2. Delete the word *who* or *whom*. There will now be a gap in thought, usually at the beginning or end but sometimes in the middle of the phrase. The words may need to be rearranged to make sense.
3. Fill the gap with *he* or *him*. If *he* completes the thought, then *who* is correct. If *him* completes the thought, then *whom* is correct. The fact that *him* and *whom* both end in *m* makes this easy to remember.

Here are some examples:

Ken is the one (who/whom) will be hired.
1. who/whom will be hired.
2. _______ will be hired.
3. he will be hired.

He completes the thought, so *who* is correct: Ken is the one who will be hired.

Ken is the one (who/whom) I will hire.
1. who/whom I will hire.
2. I will hire _______.
3. I will hire him.

Him completes the thought, so *whom* is correct: Ken is the one whom I will hire.

Give this letter to (whoever/whomever) answers the door.
1. whoever/whomever answers the door.
2. _______ answers the door.
3. he answers the door.

He completes the thought, so *whoever* is correct: Give this letter to whoever answers the door.

Give this letter to (whoever/whomever) you want to write the response.
1. whoever/whomever you want to write the response.
2. you want _______ to write the response.
3. you want him to write the response.

Here the gap is in the middle of the clause. But once it is located, determining the correct choice is easy—in this case, *him,* so *whomever* is correct: Give this letter to whomever you want to write the response.

In some sentences, a clause separates the subject and verb. Here, only the *who* clause should be isolated.

> The candidate (who/whom) smiles the most will win the election.
> 1. who/whom smiles the most.
> 2. _______ smiles the most.
> 3. he smiles the most.

He completes the thought, so *who* is correct: The candidate who smiles the most will win the election.

Whose *and* Who's

Whose is a possessive pronoun and should not be confused with *who's,* the contraction for *who is.* To determine which word to use, substitute the phrase *who is.* If the sentence makes sense, then *who's* is correct; if the sentence does not make sense, then *whose* is correct. (Keep in mind that contractions are rarely used in formal writing.)

> (*Whose/Who's*) coming to dinner?
> *Who is* coming to dinner? (This makes sense; therefore, *Who's* is correct.)

The word *whose* is a possessive pronoun.

> (*Whose/Who's*) raffle ticket is the winning one?
> *Who is* raffle ticket is the winning one? (This does not make sense; therefore, *Whose* is correct.)

THE PRETENTIOUS WHOM

Many people avoid using the word *whom* because they are uncertain about when to use it. Still others use *whom* frequently, and often incorrectly, because they think they are being grammatically correct. Even though some have complained that this pronoun is a relic from the past and have proposed its demise, *whom* seems to be here to stay.

An example of *whom's* pretentious associations is the well-mannered butler in countless British movies who answered the phone or the door and asked, "Whom shall I say is calling?" Although he sounded very proper, he was very wrong.

Its *and* It's

By far the most common pronoun error is using *it's* for the possessive pronoun *its*. *It's* is a contraction meaning *it is*. The error is frequently seen in signs, advertisements, and other printed matter created by nonprofessional writers and editors, but it's not uncommon to see *it's* used incorrectly in newspapers and magazines.

> *It's* overall environmental impact is negligible. . . . (*Rochester* [N.Y.] *Democrat and Chronicle,* March 14, 1992)

Here's how to make sure of the correct form. Substitute the phrase *it is* to determine the correct pronoun; if the sentence makes sense, *it's* is the correct form.

> Virtue is (*its/it's*) own reward.
> Virtue is *it is* own reward. (This does not make sense, so *its* is correct.)

> (*Its/It's*) a grand night for singing.
> *It is* a grand night for singing. (This makes sense, so *it's* is correct.)

Which *and* That

Both *which* and *that* are relative pronouns used to refer to places, animals, objects, ideas, and qualities. To improve clarity, many writers and editors make this distinction: The word *which* is used to introduce a clause containing informative but nonessential (nonrestrictive) information. Because the information in this clause is additional and therefore unnecessary to the meaning of the sentence, commas are placed before the word *which* and at the end of the clause. If the clause is at the end of the sentence, a comma is placed only before the clause.

In these sentences, the *which* clauses could be deleted and the meaning of the sentences would remain the same.

> This speech, *which* would have softened good Mrs. Lynde's heart in a twinkling, had no effect on Mrs. Barry except to irritate her still more. (Lucy Maud Montgomery, *Anne of Green Gables*)
> Daniel Kahnweiler's collection of cubist paintings, *which* had been taken over by the government during the war, was now to be sold. (Janet Hobhouse, *Everybody Who Was Anybody: A Biography of Gertrude Stein*)

The word *that* is used to introduce a clause containing essential (restrictive) information. Because the information in the clause is essential to the meaning of the sentence, no commas are used. Without the information in the clause, the following sentences would have a completely different meaning.

Beware all enterprises *that* require new clothes. (Henry Thoreau)
In 5 minutes, she solved the problem *that* I had been working on for 3 hours.
You know what I mean—you know it's only the showy things *that* are cheap. (Edith Wharton, *House of Mirth*)

A word of warning to editors: Not all sentences are easy to interpret; sometimes only the writer will understand the meaning well enough to know whether a clause should be introduced by *which* or *that*. Because changes in meaning can happen so easily in this kind of sentence, editors should always

---

COPYEDITORS WHO GO ON "WHICH HUNTS"

Copyeditors, whose job it is to rid manuscripts of any factual, spelling, grammar, and punctuation errors before a piece goes to the typesetter, can sometimes go a little too far in their diligence, to the vast irritation of the author or publisher or both.

"Which hunts," as one publisher has been known to call them, are an example of this problem. Some copyeditors, especially those new to the job, will mechanically search out every sentence looking for *whiches* that should be *thats* and *thats* which should be *whiches*. Three problems often result: First, if punctuated correctly, the word *which* is not incorrect in the restrictive sense, and the copyeditor not only has changed what could be the author's preference but also has made what many believe to be an optional change that will add to the time and cost of preparing the manuscript.

Second, determining whether a phrase is restrictive or nonrestrictive is not always easy. Querying the author is essential when there's doubt, especially when the meaning will be unclear to the reader. A copyeditor who blithely makes a change is not doing his or her job.

And third, as experienced copyeditors know all too well, the chance of missing out-and-out errors increases when one's mind is on the hunt.

Copyeditors are valuable protectors of the language and of the quality of the written word, but the very best ones think twice before imposing certain optional or style changes on a manuscript, especially if the author has used terms correctly and consistently. It's not always easy, but good copyeditors must strike a balance among the often conflicting demands of the publisher's time and money, the author's wishes, and the reader's needs.

---

query authors before making a change they're not absolutely sure of. For example, consider the following:

> Cracks in an airplane's fuselage which result from metal fatigue are almost undetectable when they start.

If the context of the paragraph doesn't provide a clue to the intended meaning, a query is in order. It's important to phrase the query so that the author will understand the problem and provide the needed answer. Thus, the query might read, "Do *all* cracks in the fuselage result from metal fatigue?" If the author's answer is yes, a comma should be inserted before *which* and after *fatigue.* If the answer is no, change the *which* to *that.*

Finally, writers and editors should note that it is not considered incorrect to use *which* in a restrictive clause as long as the clause is punctuated correctly—that is, with no commas. The distinction drawn for *that* and *which* was originally suggested by Fowler in 1906, who said, "If writers would agree to regard *that* as the defining (restrictive) relative pronoun, and *which* as the non-defining, there would be much gain in both lucidity and in ease." Follett and Barzun (*Modern American Usage*) favor Fowler's suggestion but point out that "no one could plausibly insist that *which* as a restrictive relative pronoun is indefensible or incorrect." Note that in no case should a comma be used before *that.*

Who *and* That

Who and *that* are both used when referring to persons. The pronoun *who* is used to refer to an individual, and *that* is used to refer to a group of people.

> The exact number of American soldiers *that* participated in the Vietnam War has never been calculated.
>
> A politician is a man *who* understands government, and it takes a politician to run a government. A statesman is a politician *who*'s been dead 10 or 15 years. (Harry S Truman)

RESTRICTIVE OR NONRESTRICTIVE: AN EASY WAY TO TELL

Sometimes grasping the concept of restrictive versus nonrestrictive isn't easy. Writing in *The Editorial Eye* newsletter (February 1989), Mary Scroggins offered another approach to decide whether *that* or *which* is correct in a sentence:

> An easy way to decide whether information is restrictive or nonrestrictive is to determine whether the information in the clause applies to *all* people or things defined or described in the clause. If the information does apply to all, the clause is nonrestrictive (it does not set limits and adds no needed information) and requires commas. If the information does *not* apply to all, the clause is restrictive (it sets limits and adds needed information) and does not require commas. Using this technique, decide which of the following sentences is correctly worded and punctuated:
>
> *Nonrestrictive:* Rules of grammar, which are purposeless, should not be followed.
>
> *Restrictive:* Rules of grammar that are purposeless should not be followed.
>
> Are all rules of grammar purposeless? If you answer *yes,* the first sentence is correct . . . because *which* (with commas) used to introduce the clause in the sentence indicates that *all* rules of grammar are purposeless. If you answer *no,* the second sentence is correct, because the restrictive clause introduced by *that* (no commas) signals the reader that *not all* rules of grammar—only the kind noted—are purposeless.
>
> These two sentences convey markedly different messages. The first advocates total abandonment of rules of grammar; the second, judicious use of them. Obviously, the second sentence is correct and conveys the generally accepted view.

5

VERBS

VERBS

In terms of sheer number, English has more verbs than any other European language, a fact it owes to its checkered past. Germanic in origin, English was first influenced by the Latin vocabulary that accompanied the introduction of Christianity and later by the conquering Vikings and Normans, who added thousands of new words to the mix. During the Renaissance, English scholars created new words derived from Greek and Latin, hoping to lend respectability to what was then a fairly vernacular language. For writers, the fortunate result of all this blending is that English often offers several verbs for a single concept—for example, the Germanic *rise,* the French *mount,* and the Latin *ascend.*

But along with their variety and vitality, verbs cause more than their share of grammar problems. The 250-odd irregular verbs—some of them dating back to the early days of English when inflections, or changes in a word's form to reflect tense, number, or gender, were more prevalent—are the first to bewilder children learning the language; "He comed to see me" makes perfect sense to a 6-year-old.

As hard as our English teachers may have tried, the only rule about verbs that most of us remember is that infinitives shouldn't be split. But that rule is no longer a rule, if it ever really was. So for many of us a fresh start may be in order.

VERB FORMS

The form of a verb—the way it is spelled—changes depending on tense, person, number, mood, and voice, all of which cause problems for writers. This chapter starts with tense and explains the uses of the various tenses, as well as which tenses to use when a sentence has two or more verbs showing

---

❧

PRESIDENT WILSON'S POVERTY OF VERBS

In *The Technique of Clear Writing,* Robert Gunning tells the story of how a leading newspaperman of the early 1900s, William Bayard Hale, wrote a small book called *The Story of a Style* that criticized President Woodrow Wilson. In it, he analyzed the president's weak prose style, saying that Wilson failed to put his message across to the American people partly because he used the verb *to be* to the exclusion of more expressive verbs and because he used far more adjectives than verbs.

To assess Wilson's prose style, Hale calculated the ratio of strong verbs to adjectives in writings by Shakespeare, Poe, Dickens, Hardy, Shaw, Mark Twain, and a few other well-known writers. He found that these writers averaged 13 strong verbs and 4.5 adjectives per hundred words—a ratio of about 3 to 1.

In his book, Hale praised verbs:

> The task of speech is to predicate, not to paint. . . . Adjectives qualify, describe, limit. . . . They are popular, because easy; they eke out effortless poverty of idea. The man who has something to tell has little need, little time, for them; he snaps out his tale in words of action. The thought that pants for deliverance bursts out in verbs. . . . The artist in language suspects an approaching adjective as he would suspect a possible rogue at the door.

---

different times. It then discusses voice and mood, describing when the subjunctive mood is called for and when it is not. The biggest problem area with verbs has a chapter of its own, Chapter 6, Subject-Verb Agreement.

Although this chapter focuses on solving problems in everyday writing, a brief review of verbs is in order. In English the *stem* of a verb is the form listed first in a dictionary; to create the *infinitive* form, place *to* in front of the stem. Verbs have four principal parts: present, present participle, past, and past participle. Regular verbs all change the form of their principal parts according to this pattern: *walk, walking, walked, (has) walked.* Irregular verbs change their form in often unpredictable ways. The principal parts of the irregular verb *throw* are *throw, throwing, threw, (has) thrown.*

Some otherwise regular verbs have alternate past forms (*dived* or *dove,* proved or *proven, burned* or *burnt, waked* or *woke*). In some cases, one form is preferred over another; a good reference for this information is *The American Heritage Dictionary,* third edition, which discusses many of these verbs in usage notes following the main entry.

VERB TENSES

Part of the power of verbs comes from their usefulness in telling time. The three basic tenses—past, present, and future—are straightforward and easy to use. But English verbs have *nine more* tenses, for a total of twelve possible ways to express specific combinations of action. Good writers make full use of all these tenses, often in original ways. Notice the shifts in tense woven into this paragraph:

> But most times, as I *say*, I'd *doze* off. Let me *give* you a sample evening. About twelve-thirty the lights of his half-ton *would come shooting* through the living room, *bouncing* off the walls, *scooting* along the ceiling when he *wheeled* into the driveway like a madman. It *was* the lights flashing in my eyes that *woke* me up most nights, and if that *didn't do* it there *was* always his grand entrance. When the old man *comes* into the house, from the sound of it you'*d think* he never *heard* of door knobs. I *swear* sometimes I'*m sure* he'*s taking* a battering ram to the back door. Then he *thunks* his

---

PROBLEMS WITH *LAY* AND *LIE*

Even the most experienced writers and editors sometimes run to their grammar books when confronted with *lay*—to put or place—and *lie*—to recline, rest, or stay. The principal parts of *lay* are *lay, laying, laid,* and *laid;* the principal parts of *lie* are *lie, lying, lay,* and *lain.* Note that the past tense of *lie* is the same as the present tense *lay,* a fact that certainly adds to the confusion over the two words.

Lay requires an object to complete its meaning.

> The worth of a new novel depends on whether you are able to *lay* it down.
> He is constantly *laying* the blame on someone else.
> I *have laid* three books on your desk.

Lie does not take an object.

> Bruce likes to *lie* in the sun while he reads; he *has lain* there for hours at a time.
> The proposal from the new client *is lying* on your desk.
> The mountain range *lay* before us as we continued west.

In deciding whether to use *lie* or *lay* in a sentence, substitute the word *place, placing,* or *placed* (as necessary) for the word in question. If the substitution makes sense, use the correct form of *lay.* If the substitution does not make sense, use the correct form of *lie.*

❧

LANGUAGE IN TRANSITION: INFINITIVES—TO SPLIT OR NOT TO SPLIT

English is the only language in which it is possible to split an infinitive because it is the only language with a two-word infinitive; in all other languages, the infinitive form is built into the word. Split infinitives were first seen in the 1400s and were accepted until a grammar book published in 1864, *The Queen's English,* strongly opposed placing words between *to* and the stem of the verb. This pronouncement became the voice of authority until 1926, when H.G. Fowler, in *Modern English Usage,* argued that personal style and clarity of meaning should take precedence. Yet almost 75 years later, many people, including teachers and grammarians, still believe that split infinitives are incorrect. Considering that split infinitives have been "wrong" for only about 60 years may help put the usage in perspective.

Here's a sentence that would read more smoothly with the infinitive split:

> At NORAD headquarters, the senior watch officer had quickly *to check* his memory to remember what a Dropshot was. (Tom Clancy, *The Cardinal of the Kremlin*)

These sentences offer examples of splits that promote readability:

> The government officials expect the nation's minimum wage *to* more than *double* in the next 10 years.
> The legislator has decided *to* all but *give up* on her child care bill.
> The president proceeded *to* sharply *admonish* the reporters who asked unanswerable questions.

---

lunch bucket on the kitchen counter and *bowls* his hard hat into the landing. This *is* because he always *comes* home from work mad. Never once in his life *has* a shift ever *gone* right for that man. [italics added] (Guy Vanderhaeghe, *Man Descending*)

The following section briefly describes each tense and then explains sequence of tenses—the science (and art) of combining tenses in a sentence to convey different layers of time.

Choosing the Right Tense

Tenses give us a way to describe past, present, and future events as well as indicate more subtle aspects of time, such as an action that is still going on, a past event that happened before another past event, or an action that will be completed a month or year from now.

To Show Action That Began in the Past and Is Continuing in the Present (Present Perfect). The auxiliary verb *has* or *have* precedes a past participle to indicate an action that began in the past and is continuing in the present or an action that shows a habitual past action.

> The Sprouds *have worked* here for the past 6 years.
>
> Birds hardly anyone *has seen* in Holland since the time of Napoleon are there now. (Barry Lopez, *Crossing Open Ground*)

The auxiliary verb phrase *has been* or *have been* with the present participle can also indicate this action (present perfect progressive). Using this form suggests continuous action in the past.

> The ozone layer *has been eroding* at a faster rate and for a longer period than experts had first predicted.
>
> Wyoming researchers *have been studying* the grizzly bear's summer diet of army cutworm moths.

To Show That One Past Action Has Occurred Before Another Past Action (Past Perfect). The auxiliary verb *had* precedes a past participle to indicate that one past action occurred before another past action.

> A state appeals court *had reversed* the conviction of a state official before the case went to federal court.

The auxiliary verb phrase *had been* with the present participle can also indicate this action (past perfect progressive). This form suggests continuous action in the past.

> The space station *had been functioning* flawlessly until a computer error shut down communications.

To Show Action That Will Be Completed by a Certain Time in the Future (Future Perfect). The auxiliary verb phrase *will have* and the past participle are used to show an action that will be completed by a certain time in the future.

> By the end of the year, I *will have jogged* 1,500 miles.

The auxiliary verb phrase *will have been* with the present participle can also indicate this action (future perfect progressive).

> By the end of January, the contractor *will have been working* on the road for 10 months.

To Show Action That Is Still in Progress (Present Progressive). The auxiliary verb *am, is,* or *are* precedes the present participle to indicate an action that is still going on.

The company *is hiring* 200 new assembly line workers.

To Show Action That Was in Progress Sometime in the Past (Past Progressive). The auxiliary verb *was* or *were* precedes the present participle to indicate an action that was in progress sometime in the past.

He *was reviewing* the facts of the murder case when his office was suddenly thrown into darkness.

To Show Action That Will Be in Progress at a Later Time (Future Progressive). The auxiliary verb phrase *will be* precedes the present participle to indicate an action that will be in progress in the future.

I *will be starting* the new project next week.

Sequence of Tenses

Understanding how the various tenses convey time differences is the first step in understanding verbs. The second is understanding how the verb in the main clause affects the tense of other verbs in the sentence, such as those in subordinate clauses or verbal phrases. This relationship is known as *sequence of tenses.* The tenses in different parts of the sentence do not have to be the same, but they must correctly reflect shifts in time. Writers and

---

LANGUAGE IN TRANSITION: *WILL* AND *SHALL*

Traditional grammarians dictated that *shall* should always be used in the first person: I *shall* meet you for lunch at noon. But few people today observe this distinction in speaking or in writing.

The language has changed to accept *will* as the auxiliary verb of choice in most situations. *Shall* is still used in certain situations, however.

To indicate a mandatory action. In some circles, this is called regulatory language. "The officer in charge shall lock the safe each night at 10:00 p.m."

To invite or offer. "Shall we dance?" "Shall we go to Europe this spring?"

---

editors often encounter sentences in which verb tenses don't seem to be quite right. The paragraphs below will help pinpoint the problems.

When verbs in the main clause and verbs in the dependent clause or clauses all describe action that happened at the same time, all verbs are in the same tense.

> When they *passed* by Gabriel's Crossing [dependent clause], the dogs in the yard below and the corralled stallions *sent* up challenges [main clause] that *echoed* faintly off the water [dependent clause]. (Alfred Silver, *Lord of the Plains*)

A verb in a dependent clause that refers to a general or universal truth or a habitual action is always in the present tense, even if the verb in the main clause is in the past tense.

> The instructor *explained* [main clause] that water *boils* at 212 degrees Fahrenheit [dependent clause].
>
> The lawyer *reminded* his client [main clause] that in this state anyone under 18 *is* a minor [dependent clause].

Because using present tense sounds odd to the ear in some sentences, an exception to the above rule is made for certain statements that show habitual action—that is, actions that describe facts or fixed events. In such cases, both clauses are in the past tense.

> We never *knew* that you *were* an architect.
>
> When *did* you find out that you *were born* in Romania?

Because English has no tense to indicate an action that is "more past" than past perfect, clauses describing one or more past events that preceded another past event are both stated in the past perfect, except as noted in the next paragraph.

> The history book *stated* that Jack Ruby *had murdered* Lee Harvey Oswald after Oswald *had assassinated* President John Kennedy.

If words denoting time (*after, before, last month,* and so on) are included in the dependent clause, the past perfect—although not wrong—is unnecessary; the past tense is sufficient.

> After he *lost* [not *had lost*] the New Hampshire primary, Paul Tsongas announced his withdrawal from the presidential race.

The infinitive shows action that happens at the same time as or later than the action of the main verb.

> Our family *went to see* the new Spielberg movie. (The going and the seeing happened at the same time.)

Our family *wants to see* the new Spielberg movie. (The wanting is in the present. The seeing will happen some time in the future.)

The auxiliary verb phrase *to have* or *to have been* and the past participle show action that happened earlier than the verb in the main part of the sentence.

The painting was thought *to have been lost.* (The loss happened before the thinking.)

Another way to show action that occurred before an action in the main verb is to use the infinitive *to have* and the past participle.

I would like *to have gone.*

The present participle shows action that happens at the same time as action in the main part of the sentence.

When Fannie Mae and Freddie Mac *buy* residential mortgages for banks and other mortgage lenders, they *are giving* the lenders funds to make more loans.

The present participle *having* and the past participle show action that was completed earlier than action in the main clause.

Because she was having severe headaches, Martha *decided* to see the doctor.

If the two actions happened relatively close together, an exception is made. Here the writer must make a subjective judgment: Did a brief or insignificant interval occur between the two actions? If so, the present participle is used because showing the levels of past events is unnecessary. It is almost as if everything happened at once, even though logically we know it didn't.

Running after the bus, he *tripped, fell,* and *broke* his leg.

Finally, the past participle shows action that happened earlier than the verb in the main part of the sentence.

Deprived by destiny of all superficial prettiness—though not devoid, in moments of animation, of a loveliness peculiar to herself—Perdita *had reached* her twenty-fifth year without anything approaching a love affair. (John Cowper Powys, *Weymouth Sands*)

I *was excited* because I was in a house with nine women who *had* once *had* awful marriages, nine women who no longer *had to obey* husbands or mothers-in-law. (Amy Tan, *The Kitchen God's Wife*)

Omitting Parts of Verb Phrases

When compound verb phrases in a sentence share a common element—either an auxiliary verb or a main verb—the common element does not have to be repeated when the verb form is the same.

I *have interviewed* three candidates and *decided* to hire the one you recommended. (The auxiliary verb *have* is shared by both main verbs, *interviewed* and *decided.*)
The counselor *can* and *will advise* the student council on proper procedure. (The main verb *advise* is shared by both auxiliaries, *can* and *will.*)

But when different forms of the main verb are needed, omitting parts of the verb phrase can lead to problems.

Incorrect: We *have* and still *are requesting* a new vacation policy.

Here, the auxiliary verb *have* cannot logically share the form of the main verb *requesting*—it makes no sense to say *have requesting.*

Correct: We *have requested* and still *are requesting* a new vacation policy.
Incorrect: I never *have* and never *will forget* how you helped me through rough times. (This is a common error with the verb *forget.* The auxiliary verb *have* cannot logically share the main verb *forget.*)
Correct: I never *have forgotten* and never *will forget* how you helped me through rough times.

MOOD

Mood is the form of a verb that shows the attitude of the speaker or writer toward the statement being made. Depending on mood, for example, a sentence may be a statement of fact, a command, a possibility, or a wish. There are three basic moods: indicative, imperative, and subjunctive. Three lesser-known moods are formed with auxiliary verbs and main verbs: the potential mood uses *may, might, can,* and *could;* the conditional mood uses *should* and *would;* and the obligative mood uses *must* and *ought.*

Indicative

The indicative mood is used to state a fact or an opinion or ask a question.

New York is the nation's largest city. (fact)
New York is a beautiful city. (opinion)
Did you enjoy your visit to New York City? (question)

Imperative

The imperative mood expresses a command or warning or makes a request. The subject of the sentence *(you)* is often omitted.

> Be wary of the man with a professional interest in justice. (Judith Rossner, *His Little Women*)
> Please return the survey by the first of the month.

Subjunctive

Using the subjunctive mood can seem like speaking English in a slightly different universe, where the basic rules of tense are reversed: present tense is used for past, past is used for present, and *be* is used for *is, am,* and *are.* Although its demise has been predicted for decades, the subjunctive mood is still widely used in three forms: in *that* clauses that express a suggestion, a demand, or a requirement; in sentences using the verb *wish;* and in sentences that state conditions that are improbable, doubtful, or contrary to fact.

Suggestion, Demand, or Requirement. When any form of the verb *to be* appears in the dependent clause, the form *be* is used with all subjects.

> I ask that the motion to pass the budget *be tabled* until we have more information. (suggestion)
> I insist that we *be assigned* to the project. (demand)
> Rules dictate that all entries *be submitted* on November 1. (requirement)

For verbs other than *to be,* the present tense is used for all subjects. An *-s* is never added to the verb, even if the subject is third person singular.

> The coach recommended that she *practice* more often. (suggestion)
> We insist that she *work* overtime to complete the project. (demand)
> It is essential that he *tell* the truth. (requirement)

WRITING IN THE IMPERATIVE MOOD

Delia Ephron, in *How to Eat Like a Child,* uses the imperative mood to instruct adults "How to Eat Chocolate Chip Cookies Like a Child":

> Half-sit, half-lie on the bed, propped up by a pillow. Read a book. Place cookies next to you on the sheet so the crumbs get in the bed. As you eat the cookie, remove each chocolate chip and place it on your stomach. When all the cookies are consumed, eat the chips one by one, allowing two per page.

❧

WATCH OUT FOR THAT *IF*

In an August 1991 story about World War II hero Raoul Wallenberg, a *Washington Post* reporter discussed the possibility that Wallenberg may still be alive. The reporter stated, "Next August Raoul Wallenberg *turns* 80, or would *were* he still *alive.*" This sentence is grammatically correct if Wallenberg is, in fact, dead. However, since there is some speculation that he is still alive, the sentence should have been written this way: "Next August Raoul Wallenberg *will turn* 80, if he is still alive."

Wish. In sentences using the verb *wish,* the verb in the dependent clause must be in the past tense to express present time.

I wish I *knew* the results of the election.
I wish that I *felt* better.

Improbable, Doubtful, or Contrary-to-Fact Statements. In sentences that state conditions that are improbable, doubtful, or contrary to fact, the verb in an *if* clause or in an *as if* or *as though* clause is in the past tense to express present time. To express past time, the verb in an *if* or in an *as if* or *as though* clause is in the past perfect tense.

If pregnancy *were* a book [contrary to fact; it's not and never will be], they *would cut* the last two chapters. (Nora Ephron)
If I *were* you [contrary to fact; I'm not and never will be], I *would be content* with the settlement.
Jane acts as if she *were* the manager of the project [doubtful; she is not and probably never will be].

Here is where deciding between the subjunctive and the normally used indicative mood gets tricky. The words *if, as if,* or *as though* do not always signal the subjunctive mood. If the information in such a clause points out a condition that is or was probable or likely, the verb should be in the indicative mood. The indicative tells the reader that the information in the dependent clause could possibly be true.

If she *was* the boss, this office *would run* smoothly. (There is a possibility that she could become the boss some day.)
If he *is drafted,* he *will be proud* to serve.
It *looks* as if [as though] the picnic *will have to be canceled.*

Finally, a few idiomatic expressions are traditionally expressed in the subjunctive: "be that as it may," "suffice it to say," and "as it were."

VOICE

Depending on their voice, action verbs show whether their subjects are acting or are being acted upon. A verb is in the active voice when the subject performs the action. A verb is in the passive voice when the subject receives the action or is acted upon. Note that these two sentences have the same meaning but say it in two different ways.

> The voters *have chosen* the delegates to the convention.
> The delegates to the convention *have been chosen* by the voters.

In the first sentence, written in the active voice, the voters are the focus; they did the choosing. The second sentence, written in the passive voice, focuses on the delegates; phrased this way, the sentence places more importance on the delegates than on the voters who chose them.

The active voice is stronger and clearer than the passive because the subject is doing the acting. In effect, the active voice assigns responsibility to the subject. The passive voice, on the other hand, emphasizes or directs attention to the receiver of the action—in the example above, the delegates.

FDR AS EDITOR

During World War II President Franklin Roosevelt received the following memo, written in the passive voice:

> Such preparations *shall be made* as will completely obscure all federal buildings *occupied* by the federal government during an air raid for any period of time from visibility by reason of internal or external illumination. Such obscuration *may be obtained* either by blackout construction or by terminating the illumination.
>
> This will, of course, require that in building areas in which production must continue during a blackout, construction *be provided,* that internal illumination may continue. Other areas, whether or not *occupied* by personnel, *may be obscured* by terminating the illumination.

The president revised the memo, ridding it of passive voice as well as jargon, to read

> In buildings where work will have to keep going, put something across the windows. In buildings where work can be stopped for a while, turn out the lights.

The passive is usually formed with an auxiliary verb (the correct form of *be*) and the past participle; other auxiliary verbs can also be used.

Although the passive voice has its uses, it can result in wordy, dull prose. Sometimes writers use the passive when the person performing the action is unknown or unimportant. At other times, writers use the passive to obscure responsibility for an action; this practice is especially common in business and government writing. For example, in the sentence "The decision *was made* to reduce the staff by 15 percent," we do not know who made this decision or who is taking responsibility for it. (See Chapter 24, Editing, which also discusses voice.)

Use the same voice within a sentence; a sudden shift from active to passive can confuse the reader.

Incorrect: She admitted that she *had recommended* her attorney for the job, but accusations of conflict of interest *were denied*.

Correct: She admitted that she *had recommended* her attorney for the job but *denied* accusations of conflict of interest.

6

SUBJECT-VERB AGREEMENT

SUBJECT-VERB AGREEMENT

In theory, subject-verb agreement is simple. If the subject is singular, the verb is singular; if the subject is plural, the verb is plural. In practice, however, agreement is sometimes confusing for two reasons: (1) locating the subject may be difficult and (2) deciding whether the subject is singular or plural may be problematic.

For easy reference, the following explanation of subject-verb agreement falls under three headings: singular subjects that require singular verbs, plural subjects that require plural verbs, and subjects that require either singular or plural verbs, depending on sentence structure or meaning.

SINGULAR SUBJECTS THAT REQUIRE SINGULAR VERBS

A singular subject requires a singular verb.

Singular Nouns and Pronouns

Singular nouns and pronouns take singular verbs.

The best *way* out *is* always through. (Robert Frost)

A *total* of 769 randomly selected adults *was* interviewed Wednesday for the latest Post-ABC News poll.

Prepositional phrases and descriptive clauses sometimes cause confusion when they come between the subject and the verb.

Typically, about *one* in three shareholders *bothers* to attend the annual meeting.

THE MOST COMMON ERROR IN WRITING

In *The Careful Writer* the language authority Theodore Bernstein claims

> Anyone who can distinguish between one and more than one—and this class of the population should include all alumni of kindergarten, even those who majored in raffia work—might normally be expected to match a singular subject with a singular verb and a plural subject with a plural verb, and to match singulars and plurals in general. Curiously enough, however, errors in agreement between subject and verb are the most common ones that writers make. So common are such mistakes that it is even more curious that the high priests of the let-'em-say-what-they-like faith, who seemingly subscribe to the odd theory that if a crime is committed commonly enough it becomes legal, have not yet decided that such mistakes are not mistakes at all.

Her *experience* in systems analysis and programming languages *makes* her well qualified for the position.

A major *problem,* decreases in productivity, *is* not being given sufficient attention by board members.

One of the qualities that often define character *is* honesty.

A singular subject followed by such phrases as *together with, as well as, in addition to, plus,* or *along with* still requires a singular verb. These phrases provide additional information and are not part of the subject.

A *footlocker* filled with a week's worth of name-tagged clothes, together with a duffel bag crammed with sheets and towels, *was stuffed* into our station wagon.

If the information in such phrases is as important as the subject, it is better to join the two pieces of information with *and,* creating a compound subject that will require a plural verb.

The following indefinite pronouns almost always require singular verbs; see Chapter 4, Pronouns, for a discussion of the exceptions.

another	much
anybody	neither
anyone	nobody
each	no one
either	nothing
every	one
everybody	somebody
everyone	someone
everything	something
many a	

Each has an idea about improving work conditions.
Much remains to be done.
Neither of the proposals *is* acceptable.
Everyone knows who fired the shot, but *no one is willing* to volunteer the information.

Note that the pronouns *anyone, everyone,* and *someone* are spelled as two words when the pronoun is followed by an *of* phrase or means "one of a number of things."

Every one of them has offered to donate money or clothing.

Depending on the sentence, the constructions *either . . . or* and *neither . . . nor* may take singular or plural verbs; see page 167 for further explanation.

Two compound indefinite pronouns joined by *and* require a singular verb.

Anyone and everyone is considered innocent until proven guilty.

Compound Subjects Modified by **Each, Every,** *or* **Many A**

Compound subjects modified by *each, every,* or *many a* require a singular verb.

Each manager and assistant manager has an idea to increase productivity.
Every nook and cranny has been searched for the missing keys.
Many a teacher has volunteered to participate in the recycling program.

For clarity, *each* should follow the verb or object when the subject is really plural.

Poor: Martha, Carol, and Stephanie *each has* $20 to spend.
Improved: Martha, Carol, and Stephanie *have* $20 *each* to spend.

When *each* follows a plural subject, the verb is plural.

They each own their own home.
The *contractors each have* a contract for us to sign.

In some sentences, *each* is unnecessary.

Poor: On the questionnaires, *each* of the items 24, 42, and 61 contains errors.
Improved: On the questionnaires, items 24, 42, and 61 contain errors.

An -ing Subject

An *-ing* verb form (gerund) acting as the subject of a sentence requires a singular verb.

Seeing is believing.
Reading is to the mind what *exercise is* to the body. (Sir Richard Steele)
Reviewing the criteria for nominating the outstanding employee of the year *has been assigned* to a committee.

Parts of a Subject That Combine to Form One Entity, Idea, or Person

When the parts of a subject refer to one entity, idea, or person, the subject requires a singular verb. The important point to remember is that the combined items must constitute a unit.

Turkey and Swiss cheese is my favorite sandwich.
The *winner and new president is* Joan Richardson.
Early to rise and early to bed makes a male healthy and wealthy and dead. (James Thurber)

Nouns That End in -s but Are Singular in Meaning

Some nouns cause confusion because they look plural—they end in *-s.* But they are singular in meaning and require a singular verb.

Mumps is an acutely contagious viral disease.
No *news is* good news.

Others include *lens, measles,* and *summons.*

Titles

The title of a book, magazine, movie, song, poem, or other work is always singular, even if the title itself is plural.

Familiar Quotations offers information found nowhere else.
The Birds, an old Alfred Hitchcock movie, *is playing* at the local theater.

A Phrase or Clause That Is the Subject of the Sentence

When a phrase or clause is the subject of the sentence, the verb should be singular.

> *To know him is* to love him.
> *Editing manuscripts takes* most of my time.
> *Whoever votes for him is voting* for a winner.
> *What had seemed impossible and therefore unreal was* now a fact clear to them all. (William Golding, *Darkness Visible*)

PLURAL SUBJECTS THAT REQUIRE PLURAL VERBS

A plural subject requires a plural verb.

Plural Nouns and Pronouns

Plural nouns and pronouns that function as subjects require plural verbs.

> Her knobby little *hands were* like tools laid upon the formica counter of the coffee bar. (Nadine Gordimer, *Something Out There*)
> *Those who stay at home* all day *live* in a world of women. (Anita Brookner, *Brief Lives*)

Compound Subjects

Two singular subjects joined by *and* or by *both . . . and* usually require a plural verb. This rule holds even if the writer has used commas to separate the parts of a compound subject. Note that this rule holds only for the conjunction *and;* see the discussion under "Singular Subjects That Require Singular Verbs" on page 162 for phrases introduced by *plus, in addition to,* and similar wording.

> *Managing the department* and *doing the weekly payroll require* attention to detail.
> *Whether the client accepts the proposal* and *whether the funds will be available are* two issues that have not been resolved.
> *Turkey* and *Swiss cheese are* two of my favorite foods.

The last example looks similar to the example on page 164—"Turkey and Swiss cheese is my favorite sandwich." But in that example, the two nouns that form the subject—turkey and Swiss cheese—combine to form one entity, a sandwich, and therefore take a singular verb.

The Unwritten and

Sometimes the word *and* is understood rather than written.

> *His face, his eyes show* the effects of a sleepless night.

Plural Nouns That Refer to a Single Item

Some plural nouns refer to a single item but still require a plural verb. Here are some examples (see also the discussion of words ending in *-ics* on page 170):

assets	premises
belongings	proceeds
credentials	quarters
earnings	riches
goods	savings
grounds	thanks
leavings	winnings
odds	

The applicant's *credentials suggest* that she is eminently qualified for the position.
The *assets are* to be liquidated.
The *odds* of winning the lottery *are* 1 in 12 million.

The following nouns are always plural unless they are preceded by the words *a pair of:*

glasses	scissors
pants	trousers
pliers	

My new *glasses are* broken. (*But:* My new *pair* of glasses *is* broken.)
The *trousers* with the pleated front *are* on sale this week. (*But:* That *pair* of trousers *is* on sale this week.)

Both, Few, Many, Others, *and* Several

The words *both, few, many, others,* and *several* always require a plural verb.

A *few* of the applicants *have* already had interviews.
Several of the employees *have* requested leave during the same week in August.
Many of the voters *are choosing* to stay home on election day.

SUBJECTS THAT REQUIRE EITHER SINGULAR OR PLURAL VERBS, DEPENDING ON THE SENTENCE

Some subjects can take either a singular or a plural verb. Usually, the sentence structure will determine which verb is correct, but sometimes the meaning will be the determining factor.

Or *or* Nor

When compound subjects are joined by *or* or *nor,* the verb agrees with the subject closer to the verb.

> The staff members or the *director is* always available to answer questions.
> The director or the *staff members are* always available to answer questions.

Placing the plural noun last in such constructions often makes the sentence read more smoothly. If following this rule results in a sentence that still doesn't sound right, the problem could be that *or* should be *and.*

Either . . . or, Neither . . . nor, Not Only . . . but Also

Subjects that are connected by *either . . . or, neither . . .nor,* or *not only . . . but also* follow the same rules as those connected by *or* and *nor.* That is, the verb agrees with the subject closer to it.

> Neither the employees nor the *owner knows* what happened to the receipts.
> Neither the owner nor the *employees know* what happened to the receipts.
> Either you or *I am* certain to be chosen.

Although this last sentence is grammatically correct, it is extremely awkward. In this case, it is better to rewrite the sentence: *One of us is certain to be chosen.*

None

None can be used with either a singular verb or a plural verb, but most grammarians and style manuals prefer the plural. The old belief that *none* means "not one" is not true in most cases; a closer look will usually show that "not any" is the thought being expressed in almost every instance.

> *None* of the reporters *were able* to interview the defendant.
> Television is the chief way that most of us partake of the larger world, of the information age, and so *none* of us completely *escape* its influence. (*The New Yorker,* March 9, 1992)

In the few cases where *none* clearly means "not one" or "no one," the verb is singular.

Incredibly, *none* of the 54 people on the train *was hurt* in the derailment.

In fact, most sentences expressing the singular aspect of *none* convey the idea more clearly when they contain "not one" or similar words.

Incredibly, *not one* of the 54 people on the train *was hurt* in the derailment.

All, Any, More, Most, Some, *and Fractional Expressions*

When *all, any, more, most,* and *some* or fractional expressions such as *one-half of, two-fifths of, a part of, a percentage of, a portion of,* or *a majority of* function as the subject of the sentence, the verb can be either singular or plural. In such cases, the meaning determines the correct form of the verb. Use a singular verb if the noun following *of* is singular and a plural verb if the noun following *of* is plural.

Some of the book *lacks* suspense.
Some of the letters *were not answered* for months.
Three-quarters of the apple *was left* uneaten.
Three-quarters of the employees *are* at a seminar today.
Part of our company *is being relocated* to Ohio.
Part of our files *were lost* in the fire.

Nouns That Do Not Change Form

Some nouns that end in *-s* (like *means, species,* and *series*) have the same form whether they are singular or plural. Other nouns, especially the names of animals like *sheep, deer,* and *moose,* also never change their form. The form of the verb used with such nouns depends on the meaning of the sentence.

One *means* of improving morale *is* offering an incentive program. (Only one means is mentioned.)
Other *means* of cutting costs *are* reducing travel funds and eliminating staff positions. (Two means are mentioned.)
The *sheep has fallen* into the hole.
The *sheep were huddled* together for warmth.

Foreign Words

Singular forms of foreign words that have passed into English require singular verbs, and their plurals require plural verbs. Here are a few to remember:

Singular	*Plural*
consortium	consortia
criterion	criteria (also criterions)
curriculum	curricula (also curriculums)
datum (rare)	data
kibbutz	kibbutzim
medium	media (also mediums)
millennium	millennia (also millenniums)
phenomenon	phenomena

The main *criterion* for selecting candidates *is* party loyalty.
The *criteria* for sainthood *include* evidence of miracles.
The *data are* remarkably consistent.
The *media are* keeping the public's interest alive.

Collective Nouns

Collective nouns require singular verbs when the group is functioning as a unit and plural verbs when the individual members of the group are considered to be acting independently. If a sentence seems awkward, the problem can be circumvented by inserting the words *members of* before the collective noun and using the plural verb. Here are some examples of collective nouns:

audience	couple	herd	public
band	crowd	jury	quartet
chorus	faculty	league	staff
class	family	membership	team
clergy	flock	mass	varsity
committee	gang	orchestra	
community	government	platoon	
council	group	press	

LANGUAGE IN TRANSITION: DATA AND MEDIA

Although *data* and *media* are plural nouns and properly take plural verbs, their use with singular verbs is becoming widely accepted. But *The New York Times Manual of Style and Usage* and *The Washington Post Deskbook on Style* both stand firmly with tradition except when these words are used with singular verbs in direct quotes. Style manuals for scientific publications also continue to treat these words as plurals. When *data* has the meaning of *information*, however, it makes sense to treat it as a singular noun.

MEDIA AND MEDIUM; MEDIAS AND MEDIUMS?

The word *media,* the plural of *medium,* is commonly used as a plural noun referring to the vehicles of mass communication such as newspapers, magazines, radio, and television. In the jargon of the advertising world, *media* is often also used as a singular noun, with *medias* the plural form, a usage that dates to the 1930s according to Richard Weiner's *Webster's New World Dictionary of Media and Communication.*

The plural *mediums* is used when referring to spiritualists; to materials of artistic expression—oils, watercolors, and the like (*media* is also correct); and to the substance in which organisms grow.

Most style guides, including those of the *New York Times* and the *Washington Post*, state that *couple* should be plural. But an informal survey revealed that this rule is often ignored.

Incorrect: The *couple has* three children. . . . (*Washington Post,* Feb. 26, 1992)

Correct: In Francis' off months, the *couple travel* together, sometimes researching locales for the next book. (*People* magazine, Nov. 23, 1992)

Here are a few other correct examples of verbs with collective nouns.

The committee is meeting to discuss its proposal for a new marketing campaign.

The *jury has reached* its verdict. (one group working together)

The *jury are going* home. (This extreme example is correct: The group does not share a home. However, most writers would say, "The jurors are going home.")

The *mass* of men *lead* lives of quiet desperation. (Henry Thoreau)

Nouns That End in -ics

Nouns that end in *-ics,* such as *acoustics, athletics, economics, politics, physics,* and *statistics,* may be either singular or plural, depending on the meaning of the sentence. An *-ics* word requires a singular verb if the noun refers to an organized body of knowledge and a plural verb if the noun refers to activities, qualities, or individual facts.

Statistics is a prerequisite for graduation.

The *statistics* derived from his research *present* a convincing argument.

Modern *physics begins* with Isaac Newton.
The *physics* of hitting a golf ball *are* quite complex.
Athletics is part of the core curriculum.
Athletics provide an excellent form of exercise.
Acoustics is an interesting field of study.
The *acoustics* in the auditorium *were* poor.
Politics is the science or art of government.
Office *politics dictate* prudence.

Clauses That Begin with Who, That, *or* Which

The pronouns *who* and *that* as subjects can be either singular or plural. To determine their number, it is necessary to find the antecedent, the noun or pronoun to which *who* or *that* refers.

Michener is a contemporary *author who writes* epic novels.

Because the antecedent for *who* is *author,* the singular *writes* is needed.

Michener is one of those contemporary *authors who write* epic novels.

Because the antecedent for *who* is *authors,* the plural *write* is needed. The sentence means that many authors write such novels, not just one.

Exception: If the sentence contains the word *only,* the singular verb is needed because the logic of the sentence requires it.

Michener is the only one of the authors on the list *who writes* epic novels.

Clauses That Begin with What

Clauses beginning with *what* may be singular or plural, depending on the meaning. The words following the verb determine whether the verb is singular or plural.

What we want is affordable housing.

A Subject That Follows the Verb

A singular subject that follows a verb requires a singular verb. If the subject is plural, the verb must be plural.

How forcible *are right words*! (Job 6:25)
All I maintain is that on this earth there *are pestilences* and there *are victims,* and it's up to us, as far as possible, to join forces with pestilences. (Albert Camus)

The Number *and* a Number

The number always requires a singular verb because the meaning is singular; *a number* always requires a plural verb because the meaning is plural.

> *The number* of employees who have dental coverage *increases* every year.
> *A number* of employees *have* recently *applied* for dental coverage.

Geographic Terms

Some geographic terms are plural in form but singular in concept. In these cases, a singular verb is required.

> The *Netherlands is* the last stop on our European tour.
> The *United States has developed* new educational programs.

Geographic terms that refer to more than one unit take a plural verb.

> The *Alps are* as accessible as they are gorgeous.
> The *Hawaiian islands are* a magnificent place to visit.

Company Names

Company names used as subjects usually require a singular verb.

> *Procter and Gamble is advertising* its new detergent.
> *JJK Associates has accepted* our proposal.

In keeping with its singular, impersonal character, a company is usually referred to with the pronouns *it* and *which*, not *they* and *who*. Some editors, however, prefer to use plural verbs with company names that contain plural words like *associates*.

> *Smith, Jones, and Associates are moving* to a new location.

Time, Money, and Quantities

When subjects refer to periods of time, amounts of money, or quantities, the verb can be singular or plural. Subjects expressing a total amount require a singular verb, but those expressing a number of individual units require a plural verb.

> The *$6,000 is* to be used as a down payment on the house.
> (*But: Thousands* of dollars *have been spent* on the renovation.)

> *Four miles is* a good distance to run in 40 minutes.
> (*But: Four miles* of road *were cleared* before the snowplow broke.)

> *Three hours is* too long to sit still.
> *Three hours were spent* in acrimonious debate.

When a number other than *one* stands alone as a noun and is the subject of the sentence or clause, the sentence requires a plural verb because a plural quantity is being expressed.

Of the top nine graduates, *four are taking* jobs on the East Coast.

Positive and Negative Subjects

When a positive subject is contrasted with a negative one, the verb should agree with the positive subject.

It is the *president,* not the vice presidents, *who makes* the final decision.

7

MODIFIERS

MODIFIERS

A modifier is a word, phrase, or clause that describes or restricts the meaning of a word. Writers must be constantly on guard because if modifiers are placed incorrectly, the results can be confusing or—worse—humorous. This chapter first explains how adjectives and adverbs work as modifiers and then offers advice on how to spot and correct misplaced modifiers in sentences.

ADJECTIVES AND ADVERBS: THE BASICS

An adjective describes a noun (a *rowdy* crowd) or pronoun (they were *rowdy*). In doing so, it answers the question what kind (*snobbish* attitude), how many (*seven* books), or which one (*recent* report). The modifier can be a one-word adjective (a *charming* woman), an adjectival phrase (a woman *of great charm*), or an adjectival clause (a woman *who has great charm*).

When the word that follows a verb modifies the subject (a noun or pronoun), an adjective is used. Also, an adjective usually follows any form of the verb *to be* and the verbs *appear, sound, look, feel, taste, seem, become,* and *smell.*

I feel *bad.* (not *badly*)
The bell sounded *loud.* (not *loudly*)
The milk smells *sour.* (not *sourly*)

An adverb answers the question when *(today)*, where *(here)*, why *(because)*, in what manner *(quickly)*, or to what extent *(very)*. The modifier can be a one-word adverb (walk *slowly*), an adverbial phrase (walk *at a slow* pace), or an adverbial clause (walk *as slowly as you want*).

The conference will begin *promptly* at nine o'clock. (*promptly* modifies the verb *will begin*)
The *very* talented author will be a visiting professor next fall. (*very* modifies the adjective *talented*)
He was not injured *very* badly in the accident. (*very* modifies the adverb *badly*)

Even though an *-ly* ending usually indicates that the word is an adverb, some adjectives also end in *-ly*: *lonely, friendly, lovely, costly, fatherly, motherly, worldly,* and *neighborly* are a few.

Mr. Wilson is well liked because he is so *neighborly*.
A *costly* lawsuit forced the company into bankruptcy.

To further confuse the issue, some *-ly* words can be either adjectives or adverbs, including *early, only, daily, weekly, monthly,* and *annually*. With these words, correct placement is important to convey the right meaning.

I read the *daily* newspaper. (adjective; it tells which newspaper)
I read the newspaper *daily*. (adverb; it tells when the newspaper is read)

Adverbs are used to qualify adjectives; one adjective cannot qualify another adjective.

Incorrect: The rock climber displayed a wonderful fearless attitude.
Correct: The rock climber displayed a wonderfully fearless attitude.

Finally, some grammarians still insist that adverbs should never be placed between compound verbs; as in the case of split infinitives, however, the sense and flow of the sentence may become overriding factors.

Ironically, the success of a highly publicized school-reform movement has *most clearly* revealed the failure of schools to meet the challenges of these times. (*Atlantic Monthly,* May 1992)

Comparative and Superlative Forms of Adjectives and Adverbs

Comparative forms of adjectives and adverbs compare two items, and superlative forms compare three or more items.

One-syllable adjectives and adverbs add *-er* and *-est* to the word to form the comparative and superlative. Adjectives and adverbs with two or more syllables use the words *more* (or *less*) and *most* (or *least*) to form the comparative and superlative. Some two-syllable adjectives can be formed either way: friendlier, more friendly; friendliest, most friendly.

Other adjectives form the comparative and superlative in an irregular way.

ADVERB OR ADJECTIVE?

Here's an easy way to decide whether an adverb or an adjective is called for. If *is, are, was, were,* or some other form of the verb *to be* can be substituted for the verb, use the adjective.

She looked *happy.*

It makes sense to substitute *is*—"She is happy"—so the adjective *happy* is correct.

She looked *happily* at her newborn child.

It does not make sense to substitute *is* in this sentence: "She is happily at her newborn child." Therefore, the adverb *happily* is correct.

Positive	*Comparative*	*Superlative*
good or well	better	best
bad or ill	worse	worst
far	farther, further	farthest, furthest
little	littler, less, lesser	littlest, least
many, much	more	most

The comparative and superlative forms of two-word adjectives containing *well* use the modifiers *better* and *best*—for example, *well dressed, better dressed, best dressed,* not *more well dressed* or *most well dressed*; and *well known, better known,* and *best known,* not *more well known* or *most well known.* (Hyphenation of comparative and superlative adjectives is discussed in Chapter 16, Hyphenation and Compound Words.)

Comparisons Within a Group

When a person or thing is being compared within the group to which it belongs, the superlative is used. When a person or thing is being compared with each individual member of the group, the comparative is used with the words *other* or *else.*

Kimberly is the *most* industrious person in the class.
Kimberly is *more* industrious than any *other* person in the class.

Without the word *other,* the second sentence would mean that Kimberly is not in the class.

Lake Superior is the *largest* of the Great Lakes.
Lake Superior is *larger* than any of the other Great Lakes.

Without the word *other,* the second sentence would mean that Lake Superior is not one of the Great Lakes.

> Doreen's idea was the *best* of all the ones discussed at the meeting.
> Doreen's idea was *better* than anyone else's. (not *anyone's*)

The word *all* (not *any*) is used with the superlative when the subject being compared belongs within the group.

> Derek Jacobi is thought by many to be the greatest of *all* living actors.

Writers should take care to compare only people or things within the same group. This sentence illogically compares books with authors.

> *Incorrect:* Charles Dickens' books are the most descriptive of all English authors.
> *Correct:* Charles Dickens is the most descriptive of all English authors.

The same rule holds true for comparisons that use the words *like* or *similar.* In this sentence, the placement of *similar* makes a difference.

> *Incorrect:* The home we purchased in Virginia is a colonial that has a similar floorplan to the home we sold in Ohio.
> *Correct:* The home we purchased in Virginia is a colonial that has a floorplan similar to the one in the home we sold in Ohio.

Absolute Qualities

When certain adjectives denote absolute qualities, logic says that no further comparisons are possible; these include words such as *unique, certain, vital, essential, final, critical, favorite, extreme, eternal, perfect, excellent, complete,* and *adequate.* Therefore, modifiers such as *more, most, very, somewhat, rather,* and *comparatively* should not be used with words denoting absolute qualities. *Unique* is often incorrectly modified.

> *Incorrect:* We ate at the *most unique* restaurant.

Something unique is one of a kind and cannot be compared.

Exceptions are possible for some absolutes, however; the following modifiers are usually acceptable: *quite, almost, nearly, really, surely, perhaps, absolutely, in some respects, not entirely,* and sometimes *not quite.*

> *Correct:* This report's findings are *not entirely complete.*
> *Correct:* The fit of that suit is *almost perfect.*

PROBLEMS WITH MODIFIERS

Misplaced Modifiers

A misplaced modifier is a word, phrase, or clause that is placed incorrectly in a sentence, thus distorting the meaning. Writers and editors should place modifiers as close as possible to the words they modify, both to ensure clarity and to avoid providing material for humorous fillers in publications like *The New Yorker.*

She came at me with the potato peeler, wearing an L.L. Bean chamois shirt, forest green, with long tuck-in tails. (Don DeLillo, *The Names*)
The new laser system is being used for the treatment of snoring in physicians' offices.
A 23-year-old Kerrville man was arrested for assault on a police officer when he allegedly tried to gore an off-duty officer with deer antlers strapped to his bicycle handlebars. (Kerrville [Tex.] *Daily Times*, Feb. 23, 1992)

Dangling Modifiers

A dangling modifier is a phrase or an elliptical clause (a clause in which some essential words are omitted) that is placed next to a word that it cannot sensibly modify. Dangling modifiers are usually found at the beginning of sentences, and often the word that should be modified by the dangler has been dropped from the sentence. All of these sentences need rewriting.

A Phi Beta Kappa graduate of Dartmouth, Jim Smith's head is bursting with ideas.
Earning his pilot's wings, his boyhood dreams had finally come true.
Electronically animated, the baseball fans enjoyed the scoreboard's graphics as much as they enjoyed the game.
Based on extensive research, the author wrote a true-to-life story.
Once considered a rising star, her political capital in Congress and within the administration has been depleted. . . . (*Time*, Nov. 29, 1993)

Sometimes dangling constructions fall elsewhere in a sentence and cause illogical or unclear relationships. Sentences like this one should also be rewritten:

Gates' testimony provided new details to earlier U.S. descriptions of the Iranian rearmament effort, estimating that. . . . (*Washington Post*, March 28, 1992)

❧

WHO HAS THE LAST WORD?

The first sentence in Norman Mailer's novel *Harlot's Ghost* contains a dangling participle:

> On a late-winter evening in 1983, while driving through fog along the Maine coast, recollections of old campfires began to drift in the March mist, and I thought of the Abnaki Indians of the Algonquin tribe who dwelt near Bangor a thousand years ago.

This sentence has the recollections driving the car. When the error was discovered, the book's copyeditor was blamed for missing it, but Mailer later claimed he made the error on purpose:

> We often live in recollections while driving a car; it can even seem as if the recollections are steering the vehicle. Dangling participles can offend a few readers intensely, but the damage caused might add up to less than the rupture occasioned by straightening out the grammar and wrecking the mood.

Squinting Modifiers

A squinting modifier is a modifying word, phrase, or clause that could refer to a word before it or after it, sometimes with hilarious results.

> The doctor delivered the baby wearing a jogging suit.

Of course, it is highly unlikely that a baby would be born clothed, but to keep the reader from stopping and wondering in sentences like these, the writer should place the modifier closest to the word or phrase it modifies.

> The doctor, wearing a jogging suit, delivered the baby.

Limiting Modifiers

This modifier is a word, phrase, or clause that limits the meaning of a preceding or a following word. Examples of limiting modifiers are *almost, exactly, hardly, just, merely, only, scarcely,* and *simply.* Writers must be careful where they place these modifiers; changing the location of the word *only* in the sentence *He said that he loved me* leads to six different meanings.

> Only he said that he loved me. (No one else said it.)
> He only said that he loved me. (He didn't mean it.)

He said only that he loved me. (That's the only thing he said.)
He said that only he loved me. (He said that no one else loved me.)
He said that he only loved me. (He didn't like me, and he didn't respect me.)
He said that he loved only me. (He didn't love anyone else.)
He said that he loved me only. (He didn't love anyone else.)

8

ARTICLES, PREPOSITIONS, AND CONJUNCTIONS

ARTICLES, PREPOSITIONS, AND CONJUNCTIONS

Nearly all English prepositions and conjunctions can be traced to our language's Germanic roots, according to Robert Claiborne in *The Roots of English*. Even though Germanic words constitute only a small part of our total vocabulary, in terms of frequency they make up most of the words we speak. Claiborne mentions a computerized study done several years ago that found that of the hundred English words used most often, every one was Germanic in origin; of the second hundred most commonly used words, 83 were Germanic.

ARTICLES

Articles, which are considered to be adjectives, are of two types: indefinite and definite. *A* and *an* are indefinite, and *the* is definite.

Indefinite Articles

The sound, not the spelling, of the word that follows the indefinite article *a* or *an* determines which word to use. The article *a* is used before all consonant sounds, including a sounded *h*, a long *u*, and an *o* with sound of *w* (as in *one*).

a book	a historian	a one-week vacation
a catalog	a historic home	a uniform
a euphemism	a house	a European country

The article *an* is used before all vowel sounds except a long *u* and before words beginning with a silent *h*.

an apprentice	an outfielder	an honor
an easel	an uprising	an heiress
an idea	an earful	an hour
an eight ball		

How an abbreviation is pronounced, not the way it is written, dictates which article to use. For some acronyms, the writer must determine whether readers pronounce the acronym as a word or say each letter.

an X-ray machine
an SAT score (or a SAT score, if the acronym is pronounced, not spelled)
a U.N.-sponsored symposium
a CEO

When an indefinite article is used in text with a series of nouns, the writer has two choices: (1) to use the indefinite article before each noun or (2) to use the indefinite article before only the first noun. The article is required before each when one requires *a* and the other *an.*

We have *a* boy and a girl.
We also have *a* cat and dog.
We have *a* townhouse and *an* apartment.

When the indefinite article is used before two nouns that create a single concept, the indefinite article is placed before the first item.

The newlyweds rode in *a horse and buggy* through Central Park.

An indefinite article is unnecessary before a word that is used as a word.

What is the definition of *seismograph*?

THIS USAGE IS HISTORY

Is it "*an* historic" or "*a* historic"? Americans use *a* before a consonant sound and *an* before a vowel sound, so "*a* historic" is correct. The confusion that often arises can be traced to two obsolete language traditions. First, years ago it was considered correct to use *an* before words that began with *h* if the first syllable wasn't stressed. Second, in the 1700s and 1800s, the *h* sound was often dropped from words like *historic* and *heroic,* but by the late 1800s most educated speakers began to pronounce the *h.* Yet many speakers and writers today prefer the sound of *an* before *historic,* which a usage note in the *The American Heritage Dictionary*, third edition, calls "a harmless adornment in formal writing."

❧

WATCH THAT *THE*

In *A Dictionary of Usage and Style,* Roy H. Copperud explains how even a small word like *the* can mislead.

> Careless use of *the* may confer a distinction that is either inaccurate, unintended, or both. Referring to John Jones as "*the* vice-president of the Smith Corporation" implies that the corporation has only one vice-president. "Laurence Olivier, *the* actor" is acceptable on the assumption that he is so well enough known that his name will be recognized. On the other hand, referring to a movie starlet, Hazel Gooch, lately of Broken Bottle, Iowa, as "*the* [rather than *an*] actress" leaves the reader with a rattled feeling that he has not recognized a name he should know, although in fact his ignorance of Miss Gooch is nothing to be ashamed of.

An indefinite article is used only in a singular sense; there is no plural indefinite article.

Definite Articles

The word *the* is called a definite article because it is usually used to refer to a definite person, place, or thing. *The* is used before both singular and plural nouns.

The word *the* should be placed before each of two nouns that are of equal grammatical weight but name different objects.

> We will discuss election procedures with *the* executive committee and *the* fundraisers.
>
> Recyclable materials are collected on *the* second and *the* fourth Wednesday of each month.

However, *the* is used only once if it precedes two adjectives modifying a plural noun.

> We will discuss election procedures with *the* executive and fundraising committees.
>
> Recyclable materials are collected on *the* second and fourth Wednesdays of each month.

In a series of three or more nouns, the word *the,* like the indefinite articles, is written either before each item or before only the first item. The choice depends on a writer's intended emphasis or the need to ensure clarity.

The word *the* should not be inserted before nouns that are meant to be indefinite in reference.

> Athletes often lose their physical prowess before they are in their thirties. (not "*The* athletes")

The article *the* can be used to distinguish one person or item from another with the same name.

> *The* Sybil Jefferson from Richmond is my cousin; I have never heard of *the* Sybil Jefferson you are referring to.

PREPOSITIONS

A preposition is a linking word that shows the relationship of a noun or pronoun to some other word in the sentence. The relationship may be one of time; space, direction, or location; possession or belonging; or association, cause, or instrumentality. The noun or pronoun following a preposition is in the objective case.

> A lawyer *with* a briefcase can steal more than a hundred men *with* guns. (Mario Puzo, *The Godfather*)
>
> Elections are won *by* men and women chiefly because most people vote *against* somebody rather than *for* somebody. (Franklin P. Adams, *Nods and Becks*)
>
> I have a fine sense *of* the ridiculous, but no sense *of* humor. (Edward Albee, *Who's Afraid of Virginia Woolf?*)

Certain prepositions are used idiomatically with certain words; see "Prepositions" in Chapter 2, Misused and Easily Confused Words, for a list of correct combinations.

WHY DO WE SAY "TRANSLATED FROM THE . . ."?

One interesting sidenote about *the:* Most credit lines on translations into English say "translated from *the* French" or whatever the language happens to be. But when something is translated *into* another language, we say it was translated into Spanish—not into *the* Spanish. Theodore Bernstein addressed the question in *The Careful Writer,* saying that the answer must be that the *the* refers to the missing word *language:* "translated from the French *language.*" He added that the *the* is unnecessary.

❧

LANGUAGE IN TRANSITION: ENDING A SENTENCE WITH A PREPOSITION

Perhaps because some scholar once noticed that *preposition* came from the Latin *prae + ponere,* meaning *to place before,* generations of students have been taught that a preposition must be placed before its object and never at the end of a sentence.

Many well-known writers disagree. E.B. White wrote a letter in 1962 to J.G. Case in which he said,

> The next grammar book I bring out I want to tell how to end a sentence with five prepositions. A father of a little boy goes upstairs after supper to read to his son, but he brings the wrong book. The boy says, "What did you bring that book I don't want to be read to out of up for?"

A strict grammarian would agree with only three of White's prepositions; *out of* is considered to be a two-word preposition, and *up* is an adverb in this sentence.

Ending a Sentence with a Preposition

Even today, some college and high school English teachers are telling their students that a sentence should not end with a preposition. But this is another "rule" that is no longer firm, if it ever really was. Ending a sentence with a preposition is acceptable, especially when the preposition is part of an idiomatic phrase. Also, the emphasis or effect that the writer desires often will determine where a preposition is placed.

A student should not be taught more than he can think *about.* (Alfred North Whitehead)
Which scene will you appear *in*?
What is this gadget used *for*?

Omitted Prepositions

Sometimes the *to* in the infinitive form of a verb can be omitted.

The computer class helped me [*to*] understand how to use the new software.
The *at* or *in* of an adverbial prepositional phrase may be omitted.
The new methods of research were developed [*in*] the same way.

Prepositions that add nothing to the meaning of a sentence should be omitted.

Where are they [*at*]?
Where did you go [*to*]?
My office is opposite [*to*] yours.

Necessary Prepositions

The preposition should not be omitted if it is needed to clarify the relationship of the phrase to the rest of the sentence.

> I could not find that type *of* reed in any music store. (not *type reed*)

The need to repeat prepositions with correlative conjunctions (*and . . . but, either . . . or,* and *neither . . . nor*) depends on the position of the conjunctions in the sentence.

> *Correct:* I was grateful *to both* my parents and my children for their help.
> *Incorrect:* I was grateful *both to* my parents and my children for their help.
> *Correct:* I was grateful *both to* my parents and *to* my children for their help.

In the first example, the preposition *to,* in its position before *both,* applies to the parents and the children. In the second example, *to* follows *both* and therefore should be repeated before *children,* as the third example shows.

Prepositions in a series should also be repeated.

> *Incorrect:* He went *to* Spain, Portugal, and *to* France.
> *Correct:* He went *to* Spain, *to* Portugal, and *to* France.
> *Better:* He went *to* Spain, Portugal, and France.

A common error is using only one preposition when two different prepositions are called for.

> *Incorrect:* You can often settle a customer's complaint by referring or citing information *from* the original order.
> *Correct:* You can often settle a customer's complaint by referring *to* or citing information *from* the original order.

Between *and* Among

Generally, the preposition *between* should be used when a relationship is being shown between two things or people. The preposition *among* should be used to indicate the relationship of three or more people or things.

> Just *between* you and me, I think these Senate hearings are an insult to the American public.
> The secretaries agreed *among* themselves who would work overtime to complete the project.

However, the preposition *between* is used when two persons or things are being considered in pairs, as well as in a group, or when three or more items are being considered individually. (See the entry for "among, between" in Chapter 2, Misused and Easily Confused Words, for further explanation.)

> You must read *between* the lines to understand that novel.
> *Between* the rows of tulips, someone had planted hyacinths.

In, Into, In To

The preposition *in* implies a position within; *into* implies entry or change of form; used together, *in* is an adverb that modifies a verb and *to* can be either a simple preposition or part of an infinitive.

> The top secret papers were locked *in* the wall safe for 20 years.
> The coach dived *into* the pool to demonstrate the new turn.
> I jumped *in to* see whether the water was deep enough for diving.

On, Onto, On To

The preposition *on* implies position or movement over. *Onto* implies movement toward and then over. Used together, *on* is an adverb that modifies a verb and *to* can be either a simple preposition or part of an infinitive.

> The map you are looking for is *on* the kitchen table.
> The gardener pushed the wheelbarrow *onto* the sidewalk.
> Let's move *on to* the next topic.

CONJUNCTIONS

A conjunction is a word that connects words, phrases, and clauses. There are three kinds of conjunctions: coordinating, correlative, and subordinating.

Coordinating Conjunctions

The coordinating conjunctions are *for, and, nor, but, or,* and *yet.* The word *coordinating* in this sense means equal. These conjunctions connect words, phrases, and clauses of equal grammatical weight. Therefore, whatever grammatical construction is on one side of the coordinating conjunction must also be on the other side.

> I cannot locate the *original or the copy.* (two nouns)
> He *ran* the race well *but came* in last. (two verbs)
> *If the weather holds and if the two coaches agree,* we can continue the game to try to break the tie. (two dependent clauses; note that the second *if* can be deleted)
> According to our records, *20 people volunteered* to help clean the schoolyard, *but only 9 actually showed up* to work. (two independent clauses)

And/or. The slash between *and* and *or* in *and/or* means *or.* Although *and/or* is sometimes used in legal writing, most editors consider it to be unacceptable in formal writing. In most cases, *or* can be substituted for *and/or;* in others, the sentence should be rewritten to clarify the meaning.

Omission of and. The word *and* may be omitted before the last item in a series to indicate that similar items could be added to the series. The omission of *and* indicates *et cetera, and so on,* and *and the like.* Note that *and* is omitted if any of these phrases is used.

> What we eat is vaguely Thai: chicken, spicy and succulent, a salad of exotic foliage, red leaves, tiny splinters of purple. (Margaret Atwood, *Cat's Eye*)
>
> Fans came together from every class, culture, and vocation, united, if only for three hours, by passions for the team, the sport, the unbroken string of victories. (*Washington Post,* Nov. 18, 1991)

See Chapter 10, Punctuation, page 259, for rules on use of semicolons with coordinating conjunctions.

Correlative Conjunctions

Correlative conjunctions are actually coordinating conjunctions used in pairs. The most common pairs are *either . . . or, neither . . . nor, both . . . and, not only . . . but also* (the word *also* may be dropped), *whether . . . or,* and *although . . . yet.* Correlative conjunctions can connect words, phrases, or clauses. Whatever grammatical structure follows one part of the correlative must follow the other.

> It is *not only* the most difficult thing to know oneself *but* the most inconvenient one, too. (H.W. Shaw)
>
> When a boy is eleven years old, you had better find something to engage his interest. I offer it as a theorem that a boy that age is *either* doing something *or* breaking something. (Jerrold R. Zacharias)
>
> The great pleasure of a dog is that you may make a fool of yourself with him and *not only* will he not scold you, *but* he will make a fool of himself too. (Samuel Butler)

Proper placement of the word *either* can help clarify the meaning of the sentence.

> *Poor: Either* the sellers will pay the points or accept a lower bid.
> *Improved:* The sellers will *either* pay the points or accept a lower bid.

Subordinating Conjunctions

A subordinating conjunction joins a dependent clause (a group of words that do not form a complete sentence) to an independent clause (a group of words that could stand alone as a complete sentence). By subordinating information, the writer is indicating that the information in the main part of the sentence is more important than the information in the subordinate clause.

Here are a few common words and phrases used to introduce subordinating clauses. Many of these words raise usage issues and are discussed in Chapter 2, Misused and Easily Confused Words.

before	unless
after	until
although	when, whenever
as if, as though	where, wherever
because	whether
even though	which
if	while
so that	who
than	whom
that	whose

See Chapter 10, Punctuation, page 249, for a discussion of commas with dependent clauses.

Conjunctive Adverbs

A conjunctive adverb is an adverb that acts as a conjunction to connect complete ideas. A complete sentence is always on either side of a conjunctive adverb. Some words frequently used as conjunctive adverbs are *therefore, nevertheless, furthermore, thus, consequently, however, otherwise,* and *moreover.*

The paralegal spent weeks researching the case; *nevertheless,* she felt that a piece of the puzzle was still missing.
You must file your income tax return by April 15; *however,* if you are unable to pay your taxes, you can set up a payment plan.

Sometimes words like *nevertheless, however,* and *therefore* are interrupters, not conjunctive adverbs. That is, a complete sentence does not appear on either side. In such cases, the interrupters are set off with commas.

It seemed, *however,* as if the atmosphere of the room had suddenly changed.
We agreed, *nevertheless,* that the show would go on.

Words like *therefore, nevertheless,* and *consequently* often function as adverbs, to add emphasis, and require no punctuation. Using commas with these words is optional.

The cost must *therefore* be less than $1,000.
The cost must, *therefore,* be less than $1,000.

LANGUAGE IN TRANSITION: CAN YOU BEGIN A SENTENCE WITH HOWEVER?

"Never, ever begin a sentence with a conjunctive adverb," insisted the English teacher to her eighth-graders about 50 years ago.

Was she right?

Theodore Bernstein, in *The Careful Writer,* said, "Forget it." The placement of *however* depends on which ideas are being contrasted; there is no hard and fast rule in grammar that prohibits placing *however* at the beginning of a sentence. The same goes for *and* and *but,* by the way.

PART THREE

STYLE

9

CAPITALIZATION

CAPITALIZATION

Writers, dictionaries, and style guides differ more often over capitalization than over any other aspect of style. There are few hard and fast rules; the key is choosing an appropriate treatment and using it consistently within a manuscript or publication.

Probably the most common error is to overcapitalize, especially in business, military, and government writing. Many writers seem to think that capitalizing a word or term increases its importance. The trend over the past 50 years, however, has been to limit the use of capitalization to proper names of people and places, certain titles, and certain events, an approach this chapter takes. Exceptions are often made within specialized fields of study, where customary preferences in capitalization should usually be followed. Because no style manual can cover every capitalization question a writer or an editor will face, we offer here some general guidelines to keep in mind when setting a style for various works.

First, select a current dictionary to serve as an arbiter for decisions on capitalization, as well as spelling and hyphenation. This will establish accepted general practice. Up-to-date almanacs and atlases are good additional resources for names of people and places that do not appear in dictionaries.

Second, in most publications the "down" style of capitalization is the safest; when in doubt, lowercase, the exceptions being proper names, trademarks, and trade names.

Finally, the introductory paragraphs to each of the topics discussed in this chapter provide some rationale for the decisions made in this book; by using the reasoning given and considering the examples that follow, editors and writers should feel free to make their own decisions when no other resource addresses the point in question.

LANGUAGE IN TRANSITION: "DOWN" CAPITALIZATION'S SLIPPERY SLOPE

William Safire, in his column "On Language" in the *New York Times* on October 7, 1991, sided with an irate reader whose manuscript had been copyedited to reflect the "down" (or lowercase) trend in capitalization.

> Modern copy editors and their stylebook conspirators have a case of the lowers, which is to say that capitalization is out. . . . This has been a two-century trend in America; if Thomas Jefferson were writing today, the Continental Congress's Committee on Style would not permit "certain unalienable Rights, that among these are Life, Liberty and the pursuit of Happiness" or even "mutually pledge to each other our Lives, our Fortunes and our sacred Honor." O.K., styles change, we don't wear powdered wigs anymore, and common nouns are not capitalized anymore except in German. . . .
>
> [But] we are not going to turn into slaves of e.e. cummings. Some of us still capitalize Hell, to gladden the heart of the Devil, when referring to a specific place and its genial host; only when using those terms in a derivative sense (what the hell, I'm devil-may-care) do we accept the lowercase. A Russian dressing is not a russian dressing; thus does capitalization differentiate.

IN SENTENCES, QUOTATIONS, AND LISTS

In Sentences

The first rule a child learns when beginning to write is, Start each sentence with a capital letter. Few other rules about capitalization are so simple to remember or so easy to apply. But sometimes a sentence has more than one "first" word, the first sentence in this paragraph being one example. When a complete sentence follows a comma or colon, the first word is capitalized. This construction frequently contains rules, as in the example above, or questions.

> The question is, Will they meet their deadline?

In the case of colons, the general rule is to capitalize the first word after the colon if the clause is a complete sentence and to lowercase the first word if the clause is a fragment.

> Here's the first lesson an editor must learn: Not every manuscript needs or deserves the same level of editorial attention.
>
> A natural reader will read anything: dictionaries, comic strips, the backs of cereal boxes.

There is often disagreement on this point; see "Colon" in Chapter 10, Punctuation, for further discussion.

Capitalization of sentences within parentheses also may vary. If an entire sentence is in parentheses, the first word is capitalized.

> The root of "idiom" is Greek *idios,* "one's own, peculiar to oneself." (Ironically, the same root is at work in "idiot.") (Willard R. Espy, *Say It My Way*)

If the sentence appears in parentheses *within* another sentence, the first word is not capitalized.

> Where the Indo-Europeans (the name is one of convenience; strictly speaking it applies to a language, not a people) lived has been a matter of speculation. (Victor Stephenson, *Words*)

But when the sentence within parentheses is a direct quotation of a complete sentence, this rule does not apply.

> Why can you still buy I.T. cheese spray ("One can of 'instant taste' will flavor more popcorn than 4 lbs. of butter") but not Finger Frosting? (David Owen, *The Man Who Invented Saturday Morning*)

Chapter 10, Punctuation, addresses other questions about parentheses.

In Quotations

The first word of a complete direct quotation is capitalized.

> Lower on the page, Romeo stares up at Juliet and says, "Inside! Eighteen new publications plus many other fine materials." (Richard Lederer, *Crazy English*)

The first word of an indirect quotation is not capitalized. Note that the word *that* frequently introduces indirect quotations.

> And Jane less graciously reported that "a young Mrs. Taylor, tho' encumbered with a husband and children, has ogled John Mill successfully so that he was desperately in love." (Phyllis Rose, *Parallel Lives*)

If words like *yes* and *no* are not direct quotations, they are lowercased.

> He answered yes to every question.

Writers and editors are free to adjust the capitalization of the first word of quoted material to fit the content of the passage into which the quotation is being integrated; placing the changed letter in brackets is unnecessary in most cases. (See Chapter 12, Quotations, for further explanation.)

In Lists

As a rule, the first words of list items in running text are not capitalized, but the first words in lists that are set apart from text (in list format) usually are.

> Freelance writers should clarify the following points before starting an assignment: the intended audience, the purpose of the writing, the resources available, the review process, and the deadline.

> Freelance writers should clarify the following points before starting an assignment:
>
> - The intended audience
> - The purpose of the writing
> - The resources available
> - The review process
> - The deadline

Many variations in capitalization and punctuation of lists are possible; Chapter 13, Lists, describes several approaches.

NAMES AND TITLES OF PEOPLE

Nationalities, Races, and Tribes

The names of races, nationalities, tribes, religions, and other groupings of people are generally capitalized; in recent years, increased awareness of the discriminatory effects of ethnic and racist terminology has led to continuing changes in both capitalization and preferred designations. (See Chapter 1, Usage, for more on this topic.) Here are a few examples of some currently acceptable terms.

> American Indian, Eskimo, Aleut (these are U.S. Bureau of the Census terms; some groups use Native American, Native Alaskan)
> African American (no hyphen is necessary, even as an adjective)
> Asian, Asian American
> Caucasian
> Hispanic (the broadest term; Latino usually refers to persons of Latin American ancestry; Chicano may be considered derogatory)
> Italian American
> Eurasian

General groupings based on color are lowercased.

> blacks
> whites

Personal Names

Proper names of individuals are capitalized.

E.B. White
Neil Armstrong

Questions on capitalization of particles (articles and prepositions) in personal names often arise. There are not always clear rules, and checking several sources or the person in question may be necessary to ensure accurate capitalization. The biographical names section in the current edition of *Merriam-Webster's Collegiate Dictionary* is a good place to start. Current editions of *Webster's New World Dictionary, The American Heritage Dictionary,* third edition, and the unabridged *Random House Dictionary of the English Language* include personal names in the general alphabetical listing of words. Here are a few general guidelines.

Family preference for the English spelling should always be followed if it can be determined; most English and American citizens capitalize particles—for example, E.I. Du Pont de Nemours, W.E.B. Du Bois, Robert La Follette, Daphne Du Maurier—but the practice varies according to personal preference—for example, Henry du Pont and Gov. Pierre S. du Pont IV.

For names of citizens of non-English-speaking countries, native usage is followed. In French names, *Du, Des, Le, La,* and *Les* are capitalized when they precede a title or a given name. The preposition *de* and its abbreviated form *d'* are always lowercased.

Marie-Madeleine de La Fayette; Mme. de La Fayette
Honoré d'Urfé

When the surname stands alone, the article is sometimes dropped altogether, as in the case of Alexis de Tocqueville, who is referred to as Tocqueville; dictionaries indicate this treatment by listing Tocqueville under the *T*'s rather than the *D*'s. In other cases, the article has been blended into the surname; Lafayette is an example. And when the surname is one syllable, the article is often retained when the surname stands alone, as in de Gaulle, found under the *D*'s in dictionaries.

In Spain and Latin America most people use a surname consisting of the family names of the father and the mother, in that order, sometimes joined by a lowercase *y*—for example, José Ortega y Gasset. The names may be shortened to one or the other name, usually but not always the father's, in second references. The telephone book lists the person by the father's name. After marriage, a woman drops her mother's family name and replaces it with *de* and her husband's name.

In Chinese names, the surname comes first, followed by the two-syllable given name. Under the original Wade-Giles transliteration system, the second name was hyphenated and its second syllable lowercased, as in Chiang Kai-shek; under the pinyin system, formally adopted by the People's Republic in 1979, given names are spelled as one word—Mao Zedong, not Mao Tse-tung. Some older names have retained the Wade-Giles treatment; check a current dictionary for proper treatment of well-known figures.

Arab names are complicated. Many use the definite article *al* or variations thereof; *al* is always lowercased. Journalists generally omit the article—Hafez Assad—whereas other editorial style guides recommend using a hyphenated version—Hafez al-Assad. In both cases, the second reference is simply Assad. (The article is used with a hyphen in names of newspapers and places: al-Ahram, el-Alamein.)

Certain Arab names—Abd (which means "servant of"), Ibn and Bin (which mean "son of"), and Abu (which means "father of")—do not stand by themselves. They may combine as in Abubakr, Abu Nidal (never referred to by Nidal alone), and Ibn Saud; ibn is not capitalized when it is preceded by other names—Abdel Faisal ibn King Aziz al-Saud, King Faisal.

For more on other aspects of treatment of foreign names, see Chapter 21, Foreign Languages.

Informal Personal Names and Appellations

Informal titles, common nicknames, or epithets are usually capitalized.

Attila the Hun
Stonewall Jackson
Sugar Ray Leonard
the First Lady

When a nickname is given with the real name for further identification of the person, the nickname is placed in quotation marks: Harry "Bing" Crosby, William Frederick "Buffalo Bill" Cody. (See "Quotation Marks," Chapter 10, Punctuation.)

Words like *mother, father, grandmother,* and *brother* are lowercased unless they precede or are used in place of a name.

my mother's house; Mother's house
Aunt Helen; my aunt
Dad's favorite movie; my dad's favorite movie

Personifications

Personifications of abstractions are often capitalized.

In the spring Nature treats us to her full glory.

Unless a word is truly being used as a personification—that is, an abstraction that is given human attributes—it is usually lowercased.

> Most children are intrigued by the mysteries of nature.
> We were taught to honor truth, beauty, and charity.

Terms Incorporating or Derived from Proper Names

When a term incorporates a proper name, the name is usually capitalized.

> Dewey decimal classification
> Hollerith code

When a term derived from a proper name becomes commonly used for a special meaning, the name is lowercased. The list that follows gives a few examples of such terms. To check whether other terms have passed into common use and therefore should be lowercased, check a current dictionary. The rules for capitalization of trademarks and trade names and for treatment of medical and geographic terms incorporating common nouns are discussed later in this chapter.

arabic numeral	mason jar
bessemer steel	melba toast
braille	murphy bed
bunsen burner	pasteurize
cesarean operation	quonset hut
chesterfield coat	roman numeral
fedora hat	roman type
kraft paper	sanforize

Titles of Address

The following guidelines are for capitalization of titles in text matter. Despite the practice popularized by *Time* magazine to capitalize any title bestowed on a person—Historian James McPherson, Poet Robert Frost—writers should resist capitalizing such titles. For advice on forms of address for correspondence, consult the section on forms of address of *Merriam-Webster's Collegiate Dictionary*, 10th edition, *The Random House Dictionary of the English Language*, or *The New York Public Library Desk Reference.*

Government, Political, Judicial, and Military Titles. Formal titles of address, both U.S. and international, are capitalized when they immediately precede a person's name—whether or not the first name is included.

> President Herbert Hoover; President Hoover; the president (but *president* is often capped when referring to the incumbent U.S. president)

Secretary of State John Foster Dulles; Secretary Dulles; the secretary
Emperor Akihito; the emperor
Prime Minister Margaret Thatcher; the prime minister
Senator Symington; the senator
President Mitterrand; the president
Governor Long; the governor
Councilwoman Richardson; the councilwoman
Congressman (or U.S. Representative) Jones; the congressman
U.S. District Judge Alice Smith; the judge
Chief Justice William Rehnquist; the chief justice
Lieutenant Colonel Armstrong; the colonel
Mayor Kathy Whitmire; the mayor
U.N. Secretary General Trygve Lie; the secretary general

Most formal titles are not capitalized when they follow the name of the person or are used alone in place of the name.

Allen Dulles, director of the Central Intelligence Agency; the director
Sam Rayburn, speaker of the House of Representatives (*but* the Speaker)
Gen. Maxwell D. Taylor, chairman of the Joint Chiefs of Staff; the chairman
Congresswoman (or U.S. Representative) Patricia Schroeder; the congresswoman

Nor are formal titles capitalized when used in apposition to a name.

the acting secretary of state Lawrence Eagleburger
Indian president Indira Gandhi
the ambassador Joseph P. Kennedy

Titles are not capitalized when used with *former*.

former president Jimmy Carter
former prime minister Thatcher

Honorific titles and forms of address are usually capitalized.

Her Majesty Queen Victoria
His Royal Highness, the Duke of Gloucester
His Eminence, Cardinal O'Malley

A title that is used in a formal toast, an introduction, an acknowledgment, or a list, however, is capitalized.

The authors wish to thank William Jones, Senior Fellow, Brookings Institution. . . .

The Secretary's Task Force consisted of the following persons: Anne White, Executive Director, Office of Planning. . . .

A title that is used informally in place of a proper name is capitalized.

Please, Judge, let me explain.
Forgive me, Excellency.

Academic Titles. Academic degrees and honors that follow a name are usually lowercased in general use; abbreviations are capitalized.

Clyde A. Johnson, doctor of law
Martin Smith, B.A., M.A., Ph.D.
John Jones, M.D.
Clarissa Matthews, J.D.

General references to academic degrees and fields of study are not capitalized.

a doctorate in public health administration
a bachelor's degree; a bachelor of arts degree
an associate degree

Academic titles follow the general rules for capitalization.

Professor Anderson; Dr. Joe Anderson, professor of history
President Cunningham; University of Texas president Cynthia H. Cunningham
Dean Reddick; DeWitt Reddick, journalism school dean

The names of endowed professorships are always capitalized. In the following example, Professor Franklin holds one endowed chair and one other teaching position.

John Hope Franklin, James B. Duke Professor Emeritus of History and professor of legal history

Descriptive titles preceding a name or following a name in apposition are lowercased.

history professor and author Walt W. Rostow
Walt Rostow, author and history professor

Religious Titles. Treatment varies among religions; here are a few examples.

John Cardinal O'Connor, archbishop of New York; Cardinal O'Connor; the cardinal
Pope John Paul II; the pope
the Reverend William C. Howland (Protestant); the Reverend Dr. Howland; the minister
Father Leo O'Donovan (Catholic); Father O'Donovan; the pastor
Rabbi David Small; the rabbi

❧

WHAT THE BOOKS DON'T TELL YOU ABOUT FORMS OF ADDRESS

Lots of books, including any good dictionary, will tell you what form of address to use in writing or speaking to people with official positions of one kind or another, but there are other troublesome situations that the books don't cover. For instance, what salutation do you use when you write to someone whose name you don't know?

You can always fall back on "Dear Sir/Madam," but the trend is toward substituting "To" for "Dear."

> To the Director of the Park Authority:
> To the head of the Permissions Department:

And what should you do when you know the name but not the sex of your correspondent? The easiest solution is to use both names and no honorific.

> Dear Meredith Baxter:
> Dear Pat Smith:

Business Titles. Most newspapers, magazines, and books consistently lowercase business titles, even though the practice in internal business documents is to capitalize titles of a company's officers and managers, presumably to add importance. To ensure consistency, however, it is better to lowercase all titles, regardless of the person's position and regardless of whether the title precedes or follows the word.

> John Jones, president of Jones Computer; Jones Computer president John Jones
> Michael Murphy, chief financial officer
> Kathy Smith, vice president for operations
> Rob Payne, copy machine operator

Nobility. Titles of royalty follow the same general rules for capitalization of titles as described above. The full title of Queen Elizabeth is Elizabeth II, queen of Great Britain and Northern Ireland and of her other realms and territories; the short title is Elizabeth II, queen of England. For Prince Charles, it is Charles, prince of Wales; for Princess Diana, it is Diana, princess of Wales.

> Queen Elizabeth; the queen
> Prince Charles; the prince

Prince Philip; the Duke of Edinburgh; the duke
Queen Elizabeth, the queen mother
Juan Carlos, king of Spain
Carl XVI Gustaf
the Duchess of Gloucester; the duchess
the shah of Iran; the shah
Emperor Claudius; the emperor

When used without a name, certain titles are traditionally capitalized: the Prince of Wales, the Queen Mother, the Princess Royal. British publications tend to capitalize all royal titles.

NAMES OF PLACES

Proper names of places are capitalized, as are nouns or adjectives that form part of the proper name. When a common noun or adjective is used alone, it is lowercased.

Pennsylvania Avenue; the avenue
George Washington National Forest; the national forest
Westchester County; the county

Specific guidelines for capitalization of political, geographic, and structural names follow.

Political

Names of countries and their divisions—such as states, counties, provinces, territories, and cities—are always capitalized. References to the division standing alone—for example, *state, republic, nation*—are not capitalized.

the United States; the States (as a whole); the 50 states
New York State; the state of New York
New York City; the city of New York
the New England states
the South, the West, the North, the East, the Southwest, the Northeast
the Province of Ontario; the province
the British Commonwealth; the Commonwealth
the Roman Empire
the Commonwealth of Independent States; or the former Soviet Union

The exact names of most countries can be found in the current *World Almanac* or the *Information Please Almanac.*

When *East* or *Eastern, West* or *Western, North* or *Northern,* or *South* or *Southern* is part of the proper name, it is capitalized; if it is merely descriptive, indicating a geographic region, it is lowercased.

North Dakota
West Indies
the South China Sea
the Eastern Shore
South Africa
eastern Africa
northern Virginia
south Texas
central Europe
West Coast
the eastern United States
the Northern Hemisphere
Western Europe, Eastern Europe (World War II period to end of cold war, 1989)
West European, East European
the North, the South (in U.S. Civil War context)

In some proper names, the definite article *the* is part of the proper name and is capitalized. Here are a few examples.

The Hague
The Dalles (Oregon)
The Gambia
But: the Netherlands

Terms that describe groups of nations in general are usually lowercased: free world, third world.

Geographic

Regions and Locales. Style guides and dictionaries vary widely in the way they capitalize the divisions of the globe. The list below reflects the practice that names of actual places as well as cultural regions (such as Western Europe) are capitalized, but certain geographic concepts, like *equator,* are not.

the Arctic, the Arctic Circle (*but* arctic climate)
the North Pole
the tropic of Cancer
the tropics
the equator
the International Date Line

the Continental Divide; the Great Divide (North America)
the East; the Orient (referring to Asian regions)
Middle East; the Mideast
Near East
the Continent (referring to continental Europe)
Western Hemisphere; the West, Western (referring to Europe and the Americas in a cultural sense)

Some publications avoid using the terms *the East* or *the Orient* to refer to Asian countries because they reflect a view of the world as seen from the "Western" point of view; the preference is to use *Asia* or the specific country name.

The names of the seven continents are capitalized.

Africa	Europe
Antarctica	North America
Asia	South America
Australia	

Terms describing locales, neighborhoods, or popularly accepted designations are usually capitalized.

Back Bay (Boston)
the Outback (Australia)
the Lake District (England)
the Left Bank (Paris)
the Bay Area (San Francisco)
Foggy Bottom (in Washington, D.C.)
the Twin Cities (Minneapolis and St. Paul)
the Deep South
Sun Belt (or Sunbelt); Rust Belt
the Wild West
New World; Old World

Sometimes shortened forms of a name are capitalized.

the Rockies
the Smokies
Florida Keys
the Himalayas
the Village (Greenwich Village in New York City)
the Channel (the English Channel)

Oceans, Rivers, Lakes, Mountains, and Other Features. When the full proper name is used, the names of natural features are capitalized.

Mississippi River
Rio Grande (not Rio Grande River, because *Rio* means "river" and would be redundant)
Lake Tahoe
Black Sea
Finger Lakes
Great Smoky Mountains
Rock of Gibraltar
Malay Peninsula
Painted Desert
Carlsbad Caverns
Indian Ocean
Gulf of Mexico
Black Forest
Lake Baikal
Mount Fuji (or Fujiyama, but not Mount Fujiyama)

If the generic term precedes the proper names, the generic term is capitalized.

Lakes Michigan and Superior

If the generic term follows the proper names, the generic term is lowercased.

Huron and Superior streets
the Blue Ridge and Massanutten mountains

When a generic term is used descriptively, it is lowercased.

the Shenandoah River valley
the Arizona desert

Terms Derived from Geographic Names. Nouns or adjectives derived from geographic names are often capitalized.

Swiss cheese, Swiss watch, Swiss steak (*but* dotted swiss)
Dutch oven, Dutch uncle, Dutch treat
German measles
Rocky Mountain spotted fever
Lyme disease

But many terms derived from geographical names have taken on common meanings and are lowercased. A partial list follows; check a current dictionary for similar terms.

anglicize (*but* Anglophile)
artesian well
baked alaska
brazil nut
brussels sprouts
french dressing, french fries
india ink
madras cloth
plaster of paris
portland cement
roman type
russian dressing
scotch plaid, scotch whisky
siamese twins
spanish omelet
venetian blinds
vienna sausage

Buildings, Structures, and Public Places

Names of buildings, structures, monuments, and public places are usually capitalized.

the Capitol, the Mall (in Washington, D.C.)
the Empire State Building
the Golden Gate Bridge
the Great Wall of China
the Jefferson Memorial
Madison Square Garden
Gorky Park
Buckingham Palace
the Plaza Hotel
the Statue of Liberty
Place de la Concorde

Note that building and place names in foreign languages do not need to be italicized.

Names of streets, highways, parks, squares, theaters, museums, offices, and rooms are capitalized only when they form part of a proper name; they are lowercased when used generically or when standing alone.

Interstate Highway 10; the highway; I-10
U.S. Route 40
Ford's Theatre (its traditional spelling); the theater
Fifty-first Street; the street
Central Park; the park
the Green Room (of the White House)
room 614 (unless part of an address)
the New Jersey Turnpike; the turnpike

Follow native practice for capitalization of international street names.

4, route des Morillons
rue de la Paix
107 Via del Serafico

NAMES OF THINGS

Literature, Periodicals, and Entertainment

Titles. The first and last words as well as all important words in titles of books, magazines, newspapers, reports, works of art, poems, plays, movies, and television shows are capitalized. Thus all nouns, pronouns, verbs (no matter how short), adverbs, adjectives, and conjunctions that introduce subordinate clauses are capitalized in titles; titles are usually set off with quotation marks or italics as well (see Chapter 11, Setting Off Words, Terms, and Names). Usually lowercased are the *to* of infinitives (*to Be, to Go*), articles, coordinate conjunctions, and prepositions of four or fewer letters. A discussion of capitalization of cultural terms, including those used in art, literature, theater, and dance, is on page 220.

The Power and the Glory
For Whom the Bell Tolls
Paul Revere and the World He Lived In (last word capped)

Monet's *Seascape, Normandy Coast* (work of art)
Robert Frost's "Fire and Ice" (poem)
Shakespeare's *Midsummer Night's Dream* (play)
"This Is Your Life" (television show)
The Bridge on the River Kwai (movie)

The Eighth Report to the U.S. Congress on Alcohol and Health
U.S. News and World Report magazine
The Washington Post Magazine

The first word after a colon in a title is also capitalized.

The Good War: An Oral History of World War II

Usage is different in most foreign languages and for many English-language scientific publications, which capitalize only the first word of the title and any proper nouns that may occur. This "down" style also generally prevails in languages other than English; if the first word in a foreign language title is an article, it and any adjective that comes before a proper noun should be capitalized.

Some authors and publishers make exceptions to these general rules for various reasons. Therefore, reasonable care should be taken to follow actual capitalization when citing the works of others.

Writing With Precision
"thirtysomething" (television show) (*but* "Thirtysomething" at the beginning of sentence)
Long Day's Journey Into Night

And no matter what the cover or title page may show, no words in a title should be spelled with all capital letters.

Compound Words in Titles and Headings. If a title or heading contains a "temporary" compound word (see Chapter 16, Hyphenation and Compound Words, for definitions) used as a modifier, both words should be capitalized.

Retailers Launch Place-Based Magazines
Plywood and Medium-Density Fiberboard

Some authorities lowercase the second element of a compound word if it is a participle modifying the first element (*Spanish-speaking People*). The second element is also usually lowercased when the first element is a hyphenated prefix (*Re-creating the Scene of the Crime*).

Only the first word in a permanently hyphenated compound—that is, one found in an up-to-date dictionary—is capitalized in headings or titles.

Jobs for Part-time Students
Cost-effective Training Methods
Soft-boiled Eggs Found to Contain Salmonella
Law-abiding Citizens Form Neighborhood Watch Group
Labor-intensive Products

Many publications capitalize only the first word and proper nouns and adjectives in headlines or subheadings; this practice eliminates the problem of deciding what to capitalize.

Do you have what it takes to be a great editor?

Shortened Titles. With names of books, newspapers, and other works, the initial article should be dropped to fit the sense of the sentence in which the title appears.

In his *Careful Writer,* Theodore Bernstein points out frequent mistakes in grammar.
I read this morning's Boston *Globe.*
Did you see the Booth cartoon in last week's *New Yorker*?

(Chapter 11, Setting Off Words, Terms, and Names, deals with the question of when to include *the* in names of periodicals.)

The Parts of a Publication. Rules for capitalization of heads and subheads generally reflect style and format considerations of the individual publication; there are no generally followed guidelines. Similarly, capitalization of words referring to various parts of a publication varies widely, but the trend is for the words *chapter, table, figure, exhibit, appendix, part,* and so on to be lowercased in all general references.

> See table 6 for a description of mortgage types.
> The full text of the Warren Commission Report appears in appendix A.

When the title follows the reference to the part, the part is capitalized.

> In Table 6, Mortgage Highlights, we explain the different mortgage types.

Parts of poems and plays are also lowercased.

> act 2
> scene 1
> stanza 14
> line 4

Passing references to a table of contents, preface, introduction, foreword, bibliography, glossary, and index of a book are usually lowercased.

> In the introduction the author explains. . . .

Cross-references to these parts within the same book, however, are usually capitalized.

> As I noted in the Preface. . . .

The words *edition, series,* and *volume* are lowercased when they are not part of a title.

Some scientific publications specify capitalizing nouns that are followed by numerals or letters denoting a specific place in a numbered series.

> Day 3 of Experiment 6
> Group A in Trial 3

But even those publications lowercase parts of books or tables followed by numbers or letters.

> chapter 10
> page 5
> column 1

Legal and Historical Titles

Titles of treaties, laws, bills, acts, government programs, historical documents, addresses, and plans are capitalized when the full title is used; the words *bill, act,* and *law* are lowercased when standing alone.

> the Bill of Rights
> the Constitution (U.S.)

the Declaration of Independence
the Versailles Treaty
Magna Carta (or Magna Charta)
the Monroe Doctrine
the Emancipation Proclamation
the Gettysburg Address
the State of the Union Address
the Strategic Arms Limitation Treaty
the Freedom of Information Act; the act
the Public Printing Law; Public Law (P.L.) 90–620; the law
the Marshall Plan; the plan
Social Security
Medicare
Medicaid

Enacted amendments to the U.S. Constitution are capitalized, but names of proposed amendments and informal names of enacted amendments are lowercased.

the Fifth Amendment
the Thirteenth Amendment
the freedom of speech amendment
the equal rights amendment

All major words in the names of legal cases are capitalized and usually italicized. The *v.* is always lowercased, and it may or may not be italicized. (See Chapter 11, Setting Off Words, Terms, and Names, for use of italics in legal citations.)

Smith v. *the County of Fairfax*

Historical Terms

The popular names of most historical periods and events are capitalized, especially when the terms might otherwise be ambiguous.

Stone Age	Victorian period
Bronze Age	Boston Tea Party
Dark Ages	Gay Nineties
Christian Era	Progressive Era
Middle Ages	Roaring Twenties
Renaissance	Great Depression
Reformation	New Deal
Enlightenment	Third Reich

The following periods and events are most often lowercased, although some authorities capitalize them.

cold war
ice age
space age
baroque period
industrial revolution (often capped)
the nineties (or 1990s)
prohibition (often capped)

General historical movements are lowercased.

gold rush
westward movement
civil rights movement

Names of battles and wars appear on page 225.

Cultural Terms

Authorities widely disagree on the capitalization of the names of literary, artistic, musical, and philosophical movements. Those that are derived from proper nouns are capitalized.

Aristotelian
Epicurean (*but* epicurean taste)
Platonic (*but* platonic relationship)
Gothic (*but* gothic tale)
Cartesian

Those that are not derived from proper nouns are usually lowercased unless they require capitalization to be distinguished from the same word used in a general sense.

art deco
classical; classicism
cubism
existentialism
hedonism
idealism
impressionism
mysticism
nihilism
pop art
realism
romanticism
rococo
surrealism
transcendentalism

Chapter 11, Setting Off Words, Terms, and Names, offers guidelines on when to use italics and quotation marks with names of sculpture, statues, paintings, music, poems, literature, plays, films, and dance.

Religious Terms

Deities, Prophets, and Other Religious Figures. Proper nouns referring to a supreme being (God, Allah) and other deities (Krishna, Venus) are capitalized. Terms that refer to prophets, apostles, and saints are also capitalized.

the Prince of Peace
the Messiah, a messiah
Father, Son, and Holy Ghost
Buddha
the Virgin Mary
the Prophet (Muhammad *or* Mohammed)
Lamb of God
Providence
Jehovah

Pronouns and derivatives generally are not capitalized:

messianism
Jesus and his disciples
godly
christological
But: Christian; Christ-like; Buddhism

To avoid sexist language, several Christian denominations and Jewish groups have begun to eliminate masculine pronouns when referring to God and to omit or change certain other male-oriented words, such as *Father, man, mankind,* and *brethren.*

Writings. Sacred works and religious writings are generally capitalized. Note that titles of religious works are not italicized, underscored, or enclosed in quotation marks.

Bible (*but* biblical)
Authorized Version (or King James Version)
New English Bible
Apocrypha
Revised Standard Version
New Testament
Torah; Pentateuch
Ten Commandments
Genesis
Revelation (no *s*)
Psalms; Psalm 122; a psalm

Gospel of Luke
Dead Sea Scrolls
Vulgate
the Tripitika
Qur'an
Tao-tê Ching
Veda; Vedic
Shruti
Upanishad
the Koran; Koranic
Talmud

Religions, Denominations, Orders, and Movements. Names of religions, denominations, orders, and movements are capitalized.

Puritans	Taoism
Catholicism	Shinto
Hinduism	Protestantism
Judaism	Zen; Zen Buddhism
Islam	Jehovah's Witnesses
Jesuit	Mormon; Mormonism

Names of churches, as both religious groups and specific houses of worship, are capitalized.

the Baptist church; First Baptist Church
the Roman Catholic Church

Other Terms. Names of creeds, synods, prayers, and meetings are capitalized.

the Apostle's Creed	Kaddish
Second Vatican Council	Salat
the Lord's Prayer	*But*: litany
Hail Mary	

Names of certain religious concepts and events are capitalized.

Diaspora	Second Coming
Resurrection	Hegira (Mohammed's)
Last Supper	

Names of services and rites are usually lowercased.

communion	baptism
evening prayer	bar mitzvah (boy); bat (or bas) mitzvah (girl)
worship service	mass (*but often* Mass, High Mass)
confirmation	

The following terms are usually lowercased.

devil	shofar
heaven	sanctuary
hell	karma
holy water	nirvana

Governmental and Political Terms

Full names of federal, state, and local government organizations, departments, agencies, and political groups are capitalized.

U.S. Congress; Congress; congressional
102nd Congress
the Senate
the House
Armed Services Committee; the committee
Department of Defense; the department
U.S. Geological Survey; the survey
National Institutes of Health
Interstate Commerce Commission; the commission
Los Angeles City Council; the council
Peace Corps
U.S. Supreme Court; the Court
Michigan Supreme Court; state supreme court
Republican party; the GOP; the party; a Republican
Democratic party; the party; a Democrat (*but* the democratic process, a democratic country)
General Assembly of Maryland; the assembly; the state senate
the Court of Appeals of the State of New York; the court of appeals
National Labor Relations Board

Also capitalized are proper names of international bodies.

U.N. Security Council; the Security Council
Common Market
European Economic Community; European Community
British Labour party
North Atlantic Treaty Organization (NATO)
General Agreement on Tariffs and Trade (GATT)

The following terms are usually lowercased. Note that social movements—social democracy—are lowercased, but specific parties—Social Democratic Party—are capitalized.

Fillmore administration; the administration
commander in chief
American embassy
city council
chamber of commerce
board of health
planning commission
federal government; federal; government
state government
executive, legislative, judicial branch
cabinet
juvenile court
left wing, right wing (*but* the Left, the Right)

communism (*but* Communist party)
fascism
socialism (*but* Socialist party)

Military Terms

The proper names of a country's military service branches and units are capitalized. Shortened forms are capitalized only when referring to U.S. service branches (the U.S. Army, the Army). Here are some examples.

U.S. Army	Royal Navy
U.S. Navy	U.S. Army Corps of Engineers
Red Army	Fifth Army
U.S. Marine Corps	Second Battalion
Green Berets	12th Regiment

Shortened forms of the U.S. forces are usually capitalized.

the Army	Army officer
the Navy	the Army Reserve
the Marines	

Informal references to international forces are not capitalized.

the British army (*but* Royal Air Force)
the French navy
the armed forces
U.N. peacekeeping force

Names of coalitions in wars are capitalized.

the Allies (World Wars I and II)
the Central Powers (World War I)
the Axis Powers (World War II)
the Federals (Northerners, the North), the Confederates (Southerners, the South) in U.S. Civil War

Military titles are capitalized when preceding a name; they are lowercased when standing alone.

We met Colonel Jones at the Pentagon. The major joined us later.

Names of medals and decorations are capitalized.

Purple Heart
Distinguished Service Medal
Medal of Honor ("Congressional" is not part of the name)
Bronze Star
Legion of Honor (Légion d'honneur)
Croix de Guerre

Full names of battles and wars are usually capitalized. *War* and *battle* are lowercased when standing alone or used in a general sense.

Battle of Hastings
Battle of Gettysburg
Battle of the Bulge
the Crusades
Thirty Years' War
Seven Years' War
American Revolution; the Revolution
Civil War (American); the war
Vicksburg Campaign
Spanish civil war
Spanish-American War
Napoleonic Wars
World War II; Second World War (British preference); the two world wars
Korean War
Vietnam War
Desert Storm
Persian Gulf War

Names of Corporate and Organizational Entities

Names of companies, corporations, and organizations are capitalized.

Polaroid Corporation
National Federation of Teachers

When referred to in the press and in nonfiction writing in general, generic names of subunits within organizations are lowercased.

the General Motors marketing department
the social science department
the biology faculty

Formal names of departments and divisions are usually capitalized in a company's own reports and publications; journalistic style is to lowercase such names.

the Midwest Sales Division (in the company's annual report)
AT&T's Midwest sales division (in a newspaper article)

In internal company documents, the name of a unit that stands alone is sometimes capitalized to avoid ambiguity.

Wait until Personnel has made a decision.

The full titles of boards of directors and trustees are capitalized; without the full name, they are lowercased.

the Board of Directors of the AAA Computer Company; the board
the Board of Trustees of Johns Hopkins University; the board of trustees, the board, the trustees

Nicknames and other alternate terms are capitalized to avoid confusion with ordinary text.

Big Blue (for IBM)
the Big Three automakers
a Big Eight accounting firm

Names of Clubs, Societies, Associations, and Institutions

Proper names of clubs, societies, associations, institutions, and similar organizations are capitalized.

Friends of the National Zoo
Boy Scouts of America
American Automobile Association
National Geographic Society
Smithsonian Institution
National Wildlife Federation
Daughters of the American Revolution
Alcoholics Anonymous
Better Business Bureau

Scientific Terms

General. Proper names in laws, theorems, and principles are capitalized, but the words *law, theory,* and *principle* are not.

Einstein's theory of relativity
law of gravity
Mendel's law
third law of thermodynamics
Avogadro's number
the Heisenberg uncertainty principle

Astronomy. The names of planets, moons, stars, constellations, and other astrological objects are capitalized.

Venus and Mars are the planets closest to Earth.

Unless they are used in connection with the names of other such objects, the words *sun, earth,* and *moon* are lowercased. (Note that *earth* is never capitalized when preceded by *the.*)

The full moon lit the yard last night.
The group is actively encouraging others to conserve the earth's resources.
Voyager 2 is heading out of our solar system into the far reaches of the Milky Way.

General meteorological terms are lowercased.

aurora borealis
northern lights
midnight sun

Geology. This subject can be tricky, and in general the author's preferences should be followed. Both the *U.S. Government Printing Office Style Manual* and *Suggestions to Authors of the Reports of the U.S. Geological Survey* provide extensive lists of geological terms. Even the words *upper* and *lower* vary in their capitalization depending on the what they are referring to—rock formations or time—and on the particular rocks or periods of time mentioned. For example, the *U.S. Government Printing Office Style Manual* lists these:

upper Eocene
Upper Devonian
lower Tertiary
Upper Jurassic
lower Oligocene

Names of formal geological terms are capitalized.

Devonian System
Morrison Formation
Pacific Mountain System
Ozark Plateau

Names of eras, periods, systems, and epochs are capitalized.

Mesozoic era
Cretaceous period
Upper Cretaceous epoch
Silurian System

Biology. The names of a kingdom, phylum, class, order, or family are capitalized when the proper name is given; the names of species are not. Genus and species names are italicized. Humans are categorized as follows: Animalis (kingdom), Chordata (phylum), Vertebrata (subphylum), Mammalia (class), *Homo* (genus), *sapiens* (species). In nontechnical use, however, Homo sapiens is usually not italicized.

Common names of plants and animals are lowercased except when a term includes a proper name.

black-eyed Susan (*Arisaema atrorubens*)
Indian paintbrush (*Castilleja* sp.)
But: jack-in-the-pulpit (*Echinocereus asterias*)

Exceptions are domestic breeds and varieties that were specially developed and may even be trademarked.

Big Boy tomato
Silver Queen corn
Baby Fordhook lima beans

Medicine. Diseases and syndromes are usually lowercased except for any proper names that are part of the term.

Alzheimer's disease
Graves' disease
Lyme disease
Epstein-Barr virus
Parkinson's disease
Down syndrome (preferred; also Down's syndrome)
acquired immunodeficiency syndrome (AIDS)
carpal tunnel syndrome
Tay-Sachs disease
degenerative joint disease
black lung disease

Adjective forms of proper names are lowercased: parkinsonian symptoms. Generic names of drugs are lowercased; trade names are capitalized.

Drugs such as diazepam (Valium) should be taken for brief periods only.

Physics and Chemistry. Chemical symbols are capitalized, but their spelled-out names are lowercased. (A list is provided in Chapter 18, Signs and Symbols.) Locants and descriptors in chemical names do not change their capitalization according to their location in a sentence.

In text: tert butyl alcohol, L-methionine
At beginning of sentence: tert Butyl alcohol, L-Methionine
In heading: tert Butyl Alcohol, L-Methionine

An excellent source of information on chemistry style for writers and editors is the *ACS* (American Chemical Society) *Style Guide;* see the annotated bibliography for more information.

Computers. Names of hardware, software, and programming languages are usually proper names and should be capitalized. Capitalization of trade names and trademarks should be followed. Many of today's trade names use mixtures of capital and lowercase letters; in the computer world this practice is known as *intercapping*. (See "Trademarks" below for further discussion.)

C programming language	netBIOS
COBOL	BASIC
Fortran	Ethernet
UNIX	ArcNET
MS/DOS	Ada
Windows	Assembler
BIOS	PostScript

Sports Terms

Names of teams, leagues, divisions, conferences, governing bodies, awards, and special sporting events are capitalized.

American League	Cotton Bowl
National Football League	Toronto Blue Jays
World Series	Stanley Cup
Super Bowl XXVII	Triple Crown
Olympic Games; the games; the Summer Olympics	Big Ten
Southwestern Conference	Davis Cup

Trademarks

Trade names and trademarks are capitalized. Use of the trademark (™) or registered trademark (®) sign is not necessary because capitalization alone identifies the name or product as being protected. The difficulty lies in determining which words or terms are trademarked and which have passed into the public domain and have become generic. The International Trademark Association in New York City at (212) 768–9887 publishes a list of current trademarks. Dictionaries, if they are reasonably current, are also sources of information about trademarks. (Chapter 18, Signs and Symbols, explains the proper use of trademarks; Chapter 23, Copyright, explains the difference between trademark and copyright.)

There is a difference between a trademark and a trade name. Trade names are corporate or business names and therefore the trademark symbol should not be used with a trade name. For example, the corporate name is Xerox Corporation, and the trade name is Xerox: "This copier is made by Xerox."

Used as a trademark, strictly speaking the name is an adjective: "This is a Xerox copier." Companies frown on the use of their trademarks as nouns or verbs ("Please Xerox this letter for me") because they fear that permitting loose usage will lead to the trademark's becoming a generic term.

The list below gives some common trademarks and their associated generic terms. Many writers prefer to use the generic term to avoid providing free advertising for a particular commercial product.

Baggies (plastic bag)
Band-Aid (adhesive bandage)
Benadryl (allergy medication)
Breathalyzer (alcoholic content-measuring apparatus)
Coca-Cola or Coke (soft drink)
Dacron (polyester fiber)
diet Coke, diet Pepsi (soft drinks)
Dolby (noise reduction system)
FedEx (overnight delivery service)
Fiberglas (textiles, etc., *but* fiberglass)
Formica (laminated plastic)
Freon (refrigerant)
Frigidaire (refrigerator)
Hide-A-Bed (sleep sofa)
Jeep (vehicle)
Jell-O (gelatin dessert)
Jockey (underwear)
Kleenex (tissues)
Levi's (jeans)
Linotronic (typesetting equipment)
Lucite (acrylic resin, paint)
Lycra (spandex fiber)
Masonite (hardboard)
Mylar (polyester film)
Novocain (anesthetic)
Plexiglas (acrylic plastic)
Post-it (note pads)
Pyrex (glassware)
Realtor (not a synonym for real estate agent)
Scotch (adhesive tape)
Sheetrock (gypsum board)
Tabasco (sauce)
Teflon (coating)
Vaseline (petroleum jelly)
Vu-Graph (slide)
X-Acto (knife)
Xerox (copier)

Some trade names and trademarks use unusual capitalization, and writers and editors should follow a company's usage. A good source for this information is a company's own advertising or product packaging; print copy produced by other sources is not always accurate. The practice is especially common in the computer industry.

CompuServe
Microsoft Word
Macintosh
PageMaker
NeXT
3Com
WordPerfect
dBASE IV

Because a sentence should always begin with a capital letter, a trade name or trademark that begins with a lowercase letter should be capitalized if it begins a sentence or the sentence should be rewritten to avoid the problem.

AllCLEAR requires a printer that supports high-resolution graphics.
The allCLEAR program requires. . . .

Writers and editors should also be aware of the difference between a logo and a trade name. A logo is the often stylistic treatment of a company's name usually found on its letterhead or products. The logo design may show the company name in all caps—WANG is an example—but the trade name is Wang Laboratories, Inc., or Wang—the founder's last name.

Miscellaneous

Prefixes. Most common prefixes attached to proper nouns or adjectives are lowercased.

anti-Semitism
neo-Nazi
non-Christian
pre-Revolutionary (U.S.)
un-American

However, some prefixes are capped:

Pan-Slavic
Pre-Raphaelite

Still other combinations have lost their hyphens and may be capped (Precambrian) or lowercased (unchristian, transatlantic). The only sure way to tell is to consult a current dictionary.

Periods of Time. Months of the year and days of the week are capitalized. Names of seasons—spring, summer, winter, autumn (or fall)—are not capitalized unless used as a personification. The scientific terms denoting times of the year, such as winter solstice and vernal equinox, also are not capitalized. Names of centuries are not capitalized: twentieth (or 20th) century.

Names of time zones are lowercased.

central standard time (CST)
Greenwich mean time (GMT)
daylight saving time (DST)

Holidays. Names of holidays are capitalized.

Bastille Day	Passover
Fourth of July	Easter
Father's Day	Yom Kippur
Christmas Day	Rosh Hashana
Veterans Day	Guy Fawkes Day

Awards, Honors, and Scholarships. Names of awards, honors, and scholarships are usually capitalized. Words that are not part of the actual name are lowercased.

Rhodes scholar
Academy Award for film direction
Nobel Peace Prize
Nobel Prize in literature
Nobel laureate
a Pulitzer Prize-winning author

Correspondence. The names and titles in the salutations of letters are capitalized.

Dear Mr. Greenspan:
Dear Ms. Randolph:

The important words in addresses are capitalized.

1603 Avenue of the Americas, Suite 204

The first word in the complimentary closing of a letter is capitalized.

Very truly yours,
Best regards,

Mottoes and Slogans. The first word and any proper names in a motto or slogan are capitalized.

Live free or die
All the news that's fit to print
In God we trust

Signs and Notices. Titles of notices and signs are usually capitalized, both on the sign or notice itself and in any reference to it.

No Smoking in the Lobby
The airplane's No Smoking sign was lit.

10

PUNCTUATION

PUNCTUATION

The ancient Greeks introduced the idea of punctuation, devising simple signs for the period, comma, colon, semicolon, and question mark. It was not until the early days of printed books, however, in the late 1400s and early 1500s, that punctuation—and even the placement of spaces between words—began to be used as a way to clarify text for the reader.

Before printing, as Daniel J. Boorstin notes in *The Discoverers,* words in manuscripts ran together, without spacing, punctuation, or paragraphing. Punctuation, then known as *pointing*, was first used in Europe after the Age of Charlemagne to guide the speakers who read text to audiences of non-readers, cueing them to stop, pause, and change intonation. As books became more popular and available, punctuation began to reflect sentence structure, not pauses in speech; Ben Jonson proposed the syntactic approach in his book *English Grammar*, published posthumously in 1640, which provided a foundation for the punctuation rules we follow today. There is still some range in punctuation usage, of which the best example is the series (or serial) comma. Book publishers tend to use this comma—every Tom, Dick, and Harry—but newspapers and some magazines, often citing space constraints, do not—every Tom, Dick and Harry. As with many other points of style, choices must be made to achieve consistency.

PERIOD

The period is the most prevalent mark of terminal punctuation, used to close all declarative and some imperative sentences. The other two marks of terminal punctuation are the exclamation point and question mark.

At the End of a Statement

The period is placed at the end of a complete sentence that makes a statement (a declarative sentence).

> There's not much to be said about the period except that most writers don't reach it soon enough. (William Zinsser)

A period is also used at the end of an expression that represents a complete statement (an elliptical expression). This type of expression usually occurs as an answer to a question or as a transitional phrase.

> Yes.
> Indeed.
> Enough about that.

At the End of a Command

A command (an imperative sentence) can be given in the form of a statement or a question. The period is used when a command is in the form of a question and the person being addressed is expected to act rather than answer the question.

> Would you please change the address on my account.

If an answer is required, a question mark should be used.

> Will you tell me how much I owe?

If it is difficult to tell how a command should be punctuated, the sentence should be rewritten to make its intent clear.

At the End of an Indirect Question

A period, not a question mark, is used in sentences containing an indirect question.

> She asked when her promotion would become effective.
> What needs to be done is clear; the question is how to get the money.

With Abbreviations

Some abbreviations require periods and some do not. Chapter 14, Abbreviations, provides general rules.

With Decimals

A period is used in decimals to separate the whole number from the decimal fraction. No space precedes or follows the period.

$53.25
87.75 percent

In Lists

See Chapter 13, Lists, for the use of punctuation in lists.

With Quotation Marks

A period is almost always placed inside quotation marks.

We will discuss Jack London's short story "To Build a Fire."

The same rule applies to single quotation marks and to single words set in quotation marks.

He said, "Tomorrow we will discuss Jack London's short story 'To Build a Fire.' "
The password is "wildflower."

There are a few exceptions to this rule. Traditionally, the period falls outside the quotation marks when single quotation marks are used with theological and philosophical terms.

His new work dealt with 'being' and 'nonbeing'.

Using italics or boldface instead of quotation marks for computer commands lets the writer avoid the problem entirely. (See Chapter 11, Setting Off Words, Terms, and Names.)

With Parentheses

When a sentence ends with information that is in parentheses, a period is placed after the closing parenthesis (like this). A period is placed inside a parenthesis only when the information within the parentheses is a complete sentence that stands alone, as follows. (See "Parentheses," page 280.)

A complete sentence enclosed in parentheses within a sentence (this is an example) does not close with a period.

QUESTION MARK

Direct Questions

A question mark is placed at the end of a direct question.

> Will you meet me for lunch today?
> How do you explain this comment, "That's news to me"?

Elliptical Questions

A question mark should be placed after a word or phrase that represents a complete question (an elliptical question).

> I understand the Murphy property is for sale. How much?

When a complete sentence and an elliptical sentence are both questions, each sentence should be punctuated separately.

> Where will the meeting be? At headquarters?

With a Command or Request

A question mark is not used after a command or request that for reasons of politeness is phrased in question form. (See "Periods," above.) But when a sentence is clearly cast as an interrogative, the question mark is used.

> Will you open the window?

With Doubtful Information

A question mark may be used to indicate doubt about the preceding information.

> Charlemagne (742?–814) was one of the greatest kings of the Middle Ages.

With a Rising Intonation

A question mark is placed after a sentence that is a statement in form but a question in intonation.

> You want to go on vacation in the middle of this crisis?

A Question Within a Statement

A short question within a statement is set off with commas, and a question mark is placed at the end of the sentence. If a short question is at the end of a sentence, a question mark is placed after it.

We can exchange the tickets, can't we, if we are unable to go?
We can exchange the tickets if we are unable to go, can't we?

There are no hard and fast rules for the use of commas or colons preceding questions within a statement, but the following examples may serve as useful rules of thumb. A long question at the end of a sentence is usually preceded by a comma, is begun with a capital letter, and is followed by a question mark.

The question is, Who will foot the bill for the reprinting?

A colon is used if the words before the question are a complete sentence.

This is the question: Who will foot the bill for the reprinting?

In a Series of Questions

A series of brief questions at the end of a sentence is usually separated by commas; however, for emphasis a writer may place question marks after each item in the series. Each question within the sentence begins with a lowercase letter.

What will be the charge for the caterer, the photographer, the florist, and the guitarist?
What will be the charge for the caterer? the photographer? the florist? and the guitarist?

A series of elliptical questions is punctuated with question marks, and each element of the series begins with a capital letter.

Has the murder case been solved? By whom? When? What was the motive?

With a series of independent questions, each independent question begins with a capital letter and is followed by a question mark.

Where will the convention take place? Who will be invited? How much will it cost?

With Quotation Marks

A question mark is placed inside the closing quotation mark if the question mark was part of the original quotation.

How it would relieve her if he said, "Ramona, what's all this for?" (Saul Bellow, *Herzog*)

A question mark is placed outside the closing quotation mark if the complete sentence is a question and the quoted material is a statement or a phrase.

Did you say, "Jane has a good idea"?

EXCLAMATION POINT

Good writers use exclamation points sparingly because so few statements are truly astonishing enough to demand them.

To Express Strong Emotion

The exclamation point is used at the end of a sentence to show urgency, surprise, enthusiasm, disbelief, or strong emotion.

> "Oh, God!" he cried, falling on his knees in the water. "I knew it was here!" (James Michener, *Centennial*)

Occasionally an exclamation point is placed in parentheses after the word a writer wants to emphasize. Exercise great caution in this usage.

> The journalist won the exclusive (!) rights to write a book about the billionaire recluse.

The exclamation point can follow a single word that is used to express strong emotion. The sentence that follows the exclaimed word is punctuated as usual.

> Congratulations! How do you plan to spend your winnings?

With Quotation Marks

An exclamation point is placed inside closing quotation marks if the words exclaimed are part of the quote; otherwise, the exclamation point is placed outside the closing quotation mark.

> "What!" The word was a hoot of astonishment, followed by laughter. (Belva Plain, *Tapestry*)
>
> I couldn't believe it when I heard the words, "You've been promoted"!
>
> The words "strange!" "singular!" and other similar expressions excited my curiosity. (Edgar Allan Poe, "The Black Cat")

COMMA

The comma, along with the apostrophe, is probably one of the most misused and controversial marks of punctuation. Many of us were taught that commas should reflect the pauses we make in speaking, but this approach leads to text littered with disruptive and unnecessary commas. In fact, commas are most valuable when they reflect the sentence's underlying grammatical structure, serving as signposts to help the reader quickly grasp the writer's meaning. For example, even though the second sentence below is long and rambling, commas help make the author's meaning clear and easy to follow.

> Rabbit liked Reagan. He liked the foggy voice, the smile, the big shoulders, the way his head kept wagging through the long pauses, the way he floated above the facts, knowing there was more to government than facts, and the way he could change direction while saying that he was going straight ahead, pulling out of Beirut, getting cozy with Gorby, running up the national debt. (John Updike, *Rabbit at Rest*)

Many comma "rules" are open to debate, however, and editors disagree among themselves more about commas than about any other aspect of punctuation. The trend for many years has been toward "open" punctuation, which means using as few commas as possible.

With Conjunctions

In Compound Sentences. In compound sentences a comma is used between the independent clauses—clauses that are complete sentences—that are joined by a coordinating conjunction (*and, but, for, or, nor, yet,* and sometimes *so*).

> It [a revolution] will originate with the individual and with culture, and it will change the political structure only as its final act. It will not require violence to succeed, and it cannot be successfully resisted by violence. (Charles A. Reich, *The Greening of America*)

If the clauses are short and misreading is unlikely, the comma between the independent clauses can be dropped, as the next example shows.

> He looked as if he would murder me and he did. (Muriel Spark, "The Portobello Road")

❧

THE COMMA AND THE PERIOD:
WHAT THEY SAY ABOUT THE WRITER

The comma is like the expressive dips of the hands we employ when making a point in friendly conversation; the period is a tap of a judge's gavel. The comma is accommodating, deferential, clement; the period is Apollonian and preoccupied. As a general rule, the fewer commas you use, the more of a tyrant you would be if placed in a position of power. It is instructive to read political theorists in this light. (Nicholas Baker, *Atlantic Monthly*, August 1984)

❧

IN THIS CASE, THE COMMA MEANT THE END

A misplaced comma cost nurse Angela Penfold her job in a health center in England. Penfold wrote to health authority officials to complain about her supervisor: "I have come to the opinion Mrs. Pepperell is out to make my life hell, so I give in my notice."

In fact, Penfold did not intend to resign. "I just meant that she was trying to get me to hand in my notice," she said. (*Boston Herald,* February 23, 1983)

To make this fact clear, Penfold should have omitted the comma.

A comma cannot take the place of the coordinating conjunction between two main clauses. This error, which produces a run-on sentence, is sometimes called a *comma splice.* In the next sentence, the comma by itself is not strong enough to separate the two main clauses; a conjunction or a semicolon is needed.

> Food was powerful, it could draw forth cravings and greedy desires which had to be met with a firm hand. (Laura Shapiro, *Perfection Salad*)

In a Series. Some writers and publishers, to ensure clarity, place a series comma before the *and* or *or* that concludes a series of three or more words, phrases, or clauses. The comma after the word *phrases* in the previous sentence is an example of a series comma, and it demonstrates the style being followed for this book. Some publications, particularly newspapers, view the series comma as unnecessary and costly (because each printed character takes up space). Regardless of the choice made, editors and writers should use—or not use—series commas consistently throughout a manuscript or publication.

> *No series comma:* After all, interviewing time is best spent getting quotes, anecdotes and other information that you can't find in books, newspapers and magazines. (Pauline Bartel, "Quick and Clean Interviewing," *Writer's Digest,* November 1992)
>
> *Series comma:* Towards that small and ghostly hour, he rose up from his chair, took a key out of his pocket, opened a locked cupboard, and brought forth a sack, a crowbar of convenient size, a rope and chain, and other fishing tackle of that nature. (Charles Dickens, *A Tale of Two Cities*)

When the conjunction *and* is placed between each element of a series, no comma is necessary.

Julia and Erika and Jenny and the others took one look at the three pit bull terriers who settled with their owners in the rented house on Buckmarsh Street and began to worry. (*Washington Post,* May 6, 1992)

When no conjunction is used, commas are used between each element of the series—and at its end.

His fortitude, his intelligence, his charisma, landed him the best job of his career.

Direct Address

In direct address a person or group is being spoken to. Set off with commas the words used in direct address.

"You laugh, Anna, but the last time he came, he had a gun. . . ." (Piers Paul Read, *On the Third Day*)

Direct Quotations and Questions

Commas usually precede direct quotations.

In *The Physics of Baseball,* author Robert K. Adair wrote, "The most important person on the team, in any one game, is the pitcher."

If a quotation is the subject, object, or complement of the sentence, however, a comma is not used.

THE ESSENTIAL COMMA

In the following sentence, did the brother go to the movies or stay home?

I went to the movies with my mother and my brother and my sister stayed home with my father.

Without a comma between the two clauses, it is unclear what the brother did. The writer could make the sentence clear by inserting a comma in one of two places, depending on the meaning intended.

I went to the movies with my mother and my brother, and my sister stayed home with my father.

I went to the movies with my mother, and my brother and my sister stayed home with my father.

She said "thanks" and left abruptly.
Our motto is "Never give up."
The seminar topic for July is "Taking on Miss Thistlebottom: Breaking the 'Rules' of Grammar."

Traditionally, however, commas precede direct questions.

The question is, Can we get there by midnight?

With Quotation Marks

A comma is placed inside closing quotation marks.

The training division will offer three seminars this month: "Stress Management," "Writing for Results," and "The Basics of WordPerfect."

"I'd forgotten you're a specialist in that sort of thing," the Colonel mused out loud. "So you'll understand," he added, "why I hope I've driven a little sense into that fellow's thick skull." (Pierre Boulle, *The Bridge Over the River Kwai*)

When single and double quotation marks are used, the comma is placed inside both marks.

"Today, we will discuss Nikki Giovanni's poem 'Revolutionary Dreams,' " announced the leader of the poetry group.

Appositives

An appositive is a word or phrase that identifies the noun or pronoun that immediately precedes it. If the information is not essential to the meaning of the sentence (nonrestrictive), the appositive should be set off with commas. Often the second comma is mistakenly omitted after long appositional phrases.

Senator Lloyd M. Bentsen, a wealthy Texas Democrat on the committee, understood completely. (Bob Woodward, *Veil: The Secret Wars of the CIA, 1981–1987*)

Mystery at Malmouth, her most recent bestseller, will be available in paperback by the end of the month.

The rule for using commas to set off appositional names is often misunderstood, although it is just a variation of the rule for punctuating restrictive and nonrestrictive information. In the next sentence the husband's name is not essential to the meaning of the sentence—Janet presumably has only one husband—and therefore the appositive is nonrestrictive and takes commas.

Janet's husband, Sam, just returned from China.

Contrast the next two examples. In the first the writer has more than one sister; the name *Margaret* is necessary to specify which sister the writer is talking about and restricts the meaning of *sister.* In the second example the writer has only one sister, so the name *Margaret* is additional information and is set off with commas.

> My sister Margaret plans to attend Wellesley this fall.
> My sister, Margaret, plans to attend Wellesley this fall.

No commas are used if the expression is essential.

> The book *Mystery at Malmouth* will be available in paperback by the end of the month.

Commas are placed incorrectly around the appositives in the next sentence.

> *Incorrect:* In the words of the famous poet, T.S. Eliot, "April is the cruelest month."

Here the comma after *poet* should be deleted because *T.S. Eliot* is a restrictive appositive. With the comma the sentence would mean that T.S. Eliot was the only famous poet.

> *Correct:* In the words of the famous poet T.S. Eliot, "April is the cruelest month."

The comma after *Eliot* is retained because it falls at the end of an introductory phrase.

Here's another example.

> *Incorrect:* For the past two decades, Fisher has been searching for the treasure off the Spanish galleon, *Nuestra Senora de Atocha.* (*Bird Talk* magazine, March 1991)

The comma after *galleon* should be deleted because there are many Spanish galleons. To help determine whether a comma is necessary in such sentences, try inserting the words *which is* or *who is* after the comma; if the sentence makes sense, a comma is necessary. The *which is* creates a meaningless sentence, and so the comma should be deleted.

> For the past two decades, Fisher has been searching for the treasure off the Spanish galleon, [**which is**] *Nuestra Senora de Atocha.*
> *Correct:* For the past two decades, Fisher has been searching for the treasure off the Spanish galleon *Nuestra Senora de Atocha.*

If the sentence read "a Spanish galleon," the comma would be correct—"a Spanish galleon," which is *Nuestra Senora de Atocha.* If the editor cannot decide for sure whether the appositive is restrictive or nonrestrictive, he or she should query the author.

When words or phrases in apposition explain or define a noun and are introduced by *or,* the appositional phrase is set off with commas.

> Samuel Clemens, or Mark Twain, was an American author who showed keen insight into human nature.

Parenthetical Words, Phrases, and Clauses

Parenthetical words, phrases, or clauses are those that interrupt the flow of a sentence and could be omitted without changing the meaning (parentheticals are often called *interrupters* or *interjections*). Some common interrupters are *however, moreover,* and *nevertheless.* Parenthetical information should be set off with commas, although dashes are sometimes used.

> On election day Smythe chose to vote for the lesser of two evils; his brother, however, chose not to vote.
>
> A great pity, now, that this unfortunate whale should be hare-lipped. (Herman Melville, *Moby Dick*)
>
> English is, in short, one of the world's great growth industries. (Bill Bryson, *The Mother Tongue*)
>
> Our most recent research, as we had predicted, proved our theory to be correct.

The use of commas around *therefore* is often a matter of preference, depending on whether the writer wants to stress *therefore.*

> Management is willing, therefore, to offer the union a compromise.
>
> She has done most of the research and therefore deserves most of the credit.

A parenthetical expression that forms a complete sentence usually requires dashes or parentheses for ease of reading.

> I puzzled for a long time over him—he might have been anything—until I saw the title of the book. (Mary Stewart, *Madam, Will You Talk?*)

Introductory Words, Phrases, and Clauses

Words. A comma is placed after such words as *yes, no, oh, well,* and *still* when they fall at the beginning or end of a sentence.

> No, he thought finally, no. She's wrong. (Irwin Shaw, *The Young Lions*)
>
> "Oh, it's utterly boring," said Sadie. (Iris Murdoch, *Under the Net*)

The word *O* is not followed by a comma, however.

O say, can you see, by the dawn's early light. . . . (Francis Scott Key, "The Star Spangled Banner")

Phrases. Commas are often necessary after introductory phrases for clarity or to prevent misreading. When an introductory phrase ends with a verb or a preposition, a comma is usually necessary for clarity.

Soon after, the vice president announced her resignation.
While eating, the children played twenty questions.

Commas are not necessary after short introductory phrases, especially of time and place.

On May 4 the cruise ship will leave the French West Indies for Miami.
After breakfast at Yaddo everyone repairs to their offices and studios for the day. (Susan Cheever, *Home Before Dark*)

No commas are needed after introductory phrases that immediately precede the verb they modify.

Between her two sons sat the matriarch of the family.
Seven miles north of our home is the George Washington National Forest.

However, when two words or numbers falling next to each other could confuse or slow down the reader, a comma is needed for clarity.

For question 16, 161 applicants gave incomplete information.
To William, Shakespeare opened new worlds.

Verbal Phrases. A comma is used after an introductory verbal phrase to set it off from the rest of the sentence. A verbal phrase can begin with a *to* form (infinitive), an *ing* form (present participle), or an *ed* or past form (past participle) of a verb.

Remembering Brinson's stern instructions and the Navy manual, Broshers gripped the torch firmly in both hands and walked down the fire alley to his twenty-year-old shipmate, Benoit. (George C. Wilson, *Supercarrier*)
Cherished for its exclusivity, St. Andrew's was the most expensive private school in Memphis. . . . (John Grisham, *The Firm*)

Clauses. A comma should follow an introductory dependent clause (an adverbial clause).

As the soup was brought in, the orchestra . . . began to play the various Viennese bird delirium waltzes that had encouraged Alessandro to eat his hors d'oeuvres rhythmically. (Mark Helprin, *A Soldier of the Great War*)

Because we have so much work, we will have to hire three temporary proofreaders for the next 6 weeks.

If the dependent clause is at the end of the sentence, no comma is necessary.

We will have to hire three temporary proofreaders for the next six weeks because we have so much work.

Transitional Words and Phrases. A comma is placed after a transitional word or phrase at the beginning of a sentence—words like *finally, first, thus, on the other hand, instead,* and *of course.*

First, the research shows that the problem is more widespread than we thought.

Instead, it was a microcosm of the most lethal equipment of modern weaponry. (Robert Ludlum, *The Bourne Ultimatum*)

Between Identical Words

When identical words fall next to each other, a comma is needed between them for clarity.

Who he is, is anybody's guess.
When I say "run," run.

There is an exception to this rule: The identical words that form the past perfect of *have—had had—*should not be separated by a comma.

Although I had had the best idea, no one was willing to implement it.

Between Adjectives That Modify the Same Noun

A comma separates two or more adjectives of equal weight (coordinate adjectives) that modify a noun. Deciding whether a comma is needed is usually simple: As a rule of thumb, if the word *and* can be used in place of the comma or if the two adjectives can be reversed and the sentence still makes sense, the comma is correct.

The room was filled with sullen, angry prisoners.

A tough, hard-swinging youngster from New York's working-class lower East Side tonight punctured the bubble of England's Aubrey Philpott-Grimes. (Edwin Newman, *Sunday Punch*)

Note that a comma is correctly omitted between *working-class* and *lower* because *working-class* modifies the phrase *lower East Side.* A comma is not used when the adjectives are not equal in weight. In the next sentence no

SPOTTING A RESTRICTIVE CLAUSE

To help decide whether a clause is restrictive or nonrestrictive, think of pairs of commas as handles. If you can lift out the information between the commas and the sentence still makes sense, the information is nonessential, and commas are required.

> My brother, who is a freshman at Harvard, had his yearly eye exam today.

If you lift the *who* clause out of the sentence, the meaning of the sentence does not change. The fact that the writer's brother attends Harvard is extra information.

> Men seldom make passes at girls who wear glasses. (Dorothy Parker)

If a comma is placed after the word *girls* and the *who* clause is lifted out of the sentence, the sentence reads as follows: Men seldom make passes at girls. In this case, the meaning of the sentence is not what Ms. Parker intended.

comma is placed after *small* or after *home-based* because *small* modifies the entire phrase *home-based computer business* and *home-based* modifies the phrase *computer business*.

> Because her small home-based computer business was expanding so rapidly, she had to rent office space.

Nonrestrictive Clauses

Commas are used to set off nonrestrictive (nonessential) clauses. A nonrestrictive clause adds extra or nonessential information to a sentence; in other words, the meaning of the sentence would not change if the information were deleted. A restrictive clause, on the other hand, supplies information that is necessary to the meaning of the sentence. Commas are not used with restrictive clauses. Sometimes only the writer knows whether a clause is essential or nonessential; if in doubt, editors should always query the author.

Notice how commas affect meaning in the next two sentences.

> All writers who love the language will enjoy reading *The Story of English*.
> All writers, who work with words daily, will enjoy reading *The Story of English*.

The first sentence restricts the group of writers who will enjoy the book to those who love the language. The second sentence says that all writers will enjoy the book; the clause *who work with words daily* is additional or nonrestrictive information.

Certain words and phrases can be used to introduce both essential and nonessential dependent clauses; others introduce only essential or only nonessential clauses. The chart shows some examples.

ESSENTIAL AND NONESSENTIAL CLAUSES: SOME COMMON INTRODUCTORY WORDS

After

Essential: The trial began after the last juror had been selected.

Nonessential: The trial began at 10:30 this morning, after the last juror had been selected.

Although, even though, though

Always nonessential: We bought the sofa that was on sale, although it was not exactly the style we had in mind.

As

Essential: The comments on the evaluations are as you thought they would be.

Nonessential: The comments on the evaluations are helpful, as you thought they would be.

As . . . as

Always essential: Cathy worked as diligently as she could.

As if, as though

Essential: He ate as if this were his last meal.

Nonessential: He ate greedily, as if this were his last meal.

Because

Always essential: The manager quit because she had a better job offer.

Before

Essential: I bought theater tickets for us before I knew you would be out of town.

Nonessential: I bought theater tickets yesterday, before I knew you would be out of town.

For

Always nonessential: He volunteered at the homeless shelter, for he wanted to do something for his community.

A comma precedes *for* when it is functioning as a conjunction to prevent confusion with its use as a preposition.

If

Essential: Please complete the application if you are interested in a position with our company.

Nonessential: She will arrive around noon, if I understood her correctly.

That

Always essential: The car that I want is out of my price range. (See Chapter 7, Modifiers, for a full discussion of *that* and *which.*)

Unless

Always essential: The gas company will discontinue our service unless we pay our bills by Friday.

Until

Always essential: Jonas will save his money until he has enough to buy a new car.

When

Essential: The new contract will become effective when the president signs it.

Nonessential: The new contract will become effective at noon tomorrow, when the president signs it.

Where

Essential: Department stores in states where winter temperatures are mild order very little cold-weather merchandise.

Nonessential: Department stores in Florida, where winter temperatures are mild, order very little cold-weather merchandise.

Which

Usually nonessential: The new medicine, which I take once a day, reduced my blood pressure immediately. (*Which* can be used to introduce essential clauses; see Chapter 7, Modifiers.)

While

Essential (when it means *during that time*): I made a few phone calls while waiting to board my flight.

Nonessential (when it means *whereas*): Harriet enjoys reading mysteries, while her sister prefers biographies.

Who

Essential: All boaters who cannot swim must wear a life jacket.

Nonessential: Cynthia, who cannot swim, must always wear a life jacket.

Whom

Essential: My daughter got an autograph from the baseball player whom she admires.

Nonessential: My daughter got an autograph from the baseball player Kirby Puckett, whom she admires.

Whose

Essential: The coach's award was given to the swimmer whose technique had improved the most.

Nonessential: The coach's award was given to Josh, whose technique had improved the most.

Incorrect Placement of Commas

With That. Commas are frequently used incorrectly with *that.* When *that* introduces a restrictive clause, commas are incorrect. If the phrase is truly nonrestrictive, *which* should be used instead of *that;* otherwise, the commas should be deleted.

> *Incorrect (if meaning is restrictive):* The house, that Jack is buying, is 175 years old.
> *Correct (if meaning is nonrestrictive):* The house, which Jack is buying, is 175 years old.
> *Correct (if meaning is restrictive):* The house that Jack is buying is 175 years old.

In constructions like those in the following examples, the comma after *that* is incorrect; however, a comma is optional *after* the *that* phrase, as the third example shows. (See Chapter 7, Modifiers, for more discussion of *which* and *that.*)

> *Incorrect:* The researchers are convinced that, with enough time and money a cure will be found.
> *Correct:* The researchers are convinced that with enough time and money a cure will be found.
> *Correct:* The researchers are convinced that with enough time and money, a cure will be found.

The authorities disagree on the last example; some believe that the *with . . . money* clause should be set off with commas on both sides. But others see the information in the clause as being essential to the meaning of the sentence; setting such clauses off with commas seems to imply that their meaning is nonessential. The comma after *money* is inserted to ensure ease of reading.

Between a Subject and Its Verb. Commas are always incorrect when they separate the subject and its verb.

> *Incorrect:* The acting chairman of the National Endowment for the Arts, told Congress yesterday that she is prepared to veto grants. . . . (*Washington Post,* May 6, 1992)

Between Phrases and Clauses Joined by a Conjunction. Phrases and dependent clauses joined by a coordinating conjunction should not be separated by a comma.

> Whether the voters will go to the polls in great numbers and whether they will vote straight tickets remain to be seen.

With For Example, Namely, *and Similar Expressions*

When expressions such as *for example* and *namely* fall in the middle of a sentence, they are set off with commas.

> During the recession many of his stocks, for example, General Motors, had to be sold.

Sometimes writers prefer to use dashes to set off the information introduced by these expressions.

> During the recession many of his stocks—for example, General Motors—had to be sold.

The comma after *for example* is retained.

To Replace Missing Words

Commas can replace missing words in sentences that have two main clauses connected by a semicolon.

> Mark is in charge of marketing; Tom, advertising.

A comma can replace the omitted word *that.*

> All I can say is, the thing I wanted most when I was a kid was to be a big-league baseball player, and the last thing I wanted was for magazines to run pictures of me in my underwear. (Roy Blount, Jr., *One Fell Soup*)
>
> Chances are, the game will have to be postponed because of rain.

A comma separates the two parts of a balancing expression that omits some words.

> First come, first served.
>
> Here today, gone tomorrow.

A comma is placed before an element that grammatically belongs to two or more phrases but is expressed only after the last one.

> We approve of, and are willing to participate in, the new 4-day work week.

In Dates

A comma should be placed before and after the year in a three-part date.

> There was evidence that Gordon Liddy and Howard Hunt had traveled to Los Angeles together under false names on September 4, 1971, and also on January 7, 1972, and February 17, 1972. (Carl Bernstein and Bob Woodward, *All the President's Men*)

No commas are necessary when a date precedes a month, a style common in U.S. military writing and in international usage.

The battalion held maneuvers from 1 April 1989 to 5 April 1989.

When only the month and year are stated, no comma is necessary.

I need the September 1993 and January 1994 issues of *Scientific American.*

With Cities, States, and Countries

A comma is placed before and after a state or country when both a city and state or country are mentioned, whether abbreviated or not.

I will attend a seminar in Duluth, Minnesota, next week and one in Bangor, Maine, the following week.
We will visit Washington, D.C., during our spring vacation.
She grew up in Utica, N.Y., and later returned there to live.

The second comma is omitted when a possessive ending is attached.

We will visit Washington, D.C.'s monuments this weekend.

The second comma is also omitted when the abbreviation forms a compound modifier.

the Fairfax, Va.-based corporation

Sentences with a string of cities and states present a challenge; in most cases, the best solution is to use semicolons to separate the city-state pairs. (See "Semicolons," page 260, for an example.)

Large Numbers

Numbers of five digits or more require a comma; commas in four-digit numbers are optional. The omission of the comma in four-digit numbers is often preferred in scientific and British usage. Exceptions to this general rule include addresses, phone numbers, page numbers, and so on (see Chapter 17, Numbers).

4,000 (*or* 4000)
40,000
400,000
4,000,000

With Jr. *and* Sr.

A comma is usually placed before *Jr.* and *Sr.* but not before *II* and *III.* Editors should be aware that some people drop the comma before *Jr.* in their names; individual preference should be followed.

John Doe, Jr. (*but* Martin Luther King Jr.)
John Doe III

If commas are used, the abbreviation or number is punctuated like a word in apposition, with a comma on each side.

John Doe, Jr., will conduct the morning staff meeting.

To avoid awkwardness, omit the second comma when a possessive end- is attached.

John Doe, Jr.'s contract expires at the end of this month.

With References

A comma is placed before and after a word or phrase that further explains a reference.

The information can be found on page 120, paragraph 3, and page 121, paragraph 1.

With Inc. *and* Ltd.

Commas are usually used to set off abbreviations such as *Inc.* and *Ltd.* unless the company preference is to drop the comma.

Time Inc.
Margaretten and Company, Inc.

When commas are used, they are placed before and after the abbreviation when it appears in a phrase or sentence.

AAA Roofing, Inc., offers a free inspection service.

No commas are used when the company name is possessive.

AAA Roofing, Inc.'s owner has filed for bankruptcy protection.

For Special Emphasis

Commas are used to set off words that are added for special emphasis.

They promise, unrealistically, that they can produce the same quality of work in less time and for less money.
I have tried, more than once, to make him understand the severity of the problem.

With Contrasting Expressions

A contrasting expression is preceded by a comma. If the expression falls in the middle of a sentence, the entire expression is set off with a pair of commas. Contrasting expressions are usually introduced with *but, not,* or *rather than.*

Success is a journey, not a destination.

Sometimes a sentence with a contrasting expression introduced by *but* is short enough to omit the commas.

It was a hectic but productive week.

These expressions should not be confused with sentences that contain correlative conjunctions, which require no commas unless the conjunction precedes an independent clause. (See Chapter 8, Articles, Prepositions, and Conjunctions, for more information.)

The budget cuts will affect not only the music and arts departments but also the physical education program.

With Adjectives and Adverbs That Follow a Quotation

A comma precedes an adjective that follows a descriptive phrase; a comma is omitted before an adverb that follows a descriptive phrase.

"Give me the gun," she said, hesitating.
"Give me the gun," she said hesitantly.

With Parentheses

A comma is placed outside a closing parenthesis.

In keeping Peggotty company, and doing all I could for her (little enough at the utmost), I was grateful, I rejoice to think, as even now I could wish myself to have been. (Charles Dickens, *David Copperfield*)

Commas are never correct before an opening parenthesis.

SEMICOLON

The semicolon tells the reader "Slow down, but don't stop." It ties together two closely related thoughts and emphasizes that relationship. Semicolons can also help readers through long or complex sentences by showing distinct breaks in thought or by separating groups of words or phrases, especially those that have commas in them. Semicolons reflect writing style as well; some writers rarely use them, while others use them so often that monotony results.

Between Main Clauses Without a Coordinating Conjunction

A semicolon can take the place of *and, but,* and other coordinating conjunctions in compound sentences—those with two main clauses.

> The first of the mourners began to arrive not long after the first rose was plundered from its bush; a light breakfast of coffee and freshly baked, buttered rolls was laid out in the small dining room. (Colleen McCullough, *The Thorn Birds*)

Between Main Clauses with a Coordinating Conjunction

Even though a comma followed by a coordinating conjunction is sufficient for connecting two main clauses in a compound sentence, some writers prefer to use a semicolon instead, especially if the sentence contains other commas. However, writers should be careful not to overuse the semicolon in this instance. A good rule of thumb is to use the semicolon if it will improve clarity for the reader.

> However, she added, Mr. Joseph was very fond of him, had called him James; and, it was said, [he] talked to him as if he were a rational being. (Virginia Woolf, "The Widow and the Parrot")

❧

THE HISTORY OF THE SEMICOLON

The Greeks first devised the semicolon sign, but its meaning was that of a question mark. The mark evolved as it moved into Latin: the dot and the comma-like curl switched places, and the curl took on slightly larger proportions, until it finally became the S-like swirl used to form the question mark as we know it.

A seventh-century Latin manuscript used a semicolon mark as we do, but a Latin manuscript two centuries later used an inverted semicolon to indicate a long pause.

A pioneer of early book publishing, the Italian scholar and printer Aldus Manutius (1450–1515) is credited with standardizing the use of the semicolon and giving it its name.

The semicolon's use to signal a pause stronger than a comma but less final than a period was further enforced by Justus George Schottelius, whose 1663 work *Detailed Treatise on the German Language* described and defined the *Strichpünktlein* ("stroke, little dot").

Between Main Clauses with a Conjunctive Adverb

A semicolon is placed before a conjunctive adverb that connects two main clauses, and a comma usually follows conjunctive adverbs like *furthermore, therefore, moreover, nevertheless, consequently, still, otherwise, besides, also, however,* or *accordingly.* A comma isn't needed after the conjunctive adverbs *hence, then, thus, so,* and sometimes *therefore.*

> Colonel Cunningham is a scholar, a valiant man, a true hero; however, encouraging him to run for political office would be a mistake.

In a Series

A semicolon helps separate items in a series when one or more items have internal punctuation.

> On the northern side were the beach, the lagoon, and the beautiful little island already mentioned; to the south, or directly inland, was the great valley of Vaipoopoo and a distant glimpse of Oro head, framed in the cliffs of the gorge; to the west lay Point Venus, with the sea breaking high on the protecting reefs; and to the east, facing the sunrise, was a magnificent view of the rocky, unprotected coast of Orofara and Faaripoo, where the surges of the Pacific thundered and spouted at the base of the stern black cliffs. (Charles Nordhoff and James Norman Hall, *Mutiny on the Bounty*)
>
> Conferences were held in Harlingen, Texas, on May 1, 1989; in Golden, Colorado, on April 14, 1990; and in San Jose, California, on July 25, 1991.

If the city name is very well known, the state name does not have to be included even if the sentence contains other city-state combinations.

> The author's book tour took him to Washington, D.C.; Atlanta; Springfield, Missouri; Chicago; and Eugene, Oregon.

With Quotation Marks

A semicolon is placed outside closing quotation marks.

> I never quite bought Coleridge's account of writing "Kubla Khan"; I don't care how good the opium was. (Arthur Plotnick, *Honk If You're a Writer*)

❧

SOME CONFLICTING THOUGHTS ON SEMICOLONS

Punctuation, [Abraham] Lincoln said to Noah Brooks, was with him a matter of feeling rather than education. The semicolon was found to be "a very useful little chap." (Carl Sandburg)

It is almost always a greater pleasure to come across a semicolon than a period. . . . You get a pleasant little feeling of expectancy; there is more to come; read on; it will get clearer. (George F. Will)

Semicolons are pretentious and overactive. . . . Far too often, [they] are used to gloss over an imprecise thought. They place two clauses in some kind of relationship to one another, but relieve the writer of saying exactly what that relationship is. (Paul Robinson)

There is a nineteenth-century mustiness that hangs over the semicolon. We associate it with the carefully balanced sentence, the judicious weighing of "on the one hand" and "on the other hand," of Conrad and Thackeray and Hardy. Therefore it should be used sparingly by writers of nonfiction today. (William Zinsser)

With Parentheses

The semicolon is placed outside a closing parenthesis.

> There *was* that time I had called her at home at midnight (I smiled faintly, remembering); I'd told her that my intention was not to be a nuisance. . . . (Richard Weizel, "A Voice from the Past," *Parenting*, October 1991)

COLON

A colon is a mark of introduction. It can precede a quotation, a list, an explanation, or a main clause. Although some writers and editors disagree on this point, the traditional view holds that the words preceding a colon must always form a complete sentence.

> Lake was aware of three sounds in the room: the gentle whoosh of an oscillating fan, a hum from the fluorescent lights, and disco music from a small radio that sat on the floor in the corner. (Margaret Truman, *Murder on Embassy Row*)

Introducing a List

A colon is always correct after a complete sentence that introduces a list.

> We will discuss three editing problems today:
>
> 1. Misplaced modifiers
> 2. Unclear antecedents
> 3. Redundancy

If the introduction is not a complete sentence, the colon should not be used—a dash or no punctuation at all is preferred. (For more information, see Chapter 13, Lists.)

A colon is incorrect after words like *such as,* between a verb and the rest of the sentence, and between a preposition and its object.

> *Incorrect:* My advice to any young writer is: become an editor. You'll do less work, have less pressure, have more influence, make more money, and best of all: you get to tell others what to do instead of having to do all that rotten research and writing yourself. (Bob Chieger)

The colon after *is* is wrong because a colon should not separate a verb from the rest of the sentence. No punctuation is necessary. The colon after *all* should be replaced with a comma.

Before a Quotation

A colon (or a comma) can be used after a main clause that introduces a quotation.

> She said it over and over under her breath: "Free, free, free!" (Kate Chopin, *The Story of an Hour*)

Before an Explanation or Description

A colon is placed after a sentence that introduces an explanation or description. This is a style issue: Most authorities state that if the words following the colon form a complete sentence, the first word following the colon is capitalized. If not, the first word is lowercased. (See Chapter 9, Capitalization, page 202.)

> It was now that she exhibited her devotion to the principle she had expounded at college: The test of a woman is how she organizes space. (James A. Michener, *Space*)
>
> Never did I realize till now what the ocean was: how grand and majestic, how solitary, and boundless. . . . (Herman Melville, *New York to Liverpool*)

However, some editors prefer to lowercase the first word of a complete sentence following a colon.

> She learned never to take the twins to the hospital at the same time: there were too many weapons in hospitals. (Larry McMurtry, *Texasville*)

Either approach is acceptable as long as consistency is maintained throughout the document or publication.

With Expressions of Time and Ratios

When hours and minutes are expressed in figures, a colon is placed between the hour and the minutes.

> 10:25 a.m.

A colon represents the word *to* in a ratio. In most nontechnical text, however, the word *to* is preferred.

> a 10:1 ratio *or* a 10-to-1 ratio
> The odds of winning are 42,500 to 1.

After Salutations

In a business letter, a colon follows the salutation. A comma is used instead of a colon when only the first name is needed, as in a less formal business letter and in informal or social correspondence.

> Dear Dr. Smith:
> Dear Mike,

With Quotation Marks

A colon is placed outside the closing quotation mark when the colon is part of the sentence, not the quotation.

> The writer had one hope for her short story "Caterpillar": to win an O. Henry Award.

DASH

Dashes come in four varieties:

- The em dash (—), formed with two hyphens in typewriter fonts, is the most common form and is used in sentences instead of a comma, a colon, or parentheses to set off information or to divide two elements when one or both of which already contain an en dash.

- The en dash (–), formed with one hyphen in typewriter fonts, represents the word *to* or *through* between two numbers or in expressions of time. It also marks the division between two elements, one or both of which already contain a hyphen.
- The 2-em dash (——), formed with four hyphens in typewriter fonts, shows that part of a name or word has been deliberately omitted.
- The 3-em dash (———), formed with six hyphens in typewriter fonts, shows that all of a word or name has been omitted; this type of dash is used to show that an author's or authors' names in bibliographies are the same as the last complete entry.

The Em Dash

The em dash is the primary form of the dash and is simply called *the dash* in this section. It is used primarily to emphasize the information that follows. Dashes are stronger than commas in sentences like this one:

> The only article of clothing he wore—a pair of ill-fitting overalls—was torn, seam-split, pinched in the rear and stiff with filth. (T. Coraghessan Boyle, *East Is East*)

A dash can also take the place of a colon.

> When I was young I enjoyed parties so much that any was better than none—the murmur of voices and clink of glasses as I came up the staircase, the smell of the women's scent, the spurts of laughter, the sparkle of lights would delight me in themselves. (Diana Athill, *Instead of a Letter*)

Words enclosed by a pair of dashes often provide an explanation or give extra or parenthetical information. By using a pair of dashes instead of parentheses, a writer emphasizes rather than deemphasizes those words.

> To speak critically, I never received more than one or two letters in my life—I wrote this some years ago—that were worth the postage. (Henry David Thoreau, *Walden*)

Appositives. Dashes are used around appositives if the use of commas might cause confusion.

> In fact, concern over the decline of three wild runs—the Snake River chinook and sockeye and the coho of the lower Columbia—is spurring petitions to the federal government for protection under the Endan-

gered Species Act. (Jere Van Duk, "Long Journey of the Pacific Salmon," *National Geographic,* July 1990)

To Show Hesitation. A dash is placed before and after a word or group of words that shows hesitation or faltering speech.

"Well, I never heard of the dev—of your claiming American citizenship," said Dan'l Webster with surprise. (Stephen Vincent Benét, "The Devil and Daniel Webster")

With a Question Mark or an Exclamation Point. When a question or exclamation is set off with dashes, a question mark or exclamation point is placed before the closing dash.

With much to-do the first old woman sat down in a rocking chair—still another piece of furniture!—and began to rock. (Eudora Welty, "A Visit of Charity")

The reception—have you heard?—has been postponed until May 1.

With a Comma. When a closing dash occurs at the same point that a comma would be used, the dash is kept and the comma is omitted.

"Gee—" said Hazel, "I could tell that one was a doozy." (Kurt Vonnegut, Jr., "Harrison Bergeron")

With a Semicolon or Colon. When a closing dash occurs at the same point that a semicolon or colon would be used, the dash is omitted.

. . . [T]he designer will also devise a format and perhaps commission or secure drawings or photographs—all this with two goals in mind: making your work readable, and visually reinforcing its message. (Judith Appelbaum, *How to Get Happily Published*)

With Parentheses. The dash is retained after a closing parenthesis.

So he took a pencil and on the back of a menu—it was from Nero's Grotto, a casino (he could not recall how it came to be in his apartment)—he began to draw pictures. (Allan Appel, *The Rabbi of Casino Boulevard*)

With Quotation Marks. A dash is placed inside the closing quotation mark to show that the writer's or speaker's words were interrupted.

"No, Walter. We only stopped for dinner. Madelyn wants to make it to New York by—" (Gail Godwin, *Father Melancholy's Daughter*)

A dash is placed outside the closing quotation mark to show that the sentence is broken off after the quoted material.

> If one more writer uses the phrase "bottom line"—

A closing dash is placed outside the closing quotation mark when the quoted material is part of the nonessential information between the dashes.

> Please get the letter from my desk—it's the one marked "Addressee Unknown"—and give it to the mail clerk.

A dash is used before and after a phrase that interrupts a quoted sentence and is not part of the direct quotation.

> "Actually"—Barbara thumped her chest with outstretched thumb—"I hate myself for what I know in my heart I must do. If I were religious, I would think of myself as a female Job." (Warren Adler, *The War of the Roses*)

With an En Dash. An em dash is used between two elements containing en dashes.

> Public Laws 85–1—85–20

With Biographical Data. An em dash is used after the birth year in a biographical reference when the person is still alive.

> Edward Kennedy (1932—), the youngest son of Joseph and Rose Kennedy, was elected to the Senate in 1962.

The En Dash

With Letters and Numerals. An en dash is used with sets of numerals, letters, or a combination of both; exceptions include numbered designations of aircraft (DC-10) and highways (I-95), which use hyphens.

> Public Law 85–1
> 1935–1937
> AFL–CIO merger
> exhibit 6–A
> appendix B–2

With Modifiers. An en dash, not a hyphen, is used to join compound modifiers formed with two-word proper nouns or already hyphenated words.

> the North Dakota–South Dakota coalition
> non-European–non-Asian population

Although it is always preferable to use the words *through* or *to* with dates, times, and days of the week in text, en dashes are sometimes used, especially in lists, tables, or other kinds of displayed information:

$5–$20
pages 38–45
Monday–Friday (*but not:* from Monday–Friday)
9:00 a.m.–3:00 p.m.
the October–December timeframe

The 2-Em Dash

The 2-em dash is used to show that a name, a part of a name, or a word has been omitted.

Dr. —— and Ms. —— are the defendants in the case.

The 3-Em Dash

A 3-em dash shows that an entire name or word has been omitted.

The two defendants in the case, ——— and ———, were escorted to the jail through a secret hallway from the courthouse.

In a bibliography, a 3-em dash takes the place of an author's name when the preceding entry is by the same author. (See Chapter 20, Reference Citations.)

APOSTROPHE

Apostrophes have many uses: They show omissions of letters and numbers, they signify possession or ownership, and sometimes they are used to form plurals of letters, numbers, and symbols. The apostrophe, especially when used to show the possessive, is often misunderstood and misused.

❧

MARK TWAIN'S APPROACH TO PUNCTUATION

Mark Twain, goes the story, didn't see the need for punctuation marks in his writing. When his editor complained, Twain sent him an entire page of punctuation marks in random order. His enclosed note said, "Put them wherever they seem to fit." His editor never raised the issue again.

Contractions

A contraction is a shortened form of a word or phrase. The apostrophe replaces the omitted letter or letters. Examples are *don't* for *do not, who's* for *who is, sec'y* for *secretary, 'twas* for *it was,* and *dep't* for *department.*

Possessives

Singular Nouns. An apostrophe is used with a noun to show ownership. Most possessives are formed by adding *'s* to the end of a noun that does not end in *s.*

my friend's house
the horse's tail

Singular Nouns That End in s. Some punctilious writers and editors hold to the traditional school of thought and place an *'s* at the end of all singular nouns, even nouns ending in an *s,* deciding on the basis of how the word is pronounced: If a new syllable is created when the possessive is formed, then an *'s* is added (the boss's decision); if the addition of another syllable would make the noun difficult to pronounce, only an apostrophe is added (Athens' temples).

Others, however, believe that adding *'s* to a word that already ends in *s* creates an excess of *s*'s. This approach is gaining acceptance and is favored by the editors of this book.

the boss' memos
the witness' statement
the hostess' chair

Certain expressions that end in *s* or the *s* sound traditionally require an apostrophe only.

for appearance' sake
for conscience' sake
for goodness' sake

Plural Nouns. The first step in forming the possessive of plural nouns is to form the plural correctly. (Chapter 15, Spelling, explains.) If the plural ends in *s,* the possessive is formed by adding an apostrophe.

boxes' sides
cartons' tops
girls' dresses
shelves' brackets

If the plural does not end in *s*, the possessive is formed by adding *'s*.

children's games
geese's pens
oxen's yokes
women's rights

If a noun uses the same form for both singular and plural, the possessive form depends on whether the noun ends with *s*. Those that end with *s* take only an apostrophe; the rest take an *s* preceded by an apostrophe.

athletics' appeal
corps' members
deer's pastures
moose's antlers
series' conclusions
sheep's wool
species' distributions

Often such phrases are improved by rewording: the appeal of athletics, the members of the corps, the distributions of species.

The possessive of *people* often causes difficulty. Notice the following two examples:

Many different peoples made up the Soviet Union. These peoples' preferences were never important to the rulers.
Johnson is the people's choice.

Although *people* itself is a noun denoting a group and takes a plural verb, it has two possessive forms. The first example indicates that the peoples of the Soviet Union may have had different preferences; therefore, the plural possessive is necessary. The second example shows that the people made a collective choice by electing Johnson; therefore, *people* takes the form of a singular possessive.

Proper Names. In most cases, the possessives of both singular and plural proper names are formed like those of any other noun.

To form the possessive of proper nouns that end in *s*, add only the apostrophe.

James' idea
Charles Addams' cartoons

For names ending in a silent *s* or *x*, the possessive is also formed by adding only an apostrophe. The *s* is pronounced in this instance.

Dumas' writings
Descartes' ideas

Most problems with forming possessives are actually problems with forming the plural.

Singular	*Plural*
Mary Adams' house	the Adamses' house
Bob Davis' house	the Davises' house
Bob Smith's house	the Smiths' house

Multisyllabic names ending in the *eez* or *z* sound, particularly Greek names, traditionally take no *s* after the apostrophe.

Socrates' most famous student was Plato.
Jesus' death occurred around A.D. 30.
Moses' name means "brought him out of the water."

Compound Nouns and Phrases. If the compound is singular, add *'s* to the last element of the expression.

attorney general's ruling
Queen Elizabeth II's reign
sister-in-law's silverware
somebody else's problem

If the compound is plural, it is best to avoid confusion by using *of* to indicate possession.

The rulings of the state attorneys general differed.
The glances of the passers-by indicated disapproval.
I covet the family heirlooms that belong to my sisters-in-law.

Personal Pronouns. A common error is to use apostrophes with possessive pronouns that end in *s.* No apostrophe is required with *hers, his, its, ours, theirs,* and *yours* because these pronouns are already possessive.

Indefinite Pronouns. Although possessive personal pronouns never require an apostrophe, some indefinite pronouns have regular possessive forms.

anyone's guess
the other's idea
the others' ideas
each other's ideas
no one's fault
someone's lucky day

An *of* phrase is used with indefinite pronouns that have no possessive form.

Although the two proposals are going to different clients, the contents *of each* are similar.

Descriptive Words. An apostrophe is not used with a descriptive word that ends in an *s*. In the examples that follow, the words *news, sales, savings,* and *measles* are adjectives, not possessives.

news flash
sales promotion
savings bank
measles epidemic

Although an apostrophe is not incorrect in terms like the following, increasingly it is omitted when the sense of the term is descriptive rather than possessive—that is, when *for* is meant rather than *of.*

teachers college	officers club
teachers union	travelers checks
boys clubs	users manual
Merchants Bank	

In some cases a slight difference in wording determines whether a word is descriptive or possessive.

2-year sabbatical	2 years' sabbatical
Nevada history	Nevada's history
the Panzer account	Bob Panzer's account
the Carpenter children	the Carpenters' children
6 months of probation	6 months' probation

Joint Possession. When two or more people jointly possess an item, the apostrophe is placed after the noun closest to the item.

Bill and Mary's house (Bill and Mary jointly own one house.)
Bill and Mary's houses (Bill and Mary jointly own more than one house.)
Tom and Harry's responsibility (Tom and Harry share the responsibility.)

When two or more people separately possess items, an apostrophe or an *'s* is added to each noun.

men's, women's, and children's bicycles
Bill's and Mary's houses (Bill and Mary each own at least one house; they may own more. Bill's ownership is independent of Mary's.)

Some phrases of joint possession may cause problems in meaning.

Awkward: Susan and Meredith's boyfriend went to the movie.

This sentence could be read two ways: Susan and Meredith share a boyfriend, or Susan went to the movie with Meredith's boyfriend. For clarity, the sentence should be recast.

Susan went to the movie with Meredith's boyfriend.

Groups. Sometimes the apostrophe is used to express something meant for two or more people or groups rather than to show true possession.

fathers' and daughters' breakfast
1992 Children's Writer's & Illustrator's Market

Geographic Names. Increasingly, mapmakers are eliminating apostrophes from place names to avoid confusion with the prime mark.

Tysons Corner
Harpers Ferry
But: Martha's Vineyard

Names of Companies, Organizations, and Publications. The possessive of a company or organization name that contains a preposition is formed by adding an *'s* if the name does not end in an *s*. If the name ends in an *s*, only an apostrophe is added.

The Bank of Virginia's trust department
The First Bank of Kansas' car loan rates

But an organization's or publication's preference should be followed.

Young Women's Christian Association
St. Elizabeths Hospital
International Ladies' Garment Workers' Union
Writer's Digest
Publishers Weekly

Abbreviations. To form the possessive, add an *'s* to a singular abbreviation that does not end in *s*. Add an apostrophe only to singular abbreviations that end in *s* and to plural abbreviations.

TWA's flight
HHS' policy
the CEOs' forecasts
the PACs' political influence

The possessive of a company name ending in an abbreviation is formed by adding an *'s* to the end of the complete name.

the Seacord Co. Inc.'s new location
Marathon Books, Inc.'s recent publication

The first example shows the name of a company with the comma omitted before the abbreviation, and the second example shows the name of a company with the comma inserted before the abbreviation.

The possessive of a personal name that ends with an abbreviation or a number is formed by adding an *'s* to the end of the complete name.

John Doe, Jr.'s speech
Charles T. Pinkerton III's trust fund

If the abbreviation is plural, only an apostrophe is added.

the John Latall, Jrs.' party

Possessives That Stand Alone. When a noun that is modified by a possessive is understood rather than stated, the possessive is formed according to the standard rules.

We have been invited to a party at the Brightons'.
This month's income far exceeds last month's.

Inanimate Possessives. Many writers claim that because inanimate objects cannot show ownership, the possessive should not be used. But others disagree, arguing that the alternative results in unnecessary wordiness. For example, some writers and editors would change "the train station's platform" to "the platform of the train station," although most today would not.

In phrases of personification of time and money, however, the possessive has always been acceptable.

this evening's storm
dawn's early light
5 days' leave
3 years' salary
6 dollars' worth
Seven Years' War

The possessive should not be used when no possessive relationship exists.

3 years ago
6 years later

Gerunds. When a noun or a pronoun modifies a gerund (a verb form that ends in *-ing* and functions as a noun), the noun or pronoun should be in the possessive. (See Chapter 3, Nouns, page 119, for more about possessive pronouns with gerunds.)

The accountant approved of our leasing the building.

Some sentences are grammatically correct but stylistically awkward and should be recast.

Awkward: To ensure his children's having a college education, he established a trust fund for each child.
Improved: To ensure that his children would have a college education, he established a trust fund for each child.

Double Possessives. A possessive modifying a possessive may result in a grammatically correct but awkward sentence. A double possessive will usually force a reader to stop in midsentence to try to figure out what the writer is trying to say. The best solution is to rewrite the sentence.

Awkward: The telephone company's president's idea was to offer discount rates to senior citizens.
Improved: The telephone company's president conceived the idea of offering discount rates to senior citizens.

Sometimes the use of an apostrophe in an *of* phrase can create a grammatically correct—but awkward—sentence. In this case, the sentence should be recast.

Awkward: A friend of mine's contract was not renewed.
Improved: My friend's contract was not renewed.

Certain idiomatic expressions, however, permit the double possessive; an example is *a friend of the girl's.*

Holidays. Possessives of names of holidays are usually singular; however, some, by tradition, are plural.

Valentine's Day
Father's Day
New Year's Day
Martin Luther King's Birthday
Presidents' Day
April Fools' Day
But: Veterans Day

Common Expressions. Several common expressions require the apostrophe to indicate possession. Most are singular.

bachelor's degree
cat's cradle
baker's dozen
confectioner's sugar
writer's block
buyer's market
dog's life
fool's gold

But:
lovers' lane
proofreaders' marks

With Quotation Marks. The apostrophe and *s* are placed outside closing quotation marks. This combination usually looks awkward; the sentence should be recast.

Awkward: "The Road Not Taken" 's last line is embedded in the memory of most high school graduates.
Improved: The last line of "The Road Not Taken" is embedded in the memory of most high school graduates.

To Indicate Omission of a Number in a Date

An apostrophe is used as a sign of omission of the first two digits in the date of a year. This usage is strictly informal.

the class of '64
the summer of '42

In Plurals of Letters and Numbers

An *'s* is added to lowercase letters to make the element plural.

1500 rpm's
He was the quintessential organization man and his *i'*s were dotted and all his sentences were diagrammed by a portentous vacuity. (Pat Conroy, *The Prince of Tides*)

Plurals of most numbers and uppercase letters do not require an apostrophe.

during the 1940s
Her SAT scores were in the 700s.
Jackson had three RBIs by the seventh inning.

(See Chapter 14, Abbreviations, for further discussion.)

In Plurals of Spelled-out Numbers and Words

The apostrophe is usually omitted in plurals of spelled-out numbers, of words used as words, and of words already containing an apostrophe.

ones, fives, and nines
yeses and nos
ins and outs
whys and wherefores

However, the apostrophe is used to indicate the plural of a word that might cause difficulty in reading.

> do's and don'ts (note that for appearance' sake the apostrophe before the *s* in *don'ts* is traditionally dropped)
> which's and that's
> or's and nor's

QUOTATION MARKS

The purpose of quotation marks is to mark the beginning and end of directly quoted words. Chapter 11, Setting Off Words, Terms, and Names, discusses when to use quotation marks for special emphasis and titles. The most frequently asked question about quotation marks is, "Where does the period (or comma or semicolon or colon) go—before or after the quotation marks?"

With a Comma or Period

The comma and period are placed *before* the closing quotation mark.

> Others might say the stock market fell, but those who work on Wall Street prefer to say that the stock market "retreated," "eased," "made a technical adjustment" or a "technical correction," or perhaps the "prices were off due to profit taking," or "off in light trading," or "lost ground." (William Lutz, *Doublespeak*)

With a Semicolon or Colon

The semicolon and colon are placed *after* the closing quotation mark.

> They said he was a "bright kid," that he would "go places"; and they made it clear that they expected him to go. (James Baldwin, *Another Country*)

With a Question Mark or an Exclamation Point

Question marks and exclamation points are placed *before* closing quotation marks when the entire quotation is a question or exclamation, and they belong *after* closing quotation marks when only words or phrases are in quotation marks.

> What is meant by "matter itself" as opposed to "apple matter" and "human matter"? (Mortimer J. Adler, *Aristotle for Everybody*)
> When you write such a thing about a character, ask yourself: "Did he really

do that? Have I ever seen *anyone* do that?" (Brenda Ueland, *If You Want to Write*)

With Direct Quotations

Quotation marks are placed around the exact words of a speaker or writer. The words may be a complete sentence, a clause, a phrase, or a word. Note how the punctuation and capitalization in the following examples vary depending on sentence structure.

> "You're off a million miles," said father. "Look alive. Walk with us." (Ray Bradbury, *Dandelion Wine*)
>
> "So what happened?" asked Tyrone. (Toni Cade Bambara, "Blues Ain't No Mockin' Bird")
>
> But then the Orkin man called out from inside the chimney. "Hey," he said, "do you know what's in here?" (Robb Forman Dew, *The Time of Her Life*)
>
> Tasha didn't protest because "I didn't want the responsibility for this man. I didn't want to be with him the rest of my life." (Sara Davidson, *Loose Change*)

Double Punctuation. Double punctuation is not used at the end of a direct quotation. If the sentence needs one type of punctuation and the direct quotation needs another type, the "stronger" punctuation should be retained. The comma and the period are the weakest marks and are usually dropped, while the exclamation point is usually—but not always—stronger than the question mark; the overall sense of the sentence must be taken into account. If the sentence and the direct quotation require the same type of punctuation, the first is retained.

> The human race is divided into two classes—those who go ahead and do something and those who sit still and inquire, "Why wasn't it done the other way?" (Oliver Wendell Holmes, Jr.)
>
> *Correct:* Who yelled, "Look out!"
>
> *Incorrect:* Who yelled, "Look out!"?
>
> *Correct:* "Did she ask, 'Where am I?' "
>
> *Incorrect:* "Did she ask, 'Where am I?'?"

In Dialogue. In the recounting of a conversation, the comments of each speaker should begin on a new line, be indented, and show opening and closing quotation marks. Note that end punctuation is placed inside a direct quotation that stands alone.

> "Hi, Mr. Hawley."
>
> "I thought you were closed today."

> "Looks like I never close. Thirty-six dollar mistake in the books. I worked till midnight last night."
>
> "Short?"
>
> "No—over."
>
> "That should be good."
>
> "Well, it ain't. I got to find it."
>
> "Are banks that honest?"
>
> "Banks are. It's only some men that aren't. If I'm going to get any holiday, I've got to find it." (John Steinbeck, *The Winter of Our Discontent*)

If one of the speakers continues for more than one paragraph, closing quotation marks are not used until the person stops speaking.

Quotations Within Quotations. A quotation within a quotation is enclosed in a pair of single quotation marks.

> "Would you want your daughter to spend her life playing with the 'living impaired'?" (Margaret Truman, *Murder on Embassy Row*)

In the rare instance when a direct quotation falls within the single quotation marks, double quotation marks are used.

With Indirect Quotations

Quotation marks are not used with an indirect quotation or with a paraphrase of a person's actual words.

> In his State of the Union Address the President promised that taxes would not be increased.

With a Direct Question

Quotation marks are optional with a direct question unless the question is a direct quotation.

> The question is, Will we meet the Friday deadline?

With Yes *and* No

Quotation marks are not placed around the words *yes* and *no* unless they are part of a direct quotation.

> I told him my answer was yes.

In Plays, Interviews, and Court Testimony

In plays, interviews, and court testimony or in any similar text where conversation is recorded, quotation marks are unnecessary because the names of the speakers are given. In his book *The Portable Curmudgeon,* Jon Winokur records the following interview with writer Calvin Trillin.

> JW: *Your wife has called you a "sausage-eating, slothful crank."*
> CT: She has. But she also says that down deep I'm really a sweetheart.
> JW: *A sweetheart, not a curmudgeon?*
> CT: I've been accused of being amiable. Good-humored is another accusation that's been made against me.

SLASH

The slash goes by many names: virgule, cancel, shilling, diagonal, slant bar, stroke, solidus, and separatrix. The slash is used in abbreviations, expressions of time, and alternatives and with fractions and serial numbers. It can also be used to indicate that a person or thing has two functions. In most cases, no space appears before or after a slash.

With Abbreviations

The slash is used in some abbreviations, such as *c/o* for *in care of.* It can replace the Latin term *per* in some abbreviations (for example, *km/h* for *kilometers per hour*).

With Expressions of Time

Slashes, as well as en dashes, are used to show a range of time:

> fiscal year 1991/92
> the January/February receipts

With Expressions of Alternatives

Although this practice is growing, many writers and editors prefer to avoid the use of a slash in formal writing to express an alternative when the slash means *or.*

Some writers use *his/her* to avoid sexist language, but there are other ways to approach this issue; see Chapter 1, Usage, for a discussion.

THE METAMORPHOSIS OF THE SLASH

The slash originated sometime in the 13th or 14th century as a form of light stop. In the late 15th century, according to the *Britannica Book of English Usage,* it "sank to the baseline, developed a curve," and became the modern comma.

To Show Two Functions

A slash may be used to combine two jobs or titles: the secretary/treasurer, the actor/director. A hyphen may also be used for this purpose.

With Fractions

In technical text or tabular material, fractions can be shown with slashes: 4/5, 2/3.

In Poetry

When part of a poem is incorporated into running text, a slash is used to show where one line ends and another begins. A space follows the slash.

> As Robert Frost said in his famous poem, "I took the one less traveled by, / And that has made all the difference."

ELLIPSIS POINTS

Ellipsis points (or marks) are a series of three dots that indicate the omission of quoted words. Chapter 12, Quotations, explains when and how to use these marks. Other uses of ellipses are to show a trailing off of thought at the end of a sentence or to show a pause, as is done with a comma or a dash.

> [S]he wore her hair this way, not that . . . she smelled like a poppy petal and not lavender cologne . . . she made the toast first and did *not* butter it when we had it with hot cocoa. . . . (M.F.K. Fisher, *Among Friends*)

PARENTHESES

Parentheses enclose information the writer does not deem important enough to stand alone. Usually this information provides extra facts, such as spelling out an acronym or providing one, explaining part of the sentence, or interjecting a thought or an aside.

Writers and editors may wish to keep the following distinctions in mind when deciding whether to use parentheses, dashes, or commas: Parentheses deemphasize information and tell readers that the enclosed words are not vital to the meaning of the sentence, dashes emphasize information and tell the reader that these words are important, and commas indicate that the information is simply part of the sentence.

Punctuation and capitalization are the biggest problems with parentheses because the rules change depending on whether the words in parentheses appear within a sentence or stand alone. The paragraphs below explain the difference.

Within a Sentence Versus Standing Alone

When a parenthetical expression appears within a sentence, the first word does not begin with a capital letter unless the first word is a proper name or proper pronoun or is a capitalized word in a direct quotation. No period is used, *even if the statement forms a complete sentence;* a question mark or exclamation point may be needed, however. The following examples are from a master of parentheses, writer David Owen, in *The Walls Around Us.*

> After holding it next to some drawings in a home-inspection guide, I became convinced that what I had in my hand was a termite. Its antennae were not elbowed (an ant's would have been).

If the statement in parentheses is just a word or two or a phrase, the same rule holds.

> During the Second World War, wooden crates left on the ground on an island in the Pacific were rapidly (and invisibly) consumed to the point where they fell apart when soldiers attempted to lift them.

But when the parenthetical expression stands on its own, outside the other sentences, it is considered to be a complete sentence and is capitalized and punctuated normally within the parentheses, as Owen demonstrates.

> [Carpenter ants] often leave visible piles of sawdust or chewed-up foam insulation near their excavations, and they can sometimes—usually at night—be heard munching and moving around inside a wall. (The stethoscope from your child's Fisher-Price medical bag is a useful instrument for detecting this activity.)

When parentheses fall within a sentence, other punctuation—commas, colons, dashes, and semicolons—is placed *after* the closing parenthesis, never before. As Owen continues,

This is true even if the lumber is labeled KDAT (kiln-dried after treatment), as it occasionally is.

If the information in parentheses falls at the end of a sentence, the necessary end punctuation also falls *after* the closing parenthesis.

To Enclose References

References (such as author, date, and title) and cross-references (such as "see figure 1") are often placed in parentheses. These references can be placed anywhere within a sentence, or they can stand alone; the rules described above for capitalization and punctuation of parenthetical phrases or sentences apply. The writer should choose one approach and use it throughout the manuscript.

> Figure 1 (see page 46) shows text and numbers on a worksheet.
> *or*
> Figure 1 shows text and numbers on a worksheet (see page 46).
> *or*
> Figure 1 shows text and numbers on a worksheet. (See page 46.)

The last two approaches are preferred because the text is not interrupted.

With Lists in Running Text

Parentheses are used in pairs around numbers or letters that precede items in a list in running text. Parentheses are unnecessary if the list is displayed, or set apart from the running text.

> Errors requiring basic marks fall into four categories: (1) surplus characters or words, to be marked for deletion; (2) omitted characters or words, to be marked for insertion; (3) wrong characters or words, to be marked for replacement; and (4) out-of-order characters or words, to be marked for transposition. (Peggy Smith, *Proofreading Manual and Reference Guide*)

In final copy, the numbers or letters should stay on the same line with the text that follows.

With Quotation Marks

The closing quotation mark is placed outside the closing parenthesis when the parenthetical information is part of the quoted material.

Bill Stott, in his book *Write to the Point,* describes information in parentheses as "a wink across the footlights, an index finger wagging for the roving camera (hi, Mom)."

Quotation marks are placed *inside* the parentheses when the quoted material is part of the parenthetical information.

At first I failed to grasp what was going on, but then I suddenly remembered what Baribhai had said ("You are looking at a single monkey"). (Leo Lionni, *Parallel Botany*)

BRACKETS

Like parentheses, brackets enclose comments or explanations. They are most frequently seen in quoted material, where they indicate corrections or comments made by an editor or another writer. The information in brackets, as in parentheses, may be a word, a phrase, or a complete sentence, and punctuation rules are the same. (Chapter 12, Quotations, further explains this use of brackets.)

The statement went on to mourn for our "unhappy country [Virginia]" which would, through Washington's resignation, receive an irreparable loss. (James Thomas Flexner, *Washington: The Indispensable Man*)

With Parentheses

Brackets are used to show another level of parenthetical information within parentheses.

. . . the conglomerate was invaded by large volumes of granitoids and monzodiorite (Algoman Group of Lawson [1913]).

Double parentheses are preferred by many publications, however.

According to the news magazine, a May poll showed that the voters are losing confidence in the President. However, a more recent poll (taken by the *Washington Post* (June 4, 1992)) indicates that the President's popularity is on the upswing.

Mathematical equations use parentheses within brackets. See Chapter 19, Mathematical Expressions, for details.

11

SETTING OFF WORDS, TERMS, AND NAMES

SETTING OFF WORDS, TERMS, AND NAMES

Italics, underscores, quotation marks, boldface, small capitals, and all capital letters—these are the typographic tools that writers, editors, and designers use to give emphasis to letters, words, names, and titles. This chapter describes the most common conventions. Overuse of any of these devices tends to diminish their effectiveness. In general, boldface and all caps are best saved for headlines and subheads. In text, they should be used sparingly, if at all; an exception is computer documentation, where commands and functions need to be instantly recognizable.

Underscores are the typewritten equivalent of typeset italics. *Typewritten* here refers to copy prepared using traditional typewriter typefaces, still common in most word processing settings; *typeset* refers to proportionally spaced type of the kind seen in books and periodicals. Underscores in typeset text, rarely used in traditional typesetting, are now being seen, probably as a result of the widespread use of desktop publishing software by those who learned to type on typewriters and word processors.

Styles vary widely on when to use italics and quotation marks to set off words and titles. Some newspapers, including the *New York Times* and the *Washington Post,* set names of periodicals in roman type—that is, standard text type—and place quotation marks around titles of books. The guidelines in this chapter, however, reflect more formal conventions.

TO SET OFF WORDS AND LETTERS

Writers are often tempted to use italics, underscores, boldface, all uppercase letters, or quotation marks to call attention to a word or phrase, and, used sparingly, these treatments help convey the writer's emphasis. Certain words and terms, such as definitions, unfamiliar terminology, and foreign words and phrases, are also often set off typographically to set them apart from standard text.

A Word Emphasized in Text

Ideally, writers should rely on sentence structure to emphasize the importance of a word or group of words; however, if the reader might not catch the emphasis on the first reading, italics may be used to show stress. Overuse of this treatment should be avoided.

> I think I was born with the impression that what happened in books was much more reasonable, and interesting, and *real*, in some ways, than what happened in life. (Ann Tyler in *The Writer on Her Work*, edited by Janet Sternburg)

The same advice applies to the use of all capital letters. Entire paragraphs set in all caps or all italics should be avoided completely because they are so difficult to read.

A Word Referred to as a Word

A word referred to as a word is usually placed in italics; however, quotation marks may also be used. Whichever form is chosen should be used consistently throughout a manuscript.

> The word *colonel* is pronounced *kernel.*

❧

ITALIC TYPE:
ONE GIANT LEAP FOR PUBLISHING

Around 1500 one of the world's first great printers, Aldus Manutius of Venice, commissioned the design of a new typeface that would take up less space and be more readable than the standard black-letter or gothic type used by Gutenberg. The compactness of this new face, which was based on cursive script, let Aldus proceed with another publishing innovation, "octavo" size books (about 6 by 9 inches), which were much more portable than the large, bulky volumes then current. The Venetian senate gave Aldus the exclusive right to print the classics in both Greek and Latin, for which he used italic type. Many other printers found this new typeface to be so pleasing and practical that they soon defied the monopoly and began printing in italics as well.

The first book Aldus printed in italics was an edition of Virgil that was dedicated to Italy, and the word *italic* was thus derived from its country of origin.

Definitions in Text

When a word is defined in text, the word is set in italics, and the meaning is placed in quotation marks. An article should not be used before the word being defined.

> When the editor checked the dictionary, she was surprised to see that the first definition of *receipt* was "recipe."

Technical and Specialized Terms

A technical or specialized term that may be unfamiliar or unclear to most readers is often set in italics or quotation marks the first time it appears in text. After the first use, the term is set in roman.

> Fixed disks are also referred to as *hard disks* because their magnetic medium is rigid. The hard disk is usually housed in the central processing unit.
>
> "Technological progress" and "technical progress" are used interchangeably to indicate increases in multifactor productivity associated with increased knowledge. (Martin Neil Baily and Alok K. Chakrabarti, *Innovation and the Productivity Crisis*)

Foreign Words and Phrases

In general, most foreign words and phrases should be set in italics.

> The French use the term *esprit de l'escalier* ("wit of the stairway") to describe the brilliant comments that occur to us just after we have left the party or meeting where they would have been appropriate. (David Grudin, *Time and the Art of Living*)

If the word or phrase is used repeatedly throughout the text, it is acceptable to italicize only the first use and use roman for subsequent occurrences. Also, more than a sentence or two of foreign language text is usually best set in roman type for ease of readability.

Anglicized Words. Many foreign words, however, have become an established part of the English language and should not be italicized; the test is whether English dictionaries list these words as entries in the main text. (Many dictionaries provide a separate list of foreign words and phrases, and words in those lists should be italicized.) These words usually lose their diacritical marks when they enter English, except in cases where confusion could result (for example, *resume* for *résumé*). Check a dictionary for guidance on diacritical marks as well.

à la carte
a priori
ad hoc
ad infinitum
auf Wiedersehen
bistro
bona fide
carte blanche
communiqué
coup d'état
cul-de-sac
de facto
détente
deus ex machina
enfant terrible
et al.
ex officio
facade
gratis
habeas corpus
ibid.
in vitro
in vivo
kibbutz
kulak
laissez-faire
modus operandi
non sequitur
nouveau riche
papier-mâché
perestroika
per se
prima facie
prix fixe
pro forma
pro rata
pro tem
quid pro quo
résumé
sans serif
sotto voce
tête-à-tête
tsunami
vis-à-vis
zeitgeist

Here are a few words and phrases that are not yet a part of English:

au fond
bon appétit
e pluribus unum
d'accord
nyet
suo jure
tristesse
wunderbar

Proper Names. Foreign language names of cities, streets, buildings, structures, organizations, government bodies, institutions, and churches are not italicized. Note that these words are usually capitalized and that the accents are retained.

Bibliothèque Nationale
Universitätsstrasse
Brandenburger Tor
Musée de Louvre
Firenze
29, rue de la Paix

Except for German, most languages tend to use lowercase in names and titles to a greater extent than we do in English. The treatment used in the language should be followed. (See Chapter 9, Capitalization, and Chapter 21, Foreign Languages.)

Letters

Letters Used as Letters. When an individual letter of the alphabet is referred to in a sentence, the letter is set in italic.

A young child may have difficulty writing an *s*.

Letters That Indicate Academic Grades. Letters representing school grades are not italicized.

She felt lucky to receive a C in first-year economics.

Letters That Indicate Shapes. A letter that designates the shape of something is set in roman, not in italics. Usually the letter is set in sans serif type to further emphasize the distinction.

an L-shaped wing of a building
a U-shaped table
an S-curve

Letters That Are "Spelled." A letter of the Latin alphabet that is spelled out to show its sound should be set in italics.

The proofreader instructed the typesetter to change the symbol zero to the letter *oh.*

Letters That Indicate Musical Notes. Musical notes are set in roman capitals.

A-minor
C-sharp minor
middle C

Letters in Mathematical Expressions. Letters representing variables and constants in mathematical expressions are set in italics; functions are set in roman. See Chapter 19, Mathematical Expressions, for further discussion of when to use italics with math.

$xy - ab = 42$

Letters in Text That Refer to Parts of an Illustration. A letter in text or a legend that refers to a letter in figures or illustrations is set in italics even if the letter in the figure or illustration is set in roman.

Point *C* in figure 1 indicates. . . .

Letters That Indicate Rhyme Scheme. When letters are used to indicate a rhyme scheme in poetry, the letters are set in italics.

The rondeau rhyme scheme is *a a b b a, a a b R, a a b b a R,* with the *R* signifying the refrain.

Sounds That Are Spelled

When a combination of letters is used to represent a sound, the letters are set in italics.

The camping family flew through the woods when they heard the *gr-r-r-r-r* of a bear.

Unspoken Thoughts

Seen most often in fiction, thoughts are often set in italics—not quotation marks—to indicate that the words were not spoken aloud.

I wonder, she thought, *will he fully understand the significance of the situation*?

After So-Called

Quotation marks are not used around words that follow *so-called.*

The so-called rings of Saturn are in fact a sea of orbiting particles that run in waves.

Irony

Sometimes writers prefer to enclose in quotation marks words that are used in an ironic sense. This convention must be used sparingly; excessive use of quotation marks often creates the impression of a Victorian girl's diary.

The "business meeting" consisted of dinner and dancing.
The idea was so "intelligent" that we lost the client.

Neologisms

Newly coined words are usually set off in quotation marks or italics until they become an accepted part of the language—that is, until they appear in dictionaries. Usually, only the first use of the word in a manuscript needs to be set off in this way.

The "buckeyball" is a molecule of pure carbon that resembles a geodesic dome.

Slang

Slang should usually not be set in quotation marks. By setting a word or phrase in quotation marks, the writer seems to be apologizing to the reader for using the expression.

Because she is such a fuddy-duddy, she rarely receives social invitations.

Generally, the use of slang and clichés should be avoided.

Nicknames

Nicknames that fall between a first and last name should be placed in quotation marks.

Charles D. "Casey" Stengel
Thomas "Stonewall" Jackson

If the nickname is in general use, the quotation marks are unnecessary.

Doctor J.
Wilt the Stilt Chamberlain
Kissin' Jim Folsom

TITLES

Books

Titles of books and other separately published literary works are usually set in italics.

The Scarlet Letter
Bless the Beasts and Children
Paradise Lost
Beowulf

Newspapers and Other Periodicals

Except in journalistic style, the names of newspapers and other periodicals are usually set in italics. For U.S. newspapers the city name is generally considered to be part of the name whether it is part of the official title or not and is italicized except where absolute accuracy is required; in such cases—perhaps in bibliographies—the official name as used in the newspaper's nameplate should be used. If the city is not well known or could be confused with another city, the state abbreviation is added.

Springfield (Ill.) *State Journal Register*
Greensboro (N.C.) *News & Record*

For newspapers, the article *the* is usually not considered to be part of the name and hence is not italicized. When it appears, *the* is lowercased unless it begins the sentence.

Did you see the story about the dog-biting man in the *Pittsburgh Press* today?

The *Atlanta Constitution* printed the president's State of the Union address in its entirety yesterday.

Some international newspapers retain the definite article as part of the name, however.

When we lived in England, I worked for *The Times* of London.
Der Tagesspiegel is one of 15 newspapers published in Berlin.

The article *the* is not used with the name of the publication in notes or bibliographies.

In their own text, most newspapers do not use italics with names of periodicals. Some prefer to capitalize the article *the* in their own name, and most newspapers drop the city name when referring to themselves.

The candidate's retraction was printed in The Washington Post yesterday.
As reported in The Post yesterday. . . .

If the official name of a periodical includes the word *magazine*, *magazine* is capitalized and italicized with the rest of the title. However, sometimes clarity demands that the word *magazine* follow the name of the publication even if it is not part of the formal name. In this case, the word *magazine* is neither capitalized nor italicized.

Alfred Hitchcock Mystery Magazine
Weight Watchers Magazine
Washingtonian magazine
Time magazine
Popular Photography magazine

Most magazines do not use *the* as a formal part of their names, and therefore the word is both lowercase and roman.

the *Washington Post Magazine*
the *Journal of the American Medical Association*

However, a few magazines use *The* as part of their title.

The New Yorker
The Nation

For consistency of treatment among names of publications and because it is not always easy to verify a periodical's official title, it is generally acceptable to lowercase and set the *the* in roman for all periodical names.

Her new novel received a favorable review in the *Atlantic Monthly* last month.

When a possessive precedes a book title that begins with an article, the article is omitted.

In John Steinbeck's *Grapes of Wrath,* the perseverance of the turtle has great significance.

In her *Finishing School,* Gail Godwin introduces Ursula, a free-spirited woman of the world.

Parts of Published Works

Quotation marks are used to set off titles of magazine, journal, and newspaper articles; columns; short stories; poems; essays; and other parts of a larger published work.

"The Black Cat" by Edgar Allan Poe
"Self-Reliance" by Ralph Waldo Emerson
"Birches" by Robert Frost
"Talk of the Town"

Unpublished Works

Titles of unpublished works, such as papers, reports, and dissertations, may be enclosed in quotation marks, although often there is no special treatment other than capitalization.

Research Report 109, The Effects of Bandwidth Compression on Image Interpreter Performance

Movies and Plays

Titles of movies and plays are set in italics.

Casablanca
Dances with Wolves
Hamlet
A Chorus Line

Radio and Television Shows

Titles of radio and television shows are set in quotation marks.

"All in the Family"
"60 Minutes"
"All Things Considered"
"Masterpiece Theatre"

Some styles italicize the names of long-running series and place quotation marks around the titles of individual programs or episodes in the series—for example, "Upstairs, Downstairs" on *Masterpiece Theatre.*

Musical Compositions

Long Compositions. When a numeral or musical key is in the title, sonatas, symphonies, and concertos are set in roman. If, however, the piece includes a descriptive phrase, the phrase is placed in quotation marks.

Serenade No. 12 in C Minor
Beethoven's Fifth Symphony
Brahms' Piano Concerto No. 2
Mozart's "Jupiter" Symphony

Ballets, oratorios, operettas, operas, and musicals are set in italics.

Swan Lake
La Bohème
The Barber of Seville
Carmen
The Pirates of Penzance
Messiah (not *The*)
Porgy and Bess

Songs. Song titles are placed in quotation marks. Note that prepositions are capitalized when they are the last word in a title.

"As Time Goes By"
"Send in the Clowns"

Works of Art

Titles of paintings, sculptures, and other works of art are usually set in italics.

Rodin's *The Kiss*
Rembrandt's *The Night Watch*
Peter Paul Rubens' *Boar Hunt*
Raphael's *The School of Athens*

Ships, Aircraft, Spacecraft, and Other Vessels

The names of ships, aircraft, spacecraft, and other vessels are set in italics. The type of aircraft or vessel and the abbreviations SS, USS, and HMS that precede a name are set in roman.

the space shuttle *Challenger*
HMS *Hornet*
USS *Wisconsin*
the liner *America*
F-15 *Eagle*

The names of trains and general types or classes of ships and aircraft are set in roman.

Metroliner
Amtrak's AutoTrain
Stealth bomber
DC-10
Concorde

CREDIT LINES

Credit lines that follow the text of an article are often set in italics to set them apart.

(*written by Dorothy Pinkham, independent consultant*)

When a credit line contains a title that would normally be set in italics, the credit line itself is set in italics and the title is set in roman.

—adapted from Editing the Small Magazine *by Rowena Ferguson*

LEGAL CITATIONS

Traditionally, names of legal cases have been printed in italics, but roman is also widely accepted. The *v.* (versus) is usually set in the contrasting typeface, although increasingly publications are setting it in the same face as the rest of the name. Consistency should be the guiding factor. If terms such as *et al.*, *ex rel.*, and *ex parte* are used, they are set in the same face as the rest of the title.

Missouri ex rel. v. *Gaines Canada, Registrar of the University of Missouri*
Sipuel v. Board of Regents of the University of Oklahoma
Roe v. Wade

RESOLUTIONS AND LEGISLATIVE ACTS

The word *resolved* in resolutions and legislative acts is italicized. The word *provided* in the body of resolutions and legislative acts is usually italicized.

> *Resolved:* That every company proposal be reviewed by each vice president. . . .

COMPUTER COMMANDS

Boldface is preferred over quotation marks, all caps, or italics for specifying computer commands in software instructions, for two reasons: It provides an obvious contrast from the text, and it avoids the confusion that often results from the use of all caps or quotation marks. The user should not have to guess about whether to include periods, commas, or other punctuation in a typed command.

> To produce a degree sign in WordPerfect, press **ctrl** and **v**, then type **6,36**.

SCIENTIFIC NAMES

The scientific names for animals and plants are in Latin because at one time Latin was the international language among scholars.

Taxonomic Names

Genus and Species. The genus or generic and species names of animals and plants, called *binomials*, are set in italics. If the name of a person who first proposed the species or subspecies is used, it appears in roman type.

> *Agave americana*
> *Asterias rubens*
> *Senecio robbinsii* Oakes

If a subspecies name is used, it follows the species name and is set in italics. If the designation *var.* (meaning variety) is used before the subspecies name, it is set in roman type. An exception to the general rule is Homo sapiens, which does not need to be italicized in general use.

Higher Divisions. Names of taxonomic divisions higher than genus, such as family, order, class, and phylum, are set in roman.

> Protozoa (phylum)
> Crustacea (class)

Common Names and Scientific Names Used in the Vernacular

The common names of plants and animals are set in roman type.

century plant
common seastar, starfish

Scientific names of bacteria and viruses that are used in general speech are also set in roman.

staphylococcus
streptococcus
salmonella

Medical Terms

Names of infectious organisms are set in italics, but the names of diseases or conditions that are derived from the original names are set in roman.

Pneumocystis carinii
serous otitis media (fluid in the ear)
Mycoplasma
salmonellosis

INDEXES

In indexes, italics are often used to indicate references to figures and illustrations, to words used as words, and to cross-references. Boldface is often used to set off main headings or to indicate pages of primary coverage of a topic. See Chapter 28, Indexing, for explanations and examples.

BIBLIOGRAPHIES

Bibliographic styles vary widely in their use of italics; writers and editors should observe internal consistency or follow an established reference style; see Chapter 20, Reference Citations.

TYPOGRAPHIC CONCERNS

Plural and Possessive Endings with Italics

The *s* or *es* plural ending and the *'s* possessive ending are not italicized in italicized names, titles, foreign words, words used as words, or letters used as words.

> I'm mailing several *Posts* to my daughter in Texas.
> The *Atlantic Monthly*'s "Word Histories" column is a favorite among editors.
> Be sure to dot your *i*'s and cross your *t*'s.
> The editor felt the writer used too many *however*s.

Quotation Marks with Italics

Quotation marks should not be used with words, phrases, or titles that are italicized or underscored. One form of special treatment is considered sufficient.

Punctuation That Follows Italics

Commas, colons, semicolons, and periods that follow a word set in italic or boldface type should be set in italic or boldface as well.

> **Note:** Read these instructions carefully.
> *The Elements of Typographic Style,* although difficult to find in bookstores, is a worthwhile addition to an editor's library.

The treatment of question marks and exclamation points depends on the context of the sentence. For example, if the question mark or exclamation point is part of the title, it should be italicized; if it is not part of the title, it should appear in roman.

> Do you have a copy of *Words Into Type*?
> Susan Sheehan won the 1983 Pulitzer Prize in general nonfiction for her book *Is There No Place on Earth for Me?*

If all of the text enclosed in brackets or parentheses is set in italics, the brackets or parentheses should appear in italics; if any or all of the words within brackets or parentheses are in roman, the brackets or parentheses should be in roman. This same rule applies to boldface.

> *(continued on page 49)*
> (for example, *The Remains of the Day*)

12

QUOTATIONS

QUOTATIONS

When used effectively—which usually means sparingly—quotations from outside sources give writers a way to call in an authority, illustrate a claim, lighten a discussion, or introduce another point of view. Quotations can also inject variety into long stretches of narrative.

Although selecting quotations never seems to be a problem, writers and editors often are stymied by style and format questions. Can capitalization ever be changed? How many ellipsis points are used at the end of a partially quoted paragraph? Can quotations be edited for grammar and style? What needs to be cited, and how? Fortunately, most authorities agree on certain conventions for copyediting and formatting quotations, and this chapter summarizes generally accepted guidelines. Other chapters address related matters. See Chapter 10, Punctuation; Chapter 20, Reference Citations; and Chapter 23, Copyright.

CAN QUOTATIONS BE EDITED?

Strictly speaking, a direct quotation is just that: actual spoken or written words. By setting off these words with quotation marks or as a separate block of text (format is discussed below), the writer is telling the reader that these are the exact words used by the cited source. The editor's freedom to make changes depends on whether the quotation is "live"—that is, taken directly from the spoken source—or is from a previously published source.

Editing "Live" Quotations

In quoting from actual speech, minor changes are both permissible and advisable. For example, when writers want to use quotations that happen to be ungrammatical, they are usually safe in correcting the speaker in print to save that person from embarrassment; in fact, it would be unkind and perhaps condescending not to do so. But in other cases, grammatical errors may be left alone if the writer's intent is to demonstrate a point, say, about the person's educational level or to demonstrate the person's speaking style.

Nevertheless, writers and editors must take care not to change the speaker's overall meaning when editing for grammatical correctness or when deleting phrases or sentences to shorten the quote. If the quotation cannot be easily and safely edited, the writer should consider paraphrasing.

Most publications allow editors to remove vulgar language; *The Washington Post Deskbook on Style* says, "Irrelevant profanities may be deleted." *The New York Times Manual of Style and Usage* also states that profanities should not appear in the newspaper, but exceptions are made for milder forms or in cases "when the printing of the objectionable word or words will give the reader an obviously essential insight into matters of great moment—an insight that cannot otherwise be conveyed." As an example of this exception, the *Times* mentioned its publication of the expletive-ridden Watergate transcripts in 1974.

Editing Previously Published Material

Changes in Grammar, Spelling, and Punctuation. When quoting from published sources, spelling, punctuation, and typographical errors may be corrected. Although many editors prefer to keep the error and insert the word *sic* (Latin for "so" or "this is the way it was") in brackets after the offending word, this treatment is usually reserved for instances when there is a good reason to preserve the error, such as to retain historical or technical accuracy. Otherwise, it is considered pedantic and even snide.

Changes in Capitalization. When a quotation is introduced by a phrase that ends with a colon, the first word is capitalized, whether or not the word was capitalized by the original source. To illustrate, consider the following advice to writers by English essayist Sydney Smith (1771–1845): "In composing, as a general rule, run your pen through every other word you have written; you have no idea what vigor it will give your style." Here are two ways a writer might incorporate that quotation:

> Sydney Smith once offered the following advice: "Run your pen through every other word you have written; you have no idea what vigor it will give your style."
>
> One way to improve your writing is to "run your pen through every other word you have written," as Sydney Smith once said.

THE SUPREME COURT RULES ON ALTERING QUOTATIONS

Can a person who was misquoted in a magazine article bring a libel suit against the writer?

Yes, ruled the U.S. Supreme Court in 1991, but only if the misquotation was deliberate and materially changed the meaning of the statement. Altering a quotation beyond correcting it for grammar and syntax does not by itself prove that the writer deliberately falsified the quotation for malicious reasons; actual malice is necessary to prove libel under the First Amendment.

In this case, *Masson* v. *The New Yorker Magazine Inc.*, Jeffrey Masson, a psychoanalyst, was the subject of a 1984 *New Yorker* profile by writer Janet Malcolm. Masson claimed that Malcolm had libeled him by attributing to him invented quotations that damaged his reputation. The Court ruled that Masson was entitled to a jury trial at which five of the quotations could be used to consider whether Malcolm published the quotations "with knowledge or reckless disregard of the alterations."

Journalists generally found the ruling sympathetic to their cause because the Supreme Court recognized that writers almost always have to "edit and make intelligible a speaker's perhaps rambling comments." The ruling protected their ability to edit quotations for grammar, syntax, and obvious errors as well as clarity, as long as the speaker's intended meaning is preserved.

Most publications have clear policies on the use of quotations that often are even stricter than the Court's ruling. In an interview with *Folio's Publishing News* (August 15, 1991), Harry Johnston, *Time* magazine's vice president and general counsel, explained *Time*'s policy:

> It is one of our rules that there can be no alteration of a quotation if it would change its meaning. It's part of a booklet of policies we have. . . . The policy states, "Quotes must be accurate. If edited or cut, there must be no alteration of the meaning or the context. If a quote is paraphrased, it must not be in quotation marks. Grammar and spelling may be corrected, but it is unacceptable to add or delete a word or phrase that alters the meaning."

To be safe, writers and editors should use direct quotations only if they can be backed up with tapes or notes from interviews. Double-checking a possibly controversial direct quotation with the speaker before publishing it is another way to ensure accuracy. Paraphrasing should be used if there is any doubt about actual wording.

In cases where absolute accuracy is called for (for example, in legal or scholarly works), the changed capitalization is noted by use of brackets:

> "[R]un your pen through every other word you have written," Sydney Smith once advised writers.

Changes in Editorial Style. Editors are divided on the question of changing a quotation to reflect the editorial style of the publication it is quoted in. Some editors believe that such changes should not be made except to correct obvious errors or to improve clarity. To them, the fact that the quotation is being portrayed as direct eliminates the need to be concerned with issues of editorial style. Others, however, would feel free to change "1990's" in a quotation to be consistent with the house style of "1990s." These editors believe that making style changes does not threaten the integrity of the quotation and ensures that the text has a consistent appearance. As with many other aspects of editing, the approach taken should consider the needs of the reader and the nature of the material being quoted.

FORMATTING QUOTATIONS

The length of the quotation and sometimes its nature—for example, poetry—are factors to consider when formatting. This section explains treatment of both run-in and block quotations and briefly explains how to format poetry. A full discussion of quotation marks in general appears in Chapter 10, Punctuation.

Run-in Versus Block

A general rule of thumb is to run quotations of a sentence or two into the text and to "block," or set apart from the running text, longer quotations; a long quotation is variously defined as anywhere from 40 to 100 words and more.

Run-in quotations are set off with quotation marks; block quotations, also called *excerpts* or *extracts*, drop the quotation marks and receive distinctive typographical treatment so that the reader sees immediately that the material is a direct quotation. Usually, block quotations are indented from the left margin (they may or may not be indented from the right margin), with paragraph indentions or the lack thereof matching the format of the running text. Often a slightly smaller typeface and decreased leading (spacing between lines) are also used.

All rules discussed in this chapter regarding capitalization and punctuation, including use of brackets and points of ellipsis, apply to both run-in and block quotations, with one exception. In run-in quotations, further quota-

GOING FROM WORD PROCESSING TO TYPESETTING: GETTING "OPENING" AND "CLOSING" QUOTATION MARKS

In most word processing programs, writers and editors use the apostrophe key to show single quotation marks and the quotation mark key to show double quotation marks. In the case of double quotation marks, the symbol is the same for both opening and closing marks, but typeset quotation marks, both single and double, curve to the left to show opening quotes and to the right to show closing quotes; the popular term for these marks is "smart quotes." At the time of this writing, most programs that convert word processed files to typeset ones can't make this distinction, and so proofreaders often see quotation marks that are turned the wrong way.

Most production departments are aware of this problem and make the required corrections, usually in some automated way. Codes that distinguish opening from closing quotation marks can also be placed in the original word processing file—for example, in WordPerfect pressing **ctrl** and **v** at the same time and then entering **4,32** creates opening quotation marks; **ctrl** and **v** and **4,31** creates closing quotation marks.

tions within the quotation are set off with single quotation marks; in block quotations, internal quotations are set off with double quotation marks.

Poetry

If lines of poetry are run in with the text, original line breaks are shown by using slashes, or virgules, followed by a space. For example,

> Dylan Thomas wrote, "In the sun that is young once only, / Time let me play and be/ Golden in the mercy of his means."

Most poetry, even just a few lines, looks best if it is displayed, however. No quotation marks are necessary, and line beginnings and endings should follow the original. If line endings are too long to fit the column, indented runover lines may be used. When more than one stanza is shown, extra space should be left to show stanza breaks. If the poem has lines that begin with quotation marks, they should be aligned with the first letters of the other lines. If lines are omitted, a line of spaced points the length of the omitted line (or the length of the longest line in the case of a multiple-line deletion) is used to show the deletion.

Eugene Field's well-known children's poem begins and ends with these stanzas:

> Wynken, Blynken, and Nod one night
>   Sailed off in a wooden shoe—
> Sailed on a river of misty light
>   Into a sea of dew.
> "Where are you going, and what do you wish?"
>   The old moon asked the three.
> "We have come to fish for the herring-fish
>   That live in this beautiful sea;
>   Nets of silver and gold have we,"
>   Said Wynken,
>   Blynken,
>   And Nod.
>
> . . . .
>
> So shut your eyes while mother sings
>   Of the wonderful sights that be,
> And you shall see the beautiful things
>   As you rock in the misty sea
>   Where the old shoe rocked the fishermen three—
>   Wynken,
>   Blynken,
>   And Nod.

ELLIPSIS POINTS

Points of ellipsis show the reader that words or paragraphs have been deleted from the work being quoted. The number of points to use—three or four—and whether to use points at all are common questions. Here are some general guidelines; for ease of illustration, the source for all the following quotations is the sixth volume of Dumas Malone's biography of Thomas Jefferson, *The Sage of Monticello.*

When deleting words from a sentence, whether at the beginning, in the middle, or at the end, insert three points of ellipsis, or dots. The period at the end of a sentence is retained, as the second example shows.

> The sale of his library to Congress enabled Jefferson to reduce his . . . debt by half.
>
> Craven Peyton, who had acted for him in this business, offered him an emergency loan, ...

In the latter example, retaining the comma after *loan* is optional.

To show deletion of entire sentences within a quotation, retain the end punctuation of the preceding sentence, usually the period, and add the three dots:

> Early in the year Jefferson's financial difficulties had been compounded by the unfavorable outcome of an arbitration. . . . The sale of fields belonging to heirs who were under age at the time had been ruled invalid, and Jefferson was ordered to make immediate payment of close to $800 for rent.

To show the deletion of paragraphs, retain the end punctuation of the sentence in the paragraph before the deleted paragraph and add the three dots.

> Shortage of cash was no new experience for Jefferson, but we may doubt if this landholder had ever been more painfully conscious of it than now. . . .
>
> When Jefferson set out for Poplar Forest in July, he seems to have had no personal forebodings. He actually forgot to renew one of his notes, and Gibson had to substitute one of his own for it.

Even though the paragraph above continued for several more sentences, it is permissible to end the quotation with a period alone, so long as the last sentence is a complete sentence. This practice holds true for both run-in and block quotations. Note also that dots are not necessary at the beginning of the second paragraph. If the beginning words or sentences are deleted from a paragraph, however, dots are used to show that the paragraph really did not start that way; for example, ". . . He actually forgot to renew one of his notes, and Gibson had to substitute one of his own for it."

In run-in quotations, ellipsis points are unnecessary before or after complete sentences:

> Speaking of the "parasite institutions" of banks to the former Secretary of the Treasury, he said: "The flood with which they are deluging us of nominal money has placed us completely without any certain measure of value, and by interpolating a false measure, is deceiving and ruining multitudes of our citizens."

Ellipsis points are also unnecessary in block quotations that begin with complete sentences, and in block quotations that are introduced by a sentence that is completed by the quotation:

> Malone explains that Jefferson
>
> > had been a close observer of financial affairs at home and abroad. Furthermore, he was familiar with the literature of the young science of political economy. He paid his respects to Adam Smith and Jean Baptiste Say in the introduction he wrote to Destutt de Tracy's treatise.

ADDING INFORMATION AND EMPHASIS TO QUOTATIONS

At times the writer or editor may want to add a comment or a note of explanation within a quotation. The standard method for handling such comments is to place them in brackets. Brackets are also used to enclose the word *sic* and to show original or correct spelling, capitalization, or punctuation.

> Being unable to resume his daily ride until nearly the end of the year [because of ill health], Jefferson had more time than usual to reflect on his precarious financial situation and the economic state of the country.

At other times a writer may want to emphasize a word or phrase in a quotation. Italics are generally used for this purpose, followed by an acknowledgment of the change in brackets at the end of the quotation.

> The eyes of the citizens were not yet open to the true cause of their troubles—*the banking system* [emphasis added].

Other phrases include "italics added" and "italics mine." Another way to call attention to this change is in a reference note or an explanation in the preceding text.

PULL-QUOTES: QUOTATIONS IN PAGE DESIGN

Long a favorite device of magazine designers, pull-quotes are words repeated from the text of an article, set in larger type, and usually set off by graphic rules or bars. They are an easy and effective way to break up columns of gray text and entice the reader into the article.

The general rule about block quotations applies to pull-quotes as well—there is no need to use quotation marks. Here are a few other guidelines for using pull-quotes:

- Although the quotations are meant to be word for word, some paraphrasing is allowable; after all, these are graphic elements, not the actual text.
- Pull-quotes are placed where they are needed to serve the design purpose; it is not necessary to place them next to or on the same page as the text from which they were drawn.
- The quotations used should capture the flavor or gist of the article; sometimes they also summarize its major themes.

CITING SOURCES

Writers must be careful to cite all direct quotations; for long quotations, permission may be needed from the copyright holder (see Chapter 23, Copyright). The extent and method of citation used also depend on the reference citation requirements of the manuscript in general. Chapter 20, Reference Citations, offers three general approaches to source citation, the most informal of which weaves the reference directly into the text. The following example is from the *Atlantic Monthly,* January 1992:

> To halt the spasm of extinction, [Edward O.] Wilson and Paul Ehrlich wrote in a special biodiversity issue of *Science* last August,
>
> > the first step . . . would be to cease "developing" any more relatively undisturbed land.

In some cases, as when quoting lines from literature and poetry, only the name of the author and perhaps the name of the work, if appropriate, are necessary; the sentence examples used in earlier chapters of this book follow this method. Formats may vary, from enclosing the reference in parentheses after the quotation to setting the information on a separate line preceded by a dash.

In more formal works, the source information can appear in one of several ways: as a complete citation in the text (as in the first example below); as a numbered footnote or endnote, with the citation located at the bottom of the page or at the end of the chapter or book; or as a parenthetical citation of author and date—or a shortened form of the title—with the complete citation in a bibliography or reference list. Here are examples showing proper placement of reference information for in-text and block quotations.

> In every book she wrote, M.F.K. Fisher described food fondly and often. "Aunt Gwen's onions were as delicate and light and apparently as digestible as gossamer might prove to be. They seemed to float onto our fingers and down our throats" (*Among Friends* [San Francisco: North Point Press, 1983]).
>
> She often reminisced about her childhood memories of food:
>
> > In the good Laguna days, though, it was an exciting promise, to warm up the pan, ready the ingredients, and make fried-egg sandwiches. Aunt Gwen insisted that we have at least two pockets somewhere on us, one for shells, stones, small fish, or lizards, and one big enough to hold these greasily wrapped, limp, steamy monsters. (Ibid., 91)

Note that the reference falls inside the period in the in-text quotation but outside the period in the block quotation. If an in-text quotation ends with a question mark or exclamation point, the reference is placed at the end of the quotation and is followed by a period.

> In *Solitude: A Return to the Self,* Anthony Storr notes that most of the writers he describes in chapter 8 had unhappy childhoods, and he raises these questions: "Did their early experience prevent them from making the kind of relationships with others which bring happiness? If so, did the exercise of their imaginative gifts bring them happiness of another kind?" (page 120).

If endnotes or footnotes are used, the numbers are placed after the end quotation marks: ". . . bring them happiness of another kind?"[1]

Also note that "ibid." (an abbreviation of the Latin *ibidem,* meaning "in the same place") is used to indicate that the quotation is from the same source; it is not italicized. In the past, "ibid." and the terms "op. cit." and "loc. cit." had distinct meanings, but the latter two terms are considered old-fashioned by most authorities and are rarely used today; "ibid." or a shortened form of the work's title is preferred (see Chapter 20, Reference Citations). Ibid., in effect, repeats all the information in the immediately preceding reference; any additional information, such as a different page number, follows after a comma (e.g., ibid., 283).

When quoting passages from long poems, plays, or the Bible, it is often easiest to note the name of the work in the text and then simply cite the relevant volume, page, act, scene, stanza, or line numbers in parentheses after each passage. A note to the reader explaining this approach is needed if the numbers' meanings aren't obvious.

> Many English sayings heard today originated with William Shakespeare; consider the following lines from *Hamlet,* written in 1600 and 1601 (the numbers in parentheses refer to act, scene, and line number):
>
> > Brevity is the soul of wit. (II, ii, 90)
> > Get thee to a nunnery. (III, i, 124)
> > The lady doth protest too much, methinks. (III, ii, 242)
> > I must be cruel only to be kind. (III, iv, 178)

QUOTATIONS IN FOREIGN LANGUAGES

Whether to include quotations written in a foreign language depends largely on the ability of most readers of the work to read and understand it. In most cases, the English translation should be used, and depending on its significance, the original version may be included, perhaps in a note or an appendix. The source of the English translation, as well as the source of the original version, should be noted. Punctuation and format, including the use of quotation marks and ellipsis points, should follow American practice as described in this chapter. (See Chapter 21, Foreign Languages, for punctuation conventions in several languages.)

13

LISTS

LISTS

Lists can make the job of presenting information easier. They break down and organize material that is difficult to explain in text, make information clearer, and provide visual relief from lines of dense text. For writers and editors, the problem is styling them consistently. This chapter offers possibilities—there are few rules—to consider when faced with trying to make lists consistent.

Lists fall into two main types—run in and displayed. Punctuation and capitalization of both depend on whether the list is introduced by a complete sentence. Several types of lists can be used in a publication, as long as each type is treated consistently throughout.

RUN-IN LISTS

Run-in lists, sometimes called paragraph lists, are series of short items run into the text. When the items are numbered or lettered, the numbers or letters are usually enclosed within parentheses.

> Three pieces of identification are necessary: (1) a valid passport, (2) a valid driver's license, and (3) a notarized copy of the birth certificate.

The main reason for using a run-in list is to emphasize the number of items or show the order of importance or occurrence. Sometimes a run-in list is the easiest way to clarify a complex sentence, even when the list contains only two items.

> The major impediments to successful marrow transplant are (1) the presence of donor T cells that can cause GVHD in allogeneic specimens and (2) the possible reinfusion of tumor cells in autologous marrow transplants.

Note that in final copy any parenthetical numbers or letters should appear on the same line as the word that follows.

If there is no need to emphasize the number or order of items or to clarify the sentence, numbers or letters are unnecessary.

Many editors believe it is grammatically incorrect to use a colon at the end of a phrase that introduces a list, although the practice is becoming more widespread. To determine whether the colon is correct, mentally replace it with a period and see whether the preceding words make a complete sentence. The rationale behind this advice is that periods and colons are both types of end punctuation and therefore are interchangeable.

> *Incorrect:* These demands can be categorized as: timber removals, land-clearing removals, or set-asides.
>
> *Correct:* These demands can be categorized as timber removals, land-clearing removals, or set-asides.

Short list items are separated by commas. Semicolons are used when a series is lengthy or has internal commas. The introductory sentence in the next example ends with a colon because it is a complete sentence. Note that the first word of each item is not capitalized.

> The membership of the committee follows: (1) private sector executives, nine; (2) holders of public office, eight; and (3) individual citizens, six.

Run-in lists work well until they become so long that readers find it difficult to remember the introductory phrase or sentence. When a list runs longer than about eight lines of manuscript type, the writer should consider displaying it.

DISPLAYED LISTS

Displayed lists, sometimes called vertical lists, should have at least three items, each of which is set on a separate line. Displayed lists may be set off by numbers, letters, bullets, or other typographical symbols.

There is no firm rule about the maximum number of items in displayed lists, but editors should keep in mind that readers can get lost in a long list. Among the possible cures are condensing the wording or integrating the material with the preceding or following text.

Bulleted Lists

Bullets, dashes, or similar typographical symbols are used when the items in the list are of equal importance and do not have to be referred to individually later in the text. For visual balance each bulleted item should be no more than about one-third of a page long; bulleted lists are usually set with hanging indention (see "Formatting" below), creating what seems to be an excessively large left margin if left unbroken by other bullets or by normal text.

Numbered or Lettered Lists

Numbers are used when the introductory text emphasizes the number of items or when the items are listed in order of importance or occurrence; numbers or letters also should be used when any of the items must be referred to later in the text.

Numbered and lettered lists look best when the numbers or letters are followed by periods. In lists with 10 or more numbers, the periods should be aligned.

> The 10 main functions of the Department of State's Overseas Citizens Service follow:
>
> 1. Assistance concerning arrests
> 2. Financial and medical assistance
> 3. Assistance with deaths overseas
> 4. Welfare and whereabouts information
> 5. Search and rescue
>
> . . . .
>
> 10. Travel advisories

Punctuation and Capitalization

Punctuation and capitalization in displayed lists may vary, depending on the writer's preference. For writers working on the same publication, however, it is usual to set guidelines.

Complete Introductory Sentence. When a displayed list is introduced by a complete sentence, that sentence may end with a period or a colon. When the introductory sentence contains such anticipatory words or phrases as *these, as follows,* and *the following,* a colon may be more appropriate.

When the list items that follow a complete introductory sentence are not complete sentences, the items may begin with either uppercase or lowercase letters and end with either periods or no punctuation. Whatever style is chosen, it should be followed throughout the publication for the same type of list.

> Once the series editor and the author have made all substantive changes, the manuscript goes through five steps:

1. Fast pass for copyediting and formatting
2. Slow pass for copyediting
3. Author's final check on manuscript or proofs
4. Final editorial and production proofreading
5. Copyeditor's checking of corrected proofs

When the list items that follow a complete introductory sentence are complete sentences, each item should begin with an uppercase letter and end with a period. The following list provides both an example and guidelines.

When the list items are complete sentences, the following method can be used:

- The introductory sentence ends with a colon or a period, whichever is appropriate.
- Each list item begins with a capital letter.
- Each list item ends with a period.

Incomplete Introductory Sentence. When a displayed list is introduced by an incomplete sentence, the sentence fragment should not end with a colon because the colon interrupts the grammatical continuity of the sentence, as explained earlier in this chapter. In fact, when combined with the introductory phrase, each list item must form a grammatically correct sentence. Watch for problems in subject-verb agreement and tense. Here's one way this type of list can be set up.

When each item of the list completes the introductory sentence,

- the introductory sentence may end with a comma, semicolon, dash, or no punctuation at all, whichever is appropriate;
- the list items can begin with lowercase letters;
- all but the last item end with a comma or semicolon;
- the second-to-last item ends with *and;* and
- the last item ends with a period.

If none of the items in the list has an internal comma, each item ends with a comma instead of a semicolon. Although no punctuation is necessary after the introductory phrase in the example below, a dash is acceptable for those who feel that the introduction looks incomplete without some punctuation. The list below shows another widely accepted approach to this type of list, in which the first word of each item is capped and end punctuation is dropped entirely.

If you want to work successfully with freelancers, you should—

- Set the stage for success in your first meeting with potential freelancers
- Treat them fairly and give them adequate support
- Recognize and try to address the limitations of freelance work

Formatting

When text is set flush left, numbers and letters may be set either flush left or indented paragraph style.

1. The numeral on this line is set flush left.

    a. The letter on this line is set paragraph style.

Bulleted list items look best when set with hanging indention, which may appear as shown or with further indention of runover lines.

    • The bullet on this line is set indented paragraph style, and the list item that accompanies it is set with hanging indention.

• The bullet on this line is set flush left, and the list item that accompanies it is set with hanging indention.

Hanging indention is preferred for numbered list items, but paragraph style is acceptable when (1) every item or almost every item is about one-third of a manuscript page long or longer or (2) the page is to be typeset in two or more columns.

Three definitions apply to this section:

1. *Radiation* includes alpha rays, beta rays, gamma rays, X rays, neutrons, high-speed electrons, high-speed protons, and other atomic particles. But this term does not include sound or radio waves, visible light, or infrared or ultraviolet light.

2. *Radioactive material* means any material that emits corpuscular or electromagnetic emanations.

3. *Unrestricted area* means any area to which access is not controlled by the employer to protect individuals from exposure to radiation or radioactive materials.

EDITING LISTS

Lists, both run in and displayed, must be grammatically parallel. An example of a *nonparallel* list follows:

Several ideas are offered that might help avoid a disaster:

- The rules should be changed so that players are not so vulnerable.
- Ejection of a player for spearing or blindsiding.
- Write a letter warning of these practices to the pertinent officials.

In this example, the three list items are structured in three different ways: the first is a complete sentence in the third-person passive, the second is a noun phrase, and the third is a verb phrase or imperative sentence. Any one of these three types of structure could be imposed on the entire list. The choice depends on the context and on the emphasis desired.

The third-person passive emphasizes what should be done and does not specify who should take action.

- The rules should be changed so that players are not so vulnerable.
- Players should be ejected for spearing or blindsiding.
- Letters warning of these practices should be written to the pertinent officials.

Noun phrases emphasize the recommended measures.

- Changes in the rules so that players are not so vulnerable.
- Ejection of a player for spearing or blindsiding.
- Letters to the pertinent officials warning of these practices.

Verb phrases emphasize what someone should do.

- Change the rules so that players are not so vulnerable.
- Eject players for spearing or blindsiding.
- Write letters warning of these practices to the pertinent officials.

Editing lists for format, parallelism, and editorial consistency often requires considerable time and effort, but the payoff is a better-looking, more readable manuscript.

14

ABBREVIATIONS

Lists of Abbreviations

ABBREVIATIONS

Abbreviations are found to some degree in every kind of writing. In standard prose and works of fiction, especially in dialogue, only the most customary abbreviations are used, for words that are rarely seen spelled out—*Mr.*, *Mrs.*, *Dr.*, *Ph.D.*, *a.m.*, *p.m.*, *RSVP*, and the like. When practical concerns take precedence—getting the most information on the page or speeding the reader through dense copy—then abbreviations are used more freely, especially in reference works, bibliographies, tables, and business, military, and technical writing.

Abbreviations appeared in the earliest manuscripts and books, devised by early scribes and typesetters to save needless repetition as well as time and space, a real concern in the days when printing materials were much costlier than they are today. Abbreviations have long been a part of American English, beginning with such abbreviations as *O.K.* and *P.D.Q.* in the early 1800s and continuing today with the proliferation of *initialisms* (abbreviations pronounced letter by letter, e.g., AFL/CIO) and *acronyms* (abbreviations that can be pronounced as a word, e.g., NATO). In fact, some groups have been known to devise a catchy or appropriate acronym and then make the spelled-out version fit—for example, MADD, for Mothers Against Drunk Driving. Another recent development is the creation of a new word as the result of a term's brief stopover as an acronym—*young urban professional* to *Y.U.P.* to *yuppie*.

In terms of style, the trend is toward fewer periods and decreased capitalization, although many traditional abbreviations will probably continue to resist change, especially those relating to titles (*Mr.*, *Dr.*) and those derived from Latin (*i.e.*, *etc.*, *a.m.*, *A.D.*). The lists at the end of this chapter provide a brief sampling; any current dictionary can also provide guidance for common abbreviations. The most comprehensive reference work for meanings of abbreviations is the *Acronyms, Initialisms, and Abbreviations*

Dictionary, published by Gale Research; it is not recommended as a style guide, however. This three-volume set contains some 480,000 definitions covering a wide range of fields; it is updated annually and can be found in most libraries.

Editors should keep in mind that an abbreviation may be acceptable in one form of writing but inappropriate in another. *Versus,* for example, is usually abbreviated as a single letter in citations of legal cases (*Starr* v. *Gorman*) or as two letters in a newspaper headline (Cowboys vs. Redskins) and is usually spelled out in normal prose (spending versus saving). In scientific and technical writing, editors should also be aware that each discipline has its own conventions, and a reader may encounter *weight percent* as *wgt. pct., wt. pct., wt pct, wt. %, wt %,* or *wt%,* depending on the style used.

In general, an abbreviation for an organization, concept, or the like should be used only if it appears often in the text; otherwise, the written-out form should be used. Most abbreviations should be defined at first use; the formal style is to write the full term, with the abbreviation following after a comma or in parentheses.

> Qualified persons can open an individual retirement account, or IRA, through most financial institutions.
>
> The sponsor was the Advisory Committee on Marine Resources Research (ACMRR).

In cases where the abbreviation is the more familiar term, the spelled-out form may, if necessary, follow in parentheses.

> The community center is offering lessons in CPR (cardiopulmonary resuscitation).

Another approach is to begin with the spelled-out term and then introduce the abbreviation in the next sentence or two; in most cases, readers will make the connection, especially if the term is fairly short.

> In 1992, the first CD-ROM version of the *Oxford English Dictionary* was released. This new format allows readers to use the *OED* in ways never before possible.

Some abbreviations, such as IBM and FBI, may be so familiar that they do not need to be defined. It is best to consider the publication's entire audience in determining whether the abbreviation is familiar.

It is not necessary to use printer's devices such as capitalization, italics, boldface, or underlining when defining an abbreviation to show how the abbreviation was derived.

> *Unnecessary:* IWEX (*I*nternal *W*ave *Ex*periment)

CAPITALIZATION

Abbreviations formed from the initial letters of a term are usually all capitals.

NATO (North Atlantic Treaty Organization)

Articles, conjunctions, and prepositions are usually not represented in the abbreviation.

HUD (Housing and Urban Development)
AFL (American Federation of Labor)

The spelled-out expression of an abbreviation is *not* capitalized unless it is a proper name.

SEM (scanning electron microscope)
HF (high frequency)
But: MIT (Massachusetts Institute of Technology)

A lowercase letter is sometimes used to distinguish what could be identical abbreviations.

FmHA (Farmers Home Administration)
FHA (Federal Housing Administration)

Many terms that were once abbreviations have now passed into conventional usage and are spelled all lowercase.

laser
radar
sonar
modem

Satellite and instrument names that are also pronounceable words are sometimes written with initial capital letters only.

Geosat
Landsat
Seasat

An authoritative source in the relevant field should be consulted to determine how to treat such abbreviations.

PUNCTUATION

Periods

Abbreviations with Periods. Most general abbreviations, with the exception of units of measurement in technical text, end in a period. Contrary to British practice, this rule holds in U.S. usage even if the last letter of the abbreviation is the last letter of the spelled-out word (*dept.*, not *dept*, for *department*).

Ariz.	chap.	Jan.	Jr.
Lt. Col.	op. cit.	app.	vol.
wt.	anon.	geog.	mgr.
univ.	pl.	misc.	au.

A single period is used if an abbreviation ends a sentence.

The conclusions are those of Wilson et al. (*not* et al..)

Abbreviations Without Periods. Initialisms—abbreviations pronounced letter by letter—usually appear without periods. Examples are IQ for intel-

---

WHAT DO MS. AND HARRY S TRUMAN HAVE IN COMMON?

The abbreviation *Ms.* and the *S* in President Truman's name don't stand for anything—they are abbreviations in appearance only. In Truman's case, the period is absent because the letter *S* alone was his middle name; traditionally, a period isn't used because its presence would indicate an abbreviation, but editors should note that Truman himself used a period "when he thought of it," according to Robert H. Ferrell, editor of *Off the Record: The Private Papers of Harry S. Truman*.

The case of *Ms.* is slightly different. *Ms.* was devised to provide an equivalent form of address to *Mr.*—an abbreviation of *monsieur* that makes no distinction as to marital status, as do the two traditional forms of address for women, *Miss* and *Mrs.* Technically, *Ms.* should not have a period because it is not an abbreviation, but the period is there nonetheless, for consistency and equivalency to *Mr.*

Interestingly, *Mrs.* was originally the abbreviation for *mistress*, back when *mistress* was used to refer to a married woman. Later, *mistress* came to be used as a form of address for unmarried women and was shortened to *Miss*.

---

ligence quotient, CPA for certified public accountant, COD for cash on delivery, and rpm for revolutions per minute.

Acronyms—abbreviations pronounced as words—also do not usually take periods. Examples are ZIP for Zone Improvement Plan, NASA for the National Aeronautics and Space Administration, COBOL for Common Business-Oriented Language, and CAD for computer-aided design.

Periods are not needed for shortened words that have come to be used as words by themselves, such as photo, exam, caps, and typo.

In scientific and technical text, units of measure tend to be used without periods. However, the abbreviations for inch and number (*in.* and *no.*) are set with periods to avoid confusion with the words *in* and *no*.

Slashes

Some abbreviations are punctuated with slashes in place of periods.

c/o
w/o
w/w
R/V

In scientific and technical contexts, the usual meaning for the slash is *per.*

l/min, lines per minute
L/s, liters per second
v/v, volume per volume

Hyphens

Isolated letters or numbers used in conjunction with an abbreviation are hyphenated; en dashes may also be used.

AE-A, Atmosphere Explorer A (satellite)
WCD-A, World Data Center A
ERS–1, Earth Resources Satellite 1

Abbreviations used as parts of modifiers are hyphenated.

Ph.D.-related study
AMA-devised test scores
Cl-forming reaction
U-shaped tube

A suffix or prefix is hyphenated where it joins an abbreviation.

NATO-like organization
O_2-rich blood
anti-HIV vaccine
non-NFL players
pre-CATV viewers
pro-ERA voters
DDT-free substance

A hyphen joins a numeral and a unit of measure used as a modifier.

20-km distance
6-in. board
60-km/s velocity (*but* 60 km s^{-1} velocity)
But: 35mm camera

In nontechnical text, the unit of measure should be spelled out when used as a modifier.

20-kilometer distance
7-foot jump

If the unit of measure is used in the plural sense, a hyphen is not used in the modifier.

38 cm ice/yr
1.5 ppm HCl (1.5 parts per million of hydrochloric acid)

A unit of measure with an exponent is not hyphenated as a modifier.

8 cm^{-1} region

AMPERSANDS

The ampersand is usually closed up with the rest of the abbreviation.

Texas A&M University
R&D (research and development)
P&I (principal and interest)
S&L (savings and loan)

ARTICLES WITH ABBREVIATIONS

If an abbreviation begins with a consonant sound, *a* is used. For a vowel sound, *an* is used.

an IQ test
a USDA-approved drug

an OPEC country
a TVA project
an NFL player

In some cases, either article is correct, depending on how the reader will pronounce the abbreviation.

an SAT score
a SAT score

It is not always necessary to use *the* before an abbreviated name of an organization; practice varies (the FBI, the IRS, the UN, NIH, NATO, UNICEF). The organization's preference should be followed.

ABBREVIATIONS AT THE BEGINNING OF A SENTENCE

Starting a sentence with an abbreviation is not recommended if the abbreviation is a partial word, a number, or a lowercase letter.

Figure 1 shows . . . (*not* Fig. 1 shows . . .)
The *t*-tests measured . . . (*not* *t*-tests *or* *T*-tests measured . . .)
The *u* in each case equals . . . (*not* *u* in each case . . .)
Carbon 14 was supplied . . . (*not* ^{14}C was supplied . . .)
December 10 is the deadline . . . (*not* Dec. 10 . . .)

Otherwise, starting a sentence with an abbreviation is acceptable.

VIP awards were announced.
Dr. Rawlings attended the ceremony.
FBI standards were discussed.

FORMATION OF PLURALS

Plural abbreviations are generally formed by adding an *s*.

UFOs	cols.
chaps.	IOUs
ISBNs	Drs.

If the abbreviation is composed of lowercase letters or a single letter or if it would otherwise be confusing if the *s* alone were added, an apostrophe is placed before the *s*.

sst's	*y*'s
A's	s.d.'s
pdf's	SOS's

Abbreviations with periods also take *'s.*

Ph.D.'s
M.A.'s

A unit of measure used in abbreviated form is the same in singular and plural.

1 in.; 6 in.
0.5 mi; 10 mi

Some abbreviations have irregular forms in the plural.

pp., pages	eqq., equations (also eqs.)
ff., following pages	vv., verses
Messrs., misters	nn., notes
Mses. *or* Mss., plural of Ms.	ss., sections
exx., examples	cc., copies

For guidance on forming plurals of numbers, see Chapter 17, Numbers.

FORMATION OF POSSESSIVES

A singular abbreviation requires an *'s* to form the possessive.

DAR's standards
FDA's policy

The possessive of a plural abbreviation requires an apostrophe after the *s.*

RNs' schedules
VIPs' thanks
WAVES' contributions
But: the Oakland A's winning streak

For an organization whose final initial is *S,* the possessive is formed by adding an apostrophe only, unless the organization itself adds an apostrophe *s.*

EDS' employees (apostrophe only)

LATIN WORDS AND TERMS

Latin terms that are commonly recognizable are abbreviated in text, set with periods, and not italicized.

e.g.	etc.
A.D.	ibid.

op. cit.	viz.
i.e.	et seq.
ca.	et al.
P.S.	id.

The abbreviation *etc.* should be used sparingly in text and is redundant when used in conjunction with *such as* or *for example.*

Incorrect: Flooding was caused by several factors (e.g., low grade, cutbanks, high water table, etc.).
Correct: Flooding was caused by several factors (e.g., low grade, cutbanks, and a high water table).

In text that is heavy with reference citations, *et al.* may be used in place of citing three or more authors (for example, Jones et al. instead of Jones, Mason, and Smith) after all names are given at first reference. The phrase *Jones and others* is preferred in some disciplines.

The terms *post, infra,* and *supra* are italicized when part of a legal citation but are not italicized in nonlegal text.

DIALOGUE

When considering the use of abbreviations in dialogue, writers and editors must decide how the speaker would actually pronounce the term. For acronyms and initialisms, the decision is fairly straightforward because these abbreviations are usually pronounced, either as a word or as letters:

Jane yelled, "I passed my CPA exam!"
"Sam is waiting for you at the TWA terminal," Cynthia said.

It is also standard practice to allow the use of certain traditional abbreviations in dialogue.

"Please call Dr. O'Hara to confirm your appointment," she reminded.
"We'll meet you in front of the UN building at 9 a.m.," Steve said.
"OK, I'll look for you and Ms. Jones there," Victoria agreed.

In most cases, however, abbreviations are not considered acceptable in dialogue; spelled-out forms more realistically represent actual speech.

"He's six-foot-one and weighs one hundred eighty-five pounds," she bragged.
"Dow Jones and Company's offices are on Lexington Avenue," he offered.

TITLES AND ACADEMIC DEGREES

Titles in Front of a Name

Some titles are always abbreviated when used with a proper name.

Mr.	Mrs.
Dr.	Jr.
Ms.	Sr.

Other than these, titles used with a surname only are spelled out.

General MacArthur
Professor Nelson

With full names, most titles are abbreviated.

Lt. Col. Neil Henderson
Sen. Edward Kennedy
Hon. Rebecca A. Holden
Rev. George Cleaver

The titles *Honorable* and *Reverend* are spelled out when used with *the.*

the Honorable Rebecca A. Holden
the Reverend George Cleaver

For military ranks, two styles are used: general use calls for initial capitals and periods, whereas the military branches prefer to use all capitals and no periods.

Adm., ADM, admiral
Brig. Gen., BG, brigadier general
Capt., CPT, captain
Col., COL, colonel
Comdr., CDR, commander
Cpl., CPL, corporal
CWO, CWO4, chief warrant officer
Ens., ENS, ensign
Lt. Col., LTC, lieutenant colonel
Lt. Comdr., LCDR, lieutenant commander
Lt. Gen., LTG, lieutenant general
Lt. (jg), LTJG, lieutenant junior grade
2d Lt., 2LT, second lieutenant
Maj., MAJ, major
Pfc., PFC, private first class
Sfc., SFC, sergeant first class

Sp4c., S4, specialist fourth class
Vice Adm., VADM, vice admiral
WO, WO1, warrant officer

Titles That Follow a Name

The title *Esq.* is never used in conjunction with another title.

Incorrect: Mr. Thomas Moreland, Esq.
Correct: Thomas Moreland, Esq.

Academic, military, or civil honors follow a name and are preceded with a comma. Other titles such as *Mr., Mrs.,* and *Dr.* are dropped.

Ron Travis, Ph.D.
Darryl Walker, CPA
Jane Bourne, M.D.

Academic degrees are abbreviated in uppercase with periods.

B.D., bachelor of divinity
J.D., *juris doctor* (doctor of law)
LL.B., *legum baccalaureus* (bachelor of law)
M.S., master of science

A list of academic degrees is provided at the end of this chapter.

Civil titles are abbreviated in uppercase with no periods.

CLU, chartered life underwriter
OBE, Order of the British Empire

PERSONAL NAMES

It is no longer acceptable to abbreviate proper names in writing. For example, *George* and *Charles* should be used rather than *Geo.* and *Chas.*

Initials are used in place of first names when brevity is required, as in a bibliography. When two or more initials are used, the space between them should be closed up. One practical reason for this style is that if a space is inserted, a "hard space" code is created in word processing and desktop publishing software. This code permanently separates the letters and can result in a sentence that breaks between the initials.

In their classic book on usage and style, William Strunk, Jr., and E. B. White offer valuable advice to writers and editors.

Many publications have begun to close up these spaces, just as the space is closed in other kinds of abbreviations.

P.R. Newton
C.R. Jones

No periods are needed for initials that have fallen into familiar usage.

JFK
LBJ
FDR

NAMES WITH *SAINT*

Preceding the name of a saint, *Saint* is usually spelled out except in tabular material or lists. *Saint* is not used before the names of the apostles. In place names and for names of churches, streets, and squares, *Saint* is abbreviated as *St.* (plural *SS*) in text.

Saint Mary
St. Patrick's Cathedral
St. Louis, Missouri

When *Saint* forms a part of a personal name, the bearer's preference should be followed.

Susan Saint James
Adela Rogers St. John
Yves Saint-Laurent
Buffy Sainte-Marie

COMPANY NAMES

Words that form part of a company's legal name, such as *company, corporation, incorporated,* or *limited,* are usually abbreviated; these terms are often dropped completely when the context does not require the formal and complete name of the company.

Atlantic Richfield Co.
Synergen Inc.
Ameritech Corp.

The word *corporation* is never abbreviated in names of federal government units.

Commodity Credit Corporation

PLACE NAMES

Countries

United States is spelled out as a noun but is usually abbreviated as an adjective.

> The population of the United States is nearly 250 million.
> The median age of the U.S. population is 32.9 years.

Names of foreign countries should not be abbreviated except in such space-restrictive formats as tables, graphs, and catalogs.

Mex.	Ger.
Phil.	N.Z.
UAR	It.
Can.	Scot.
Rom.	U.K.
Swed.	Fr.

States and Provinces

When and how to abbreviate state names depends on the formality of the publication and personal preference. When the state name and city name are used together, the state name may be spelled out in full, the traditional abbreviation may be used, or—primarily in informal writing and in lists—the U.S. Postal Service two-letter address code can be used. When the state name stands alone, it is always spelled out.

> The Basketball Hall of Fame is in Springfield, Massachusetts. (or *Mass.* or *MA*)
> *But:* Boston is the capital of Massachusetts.

The two-letter Postal Service abbreviation is always used with ZIP codes: Boston, MA 02100.

State	*Traditional*	*Postal*
Alabama	Ala.	AL
Alaska	—	AK
Arizona	Ariz.	AZ
Arkansas	Ark.	AR
California	Calif.	CA
Colorado	Colo.	CO
Connecticut	Conn.	CT
Delaware	Del.	DE
Florida	Fla.	FL
Georgia	Ga.	GA
Hawaii	—	HI
Idaho	—	ID
Illinois	Ill.	IL
Indiana	Ind.	IN
Iowa	—	IA
Kansas	Kan.	KS
Kentucky	Ky.	KY
Louisiana	La.	LA
Maine	Me.	ME
Maryland	Md.	MD
Massachusetts	Mass.	MA
Michigan	Mich.	MI
Minnesota	Minn.	MN
Mississippi	Miss.	MS
Missouri	Mo.	MO
Montana	Mont.	MT
Nebraska	Neb.	NE
Nevada	Nev.	NV
New Hampshire	N.H.	NH
New Jersey	N.J.	NJ
New Mexico	N.M.	NM
New York	N.Y.	NY
North Carolina	N.C.	NC
North Dakota	N.D.	ND
Ohio	—	OH
Oklahoma	Okla.	OK

State	*Traditional*	*Postal*
Oregon	Ore.	OR
Pennsylvania	Pa.	PA
Rhode Island	R.I.	RI
South Carolina	S.C.	SC
South Dakota	S.D.	SD
Tennessee	Tenn.	TN
Texas	Tex.	TX
Utah	—	UT
Vermont	Vt.	VT
Virginia	Va.	VA
Washington	Wash.	WA
West Virginia	W. Va.	WV
Wisconsin	Wis.	WI
Wyoming	Wyo.	WY
Canal Zone	—	CZ
District of Columbia	D.C.	DC
Guam	—	GU
Puerto Rico	P.R.	PR
Virgin Islands	V.I.	VI
Canadian Province		
Alberta	Alta.	AB
British Columbia	B.C.	BC
Labrador	Labr.	LB
Manitoba	Man.	MB
New Brunswick	N.B.	NB
Newfoundland	Nfld.	NF
Northwest Territories	N.W.T.	NT
Nova Scotia	N.S.	NS
Ontario	Ont.	ON
Prince Edward Island	P.E.I.	PE
Quebec	P.Q.	PQ
Saskatchewan	Sask.	SK
Yukon Territory	Y.T.	YT

Canadian provinces are commonly abbreviated unless they appear alone in text.

The 50-story Benkers Hall is the second tallest building in Calgary, Alta.
Ontario and Quebec were originally called Upper and Lower Canada.

Addresses

Words that are part of an address are spelled out in straight text and abbreviated in tables, footnotes, bibliographies, and graphs.

Empire State Building (*or* Bldg.)
211 East 51st Street (*or* St.)

If the word *street* or *avenue* is part of a proper name, it is always spelled out.

14th Street Bridge (*not* St.)

The words *county, fort, mount, point,* and *port* are not abbreviated in text, but *Saint* (St.) and *Sainte* (Ste.) are abbreviated in geographical references.

Mount McKinley
Lake St. Clair
Franklin County
St. Petersburg

Sectional divisions of a city (NW, SW, NE, and SE) are abbreviated as part of an address and are set without periods.

1131 Florida Ave., NW
104 East Capitol St., SE

The designation *North, South, East,* or *West* before a street name should be spelled out.

Geographic Terminology

The terms *latitude* and *longitude* are written out in text but abbreviated in tables and footnotes.

text: latitude 10°20′03″N *or* 10°20′03″ north latitude
table: lat. 10°20′03″N

The symbols used to designate latitude and longitude are degree (°), arc minute (′), and arc second (″).

Compass directions are set without periods or spaces.

N
E
S
W
SE
NNW
SSW

Compass directions that are a single letter can be spelled out in straight text even when abbreviations are used in the same sentence.

The most frequent wind direction was WNW at night and south in the daytime.
Lakes occupied the NE and SE sectors, but meadow was predominant in the west.

TIME AND DATES

The standard abbreviations for the time of day, *a.m. (ante meridiem)* and *p.m. (post meridiem)*, are used with numerals. These abbreviations are set in lowercase or small caps, with periods and no spaces.

It's important to know that 12:00 p.m. means midnight.
The President will speak at 8:00 p.m. EST.

The abbreviations *A.D.* (*anno Domini,* in the year of our Lord) and *B.C.* (before Christ) are used with years to prevent confusion or to ensure historical accuracy. Capital letters and periods are used, and italics and spaces are not used, with these and other common chronological designations. Abbreviations that begin with the letter *A* precede the year number, and all other abbreviations follow the year number (A.D. 340, 2300 B.C.).

A.H. *(anno hegirae)*, in the year of the Hegira (A.D. 622)
A.M. *(anno mundi)*, in the year of the world

B.C.E., before the common era
B.P., before the present
C.E., common era

Names of the days and months should be spelled out in text and abbreviated only in such formats as tables, graphs, and catalogs, where space is a consideration.

Jan., Ja, J	July, Jl, J	Sun., Su
Feb., F	Aug., Ag, Au, A	Mon., M
March, Mar., Mr, M	Sept., S	Tues., Tu
April, Apr., Ap, A	Oct., O	Wed., W
May, My, M	Nov., N	Thurs., Th
June, Je, J	Dec., D	Fri., F
		Sat., Sa

Dates in military format are written as 1 Nov 85 or 1 Nov. 1985.

Shortened formats such as 1/6/82 are not considered acceptable in any text, in part because American and European usage differs. To Europeans, 1/6/82 means June 1, 1982; to Americans, it means January 6, 1982.

UNITS OF MEASURE

Units of measure are usually spelled out in nontechnical writing; when they are abbreviated, however, periods are usually used. In contrast, periods are dropped from most abbreviated units of measure in scientific and technical writing. The examples that follow reflect the latter style, since abbreviated units of measure are much more prevalent in technical text.

A unit of measure is abbreviated only when used with a number value. Abbreviations for units of measure are the same in the singular and plural.

0.5 ms	24 min
4 ft	45 in. (note period)
66 mi	200 m

A few units of measure may look like abbreviations but are not; for these, an *s* is added to create the plural form.

mho, mhos
ohm, ohms
Gal, Gals (unit of acceleration)
rad, rads (radiation units)
bar, bars
But: 5 mbar (the prefix *m* makes the unit an abbreviation, which is the same in singular and plural)

Abbreviations formed from a proper name are usually capitalized, although the spelled-out version of the measurement is not.

Ein, einstein unit
H, henry
J, joule
W, watt
Hz, hertz
A, ampere

A unit of measure is not repeated within a series or parallel structure unless it is normally printed closed up to the number value.

between 5 and 6 ms
from 1.2 to 1.8 m
heights of 5, 10, and 20 cm
But: a change from 90% to 99%
28mm to 80mm lens

Abbreviated prefixes are used with metric units of measure to show that the unit has been multiplied by some power of 10.

a, atto (=10^{-18})
c, centi (=10^{-2})
d, deci (=10^{-1})
da, deka (=10^{1})
f, femto (=10^{-15})
G, giga (=10^{9})
h, hecto (=10^{2})
k, kilo (=10^{3})
M, mega (=10^{6})
m, milli (=10^{-3})
μ, micro (=10^{-6})
n, nano (=10^{-9})
p, pico (=10^{-12})
T, tera (=10^{12})

In such terms, the entire abbreviation is closed up.

μmol, micromole
Mt, megaton
dB, decibel
Tg, teragram
kV, kilovolt

INTERNATIONAL SYSTEM OF UNITS

The International System of Units (*Système international d'unités*, abbreviated SI) is used in medical, scientific, and technical fields worldwide. The system consists of seven base units:

Unit	*Abbrev.*	*Type of Measure*
meter	m	length
kilogram	kg	mass
second	s	time
ampere	A	electric current
kelvin	K	thermodynamic temperature
mole	mol	amount of substance
candela	cd	luminous intensity

Prefixes, such as micro and centi, are added to these base units to form derived units (microseconds, centimeters). (See Chapter 17, Numbers, for definitions of metric prefixes.) When figures are used with SI units, the custom is to use only numbers between 0.1 and 1,000 (10,000 meters is expressed as 10 km rather than 10,000 m). SI abbreviations are lowercase, except those for kelvin and ampere, and use no periods. *The American Heritage Dictionary*, third edition, provides a listing of SI units under the entry heading "Measurement Table."

LISTS OF ABBREVIATIONS

GENERAL

aa	author's alteration
aac	average annual cost
aae	average annual earnings
A.D.	*anno Domini* (Latin, in the year of our Lord)
aet.	*aetate* (Latin, aged)
a.m.	*ante meridiem* (Latin, before noon)
anon.	anonymous
app.	appendix
ASAP	as soon as possible
ATV	all-terrain vehicle
aux.	auxiliary
B&B	bed and breakfast
B.C.	before Christ
B.C.E.	before the Christian (or common) era
B.P.	before present
Bros.	Brothers
c., ca.	*circa* (Latin, about)
CEO	chief executive officer
cf.	compare
ch.	chapter
CLIN	contract line item number
CLU	chartered life underwriter
c/o	in care of
Co.	Company
COD	cash on delivery

COO	chief operating officer
Corp.	Corporation
CPA	certified public accountant
CST	central standard time
D.A.	district attorney
DOA	dead on arrival
DSM	Distinguished Service Medal
DST	daylight saving time
ed.	edited, editor, edition
EEO	equal employment opportunity
EST	eastern standard time
f., ff.	and following, pages following
FICA	Federal Insurance Contributions Act (Social Security)
FLIP	Federal Loan Insurance Program; floating instrument platform
f.o.b.	free (or freight) on board
f/t	full time
f/x	special effects (movies)
FYI	for your information
GIGO	garbage in, garbage out
GMAT	Graduate Management Admission Test
GMT	Greenwich mean time
GRAD	Graduate Resume Accumulation and Distribution
GRE	Graduate Record Examination
HMS	his/her majesty's ship
HQ	headquarters
HRH	his/her royal highness
Inc.	Incorporated
IQ	intelligence quotient
IRA	individual retirement account
ISBN	International Standard Book Number
KO	knock out
l.c.	lowercase
LPN	licensed practical nurse

LSAT	Law School Admission Test
Ltd.	Limited
LVN	licensed vocational nurse
m.	married
M.	*meridies* (Latin, noon)
MC	master of ceremonies
M.O.	money order; *modus operandi* (Latin, mode of operation)
M.P.	member of Parliament; military police
MS, ms., mss.	manuscript, manuscripts
N/A	not applicable, not available
no.	number
NP	notary public
o/t	overtime
p., pp.	page, pages
PA	public address
PAC	political action committee
PERT	program evaluation and review technique
PET	parent effectiveness training
PIN	personal identification number
PIRG	public interest research group
PITI	principal, interest, taxes, and insurance
P&I	principal and interest
P&L	profit and loss
p.m.	*post meridiem* (Latin, after noon); prime minister
P.S.	postscript
PX	post exchange (military)
Q-T-D	quarter-to-date
R&B	rhythm and blues
rbi	runs batted in (baseball)
R&D	research and development
RFD	rural free delivery
RFQ	request for quotation
RIP	*requiescat in pace* (Latin, rest in peace)
RN	registered nurse
RR	railroad
R&R	rest and relaxation (military)
RSVP	*répondez s'il vous plait* (French, respond if you please)

SASE	self-addressed stamped envelope
SAT	Scholastic Aptitude Test
s.c.	small capital letters; subcutaneous
scuba	self-contained underwater breathing apparatus
SIG	special interest group
S&L	savings and loan
SOS	international distress signal
SS	Social Security; steamship; supersonic
TD	touchdown (football)
u.c.	uppercase
UFO	unidentified flying object
USS	United States ship
VIP	very important person
vol.	volume
V.P.	vice president
WASP	white Anglo-Saxon Protestant
WIN	work incentive program
W-I-P	work-in-progress
Y-T-D	year-to-date
yuppie	young urban professional
ZIP	Zone Improvement Plan (U.S. Postal Service)

MEASUREMENT

Note: In technical literature, a letter abbreviation can mean different things depending on whether it is in italics, is in full caps, or is lowercase. The *ACS Style Guide* (see annotated bibliography) is a useful guide for many scientific abbreviations.

A	ampere
Å	angstrom
a.	acre
atm	standard atmosphere
at wt	atomic weight
bbl.	barrel
bd ft	board foot

BeV	billion electron volts
Btu	British thermal unit
bu.	bushel
C	centigrade, Celsius; coulomb
C.	curie
Cal	large calorie (kilocalorie)
cal, c	calorie
cc	cubic centimeter
cd	candela
cg	centigram
cgs	centimeter gram second
cl	centiliter
cm, c	centimeter
cp	candlepower
CPS	cycles per second
cu. ft.	cubic foot
cu. in.	cubic inch
cwt.	hundredweight
d.	day
dag	decagram
dam	decameter
dB	decibel
dg	decigram
dl	deciliter
dm	decimeter
doz.	dozen
dr.	dram; drachma
dwt.	pennyweight
F	Fahrenheit; farad; fermi; formal (concentration)
fps	foot pound second
ft	foot
ft-lb	foot-pound
G	gauss
g	gram (also seen as gm); gravity
gal.	gallon
gi.	gill
gr.	grain; gross
h, hr.	hour
ha	hectare

hg hectogram
hhd. hogshead
hl hectoliter
hm hectometer
hp horsepower
Hz hertz

i.d. inside diameter
in. inch
IU international unit

J joule

K 1,000; kelvin
k. karat
kbar kilobar
kc kilocycle
kg kilogram
kl kiloliter
km kilometer
kn knot
kph kilometers per hour
kV kilovolt
kW kilowatt
kWh kilowatt-hour

L liter
lat. latitude
lb, lb. pound
l/min lines per minute
long. longitude
L/s liters per second

M mega; molar
m meter; molal
mA milliampere
Mc megacycle
mCi millicurie
MeV million electron volts
mg milligram

MHz	megahertz
mi.	mile
min.	minute; minimum
ml	milliliter
mm	millimeter
μm	micrometer
mmHg	millimeters of mercury
mmol	millimole
μmol	micromole
mo.	month
mol	mole
mol wt.	molecular weight
mp	melting point
mpg	miles per gallon
mph	miles per hour
ms, msec	millisecond
Mt	megaton
MW	molecular weight
myg	myriagram
myl	myrialiter
mym	myriameter
N	Newton; normal (concentration)
ng	nanogram
NM	nautical mile
nm	nanometer
ns	nanosecond
Ω	ohm
o.d.	outside diameter
oz.	ounce
Pa	pascal
pH	negative log of the hydrogen ion concentration
pk.	peck
ppb	parts per billion
ppm	parts per million
psi	pounds per square inch
pt.	pint
q	quintal
qt.	quart

r, R	roentgen
rd.	rod
rpm	revolutions per minute
s, sec.	second
scfh	standard ft^3/h
SD	standard deviation
SE	standard error of the mean
sp gr	specific gravity
sp ht	specific heat
sp vol	specific volume
sq.	square
T	ton; tesla
t	temperature, °C
T	temperature, K
tbsp	tablespoonful
Tg	teragram
tsp	teaspoonful
V	volt
v/v	volume per volume
vol	volume
vol %	volume percent
W	watt
wgt. pct., wt %	weight percent
wk.	week
w/v	weight per volume
yd.	yard
yr.	year

MEDICAL

aa	*ana* (Latin, of each alike)
AAS	atomic absorption spectroscopy
abd	abdominal
abs	absolute
Ac	acetyl
a.c.	*ante cibum* (Latin, before meals)
ACTH	adrenocorticotropic hormone

AD	Alzheimer's disease
ADH	antidiuretic hormone
ADNase	antideoxyribonuclease
ADP	adenosine diphosphate
AES	atomic emission spectroscopy
AFB	acid-fast bacilli
AFP	alpha fetoprotein
A/G	albumin-globulin
Ag-Ab	antigen antibody
AHF	antihemophilic factor
AIDS	acquired immunodeficiency syndrome
ALD	aldolase serum
AMA	antimitochondrial antibody; American Medical Association
ANA	antinuclear antibody
anhyd	anhydrous
AO	atomic orbital
AP	anteroposterior
APA	antiparietal antibody
aq	aqueous
aq.	*aqua* (Latin, water)
ARC	AIDS-related complex
ASH	antistreptococcal hyaluronidase
ASLO	antistreptolysin O
ASMA	anti-smooth muscle antibody
ASTO	antistreptolysin O titer
ATP	adenosine triphosphate
ATR	attenuated total reflection
AV	atrioventricular
av	average
BEI	butano-extractable iodine
BFT	bentonite flocculation test
b.i.d.	*bis in die* (Latin, twice a day)
biol	biological(ly)
BMR	basal metabolic rate
BOD	biological oxygen demand
Br	bromine
BSP	bromsulphalein
BU	Bodansky unit
Bu	butyl
BUN	blood urea nitrogen
Bz	benzoyl

C-A	carbonic anhydrase
calcd	calculated
cAMP	cyclic adenosine monophosphate
CAT	computed axial tomography
CBC	complete blood count
Cbz	carbobenzoxy
CD	circular dichroism
CE	Cotton effect
CEA	carcinoembryonic antigen
CF	complement fixation
CFA	complement-fixing antigen
CI	color index (of blood); chemical ionization; configuration interaction
CIDEP	chemical-induced dynamic electron polarization
cmc	critical micelle concentration
CNDO	complete neglect of differential overlap
CNS	central nervous system
CoA	coenzyme A
coeff	coefficient
compd	compound
concd	concentrated
concn	concentration
const	constant
cor	corrected
CP	chemically pure; cross-polarization
Cp	cyclopentadienyl (also, cp)
CPC	clinical pathological conference
CPE	controlled potential electrolysis
CPK	creatine phosphokinase; Corey-Pauling-Koltun (models)
CPL	circular polarization of luminescence
CPR	cardiopulmonary resuscitation
crit	critical
cRNA	chromosomal ribonucleic acid
CRP	C-reactive protein
CRU	constitutional repeating unit
cryst	crystalline
C&S	culture & sensitivity
CSF	cerebrospinal fluid
CT	charge transfer
CVA	costovertebral angle
CW	continuous wave; constant width
D&C	dilation and curettage

diam	diameter
dil	dilute
distd	distilled
DNA	deoxyribonucleic acid
DSC	differential scanning calorimetry
DTA	differential thermal analysis
DTs	delirium tremens
ECHO	enteric cytopathogenic human orphan (virus)
ED	effective dose
EDTA	ethylenediaminetetraacetic acid
EEG	electroencephalogram
EFG	electric field gradient
EI	electron impact; electron ionization
EKG	electrocardiogram
EM	electron microscopy
emf	electromotive force
ENDOR	electron (external) nuclear double resonance
Eq	equivalent (chem)
eq.	equation
equiv	equivalent (math)
EPR	electron paramagnetic resonance
ESCA	electron spectroscopy for chemical analysis
ESR	erythrocyte sedimentation rate; electron spin resonance
Et	ethyl
EU	enzyme unit
eu	entropy unit
expt(l)	experiment(al)
FAD	flavin adenine dinucleotide
FAFS	flame atomic fluorescence spectroscopy
FANA	fluorescent antinuclear antibody
FBS	fasting blood sugar
FI	field ionization
FSH	follicle-stimulating hormone
FT	Fourier transform
FTA	fluorescent treponemal antibody
FTI	free thyroxine index
fwhm	full width at half-maximum
g	gas; gram
GC	gas chromatography
GFR	glomerular filtration rate

GG	gamma globulin
GH	growth hormone
GLC	gas-liquid chromatography
GPC	gel permeation chromatography
GPT	glutamic pyruvic transaminase
G6PD	glucose-6-phosphate dehydrogenase
GSH	glutathione
gt.	*gutta* (Latin, drop)
GTT	glucose tolerance test
h	Planck constant
HAE	hereditary angioneurotic edema
HBD	hydroxybutyric dehydrogenase
HCG	human chorionic gonadotropin
HCS	human chorionic somatomammotropin
Hct	hematocrit
H&E	hematoxylin and eosin
HF	Hageman factor
Hg	hemoglobin
HGF	hyperglycemic glycogenolytic factor
HIAA	hydroxyindoleacetic acid
HIV	human immunodeficiency virus
HOMO	highest occupied molecular orbital
HPF	high-power field
HPLC	high-pressure liquid chromatography; high-performance liquid chromatography
IBC	iron-binding capacity
ICR	ion cyclotron resonance
ICSH	interstitial cell-stimulating hormone
IE	ionization energy
IEC	ion-exchange chromatography
IF	infective dose
IHA	indirect hemagglutination
II	icterus index
IM	intramuscularly (also, im)
INH	isonicotinic acid hydrazide
INO	iterative natural orbit
insol	insoluble
IP	ionization potential; intraperitonially (also, ip)
IR	infrared
IV	intravenously (also, iv)
K	potassium
KAU	King-Armstrong unit

LCAO	linear combination of atomic orbitals
LD	lethal dose
LDH	lactic (acid) dehydrogenase; lactate dehydrogenase
LE	lupus erythematosus
LFER	linear free-energy relationship
LIS	lanthanide-induced shift
LOA	left occipitoanterior
LPF	low-power field
L/S	lecithin-sphingomyelin
LSD	lysergic acid diethylamide
LTH	luteotropic hormone
LUMO	lowest unoccupied molecular orbital
max	maximum
MCH	mean corpuscular hemoglobin
MCHC	mean corpuscular hemoglobin concentration
MCV	mean corpuscular volume
Me	methyl
MED	minimal effective dose
mEq/L	milliequivalents per liter
min	minimum
MLD	minimum lethal dose; median lethal dose
mM	millimolar
mmol	millimole
mmp	mixed melting point
MO	molecular orbital
MR	molecular refraction
MRI	magnetic resonance imaging
mRNA	messenger ribonucleic acid
MS	mass spectroscopy
MSG	monosodium glutamate
MSH	melanin-stimulating hormone
MU	mouse unit
N	normal
NA	nuclear antibody
NAD	nicotinamide adenine dinucleotide
NADH	reduced NAD
NANA	*N*-acetylneuraminic acid
NIR	near infrared
NMR	nuclear magnetic resonance (spectroscopy)
NOCOR	neglect of core orbitals
NOE	nuclear Overhauser effect
NPN	nonprotein nitrogen
NQR	nuclear quadruple resonance

nRNA	nuclear ribonucleic acid
NSQ	not sufficient quantity
obsd	observed
OCT	ornithine carbamoyltransferase
OHCS	hydroxycorticosteroid
ol.	*oleum* (Latin, oil)
ORD	optical rotary dispersion
osM	osmolar
ox	oxidized or oxidation
PABA	*para*-aminobenzoic acid
p.ae.	*partes aequales* (Latin, equal parts)
PAH	*para*-aminohippurate
PAS	*para*-aminosalicylic acid
PBG	porphobilinogen
PBI	protein-bound iodine
p.c.	*post cibum* (Latin, after meals)
PCV	packed cell volume
Ph	phenyl
PKU	phenylketonuria
PMN	polymorphonuclear neutrophilic leukocyte
PPD	purified protein derivative
PPLO	pleuropneumonia-like organism
ppt	precipitate
Pr	propyl
prepn	preparation
p.r.n.	*pro re nata* (Latin, as necessary)
py	pyridine
q.h.	*quaque hora* (Latin, every hour)
q.i.d.	*quater in die* (Latin, four times a day)
q.l.	*quantum libet* (Latin, as much as you please)
q.pl.	*quantum placet* (Latin, as much as seems good)
q.s.	*quantum sufficit* (Latin, a sufficient quantity)
q.v.	*quantum vis* (Latin, as much as you will)
RBC	red blood cell; red blood (cell) count
recryst	recrystallized
red	reduced or reduction
redox	reduction-oxidation process
REM	rapid eye movement
RNA	ribonucleic acid
RQ	respiratory quotient
rRNA	ribosomal ribonucleic acid
Rx	prescription

s	sedimentation coefficient
S	svedberg unit
SA	sinoatrial
SAR	structure-activity relationship
SCF	self-consistent field
SGOT	serum glutamic-oxaloacetic transaminase
SI	International System of Units (Système International)
SK-SD	streptokinase-streptodornase
sol	soluble
soln	solution
std	standard
STH	somatotropic hormone
STO	Slater-type orbital
sym	symmetrical
temp	temperature
t.i.d.	*ter in die* (Latin, three times daily)
TLC	thin-layer chromatography
TMV	tobacco mosaic virus
tRNA	transfer ribonucleic acid
TSH	thyrotropic hormone
ut dict.	*ut dictum* (Latin, as directed)
UV	ultraviolet
VPC	vapor pressure chromatography
VSIP	valence state ionization potential
WBC	white blood cell; white blood (cell) count
XRD	X-ray diffraction
zfsc	zero-field splitting constant

SCIENTIFIC AND TECHNICAL

A	ampere
AC	alternating current
Ac	actinium
ACC	automatic chroma control
ACM	advanced cruise missile
A/D	analog-to-digital converter
ADM	air defense missile
AF	audiofrequency
AFC	automatic frequency control
AFT	automatic fine tuning
Ag	silver
AGC	automatic gain control
agl	above ground level
AGM	air-to-ground missile
Al	aluminum
ALCM	air-launched cruise missile
ALSAM	air-launched surface attack missile
AM	amplitude modulation
Am	americium
APC	automatic phase control
APL	average picture level
Ar	argon
As	arsenic
At	astatine
ATU	antenna tuning unit
Au	gold
B	boron
Ba	barium
bar	barometer, barometric
BCD	binary coded decimal
Be	beryllium; Baume
BHP	brake horsepower
Bi	bismuth
bionics	biology and electronics
Bk	berkelium
bp	boiling point
Br	bromine
C	carbon
Ca	calcium
Cb	columbium

CCD	charge coupled device
Cd	cadmium
cd	candela
CD-4	four-channel recording
Ce	cerium
Cf	californium
Cl	chlorine
Cm	curium
CMRR	common mode rejection ratio
Co	cobalt
cp	candlepower
Cr	chromium
Cs	cesium
Cu	copper
d	deuteron
D	deuterium
DA	distribution amplifier
DASH	digital audio stationary head
DAT	digital audio tape
DBS	direct broadcast satellite service
DC	direct current
DMA	dropping mercury electrode
DOF	degrees of freedom
DTA	differential thermal analysis
Dy	dysprosium
EARS	Electronic Airborne Reaction System; Electronically Agile Radar System; Emergency Airborne Reaction System
eff	efficiency
EMF	electromotive force
ENDEX	Environmental Data Index
Er	erbium
Es	einsteinium
Eu	europium
eV	electron volt
F	fluorine
f	focal length
fcc	face-centered cubic
Fe	iron
FET	field effect transistor
FIR	finite impulse response

FM	frequency modulation
Fm	fermium
fp	freezing point
Fr	francium
Ga	gallium
Gd	gadolinium
Ge	germanium
GEOS	geodetic Earth-orbiting satellite
GeV	billion electron volts (also, BeV)
H	hydrogen
Ha	hahnium
HCl	hydrochloric acid
He	helium
hex	hexagonal
HF	high frequency
Hf	hafnium
Hg	mercury
Ho	holmium
I	iodine
ICE	in-circuit emulator
ICPM	incidental carrier-phase modulation
IIR	infinite-impulse response
In	indium
INLAW	infantry laser weapon
INTELSAT	intelligence satellite
IPA	intermediate power amplifier
IPL	interprocessor link
IR	infrared
Ir	iridium
IRC	interval-related carrier
K	potassium
Kr	krypton
La	lanthanum
LF	low frequency
Li	lithium
LNA	low noise amplifier
LO	local oscillator
LORAN	Long-Range Aid to Navigation
Lr	lawrencium

Lu	lutetium
lx	lux (unit of illuminance)
MAD	mutually assured destruction
Mc	megacycle
Md	mendelevium
Mg	magnesium
Mn	manganese
mn	monoclinic
Mo	molybdenum
mp	melting point
MS	mass spectrum, mass spectroscopy
MSL	mean sea level
Mx	maxwell
N	nitrogen
Na	sodium
NaCl	sodium chloride
Nb	niobium
Nd	neodymium
Ne	neon
Ni	nickel
No	nobelium
NOMAD	Navy oceanographic and meteorological device
Np	neptunium
NRZ	nonreturn to zero
NS	not significant
O	oxygen
Os	osmium
ox	oxidant
P	phosphorus
p	probability
Pa	protactinium
Pb	lead
Pd	palladium
pH	measure of acidity
PLD	programmable logic device
Pm	promethium
Po	polonium
pos	positive
ppt(d)	precipitate(d)
Pr	praseodymium

Pt	platinum
Pu	plutonium
PZE	piezoelectric
R, r	roentgen (X-ray exposure)
Ra	radium
RADAR	radio detecting and ranging
Rb	rubidium
R-DAT	rotary head digital audio tape
Re	rhenium
red	reductant
RF	radiofrequency
Rf	rutherfordium
RFI	radiofrequency interference
Rh	rhodium
rms	root mean square
Rn	radon
RTL	resistor-transistor logic
Ru	ruthenium
S	sulfur
SAFE	system for automated flight efficiency
SAW	surface acoustic wave
Sb	antimony
Sc	scandium
SCPC	single channel per carrier
Se	selenium
SEM	scanning electron microscope
Si	silicon
Sm	samarium
SMOW	standard mean ocean water
Sn	tin
SOS	silicon on sapphire
sp gr	specific gravity
sp ht	specific heat
sq	square
Sr	strontium
SS	sum of squares
std	standard
STP	standard temperature and pressure
STPA	standard temperature and pressure, absolute
STPG	standard temperature and pressure gauge

T	tritium
Ta	tantalum
TAG	transatlantic geotransverse
Tb	terbium
Tc	technetium
Te	tellurium
temp	temperature
Th	thorium
THD	total harmonic distortion
Ti	titanium
Tl	thallium
TLC	thin-layer chromatography
Tm	thulium
T.N.T.	trinitrotoluene
TTL	transistor-transistor logic
TVRO	television receive only
TWT	traveling wave tube
U	uranium
u	atomic mass unit
UHF	ultrahigh frequency
UT	universal time
V	vanadium
VCO	voltage-controlled oscillator
VHF	very high frequency
VITC	vertical-interval time code
VITS	vertical-interval test signal
VSWR	voltage standing wave ratio
W	tungsten
Wb	Weber
Xe	xenon
Y	yttrium
Yb	ytterbium
Z	zinc
Zr	zirconium

ORGANIZATIONS

AAA	American Automobile Association
ACTION	American Council to Improve Our Neighborhoods
AEF	American Expeditionary Force (World War I)
AFL	American Federation of Labor
AID	Agency for International Development; American Institute of Decorators
ALCOA	Aluminum Company of America
AMA	American Medical Association
AMEX	American Express Company
AMOCO	American Oil Company
ANSI	American National Standards Institute
ASCAP	American Society of Composers, Authors, and Publishers
ASPCA	American Society for the Prevention of Cruelty to Animals
BART	Bay Area Rapid Transit
BASS	Bass Anglers Sportsman Society
BBB	Better Business Bureau
BIB	Bureau of International Broadcasting
BSA	Boy Scouts of America
CAB	Civil Aeronautics Board
CALM	Citizens Against Legalized Murder
CARE	Cooperative for American Relief Everywhere
CCC	Civilian Conservation Corps
CIA	Central Intelligence Agency
CIO	Congress of Industrial Organizations
COMEX	Commodities Exchange (New York)
CORE	Congress of Racial Equality
CURE	Citizens United for Racial Equality
DAR	Daughters of the American Revolution
DEA	Drug Enforcement Agency
DELCO	Dayton Engineering Laboratory Company
DISCO	Defense Industrial Security Clearance Office
DOD	Department of Defense
DSO	Distinguished Service Order
DYNAMO	Dynamic Action Management Operation
EPA	Environmental Protection Agency
EPCOT	Experimental Prototype Community of Tomorrow
EXIMBANK	Export-Import Bank of the United States

FAA	Federal Aviation Administration
FBI	Federal Bureau of Investigation
FCC	Federal Communications Commission
FDA	Food and Drug Administration
FDIC	Federal Deposit Insurance Corporation
FEW	Federally Employed Women
FHA	Federal Housing Administration
FmHA	Farmers Home Administration
FRS	Federal Reserve System
FTC	Federal Trade Commission
GAG	Graphic Artists Guild
GAO	General Accounting Office
GARB	Garment and Allied Industries Requirements Board
GLAD	Gay and Lesbian Advocates and Defenders
GOP	Grand Old Party (Republican party)
GPO	Government Printing Office; general post office
GSA	Girl Scouts of America
GSFC	Goddard Space Flight Center
HART	Honolulu Area Rapid Transit
H.R.	House of Representatives
HUD	(Department of) Housing and Urban Development
ICC	Interstate Commerce Commission
INS	Immigration and Naturalization Service
INTERPOL	International Criminal Police Organization
INTERTELL	International Intelligence Legion
IRA	Irish Republican Army
IRS	Internal Revenue Service
JOBS	Job Opportunities in the Business Sector
LC	Library of Congress
MADD	Mothers Against Drunk Driving
MOMA	Museum of Modern Art (New York)
NAACP	National Association for the Advancement of Colored People
NAM	National Association of Manufacturers; National Air Museum
NAPA	National Automotive Parts Association
NARCO	United Nations Narcotics Commission

NASA	National Aeronautics and Space Administration
NASCAR	National Association of Sports Car Racing
NATO	North Atlantic Treaty Organization
NECCO	New England Confectionary Company
NORAD	North American Air Defense
NOW	National Organization for Women
NRA	National Rifle Association; National Recovery Administration
NRC	Nuclear Regulatory Commission
NSC	National Security Council
NYPL	New York Public Library
NYSE	New York Stock Exchange
ODECO	Ocean Drilling and Exploration Company
OPEC	Organization of Petroleum Exporting Countries
OSHA	Occupational Safety and Health Administration
OXFAM	Oxford Famine Relief
PAC	Pacific Air Command
PATCO	Port Authority Transit Corporation
PATH	Port Authority Trans-Hudson
PEN	Poets, Playwrights, Editors, Essayists, and Novelists
PTA	Parent-Teacher Association
R.A.	Royal Academy
RIF	Reading Is Fundamental
ROTC	Reserve Officers' Training Corps
SAC	Strategic Air Command
SALT	Strategic Arms Limitations Talks
SDI	Strategic Defense Initiative
SDS	Students for a Democratic Society
SEATO	Southeast Asia Treaty Organization
SEC	Securities and Exchange Commission
Sen.	Senate
S.J.	Society of Jesus (Jesuits)
SPCA	Society for the Prevention of Cruelty to Animals
TAC	Tactical Air Command
TVA	Tennessee Valley Authority
U.N.	United Nations
UNESCO	United Nations Educational, Scientific, and Cultural Organization

UNICEF	United Nations International Children's Emergency Fund
USA	United States Army
USAF	United States Air Force
USCG	United States Coast Guard
USDA	United States Department of Agriculture
USIA	United States Information Agency
USMC	United States Marine Corps
USN	United States Navy
VA	Department of Veterans Affairs (formerly Veterans Administration)
VFW	Veterans of Foreign Wars
VISTA	Volunteers in Service to America
WAC	Women's Army Corps
WAVES	Women Accepted for Volunteer Emergency Service (Navy)
WCTU	Woman's Christian Temperance Union
WHO	World Health Organization
WUDO	Western European Defense Organization
YMCA	Young Men's Christian Association
YMHA	Young Men's Hebrew Association
YWCA	Young Women's Christian Association
YWHA	Young Women's Hebrew Association

SCHOLARLY

A.B.	*artium baccalaureus* (Latin, bachelor of arts)
abbr.	abbreviated, abbreviation
ab init.	*ab initio* (Latin, from the beginning)
abl.	ablative
abr.	abridged
acc.	accusative
act.	active
ad inf.	*ad infinitum* (Latin, to infinity)
ad init.	*ad initium* (Latin, at the beginning)
ad int.	*ad interim* (Latin, in the meantime)
adj.	adjective
ad lib.	*ad libitum* (Latin, at will)
ad loc.	*ad locum* (Latin, at the place)
adv.	adverb

aet.	*aetatis* (Latin, aged)
AF	Anglo-French
A.M.	*artium magister* (Latin, master of arts)
AN	Anglo-Norman
anon.	anonymous
app.	appendix
art.	article
AS	Anglo-Saxon
b.	born; brother
B.A.	bachelor of arts
B.D.	bachelor of divinity
bibl.	*bibliotheca* (Latin, library)
bibliog.	bibliography, -er, -ical
biog.	biography, -er, -ical
biol.	biology, -ist, -ical
bk.	block; book
B.S.	bachelor of science
bull.	bulletin
c.	chapter (in legal citations)
c., ca.	*circa* (Latin, approximately)
Cantab.	*Cantabrigiensis* (Latin, of Cambridge)
cf.	confer (Latin, compare)
chap.	chapter
col.	column
colloq.	colloquial, -ly, -ism
comp.	compiler; compiled by
compar.	comparative
con.	*contra* (Latin, against)
conj.	conjunction; conjugation
cons.	consonant
constr.	construction
cont.	continued
contr.	contraction
copr.	copyright
d.	died; daughter
dat.	dative
D.B.	*divinitatis baccalaureus* (Latin, bachelor of divinity)
D.D.	*divinitatis doctor* (Latin, doctor of divinity)
def.	definite, definition
dept.	department
deriv.	derivative

dial.	dialect
dict.	dictionary
dim.	diminutive
dist.	district
div.	division
D.O.	doctor of osteopathy
do.	ditto
D.V.M.	doctor of veterinary medicine
ea.	each
ed.	editor; edited by; edition
eds.	editors
EE	Early English
e.g.	*exempli gratia* (Latin, for example)
encyc.	encyclopedia
Eng.	English
engg.	engineering
engr.	engineer
eq.	equation
esp.	especially
Esq.	esquire
et al.	*et alii* (Latin, and others)
etc.	et cetera (Latin, and so forth)
et seq.	*et sequentes* (Latin, and the following)
ex.	example
f., fem.	feminine, female
ff.	and following
fasc.	fascile
fig.	figure
fl.	*floruit* (Latin, flourished)
fol.	folio
Fr.	French
fr.	from
FRS	Fellow of the Royal Society
fut.	future
f.v.	*folio verso* (Latin, on the back of the page)
Gael.	Gaelic
gen.	genitive; genus
geog.	geography, -er, -ical
geom.	geometry, -ical
Ger.	German
ger.	gerund

Gr. Greek

hist. history, -ian, -ical

ibid. *ibidem* (Latin, in the same place)
id. *idem* (Latin, the same)
IE Indo-European
i.e. *id est* (Latin, that is)
imper. imperative
incl. inclusive, including, includes
indef. indefinite
indic. indicative
inf. *infra* (Latin, below)
infin. infinitive
infra dig. *infra dignitatum* (Latin, undignified)
in pr. *in principio* (Latin, in the beginning)
inst. instant; institute; institution
instr. instrumental
interj. interjection
intrans. intransitive
intro. introduction
irreg. irregular
It. Italian

J.D. *juris doctor* (Latin, doctor of law)
J.P. justice of the peace

L Latin
L. left (in stage directions)
l. line
LG Low German
L.H.D. *litterarum humaniorum doctor* (Latin, doctor of humane letters)
lit. literally
Litt.D. *litterarum doctor* (Latin, doctor of literature)
ll. lines
LL.B. *legum baccalaureus* (Latin, bachelor of law)
LL.D. *legum doctor* (Latin, doctor of law)
loc. locative
loc. cit. *loco citato* (Latin, in the place cited)
loq. *loquitur* (Latin, he/she speaks)

m., masc. masculine
M.A. master of arts
marg. margin, -al
math. mathematics, -ical

M.D.	*medicinae doctor* (Latin, doctor of medicine)
ME	Middle English
med.	median; medical; medieval; medium
memo	memorandum
mgr.	manager
MHG	Middle High German
misc.	miscellaneous
ML	Middle (or Medieval) Latin
MM	Maelzel's metronome (tempo indication)
m.m.	*mutatis mutandis* (Latin, necessary changes being made)
Mod. E.	Modern English
M.P.	member of Parliament
M.S.	master of science
MS, ms.	manuscript
mss.	manuscripts
mus.	museum; music, -al
n.	*natus* (Latin, born); note, footnote; noun
nat.	national; natural
N.B.	*nota bene* (Latin, note well)
n.d.	no date
neg.	negative
neut.	neuter
N. Gr.	New Greek
NL	New Latin
nn.	notes
no.	number
nom.	nominative
non obs.	*non obstante* (Latin, notwithstanding)
non seq.	non sequitur (Latin, it does not follow)
n.p.	no place; no publisher
N.S.	New Style (dates)
n.s.	new series
ob.	*obiit* (Latin, died)
obs.	obsolete
OE	Old English
OF	Old French
O. Gael.	Old Gaelic
OHG	Old High German
ON	Old Norse
op. cit.	*opere citato* (Latin, in the work cited)
O.S.	Old Style (dates)
o.s.	old series
Oxon.	*Oxoniensis* (Latin, of Oxford)

p.	page; past
par.	paragraph
part.	participle
pass.	*passim* (Latin, throughout); passive
path.	pathology, -ist, -ical
perf.	perfect; perforated
perh.	perhaps
pers.	person, personal
Pharm.D.	doctor of pharmacy
Ph.B.	*philosophiae baccalaureus* (Latin, bachelor of philosophy)
Ph.D.	*philosophiae doctor* (Latin, doctor of philosophy)
Ph.G.	graduate in pharmacy
pl.	plural; plate
p.p.	past participle
pp.	pages
prep.	preposition
pres.	present
pron.	pronoun
pro tem.	*pro tempore* (Latin, for the time being)
prox.	*proximo* (Latin, next month)
pt.	part
pub.	publication, publisher, published by
Q.E.D.	*quod erat demonstrandum* (Latin, which was to be demonstrated)
quart.	quarterly
q.v.	*quod vide* (Latin, which see)
R.	*rex* (Latin, king), *regina* (Latin, queen); right (in stage direction)
r.	reigned; recto
refl.	reflexive
repr.	reprint, reprinted
rev.	review; revised, revision
R.I.P.	*requiescat in pace* (Latin, may he/she rest in peace)
s.	substantive
s.a.	*sine anno* (Latin, without year); *sub anno* (Latin, under the year)
sc.	scene; *scilicet* (Latin, namely); *sculpsit* (Latin, carved by)
s.d.	*sine die* (Latin, without setting a day for reconvening)
sec.	section; *secundum* (Latin, according to)
seq.	*sequentes* (Latin, the following)
ser.	series

sing.	singular
s.l.	*sine loco* (Latin, without place)
sociol.	sociology
Sp.	Spanish
st.	stanza
subj.	subjective
subst.	substantive
sup.	*supra* (Latin, above)
superl.	superlative
suppl.	supplement
s.v.	*sub verbo, sub voce* (Latin, under the word)
syn.	synonym, -ous
theol.	theology, -ian, -ical
trans.	transitive; translated, -or
treas.	treasurer
ult.	*ultimo* (Latin, last month)
univ.	university
ut sup.	*ut supra* (Latin, as above)
v.	verse; verso; *vide* (Latin, see); verb
v.i.	verb intransitive
viz.	*videlicet* (Latin, namely)
voc.	vocative
vol.	volume
vs.	versus (Latin, against)
v.t.	verb transitive
yr.	your; year

COMPUTERS

ABIOS	Advanced Basic Input Output System
ACB	asynchronous communications base
ACL	access control list
ACU	automatic calling unit
A/D	analog to digital
ADA	automatic dynamic analyzer
ADE	automatic dialing equipment
ADLC	asynchronous data line controller
ADPE	automated data processing equipment
AI	artificial intelligence

AIS	automated information systems
ALGOL	algorithmic-oriented language
Alt	alternate
ALU	arithmetic logic unit
ANSI	American National Standards Institute
AOC	automatic operation controller
APA	all points addressable
API	application program interface
APL	A programming language
ASCII	American Standard Code for Information Interchange
ASPI	asynchronous serial printer interface
ASR	automatic send-receive
ATG	arithmetic test generator
AUX	auxiliary
BASIC	Beginner's All-Purpose Symbolic Instruction Code
BBS	bulletin board system
BCCD	bar code controller-decoder
BCD	binary coded decimal
BCDIC	binary coded decimal interface code
BCM	basic control monitor
BFAS	basic file access system
BIOS	basic input-output system
bit	binary digit
BITNET	Because It's Time Network
BIZNET	American Business Network (database of U.S. Chamber of Commerce)
BLT	basic logic test
BMC	bulk media conversion
BOLD	Bibliographic On-Line Display (document retrieval system)
BPM	batch processing monitor
bps	bits per second
BSC	binary synchronous communications
BSN	block sequence number
BTM	batch time-sharing monitor
byte	eight bits
CAD	computer-aided design
CAD/CAM	computer-aided design/computer-aided manufacturing
CADD	computer-aided design and drafting
CAI	computer-aided instruction
CAL	course authoring language
CAS	computer-aided software engineering

CBT	computer-based training
CCU	combined card unit
CD	compact disc
CDEV	control panel device
CD-ROM	compact disc—read-only memory
CDU	cartridge disk unit
CFF	common files facility
CGA	color graphics adapter
CGKVDU	color graphics keyboard video display unit
CGM	color graphics metafile
CIF	central information file
CISC	complex instruction set computer
CIU	channel interface unit
CLASSMATE	Computerized Language to Aid and Stimulate Scientific, Mathematical and Technical Education
CLM	configuration load manager
CMD	cartridge module disk
CMI	computer-monitored instruction
CML	current mode logic
CMOS	Complementary Metal-Oxide Semiconductor
CNC	communication network configurator
COBOL	Common Business-Oriented Language
COM	communications
COMDEX	Communications and Data Processing Exposition
COTS	commercial off-the-shelf
CP	central processor
cpi	characters per inch
CPL	console power and logic
CPM	critical path method
CP/M	Control Program for Microprocessors
cps	characters per second
CPU	central processing unit
CRC	cyclic redundancy check
CRP	capacity requirements planning
CRT	cathode ray tube
CRU	card-reader unit
CSCI	computer software configuration item
CSMA/CD	carrier sense multiple access with collision detect
CSU	console system unit
Ctrl	control
DA	desk accessory
DAC	direct-access communications
DAI	direct adaptor interface

DAS	direct access storage
DASD	direct access storage device
DAT	digital audio tape
DBA	database administration
DBDL	database definition language
DBMS	database management system
DBS	database system
DCC	data communications controller
DCD	data communications device
DCL	direct coupled logic
DD/DS	data dictionary/dictionary system
DDL	data definition language
DDP	distributed data processing
DEL	delete
DES	Data Encryption Standard
DHP	document handler processor
DHU	document handler unit
DIF	data interchange format
DIP	dual in-line package
DLC	data line controller
DLI	direct line interface
DMA	direct memory access
DML	Data Management Language; Data Manipulation Language
DMS	data management system
DMU	display monitor unit
DOS	disk operating system; digital operating system
DP	data processing
dpi	dots per inch
DRAM	dynamic random-access memory
DSAC	distributed system administration and control
DSS	disk storage subsystem
DST	distributed systems terminal
DTE	data terminal equipment
DTL	diode-transmitter logic
DTP	desktop publishing
DTS	direct timing source
DVI	digital video interactive
DVT	design validation testing
EARN	European Academic Research Network
EBCDIC	Extended Binary Coded Decimal Interchange Code
ECC	error correcting code

ECL	emitter coupled logic; Execution Control Language
ECSL	Extended Control and Simulation Language
EDAC	error detection and correction
EDI	electronic data interchange
eEGA	enhanced EGA
EEMS	enhanced expanded memory specifications
EGA	enhanced graphics adapter
EIS	extended instruction set
EISA	Extended Industry Standard Architecture
EL	electroluminescent
E-mail	electronic mail
EMI	electromagnetic interference
EMMU	extended main memory unit
EMS	expanded memory specification
EOF	end of file
EOJ	end of job
EOL	end of line
EPROM	erasable programmable read-only memory
EPS	encapsulated PostScript
EPU	execution processing unit
EQ	example query
EQUAL	Extended Query and Update Access Language
ES	expert system
Esc	escape
ESDI	Enhanced System Device Interface; enhanced small device interface
ESS	executive support system
ETS	extended time-sharing
FACT	file access control table
FAT	file allocation table
FCB	file control block
FDDL	file data description language
FEDLINK	Federal Library Information Network
FEP	front-end processor
FIB	file information block
FIFO	first-in/first-out
FILO	first-in/last-out
FMS	file management supervisor
FNPS	front-end network processor support
FORTRAN	Formula Translation (programming language)
FPL	forms processing language
FTF	file transfer facility
FTP	file transfer protocol

GCR	group character recording (Apple)
GFRC	general file and record control
GIPSY	General Information Processing System
GMAP	General Macro Assembler Program
GPI	graphics programming interface
GPIB	general purpose interface bus
GUI	graphical user interface
HFS	Hierarchical File System
HGC	Hercules graphics card
HHBCR	hand-held bar code reader
HSLA	high-speed line adapter
IAS	immediate access storage
IBS	Interactive Business Storage
IC	integrated circuit
ICCU	intercomputer communications unit
ICU	integrated control unit
IDI	intelligent device interface
Ins	insert
INTERMARC	International Machine-Readable Catalog
I/O	input/output
IOF	Interactive Operation Facility
IOM	input-output multiplexer
IOP	input-output processor
IORB	input-output request block
IPS	interactive processing system
IQ	interactive query
IQF	interactive query facility
IQL	interactive query language
IRDS	Information Resource Dictionary System
IRM	inventory record management
ITC	intelligent transaction controller
ITP	integrated transaction processor
IURP	integrated unit record processor
JCL	job control language
KDS	keyboard/display station
KDT	keyboard/display terminal
KSR	keyboard send/receive
KVDU	keyboard/video display unit
LAN	local area network

LANC	local area network controller
LCD	liquid crystal display
LDM	limited distance modem
LED	light-emitting diode
LFN	logical file number
LIFO	last-in/first-out
LIPS	laser printer image processing system
LISP	LISt Processing language
LPH	line protocol handler
LRC	longitudinal redundancy check
LRN	logical resource number
LSI	large-scale integration
LTD	live test demonstration
LUD	logical unit designator
MARC	machine-readable cataloging
MCA	microchannel architecture
MCGA	multicolor graphics array
MCP	multi-chip package
MDA	monochrome display adapter
MFM	modified frequency modulation
MFP	multi-function processor
MFU	multi-function unit
MICR	magnetic ink character recognition
MIDI	musical instrument digital interface
MIPS	million instructions per second
MIS	management information system
MIU	multiple interface unit
MMU	main memory unit
MOC	message-oriented communications
MOLTS	mainframe online test subsystem
MOS	metal oxide semiconductor
MPC	microprogrammed peripheral controller
MPP	microprogrammed peripheral processor
MPS	mathematical programming system
MRS	magnetic reader/sorter
MSC	mass storage controller
MSI	medium-scale integration
MSP	mass storage processor
MSR	mass storage resident
MSS	mass storage subsystem
MSU	mass storage unit
MTBF	mean time between failures
MTC	magnetic tape controller

MTP	magnetic tape processor
MTS	magnetic tape subsystem
MTU	magnetic tape unit
NASF	network administrator storage facility
NAU	network administration utilities
NCS	network control supervisor
NLQ	near letter quality
NOI	node operator interface
NPS	network processing supervisor
OAS	office automation system
OBCR	optical bar code reader
OCL	Operator Control Language
OCR	optical character recognition
ODESY	On-Line Data Entry System
OEM	original equipment manufacturer
OLTD	online tests and diagnostics
OMR	optical mark read
OMS	office management systems
OOPS	object-oriented programming system
OPPM	outside principal period of maintenance
ORU	optimum replaceable unit
OS	operating system
OSI	open system interconnection
OVE	other vendor equipment
PC	personal computer
PCB	printed circuit board
PCF	program checkout facility
PCL	Peripheral Conversion Language; printer command language
PDL	page description language
PDN	Public Data Network
PDSI	peripheral device serial interface
PDU	power distribution unit
PE	phase-encoded
PIM	personal information manager
PIN	personal identification number
PLN	product line notice
PM	preventive maintenance
POL	Procedure-Oriented Language
POLTS	Peripheral Online Test Subsystem

PPM	principal period of maintenance
PPS	Page Printing System
PROM	programmable read-only memory
PrtSc	print screen
PSDN	Packet Switched Data Communication Network
PSI	peripheral subsystem interface
QA	quality assurance
QBE	query by example
QLT	Quality Logic Test
QUICKTRAN	Quick FORTRAN (computer language)
RAD	rapid access data
RAM	random-access memory
RBM	real-time batch monitor
RBT	remote batch terminal
RBTS	remote batch terminal system
RDBMS	relational database management system
RDBSQL	Relational Data Base Structured Query Language
READ	real-time electronic access and display
RFF	remote file facility
RFI	radio frequency interface
RGB	red, green, and blue video in real time
RIP	raster image processor
RIS	resources information system
RISC	reduced instruction set computing
RJE	remote job entry
RLL	run length limited
RLP	remote line printer
RMC	remote message concentrator
RMS	remote maintenance system
RO	receive-only
ROLTS	Remote Online Test System
ROM	read-only memory
RSUF	Remote Software Update Facility
RTE	remote text editor
r/w	read/write
SAA	System Application Architecture
SAF	short address format
SCF	System Control Facility
SCSI	Small Computer System Interface
SCU	System Control Unit
SDCB	software disk cache buffer

SF	scalable font
SGML	Standard Generic Markup Language
SIMM	single in-line memory module
SIP	scientific instruction processor; single in-line package
SL	Simulation Language
SLIP	serial line interface protocol
SLT	self-loading tape
SMD	storage module device
SMS	shared mass storage
SNA	Systems Network Architecture
SNOBOL	string-oriented symbolic language
SPARC	scalable processor architecture
SPD	shared program display
SPG	sort program generator
SQL	Structured Query Language
SRAM	static random access memory
SRB	Software Release Bulletin
SSI	small-scale integration
SSLC	synchronous single-line controller
SSU	system support unit
SYSOP	system operator
TAC	technical assistance center
TCB	task control block
TCL	Transaction Compiler Language
T&D	test and diagnostics
TDG	test data generator
TDP	terminal display processor
TED	text editor
TEMPEST	Transient Electromagnetic Pulse Emanations Standard
TeX	public-domain page description language
TIFF	tagged-image file format
TIM	terminal interface manager
TPR	transaction processing routine
TRB	task request block
TSA	trap save area
TSM	transaction screen management
TSR	terminate and stay resident
TSS	time-sharing system
TTY	teletype
T&V	test and verification
UART	Universal Asynchronous Receiver/Transmitter
UM	users manual

UNIVAC	universal automatic computer
UPC	universal product code
UPF	user productivity facility
UPS	uninterruptible power supply
URP	unit record processor
USI	user system interface
VAN	value-added network
VAR	value-added reseller
VCAM	Virtual Communications Access Method
VDT	video display terminal
VDU	video display unit
VFU	vertical format unit
VGA	video graphics array
VIP	visual information projection
VLSI	very large scale integration
VOL	volume
VRAM	video RAM
WAN	wide area network
WATS	Wide-Area Telecommunications Service
WORM	write once/read many
WP	word processing
WYSIWYG	what you see is what you get
XCFN	external function
XCMD	external command
YMCK	yellow, magenta, cyan, black
ZBR	zone bit recording

15

SPELLING

SPELLING

Spelling is an ongoing challenge for even the best writers and editors, for reasons that can be traced to the evolution of the English language. English words have come from a multitude of other languages over the centuries, and those that have kept their original form *(champagne, chassis, chamois)* are often pronounced in ways that provide no clue to their spelling. The spelling of many other words can be traced to the countless people who recorded early modern English. Before dictionaries were created, writers, scribes, and printers often made their own spelling decisions, based on pronunciation or personal preference.

To confound the problem, pronunciation of certain letters, especially vowels, has changed over the years. We don't pronounce words the same way early English speakers did. So today we not only use the same letter to denote different sounds (*c* pronounced both as *see* and *kay,* as in *center* and *catch*), but we also use different letters to create similar sounds. For example, *c, s, ss,* and *sc* all carry the *s* sound (*reliance, defense, digress,* and *coalesce*); the *sh* sound is made with the letters *s, ci* and *sci, si,* and *ti* (*sure, precious, conscience, occasion,* and *discretion*); and the *f* sound is heard in the letter combinations of *gh* and *ph* (*cough* and *phone*). The list goes on and on.

To add to the confusion, those same early typesetters often changed spellings to fill out a line or balance the page; the final *e* in many words can be traced to this practice.

Finally, there are spelling differences between American and British English. American usage calls for dropping *l*'s—*traveler, canceled, jeweler*; for dropping *u*'s in *-our* words *(honor, color, humor)*; and for dropping *e*'s (*judgment, acknowledgment*). There are also a few other miscellaneous forms—*aluminum, gray,* and *curb*—that differ. In general, most copyeditors are free to change the spellings in British manuscripts for publication in

SPELLING REFORM: IF AT FIRST YOU DON'T SUCCEED . . .

In *Death by Spelling: A Compendium of Tests, Supertests, and Killer Bees*, author David Grambs devotes a chapter to spelling reform. In a summary of failed attempts in American spelling reform over the past century, he describes how a U.S. president became involved.

> 1906. The Simplified Spelling Board is organized with a supportive subsidy from Andrew Carnegie and issues a list of three hundred proposed spellings. President Theodore Roosevelt orders their adoption by the Government Printing Office (GPO), causing great official and public outcry. Ultimately, and briefly, only the White House uses the new spellings—twelve of them. When Taft becomes President, the New York *Sun* refers to the defeated candidate Roosevelt with a one-word headline: "THRU."

Grambs suggests that a reason for the failure of the many reform movements is that "one of the things that people cherish about English is that its spellings reflect its rich and varied history."

And, in the long run, most people realize that spelling reform is impractical, not to mention humorous. Grambs quotes H.L. Mencken as saying, "When the Simplified Spelling Board began making its list longer and longer and wilder and wilder, the national midriff began to tickle and tremble, and soon the whole movement was reduced to comedy."

the United States, but they usually don't touch other aspects of British usage. Software programs that spot British spellings in word processing files are available.

As illogical and nonphonetic as English words can be, all proposals to reform spelling over the years have met with defeat, and even the simplest change in the accepted spelling of a word can arouse surprising passion.

THE "RULES" OF SPELLING

Almost everyone who has studied spelling remembers at least a couple of spelling "rules"—probably those that provide tips in mnemonic form, such as the jingle that begins "*I* before *e* except after *c*." The next thing people remember is that each so-called rule has exceptions. The exceptions, of course, are the "catch" that makes learning to spell considerably more than child's play. To add to the confusion, there is more than one "right" way to spell some words. Most publishers of newspapers, magazines, and books choose a particular dictionary as their authority and decide that the first spelling given is their preferred one. Today there is also a tendency to prefer the shorter or "less foreign" form of a word.

The words in this section probably appear on everyone's list of hard-to-spell words. Because they are relatively few, it may be simpler to learn the words themselves than to master a set of rules to cover them.

The first group is words that end in the "seed" sound. The *only* word that ends in *-sede* is *supersede* (a super spelling demon; it does not come from the same Latin root as the other "seed" words). Only three words end in *-ceed: exceed, proceed,* and *succeed.* The other words end in *-cede: concede, intercede, precede, recede,* and *secede.*

Next, the *-ery* ending is much rarer than *-ary.* Here are a few of the words that end with *-ery.*

adultery
beanery
celery
cemetery
confectionery
delivery
distillery
dysentery
eatery
millinery
monastery
stationery (writing materials)
winery

. . . TRY, TRY AGAIN

Back in 1974, the *Washington Post* stylebook called for the short spelling *employe* rather than the traditional *employee.* For years, the practice aroused readers' ire, as expressed in letters like the following.

> I find The Post's policy of misspelling "employee" as "employe" very irritating. To be consistent it should write of "a guarante of the safety of the soccer refere, who is fond of lyche nuts, was reported by the newspaper edited by Benjamin C. Bradle, who drinks coffe in the land of the fre."

In 1988, the newspaper capitulated and returned to *employee.*

THE TOP 50 MISSPELLED WORDS

Here we include our candidates for the 50 most commonly misspelled words. Not included are words that are troublesome pairs with similar spellings but different meanings—principle/principal, affect/effect, complement/compliment, stationery/stationary, and capital/capitol. Those words and others like them are explained in Chapter 2, Misused and Easily Confused Words.

accommodate
acknowledgment
argument
auxiliary
commitment
connoisseur
conscience
consensus
deductible
defendant
definitely
dependent
desiccate
embarrass
existence
exorbitant
fluorescent
forcible
foreword
grammar
harass
hygiene
hypocrisy
idiosyncrasy
inadvertent
indispensable
inoculate
jewelry
judgment
liaison
license
lightning
millennium
minuscule
occasion
occurrence
perseverance
personnel
prerogative
privilege
proceed
queue
rhythm
sacrilegious
separate
supersede
threshold
transferable
weird
withhold

The *-ar* ending is also rare. Here are a few of the small number of words that end with *-ar*.

basilar
beggar
binocular
bulbar
Bulgar
calendar (dates)
collar
dollar
jocular
lenticular
lobar
monocular
regular
singular
ventricular

Even someone who could spell every word in the dictionary would not "know" how to spell. Spellings change when singular forms become plural, when nouns or pronouns become possessive, and when prefixes or suffixes are attached to words. One of the obstacles to learning to spell the various forms may be the fact that (with the exception of prefixes) the rules deal with the *ends* of words. From "A is for apple" onward, people are more comfortable with how words begin than they are with how they end. The next sections offer some guidelines.

PLURALS

The plural of most nouns is easily formed by adding *-s*. If a noun ends in *-ch,-sh, -s, -x,* or *-z,* the plural is formed by adding *-es* (boxes, churches, fezes, flashes, gases). Adding *-es* also adds another syllable to the word and makes it easy for English speakers to pronounce. Note that verbs reverse this rule. The singular adds *-es* when the verb ends in *-ch*, *-sh*, *-s*, *-x*, or *-z*.

A few nouns form irregular plurals; most of them are so common that few people over 3 years old need to think about them—children, feet, geese, lice, men, mice, oxen, teeth, women.

Some nouns have the same form in both singular and plural (athletics, buffalo, chassis, corps, deer, ethics, moose, series, sheep, species, swine).

A WORD ABOUT SPELLING CHECKERS

A common perception today is that in a few years no one will need to know how to spell because computers will take care of spelling. It's certainly true that the spell-checking features available on most personal computers are useful aids. They do indeed catch many spelling errors as well as typos, and it is wise to use a spelling checker if one is available. But until spelling checkers can be combined with the sort of artificial intelligence that will enable the program to understand word usage, they will miss all of the myriad typos that result in words—and/an, not/now, the/they, etc. Nor can a computer recognize the incorrect use of a correctly spelled word—effect/affect, except/accept. And only by reading the text word for word is it possible to catch missing words or lines, errors that have become more commonplace with desktop publishing.

CAN YOU SPELL "MNEMONIC"?

Over the years, many have tried to devise simple rules or mnemonic devices to help the rest of us spell better. Unfortunately, English spellings originated from such diverse sources that no single "trick" comes without a string of exceptions.

One of the best devices is the *ie/ei* rule:

I before *e*
Except after *c*
Or when sounded like *a*
As in *neighbor* and *weigh*.

But it has several notable exceptions: deify, height, ancient, foreign, forfeit, heir, leisure, neither, seismic, seize, and sleight. To remember some of these, another device is available:

> The weird foreign heir seizes neither sleight leisure nor seismic pleasure at their height.

Confusion over the suffixes *-ible* and *-able* results in many spelling errors. Several have tried to come up with rules to simplify the choice, but most rules work so unreliably that a trip to the dictionary would be necessary just to see if the trick worked.

Most English words ending in *-ible* derive chiefly from Latin verbs that end in *-ēre*, *-ere,* and *-ire,* which form their Latin adjectives with *-ibilis—horribilis*. Many *-able* words come from Latin *-are* verbs by way of French and form their adjectives with *-abilis—mirabile dictu*. In French, the regular ending *-able* is used for adjectives derived from all Latin verbs. Today *-able* is a living suffix used for nearly all coined words—for example, readable, scannable, programmable, fixable.

There is one mnemonic, however, that is both foolproof and easy to remember: deductible takes an *i* as in IRS.

Nouns That End in -f *or* -fe

Most nouns form the plural simply by adding *-s* (dwarfs, puffs, roofs, safes), but there are quite a few exceptions.

calves	leaves	shelves
elves	lives	thieves
halves	loaves	wives
knives	selves	wolves

Nouns That End in -is

These nouns form the plural by changing *-is* to *-es.* Both these and nouns that end in *-ix* originated in Latin and have kept their Latin plural forms.

basis, bases
crisis, crises
ellipsis, ellipses
hypothesis, hypotheses
parenthesis, parentheses
thesis, theses

Nouns That End in -ix

Many nouns that end in *-ix* form the plural by changing the *-ix* to *-ces.* Dictionaries often give two acceptable plural forms for such nouns, but the trend is toward using the *-ixes* ending. In the case of *index,* the different plurals have different meanings.

appendix, appendices or appendixes
calix, calices
helix, helices or helixes
index, indexes (to books); indices (in math or science)
matrix, matrices or matrixes
radix, radices or radixes
thorax, thoraxes
vortex, vortices or vortexes

IS IT MICE OR MOUSES?

When the word *mouse* refers to something other than the common rodent, editors are sometimes puzzled about how to form the plural; with no better solution available than to rewrite in the singular, most editors have given in and now refer to more than one computer mouse as *mice.*

But other problems can and do arise. One of the editors of this book was briefly stumped when her two children both wanted an ice cream novelty called a Mickey Mouse. Being a conscientious editor, she couldn't bring herself to ask for "two Mickey Mice," but "two Mickey Mouses" also sounded wrong. So, as editors must often do, she "wrote" around the problem: "A Mickey Mouse for each child, please."

MUSICAL TERMS

Many musical terms came to English from Italian. Although words that end in *o* form the plural by adding *-i* in Italian, in English add *-s:* altos, cantos, cellos, concertos, falsettos, maestros, pianos, piccolos, solos, sopranos, virtuosos. Listen carefully at the next concert, opera, or ballet you attend, however, and you may hear some enthusiastic "Bravi!"

The plural of *axis* is *axes,* pronounced with a long *e* to distinguish it from the plural of *ax.*

Nouns That End in a Consonant Plus -o

The plural of most nouns ending in *-o* is formed by adding *-s.* Exceptions are listed below.

echo, echoes
hero, heroes
hobo, hoboes
potato, potatoes
tomato, tomatoes

Nouns That End in a Consonant Plus -y

These nouns form the plural by changing the *-y* to *-ies.*

county, counties
fly, flies
ditty, ditties
ecstasy, ecstasies
story, stories
tragedy, tragedies

Nouns That End in a Vowel Plus -y

These nouns form the plural by adding *-s.*

attorney, attorneys
boy, boys
money, moneys or monies
valley, valleys

An exception is the *qu-* combination, which is treated like a consonant in forming the plural.

colloquy, colloquies
soliloquy, soliloquies

Nouns of Foreign Origin

A number of foreign-derived words retain their original plural forms, although the tendency simply to add *-s* to the singular form grows stronger with the passage of time. For example, *memorandums* is cited in *Merriam-Webster's Collegiate Dictionary*, 10th edition, as the more common plural, although *memoranda* is also given. As the list below shows, the original spellings of plural forms are especially likely to be retained in scientific usage. A few plurals, like *data* and *media*, are often used as singular nouns; see Chapter 6, Subject-Verb Agreement, for further discussion.

addendum, addenda
alga, algae
alumna, alumnae (fem.)
alumnus, alumni (masc.)
antenna, antennas, antennae (zoology)
bandeau, bandeaux
bateau, bateaux
blin, blini
coccus, cocci
consortium, consortia
criterion, criteria
datum, data
desideratum, desiderata
equilibrium, equilibriums, equilibria (scientific)
erratum, errata
fungus, fungi
genus, genera
kibbutz, kibbutzim
larva, larvae
lira, lire
locus, loci
madam, mesdames
medium, mediums, media
minutia, minutiae
monsieur, messieurs
nucleus, nuclei
opus, opera (pronounced with a long *o* and three syllables)
phenomenon, phenomena

phylum, phyla
radius, radii
stimulus, stimuli
stratum, strata
symposium, symposia, or symposiums
terminus, termini, or terminuses
thesaurus, thesauruses, thesauri
vertebra, vertebras, vertebrae (zoology)

Plurals of Compound Terms

In compound terms, the most significant word—generally the noun—takes the plural form. The significant word may be at the beginning, middle, or end of the term. These compounds have the significant word at the beginning:

adjutants general
aides-de-camp
attorneys at law
billets-doux
bills of fare
brothers-in-law
charges d'affaires
chiefs of staff
coats of arms
commanders in chief
comptrollers general
courts-martial
crepes suzette
grants-in-aid
notaries public
rights-of-way
senators-elect
sergeants at arms

In these examples, the significant word is in the middle:

assistant attorneys general
joint chiefs of staff

When no single word is of great significance or when neither word is a noun, the plural is formed on the last word.

also-rans
come-ons
forget-me-nots
go-betweens
hand-me-downs
higher-ups
jack-o'-lanterns
pick-me-ups
run-ons
show-offs
tie-ins
will-o'-the-wisps

When a noun is joined with an adverb or preposition with a hyphen, the plural is formed on the noun.

comings-in
fillers-in
goings-on
hangers-on
listeners-in
lookers-on
passers-by

Nouns That End in **-ful**

These nouns form the plural by adding *-s.*

> I have several *armfuls* of clothing to contribute to the yard sale.
> Add five *bucketfuls* of sand to the cement.
> The recipe calls for two *cupfuls* of sugar.

Plurals of Abbreviations

Chapter 14, Abbreviations, explains how to form these plurals. The question of how to form plurals of abbreviations is largely stylistic, and authorities differ over whether to use an apostrophe before the *s*. Since the apostrophe plus *s* generally signals the possessive rather than the plural, this book recommends using only the *s* to form plurals of abbreviations, initialisms, and acronyms—HMOs, YMCAs, WASPs—but with the following exceptions to ensure clarity: abbreviations with periods (M.A.'s) and abbreviations that are single letters (A's) or all lowercase letters (rpm's).

Plurals of Numbers

Plurals of numbers are formed by adding *-s.*

> 1s and 2s
> 10s and 100s
> the 1890s

Plurals of Names

The plurals of proper nouns (names) are formed by adding *-s* or *-es*. The spelling of the name itself must be preserved, so the guideline for changing *-y* preceded by a consonant to *-ies* does not apply.

Charleses	Jerrys
Georges	Lees
Harrys	Marys
Jameses	

POSSESSIVES

The frequent errors seen with possessives probably arise from the fact that both the letter *s* and the apostrophe, which are used together to form possessives, pull double duty in English. As discussed above, *-s* is used to form plurals; the apostrophe is used to form contractions. Chapter 10, Punctuation, addresses possessives in detail.

PREFIXES

Prefixes usually cause few spelling problems. When a prefix is added to a root word, both the prefix and the root retain their original spellings, with no letters dropped or added.

dis + appoint = disappoint
mis + spell = misspell
trans + plant = transplant
un + named = unnamed

The chief spelling problem associated with prefixes is the question of when to use the hyphen. Some style guides recommend that a hyphen be used to avoid doubling a vowel (*anti-inflammatory*). But as words formed with prefixes become widely accepted, the hyphens tend to disappear. For this reason, it is not always necessary to hyphenate a prefix simply because the prefix ends in a vowel and the root word begins with the same vowel.

bio + optics = biooptics
re + elect = reelect

To avoid misreading, a few words formed with prefixes should retain their hyphens; for example,

multi-ply	re-sort
pre-position	un-ionized
re-creation	

A hyphen (or sometimes an en dash; see Chapter 10, Punctuation) is used between a prefix and a capitalized word or a number.

anti-American	pre–World War II
post-1918	pro-French

A hyphen is usually used when a prefix is added to a multiword term, although some styles and dictionaries recommend closing the prefix (see Chapter 16, Hyphenation and Compound Words).

non-alcohol-related dementia
non-English-speaking students
pre-school-aged children

The prefix *ex-* (meaning "former") takes a hyphen to distinguish its use from the many nonprefixed words that begin with the letters *ex*.

ex-champion
ex-senator
ex-spouse

SUFFIXES

Because suffixes are added to the ends of root words, they, like plural forms, can cause spelling changes. Indeed, the range of suffixes and the variety of spelling guidelines associated with them probably cause more spelling problems than any other area. This section offers some general guidelines for spelling words formed with suffixes. Some specific suffixes are covered in "Problem Suffixes," page 401.

Root Words That End in Silent -e

If the root word ends with a silent *-e* preceded by a consonant and if the suffix begins with a consonant, the silent *-e* is usually retained.

absolute, absolutely
complete, completely, completeness
hope, hopeful
nine, nineteen, ninety
sincere, sincerely
stale, staleness

If the root word ends with a silent *-e* preceded by a consonant and if the suffix begins with a vowel, the silent *-e* is usually dropped.

come, coming
deceive, deceivable, deceived, deceiving
dose, dosage, dosed, dosing
fame, famed, famous
love, lovable, loved, loving
size, sizable

Exceptions are *bingeing* and *singeing* (to distinguish from *binging* and *singing*).

If a root word ends in a soft *c* or *g* followed by a silent *-e,* the silent *-e* is usually retained before suffixes that begin with *a* or *o,* as well as before suffixes that begin with a consonant.

arrange, arrangeable, arrangement
courage, courageous
encourage, encouragement
knowledge, knowledgeable
notice, noticeable
peace, peaceable, peaceful

Two notable exceptions, in American but not in British English, are *acknowledgment* and *judgment.*

If the root word ends in a silent *-e* preceded by a vowel and if the suffix begins with a vowel, the silent *-e* is usually dropped before the suffix.

argue, argued, arguing
issue, issued, issuing
value, valuable, valuing

Here are a few exceptions:

canoe, canoeing
dye, dyeing (to distinguish it from *dying*)
eye, eyeing
hoe, hoeing

Root Words That End in Other Vowels

If the root word ends in *-ie* and if the suffix is *-ing*, the *-ie* is usually changed to *-y*.

die, dying
lie, lying
tie, tying

If a root verb ends in *-y* preceded by a vowel, the spelling usually does not change to form the past participle of the verb.

assay, assayed
play, played

Here are some exceptions:

lay, laid
pay, paid
say, said

If a word ends in *-y* preceded by a consonant and the suffix begins with *e*, the *-y* is usually changed to *i* before the suffix.

cry, cried, cries
deny, denied, denies
reply, replied, replies

Such words retain the *y* before the suffix *-ing*.

crying
denying
replying

Root Words That End in a Consonant

If a one-syllable word or a word that is accented on the last syllable ends in a single consonant and if the suffix begins with a vowel, the last consonant of the root word is usually doubled.

> beg, beggar, begging
> flat, flatten, flatter
> knit, knitter, knitting
> mad, madden, maddest
> admit, admitted, admitting
> control, controller, controlling
> recur, recurrence, recurring

An exception is *bus, bused, bussing*. Other exceptions are words that end in *-k, -v, -w, -x,* and *-y*, which do not double the final consonant.

> box, boxed, boxing
> dew, dewy
> display, displayed, displaying
> enjoy, enjoyed, enjoying
> fox, foxy
> sow, sowed

An exception to this exception is *rev, revved, revving*.

If a multisyllable word that ends in a single consonant is accented on a syllable other than the last, in preferred American spelling the final consonant is not doubled when a suffix is added.

> benefit, benefited, benefiting
> cancel, canceled, canceling (*but* cancellation)
> develop, developer, developing
> differ, different, differing
> model, modeled, modeling
> travel, traveled, traveling

Problem Suffixes

Of the large array of word-forming suffixes available in English, a handful cause most of the spelling problems. This section addresses the worst offenders.

-able *Versus* -ible. Every effort to provide useful guidelines for these suffixes founders in a sea of exceptions. The best approach is to look up the word in question.

-ally *Versus* -ly. Of these two adverb-forming suffixes, *-ly* is far more common. It can be added to most root words, including those that end in *-l* or silent *-e*, without changing the spelling of the root word.

complete, completely
definite, definitely
fundamental, fundamentally
immediate, immediately
monumental, monumentally
sincere, sincerely
useful, usefully

Exceptions are root words that drop the silent *-e* before *-ly*.

due, duly
true, truly
whole, wholly

Root words that end in *-ic* (or *-ics*) take the suffix *-ally*.

academic, academically
athletics, athletically
basic, basically
classic, classically
lyric, lyrically
magic, magically
mathematics, mathematically

One exception comes to mind: public, publicly.

-ance *Versus* -ence. These suffixes do not lend themselves readily to analysis. Only one useful guideline can be offered: If the root word ends in a vowel followed by *r* and if the last syllable is accented, then the suffix is *-ence*.

abhor, abhorrence*
confer, conference
infer, inference
occur, occurrence*
prefer, preference
recur, recurrence*
refer, reference

* Note: If the accent in the new form stays on the same syllable as in the root word, the *r* is doubled. If the accent shifts, the *r* is not doubled.

-efy *Versus* -ify. This is an easy one. Only four root words take the *-efy* suffix.

liquid, liquefy
putrid, putrefy
rare, rarefy
stupid, stupefy

-ise *Versus* -ize. The spelling *-ize* is used for most words in American English; obvious exceptions are *advertise, merchandise,* and *surprise.* British preference is *-ise,* even though, strangely enough, the *Oxford English Dictionary* calls for *-ize* in most cases.

ANGLICIZED AND FOREIGN WORDS

There is continual two-way traffic between English and other languages. English is swift to incorporate foreign words, but at the same time words of English origin are increasingly becoming part of the vocabulary of many world languages.

For the writer and editor, borrowed words raise two questions: Should the words be italicized, and should they retain diacritical marks? Chapter 11, Setting Off Words, Terms, and Names, addresses these questions. In general, the more widely used a foreign word becomes, the less need there is to italicize it. By the time a word appears in an American dictionary, italicizing not only is unnecessary but may seem somewhat pretentious.

The use of diacritical marks in borrowed words is more complex. Most modern languages written in the Latin alphabet use such marks; in only a very few cases, however, where confusion could result, does English retain them—*résumé* is one example. Diacritical marks also are not used in English transliterations of languages using nonromanized alphabets. Chapter 21, Foreign Languages, provides guidance on diacritical marks in several languages.

Editors also need to be aware of rules regarding spellings of foreign proper and place names. Articles and particles that form proper names can vary in treatment; see Chapter 28, Indexing, for more information. Each language also has its own rules for capitalization, punctuation, and word division (see Chapter 21, Foreign Languages, for guidelines).

16

HYPHENATION AND COMPOUND WORDS

HYPHENATION AND COMPOUND WORDS

The hyphen is used to show a connection, either between words or between the syllables of a word. The use of hyphens between syllables raises no controversy, although dictionaries differ on how some words are divided. The use of hyphens between words, however, always generates questions and debate. A well-placed hyphen can instantly clarify meaning for the reader; too many hyphens can be distracting and unnecessary. This chapter provides a few basic guidelines on both uses of the hyphen.

WORD DIVISION

Computerized Hyphenation

Gone are the days when human typesetters decided when and how to divide words at the ends of lines. Today's computers make those decisions in one of two ways: by using a dictionary built into the word processing or publishing software (usually the same dictionary used for the spelling checker) or by applying a program containing hyphenation rules, or algorithms.

These programs vary in the amount of control and customization available. Some let the user build a customized list of exceptions and additions, and most allow manual override and control over the degree of hyphenation, from the sparing hyphenation found in unjustified ("ragged right") columns to the frequent word breaks necessary in narrow-width text. Writers and editors should read the section on hyphenation in their word processing or desktop publishing software manuals to understand better the features and limitations of each program.

Examples of poor computer hyphenation are plentiful, especially in the daily press, where editors have little time to correct the computer's seemingly mindless decisions. Checking hyphenation in final copy is more impor-

HOW DICTIONARIES DIFFER

For the most part, American dictionaries divide words according to the way they are pronounced. But dictionaries don't always agree, probably because the pronunciation of distinct syllables is not always clear-cut (for example, *eighteen, performance, service,* and *atmosphere*). Some take the approach of retaining the appearance of the original root word; this is apparently the rationale of *The American Heritage Dictionary,* third edition, for specifying *eight-een* and *perform-ance*, whereas *Merriam-Webster's Collegiate Dictionary*, 10th edition, prefers to divide between consonants for those words—*eigh-teen* and *perfor-mance*. Over the years, dictionary editors and typesetters have established certain rules for word division (see this chapter for a summary of some of these rules) to take care of problems like this.

Most editors and proofreaders adopt a particular dictionary as their single authority for both spelling and hyphenation. But problems will arise if the dictionary built into their word processing, desktop publishing, or typesetting software conflicts with their dictionary of choice. One solution is to see whether the spell-checking or hyphenation software can be edited to reflect in-house preferences. If that is not possible, editors must either accept the computer's preferences or mark for manual word breaks to be made. It is usually best to keep manual breaks to a minimum because each changed word may cause the text to reflow, introducing the possibility of new hyphenation problems in the next version.

tant than ever simply because no computer program to date is perfect, especially for words that are spelled alike but pronounced differently—*pro-ject* and *proj-ect,* for example—or breaks that lead the reader to mispronounce the word—such as *capa-city* and *Wed-nesday.*

General Principles

In general, word divisions are made at syllable breaks, but not all syllables are appropriate places for word breaks; pronunciation, including avoidance of misleading pronunciation, and the appearance of the page should be the overriding factors. Here is a summary of some of the traditionally accepted hyphenation rules that many typesetters and dictionary editors follow.

- Short words—those of five letters or fewer—should not be broken if possible.

- One-syllable words *(fenced, jogged, prayer)* should not be broken.
- Words should not be divided at single letters, at either the beginning or the end of a line *(over, even, iris)*. End syllables of two letters should not be carried to the next line *(dowel, clinic, barker)*.
- Words, when possible, should be divided after prefixes and at the natural breaking point for solid compound words *(pre-cursor, lumber-yard, hand-kerchief)*. Also, when pronunciation allows, words containing Latin and Greek roots should be divided at those roots *(anti-biotic, petro-chemical, centi-meter, heli-copter)*.
- Hyphenated compound words should be broken only at the hyphen, although this is not always possible in narrow-width copy.
- Words should be divided between adjoining consonants *(eigh-teen, cinnabar, don-key)*; if a word has three or more consecutive consonants, keep one consonant with the preceding vowel *(dis-tribute, atmos-phere)* unless the break results in mispronunciation.
- Words ending in *-ing* are divided on the base word *(sing-ing, writ-ing)* except when the final consonant is doubled to form a participle *(referring, admit-ting, begin-ning)*. If the original verb ends in *-le,* one or more of the preceding consonants are usually carried over with the *-ing* *(puz-zling, whis-tling)*.
- Words of three or more syllables are divided on the vowel if pronunciation allows *(lati-tude, harmo-nize, demonstra-tor)*.

COMPUTERS AND HYPHENS, CONTINUED: AVOIDING MIDDLE-OF-THE-LINE WORD BREAKS

Most computer programs let the user hyphenate end-of-line words manually by offering choices within the hyphenation program; these hyphens are often referred to as "soft" hyphens and will disappear if revisions cause the text to reflow. "Hard" hyphens, on the other hand, result from using the hyphen key to place a hyphen; these hyphens are permanent and will stay with the word until they are deleted (compound modifiers are one example).

Most of us have seen published text that has words divided in the middle of a line; they look some- thing like this. This error is the unfortunate result of (1) poor proofreading or (2) someone's trying to override the computer's hyphenation program by using the hyphen key. For this reason, most publishers ask writers and editors not to worry about word division while the manuscript is in the word processing stage.

- Words ending in *-ible* and *-able* are broken before those suffixes except when the root word loses its original form when *-ible* or *-able* is added *(cita-ble, palpa-ble, negotia-ble).*
- These endings are never divided: *-ceous, -cial, -cient, -cion, -cious, -scious, -geous, -gion, -gious, -sial, -tial, -tion, -tious,* and *-sion.*
- Contractions should not be divided *(doesn't, couldn't).*
- Proper names should not be divided unless absolutely necessary, and a person's initials or an abbreviated title or part of a name (such as *Mr., Dr., III,* or *Jr.*) should not be separated from the name.
- Abbreviations are never hyphenated *(Ph.D., i.e.).*
- Numbers should not be divided, but when long numbers make division unavoidable, they should be divided at the comma, retaining the comma. Numbers should stay on the same line with abbreviated units of measurement *(640 MB)* and with symbols, such as degree signs *(72°F).*

A few hyphenation problems can be fixed only by editing the line or previous line to cause the text to reflow completely. This is usually a last resort, and proofreaders must be especially cautious when considering this step.

When looking at the final typeset page, proofreaders should also be aware of these typographic traditions:

- No more than two consecutive hyphens should fall at the ends of lines.
- The last word in a paragraph should not be divided; if the break is unavoidable, then the majority of the word should carry to the last line.
- The last word on a right-hand page should not be divided.

Hyphenation of foreign words should follow the rules for hyphenation in the language itself; this is discussed in Chapter 21, Foreign Languages. Writers and editors should be aware that foreign language modules for spelling and hyphenation are available in some high-end word processing and desktop publishing packages.

COMPOUND WORDS

Two or more words that express a single idea are called *compound words*. When these words work as nouns, their appearance, with or without hyphens, tends to be permanent; they can be found in a dictionary. These are words like *keyboard, softball, sister-in-law, six-pack,* and *redhead.*

When compounds work as adjectives, they can remain open, or unhyphenated; be joined in a single word; or be hyphenated. Some of these are called temporary compounds—we make them up as we go along—and they include unlimited combinations of modifiers like *raspy-voiced, reduced-sodium, passion-filled, nerve-jangling,* and *power-sharing.*

Many compound words evolve through three stages: from separate words (open compound), to words joined by a hyphen (hyphenated compound), to a single word (closed or solid compound). The more widely a compound is used, the more likely it is to evolve into a closed compound. Thus, *spaceship* has become a solid compound, while *moon rocket* is still open. In recent years, this evolution has often been quick; for many words, the hyphenation step is skipped entirely.

In general, the use of hyphens with *compound nouns* is not a source of confusion. If a compound noun is listed as closed in the dictionary, the hyphen is unnecessary. If it is listed as hyphenated, a writer shouldn't agonize over the matter. Such compounds are considered "permanent" in that their form has been accepted into the lexicon.

Compound modifiers—words used as adjectives—are another problem entirely. Trying to decide whether to hyphenate makes most writers and editors wish for a hyphen hotline. No dictionary can list all the possible combinations of adverbs, adjectives, participles, and nouns that can be used as modifiers. Style guides are likely to go to one of two extremes—some offer a handful of general principles and leave the writer to deduce particular usages; others try valiantly to cover every possible contingency—The *U.S. Government Printing Office Style Manual* offers 52 rules and a list of 9,000 words. The "general principles" tactic can leave a writer feeling insecure; the comprehensive approach may go to mindboggling lengths and still not cover the usage the writer has in mind. And a writer who finds a particular style guide congenial must realize that other style guides treat hyphens differently. As John Benbow said in *Manuscript and Proof* (1937), "If you take hyphens seriously, you will surely go mad."

This chapter attempts to strike a middle ground, with brief descriptions of the general principles followed by a chart showing frequently questioned compounds. There are few hard-and-fast rules; common sense and consistency within a manuscript should prevail.

Compounds That Don't Need Hyphens

Some words simply go together naturally. Even though they appear as two separate words, they are thought of as a unit: *post office, real estate, blood pressure, data processing, income tax, life insurance,* and *civil rights* are just a few. When used to form compound modifiers, these words rarely need hyphens, for their meaning is clear—*post office box, data processing center, life insurance policy.*

Compounds That Are Always Solid

Certain pairs of nouns and adjectives have acquired a distinct meaning. They are always seen together because they could mean something else when separated. These are words like *gentleman, cupboard, bookworm, bonehead, greenback, graybeard, hellbent, heartache,* and *handbag.* These words usually are spoken with equal stress on both parts. Most are found in dictionaries.

Compounds Formed with Verbs and Adverbs

As modifiers and sometimes as nouns, words like *runoff, holdup, setup,* and *breakdown* are written as one word.

> The *runoff* election is next Tuesday.
> The table *setup* pleased the conference attendees.

As verbs, however, they revert to their two-word form.

> Please *run off* the new mailing list for me.
> They *set up* the tables according to the manager's directions.

Compound Modifiers Formed to Promote Clarity

Writers who automatically insert a hyphen between unit modifiers may contend that, although not essential, the punctuation aids readability and enhances consistency. But frequent and unnecessary hyphenation can be distracting.

When a compound modifier consists of more than two words, hyphens can contribute to clarity. Conversely, they may also call attention to themselves and make the modifier look ungainly. When writing for a highly technical audience, many science and technical writers hyphenate sparingly to avoid hyphen overload (*high pressure liquid chromatography, nuclear magnetic resonance spectroscopy*). Even in nontechnical writing, a writer should pause before hyphenating modifiers like *balance of payments issue* and *cost of living index.* One rule of thumb is to ask whether a compound could have another meaning; consider *old furniture dealer. Old-furniture dealer* clarifies that the person being described deals in old furniture, whereas *old furniture dealer,* with no hyphen, may be indicating the person's age.

Nevertheless, a writer or editor who stops to consider whether to hyphenate should realize that the reader may also pause—and perhaps lose track of the writer's point in the process. In such cases, a hyphen may be needed to help the reader grasp the thought quickly and easily.

Most style guides agree that most modifiers formed with a present or past participle (a verb ending in *-ing* or *-ed*) should be hyphenated when they fall before the noun. Other combinations of adverbs, adjectives, and nouns are also traditionally hyphenated. Here are a few examples:

law-abiding citizen	fiery-tempered teenager
agreed-upon rules	fire-engine-red car
long-term contract	state-of-the-art computer
high-speed train	part-time employee
U.S.-sponsored resolution	12-inch-wide board
fire-resistant material	pale-faced boy

When these same compounds follow the noun they modify, however, they appear without a hyphen.

The material is fire resistant.
The board is 12 inches wide.
The new rules were agreed upon by the members.

Comparative and Superlative Forms of Adjectives

When comparative and superlative adjectives—usually words ending in *-er* or *-est*—are used with a modifier, hyphens are used. Examples are *highest-priced house, best-qualified person, longer-term impact*.

Adverbs: Very *and Words Ending in* -ly

Although a few style guides allow it, most editors do not hyphenate *-ly* words used as modifiers. Examples are *wholly owned subsidiary, publicly held stock,* and *radically new idea.* If the modifier includes the word *very,* most guides agree that no hyphen is used: *very respected author, very well known man.* Note that *well known* is not hyphenated in the last example even though it would be without *very* (a *well-known man*).

Proper Names Used as Modifiers

Most proper names used as modifiers are hyphenated when combined. Examples are *Mexican-American trade, Iran-Iraq war,* and *Dallas-Fort Worth area.* The hyphen indicates that both nouns carry equal value. Hyphens are not used when a proper noun is two words in its original form: *Latin American countries, Middle East conflicts, French Canadian companies.*

Sometimes the presence or absence of a hyphen takes on social or political overtones; the current preference for *African American* (without the hyphen) is an example, reflecting the desire of American citizens of

African ancestry not to be considered "hyphenated Americans." (See Chapter 1, Usage.) In fact, the absence of the hyphen in a term describing citizens of a certain ancestry has been used for years by French Canadians. In these uses, the words *African* and *French* are adjectives, not nouns of equal weight. One well-known authority, *Words Into Type* (1974), suggests that hyphenated terms such as Italian-American and Japanese-American should probably be reserved to refer to the ancestry of a person each of whose parents was born in a different country. Of course, words formed with prefixes—such as Anglo-American and Afro-American—are always hyphenated.

Foreign Phrases

Hyphens are not needed in foreign phrases used as modifiers unless the phrase is hyphenated in the original language; laissez-faire is one of the few exceptions. Many of these phrases are anglicized Latin words—bona fide, ad hoc, per capita, and ex officio.

Prefixes and Combining Forms

Only two prefixes are usually hyphenated: *self-* and *quasi-*. The prefix *ex-* is hyphenated with titles and occupational descriptions (for example, *ex-president, ex-teacher*). The following prefixes and combining forms are printed solid unless (1) they are combined with a capitalized word or (2) there is a possibility of two meanings or mispronunciation (for example, *un-ionized* and *unionized, re-cover* and *recover, re-creation* and *recreation,* and *multi-ply* and *multiply*). Also, a hyphen is sometimes used if the combination results in a double identical vowel (particularly two *i*'s) and is always used if it results in a triple consonant; check a current dictionary to be sure.

after	inter	post
ante	intra	pre
anti	intro	pro
bi	iso	pseudo
by	macro	re
co	meso	semi
contra	micro	step
de	mis	sub
demi	mono	super
extra	multi	trans
fore	neo	tri
hyper	non	ultra
hypo	off	un
in	out	under
infra	over	

When *non* or *un* starts off a three- or four-word modifier, it is often best to hyphenate those prefixes, for example, *un-self-conscious attitude* and *non-load-bearing wall.* The logical reason for this practice is that the prefix applies to the entire idea of the modifier, not just its first word. Some editors don't make this distinction, resulting in hard-to-read phrases like "an unself-conscious attitude" and "a nonload-bearing wall."

In the rare cases where they can't be avoided, duplicated prefixes should also be hyphenated: *sub-subheading, re-redesign.*

Suffixes and Combining Forms

These suffixes and combining forms are usually seen with their roots as one word:

-able	-less
-fold	-like
-ful	-ship
-gram	-ward
-hood	-wise

Modifiers Formed with Numbers or Letters

Numbers and letters used to form modifiers are usually hyphenated, although there are a few notable exceptions, including terms used in the possessive: *3 weeks' vacation* or *3-week vacation,* not *3-weeks' vacation.* Another exception is with amounts of money: *$10 million project,* not *$10-million project.* Other closed-up number forms include words ending in *-fold* or *-some* when numbers are spelled out: *threefold, foursome.*

Numbers expressed with two or more words (for example, *twenty-one*) and fractions (for example, *two-thirds*) are hyphenated whether standing alone or modifying a noun.

Numbers, whether spelled out or shown as numerals, are hyphenated when they form modifiers—a *48-inch ruler,* a *24-hour day,* a *four-in-hand tie,* a *sixth-grade teacher,* a *10-year-old child,* a *20-cent surcharge.* The number style followed determines whether words or figures are used; see Chapter 17, Numbers, for guidelines. Exceptions to this rule are modifiers using the word *percent*—a *5 percent increase,* not a *5-percent increase*—and large numbers spelled out *(two hundred sixty-four,* not *two-hundred-sixty-four).*

A general rule for letters used with modifiers is a little trickier. If the letter precedes the word, it is usually hyphenated—*A-frame, I-beam, T-square*—although there is wide disagreement on this point. If a letter follows a word, it is usually left open—*grade A milk, title IV grant, vitamin C tablet.*

Suspended Compounds

In "suspended compounds" such as the following, hyphens serve as placeholders for the omitted part of the compound.

> The school admits 3-, 4-, and 5-year-old children.
> I can afford a second- or third-class ticket.

The ability to hyphenate suspended compounds is not a license for overusing them. They force readers to pause and perhaps glance ahead to find the end of the compound, thus interrupting the flow of ideas.

A Final Word

The chart that follows attempts to cover the topics just discussed, as well as a few others. Of all the aspects of style, the most slippery is compounding, with fashions changing from year to year and disagreement among writers and editors commonplace. Perhaps the best that can be expected is that hyphens will be used consistently when they are necessary and avoided when unnecessary, that the reader's needs will be served, and that reason will be the ultimate guide.

GUIDE TO COMPOUNDING

TYPE OF COMPOUND	EXAMPLE	EXCEPTIONS	COMMENTS
Nouns			
Two nouns of equal value	stockbroker, database, football		Solid, as a result of common use
	city-state		Hyphenated, two equal titles or functions
	blood pressure		Open, words go together naturally
Family relationships	great-aunt, mother-in-law	grandfather, stepmother, half sister	Hyphenated, except with *grand* and *step*; open with *half*
Occupations	salesperson, congresswoman		Closed
Titles	attorney general, sergeant major, vice president, commander in chief		Open describing one function
	secretary-treasurer, soldier-statesman		Hyphenated describing dual function
Proper nouns	Baltimore-Washington corridor, Italian-American heritage, the Army-Navy game	Central American countries, Air Force procedures	Hyphenated as modifier except when original form has two words
	New Jersey–New York trains		Use en dash to connect two or more proper nouns, one of which has two words

GUIDE TO COMPOUNDING
(continued)

TYPE OF COMPOUND	EXAMPLE	EXCEPTIONS	COMMENTS
Possessives	bull's-eye, crow's-feet	menswear	Hyphenated with nonliteral expressions
Prepositional phrases	jack-in-the-box, grant-in-aid	next of kin, friend of the court	Hyphenated with three or more words that form a compound noun
Object with gerund	problem solving, decision making (noun)		Open used as noun
	decision-making, policy-making (adj.)		Hyphenated used as adjective
Technical measurement and chemical terms	light year, person hour, fiscal year, kilowatt hour, carbon dioxide		Open as noun
Nouns and adjectives formed with letters	A-frame, I-beam, T-square, V-neck, X-ray	grade A milk	Hyphenated except when letter follows adjective
Adjectives			
Adverb with participle	much-praised act, well-kept secret	wholly owned subsidiary, hardly touched food, very much liked man, longer than usual wait	Hyphenated with adverb and participle except *-ly* words, with the word *very*, and with three or more adverbs
Object with present participle	English-speaking nation, ear-splitting scream		Hyphenated
Colors	off-white paint, gray-blue dress, bluish-gray sky	bluish gray	Hyphenated as modifier; open when standing alone

TYPE OF COMPOUND	EXAMPLE	EXCEPTIONS	COMMENTS
Numbers and fractions	2-year loan, 1-inch margin, 40-odd dissenters, 4-, 5-, and 6-foot boards, two-thirds, twenty-five	2 inches wide, twofold plan, 20 percent discount, $10 rebate offer, 2 to 1 ratio	Hyphenated as modifier and with spelled-out numbers and fractions; open as noun, with *percent*, with money, with ratios; closed with *-fold*
	2-week vacation	2 weeks' vacation	Open with possessive
Scientific and medical terms	squamous cell carcinoma, birth control device, ammonium chloride, structural glucose polymer	carbon-12, 4-chloro-*m*-cresol	Open except with figures
Words starting with—			
all-	all-city champions		Hyphenated
cross-	cross-country skier, cross-stitched sampler, cross-sectional	crossbred species	Hyphenated except in certain technical terms
ex-	ex-teacher	ex officio, excommunicate	Hyphenated except when used in Latin phrase or as part of normally prefixed word
high-, low-	high-level meeting, low-wattage bulb	high school student, low maintenance vehicle	Hyphenated as modifier; open when meaning is clear
in-	inhouse rule, inpatient treatment	in-service	Usually closed

GUIDE TO COMPOUNDING
(continued)

TYPE OF COMPOUND	EXAMPLE	EXCEPTIONS	COMMENTS
Words starting with—(continued)			
large-, small-	large-scale drawing, small-size car	largemouth bass	Usually hyphenated
over-, under-	overrepresented group, underserved population		Usually closed; check dictionary
quasi-	quasi-governmental		Hyphenated
self-	self-conscious, self-restraint		Hyphenated
well-, ill-, better-, best-, little-, lesser-	well-made suit, ill-fated voyage, better-looking brother, best-selling book, little-known village, lesser-known politician	very well made suit	Hyphenated; open with additional modifiers; open when following verb *to be*; check dictionary for permanent compounds
first-, second-, third-, etc.	first-rate mind, second-ranking scholar, third-world issues		Hyphenated
Words ending with—			
-book	notebook, handbook	reference book	Usually closed
-elect	mayor-elect Jones		Hyphenated
-fold	twofold increase	20-fold increase	Closed with spelled-out numbers, hyphenated with numerals
-like	lifelike statue	Madonna-like presence; bell-like sound	Closed except with proper name and with triple consonant

TYPE OF COMPOUND	EXAMPLE	EXCEPTIONS	COMMENTS
Words ending with—*(continued)*			
-ly	happily married man, easily grown plant		Open in all cases
-wide	worldwide epidemic, statewide policy	London-wide blackout, Army-wide policy	Closed except with proper noun
Foreign phrases	ad hoc committee	laissez-faire, postmortem study	Open unless hyphenated in original language or listed as solid in dictionary
Words in quotation marks	"go for broke" mentality		Open
Phrases preceded by—			
very	very much admired woman		Open
already	already named opponent		Open
most	most loved child, most favored nation status		Open
less, least	least liked alternative, less expensive tour, least favorable terms		Open
ever	ever-faithful		Hyphenated
still	still-youthful		Hyphenated
Prepositional phrases	up-to-the-minute account, off-the-record statement		Hyphenated

17

NUMBERS

NUMBERS

The treatment of numbers in text is open to more variations than almost any other aspect of style, and writers and editors should always consider the needs of the reader when deciding on an approach. In less hurried times, people could linger over deciphering *two hundred seventy-five thousand votes* and reading about *twenty-five cent fares* and *thirty three-story* buildings. As the pace of life has quickened and the content of much that is published has become more technical, the trend is toward using numerals whenever they can be justified in almost any writing except the most formal.

This chapter provides a simplified approach to number style that writers and editors can use as it stands or as a basis for deciding on a style that suits the audience and the purpose, tone, and style of the manuscript; our approach is based on a system that uses numerals for numbers 10 and higher. Keep in mind, however, that in most "humanistic" or nontechnical text, as opposed to scientific, technical, and journalistic text, numbers are generally spelled out up to 100. Exceptions include any series of numbers that includes at least one with three digits and any thick clusters of numbers, whatever their size. The spelling out of numbers in this style extends to all approximate numbers, even very large ones, and all numbers in dialogue. Numerals are, however, usually used with *percent* and *million* and *billion*.

More important than the scheme used is the need for consistency in treatment of numbers. Consistency is an elusive goal, but one worth striving for, within reason. Just as readers are slowed down by large spelled-out numbers, so are they distracted by a mix of numerals and spelled-out numbers in the same sentence or paragraph: "It took people five or 10 minutes to realize what had happened," as many journalistic styles dictate.

The chart on the next page offers a quick reference to basic guidelines for number style; note that it reflects the approach taken in this chapter,

NUMBER STYLE QUICK-REFERENCE GUIDE

SPELL OUT NUMBERS ZERO TO NINE	**USE NUMERALS FOR NUMBERS 10 AND OVER**
Examples	*Examples*
eight children, one-time offer, nine applicants	49 states, 200,000 people, 4 million residents (spell *million, billion, trillion*)
ordinal numbers first to ninth	ordinal numbers 10th and above (21st birthday, 18th century, 13th edition)
Exceptions	*Exceptions*
Use figures—	Spell out at beginning of sentence or list item—Forty women helped; Nineteen ninety-nine will be a year to remember.
With numbers nine and below grouped for comparison in the same sentence or paragraph with numbers 10 and above—3 of 21 students, 9th and 12th grades	Spell out all numbers in dialogue—"Meet me in forty-five minutes."
With numbers preceding units of measure, symbols, and abbreviations—5-inch border, 8°C, 4 MB RAM, 5-mg dose	Spell out to clarify back-to-back modifiers—20 six-year-olds, 12 thirty-minute segments, 100 twenty-nine-cent stamps
With names of parts of books, series, tables, etc.—chapter 2, volume 7, row 9, grade 3	Spell out decades—the sixties *or* the 1960s *or* the '60s
With percentages—1 percent; mixed fractions—2½ years; decimals—1.3 times; and ratios—2 to 1	
With ages—2-year-old child, 9 years old	
With sums of money—4 cents, $5.25, $7 million	
With dates and times—6 hours, 3 weeks, 5-year plan, 21st century, *but* two centuries, five decades	

which uses numerals for numbers 10 and above. The text that follows expands on these guidelines and addresses many other aspects of number style, including alphabetization, plurals, and punctuation.

GENERAL GUIDELINES

The first general guideline is to spell out numbers zero to nine and use numerals for 10 and above, with certain exceptions and special treatments, as noted in the chart and explained in the following paragraphs.

Numbers Grouped for Comparison

If a sentence or paragraph compares numbers in a particular category—for example, the numbers of exhibitors in the sentence below—figures are used for all numbers in that category.

> Exhibitors from five states came to the fair: 23 from Illinois, 9 from Michigan, 7 from Idaho, 46 from Texas, and 12 from Kansas.

Adjacent Numbers

Numbers that would otherwise be numerals may be spelled out to clarify back-to-back modifiers.

> The movie was interrupted by fifteen 3-minute commercials.

Or:

> . . . 15 three-minute commercials.

But not:

> . . . 15 3-minute commercials.

A general rule of thumb in such cases might be to spell out the smaller number.

Beginning of a Sentence

Numbers that begin a sentence are always spelled out.

> Nineteen sixty-nine was a landmark year for the U.S. space program.
> One hundred twenty-three people responded to the questionnaire, but only 119 of the responses were valid.

Both sentences, of course, can easily be rewritten to avoid spelling out large numbers:

> The year 1969 was memorable. . . .
> A total of 123 people responded. . . .

THE LANGUAGE OF MATHEMATICS

Many writers and editors share a distaste for things mathematical. But by viewing math as a language of sorts, where numbers and symbols replace letters and symbols, we can begin to appreciate how math can provide us with fascinating glimpses into the natural world.

One of the most interesting mathematical phenomena is the Fibonacci series, in which the next number in a sequence of numbers is formed by adding the two previous numbers: 1, 1, 2, 3, 5, 8, 13, 21, and so on. In *Et Cetera, Et Cetera,* Lewis Thomas explains a few of the intriguing aspects of the series.

> . . . As the numbers increase, the relationship of each number to the following one begins to approach the irrational number 1.6180339. . . . The number 610, for example, is the fifteenth in the series (F15) and the next up is 987. Divide 987 by 610, you get 1.6180327. Further on, F26 is 121,393, followed by F27, 196,418; divide F27 by F26, you get 1.6180339 . . . , which is about as close to the "golden ratio" as you will ever get. Generations of mathematicians have speculated about the significance of this ratio, for it keeps turning up in unexpected places. It is the harmonious proportion of one length to another in the structure of the Parthenon, it describes the relationship of the spirals of seeds going clockwise in a sunflower compared with those going counterclockwise; it can be seen in the arrangement of fronds on a pine cone or chambers in a nautilus shell. . . . It may, indeed, represent the best way to pack things closely together in nature, when no other way will do.

Approximate Numbers

Approximate or round numbers follow the same guidelines as those for specific numbers.

> Her personal library contained almost 7,500 volumes.

When very large approximate numbers are mentioned—amounts in the millions, billions, trillions, and above—a figure is used, followed by the word *million, billion,* and so on.

> The federal deficit is approaching $5 trillion.

"Approximately" and "about" should not be used—they just don't make sense—when a specific number is known.

> *Incorrect:* About 143 people attended the lecture.
> *Incorrect:* He had approximately $753.47 in his account.
> *Correct:* He had $753.47 in his account.

Dialogue

Numbers in dialogue are spelled out.

> "Meet me under the clock in forty-five minutes," he whispered.
> "But this is the nineties!" she exclaimed.
> "I'll be there at twelve," he promised.

Exceptions are sometimes made for large amounts.

> "It'll cost you $250,000," she sneered.

Figures of Speech and Common Expressions

Numbers in figures of speech or certain common expressions are spelled out.

> Ten Commandments
> top ten
> Fourth of July
> Gay Nineties
> a fifty-fifty chance
> I wouldn't touch that with a ten-foot pole!

Ordinal Numbers

Ordinal numbers are treated the same as cardinal numbers. Spell out first through ninth, and use figures for 10th and above.

> He passed the bar exam on his fourth attempt.
> The 21st century is just a few years away.

In reference lists, footnotes, and tables, however, figures are usually used to save space.

> 2nd [or 2d] ed.
> 5th rev. ed.

Lists

Numbers that begin a sentence or phrase in a list are usually spelled out; see Chapter 13, Lists, page 317, for treatment of numbers in lists.

Alphabetizing Numbers

Numerals are usually alphabetized as if they were spelled out. (See Chapter 28, Indexing, for guidelines on alphabetization.)

Namibia in Transition
1970s: Time of Crisis
Noriega and the DEA

Plurals

Plurals of spelled-out numbers, like plurals of other nouns, are formed by adding *-s* or *-es*. No apostrophes are necessary.

The winning lottery ticket was two sixes followed by three eights.

Plurals of figures are also formed by adding *s*.

1920s
F-15s
1040s

Punctuation

Commas. In sentences containing the month, day, and year, commas are placed before and after the year.

President John F. Kennedy was assassinated on November 22, 1963, in Dallas, Texas.

In military and British usage, the day is given before the month and no commas are used.

The Persian Gulf War began on 2 August 1990.

If only the month and year are mentioned, no comma is used.

The highest average temperatures for the decade occurred in July 1978.

Commas are generally used with figures of four digits or more.

3,000
345,078
2,345,524

Obvious exceptions to this rule include years, page numbers, addresses, serial numbers, and phone numbers. Some technical publications do not use commas with four-digit numbers: 3400.

Certain styles, including some European styles and the American Medical Association style, use thin spaces rather than commas.

254 869
3 486 876

Neither commas nor spaces are used with binary numbers.

110010

Hyphens. Hyphens are used in compound modifiers with numbers.

8-foot ceiling
18-year-old student

A hyphen is used when spelling out numbers twenty-one through ninety-nine.

Forty-five days passed without a drop of rain.

Neither a hyphen nor the word *and* is used when spelling out numbers in the hundreds and thousands.

one hundred sixty applicants (*but* one hundred sixty-one)
two thousand five hundred cars

A hyphen is used to express fractions when they stand alone or are used as compound adjectives.

two-thirds
three-eighths
one-third red
two-tenths point

When *-fold* is used, a hyphen is required with a figure but not with a spelled-out number.

fourfold
20-fold

En Dashes to Show Inclusive Numbers. Where a range of numbers is indicated, as with years or page numbers, an en dash is used. A hyphen may be used when an en dash is not available, as in typewritten text. (See Chapter 10, Punctuation, for a complete discussion of en and em dashes.) Although the common element is often omitted from the second number—for example, pages 245–48, 1234–9—the preferred style is to include all numbers to ensure clarity.

1985–1993
pp. 9–10, 85–89, 101–150, 1362–1368
485–456 B.C.

Note that use of the en dash with numbers should be avoided in most formal writing.

from 1985 to (or through) 1994
between 1985 and 1993
Not: from 1985–1993 *or* between 1985–1993

Because it is unclear whether the hyphen means "from . . . to" or "from . . . through," this use should be avoided:

Incorrect: From 1978–1979 the crop yield was at a record low.

An en dash or a slash is used to indicate a fiscal year or a season that extends over two calendar years.

winter 1992–93 (*or* 1992/93)
fiscal 1978/79

Mathematical Expressions

See Chapter 19, Mathematical Expressions, for a complete discussion of punctuation with mathematical text.

Titles and Headings

Number style for book and chapter titles and subtitles, headings, and subheadings usually follows the style used in the text, although space limitations may dictate the use of numerals. In some publications, numerals are permissible at the beginning of a title or headline:

1980: The Cuban Boatlift

Book titles that contain years usually use numerals.

1984, by George Orwell
2081: A Hopeful View of the Human Future, by Gerard K. O'Neill
2001: A Space Odyssey, by Arthur C. Clarke

THE BEST PART OF ALGEBRA IS ITS ROOTS

In his entertaining book *Beyond Numeracy: Ruminations of a Numbers Man,* John Allen Paulos describes the discovery of algebra in the ninth century by Al-Khowarizmi, a Baghdad mathematician, from whose name our word *algorithm* comes. He wrote an important book on the subject called *Al-jabr wa'l Muqabalah,* from which our word *algebra* is derived. To our knowledge, no English word was ever spun off from *muqabalah.*

Names of Parts of Books

Figures are usually used with names of chapters, sections, series, tables and exhibits, and the like.

chapter 5	figure 4
row 10	volume 7

When the complete name of the chapter, volume, figure, and so on is included, the treatment is

Chapter 10, Conclusion
Figure 4, Effects of Moonbeams on Laboratory Rats

See Chapter 9, Capitalization, and Chapter 22, Parts of a Book, for further explanation.

Roman numerals are generally considered out of fashion for chapter and figure numbers, but they are sometimes helpful for differentiating volumes or parts of books (volume III, part I) from chapters (chapter 12).

SPECIFIC GUIDELINES

Units of Measure

Except in literary works and very formal writing, figures are used with units of measure.

3 miles	5 acres
1,000 pixels	6 gallons
17 kilometers	30 minutes
10 years	1 ounce

Ages. Ages of people and things are usually expressed in figures.

3-year-old child
9 months old
mid-40s

Abbreviations and Symbols. Figures are used with abbreviations and symbols.

73 m	75 V
5°C	9 MHz
5 bu	5′4″
23° latitude	

Note that the symbol is repeated with each number.

4″ × 6″

(See Chapter 18, Signs and Symbols, for details.)

METRIC CONVERSION CHART

	When you know	*You can find*	*If you multiply by*
Length	inches	millimeters	25
	feet	centimeters	30
	yards	meters	0.9
	miles	kilometers	1.6
	millimeters	inches	0.04
	centimeters	inches	0.4
	meters	yards	1.1
	kilometers	miles	0.6
Area	square inches	square centimeters	6.5
	square feet	square meters	0.09
	square yards	square meters	0.8
	square miles	square kilometers	2.6
	acres	square hectometers (hectares)	0.4
	square centimeters	square inches	0.16
	square meters	square yards	1.2
	square kilometers	square miles	0.4
	square hectometers (hectares)	acres	2.5
Mass	ounces	grams	28
	pounds	kilograms	0.45
	short tons	megagrams (metric tons)	0.9
	grams	ounces	0.035
	kilograms	pounds	2.2
	megagrams (metric tons)	short tons	1.1
Liquid Volume	ounces	milliliters	30
	pints	liters	0.47
	quarts	liters	0.95
	gallons	liters	3.8
	milliliters	ounces	0.034
	liters	pints	2.1
	liters	quarts	1.06
	liters	gallons	0.26

METRIC PREFIXES

Prefixes expressing numbers that are both larger than we can imagine and smaller than we can believe have become part of everyday language. Here's a quick translation table.

Large Numbers

Prefix	*Factor*	*Common Term*	*Symbol*
kilo-	10^3	thousand	k
mega-	10^6	million	M
giga-	10^9	billion	G
tera-	10^{12}	trillion	T
peta-	10^{15}	quadrillion	P
exa-	10^{18}	quintillion	E
zetta-	10^{21}	sextillion	Z
yotta-	10^{24}	septillion	Y

Small Numbers

Prefix	*Factor*	*Common Term*	*Symbol*
centi-	10^{-2}	one-hundredth	c
milli-	10^{-3}	one-thousandth	m
micro-	10^{-6}	one-millionth	μ
nano-	10^{-9}	one-billionth	n
pico-	10^{-12}	one-trillionth	p
femto-	10^{-15}	one-quadrillionth	f
atto-	10^{-18}	one-quintillionth	a
zepto-	10^{-21}	one-sextillionth	z
yocto-	10^{-24}	one-septillionth	y

Ten raised to the hundredth power—10^{100}, or a number with 100 zeros—is called a *googol*, a word suggested by the 9-year-old nephew of mathematician Edward Kasner. To get an idea of how large this number really is, consider that some physicists have speculated that there are 10^{87} electrons in the entire known universe. A googolplex is incredibly larger still—10^{googol}.

Percentages, Fractions, and Decimal Fractions

Percentages. Figures are used with both the percent sign in technical or tabular text and the word *percent.*

Results revealed that 1 percent of the subjects had symptoms of the disease.
Her blood alcohol content was 0.15%.

Fractions. Common fractions used alone, without a whole number preceding, are usually spelled out. Such common fractions include

one-half
three-quarters
one-eighth
two-thirds

The suffixes *-nds* and *-ths* are unnecessary.

Correct: 3⁄8 inch	9⁄32 inch	7⁄16 inch
Incorrect: 3⁄8ths of an inch	9⁄32nds	7⁄16ths

Figures are used to express mixed numbers. When available, *case* fractions (½, ¼) should be used instead of slashes and hyphens (3-3/4), the typewritten substitute for typeset fractions. Stacked fractions, along with many other typographic signs and symbols, are available in almost all word processing and desktop publishing programs.

The photo was enlarged to 2½ (or 2-1/2) times its original size.

When whole numbers and fractions are mixed, all numerals are used.

The book measured 6½ by 9 inches.

In formal writing, mixed-number fractions are spelled out.

The photo was enlarged to two and one-half times its original size.

Decimal Fractions. Figures are used with decimal fractions.

The typical American household has 1.9 persons.

In text that mixes decimals and whole numbers, a trailing zero is added to the whole numbers—2.9, 3.5, and 4.0. If any decimal number is less than one, a leading zero is added—0.2. However, if the quantity will never be greater than one, as is the case with probabilities, the zero is not added.

$p < .01$
.45 caliber

Ratios, Proportions, and Odds

Except in formal writing in which most numbers are spelled out, figures are used to express ratios, proportions, and odds.

The proportion is 7 to 2.
The horse was favored by odds of 9 to 1.

EARLY UNITS OF MEASURE

Early measurements were based on different parts of the human body. A cubit was the distance from the elbow to the middle fingertip; a fathom the distance from fingertip to fingertip of a sailor with outstretched arms. Because sailors obviously varied greatly in size, such measurements were based on the reigning monarch.

The foot was literally the length of Charlemagne's foot, an imposing man both in legend and in fact. The yard was the distance from King Henry I's nose to the tip of his outstretched thumb.

The problem with these units of measurement was that they were hardly fixed and universal. By the late 1790s the French proposed a more convenient and objectively based form of measurement—the metric system.

The idea behind the metric system is to have just a few base units from which all other units are derived. The French decided to set the base for the unit of length as one ten-millionth of the distance, at the earth's surface, from the North Pole to the equator. This unit was called a *metre*, from the Greek word *metron*, meaning "a measure." By 1799, after several years of surveying, initial standards were set for several base units, and the French government took on the challenge of persuading other nations to adopt the system.

Use of a colon to express ratios and odds—70:1—is found only in informal or technical writing.

Currency

Except in some literary works and other formal writing, figures are used to express currency.

$5 (*but* five dollars, if spelled out)
75¢ *or* 75 cents *or* $0.75 (if dollar amounts also appear)
$14,500
$120 million

If there is a mixed dollar-and-cent figure in a paragraph, all other references to currency should take the same format. For consistency, trailing zeroes should be added to any whole numbers, and amounts less than one dollar should be preceded by a dollar sign and a zero before the decimal point.

His grocery bill totaled $126.98. The lettuce was a bargain at $0.59, but the prime rib cost $35.00.

7/4/94 OR 4/7/94?

Not only is the format *7/4/94* considered too informal for most published material, but it also can lead to confusion. Depending on the style you or your readers are used to, it could be read as either July 4, 1994, or April 7, 1994.

Americans are accustomed to seeing dates in month-day-year format. However, military and British styles reverse the day and month, using day-month-year order. So does Continental style, which is 4.vii.94 for 4 July 1994 (the *vii* stands for the seventh month).

In foreign currencies, a space appears between the abbreviation and the number except when a symbol is used.

Fr 25 million
DM 406.86
US$55
Can$15
£55

Most almanacs list standard abbreviations for foreign currencies.

Periods of Time

Dates. The day of the month is treated as a cardinal number unless the month is not mentioned.

February 21
But: on the 21st

Decades and Centuries. When specific years are mentioned in a paragraph, any references to decades should take the same form.

We were married in 1962, our daughter was born in 1966, and we moved to France in 1968. The 1960s were years of great change for us.

When specific years are not mentioned, references to decades may take one of three forms; consistency of treatment is important.

The seventies [*or* 1970s *or* '70s] were a time of crisis in American society; the eighties [*or* 1980s *or* '80s (in informal uses)] were calmer days.

Note that *eighties* is lowercase. Decades are capitalized only when they form a term such as Roaring Twenties.

Following the general guidelines for numbers, references to decades and centuries nine and below are spelled out; figures are used for those 10 and above.

15 centuries
two decades
mid-18th century
ninth century

Eras. Figures are used with era designations.

A.D. 72
25 B.C.

Time of Day. When the exact time is specified, figures are used. The designations *a.m.* and *p.m.* are usually set lowercase, with periods and no space between the letters; they may also be set in small capital letters (A.M., P.M.).

The class begins at 7:30 a.m.
The launch is scheduled for 11:42 a.m. EST.

In literary works and formal writing, the time of day is usually spelled out when referring to the hour, half hour, or quarter hour. No hyphens are necessary.

He crossed the border at quarter to seven and reached Vienna by eleven thirty.
She'll be home in half an hour (*or* in a half hour).

When time of day is already evident from the context of the sentence, it is not necessary to add *in the evening,* or *p.m.*

When referring to 12 a.m. or 12 p.m., eliminate confusion by specifying 12:00 noon or 12:00 midnight.

When *o'clock* is used, the hour is spelled out and *a.m.* or *p.m.* is omitted.

nine o'clock

Twenty-four-hour Time. No punctuation is used to separate the hours and minutes of 24-hour time.

1430
0800

ROMAN NUMERALS

I	1	XVIII	18	DCCC	800
II	2	XIX	19	CM	900
III	3	XX	20	M	1000
IV	4	XXX	30	MC	1100
V	5	XL	40	MCC	1200
VI	6	L	50	MCCC	1300
VII	7	LX	60	MCD	1400
VIII	8	LXX	70	MD	1500
IX	9	LXXX	80	MDC	1600
X	10	XC	90	MDCC	1700
XI	11	C	100	MDCCC	1800
XII	12	CC	200	MCM	1900
XIII	13	CCC	300	MM	2000
XIV	14	CD	400	MMM	3000
XV	15	D	500	$M\overline{V}$	4000
XVI	16	DC	600	$\overline{V}$	5000
XVII	17	DCC	700	$\overline{V}M$	6000

Note: A line over the top of a roman numeral indicates that the original value is multiplied by 1,000.

Roman Numerals

Roman numerals, especially those expressing numbers over 20 (XX), are considered somewhat pretentious and are best avoided except in part and volume titles and in front matter page numbering. Large numbers expressed in roman numerals are hard to interpret, and it's been claimed that producers often use them in copyright dates to obscure the age of a film. The chart above can be used to translate or interpret dates, page numbers, and Super Bowl designations.

Family Names. When capital roman numerals are used in family names, no comma separates the number from the surname.

Robert Banks Smith III

Personal preference may dictate this treatment:

Robert Banks Smith 3rd (*or* 3d)

Possessives of these surnames are formed as follows:

Robert Banks Smith III's (or 3rd's) company (singular)
the Robert Banks Smith IIIs' (or 3rds') home (plural)

Monarchs. Capital roman numerals follow the names of monarchs, emperors, popes, and sovereigns.

Elizabeth II
Henry VIII
Pope Paul VI

Addresses

Streets. Common sense and general local usage may dictate whether to use figures or spell out street numbers; as a general rule, spell out numbered streets of nine and below, and use ordinal or cardinal numbers (a more recent trend) for streets numbered 10 and higher.

222 Third Avenue
234 West 73rd Street *or* 234 West 73 Street
But: 813 Forty-fourth Street (to avoid confusion that could result from adjacent numerals)

Buildings. Occasionally the name of the building is also its address, in which case the number should be spelled out.

Ten Dupont Circle
One Place de Lafayette

Room numbers, suite numbers, and the like are expressed in numerals.

Suite 200
Room 7659
Apartment 306

Highways. Federal, state, county, and local highways and road numbers are expressed in numerals.

I-410
County Road 34
U.S. 40

Organization Names

Military, Governmental, and Political Designations. Numbers that form the names of military, governmental, and private organizations follow the general guidelines for ordinal numbers.

IF WE STAY ON ROUTE 66, WE'LL NEVER GET TO CANADA

When the interstate highway system was established, the American Association of State Highway and Transportation Officials designated odd numbers for interstate routes generally running north and south and even numbers for routes running east and west.

West Coast roads have the lowest odd numbers. For instance, I-5 runs from San Diego in southern California to Vancouver; on the East Coast, I-95 runs north and south between Maine and Florida.

Roads in the south have the lowest even numbers. Route I-4 runs between Tampa on the west coast of Florida and Daytona Beach on the east coast. The highest even-numbered road is I-94, which runs in the northern tier of states from Michigan to Montana.

The main routes of the interstate system have one- and two-digit numbers. Three-digit route numbers, such as I-395, I-380, and I-505, are given to roads in metropolitan areas. These are roads that connect to main routes; for example, I-395 connects to I-95.

Third Congress *but* 110th Congress
Fifth Army *but* 49th Battalion
Third Ward *but* 14th Precinct
Fourth Circuit Court *but* Court of Appeals for the 11th Circuit Court

Churches. When a number is part of the name of a church, the number precedes the name and is spelled out.

First Baptist Church

Lodges and Unions. To indicate the particular number of a lodge or union branch, an arabic numeral follows the name.

Local Mine Workers No. 16
American Legion Post No. 3245

Telephone Numbers

For seven-digit phone numbers, a hyphen separates the first three digits from the last four.

365-8764

When the area code is added, four choices are acceptable:

999-555-8740
(999) 555-8740
999/555-8740
999.555.8740

No. or #

If the word *number* is abbreviated, *no.* is preferred to the sign for number (#). If it appears at the beginning of the sentence, *Number* is spelled out.

My insurance policy is no. A-78590-BC-8765.
Number UT-580597 has been changed to no. UU-580597.
D&C Red No. 36 has been approved for general use in drugs.

Sports Scores and Voting Results

Figures are used to report sports scores and voting results. As the comparative term, *to* is more formal; when *to* is not used, however, an en dash is preferred over a hyphen.

The Packers beat the Bears 24 to 3 (*or* 24–3).
She scored 87 out of a possible 110 points.
The vote was 23 to 2 (*or* 23–2) in favor of the amendment.
Jones, with an 8 handicap, easily birdied the par 3 tenth hole.

18

SIGNS AND SYMBOLS

SIGNS AND SYMBOLS

A *symbol* is a notation representing elements, relations, quantities, operations, or qualities; it can be a letter or letters, a character, or a sign. A *sign* is a notation other than a number or letter of the alphabet.

In nontechnical documents, signs and symbols are usually limited to illustrations, tables, lists, and other graphic aids. Symbols are almost always acceptable in technical text, but writers and editors should take care to define at first mention any signs or symbols that the reader may not know or that may have different meanings in different fields. Lists of commonly used signs and symbols follow; style guides and dictionaries for specialized fields usually provide detailed lists of signs and symbols.

COPYRIGHT AND TRADEMARK SYMBOLS

Copyright and trademark symbols are often misused and misunderstood. One frequent editorial concern is the proper way to format the copyright notice. According to the U.S. Copyright Office, the correct way is to place first the symbol © (which is preferred, although the word *copyright* or the abbreviation *copr.* is also acceptable), immediately followed by the year, the word *by,* and the name of the copyright holder:

© 1994 by The Stonesong Press, Inc.

In newspaper and magazine articles, the copyright notice usually appears at the end of the piece. In books, the notice usually appears on the back of the title page (see Chapter 22, Parts of a Book, for details; see Chapter 23, Copyright, for an explanation of copyright law).

Trademarks are used to distinctively identify a business' products or services. A trademark can be a word, a symbol, a logo, a design, or any combination of these. Three symbols are used: ® means that the trademark is registered with the U.S. Patent and Trademark Office; ™ and ℠ (service mark) are used when a trademark (for a product) or a service mark (for a service) is not registered; registration is not required for protection under the law. These marks are not interchangeable, and the owner's use, as shown on packaging or in written product materials, should be followed.

When writers and editors use the names of trademarked products in their own manuscripts or publications, however, they do not have to use the trademark symbol—the only requirement is to capitalize the term. In their own advertising and publications, however, companies almost always use the trademark symbol to reinforce publicly the fact that those names and products are their property. Chapter 9, Capitalization, provides a list of common trademarks.

SYMBOLS USED WITH NUMBERS

Such symbols as the percent sign and the degree sign are generally used only in tables, graphics, and technical text; the spelled-out form is used in most general writing—*a 20 percent increase*.

The two most common style concerns are whether to use a space between a number and a sign or symbol and whether to repeat a sign or symbol with a pair or series of numbers—for example, *15 to 20%* versus *15% to 20%*. The following paragraphs describe the usual practice in most publications.

Percent Sign

When used in technical text, the percent sign (%) is placed directly next to the number, and the sign is repeated in pairs of numbers or numbers in a series.

1%
15% to 20% (or 15%–20%)
20%, 30%, and 40%

When a percentage is used as a unit modifier, no hyphen is necessary.

a 50% drop in revenue
a 10% to 15% increase in prices (or an increase of 10% to 15%)

Decimals, not fractions, should be used with the percent sign.

8.37%
0.25%

SIGNS FROM THE PAST

Most signs and symbols have interesting origins; here are the stories behind a few.

The percent sign (%) had an early form that looked like this: N°/c, which was derived from the Italian *numero per cento,* or "to this number in a hundred." Over time, the *c* turned into an *o* and the *N* was dropped, resulting in °/o or %.

The ampersand (&) is derived from the Latin word for *and,* which is *et.* The symbol is formed by entwining a cursive capital *E* and a lowercase *t.* As William and Mary Morris explain in the *Dictionary of Word Phrases and Origins* (Harper & Row, 1977), British schoolchildren traditionally included the symbol for the word *and* at the end of their recitation of the alphabet, saying "X, Y, Zed *and per se* [meaning "by itself"] *and.*" Those words eventually were run together, resulting in *ampersand.*

The pound sign (#) is derived from the abbreviation *lb.*, which can be traced back to the Italian word *libbra,* which came from the Latin *libra* meaning "balance" and was a weight just about equal to the avoirdupois pound in England. An early form of the abbreviation included a line drawn under *lb,* which later moved toward the top of the abbreviation and eventually became the hatchmark we use for both pound and number today.

The dollar sign, used for U.S. and several other nations' currencies, was first used with Spanish currency that Americans called the "Spanish dollar." This silver coin was minted in the West Indies and used by the Spaniards in the Americas in the 1700s. It was well-known to the American colonists, who referred to the coins as pieces of eight because they bore the numeral 8, referring to its equivalence to eight Spanish reals.

Thomas Jefferson proposed using the dollar as the basis for U.S. currency both because it was a term already familiar to U.S. citizens and because he wanted to avoid using anything resembling the British pound. The first U.S. dollar was minted in 1794.

Its evolution as a symbol went like this: 8° /8/ 8/ $/ $ $

By a fortunate coincidence, the dollar sign looks as if it could have been formed by superimposing the letters *U* and *S,* giving the sign a particularly patriotic meaning.

Degree Sign

When used to express temperature, the degree sign is placed between the number and the symbol *F* or *C;* no spaces are used.

32°F
23°C

In a pair or series, the degree sign (but not the F or C) is repeated with each number.

68° to 72°F
25°, 29°, and 32°C

Monetary Signs

Currency signs are always placed directly next to the number, either before or after, depending on customary usage.

$500
59¢
£150

A space is left after most foreign currency abbreviations, however.

Fr 49 (French francs)
DM 200 (German deutsche marks)
But: Can$2,400
US$5,000 (use *US* only when clarity requires)

The *U.S. Government Printing Office Style Manual* and *The American Heritage Dictionary*, third edition, each provide an extensive list of foreign currency signs.

The sign is repeated with each number in a pair or series, and no hyphens are used when a range of monetary amounts is used as a compound modifier.

$100 to $150
the $190,000 to $220,000 price range

Chapter 17, Numbers, offers guidance on when to spell out monetary signs.

Units of Measurement

In technical and tabular text it is acceptable to use the signs for inches and feet. Again, the sign is placed directly next to the number and repeated with each number, and hyphens are not needed when such measurements are used as unit modifiers. When the symbol for *by* (× or x) is used, a space is left on either side.

8½″ by 11″ *or* 8½″ × 11″ *or* 8½″ x 11″
11″ by 17″ paper
12′ by 22′ room

When the symbol × is used to show degree of magnification, the symbol is placed next to the number: a 3× lens. To indicate "crossed with" to show breeding in biology, a space is left on either side of the symbol: Early June × Bright.

Mathematical Signs

Spaces are placed on either side of mathematical signs.

1 + 2 = 3
4 × 10 = 40
50 ÷ 10 = 5
10,000 ± 1,000

See Chapter 19, Mathematical Expressions, for information on typographical treatment of equations.

SYMBOLS FOR THE 21ST CENTURY?

The explosion in home and business personal computers has brought with it an entirely new set of informal symbols, developed starting in the 1980s by users of electronic bulletin boards and electronic mail. Called *smileys* or *emoticons,* they are symbols made up of punctuation marks and other characters to evoke the emotions used in spoken communication on the computer screen. One of the most prevalent is a sideways version of the 1970s smiley face, :-). There are hundreds of variations; *Dvorak's Guide to PC Telecommunications* has a four-page list of such symbols.

COMMON SIGNS AND SYMBOLS

General

The first four symbols shown in the next list can be used to denote footnotes in text and tables; they are placed in the order shown and may be doubled or tripled if more symbols are needed. For ease of readability, however, it may be best to replace symbols with numbers or letters if many footnotes are used.

*	asterisk	™	trademark
†	dagger	®	registered trademark
‡	double dagger	℠	service mark
§	section	℞	prescription
¶	paragraph	℅	care of
•	round bullet	*f*	function
■	square bullet	¢	cent
@	at, each	$	dollar
©	copyright	£	pound
		¥	yen

Chemical Elements

The symbols for chemical elements are used without periods in text, tables, equations, and formulas. Inferior numbers are used after the symbol of the element to denote the number of atoms in a molecule: H_2O.

In international use, the mass number is placed to the left of the symbol in a superior position: ^{14}C, ^{235}U. Also permissible are uranium 235, U-235, or U^{235}.

Ac	actinium	C	carbon
Ag	silver	Ca	calcium
Al	aluminum	Cb	columbium
Am	americium	Cd	cadmium
Ar	argon	Ce	cerium
As	arsenic	Cf	californium
At	astatine	Cl	chlorine
Au	gold	Cm	curium
B	boron	Co	cobalt
Ba	barium	Cr	chromium
Be	beryllium	Cs	cesium
Bi	bismuth	Cu	copper
Bk	berkelium	Dy	dysprosium
Br	bromine	Er	erbium

Es	einsteinium
Eu	europium
F	fluorine
Fe	iron
Fm	fermium
Fr	francium
Ga	gallium
Gd	gadolinium
Ge	germanium
H	hydrogen
Ha	hahnium
He	helium
Hf	hafnium
Hg	mercury
Ho	holmium
I	iodine
In	indium
Ir	iridium
K	potassium (kalium)
Kr	krypton
La	lanthanum
Li	lithium
Lr	lawrencium
Lu	lutetium
Md	mendelevium
Mg	magnesium
Mn	manganese
Mo	molybdenum
N	nitrogen
Na	sodium (natrium)
Nb	niobium
Nd	neodymium
Ne	neon
Ni	nickel
No	nobelium
Np	neptunium
O	oxygen
Os	osmium
P	phosphorus
Pa	protactinium
Pb	lead
Pd	palladium
Pm	promethium
Po	polonium
Pr	praseodymium
Pt	platinum
Pu	plutonium
Ra	radium
Rb	rubidium
Re	rhenium
Rf	rutherfordium
Rh	rhodium
Rn	radon
Ru	ruthenium
S	sulfur
Sb	antimony (stibium)
Sc	scandium
Se	selenium
Si	silicon
Sm	samarium
Sn	tin
Sr	strontium
Ta	tantalum
Tb	terbium
Tc	technetium
Te	tellurium
Th	thorium
Ti	titanium
Tl	thallium
Tm	thulium
U	uranium
V	vanadium
W	tungsten (wolfram)
Xe	xenon
Y	yttrium
Yb	ytterbium
Zn	zinc
Zr	zirconium

Mathematics

$+$	plus
$\pm\!\!\!+$ (++)	double plus
$-$	minus
$\pm$	plus or minus
$\times$	multiplied by (or •)
$\div$	divided by
$=$	equal to
$\neq$	not equal to
$\approx$	approximately equal to
$\equiv$	identical with; congruent
$>$	greater than
$<$	less than
$\not>$	not greater than
$\not<$	not less than
$\geq$	greater than or equal to
$\leq$	less than or equal to
$\lesseqgtr$	less than or greater than
$\not\equiv$	not equivalent to
$\gg$	much greater than
$\ll$	much less than
$\rightarrow$	approaches a limit
$\simeq$	asymptotically equal to
$\cong$	congruent to
$\approx$	approximately equal to
$\sim$	proportional to
$\subset$	included in
$\supset$	excluded from
$\cup$	union
$\cap$	intersection; logical product
$\in$	is an element of
$\notin$	is not an element of
$\varnothing$	null set
$!$	factorial
$\perp$	perpendicular to
$\vdash$	assertion
$\parallel$	parallel
$\nparallel$	not parallel
$\angle$	angle
$\measuredangle$	angle
$\llcorner$	right angle
$\veebar$	equal angles
$\triangle$	triangle
$\frown$	arc
⌓	sector
⌓	segment
$\bigcirc$	circle
O	ellipse
$\varnothing$	diameter
$\square$	square
▭	rectangle
⊞	cube
▱	rhomboid
⬠	pentagon
⬡	hexagon
$:$	ratio
$\therefore$	therefore
$\because$	because
$::$	proportion
∞	infinity
$'$	prime; minute
$''$	double prime; second
$'''$	triple prime
$\sqrt{\ }$	square root
$\sqrt[3]{\ }$	cube root
$\surd$	radical
e	base of natural logarithm
Σ	summation
Π	product
$\int$	integral
$\oint$	contour integral
⌠ (horizontal)	horizontal integral
∂	partial differential; round dee
Δ	delta
∇	nable; del
h	Planck's constant
k	Boltzmann constant
δ^i_j	Kronecker delta
$\mid\ \mid$	absolute value

19

MATHEMATICAL EXPRESSIONS

MATHEMATICAL EXPRESSIONS

One of the most difficult and tedious copyediting tasks is marking mathematical expressions for the typesetter. Mistakes are easily made, from misreading an author's handwritten symbols to overlooking a closing bracket or parenthesis in a complex formula.

Until the late 1970s, most mathematical copy had to be typeset in Monotype. Each character was set as a separate piece of metal type, and corrections had to be made by hand. In the past 20 years, phototypesetting systems have automated this task, but until recently typesetters experienced with mathematical copy were still setting most of this type. Today, however, "equation editors" are available on desktop publishing and word processing programs, giving anyone with the software—and the willingness to learn—the capability to create complex equations. Because so many more people are setting type today, copyeditors need to be even more careful to mark mathematical copy clearly and thoroughly to keep typesetting errors to a minimum.

This chapter explains, in a general way, how these systems work; suggests ways to ensure clarity and accuracy; and provides an overview of the principles and conventions of editing and typesetting mathematical copy. For a more detailed explanation of this subject, readers are referred to *Mathematics into Type* by Ellen Swanson (American Mathematical Society, 1979).

SELECTING, DEFINING, AND USING SYMBOLS

A symbol is a letter of any alphabet or any special character used to represent a quantity, operation, element, quality, or relation. Symbols are the building blocks of mathematical expressions. Editors must make sure that symbols

THE LANGUAGE OF MATH

Here are brief definitions of the terms used in this chapter:

array. Mathematical elements arranged in horizontal rows and vertical columns

built-up equation. An equation with fractions in which horizontal rules are used to show division

collapsed equation. An equation with fractions in which a solidus (or slash) is used instead of a horizontal rule to show division

collective signs. A term describing a group of mathematical symbols including summation Σ, union ∪, product Π, and integral ∫

determinant. A square array enclosed by vertical rules

displayed equation. An equation that is usually centered and is set off from the text by extra space above and below it

elision. A series of three ellipsis points indicating omission within a mathematical expression

embellishment. Dots, bars, tildes, or other accent marks used to distinguish a symbol

entries. Mathematical elements in a matrix

exponent. A superscript symbol to the right of a mathematical expression; the exponent indicates raising to a power

fence. Signs used primarily to group elements of an equation, including {[()]}; also called *sign of aggregation*

indices. Numbers or symbols that are superscript or subscript

matrix. A square or rectangular array enclosed in brackets (sometimes parentheses)

multilinear equation. An equation that extends over more than one line

nomenclature. A list of symbols defined in a glossary format

operator. A mathematical function that links mathematical expressions

radical. An expression that indicates a root by means of a radical sign

sign. A symbol that is not part of an alphabet

signs of aggregation. See *fence*

solidus. A diagonal rule, or slash, used between the numerator and the denominator of a fraction

subscript. A sign or symbol placed below the line in a smaller type size

superscript. A sign or symbol placed above the line in a smaller type size

tensor. A generalized vector with more than three components

vector. A quantity that has magnitude and direction

are used correctly and consistently throughout the manuscript. To help both readers and the manuscript's editor, authors should take care to

- Select symbols that reflect the standard usage in the particular field
- Define symbols carefully
- Use symbols consistently, being careful not to abbreviate in some places and spell out in others or to use different modifiers to denote the same meaning

Selecting Symbols

When authors select a symbol, they choose a letter of an alphabet, usually the first letter of the quality or quantity being represented (e.g., P is often used to represent pressure). This is often known as the *base* or *stem*. Authors then choose subscript or superscript numbers or letters to serve as "modifiers" that further describe the quality or quantity being represented (e.g., P_{max} represents maximum pressure).

Although an author generally has a great deal of freedom in selecting symbols, many symbols are standard in a particular field, and the author should follow convention whenever possible.

Defining Symbols

By defining the symbols used in a manuscript, the author ensures that the reader will understand exactly what the symbols represent. Definitions can be given in one of four ways:

1. In a nomenclature that precedes or follows the running text
2. At first use in the text
3. In a short nomenclature within the text
4. Within displayed equations

These methods are not mutually exclusive. Any or all may be used, but the editor should be sure that each symbol is defined only once in the text. Some publishers require that symbols be defined at first use in each different part of a paper, such as figure captions, tables, or the abstract. The following paragraphs explain each approach.

Nomenclature. A nomenclature is a list of symbols defined in a glossary format. Symbols are listed in alphabetical order (English alphabet first), equal signs are used between the symbol and its definition, and definitions are given in short phrases.

Running Text. Symbols in the running text are defined at first use. If a symbol immediately follows its definition, it should not be set off by commas or parentheses.

The initial time t_0 is. . . .

If another phrase separates the symbol from its definition, the symbol is set off by commas or parentheses.

The initial time at which the reaction occurs, t_0, is. . . .

Often definitions in the text follow the displayed equation in which they first occur and are introduced by the word *where:*

$$I = \varepsilon_b + \tau I_0$$

where I is the intensity, ε is the monochromatic flame emissivity, the subscript b denotes the blackbody, τ is the monochromatic flame transmissivity, and I_0 is a proportionality constant.

Short Nomenclature. A short nomenclature in the text is effective if an author wants to call attention to the definitions of symbols used in a particular displayed equation but the symbols are so numerous that defining them in sentence form would be awkward. A short nomenclature follows the same format as a nomenclature that precedes or follows the running text except that the symbols are listed in the order in which they are given in the equation instead of in alphabetical order:

$$\Delta\theta = 2 \int_{r_{\min}}^{r_{\max}} \frac{(l/r^2)\, dr}{\sqrt{2\mu[E - U - l^2/(2\mu r^2)]}}$$

where

$\Delta\theta$ = angle swept out by orbiting mass
r_{max} = maximum distance from force field center
r_{min} = minimum distance from force field center
l = constant
μ = mass of object
E = total energy
U = potential energy

Definitions Within Displayed Equations. Definitions within displayed equations should be avoided because they take up more space and make typesetting the equation more difficult. The expression

$$\frac{\partial \mathbf{v}}{\partial t}$$
continuity

can be changed to

$$\text{Continuity: } \frac{\partial \mathbf{v}}{\partial t}$$

Using Symbols

Symbols should be used consistently within a publication. Different modifiers should not be given for the same concept (P_{av}, P_{avg}). A practical method of ensuring consistency is to develop a style sheet giving the symbol, its definition, and the first page on which it is used. Special fonts and symbols can also be marked on the style sheet to aid the typesetter.

TYPOGRAPHIC CONVENTIONS

Avoiding Symbol Confusion

Because today's desktop publishing and word processing programs offer the capability to typeset equations, many more people are setting mathematical type. Thus, the copyeditor should not assume that the typesetter is fully experienced in setting mathematical copy. To reduce the chances for error or misunderstanding, the copyeditor should mark copy as clearly and completely as possible. For example, all spaces should be noted, typefaces and type sizes should be specified, and any confusing or ambiguous symbols and signs should be spelled out in marginal notes.

See the sidebar list of ambiguous symbols for frequently misread or misinterpreted symbols that copyeditors should define in marginal notes.

Equation Software

Text-Oriented Software. Many equation programs require the typesetter to key in English-style commands, such as *over* to create the horizontal bar showing division and *sqrt* to create a square root sign. In one program, for example, Greek letters are set by typing in their names—*theta, omega,* and so on. Special characters are also set this way: *int* creates an integral sign; *approx* creates a wavy equals sign; and *left* coupled with *right* creates brackets, braces, bars, and parentheses, with the signs growing automatically in length to fit the expression. In essence, the typesetter creates a set of

AMBIGUOUS SYMBOLS

Here is a list of frequently misread or misinterpreted mathematical symbols that copyeditors should define in marginal notes to ensure accuracy.

Marginal Note	*Typeset Character*
lc "aye"	a
lc Gr. alpha	α
variation sign	∝
infinity	∞
cap "bee"	B
lc Gr. beta	β
lc "dee"	d
lc Gr. delta	δ
partial differential, "round dee"	∂
cap "kay"	K
lc "kay"	k
lc Gr. kappa	κ
lc "ell"	l
lc script "ell"	ℓ
one	1
lc "en"	n
lc Gr. eta	η
cap "oh"	O
lc "oh"	o
zero	0
degree sign	°
lc "pee"	p
lc Gr. rho	ρ
lc "you"	u
lc Gr. mu	μ
cap "vee"	V
lc "vee"	v
lc Gr. nu	ν
lc "double-you"	w
lc Gr. omega	ω
cap "ex"	X
lc "ex"	x
mult. sign	×
lc Gr. chi	χ

Marginal Note	*Typeset Character*
cap "zee"	Z
lc "zee"	z
two	2
lc Gr. epsilon	ϵ
"element of" sign	$\in$
lc Gr. theta	θ
cap Gr. theta	Θ
lc Gr. pi	π
cap Gr. pi	Π
product sign	$\prod$
cap Gr. sigma	Σ
summation sign	$\sum$
cap Gr. psi	Ψ
lc Gr. psi	ψ
centered dot	$\cdot$
period	.

commands that reflect the way an equation is spoken, so it is important for the copyeditor to be sure all marks are understandable and unambiguous.

Graphic-Oriented Software. Other programs are graphically oriented, allowing the equation to be constructed on the screen as it will appear in print.

Typeface

Many of the standard rules for typesetting mathematical material are built into the programs themselves, including rules for typefaces and type sizes. This section explains some of these rules as they are traditionally used.

Italics. Most mathematical symbols that are letters of the English alphabet are set in italics. Symbols should be marked for italics in the running text, but it is not necessary to mark them in displayed equations because most equation programs automatically provide italics for letters used as symbols. Symbols that are already italicized in the running text of a manuscript should not be marked for italics.

Roman. The following functions are usually set in roman type:

arg (argument)
cos (cosine)

cosh (hyperbolic cosine)
cot (cotangent)
coth (hyperbolic cotangent)
csc (cosecant)
csch (hyperbolic cosecant)
det (determinant)
exp (exponential)
Im (imaginary)
inf (inferior)
lim (limit)
lim inf (limit inferior)
lim sup (limit superior)
ln (natural logarithm; script is also used for this symbol)
log (logarithm)
max (maximum)
min (minimum)
Re (real)
sec (secant)
sech (hyperbolic secant)
sin (sine)
sinh (hyperbolic sine)
sup (superior)
tan (tangent)
tanh (hyperbolic tangent)
tr (trace)

Other symbols that are usually set in roman type include numbers, units of measure, chemical symbols (see Chapter 18, Signs and Symbols), and indices that consist of entire words or multiletter abbreviations of these words:

v_{final} v_{fin}
i_{internal} i_{int}

If these symbols are italicized anywhere in a manuscript, they should be circled to indicate that they should be set in roman type.

Boldface. Symbols indicating vectors, tensors, and matrices are often set in boldface. If both vectors and tensors are used together, vectors are usually set in boldface italics, and tensors are usually set in boldface roman or Gothic (sans serif) to distinguish them from vectors. Indices and components of vectors and tensors should be set in roman. Symbols representing matrices are usually uppercase and can be either italic or roman. If an author has used an arrow over a symbol to indicate a vector, the arrow should be deleted and replaced with the standard boldface indication, a wavy line beneath the word to be bold.

Script. Script is another typeface that is often used for mathematical symbols. For example, $\mathcal{O}$ (order of) and ℓn (natural logarithm) are symbols that are often used in mathematical notation.

Other Alphabets. Greek and Cyrillic alphabets are also used in mathematical notation. Chapter 21, Foreign Languages, lists these alphabets.

Embellishments

Common embellishments include overbars, tildes, and carets. Multiple embellishments and embellishments over or under groups of letters often pose a problem for the typesetter because these marks may run into descenders and often require setting by hand. Proofreaders should ensure that the typesetter has centered any embellishments over the symbols.

Type Size

Mathematical material is usually set in 9- or 10-point type. Indices and some special symbols are exceptions; indices are set in smaller type, and some special symbols (especially collective signs) require larger type. In general, a smaller point size should be used for alphabetic indices than for numeric indices because alphabetic indices have descenders that could interfere with the next line (e.g., P_2 versus P_y).

CONVENTIONS FOR COMMON NOTATIONS AND EXPRESSIONS

This section addresses the conventions that apply to different kinds of mathematical notations, expressions, and symbols.

Arrays

Arrays are simply numbers or symbols arranged in horizontal rows and vertical columns. Matrices (a) are arrays set within brackets (parentheses in some texts). Determinants (b) are arrays set within vertical straight lines.

$$\mathbf{A} = \begin{bmatrix} a_{11} \; a_{12} \\ a_{21} \; a_{22} \end{bmatrix} \qquad \text{(a)}$$

$$|\mathbf{B}| = \begin{vmatrix} b_{11} \; b_{12} \\ b_{21} \; b_{22} \end{vmatrix} \qquad \text{(b)}$$

All arrays must be displayed so that there is absolutely no doubt as to which position within the "grid" of the array is occupied by any particular symbol.

Two-by-Two Matrices. Simple two-by-two matrices (matrices with two elements across and two elements down) can appear within running text by setting the elements of the matrix as indices $\binom{a\ c}{b\ d}$. Obviously, this may not be done if the elements of a two-by-two matrix have indices themselves.

The "col" Function. The "col" function can be used to avoid excess leading for simple column matrices. This function allows a vertical matrix to be written horizontally. Braces may also be used for this purpose:

$$\begin{bmatrix} x \\ y \\ z \end{bmatrix} = \mathrm{col}(x, y, z) \quad or \quad \{x, y, z\}$$

Binomial Coefficients

The symbols within the binomial coefficient may be set as indices $\binom{a}{b}$ for equations within the running text.

Collective Signs

Collective signs are the integral (a), product (b), summation (c), and union (d) signs. They must be set in larger type sizes than the rest of the equation, typically 12 point for product, summation, and union and 18 point for the integral sign.

$$\underset{(a)}{\int} \quad \underset{(b)}{\Pi} \quad \underset{(c)}{\Sigma} \quad \underset{(d)}{\cup}$$

All of these symbols may have associated limits, which appear in superscript and/or subscript form. (These limits give the range of values over which the expression is to be evaluated.)

Equations Within the Running Text. In these equations, the limits follow the collective signs to avoid excess leading:

$$\int_0^t \quad \prod_{n=1}^{\infty} \quad \sum_{n=1}^{\infty} \quad \bigcup_{n=1}^{\infty}$$

Displayed Equations. In displayed equations, limits for product, summation, and union appear above and below the sign:

$$\prod_{n=1}^{\infty} \quad \sum_{n=1}^{\infty} \quad \bigcup_{n=1}^{\infty}$$

However, the limits still follow the integral sign in displayed equations, except where multiple integrals are used. In the case of multiple integrals, limits appear above and below the sign:

$$\int_0^t \quad \textit{but} \quad \int\limits_0^t \int\limits_0^y$$

(Some equation programs do not allow limits to be set above and below multiple integrals.)

Exponents, Exponential Functions, and Powers

$$(x + 2)^{3y}$$

In the expression above $(x + 2)$ is the base and $3y$ is the exponent. The expression would read, "the quantity x plus 2 raised to the power $3y$." Exponents are indices and are always superscripts. If fractions appear in the exponent, they should be collapsed. (See "When to Collapse a Fraction," page 472.)

Using Exponents Consistently. The author should not use 0.23×10^5 in one place and 0.023×10^6 in another, although both represent the same value. If possible, the same exponent should be used for different values if they occur in close proximity: 1.3×10^5 and 0.2×10^6 on the same line or within the same paragraph could be changed to 1.3×10^5 and 2.0×10^5, or 0.13×10^6 and 0.2×10^6.

Scientific Notation. This is a method for expressing all numbers in the form $a \times 10^b$, where a is a decimal number with one digit to the left of the decimal point and b is a whole number. It is especially useful for very large and very small numbers.

$$4{,}260{,}000 = 4.26 \times 10^6$$
$$0.000\,432 = 4.32 \times 10^{-4}$$

In scientific notation, as in all multiplication by powers of 10, a multiplication sign (×) should be used:

4.26×10^9 *not* $4.26 \cdot 10^9$ *or* $4.26(10^9)$

Exponential Functions. When *e* is raised to a power, it is called an exponential function. (The quantity *e*, like π, occurs frequently in mathematics; its value is approximately 2.7.) The expressions e^a and $\exp a$ are identical in meaning, but one may be preferable to the other in certain contexts:

- Use e^a if the expression of the power is short and does not contain built-up fractions or collective signs or have indices itself.

e^{2a} e^{a-b} e^{3a+4}

- Use $\exp a$ if the expression of the power is long, has indices itself, or contains built-up fractions or collective signs.

$\exp(2a_i)$ $\exp(3a^2 + 4)$ $\exp\left(\dfrac{a-b}{c^2+d}\right)$

Fences (Signs of Aggregation)

These symbols are usually employed simply to group mathematical material. However, they may be used to denote a particular mathematical meaning and should be changed only with utmost caution. Fences include

$$\Bigg\{\Bigg[\Bigg(\ \Bigg)\Bigg]\Bigg\}$$

$$\{\ [\ \langle\ (\ |\ \|\ \|\ |\ )\ \rangle\ ]\ \}$$

Fences Used to Group Mathematical Material. Fences are necessary to make clear the order in which mathematical operations are to be performed. For example,

$4 \times 5 + 4 = 24$
but $4 \times (5 + 4) = 36$

Additional types of fences are required if fences are "nested" within an expression. For example, $\{[ab(x + y)(x + y)]^2 + 1\}^3$ is easier to read than $((ab(x + y)(x + y))^2 + 1)^3$. Generally speaking, fences are nested in the following order: { [( )] }.

The most common error made with fences is omitting the opening or closing fence of a pair. Except in cases of particular meaning such as $(a, b]$ or $[b, a)$, each fence that is opened must be closed. An equation with an omitted fence not only is of incorrect form, but also may be highly ambiguous; for example, $3y[a + (b - d)^2$ might have been intended to mean $3y[a + (b - d)]^2$ or $3y[a + (b - d)^2]$.

Specific Meanings of Fences. In addition to grouping mathematical material, fences have particular mathematical meanings:

- *Parentheses* enclose the coordinates of a point (a, b); indicate binomial coefficients $\binom{a}{b}$; are required around quantities following f or $\mathcal{O}$: $f(x)$ and $\mathcal{O}(17)$; are required to indicate functions of products and fractions: $\sin(xy)$, not $\sin xy$, and $\sin(x/y)$, not $\sin x/y$; and are required for the functions of negative expressions: $\sin(-xy)$, not $\sin -xy$.
- *Brackets* are used to indicate matrices:

$$\begin{bmatrix} 7 & 9 & b \\ a & 3 & 2 \end{bmatrix}$$

- *Vertical bars* are used to indicate determinants or absolute value. For this reason, they are rarely used to group mathematical material. Such use may lead to confusion.

determinant: $\begin{vmatrix} a & b \\ c & d \end{vmatrix}$ $|\mathbf{A}|$

absolute value: $|-4|$ $|a|$

Fractions

There are two types of fractions: stacked or built-up (a) and collapsed (b). Since built-up fractions require more vertical space and are therefore more costly, collapsed fractions are preferred. However, collapsing should not be done at the expense of legibility. This section explains the procedure for collapsing fractions.

$\dfrac{a}{b}$ (a)

a/b *or* ab^{-1} (b)

When Not to Collapse a Fraction. Fractions within equations should remain in built-up form when

- Collapsing them would take up more lines
- The equation contains derivatives
- The equation contains collective signs
- The equation contains an array

Only short fractions should be collapsed because collapsing a long fraction can make the equation difficult to read:

$$\frac{4ab(x+y)}{(n+y)(x+y)^2} \quad \text{should } \textit{not} \text{ be changed to} \quad 4ab(x+y)/[(n+y)(x-y)^2]$$

$$\textit{but} \quad \frac{3}{4b} \quad \text{should be changed to} \quad 3/(4b)$$

Fractions containing derivatives should not be collapsed unless the derivative stands alone and occurs often.

$$\mathbf{v} = \frac{dx}{dt} \quad \text{may be changed to} \quad \mathbf{v} = dx/dt$$

$$\textit{but} \quad F_{\text{ext}} = M\frac{dv_{\text{cm}}}{dt} \quad \text{should } \textit{not} \text{ become} \quad F_{\text{ext}} = M(dv_{\text{cm}}/dt)$$

The fractions in an equation that contains collective signs should not be collapsed because these signs take up extra space themselves and collapsing the fraction saves no space.

$$\sum_{n=1}^{\infty} dx\left(\frac{n-1}{w+1}\right) \quad \textit{not} \quad \sum_{n=1}^{\infty} dx[(n-1)/(w+1)]$$

Arrays cannot be collapsed and, as above, collapsing fractions around them saves no space.

$$4\begin{vmatrix} a & x \\ y & b \end{vmatrix}\left(\frac{a+b}{xy^2}\right) \quad \textit{not} \quad 4\begin{vmatrix} a & x \\ y & b \end{vmatrix}(a+b)/(xy^2)$$

When to Collapse a Fraction. If the fraction is not so long that collapsing it would add extra lines and the equation within which it occurs does not contain derivatives, collective signs, or arrays, the fraction may be collapsed by means of a solidus (/), also known as a virgule, shilling mark, diagonal, or slash. It may also be collapsed with the use of a negative exponent.

$$\frac{a}{b} \Rightarrow ab^{-1}$$

However, if there is any chance that the author's mathematical meaning could be altered, collapsing should not be done. Fractions should be collapsed only by a knowledgeable copyeditor.

Adding Fences. Collapsing fractions often requires the appropriate insertion of fences to preserve meaning:

$$\frac{3+5}{8} \neq 3 + 5/8 = 3\tfrac{5}{8}$$

$$\frac{3+5}{8} = (3+5)/8 = 1$$

Fences should be added when a fraction that contains a plus or minus sign in the numerator or denominator is collapsed:

$$\frac{3x}{y-n} \Rightarrow 3x/(y-n)$$

Fences should be added when a built-up fraction that precedes a number or symbol is collapsed:

$$\frac{x}{y}n \Rightarrow (x/y)n$$

Signs of aggregation are not necessary when a built-up fraction that follows a number or symbol is collapsed:

$$n\frac{x}{y} \Rightarrow nx/y$$

"Uncollapsing" Fractions. Building up a collapsed equation often requires eliminating the fences:

$$(xy+1)[d(xy)/d(ty)] \Rightarrow (xy+1)\frac{d(xy)}{d(ty)}$$

However, eliminating fences should be done with great caution, since the author could be using them to denote a special meaning.

Case Fractions. Simple numerical fractions may be collapsed into case fractions, which are set as one-character symbols: $\frac{1}{2}$, $\frac{1}{4}$, $\frac{1}{8}$. In running text, case fractions are the rule. In displayed equations, avoid mixing case fractions with stacked fractions:

$$\frac{1}{4}y + \frac{7}{10}x^2 + \frac{5}{9}z \quad \textit{not} \quad \tfrac{1}{4}y + \frac{7}{10}x^2 + \frac{5}{9}z$$

Compound Fractions. Compound fractions contain a fraction in the numerator or denominator:

$$F = \frac{(1/n) + y}{E_n - B_n} \quad \textit{not} \quad F = \frac{\dfrac{1}{n} + y}{E_n - B_n}$$

These "subfractions" should be in collapsed form. A built-up fraction should not contain another built-up fraction in its numerator or denominator.

Fractions in Subscript and Superscript. Fractions in subscript and superscript are usually collapsed to improve legibility and ease of typesetting:

$$X^{a/2} \quad \textit{not} \quad X^{\frac{a}{2}} \qquad q^{(a-b)/(xy)} \quad \textit{not} \quad q^{\frac{a-b}{xy}}$$

Limits

Certain notations are used to describe what happens as a variable gets close to a specified value, or limit: lim, lim sup, lim inf, max, sup. Often these functions appear with a given limit, which is set in subscript.

$\lim_{x\to 0} y$

Running Text. In the running text, the limit follows the function:

$\lim_{x\to 0} xn^3 \qquad \limsup_{x\to\infty}$

Displayed Equations. In displayed equations, the limit appears below the function:

$$\lim_{x\to 0} xn^3 \qquad \limsup_{x\to\infty}$$

Collective Signs. Limits as applied to collective signs are covered in "Collective Signs" (above).

Multiplication Signs

Mathematics has several ways of showing multiplication. Generally, no sign at all is used: *ab*, 22*i*, 3*xy*. In fact, using a lowercase x to signify multiplication could lead to confusion where *x* is also used as a variable: 3 x *x* = 9.

$$2 \times 3$$
$$2(3)$$
$$2 \cdot 3$$

When an opening fence and a closing fence are adjacent, multiplication is implied: $(x + 3)(y - 2)$.

Situations where a multiplication sign is used include the following:

Multiplying by Powers of 10. If a quantity is multiplied by 10 raised to some power, a multiplication sign is used to show multiplication: 2.3×10^4.

Multiplying Factorials. If two factorials are being multiplied, a centered dot is used:

$$a! \cdot b!$$

Breaking an Equation. When an equation is broken between two fences, a multiplication sign or centered dot is inserted on the continuing line; an acceptable break point is shown below with a slash. (See "Breaking Equations" later in this chapter.)

$$A = (c + 3)/(a - b) \Rightarrow A = (c + 3) \qquad or \quad A = (c + 3)$$
$$\cdot\, (a - b) \qquad\qquad \times\, (a - b)$$

Radicals

Radical signs indicate that the root of an expression or number should be taken. A radical sign with no delimiter is taken to mean "the square root of." "The square root of 4*b*" is written $\sqrt{4b}$.

$$\sqrt[3]{a}$$
$$\sqrt{81}$$

A radical sign with an index indicates that a higher-order root is to be taken. "The cube root of $(a + b)$" is written $\sqrt[3]{a+b}$. "The fifth root of $16z$" is written $\sqrt[5]{16z}$.

Changing Radical Signs to Exponents. Exponents may substitute for radical signs as shown below. The exponent is equal to 1/(order of the root):

$$\sqrt[3]{a+b} = (a+b)^{1/3} \qquad \sqrt{4b} = (4b)^{1/2}$$

Note that fences must be added to the expression.

Omitting the "Roof" from a Radical Sign. Omitting the roof from a radical sign avoids excess leading within the running text. Note that fences must enclose the expression affected by the radical sign. Some equation programs will not allow a roof to be omitted from the radical.

$$\sqrt{2(x+y)} \Rightarrow \surd[2(x+y)]$$

Superscripts and Subscripts

Superscripts and subscripts occur frequently in mathematical expressions. They are given the general term *indices.* Common uses include

- With collective signs to designate limits (see "Collective Signs" earlier in this chapter)
- As exponents (see "Exponents, Exponential Functions, and Powers" earlier in this chapter)
- In limit expressions (see "Limits" earlier in this chapter)

$$\sum_{n=0}^{4}$$

$$m_i^2$$

$$\lim_{x\to 0}$$

Marking Indices. In general, indices should be marked for the typesetter only if there are multilevel indices or if they appear ambiguous. For example, V_{t0} should be marked to indicate to the typesetter whether it should be set as V_{t0} or V_{t_0} or Vt_0.

Expressions with Both Subscripts and Superscripts. Superscripts and subscripts should not be marked to be aligned ("stacked"); the typesetter should do this automatically. However, they should be marked if staggering is necessary (as can happen in tensor notation).

$\mathbf{X}_{y}{}^{n}$

Fractions in Indices. Fractions in indices should be collapsed (see "Fractions" earlier in this chapter).

$X^{3a/2}$ *not* $X^{\frac{3a}{2}}$

Too Many Indices. Notations like $V_{av_i}^{\Sigma t_i}$ should be avoided because they are difficult to set and difficult to read.

Special Superscript Symbols. Asterisks, degree symbols, and primes must be set beside a symbol, not outside the symbol and its superscripts or subscripts:

B_2^* $\quad a_i^\circ$

T_k' *not* $T_k{}'$

Sequences and Series

Sequences and series are common in mathematics. In sequences (a), the terms are separated by commas. In a series (b), the terms are separated by operators.

$X_1, X_2, X_3, \ldots$ (a)

$X_1 + X_2 + X_3 + \cdots$ (b)

Elisions. An elision is a series of ellipsis points used to indicate omitted terms within series and sequences. Elisions contain a space after the first symbol, a space after each comma, and a space after each ellipsis point. Ellipsis points are placed on line for elisions that contain commas and are often centered vertically for elisions that contain operators or no punctuation.

$a_0, a_1, a_2, \ldots, a_n \qquad a_0 + a_1 + a_2 + \cdots + a_n$

The comma or operator must occur both before *and* after the ellipsis points.

Some equation programs will not center ellipsis points vertically, and some programs will not provide spaces after the commas and ellipsis points.

Vectors

Vectors are quantities that contain information about direction. Velocity, for example, is a vector; speed is not. The speed of a car might be 50 mph, but its *velocity* would be 50 mph *north.*

$$\mathbf{V} \quad \vec{V}$$

Notation. Vectors are set in boldface to differentiate them from scalar quantities (such as speed). In handwritten copy, vectors are often denoted by an arrow over a symbol.

Vectors written out with their components usually take these forms:

$$\mathbf{V} = (a, b, c) \quad or \quad \mathbf{V} = \begin{pmatrix} a \\ b \\ c \end{pmatrix}$$

Multiplication. There are two kinds of vector multiplication: dot products (a) and cross products (b). Each has its particular multiplication symbol, and they are *not* interchangeable.

$$\mathbf{V} \cdot \mathbf{Z} \ \ \text{(a)} \qquad \mathbf{V} \times \mathbf{Z} \ \ \text{(b)}$$

Tensors. Tensors are a "generalized vector" with more than three components. When vectors and tensors appear together, vectors are often set in boldface italic to distinguish them from tensors.

SPACING BETWEEN ELEMENTS OF EQUATIONS AND EXPRESSIONS

Correct spacing between the elements of mathematical expressions is essential. This section sets out a number of these rules; see *Mathematics into Type* for a fuller discussion.

Spacing Rules Versus Software Limitations

Many equation programs have spacing rules built into them. In some programs, these rules may be overridden if necessary. Editors should be aware that equation programs and word processors emulate traditional typesetting with varying degrees of faithfulness. Thin spaces, thick spaces, em spaces, and 2-em spaces may or may not be available in some software packages, particularly ones devoted primarily to word processing.

In the guidelines given below, a regular letter space is acceptable in place of the thin and thick spaces. Maintaining a consistent spacing scheme within the text is more important than the exact width of the spaces used.

Adjectives Versus Operators

Some spacing rules depend on a symbol's function within the particular equation—that is, on what "part of speech" it is within the equation.

Relational Symbols. Relational symbols describe the relation between one expression and another. They include

$= \neq \equiv \not\equiv \approx < > \leq \geq \subset \in \notin \rightarrow \leftarrow \leftrightarrow \simeq \cong$ and $\Rightarrow$

An equation without a relational symbol is like a sentence without a verb; both are fragments that make no statement. Relational symbols can be read like verb phrases:

$x + 4 = 7$	"x plus 4 *is equal to* 7"
$3y > 4$	"3 times y *is greater than* 4"

Operators. An operator describes a mathematical operation, or procedure, that is to be carried out. These include $+$ $-$ $\pm$ $\cdot$ $\div$ $/$ $\cup$ and $\cap$.

Adjectives: Dual Functions of Some Operator Symbols. Symbols such as $+$, $-$, and $\pm$ can function as adjectives in addition to operators. When these modify the value of a number or variable, they are adjectives (e.g., "the temperature is -3°C," or "$y = -3$"). However, when these describe an operation that is to be performed, they function as operators (e.g., $5 + 4 = 9$).

No Space

No space is required

- Between a number and the symbol it multiplies

$3x$ $10y$

- Between two symbols being multiplied

ab xy

- Before or after fences, except when the fence is adjacent to a relational symbol

$(x + y)c \quad 3(x + y) \quad 4[z]$
but $2(a + 4) = z$

- Before or after subscripts or superscripts

$\cos^2 x \quad a_i^2 y \quad A_i l^2$

- Before or after vertical arrows

$x\uparrow b \quad y\downarrow 0$

- Before or after operator and relational symbols within expressions that act as indices. (Note that some equation editor programs automatically provide spaces around operators, even when they appear within indices.)

$x^{3+y} \quad \lim_{a\to 0}$

Thin Space (1/6-Em Space)

Generally, assume that a thin space occurs before and after a symbol, except as otherwise noted here and above. Thin spaces, which are shown by carets in the following examples, are traditionally used

- Before but not after +, −, and ± when used as adjectives

$a + b =_\wedge -z$

- Before and after operators

$a_\wedge +_\wedge 3 \quad \mathbf{p}_\wedge \cdot_\wedge \mathbf{n}$

- Before and after relational symbols

$x_\wedge =_\wedge 4 \quad y + 3_\wedge >_\wedge 4$

- Before and after functions set in roman type, *except* when preceded or followed by indices or fences

$2_\wedge \cos_\wedge x \quad \exp_\wedge x^n$

but $\cos^2 a \quad (x + y)\tan_\wedge y \quad [x + y]\tan^2 y$

- Before and after collective signs
- Before and after differentials: dx, dy, and other combinations of d with another symbol following

  $4_\wedge\int_\wedge f(y)_\wedge dy_\wedge + c$

- Before and after vertical rules appearing singly (not used as fences)

  $x_\wedge|_\wedge y$

- Before and after colons used as mathematical symbols

  $3_\wedge:_\wedge x$

- Before back inferiors (subscripts that modify the symbol following them)

  $b_\wedge{}_3xc^2$ $b_\wedge{}_1x_2q$

Thick Space (1/3-Em Space)

A normal letter space (#) is generally equivalent to a thick space. A letter or thick space, shown by the space sign in the following examples, may be used in place of a thin space as described above and is always used

- After commas in sets of symbols, sequences of fractions, coordinates of points, and components of vectors

  $(a,^{\#}b)$

  $(a_1,^{\#}a_2,^{\#}a_3,^{\#}a_4)$

- Between a symbolic expression and a verbal expression in running text

  $g > 0$ # for some t

Em Space

Many equation editor programs do not offer em spaces as such, and the spaces may have to be set visually. Em spaces are used only in displayed equations; in running text, variable word spacing or a letter space is used. An em space, shown as a small square in the following examples, is used

- Between a symbolic expression and a verbal expression in display

$$g > 0 \square \text{for some } t$$

- Before and after a conjunction or a linking phrase that separates two equations or expressions

$$F = (x + n)z \square \text{and} \square F = (x + z)n$$

Two-Em Space

Like the em space, the 2-em space is not offered in many equation editor programs, and 2-em spaces may have to be visually set. Two-em spaces are used only in displayed equations. In running text, variable word spacing or a letter space is used. Two-em spaces are used

- Between two equations or expressions on the same line of a display that are not separated by a conjunction or linking phrase

$$F = (x + n)z; \square\square\; F = (x + z)n$$

- Between a symbolic statement and a condition on the statement

$$a_n - b_n \square\square\; (n = 0, 1, \ldots, z)$$

BREAKING EQUATIONS

When an equation will not fit on one line, it should be broken and set on two lines. Breaking may occur in both displayed equations and equations in running text. For definitions of operator and relational symbols, see "Adjectives Versus Operators" earlier in this chapter.

Where Breaks Occur

In general, equation breaks should occur before an operator or relational symbol. Acceptable break points are shown with a slash:

$$y(t) = A_0 / + A_1 \sin(\omega t) / + A_2 \sin(2\omega t) \qquad a + b / = y(3 - c^2)$$

$$c = 4z^2 / - BT^2 \qquad y^2 - 7 / \geq 4x^2 y$$

In running text only, the break may also appear after the operator or relational symbol:

$$y(t) = A_0 + / A_1 \sin(\omega t) + / A_2 \sin(2\omega t) \qquad a + b = / y(3 - c^2)$$

$$c = 4z^2 - / BT^2 \qquad y^2 - 7 \geq / 4x^2 y$$

Equations may be broken between sets of fences; in this case, a centered dot or a multiplication sign should be inserted:

$$A = (c + 3) / (a - b) \Rightarrow A = (c + 3) \cdot (a - b) \quad \text{or} \quad A = (c + 3) \times (a - b)$$

Where Breaks Should Not Occur

Equation breaks should not occur

- Within fences, fractions, or radicals

  no break allowed: $\sqrt{1 - x^2 + 4y^2} \qquad \frac{x + y}{3 + 4z} \qquad (x^2 + 3y)$

- After collective signs. No break may occur after the integral sign until the differential is reached (*dx* or *dy*, and other combinations of *d* with another symbol following).

$$\sum (4z + 1) / - abc \int (a^2 x + 4)\, dx / + y$$

Alignment for Broken Equations in Display

See “Displayed Mathematical Expressions” below.

MATHEMATICAL EXPRESSIONS IN RUNNING TEXT

Only simple mathematical expressions should be used in running text. If an expression is long or has built-up fractions, collective signs with limits, or arrays, the expressions should be displayed (see “Displayed Mathematical Expressions,” below).

Numbering Expressions

Equations in the running text should not be numbered.

Punctuation

Mathematical expressions in text should be punctuated according to their function in the text:

Therefore, $a + b = c$, since $x + y = z$.

A lowercase symbol should not be used to begin a sentence. A symbol directly following its definition should not be set off by commas or parentheses:

Incorrect: e is the base of the natural logarithms.
Correct: The number e is the base of the natural logarithms.

Incorrect: The initial acceleration, $a_0 = dv/dt$ at $t = 0$.
Correct: The initial acceleration $a_0 = dv/dt$ at $t = 0$.

DISPLAYED MATHEMATICAL EXPRESSIONS

A displayed equation should be centered on the page with extra space above and below it. Because displayed equations are usually complex and require more space, typesetting can be costly. The types of equations that should be displayed are

- Long equations
- Equations with built-up fractions
- Equations with collective signs
- Equations with arrays

Long equations should be displayed because they look awkward in running text and the typesetter may have difficulty breaking them at the end of a line. (Guidelines are given in "Breaking Equations," above.)

Equations with built-up fractions, collective signs, or arrays should be displayed because they require extra vertical space and will not fit on the text line. Instructions for when and how to collapse fractions are given in "Fractions," above.

Alignment of Displayed Equations

Displayed equations are indented uniformly or centered on the page.

Several One-Line Equations. Sequential one-line equations should be aligned on the first relational symbol in each equation. They are considered to constitute one display.

$$\int sec^2ax\ dx = \frac{1}{a}\tan ax + c$$

$$at^2 \geq \frac{1}{2}mv^2 - mgh$$

$$ax < \pi$$

If any word or words separate two equations, the display is considered broken, and each equation is centered independently.

$$\int sec^2ax\ dx = \frac{1}{a}\tan ax + c$$

and

$$at^2 \geq \frac{1}{2}mv^2 - mgh$$

with

$$ax < \pi$$

Alignment of Multilinear Equations. A single equation that occupies more than one line is also considered one display. A new line that begins with a relational sign is aligned with any relational sign in the preceding line. Operators that begin a new line are aligned to the right of the relational signs.

$$\begin{aligned}\int \frac{dx}{\sqrt{a^2+x^2}} &= \sinh^{-1}\frac{x}{a} + c \\ &= \ln\left|x + \sqrt{a^2+x^2}\right| \\ &\quad + c\end{aligned}$$

If this is not possible, overruns for a multilinear equation can be set either flush right or with a standard indent (at least a 1-em space) from the left margin.

$$\begin{aligned}F(n) = a_0 - a_1n + a_2n(n-1) - a_3n(n-1)(n-2) \\ + a_4n(n-1)(n-2)(n-3) + \delta\end{aligned}$$

$$\begin{aligned}&F(n) = a_0 - a_1n + a_2n(n-1) - a_3n(n-1)(n-2) \\ &\quad + a_4n(n-1)(n-2)(n-3) + \delta\end{aligned}$$

Numbering Displayed Equations

Often authors assign numbers to their equations if they have many equations or if they cross-reference the equations. Equation numbers are usually

Arabic numbers enclosed in parentheses or brackets and are usually placed flush right:

$$A = ab + ay \qquad (1)$$

Equations should be in numerical order. If equation numbers are out of order, the author should be queried unless it is clear that the author simply made a mistake in numbering.

Multilinear Equations. An equation number is usually placed on the bottom line of a multilinear equation:

$$\begin{aligned} F(n) = a_0 - a_1 n + a_2 n(n-1) - a_3 n(n-1)(n-2) \\ + a_4 n(n-1)(n-2)(n-3) + \delta \qquad (1) \end{aligned}$$

However, if the equation contains an array, the equation number should be centered vertically:

$$\mathbf{I} = \begin{bmatrix} i_{11} \; i_{12} \; i_{13} \\ i_{21} \; i_{22} \; i_{23} \end{bmatrix} \begin{bmatrix} x \\ y \\ z \end{bmatrix} = \begin{bmatrix} b_1 \\ b_2 \end{bmatrix} \qquad (1)$$

Groups of Equations. The number for groups of equations that are referred to by a single equation number can be (a) centered vertically, (b) placed beside the last equation in the group, or (c) repeated beside each equation, but with letters added.

$$\begin{array}{ll} x + y = 0 & \\ x + z = 0 & (1) \\ z + y = 0 & \end{array} \qquad \begin{array}{ll} x + y = 0 & \\ x + z = 0 & \\ z + y = 0 & (1) \end{array} \qquad \begin{array}{ll} x + y = 0 & (1a) \\ x + z = 0 & (1b) \\ z + y = 0 & (1c) \end{array}$$

(a) (b) (c)

The second method should be avoided because, unless punctuation is used at the end of the equations, it appears that the equation number refers only to the last equation in the group. The third method is preferred and is especially useful if the author cross-references individual equations within the group—"Eq. 3a" is preferable to "the first equation in Eqs. 3."

Punctuating Displayed Equations

The addition or deletion of punctuation before, within, or after a displayed equation should not alter the mathematical meaning. If there is any chance that altering the punctuation could change the meaning, the author should be queried or the changes should not be made.

Words or Phrases Preceding Equations. Words or phrases immediately preceding an equation should not end with a period or semicolon but can end with a comma if the following mathematical material is nonrestrictive, no punctuation if the following mathematical material is restrictive, or a colon if a stop is needed.

The ideal gas equation,

$$PV = nRT$$

which shows the relationship among pressure, volume, and temperature, is . . .

OR

The equation

$$PV = nRT$$

is a useful method of describing . . .

OR

The following equation can be called the ideal gas equation:

$$PV = nRT$$

Words in or Between Equations. Words in equations are punctuated as if the equation were in sentence form. They are usually capitalized if they begin an equation:

$$\text{Lift} + va = \alpha^{-1/2}$$

Words between equations on the same line are punctuated according to their function in a sentence:

$$x < 0; \text{ therefore, } y \to 0$$

Words used to link displayed equations are usually flush left, with a line break between them and the equation they precede:

$$(x + n)yzt = \frac{1}{2}xt$$

and

$$(x + z)ynt = \frac{1}{2}xt$$

Words or Phrases Following Equations. Words or phrases immediately following displayed equations that complete the sentence begin with a lowercase letter (a). Words or phrases that introduce a new concept should begin with an uppercase letter (b).

$$d = v_0t + \frac{1}{2}at^2$$

when acceleration is constant. (a)

$$d = v_0t + \frac{1}{2}at^2$$

However, an integral must be used for varying acceleration. (b)

End Punctuation. Punctuation at the end of a displayed equation is optional but should be styled consistently in a manuscript:

$$x + y = 0,$$
$$x + z = 0,$$
$$z + y = 0.$$

Equations Not Linked by Words. If two equations occur on the same line and are not linked by words, a comma or semicolon should be placed between them:

$$F = (x + n)z; \qquad F = (x + z)n$$

Spacing. Spacing rules regarding words and punctuation within displayed equations are given in "Spacing Between Elements of Equations and Expressions," page 478.

20

REFERENCE CITATIONS

REFERENCE CITATIONS

Most nonfiction authors find they must cite sources of information to some degree. From an entertaining feature article in the *New York Times* to a research paper in an academic journal, authors establish their arguments and give them credibility by stating the sources of direct quotations, paraphrases, facts, and ideas other than their own.

The kind of documentation needed and its format vary according to the audience and the nature of the topic. At one end of the spectrum is scholarly writing, in which documentation takes the form of detailed reference lists, endnotes, footnotes, or bibliographies. These sources let the reader assess the quality and timeliness of the research.

Newspaper and popular magazine articles fall at the other end of the spectrum, with trade nonfiction—everything from how-to books to biographies—and special-interest periodicals covering the vast middle range. Here, footnotes, endnotes, and other formal types of citation are considered intrusive and not always necessary. Instead, attribution is done in a variety of ways, including informal mentions in the text or lists of sources at the end of the article or book.

As with all other style issues, consistency of documentation is more important than the actual editorial choices made. Writers and editors should be aware that many publishers and organizations issue guides to reference style and format, and they should follow the house style when working on manuscripts for those groups. (An annotated bibliography of several widely used style manuals appears at the end of this chapter.) If no particular style is required, editors should respect any consistent, reasonable style used by the author and limit editorial changes to those essential for clarity and consistency. Near the end of the chapter, preceding the annotated bibliography, we offer suggested forms for several commonly encountered reference types; these forms may be used as a general guide in the absence of other instructions.

PLAGIARISM DEFINED

What is plagiarism exactly? We all know that it means word-for-word copying from another source without credit, but in fact the concept is somewhat broader. The *MLA Handbook for Writers of Research Papers* defines plagiarism as "the act of using another person's ideas or expressions in your writing without acknowledging the source. . . . In short, to plagiarize is to give the impression that you have written or thought something that you have in fact borrowed from someone else."

This means that paraphrasing another's words without attribution can also qualify as plagiarism. Making slight variations in syntax and wording may not spare a writer from this charge, which has ruined more than a few careers.

Copyright infringement and plagiarism are sometimes confused; see Chapter 23, Copyright, for a full discussion.

This chapter explains three basic levels of documentation, offers a basic bibliographic style, and discusses a few knotty problems writers and editors often face.

MINIMAL DOCUMENTATION: FOR THE CASUAL READER

The least formally documented writing appears in newspapers and popular magazines like *Newsweek, The New Yorker, McCall's,* and *Esquire*. The articles are meant to entertain as well as to inform and are usually not in-depth studies. Any "outside" sources of information are usually included in the text.

> According to J. Robert Wills, dean of fine arts at the University of Texas, ...

This kind of journalistic phraseology makes the source of the information clear without cluttering the text with formal documentation. Sources for original or controversial ideas, facts, and statistics, as well as attribution for all quotations, should be identified in this way.

MODERATE DOCUMENTATION: FOR THE EDUCATED READER

Between journalistic and scholarly writing lies a vast middle ground ranging from a cover story in the *Atlantic Monthly* to a wide array of nonfiction books aimed at a nonacademic but educated audience. These writings may

❧

WHERE HAVE ALL THE FOOTNOTES GONE?

The tremendous variation in reference styles used today ranges from no notes at all to lengthy bottom-of-the-page citations. A random sampling of one editor's bookshelf revealed the following schools of thought on the matter.

The Guess If You Can School

In *Eminent Victorian Soldiers: Seekers of Glory* (Norton, 1985), Byron Falwell uses quotations freely but no notes, only a "Select Bibliography." John Tebbel and Sarah Miles Watts also use quotations liberally throughout *The Press and the Presidency: From George Washington to Ronald Reagan* (Oxford, 1985), omit notes, and list only a bibliography divided by parts. Michael Holroyd, in *Bernard Shaw: The Search for Love,* Vol. 1 (Random House, 1988), cites no sources but promises to cite some when the last volume is completed. In his third volume, Holroyd explains why he avoids citations: "I wanted to present a 'pure' narrative that was neither interrupted by sequences of numbers nor undermined by a series of footnotes."

The No Superscript Callout but Specific Citation School

The variations on this style seem endless, beginning as early as 1975 with *Bodyguard of Lies* (Harper & Row) by Anthony Cave Brown. The text contains no indication that the book has notes, but in a section at the back called "Sources and Notes," Brown discusses the sources for each chapter before presenting notes page by page, keyed to phrases in quotation marks:

> page 52. "We are entering. . . ." Churchill, *The Second World War,* Vol. 2, p. 493.

Linda H. Davis, in *Onward and Upward: A Biography of Katherine S. White* (Harper & Row, 1987), keys her notes to a page number and a boldface phrase:

> 22 **I was the youngest:** KSW, "Books," NYer, 12/7/46

Two other variations are to skip the page numbers entirely and key the references to italicized phrases, by chapter, and to list notes by chapter, page, and line:

> [under Chapter 2] *Find a lawyer as easily in England as here:* Patrick Atiyah, "Tort Law and the Alternatives: Some Anglo-American Comparisons," 1987 *Duke Law Journal* 1002, 1017

> 30:1 Maritain 1960, 2, 39

WHERE HAVE ALL THE FOOTNOTES GONE?
(continued)

The latter note translates into page 30, line 1, Jacques Maritain, *Education at the Crossroads* (New Haven: Yale University Press, 1960), pages 2 and 39; the full citation appears in the bibliography that follows the notes.

The Endnote School

This is still the most common style. Superscripts in the text match numbered notes listed by chapter at the back of the book. Each reference gives full publication information at first mention and abbreviates it thereafter; the book also contains a detailed bibliography. Recent books sometimes place notes at the end of each chapter.

Old-Fashioned References

Despite the appearance of some newer-fangled styles, bottom-of-the-page notes are not dead. In David Hackett Fischer's *Albion's Seed: Four British Folkways in America* (Oxford, 1989), the footnotes commonly take up half the page, and the same is true of Robert V. Remini's *Henry Clay: Statesman for the Union* (Norton, 1991).

Author-Date Citations in Text, Reference List at the Back

Only the most unabashedly scholarly books—those whose authors do not intend to appeal to a general audience—seem to use this style.

Conclusion

Publishers apparently are not picky about the style of source citations; they seem to accept whatever style their authors come up with as long as it's more or less consistently carried out in the manuscript. And increasingly, authors who are trying to avoid the appearance of being pedantic are using no in-text referents for their notes.

(Adapted with permission from Priscilla Taylor, "The Watchful Eye." *The Editorial Eye*. EEI, Alexandria, Va., August 1992:6–7)

---

be as thoroughly researched as academic books and journal articles, but their appeal is more general. One can place sources of facts and figures, of direct quotations, and of original ideas in an occasional footnote or weave them into the text, even adding publishing information if desired.

> Kenneth G. Wilson, on the other hand, sees the total elimination of sexism in writing as a slow and time-consuming process (*Van Winkle's Return*, University Press of New England, 1987, p. 113).

Various formats are possible, depending on whether the author's name or book title is mentioned in the sentence itself; for example, the last example could also read as follows:

> In his book *Van Winkle's Return* (1987), Kenneth G. Wilson sees the total elimination of sexism in writing as a slow and time-consuming process.

Page numbers may not be necessary, especially if the writer is referring to a work as a whole. If the author quotes directly, however, a page number should be cited.

Sometimes an informal list of sources is included. For example, near the end of each issue the *Smithsonian* magazine lists "Additional Reading" suggestions on its article topics. Many nonfiction books also list sources at the end of the book, making it possible for readers to concentrate on the text without tripping over footnotes or strings of source citations in text.

Such source listings may vary widely in format. If only two or three published sources are consulted, the writer will probably incorporate them into the wording of the text. But a biographer who consulted many books, periodicals, or personal papers and conducted hundreds of interviews should list those sources at the end of the book. Such a list can be organized by chapter, topic, or type of source. The format chosen depends on the nature of the sources. It can be narrative, or references can be cast in a formal bibliographic style.

Informal: Information about Faulkner's foray into screen writing comes from the reminiscences of fellow writers James Smith and John Jones.

Formal: Jones, John. Screenwriter, Metro-Goldwyn-Mayer, 1939–1958. Personal interviews July 7–10, 1969.

Smith, James. Screenwriter, freelance, 1949–present. Letter, June 30, 1970.

Again, the format is secondary to the content; no one style is necessarily better than another. The entries must be consistent, accurate, and complete, however, so that the reader can readily locate the source independently.

COMPLETE DOCUMENTATION: FOR THE PROFESSIONAL READER

Manuscripts that describe an author's research require the most meticulous and complete documentation. Writers must exercise a certain amount of judgment as to what to put in a note or footnote, however; to be on the safe side, many inexperienced writers tend to document too heavily, and the result is a paper or article that is tedious to read. Many facts of a general nature—such as those that can be found in a number of sources—do not need to carry source citations. Also, any notes and comments that are important enough to mention should probably be worked into the text itself, not automatically relegated to note or footnote status.

Social Sciences and the Humanities

Writers in the social sciences and humanities are most likely to include "full" documentation—that is, notes keyed to the text by superscript or parenthetical numbers and explained in footnotes or endnotes, which are really footnotes grouped at the end of an article, chapter, or book. These notes identify the exact source of quotations, paraphrased passages, facts and figures, and ideas.

Traditional notes include the full name of the author and the title of the source material, complete publication information, and page numbers (the abbreviation *pp.* is being used less frequently, except when clarity demands it). Subsequent citations from the same source are shortened to the author's last name, a simplified rendering of the title (if more than one of an author's works are cited), and the page number. If the source is the same as the one immediately preceding, the abbreviation ibid. (now considered English and hence no longer italicized) may be used instead of the author's name and shortened title. Although ibid. is still in use, most authorities have abandoned the two other traditional bibliographic abbreviations—op. cit., meaning "in the same work," and loc. cit., meaning "in a location previously cited." The following list illustrates these conventions.

1. Brian Lamb, *C-SPAN: America's Town Hall* (Washington, D.C.: Acropolis Books, 1988), 123–124.
2. Barton Gellman, "Law and Order," *Washington Post Magazine,* Nov. 17, 1991, 13.
3. Lamb, 17.
4. Ibid., 212–213.
5. Gellman, 13.

When a simpler, less formal documentation style will do, notes may include only enough information to identify the full source in the bibliography; this is usually the last name of the author, a shortened title if appropriate, and the page number.

In addition to providing sources, notes can also include informational asides that do not readily fit in the main text. Such notes might identify sources for further reading on the topic at hand or mention a source that contradicts a point made in the text. Sometimes notes provide examples of computations or statistical information that is important to the topic but would interrupt the flow of the main text.

The use of footnotes versus endnotes is often as much a production issue as an editorial decision. Without sophisticated typesetting software, placing footnotes correctly can be time consuming and costly. If many informational footnotes are used, the resulting book pages can have an unbalanced look. For these reasons endnotes have become the norm for all but the most traditional publishers.

The bibliography—the list of sources used by the writer—is placed at the end of the article or book. Sources are listed alphabetically by the last name of the author and include full titles and publication information. All sources used, not just those directly quoted or cited in notes, are included. In an extremely long bibliography or one that includes many different kinds of sources other than published works, sources may be grouped into separate alphabetical lists of books, periodical articles, letters and personal papers, and interviews.

An individual bibliographic entry traditionally includes the author's name, the complete title of the source, and full publication information: for books, the city (and state or country when necessary to prevent confusion), publisher's name, and year of publication; for articles in periodicals, the periodical name, volume number, inclusive page numbers, and date of publication. Any additional information that will help the reader locate the source should also be included: edition, volume number, series or book editor, and the like.

The exact arrangement of elements in a bibliography is fairly standard. If the manuscript was edited using a particular style manual, the bibliographic format recommended by that style manual should be used. If no particular style manual is specified, consistency in punctuation and order of the elements become the most important considerations. The last section of this chapter offers a simple and fairly traditional approach for styling the most common types of sources.

Scientific and Technical Material

Formal documentation is an essential part of scientific and technical literature, which may take the form of papers presented at a conference, a chapter in a monograph or textbook, or articles in a professional journal. Here, reference lists are nearly as important as the text itself; previously published research findings are usually the springboard for new studies, and their careful citation not only provides a context for the new research but also lends legitimacy. Inaccurate citation of sources may create an impression of sloppiness that could cast doubts on the accuracy of the original research. Every citation in the text must have a corresponding entry in the reference list, and, conversely, every entry in the reference list must be cited in the text.

The format of text citations and bibliographic entries is most often dictated by the organization or publication that publishes the research. Professional journals usually provide style guidelines for authors. Book publishers may also issue style sheets. In the absence of a specified style, a back issue of a journal or another book in a monograph series can provide samples of editorial style decisions, including how to cite references in text and how to style the reference list itself. Writers may choose to follow a style manual used in a particular field, such as the *American Medical Association Manual of Style* for medical topics or the *CBE* (Council of Biology Editors) *Style Manual* for the life sciences.

There are two popular formats. The *name-date* style uses an alphabetical reference list and parenthetical text citations that give the last name of the author and the year of publication. Absolute consistency between the text citation and the entry in the reference list is required: names must have the same spelling, and years must be the same. Every entry in the reference list must be cited in the text. If reference entries have identical first authors and years, they may be distinguished from each other by adding the name of the second author (if different) or by adding *a* and *b* to the years in both the text citation and the reference list entry. Some sample name-date text citations follow.

(Kraft 1992)
(Haynes and Higgins 1992)
(Weidner et al. 1992)
(Caudill, Richards, et al. 1991; Caudill, Lill, et al. 1991) *or* (Caudill et al. 1991*a,* 1991*b*)

The *numbered* style features references numbered in the order in which each is first mentioned in the text and cited by superscripts or numbers in parentheses immediately following the referenced information (not necessarily the end of a sentence). This style leaves the text relatively uncluttered with names and dates. References appear only once in the reference list but can be cited many times in the text, always by the same number. First mentions of references are numbered consecutively throughout the article or chapter; no number gaps are allowed. Any author names that have been used in the text should match the reference exactly. Examples of the two formats for numbered text citations follow.

Recent studies[41–44]. . . . *or* Recent studies (41–44). . . .
Examples were published elsewhere[3,7,9–11]. . . . *or* Examples were published elsewhere (3,7,9–11). . . .

The parenthetical number style is recommended for statistical or scientific papers featuring mathematical expressions because exponents might be confused with superscript reference callouts.

Punctuation with superscript footnotes follows the same general rules as punctuation with quotation marks: Superscript numbers are placed inside colons and semicolons and outside commas and periods.

. . . are examples of recent studies.[41–44]
. . . are examples of recent studies[41–44]; others are described below.

KNOTTY PROBLEMS IN DOCUMENTATION

Callout Placement

Careful placement in text of the name-date citation is important. In the first example below, the name-date placement implies that the information in the sentence can be found in both the Frantzich and the Lamb sources. The second example makes clear that part of the sentence is based on the Frantzich source and the rest is based on Lamb's.

The revolution in information processing and the televising of congressional hearings and general sessions have changed the political process forever (Frantzich 1990; Lamb 1988).

The revolution in information processing (Frantzich 1990) and the televising of congressional hearings and general sessions (Lamb 1988) have changed the political process forever.

Order of Name-Date Citations

When several name-date citations appear in one set of parentheses, they should be arranged either chronologically from oldest to most recent or alphabetically. Citations of several works by the same author are arranged with single author citations first (listed chronologically if there is more than one such citation), citations by the same author with one other author next (arranged alphabetically by the second author, if there is more than one such citation), and then citations by the same author et al. (arranged chronologically). The same string of citations arranged in the two styles is shown in the following examples.

Alphabetical: (Barton 1980; Barton and Mentzer 1972; Barton and Miller 1979; Barton et al. 1979; Lill and Richards 1990, 1992; Richards 1989*a*, 1989*b*)

Chronological: (Barton and Mentzer 1972; Barton and Miller 1979; Barton et al. 1979; Barton 1980; Richards 1989*a*, 1989*b*; Lill and Richards 1990, 1992)

LAST NAME FIRST; FIRST NAME, MIDDLE NAME LAST

Last name first. That sounds simple enough until names complicated by particles (de, van, Le), hyphenation, and two-word surnames appear. Here are some hints: Keep hyphenated names intact (Sackville-West, Victoria; Saint-Gaudens, Augustus); generally include particles as part of the last name (Le Carre, John); place Jr. and III after the first name (Harvey, Paul Jr.); watch for two-word surnames (Conan Doyle, Arthur; Garcia Marquez, Gabriel); and do not invert Chinese names—they are already arranged with the surname first (Chan Tai-chien). See Kate Turabian's *A Manual for Writers of Term Papers, Theses, and Dissertations* and the *CBE Style Manual* for more examples of how to handle foreign language names in name-date text citations and reference list entries.

Multiple Sources by the Same Author

Multiple sources by the same first author are no problem if a manuscript has notes or a numbered reference list and text citations. They do, however, create potential complications for alphabetical reference lists with name-date citations. There are two ways to handle this problem: add *a, b, c,* and so on to the date in both reference and citation if more than one reference would need a citation with the identical name and date, or add the second authors' names (or as many additional as needed to distinguish between the entries) to the citations. Note the following examples.

(Kraft et al. 1991*a*, 1991*b*, 1991*c*) *or* (Kraft, Daniels, et al. 1991; Kraft, Higgins, Hoge 1991; Kraft, Higgins, Mentzer 1991)

Alphabetizing the Reference List

Reference lists and bibliographies are always arranged last name first and alphabetized letter by letter for at least the first author within an entry. But what if several entries have the same first author? Most styles continue the alphabetizing to the next authors as far as needed to determine the correct order. Such a scheme first lists the entries by an author alone (these will be chronological if more than one), followed by the same author and coauthors. Any entries with identical authors, regardless of the number of authors, are arranged chronologically.

Another approach is to arrange all works by the same first author in chronological order. Again, the works by the first author alone will be first, followed by works by that author and others arranged in order of date, from oldest to most recent.

Yet another style is to group the works into three categories: first the author alone, next the same author with one other author, and last the author with two or more other authors (the "et al." citations).

Page Numbers

Page numbers in bibliographic entries are included to help a researcher find the exact source. Thus, the inclusive page numbers of a journal article or book chapter should be given. Armed with these page numbers, the researcher can go immediately to the specific article or chapter without having to search the table of contents.

The exact location of quoted passages or figures or tables must be supplied. The pages on which this material is to be found in the original source should be included in the text, not in the bibliography or reference list entry. Exactly how the page number is cited depends on the format of the text citations. The page number can be included within the parentheses with the author-date citation, added to the number citation, or worked into the wording of the text. Note the following examples.

(Rea and Lanpher 1992, p. 93)
Rea and Lanpher[45, p.93]
In their treatise on college admissions, Rea and Lanpher suggest (p. 93) that. . . .

Inclusive page numbers can be shown in a variety of ways depending on how the second number is written. The clearest uses the full page number (pp. 458–467); the most concise shortens the second number as much as possible without obscuring its meaning (pp. 345–9, 945–53, 1215–7, 1356–67). Examples in this chapter use the former style.

The 3-em Dash in Bibliographies

To save keyboarding, the 3-em dash is often used in bibliographies instead of repeating the names of the authors. This device should be used only if the author information is exactly the same for each succeeding entry; if the first author is the same but any subsequent author is different, the 3-em dash should not be used—all names should be listed.

Stoller, Robert. Primary femininity. *Journal of the American Psychoanalytic Association* 24(5):59–78, 1979.

———. A different view of Oedipal conflict. In *Infancy and Early Childhood,* Vol. 1. of *The Course of Life*. DHHS pub. no. (ADM)80–786. Washington, D.C.: U.S. Government Printing Office, 1980:534–563.

Stoller, Robert, and Gilbert Herdt. The development of masculinity: A cross-cultural contribution. *Journal of the American Psychoanalytic Association* 28(4):29–59, 1983.

HOW TO STYLE REFERENCES

Book with one author

Jerome, John. *The Writing Trade: A Year in the Life.* New York: Viking, 1992.

Book with more than one author

Lass, Abraham H., David Kiremidjian, and Ruth M. Goldstein. *The Facts On File Dictionary of Classical, Biblical, and Literary Allusions.* New York: Facts On File Publications, 1987.

Book with an organization as author

American Psychiatric Association. *Diagnostic and Statistical Manual of Mental Disorders,* 3rd ed. Washington, D.C.: American Psychiatric Association, 1980.

Compilation or anthology

Cohn, Ruby, and Bernard F. Dukore, eds. *Twentieth Century Drama: England, Ireland, the United States.* New York: Random House, 1966.

Book with more than one volume

Blair, Walter, Theodore Hornberger, Randall Stewart, et al., eds. *The Literature of the United States,* 3rd ed., 2 vols. Chicago: Scott, Foresman, 1966.

Book in a series

Spooner, F.C. The European Economy 1609–50. In *The Decline of Spain and the Thirty Years War 1609–48/59,* Vol. 4 of *The New Cambridge Modern History,* edited by J.P. Cooper. New York: Cambridge University Press, 1970.

Chapter in a book with more than one author

McKibbin, Warwick J., and Jeffrey D. Sachs. Implications of Policy Rules for the World Economy. In *Macroeconomic Policies in an Interdependent World,* edited by Ralph C. Bryant et al. Washington, D.C.: International Monetary Fund, 1989:151–194.

Item from an anthology

Franklin, Benjamin [1773]. Rules by Which a Great Empire May Be Reduced to a Small One. In *The Literature of the United States,* 3rd ed., edited by Walter Blair et al. Chicago: Scott, Foresman, 1966:310–315.

In the above example, notice the date in brackets after the author's name. This refers to the original publication date of the Franklin essay and is included because if this reference is cited in the text in the author-date style, it should read "(Franklin 1773)"; without the original publication date, the text citation would read "(Franklin 1966)," which would be inaccurate and confusing.

Book in a foreign language

Marinesco, G., and A. Kreindler. Les reflexes conditionnels [The conditioned reflexes]. In *Oeuvres choisies.* Bucharest: Editions de l'Académie de la République Populaire Roumaine, 1963:485–555.

Translation

Kafka, Franz. *Letters to Milena.* Edited by Willi Hoas, translated by Tania and James Stern. New York: Schocken Books, 1962.

Article in a scientific journal

Caroff, Stanley N., and Henry Rosenberg. Data in case reports questioned (letter). *Clinical Pharmacy* 3:588, 1984.

Hyman, Steven E. Recent developments in neurobiology: Part I. Synaptic transmission. *Psychosomatics* 29:157–165, 1988a.

Hyman, Steven E. Recent developments in neurobiology: Part II. Neurotransmitter receptors and psychopharmacology. *Psychosomatics* 29:254–263, 1988b.

Include the issue number only if the journal begins each issue with page 1 rather than numbers consecutively throughout the volume; for example, 45(6):13–17.

Article in a popular magazine

Owen, David. Profiles: Opening Windows. *The New Yorker,* Dec. 2, 1991:48–64, 101–115.

Article in a newspaper

Richards, Evelyn. IBM Restructuring Won't Necessarily Revamp Computer Industry. *Washington Post,* Nov. 30, 1991:C1.

Anonymous author

Community Policing: Wave of the Future or Same Story? (editorial). *Montgomery* [Md.] *Journal,* Nov. 29, 1991:A10.

If no author is listed, begin the reference with the title. Do not use *anon.* or *anonymous.*

Book review in a magazine

Tinder, Glenn. Capitalism Versus Conservatism (review of *Doing Well and Doing Good: The Challenge to the Christian Capitalist* by Richard John Neuhaus). *Atlantic Monthly,* Dec. 1992:143–147.

Item in a reference work

Chinese Eastern Railway. *The New Encyclopaedia Britannica,* 15th ed. (Micropedia), 1990;3:233.

Government document

U.S. Department of Health and Human Services. Public Health Service. National Institutes of Health. Office of Science Policy and Legislation. *Academic Research Equipment and Equipment Needs in the Biological Sciences: 1990.* Washington, D.C.: DHHS, Sept. 1991.

Map or chart

National Geographic Society. *World War II: Europe and North Africa* (map). Washington, D.C.: National Geographic Society, Dec. 1991.

Paper presented at a professional meeting

Frantzich, Stephen. Legislatures and the Revolution in Communications and Information Processing: Untangling the Linkage Between Technology and Politics. Paper presented at annual meeting of American Political Science Association, San Francisco, Aug. 1990.

Unpublished report

Von Horner, Sebastian. Where Is Everybody? Internal report, National Radio Astronomy Observatory, Green Bank, W. Va., n.d.

Thesis or dissertation

Caudill, Gordon R. *The Correlation of Theory and Practice in the New Stagecraft Movement as Observed in the Theories and Practices of Robert Edmund Jones and Lee Simonson.* Unpublished master's thesis, Kent State University, Kent, Ohio, 1966.

Interview

Michaelson, Mike, vice president, C-SPAN. Personal interview, Nov. 27, 1991.

Personal correspondence

Stepper, Leo. Personal correspondence with the author. Takoma Park, Md., Feb. 2, 1993.

Videocassette

Schmidt, Warren S. Managing Stress, 2nd ed. Carlsbad, Calif.: CRM Films, 1989. (videocassette)

Software documentation

Novell, Inc. *NetWare 286 Maintenance: Manual Revision 1.01 for Software Version 2.0a and Above.* Provo, Utah: Novell, Dec. 1986.

Note: The examples that follow show how to cite references for various forms of electronic media; because it may be hard to tell the type of source from the context of the citation, the nature of the source appears in parentheses at the end of the citation. This area is in a state of flux as standards and new forms of communication are developed. The best approach is to provide enough information for the reader to know where you obtained your information and then treat each similar source consistently. For more details, see *Electronic Style: A Guide for Citing Electronic Information,* by Xia Li and Nancy B. Crane (Meckler, 1993).

Software program

Pro-Cite, ver. 1.4. Ann Arbor, Mich.: Personal Bibliographic Software, August 1988. (software program)

Entire database

Medline. Bethesda, Md.: National Library of Medicine, 1989—. Available through National Library of Medicine, BRS Information Technologies, and DIALOG Information Services. (online database)

Books In Print Plus, ver. 3.5. 5th ed. New York: R.R. Bowker Electronic Publishing, 1986—. Updated quarterly. (database on CD-ROM)

Part of a database

MESH Vocabulary File. Bethesda, Md.: National Library of Medicine, cited Oct. 10, 1990. Acquired immunodeficiency syndrome. Identifier D000163. (online database)

Individual contribution to a database

Jimenez, M.A., and D.R. Jimenez. Training volunteer caregivers of persons with AIDS. *Social Work Health Care* 14(3):73–85, 1990. In PsycINFO. Arlington, Va.: American Psychological Association, cited Dec. 7, 1990. Accession no. 77-31957. Available through BRS Information Technologies. (online database)

Electronic bulletin board

GRATEFUL MED BBS. Bethesda, Md.: National Library of Medicine, 1989—. (electronic bulletin board)

Newhouse, Eric. The Risk List. In ALIX (Automated Library Information Exchange). Washington, D.C.: Federal Library and Information Center Network, cited Nov. 20, 1990. Shareware Conference 1. (electronic bulletin board)

Electronic mail

Jones, William R. Culture technique. E-mail message to James Larson, Nov. 15, 1990.

ANNOTATED BIBLIOGRAPHY OF STANDARD STYLE MANUALS

The ACS Style Guide: A Manual for Authors and Editors. Washington, D.C.: American Chemical Society, 1986. The ACS guide stresses "those principles and practices that are desirable throughout the scientific literature" (foreword, p. xv), not just for ACS publications. The brief section on references, nine pages, includes a two-page list of preferred journal name abbreviations, as well as many examples of both in-text reference citations and reference list entries.

American Medical Association Manual of Style, 8th ed. Baltimore: Williams & Wilkins, 1989. The AMA guide "relates primarily to medical communications, where clarity is of the utmost importance" (foreword, p. v). In addition to the usual book and journal article examples, the discussion of references includes sections on how to handle foreign language titles and special materials such as legal cases and government documents. The guide also has extensive lists of abbreviations used in the biomedical sciences.

CBE Style Manual: A Guide for Authors, Editors, and Publishers in the Biological Sciences, 5th ed., revised. Bethesda, Md.: Council of Biology Editors, 1983. The chapter on references contains a useful section on treatment of names of foreign authors, followed by several pages of sample citations for journal articles, books and monographs, technical reports, conference proceedings, and miscellaneous publications. A revised edition was published in 1994.

The Chicago Manual of Style, 14th ed. Chicago: University of Chicago Press, 1993. This edition devotes two lengthy chapters to documentation. Chapter 15, Documentation 1, presents the documentary-note style favored for writing in literature, history, and the arts. Chapter 16, Documentation 2, discusses the more economical author-date system recommended for the natural sciences and most social sciences. Citing the practicality of the author-date system, the Chicago Press even encourages authors in other fields to use that style if possible. Both chapters feature explanations of style points and numerous examples.

The MLA Handbook for Writers of Research Papers, 3rd ed. New York: Modern Language Association of America, 1988. This guide addresses conventions used to prepare scholarly research papers and reports. Chapter 4 provides more than 200 sample entries illustrating bibliographic style, and chapter 5 explains what to document.

Publication Manual of the American Psychological Association, 3rd ed., revised. Washington, D.C.: The American Psychological Association, 1984. The APA manual recommends the author-date citation style and provides many pages of examples of how to cite various publications in a bibliography. The style is basically scientific.

Turabian, Kate L. *A Manual for Writers of Term Papers, Theses, and Dissertations,* 5th ed., revised. Chicago: University of Chicago

Press, 1987. This little book has been used for decades by college students. It features a simple bibliographic style based on the Chicago manual and has a particularly detailed section on how to cite government documents.

Words Into Type, 3rd ed., revised. Englewood Cliffs, N.J.: Prentice Hall, 1974. Known as much for its explanations of the production process as for its editorial sections, this guide has a brief section that answers most of the common questions about reference style.

21

FOREIGN LANGUAGES

FOREIGN LANGUAGES

Many writers and editors need, on occasion, some knowledge of how foreign languages are set into type. Although knowledge of the language in question is always helpful, with some guidance editors can often manage basic capitalization, punctuation, word division, and use of accents and diacritics, especially in languages that use the Latin alphabet. For languages that do not use the Latin alphabet—for example, Arabic, Hebrew, Russian, Chinese, Japanese, and Greek—scholars have developed ways to reproduce the sounds of those alphabets with letters of the Latin alphabet. These are known as transliteration or romanization systems. Many languages have more than one accepted transliteration into English—for example, Wade-Giles and pinyin for Chinese. Depending on the level of scholarliness and the intended readers, transliteration systems may vary. For example, diacritics are rarely used in transliterated versions meant for a general audience. On the other hand, if the intended readers are likely to know the original language, care is taken to transliterate as explicitly as possible, indicating with diacritics the letters of the original language.

This chapter has two parts: In the section on languages that use the Latin alphabet, we discuss Danish, Dutch, Finnish, French, German, Hungarian, Italian, Latin, Norwegian, Polish, Portuguese, Spanish, Swedish, and Turkish. In the section on transliterated languages, we cover Arabic, Chinese, classical Greek, Hebrew, and Russian. For more details on each language covered here, except Arabic and Chinese, consult the *U.S. Government Printing Office Style Manual* and the sources cited therein. For a comprehensive treatment of 140 languages that do not use the Latin alphabet, including Japanese, Korean, and Persian, see *ALA-LC Romanization Tables: Transliteration Schemes for Non-Roman Scripts,* published by the Cataloging Distribution Division of the Library of Congress.

A few comments about foreign languages in general are in order. If a foreign language word or phrase appears in an English text, the editor should first check the main section of a recent English dictionary to determine whether the word or phrase has been incorporated into English. If it has, the dictionary's recommendations for capitalization, plurals, accents, and word division should be followed. Also, once the word is part of English, it is not necessary to set it in italics. If the word has not been anglicized, it should be set in italics; this rule does not apply to names of cities, places, and people. Note, however, that *all* examples of foreign words in this chapter are italicized whether or not they are proper names. Also, to improve readability, if foreign language text runs for more than a sentence or two, it should not be italicized.

Most Latin alphabet languages and transliterated languages use diacritics—marks that show phonetic values or distinguish words that are otherwise identical. Usage varies from language to language as to whether diacritics are retained when a letter is capitalized. The notes on the alphabets and special characters that follow are intended primarily to alert writers and editors to the various complexities that exist in certain languages.

Capitalization practice varies widely, but most languages use fewer capital letters than English. For example, in most languages the days of the week and months of the year, the personal pronoun *I*, and adjectives derived from proper names are seldom capitalized. As a general rule, in titles of books and articles, only the first word and any proper nouns are capitalized. Names of foreign periodicals, however, are generally capitalized as in English. Capitalization of some transliterated languages is often arbitrary because lowercase and uppercase letters may not be part of the language, as in Chinese and Arabic.

Punctuation in foreign languages is often quite different from English usage. For example, many European languages use commas around all subordinate clauses, restrictive and nonrestrictive; many use no series comma; a number use the em dash to introduce dialogue; and alternative quotation marks range from the French guillemets (« ») to the German double prime (″) or inverted quotation marks („ “). Readers unfamiliar with Spanish punctuation marks may be surprised to see upside-down question marks and exclamation points.

Word division is often tricky in English and can be more so in other languages. Here we give basic information on combinations that should not be divided and stress the general rule that at least two or three letters should be carried over to the next line whenever possible. For several languages, the guidance states to "keep prefixes and suffixes intact, and divide compound words on their component parts," a decision that may be difficult for those who do not know the language being used; in some cases, an educated guess, backed up by looking up the word in a dictionary of the language, may provide enough information to solve the problem, but the best approach is to check with a person who knows the language.

One final note: The guidance provided here is basic and intended to answer simple questions; to ensure accuracy, consult an expert on the language in question.

DIACRITICS

Knowing the correct terms for diacritics can be helpful when dealing with typesetters or language experts; you may be tempted to call the mark over an *n* in Spanish a short squiggly line, but it's usually better to ask for a tilde. Here's a selected list of definitions and the diacritics with sample letters. Many word processing and desktop publishing programs allow placement of these marks in text, and most laser printers will print them; it's a good idea to carefully check final printouts for proper placement, however.

Mark	*Example*
acute	í
double acute	ő
caron, hachek	ž
cedilla	ç
centered dot	l·
circumflex	â
crossbar	ŧ
dot above	ċ
grave	è
macron	ū
ogonek	ą
ring above, angstrom	å
slash	ø
stroke	ł
tilde	ñ
umlaut, dieresis	ü

LANGUAGES THAT USE THE LATIN ALPHABET

Danish

Alphabet and Special Characters. Danish uses the Latin alphabet plus these special characters: *æ, ø,* and *å* and their capitals. *Aa* and *aa* can be used instead of Å or å. The letters *c, q, x,* and *z* are used only in foreign words and proper names. The character *å* usually falls after the *Zs* in alphabetical listings.

Capitalization. Danish nouns are not capitalized, but the polite personal pronouns *De, Dem, Deres,* meaning *you,* and the familiar form of *I* are capitalized. The pronouns for *he, she,* and *it* (*de, deres, dem*) are not capitalized.

Punctuation. Use commas to set off restrictive and nonrestrictive clauses.

Word Division. Carry over at least three letters to the next line. Keep prefixes and suffixes intact, and divide compound words on their component parts.

Divide words before a consonant standing between vowels. Do not divide the combinations *gj, kj, kv, lj, skj, sk, sp, spr, st, str,* and *sv.* They belong with the following vowel.

Dutch

Alphabet and Special Characters. Dutch uses the Latin alphabet and has no special characters except for limited use of accents on *a, e, i,* and *o.* The letters *ij* are equivalent to the English *y* and are treated like a ligature; both letters must be uppercased when they begin a capitalized word: *IJsland.* The letters *q, x,* and *y* appear only in foreign words.

Capitalization. Capitalize the pronouns *U* (*you*), *Uw* (*your*), and *Gij* (*you*) in personal correspondence.

Capitalize proper adjectives as in English.

Lowercase *ik* (*I*).

Lowercase the months of the year and the days of the week.

Lowercase single letters that begin a sentence, but capitalize the next word.

Lowercase *de, ten,* and *van* in family names only when used with the given name; capitalize these particles when the given name is not used: *Kees van Dongen,* but *Van Dongen.*

Punctuation. Punctuation is similar to that of German, except that apostrophes are used to show the plural and possessive of foreign loanwords: *sofa's.* Quotation marks are set like this: „*Jan.*"

Word Division. Carry over at least three letters to the next line.

Divide compounds according to their component parts.

Divide words on a vowel or before a consonant standing between vowels.

Do not divide *ch;* keep it with the vowel that follows.

In a group of two or more consonants, divide before the last consonant.

Finnish

Alphabet and Special Characters. Finnish uses the Latin alphabet with two umlauted characters: Ä, *ä* and Ö, *ö*. The letters *b, c, f, q,* and *z* do not occur in native Finnish words.

Capitalization. Capitalize proper names, references to God (*Jumala*), names of foreign countries but not names of nationalities or languages, and all main words in names of periodicals and titles of unique literary works: *Ussi Testamentii, Vanha Kalevala.* Days of the week and months of the year are lowercased.

The personal pronoun *sinä* is capitalized when referring to relatives, children, or close friends or in poetry. The personal pronoun *te* is capitalized when used to address a third person or a group of persons with a mark of respect.

Punctuation. The period is used to separate parts of dates: 4.30.1994 is April 30, 1994.

The colon is used to replace letters in abbreviations: *k:lo* for *kello,* meaning "o'clock."

The apostrophe is used to show omission of a letter and in foreign words and names that end in a vowel sound to separate the end of the name from the Finnish case ending: *Loti'n* ("of Loti").

The hyphen is used in compound words between two identical vowels (*raha-apu*) and in compounds formed with numbers or abbreviations (*30-vuotias*).

Word Division. Rules for word division are quite detailed in Finnish; see the *GPO Style Manual* for more information. In general, divide between vowels that do not form diphthongs, and do not separate a single vowel, especially at the beginning of a word, from the rest of the word.

Divide on a vowel or on a diphthong before a single consonant. Divide between double letters of a consonant or two different consonants. Divide between the last consonants of two or more consonants that appear together.

Divide compound words on their component parts.

French

Alphabet and Special Characters. French uses the Latin alphabet, except for *w* (although it may occur in words of foreign origin), plus these special characters: *à, â, ç, é, è, ê, ë, î, ï, ô, œ (oe), ù, û, ü.* Accents may be omitted from capital letters; *à* never carries the accent when capitalized, but *È* often does.

Capitalization. Capitalize the first words of sentences, phrases, verses, speeches, and citations.

Capitalize proper names of people, families, and dynasties; names of the deity; the names of stars, constellations, and planets; and the names of mythological divinities and abstractions. Capitalize place names and names of streets, squares, buildings, ships, monuments, and the like. Note that the proper name is capped, but the article is lowercased, as are common noun elements such as *place, mer, mont: la rue de Tuileries, la place de la Concorde, le Parthénon, le Titanic.*

Capitalize only the first major word of names of institutions and organizations (*la Légion d'honneur, l'Académie française*); however, if names are hyphenated, both words are capped (*la Comédie-Française, les Etats-Unis*).

Capitalize names of holidays (*la fête de Noël*); names of historical events and periods (*la Renaissance, la Révolution*); names of nationalities (*un Anglais*); titles (*sa Majesté, le General de Gaulle, M. le Duc*).

Capitalize only the first word and any proper nouns in the titles of books, articles, and other works.

Lowercase the names of the days and months: *lundi, avril;* nouns or adjectives derived from proper names (*l'Académie française*); the word *saint* when referring to the saints themselves, but not when used in a place name (*Mont-Saint-Michel, rue Sainte-Catherine*); the titles *monsieur, madame,* and so on in direct address; and names of most religious groups and their members (*un protestant, les catholiques, un chrétien*), but *un Juif.*

Punctuation. Commas are used sparingly; do not use series commas or commas to set off nonrestrictive clauses.

Numbers with four or more digits are separated by thin spaces or periods, not commas: 7 423, 7.423.

A comma is used instead of a decimal point: 1,2 percent.

French texts often use English-style quotation marks, particularly when French and English are mixed in a text. The traditional French quotation marks (« ») are called *guillemets*. They are used less often than are quotation marks in English text. An em dash often replaces the guillemets in dialogue:

—Quand veux-tu partir?
—Tout de suite.

If a quotation is just a word or phrase, any punctuation falls outside the guillemets. Otherwise, guillemets are used much as quotation marks are used in English: to announce a long quotation and to indicate the end of that quotation, to indicate a quotation within dialogue that begins with an em dash, and to show a quotation within a quotation (in this last case, any runover line begins with opening guillemets; only one pair of guillemets is used at the end).

Ellipsis marks are used as they are in English, except that a space is used after but not before them.

Hyphens are used much more frequently in French than in English to combine words—for example, between inverted verbs and pronouns in questions, in spelled-out numbers, in geographic names, and in certain common expressions and phrases. Care should be taken not to mistake end-of-line hyphens for hyphens that should be retained.

Word Division. Divide on a vowel whenever possible. In French, a consonant that falls between two vowels starts a new syllable, with these exceptions: a silent *e* following a vowel does not form a syllable, nor do *i, y, o, ou,* and *u* when they precede other vowels and are sounded as consonants (*bien, loin, ouest*).

Words containing apostrophes should not be divided at the apostrophe.

Division should be avoided before *x* or *y* and after *x* or *y* before a vowel or *h*.

Divide any two consonants, with these exceptions: *gn*, which should not be divided unless each letter has a separate sound, and *bl, br, ch, cl, cr, dr, fl, gl, gr, gh, ph, pl, pr, th, tr,* and *vr.*

As a rule, do not separate two vowels.

Divide foreign words according to the rules of their language and technical terms and compound words according to their component parts.

German

Alphabet and Special Characters. German uses the Latin alphabet with these special characters: *ß* (representing *ss*) and the umlauted vowels *ä, ö,* and *ü* and their capital letters. If the ligature *ß* is not available, *ss* may be used. Instead of an umlaut over a capital letter, a lowercase *e* may be inserted after the capital.

Capitalization. Capitalize all nouns and words used as nouns (*Gasthof, Krankenhaus*) except when used to form part of an adverbial phrase: *heute abend* (*tonight*).

Capitalize the pronouns *Sie, Ihr,* and *Ihnen* (*you*), but lowercase *ich* (*I*). In correspondence, capitalize *Du, Dein,* and their various forms.

Lowercase proper adjectives.

Punctuation. The apostrophe shows the colloquial omission of *e.* Most proper names in German use no apostrophe to show possession, but simply add an *s;* after proper names ending in *s, ß, x,* and *z,* however, the *s* is replaced by an apostrophe.

Quotation marks are pairs of double prime marks (″ ″) or inverted quotation marks („ “). Punctuation that belongs to the sentence or phrase being quoted falls inside the quotation marks.

The comma is used to set off all subordinate clauses, restrictive and nonrestrictive alike.

The series comma is not used.

Footnotes precede end punctuation.

Numbers with four or more digits are set off in groups of threes, divided by thin spaces or periods, not commas: 250 000, 250.000.

A comma is used instead of a decimal point: 49,5 percent.

Periods, commas, and semicolons fall outside closing quotation marks that set off words or phrases, but they fall inside quotation marks that set off an entire sentence.

Word Division. Divide on a vowel whenever possible.

Carry over only the last consonant if two or more consonants come between vowels.

Do not separate the letter groups *ch, sch, ph, st,* and *th* unless the letters belong to different syllables.

If *ck* must be divided, use *k-k: Hacke* is divided *Hak-ke.* Remember to restore the original spelling if the type is reset and the word is no longer broken.

Divide compound words according to their component parts, except if the first word ends in *s* and the second begins with *t: Reichs-tag.*

Do not divide a word so that a single letter is separated from the rest.

Hungarian

Alphabet and Special Characters. Hungarian uses the Latin alphabet and these special characters: *Á, á, É, é, Í, í, Ó, ó, Ö, ö, Ú, ú, Ü, ü,* and *Ű, ű.*

Capitalization. Capitalize proper names and names referring to God, but lowercase adjectives formed from proper names. Lowercase months of the year and days of the week.

Capitalize all main words in names of periodicals and titles of publications like dictionaries, handbooks, and encyclopedias, and capitalize the first word only and proper names in titles of poems, books, and monographs.

Capitalize second and third person personal pronouns in correspondence and public addresses: *Te, Ön.*

Lowercase names of nationalities, ethnic groups, and religious units.

Punctuation. The *GPO Style Manual* offers much detail on word division in Hungarian. A few general guidelines follow.

Use periods in dates, which appear in year, month, and day order: 1994.IV.30 is April 30, 1994.

Use commas to separate the parts of compound and complex sentences.

In correspondence use the exclamation mark, not the comma, after the salutation.

In works of fiction, use dashes to introduce dialogue.

Place opening quotation marks on the lower level of the line and closing quotation marks on the upper level („ ... ”); use guillemets to show a quotation within a quotation.

Word Division. Every word has as many syllables as it has vowels; consonants alone do not constitute syllables.

Do not leave one letter at the end of a line or alone at the beginning of the next line.

In words with only one consonant between two vowels, keep the consonant with the second syllable.

Do not divide compound letters (for example, *asz-tal*). See the *GPO Style Manual* for more details.

Italian

Alphabet and Special Characters. Italian uses the Latin alphabet, with the exception of *k, w, x,* and *y,* which are used only in words of foreign origin and in certain Italian surnames. The grave accent is used on accented open *e*'s and open *o*'s at the ends of words (*caffè, amò*); on accented *a*'s, *i*'s, and *u*'s at the ends of words (*sarà, finì, Gesù*); and to distinguish between *e* (meaning "and") and *è* (meaning "is"). The acute accent is used on accented closed *e*'s at the ends of words (*perché, cosicché*).

Capitalization. Capitalize words at the beginning of a sentence or after a period; also capitalize the first word after a colon when the sentence indicates direct discourse of the speaker before the colon.

Capitalize proper names, surnames, and nicknames; the titles of dignitaries and high offices (*il Papa, il Ministro, il Prefetto, il Sindaco, il Vescovo, l'Eccellenza*); the names of sacred persons (*Dio, la Vergine, lo Spirito Santo*); the names of centuries and holidays (*il Trecento, il Natale, la Pasqua, l'Assunzione*).

Do not capitalize the days of the week or months of the year.

Capitalize the names of streets and institutions: *la Via del Piombo, il Liceo Parini, l'Università, l'Accademia.*

Capitalize the names of peoples but not the adjectives derived from those names: *gli Italiani, gli Inglesi, i Romani* (the Italians, the English, the Romans) but *gli scrittori inglesi* (the English writers).

Capitalize the titles of books and works of any type: *la Divina Commedia, la Pietà, il Barbiere di Siviglia, il Cinque Maggio.* Capitalize the first word only and any proper names in titles and heads. Capitalize all words in the names of periodicals, however.

Capitalize only the first letter of acronyms: *Usa, Bnl.*

Capitalize the formal pronouns for *you* (*Ella, Lei, Loro*).

Punctuation. Use commas to set off restrictive and nonrestrictive clauses.

Use commas in the salutation of a letter, even when a colon would be used in English.

Use commas in addresses, between the name of the street and the number: *Via Roma, 15.*

Use the apostrophe only to indicate vowel elision.

Use guillemets for quotation marks (see "French" above).

Use ellipsis points as they are used in English.

Word Division. Carry over at least three letters to the next line. If a single consonant falls between two vowels, it belongs with the following vowel.

Do not divide the combinations *ch, gh, cl, fl, gl, pl, gn, s* plus a consonant, and *r* plus a consonant, except for an *s* that forms a prefix.

Words may be divided between double consonants.

If *l, m, n,* or *r* is the first of two or more consonants in the middle of a word, it belongs with the preceding vowel, and the remaining consonants are kept with the following vowel.

Do not separate two adjacent vowels unless the second is accented.

In a compound formed with an apostrophe, do not divide after the apostrophe.

Latin

Alphabet and Special Characters. The Latin alphabet uses no special characters. Elementary texts may mark long vowels with a macron (*ā, ē, ī, ō, ū*).

Capitalization. Because the Romans used all capital letters, capitalization in modern times generally follows English practice. In titles and headings, capitalize only the first word and any proper nouns and adjectives.

Punctuation. Follow English practice.

Word Division. Follow English practice for division of Latin scientific names.

Carry over at least three letters to the next line.

Divide compound words according to their component parts, and keep prefixes and suffixes intact.

Words may be divided between vowels that are not diphthongs in that word: *pu-er.*

Divide before a consonant that stands between two vowels.

Do not divide the consonant combinations *qu, ch, ph,* and *th.* Doubled consonants may be divided.

Divide before *bl, br, ch, cl, cr, dl, dr, fl, fr, gh, gl, gr, pl, pr, th, tl,* and *tr* unless the second letter is the first letter in the second part of a compound word.

Divide other combinations of two or more consonants after the last consonant.

Do not divide a word immediately after an apostrophe.

Norwegian

Alphabet and Special Characters. There are two official Norwegian languages—*Bokmål*, used by the majority in Norway, and *Nynorsk,* based on rural Norwegian dialects. Both have 29 letters, consisting of the Latin alphabet plus *æ, ø,* and *å* or *aa.* In alphabetic listings, these letters follow Z. The letters *c, q, w, x,* and *z* are used only in foreign words and proper nouns.

Capitalization. Capitalize proper nouns, but not the adjectives derived from them.

Capitalize the polite personal pronouns *De, Dem,* and *Deres.*

Capitalize the first word and proper names in titles and headings.

Lowercase the days of the week and the months of the year.

Punctuation. Series commas are not used. Commas are sometimes used for decimal points; commas are not used between thousands: 100 000.

Word Division. Carry over at least three letters to the next line.

Divide compounds according to their component parts, and keep prefixes and suffixes intact.

Divide simple words before a consonant standing between vowels.

If a word has two or more consonants, divide before the last consonant, except for *kv, sk, skj, sp, st,* and *str;* these combinations cannot be separated and should be kept with the following vowel.

Polish

Alphabet and Special Characters. Polish uses the Latin alphabet with the exception of *q, v,* and *x.* It uses these special characters: *a, ć, e, ł, ń, ó, ś, ź,* and *ż.* These are alphabetized as separate characters following the unaccented forms.

Capitalization. Capitalization is similar to that in English, except that proper adjectives, days of the week, and months of the year are lowercased. Capitalize the first word and all important words in names of periodicals.

Punctuation. Follow English practice in general; the comma is used with restrictive as well as nonrestrictive clauses.

Word Division. Carry over at least three letters to the next line.

Divide compound words according to their component parts, and keep prefixes and suffixes intact.

Divide a word before a consonant standing between vowels.

Never divide these consonant combinations: *ch, cz, dz, dź, dż, rz, sz, szcz, ść.*

These consonant combinations make up one syllable and should not be divided if possible: *bl, bł, br, brz, chl, chł, chr, chrz, chw, dl, dł, dr, drź, dw, fl, fr.*

Do not divide these vowel-consonant combinations: *bi, fi, gi, gie, ki, kie, mi, ni, pi,* and *wi.*

Portuguese

Alphabet and Special Characters. Portuguese uses the Latin alphabet except for *k, w,* and *y,* which are used only in special cases, and these special characters: *á, â, à,* and *ä.* The tilde (˜) is used over the letters *n* and *o* to indicate nasalization. The dieresis is used with the letter *u* (*ü*) to show that it has the value of *w*. The cedilla is used with the letter *c* (*ç*) to indicate the value of *s* before *a, o,* and *u*. Accents are not required on capital letters except in headlines.

Capitalization. Capitalization follows English style except that the days of the week and the months of the year and all proper adjectives are lowercased.

Punctuation. Punctuation marks are like those used in English. The apostrophe is no longer used as a sign of contraction between prepositions and pronouns.

Word Division. Portuguese word division can be quite complicated; the following are basic principles.

Carry over at least three letters to the next line.

Divide before a consonant standing between vowels.

Do not divide the following consonant combinations: *bl, br, ch, chr, cl, cr, ct, dl, dr, fl, fr, gl, gr, gu, lh, nh, ph, pl, pr, ps, pt, qu, sc, sp, st* (may be divided following a consonant), *th, tl, tr, vl, vr.*

Spanish

Alphabet and Special Characters. Spanish uses the Latin alphabet plus *Ñ* and *ñ*. The combinations *ch, ll,* and *rr* are considered to be single letters, and in a dictionary words beginning with these letters will fall at the end of the *C, L,* and *R* listings, respectively.

The acute accent is sometimes used over a vowel to show stress or to distinguish words identical in form but different in meaning. The *u* with the dieresis (*ü*) is seen with *gue* and *gui* when the *u* is pronounced. Accent marks are unnecessary over capital letters.

Capitalization. Capitalize proper names, names of the deity, and titles of honor.

Capitalize only the first words and proper nouns in titles of books and other works and in headings and captions.

Capitalize the first word and all major words in the names of periodicals.

Lowercase the names of the months of the year and days of the week.

Lowercase titles that stand alone (*señor*) as well as titles with proper names: *el presidente Clinton, el general Humberto Ortega.*

Lowercase proper adjectives or names derived from proper nouns (*teatro español*).

Punctuation. With a few notable exceptions, punctuation is similar to that in English. The most obvious difference is the use of inverted exclamation points and question marks at the beginning of a question or exclamation, even within a sentence.

Si quiere visitar el México, ¿por qué no estudia español?

Series commas are not used.

Quotation marks are used as they are in English except for dialogue, for which em dashes are preferred at the beginning of each speaker's words. Guillemets are also seen, as they are in French. Periods and commas are placed outside quotation marks.

Hyphens are used only in word division, and apostrophes are not used in modern Spanish.

Word Division. Divide on a vowel or group of vowels wherever possible. The hyphen follows the vowel if the next letter is a single consonant. Do not divide two or more adjacent vowels. Do not leave a single vowel at the end of a line. Try to carry over at least two letters.

Compound words are divided on their component parts, and prefixes and suffixes are considered separate syllables.

Keep a single consonant with the following vowel.

The letters *l* and *r,* when preceded by a consonant (except for *rl, sl, tl,* and *sr*), should not be separated from that consonant except to keep a prefix intact: *Ro-dri-guez.* Other combinations of consonants may be divided except for *ch, ll,* and *rr.*

Swedish

Alphabet and Special Characters. Swedish uses the Latin alphabet and these special characters: *Å, å, Ä, ä,* and *Ö, ö.*

Capitalization. Capitalization is similar to that in English except that proper adjectives and days of the week, months of the year, and names of holidays are lowercased.

Capitalize only the first word of a compound name: *Föenta staterna* (*the United States*).

Capitalize second person pronouns (*Ni, Eder,* and *Er*) in correspondence.

Punctuation. Punctuation is also similar to that in English except that the comma is used more often. The apostrophe is not used to show possession except in foreign names.

Word Division. Divide on a vowel or a diphthong before a single consonant, a digraph, or a consonantal unit (*kv, sk, sp, st,* and *str*). In a group of two or more consonants, divide before the last.

Keep certain suffixes and adverbial prefixes intact (see the *GPO Style Manual* for a list).

Divide compound words on their component parts.

Keep the letter *x* and the nasal *ng* with the preceding syllable.

Turkish

Alphabet and Special Characters. Turkish uses the Latin alphabet and these special characters: *Â, â, Ç, ç, Ğ, ğ, İ, ı, Ö, ö, S, ş, Û, û,* and *Ü, ü.* The circumflex (ˆ) is often used over the vowels *a* and *u*. The ligature *fi* should not be used because *ı* and *i* are different letters.

Capitalization. Capitalization is similar to that in English; capitalize the days of the week and the months of the year.

Punctuation. Punctuation is also similar to that in English, except that commas and dashes are used more frequently. Guillemets (see "French" above) are used as quotation marks.

Word Division. Turkish has no groups of vowels or consonants that may not be divided, but the following general practices apply.

Divide on a vowel before a single consonant; in a group of two or more consonants, divide before the last consonant.

Divide compound words on their component parts; Turkish has no prefixes as such, but the negative particle *gayri* acts as a prefix and is kept intact: *gayri-matbu.*

Divide on the apostrophe indicating hiatus: *mes'-ul.*

LANGUAGES THAT USE NON-LATIN ALPHABETS

Arabic

Because Arabic is spoken—with variations—in so many different regions and countries and because several transliteration systems are used, transliterating Arabic into English is not easy. Inconsistencies among the different transliteration systems are common and include variations in spelling, capitalization (since Arabic does not distinguish between uppercase and lowercase letters), and even the Latin letters chosen to represent certain phonetic sounds. For general purposes, a system that uses the fewest diacritics is preferred. For scholarly works, see the system outlined in the Library of Congress' *ALA-LC Romanization Tables.*

Alphabet and Special Characters. Special characters include the soft sign or prime (*Ad'ham*), the *alif* or hamzah (*mas'allah*), and the *ayn* (*ma'nan*). The acute (*kubrá*), macron (*billāh*), and dot below (*al-aṣl*) marks also appear. Diacritical marks are used with both uppercase and lowercase letters. Diacritics are usually used only in scholarly works addressed to readers with a knowledge of the language.

Capitalization. Use the rules for capitalization in English, except lowercase the definite article *al* unless it is the first word in a sentence or title. Capitalize only the first word and proper names in book and article titles.

When alphabetizing personal names, ignore the article; an index entry would read *Kashshaf, Ishaq al-*.

Certain Arab name prefixes—*Abd* (meaning "servant of"), *Ibn* and *Bin* (meaning "son of"), and *Abu* (meaning "father of")—should always combine with the personal name. Examples are *Abubakr* and *Abu Nidal* (never *Nidal* alone) and *Ibn Saud; ibn* is not capitalized when it is preceded by other names, such as *Abdel Faisal ibn King Aziz al-Saud,* or *King Faisal*. In indexes and other alphabetical listings, Abu, Ibn, and Bin are considered to be part of the name: *Ibn Saud, Ishaq*.

Punctuation. Use a hyphen to connect the definite article *al* to the following word: *al-asl.* Also use a hyphen between *Bin* and the following element in personal names when they are written in Arabic as a single word (*Bin-'Abd Allah,* but *Bin Khiddah*).

Chinese

Alphabet and Special Characters. Until the late 1950s the Wade-Giles system was used to transliterate Mandarin Chinese characters into the Latin alphabet. At that time the pinyin system began to come into use; its advantages were simplification and a more accurate rendering of Chinese pronunciation. The new spellings differ significantly from the old—*Peking* (Wade-Giles), *Beijing* (pinyin)—with single letters replacing consonant clusters when possible; hyphens and apostrophes are usually omitted in the names of people and places. Old spellings are often retained for most geographical names long familiar in the West and for names of persons who are dead, such as *Sun Yat-sen*. Sometimes both styles are given; here Wade-Giles comes first: *Mao Tse-tung* (*Mao Zedong*). When syllables are run together, an apostrophe may still be needed to avoid ambiguity.

The following table offers a summarized conversion list of the two systems, but editors should be aware that the Chinese language is quite complex, and an expert should be consulted to ensure accuracy.

CHINESE

Initial Letters

Wade-Giles	**Pinyin**
p	b
tś’, tź’	c
ch’ (before a, e, ih, o, u)	ch
t	d
f	f
k	g
h	h
ch (before i or ü)	j
k’	k
l	l
m	m
n	n
p’	p
ch’ (before i or ü)	q
j	r
s, sz	s
sh	sh
t’	t
w	w
hs	x
y	y
ts, tz	z
ch (before a, e, i (ih), o, u)	zh

Final Letters

Wade-Giles	**Pinyin**
a	a
ai	ai
an	an
ang	ang
ao	ao

Final Letters (cont’d)

Wade-Giles	**Pinyin**
e, o	e
ei	ei
en	en
eng	eng
erh	er
i, ih, u	i
ia (ya)	ia
ien (yan, yen)	ian
iang (yang)	iang
iao (yao)	iao
ieh (ye, yeh)	ie
in	in
ing	ing
iung (yong, yung)	iong
iu (you, yu)	iou, iu
o	o
ung	ong
ou, u (after y)	ou
u	u
ua (wa)	ua
uai (wai)	uai
uan (wan)	uan
uang (wang)	uang
ui, uei	ui
un	un
uo, o	uo
ü	ü
üan	üan
üeh	üe
ün	ün
ü	yu

Source: Chinese alphabet. *Colliers Encyclopedia*, 1987;6:334.

Capitalization. Capitalize proper and place names and names of dynasties, the first word of corporate names, and the first syllable of hyphenated names. Capitalize the first word only of titles of books, periodicals, or series.

Punctuation. Use a comma for a centered point (·) indicating coordinated words. Use quotation marks (“ ”) for brackets used as quotation marks.

ASIAN PERSONAL NAMES—A BRIEF GUIDE

In Chinese names, the surname comes first, followed by the two-syllable given name, which is spelled as one word under the pinyin system of transliteration.

In Vietnamese names, the surname precedes two given names *(Ngo Dien Diem),* but a second reference is generally shortened to the last part of the name: *Diem. Ho Chi Minh,* however, is always referred to as *Ho*. Just to confuse things, an index would list *Ngo Dien Diem* under the N's.

The Japanese increasingly use the Western style, in which the given name precedes the surname: *Mamoru Shigemitsu,* and a second reference would be *Shigemitsu.* But some Western authors writing about the Japanese use the traditional order, with surname first, so the name should be verified before a shortened reference is used.

The Thais place a given name before the family name but normally use the given name; thus, *Thanat Khoman* would be referred to as *Thanat,* and the telephone book might list either name first.

The Burmese do not use family names. Some Burmese have only one name—*Nu, Thant* (with the name usually preceded by the honorific *U* for a man and *Daw* for a married woman)—whereas others have more—*Aung San*. In the latter case, both names are used on second reference. The honorifics are dropped when other titles *(Dr.)* are used.

Laotian names assume such a variety of forms that the safest course is to use the name in full in all references.

Classical Greek

Alphabet and Special Characters. The Greek alphabet and a transliteration table follow.

Greek uses three accent marks—the acute, the circumflex, and the grave—plus two breathing marks. The circumflex is used on one of the last two syllables; the acute should be changed to a grave on the last syllable of a word when another accented word immediately follows in the same clause.

When text is set in Greek characters, the font must contain all accents and breathing marks, both lowercase and uppercase. Typesetters should be careful not to use a single quotation mark in place of a breathing mark. Transliterated Greek does not require accents or breathing marks, but the

CLASSICAL GREEK

Letters	*Name*	*Transliteration*
Α α	alpha	a
Β β	beta	b
Γ γ	gamma	g
Δ δ	delta	d
Ε ε	epsilon	e
Ζ ζ	zeta	z
Η η	eta	ē
Θ θ	theta	th
Ι ι	iota	i
Κ κ	kappa	k, c
Λ λ	lambda	l
Μ μ	mu	m
Ν ν	nu	n
Ξ ξ	xi	x
Ο ο	omicron	o
Π π	pi	p
Ρ ρ	rho	r
Σ σ, ς*	sigma	s
Τ τ	tau	t
Υ υ	upsilon	u (except *after* a, e, ē, i, *often* y)
Φ φ	phi	ph
Χ χ	chi	ch
Ψ ψ	psi	ps
Ω ω	omega	o

* The letter σ is used at the beginning or in the middle of a word, and ς is used at the end of a word.

macron is used to distinguish the long vowels *eta* and *omega* (*ē* and *ō*) from the short vowels *epsilon* and *omicron* (*e* and *o*).

Capitalization. Editors differ in their approaches to the capitalization of classical Greek; the Greeks themselves used only capital letters. In general, capitalize the first words of sentences, direct quotations, proper names, and the first word in a stanza of poetry but not the first word of each line.

Punctuation. The ancient Greeks did not use punctuation; except for the following substitutions, most editors use English punctuation as necessary. The period and comma are the same in Greek as in English.

Use a semicolon for a question mark.

Use a raised period (·) for a colon or semicolon.

Use the apostrophe to show omission of a vowel at the end of a word before a second word beginning with a vowel.

In English text, no quotation marks are used around quotations set in Greek.

Word Division. Retain at least two letters at the end of a line, and carry over at least three letters to the next line.

Divide before a single consonant that falls between two vowels.

Divide after the first consonant if a word has a doubled consonant.

Divide after a liquid (λ or ρ) or nasal (μ or υ) if either begins a combination of two or more consonants.

Keep suffixes and prefixes intact, and divide compound words according to their component parts.

Hebrew

Alphabet and Special Characters. The Hebrew alphabet and a transliteration table follow. Hebrew is read from right to left and has 22 letters, all consonants. Vowels are represented by vowel signs, or points, placed above or below the consonant.

When Hebrew is transliterated, the macrons over and the dots under letters, as well as ʾ and ʿ, are often omitted; ʾ is also printed as ʿ. *Ph* is often used for *f*, *s* is often used for ś, and the letter *samech* is sometimes represented by ṡ. For *sh*, š may be used, especially in scholarly works.

Capitalization. Hebrew does not use capital letters at the beginnings of words, even proper names.

Punctuation. Most Hebrew punctuation, including italics and quotation marks, follows English usage. Scriptural Hebrew uses 21 accent marks to indicate stress, to direct cantillation, and to show distinctions in word meanings.

Word Division. Divide between syllables of three or more letters.

Russian

Alphabet and Special Characters. The table on page 534 shows the Cyrillic alphabet and its Latin transliteration.

Capitalization. Russian practice is similar to English, except that proper adjectives, days of the week, and months of the year are lowercased.

Capitalize only the first word and proper nouns in titles, headings, and names of periodicals.

Capitalize geographical names only when they refer to formal political units or institutions.

HEBREW

Transliteration and Pronunciation	*Name of Letter*	*Book Print*
Silent	aleph	א
b as in boy	bet	בּ
v as in vine	vet	ב
g as in girl	gimel	ג
d as in door	dalet	ד
h as in house	hey	ה
v as in vine	vav	ו
z as in zebra	zayin	ז
ch as in Bach	chet	ח
t as in tall	tet	ט
y as in yes	yod	י
k as in kitty	kaf	ך כּ
ch as in bach	kaf	כ
l as in look	lamed	ל
m as in mother	mem	ם מ
n as in now	nun	ן נ
s as in sun	samech	ס
Silent	ayin	ע
p as in people	pey	ף פּ
f as in food	fey	פ
ts as in nuts	tsade	ץ צ
k as in kitty	qof	ק
r as in robin	resh	ר
sh as in shape	shin	שׁ
s as in sun	sin	שׂ
t as in tall	tav	ת

Source: Simon, Ethelyn, et al., *The First Hebrew Primer for Adults.* Oakland, Calif.: EKS Publishing Co., 1983.

Punctuation. Although similar to English, Russian punctuation has a few differences. Commas set off restrictive and nonrestrictive clauses. An em dash is sometimes used between a subject and a complement to show the omission of the verb *to be* or of an identical adjacent verb and also before a clause to show the omission of the conjunction *that.*

Dialogue is shown by em dashes rather than quotation marks, and quoted material is shown primarily in the French way, with guillemets (« »), but sometimes in the German way, with inverted quotation marks („ “).

Word Division. Transliterated Russian should be divided according to the rules used in the Cyrillic original.

RUSSIAN

Alphabet		*Transliteration*
А	а	a
Б	б	b
В	в	v
Г	г	g
Д	д	d
Е	е	ye, e[1]
Ё	ё	yë, ë[2]
Ж	ж	zh
З	з	z
И	и	i
Й	й	y
К	к	k
Л	л	l
М	м	m
Н	н	n
О	о	o
П	п	p
Р	р	r
С	с	s
Т	т	t
У	у	u
Ф	ф	f
Х	х	kh
Ц	ц	ts
Ч	ч	ch
Ш	ш	sh
Щ	щ	shch
Ъ	ъ	”
Ы	ы	y
Ь	ь	’
Э	э	e
Ю	ю	yu
Я	я	ya

[1] *ye* initially after vowels, and after ъ, ь.

[2] *yë* as for *ye*. The sign *ë* is not considered a separate letter of the alphabet, and the ¨ is often omitted. Transliterate as *ë*, *yë* when printed in Russian as *ë;* otherwise use *e*, *ye*.

Source: U.S. Government Printing Office Style Manual. Washington, D.C. Government Printing Office, 1984.

Do not divide on a single letter.

Keep prefixes intact, and divide compound words at their component parts.

Divide after a vowel or diphthong before a single Cyrillic consonant.

Divide between two or more consonants that fall between vowels.

Divide between doubled consonants.

Never divide *ct.*

Do not divide combinations that make up original Cyrillic characters: *ye, yë, zh, kh, ts, ch, sh, shch, yu, ya.*

Do not divide combinations of a vowel plus a short *i* (transliterated *y*): *ay, ey, yey,* and so on.

Do not divide these transliterated consonant combinations: *bl, br, vl, vr, gl, gr, dv, dr, zhd, kl, kr, ml, pl, pr, sk, skv, skr, st, stv, str, tv, tr, fl, fr.*

Divide on a vowel or on a diphthong before a single consonant or consonant combination.

Divide before the last consonant or consonant combination in a group of two or more consonants.

PART FOUR

PREPARING THE TEXT

22

PARTS OF A BOOK

PARTS OF A BOOK

The earliest books—rolled-up sheets of papyrus pasted together and rolled into scrolls called *volumes*—had a few basic drawbacks. They were awkward to handle and had to be rerolled after each use. They had no page numbers, which, of course, meant that tables of contents and indexes were impossible to create. Locating a particular passage was time consuming and often not worth the effort. Around the second century B.C., after the Egyptians cut off their supply of papyrus, the Greeks developed parchment, made from the skins of sheep and goats. This led to the invention of the codex, a book

---

❧

THE ORIGIN OF *FOLIO*

In today's language of printing, a folio is a page number, although in the early days of printing *folio* referred to the page itself, or the *leaf* formed by folding a printed sheet for binding. The word is derived from the Latin *folium,* meaning "leaf."

In the 1500s, when commercial book printing began in earnest, paper came in oblong sheets measuring 22 by 15.75 inches. When these sheets were folded in half once, they formed two leaves of a standard book size called a *folio;* when these sheets were folded in half twice and cut, producing four pages or leaves, the book size was referred to as *quarto;* and when folded in half three times and cut, producing eight pages, an *octavo* book resulted.

The word *leaf* is still used to refer to certain kinds of pages: An overleaf is the back of a page within a signature, and a flyleaf is a blank page at the front or back of a book.

---

in which the pages, or sheets of parchment, were folded and sewn, a technique not possible with papyrus, which cracked easily.

It wasn't until printed books were first mass produced that certain elements we take for granted today became common. The first book with consecutive page numbers appeared in 1499, but it was another hundred years before this became common practice. Tables of contents and indexes soon followed, and fast and easy retrieval of information became possible.

Today's electronic books, with their many search possibilities, have improved on these traditional tools, offering the first real advance in retrieval of published information in almost 500 years. But as long as there are printed books, certain traditions and conventions apply to their form and content.

SEQUENCE OF THE BOOK

Although there are some conventions for the placement of elements and sections of books, few rules apply to *all* books. The front matter may include an introduction, a preface, acknowledgments, or a dedication—or all four. The back matter may include a glossary, an appendix, and an index—or none of these elements. Sometimes all main elements of the front matter start on a right-hand page, although some publishers do not allow for any blank pages in the front matter. The format of a book is determined by the publisher's style, the subject matter, and the way the book will be used.

The list below shows a fairly traditional way to set up a book; be aware that not all books have all of these elements, and a quick survey of several recently published books reveals that publishers vary both the order and the inclusion of these elements. Definitions and descriptions of the contents of these pages follow; note that assignment of page numbers can and does vary from book to book and publisher to publisher. *Recto* means a right-hand page, *verso* a left.

Page	*Description*
recto (no page number)	blank (optional)
verso (no page number)	list of author's other works or blank
recto (no page number or page i)	bastard or half title
verso (no page number)	back of half title; blank
recto (page i or iii)	title page
verso	copyright and other publication data
recto	dedication
verso	back of dedication; blank

recto	contents, including list of illustrations and list of tables (these lists may also be separate, particularly if they run for several pages)
recto	foreword
recto	preface, acknowledgments
recto	introduction (unless part of main text)
1	repeat of the half title, backed by blank, or first full page of main text

Front Matter

Front matter pages, also called *preliminary pages* or *prelims,* are usually numbered with lowercase roman numerals starting with the half title page or title page, which is page i. The page number does not actually appear on this page, nor do numbers appear on the pages containing the list of the author's other works, copyright information, or the dedication or on any blank pages; all of these are called *blind folios,* although they are, of course, counted in the total number of pages for production purposes. Main elements usually begin on right-hand pages, although this is not a hard and fast rule. Much depends on the number of front-matter elements, their length, and whether combining elements onto one page would save the publisher from having to print an additional signature. (See Chapter 33, Printing, for an explanation of signatures.) Here are the most common front-matter elements, listed in the order in which they usually appear:

Bastard or Half Title Page. This first page gives only the title of the book; it does not give the subtitle, edition number, author's name, or publisher's imprint.

Frontispiece or List of the Author's Other Works. A frontispiece is an illustration that appears opposite the title page. If there is no frontispiece, this page may contain a list of the author's other works or information about other books in the series. This page is called the *card page* in trade books or the *series page* in textbooks.

Title Page. This page carries the full title, the author's name with title or affiliation, the edition number, the publisher's name and location, and sometimes the publisher's trade symbol or logo.

A STONESONG PRESS BOOK

The name "The New York Public Library" and the representation of the lion appearing in this work are registered trademarks and the property of The New York Public Library, Astor, Lenox, and Tilden Foundations.

THE NEW YORK PUBLIC LIBRARY WRITER'S GUIDE TO STYLE AND USAGE. Copyright © 1994 by The New York Public Library and The Stonesong Press, Inc. All rights reserved. Printed in the United States of America. No part of this book may be used or reproduced in any manner whatsoever without written permission except in the case of brief quotations embodied in critical articles and reviews. For information address HarperCollins Publishers, Inc., 10 East 53rd Street, New York, NY 10022.

HarperCollins books may be purchased for educational, business, or sales promotional use. For information, please write: Special Markets Department, HarperCollins Publishers, Inc., 10 East 53rd Street, New York, NY 10022.

FIRST EDITION

Designed by Abigail Sturges

Library of Congress Cataloging-in-Publication Data

The New York Public Library writer's guide to style and usage. — 1st ed.
p. cm.
"A Stonesong Press book."
Includes bibliographical references and index.
ISBN 0-06-270064-2
1. English language—Style. 2. English language—Usage. I. New York Public Library.
PE1421.N46 1994
808′.027—dc20 93-33255

94 95 96 97 98 PS/RRD 10 9 8 7 6 5 4 3 2 1

Figure 22–1. A portion of the copyright page of this book.

Copyright Page. The copyright page backs the title page (see Figure 22–1 for an example). Copyright law once required that copyright information appear on either the front or back of the title page. Although no longer a requirement, this is still the traditional page for copyright data notices. This page usually contains the following elements:

- *Copyright line.* This line gives the year of the copyright and the name of the copyright holder, preceded by the copyright symbol—©—or the word *copyright* spelled out; it is not necessary to use both the word and the symbol. To ensure that the publisher can recover damages if a copyright infringement occurs, the publisher must register the copyright with the Library of Congress Register of Copyrights. Registration forms can be obtained by writing to the Register of Copyrights, Library of Congress, Washington, DC 20559, or by calling (202) 707-9100.
- *Publisher's copyright notice and publisher's address.* This notice explicitly states the limits of the copyright. The wording of the notice varies

according to the preferences of the publisher but usually contains some form of this statement:

> All rights reserved. No part of this publication may be reproduced or transmitted in any form or by any means electronic or mechanical, including photocopying, recording, or any information storage and retrieval system, without permission in writing from the publisher.

- *Library of Congress Cataloging in Publication (CIP) data.* This information is used by libraries and booksellers as an aid to cataloging. For CIP data, publishers must submit manuscripts, galleys, or, at a minimum, the front matter of upcoming publications to the Library of Congress' CIP Division. (It is not necessary to wait for final galleys of the entire book.) From the pages submitted, the CIP Division creates a bibliographic record and mails this record to the publisher so it can be included on the copyright page of the book. In exchange for participation in the CIP program, the publisher must send a copy of the book to the CIP Division once it is printed.
- *Printing history.* The dates of printings are indicated here, sometimes expressed in the publisher's printing code (a series of numbers that starts with the year of the printing). To save the expense of resetting the page each time a new printing occurs, many publishers list a series of years in ascending order from the current date and, in descending order, numbers representing the printing; when a book goes into a second printing, the number 1 (and the previous printing year, if used) is simply blocked out on the printing plate.

94 95 96 97 98   10 9 8 7 6 5 4 3 2 1

- *Copyright notices for photographs, illustrations, or other material.* These notices are listed here if material in the publication is copyrighted by another source and is being used with permission. If the list of permissions is long, it can run at the back of the book, with a note to that effect here.
- *Country where published.* Before 1986, it was required that the country of publication be listed on the copyright page. Although no longer a requirement, it is often listed here.
- *International Standard Book Number (ISBN).* The ISBN is a 10-digit number unique to each book. The number is a code that tells where the book was published, identifies the publisher, and includes other numbers that differentiate the book's ISBN from all others. When there are different editions of the same book (for example, hardcover and paperback), each edition must have its own ISBN. Multivolume sets have several ISBNs—the set itself has one, and each volume within the set

APPLYING FOR CIP DATA

Applying for CIP data is surprisingly simple. The publisher must first register with the CIP program by filling out a Publisher's Response/ Publishing History form, which can be obtained from the Library of Congress' Cataloging in Publication Division at the address given below. The CIP Division will then assign the publisher a CIP Publisher Liaison, who will be the point of contact for all future publications.

To apply for CIP data for an individual publication, the publisher must fill out a CIP Data Sheet for Books and send it to the CIP Division, which requires 10 working days for processing. According to the *CIP Publishers Manual*, certain categories of publications are not entered into the CIP program:

- Books not published in the United States
- Serial publications, such as periodicals or annuals, that are issued regularly under the same title
- Books subsidized by individual authors or books from a publisher that publishes the works of only one author
- Religious instructional materials
- Expendable educational materials such as workbooks
- Consumable publications such as catalogs, telephone books, cut-out books, coloring books, etc.
- Translations from one language to another (other than Spanish)
- Mass market paperbacks
- Single articles reprinted from periodicals
- Audiovisual material and computer software
- Textbooks for readers below the secondary school level
- Most musical scores
- Microforms, except titles originally published in and appearing only in microform

For a copy of the *CIP Publishers Manual*, write to the Cataloging in Publication Division, Library of Congress, Washington, DC 20540, or call (202) 707-6372.

For those who prefer not to participate in the CIP program, there is an alternative. Quality Books Inc. provides the same service, but for a fee. Its rate structure is based on the number of books submitted and the turnaround time requested. A complete description of the services can be obtained by writing to Quality Books Inc., 918 Sherwood Drive, Lake Bluff, IL 60044-2204 or by calling (708) 295-2010.

has its own. Serial publications such as monographs or journals carry International Standard Serial Numbers (ISSNs). The ISSN is an eight-digit number that stays the same for each issue of the series.

- *Statement about acid-free or recycled paper.* Publishers who choose to note the paper used often do so on this page or at the end of the text, as part of the colophon. Acid-free paper lasts longer and is often used in books that will be used over a period of years. (See Chapter 33, Printing, for a discussion of the symbols used to denote recycled and recyclable paper.)
- *Credits and permissions.* These may also be given in the preface or acknowledgments sections, in which case they are not duplicated here.
- *Information on the book's translation history.* If the book is a translation of another published work, the publication information about the original work is given here.

See Chapter 23, Copyright, for more information.

Dedication or Epigraph. An epigraph is a quotation relevant to the book. If an epigraph is used, the source is given beneath it. It is not necessary to list complete bibliographic information about the source of the quotation.

Acknowledgments. Here the author lists and thanks contributors, often including the editor, the designer, and any colleagues or experts who reviewed the manuscript. This information is sometimes included in the preface instead.

Foreword. This section is written not by the book's author but by another expert in the field. The foreword serves as an endorsement. It is often signed with the name and affiliation of its author and the date it was written.

Preface. In the preface, the author addresses the reader directly. The author may state the purpose of the book or explain what the reader will learn from it. The author may also thank people who have contributed to the work. The preface usually ends with the author's initials, sometimes followed by the place where the writing was completed and the date. If the book has both an editor's preface and an author's preface, the editor's preface comes first. The preface sometimes comes directly after the table of contents.

Table of Contents. The table of contents lists front matter, chapter or section titles, and back matter. Depending on the type of book, subsections may also be listed. Subsections are indented to set them off from the main sections. The table of contents is simply headed *Contents*, not *Table of Contents* or *List of Contents.* Page numbers should be listed either directly

MORE ABOUT THE ISBN

The International Standard Book Numbering Agency for U.S. publishers is operated by the R.R. Bowker Company. When a publisher registers with this agency, it is given a four-digit identification number that becomes part of the ISBN numbers for all of its publications. Unlike CIP data, the ISBN number can be assigned in the earliest stages of the publishing process. In fact, the ISBN must be assigned first because it becomes part of the CIP data. The agency will issue a publisher a series of ISBN numbers that can be assigned to future books. The publisher then notifies the agency as the numbers are used, rather than repeating the application process each time.

The ISBN also appears as part of the bar code—or Universal Product Code—placed on the bottom of a book's back cover; the other numbers on the bar code represent the Bookland EAN, an international numbering scheme for the book trade. The digits 978 form the prefix to this number, followed by the book's ISBN; an additional five-digit code can be used to show price and currency. These bar codes speed the purchasing and inventory process for wholesalers and booksellers.

For more information, contact the International Standard Book Numbering Agency, R.R. Bowker, 121 Chanlon Road, New Providence, NJ 07974, (908) 665-6770.

after their headings or set flush right and connected to their headings by dot leaders. If the table of contents is set in two columns (chapters on the left, page numbers on the right), the columns do not need headings. Figures and tables may be listed separately if it is likely that the reader will refer to them individually. Figure legends or captions may be abbreviated as long as the references are clear to the reader. If there are different kinds of illustrations (maps, photos, and so on), they may be grouped in the list of illustrations.

Introduction or Prologue. Unlike the preface, the introduction deals with the text of the book rather than its purpose. The introduction is actually an integral part of the main text, even though it is considered front matter. Some authors use the introduction to summarize the book; others use it to pique the reader's interest.

Main Text

The main text can be divided into chapters, sections, or both. For books that are divided into sections, a section title page appears after the front matter and before the main text. Section title pages are always right-hand pages and are almost always blank on the back. The main text begins on a right-hand page. Neither the front nor the back of the section title page carries a page number, although both are counted in the pagination. Chapters usually start on right-hand pages but usually are not separated by divider pages.

Back Matter

Like the front matter, the back matter elements can be ordered in a variety of ways. Decisions about the back matter are usually the author's. If the material in the appendixes is closely tied to the main text, it should follow it directly. If the reader should scan the glossary before reading the main text, the glossary should be included with the front matter instead of the back matter. The back matter elements should always be listed in the table of contents. A description of common back matter elements follows.

Appendixes. Appendixes usually have additional information about topics covered in the main text or data used to reach the conclusions drawn in the text. The appendix begins on a right-hand page and is often preceded by a title page. If there is more than one appendix, they are labeled *Appendix A, Appendix B,* and so on and given individual titles. If there is only one appendix, it is simply called the *appendix.*

Notes or Endnotes. Notes come after the appendix and before the bibliography. They are often grouped by chapter or section.

Glossary. Glossaries are provided in books that use technical terminology or other vocabulary that may not be familiar to the readers. Terms are listed in alphabetical order, not in the order that they appear in the book.

Bibliography. The bibliography lists all the sources the author used in writing the book, whether or not they are actually cited in the text. Bibliographies differ in level of detail, depending on the preferred style of the publisher. An annotated bibliography includes a description of the source after each entry. A selected bibliography or recommended reading list gives other sources that can provide additional information on the subject of the book; these sources may not be referenced in the text. Sources in a selected bibliography may be grouped by subject.

Index. There may be one or several indexes in a book, depending on how readers are likely to look up information. Some books give both a subject index and an author index; others give additional specialized indexes.

Colophon. The colophon is a short description of the book's design and typography. This Greek word, meaning "finishing touch," originally referred to the publisher's trade symbol, which traditionally appeared on the last page of the book. Trade symbols now appear on the book's spine and on the title page. The colophon sometimes appears on the copyright page instead of at the end of the book. Not all books carry colophons.

FORMAT OF THE PAGE

Page Numbers

Probably the most frequently asked question about page numbering is "Where is page 1?" By tradition, arabic page 1 is always a right-hand page, generally the first page of the main text. Lowercase roman numerals are usually used to number the front matter.

Page Number Placement. The placement of page numbers depends on the book's design, but the most common position in works of nonfiction is the outer edge of the top or bottom of the page. Left-hand pages have page numbers on the left side of the page, and right-hand pages on the right; most publishing software handles this task automatically. Designers have some latitude in determining the size and positioning of page numbers, especially in novels and such publications as newsletters and brochures, so the number may also be centered or appear elsewhere on the page.

Traditionally some pages are not numbered. These are known as *blind folios* and may include some or all of the front matter, the divider pages that separate parts and chapters, and back matter title pages.

Page numbers that appear at the bottom of the page are called *drop folios.* Drop folios are used on the first page of each main section of both the front matter and the main text and on chapter openers even if all other page numbers appear at the top of the page.

Different Approaches to Page Numbering. There are a few instances in which numbering the pages consecutively throughout the book doesn't help the reader. For example, in books with several sections of back matter, such as appendixes, these sections may stand out better if the pages are numbered to correspond to appendix number (for example, A–22, C–34). Another exception is looseleaf manuals and other technical documents, which are more easily updated when the pages are numbered within each chapter or section (3–17, II–41) so that new pages can be easily inserted and the old pages discarded without disturbing the overall pagination.

Multivolume works also present page numbering challenges. The pagination of such publications—consecutive in each volume or consecutive throughout all volumes—depends on how the volumes will be sold and used. For multivolume books that are paginated consecutively, the front matter is paginated separately in all volumes; the consecutive numbering picks up with the next odd number after the last number in the previous volume, since the main text of each volume always begins on a right-hand page. For instance, if volume I ended on page 501, volume II would begin on page 503, page 502 being the blank backing page 501 in volume I. If a multivolume book has a single index, which most do, the index entries should indicate the volume number as well as the page number.

Running Heads

Running heads appear at the tops of pages, enabling readers to see at a glance which part of a book they have opened to. They can be centered (as in this book) or set flush with the margin: left-hand running heads are flush left; right-hand running heads are flush right. Editors select running heads, but they follow general guidelines. In nonfiction books the left running head usually gives the title of the book or the title of the main section. The right running head can give the title of the chapter or subsection. A book with many subdivisions may use the chapter title on left pages and first-level subheadings on the right, the scheme used in this book. For books with chapters written by different authors, the left running head can be the name of the author, and the right can be the title of the chapter. For books with many numbered sections, it is helpful to include both the section number and the title in the running head, particularly if the section numbers are cross-referenced frequently in the text. Running heads in front matter and back matter are the same regardless of page side; for example, the running head *Index* would appear on both the left and right pages. Long titles are usually abbreviated to fit on a single line. Running heads do not appear on title pages or divider pages and are sometimes not included on the front-matter and back-matter pages.

Footnotes

Except in scholarly publications, footnotes are used less frequently than they once were, mainly because they interrupt the flow of text and complicate the production process. In most books, articles, and reports, writers should try to incorporate footnote information into the text.

FOOTNOTE PHOBIA

The word *footnote* often strikes fear in the hearts of typesetters, proofreaders, and other book production workers because there are so many things that can go wrong with footnotes.

If notes are added or deleted, writers and editors must remember to renumber the other notes and the references in the text. Any notes that are added or revised after the pages have been set can cause the text to reflow, which is particularly cumbersome if the new or revised note is located near the beginning of the document or chapter. Although most desktop publishing programs have an automatic feature for placing footnotes, footnotes can still add to the time and cost of production. In some of the more primitive desktop publishing programs, the notes have to be moved manually and the text adjusted accordingly. And no software program can solve the problem caused by footnote numbers that fall near the end of the page, since the footnote must always begin on the page where it is referenced.

For manuscripts with many reference citations, endnotes offer several advantages over footnotes. Page design is not disrupted, and endnotes can appear at the end of each chapter or at the end of the book, which helps lower production costs. Endnotes are not appropriate, however, for note material that is an integral part of the text rather than supplementary in nature; the reader should not have to keep flipping back and forth for important information.

When footnotes are necessary, they should be used sparingly. They can be keyed to the text with symbols, usually asterisks and daggers, or with numbers. Footnote numbers are set as superscripts, in a point size smaller than that of the body text. The superscripts appear at the end of the sentence, after the punctuation, unless the note discusses only a particular word in the sentence. Notes to tables should be indicated with a different system from that used for notes in the text; italicized lowercase letters are often used. Footnote numbers should be avoided in headings because headings serve only to introduce the material that follows; the footnote number should be keyed directly to the text itself. Finally, footnotes are usually numbered consecutively within each chapter.

Footnotes run at the bottom of the page and can be set off from the text by a rule, either a short rule 2 to 3 inches long or one that extends from margin to margin. If footnotes appear on a page that is not full—for example, the last page of a chapter—the notes follow the text directly rather than appearing at the bottom of the page.

OUTSIDE OF THE BOOK

The elements that form the outside of a book can vary greatly. However, most publishers follow certain conventions to attract readers to the book.

Cover and Dust Jacket

Paperback books have a soft cover, which is made of a heavier paper than that used for the text pages and is usually coated with varnish to protect the surface. Hardcover books, also referred to as *casebound,* have covers—or cases—that are made of heavy cardboard covered with fabric, paper, leather, or vinyl. Many hardcover books also come with a dust jacket, which carries the elements that appear on the covers of paperbacks. For books with jackets, the actual cover, or case, is usually blank, except for the spine. The jacket displays the book's title, the author's name, and often a brief phrase or statement about the book's contents. The most important part of the front jacket cover is its overall design; attractive typography and graphics or photographs help convey the book's tone and contents and draw prospective readers to the book. The inside front flap introduces or summarizes the book and often lists the price at the top corner. The inside back flap can be a continuation of the summary and may also contain a brief biography of the author, sometimes with a photo. This material generally appears on the back of a paperback book. The jacket or cover credits—naming the designer or artist—appear there and not in the book itself.

Spine

The spine of the book is an important element and should not be treated as an afterthought. The spine must be easy to read and eye-catching, since it is often the first part of the book a potential reader sees. The spine of a paperback and the spine portion of the jacket of a hardcover carry the title of the book, the author, the name of publisher, and sometimes the publisher's trade symbol. The type on the spine should be printed so that the tops of the letters face the top of the book or the right edge of the spine. The type should be large enough to be read when the book is shelved.

The spine should not be too cluttered; the name of the publisher and the publisher's trade symbol may be omitted if necessary. For hardcover books, the spine of the case, which is covered by the jacket, is usually printed or foil-stamped with the same information that appears on the spine of the jacket.

Back Cover

The back of a book—whether of the jacket or, in the case of paperbacks, the cover—is almost as important as the front. It is one of the first places that browsers look when they want more information about the book. For this reason, many publishers use this space for advance quotations about the book or favorable reviews of other books by the same author.

The back cover also carries the bar code, a requirement for books that are to be carried by bookstores. On paperbacks the bar code sometimes appears on the inside front cover. The bar code includes the ISBN, the Bookland EAN (European Article Number), and sometimes the price. Bar codes are scannable and enable bookstores to ring up customers' purchases quickly and to track inventory automatically. Publishers can generate their own bar codes or get them from companies that supply camera-ready or film bar codes for a fee. Most bar codes are black on a white background. However, the background can be another color, as long as it does not contain any blue or black—these colors interfere with the scanner's ability to read the bars. The bars themselves can be any dark color.

Figure 22–2. A sample bar code and Bookland EAN.

ERRATA SHEETS

An errata sheet lists errors that were discovered too late in the production process to correct in the book. (If there is only one error, the list is called an *erratum sheet.*) If the errors are discovered after typesetting but before printing, the errata sheet is placed after the table of contents. If the errors are discovered after the book is printed, the sheet is either pasted or inserted at the end of the book.

In standard format, errata sheets list the page number of the error followed by a colon. Then the incorrect text is repeated as it stands, followed by the correct text:

Page 312, line 7: *For* ounces, *read* gallons
Page 357, line 4: *For* pounds, *read* tons

The words *for* and *read* are italicized. The text that follows them is not set off with single quotes, nor is it underscored. Errata sheets are used to correct only critical substantive errors, not minor typographical errors.

23

COPYRIGHT

COPYRIGHT

Copyright law affects writers and editors in two basic ways: when they wish to protect their rights to a work they have created, whether it is a book manuscript, a feature article, or a newsletter, and when they wish to use the words or creations of others. This chapter addresses the most frequently asked questions about protection and permission with regard to written works. Copyright law is quite complex and, like all law, is constantly being reinterpreted. In addition, changes in technology are raising new copyright issues before Congress and in the courts; for up-to-date answers to specific concerns, readers should query the Copyright Office or consult an attorney experienced in the field.

WHAT DOES COPYRIGHT PROTECT?

Federal copyright protection gives creators of original works—authors, artists, and songwriters, to name a few—exclusive control over their works in five general ways: the production of copies of the work, the sale or distribution of those copies to the public, the public performance of the work (which can include broadcasts as well as readings), the display of the work in public (which includes display on electronic bulletin boards), and the creation of adaptations of the work. Authors can sell these rights, lend them, grant limited licenses for their use, or give them away. Each of the five exclusive rights that make up a copyright can be split many different ways: by geographic or time limitations, by type of publication right (for example, book as opposed to periodical rights), or by any other conceivable division. Protection can also apply to a portion of a work as well as to the entire work.

HOW COPYRIGHT WORKS

U.S. copyright law has its basis in Article I of the Constitution, which mandates that Congress protect the rights of authors to their work for limited times. The rationale for this authority is "To promote the Progress of Science and the Useful Arts," and it creates a balancing act between encouraging the creation of new ideas by allowing authors to profit from their works for a reasonable length of time and encouraging the spread of knowledge by ultimately placing protected works in the public domain for others to build upon.

Under U.S. law, copyright protection is automatic once an original work is recorded in any form. However, the date of the work's first publication generally determines the length of time the work will be protected.

Works first published since the Copyright Act of 1976 took effect on January 1, 1978, receive copyright protection from the date of creation until 50 years after the author's death. (Works written by joint authors are protected until 50 years after the death of the last surviving author.)

Any work first published before January 1, 1978, falls under the prior law, the Copyright Act of 1909, which provided statutory copyright for 28 years, beginning with either publication or, for some unpublished works, registration with the Copyright Office (unregistered unpublished works received state common law protection). Owners of copyright in these works needed to make a formal renewal with the Copyright Office in the final year of the first term to obtain a second term of protection. This was formerly 28 years, but it has been extended to 47 years for works still under copyright protection when the 1976 law was passed. Now works still in their first term of copyright are renewed automatically, although legal incentives exist for making a formal renewal. Works created before January 1, 1978—but not published and not registered for copyright—now receive the same life-plus-50-year copyright term as works created after that date, but in no case do their copyrights expire before December 31, 2002, even if the author has been dead for centuries; if such works are published before that date, their copyright protection endures until the end of 2027. Anonymous or pseudonymous works that come under the 1976 law are protected for 75 years from the date of publication or 100 years from creation, whichever is shorter. However, if the author is identified to the Copyright Office, the normal life-plus-50-year duration applies. Finally, the copyright owner of a work for hire, which is a work created by an employee in the course of employment or which meets the stringent legal requirements of a work-for-hire agreement, is protected for 75 years from the date of publication or 100 years from creation, whichever is shorter. (Work for hire is an important issue for writers and editors; see "Who Owns the Copyright?" later in this chapter.)

Under the 1909 law, state common law protected original work until publication. At the moment of publication, a work came under federal law, but only if a proper and complete copyright notice had been affixed to the published work. If a work published before 1978 did not carry a copyright notice or carried an erroneous or incomplete notice, the work fell into the public domain. The 1976 law eased that aspect of the 1909 law; an omitted, incomplete, or defective copyright notice no longer consigned works to the public domain provided that certain conditions were met.

Another major difference in the 1976 law is that to secure a copyright, the author no longer has to publish the work or register it with the Copyright Office to obtain statutory copyright, as required by the Copyright Act of 1909. And since March 1, 1989, when the United States joined the Berne Convention, a multinational copyright treaty, a published work does not need to bear any copyright notice to be protected. Nevertheless, placing the copyright notice on a work is still recommended, as is registering with the Copyright Office, preferably within 3 months of publication. This act conveys certain advantages if the copyright is infringed. Registering is a relatively easy procedure; a later section, "Copyright Registration," offers details.

WHAT CAN BE COPYRIGHTED?

Copyright law in the United States requires only that an author express original material in a tangible medium of expression, whether on paper, computer disk, audiotape, videotape, or highway billboard. Authors and artists can copyright books, articles, short stories, poems, essays, and the like; photographs, illustrations, maps, and sculpture; musical and dramatic works; pantomimes and choreographic works; video and audiovisual works and sound recordings; computer software; and architectural designs.

For a work to be considered original, the author must demonstrate at least minimal creativity; a simple alphabetical directory of an entire area's residents, for example, is an obvious and unoriginal grouping of facts and so cannot be protected, but a more selective list broken down into other, less obvious groupings might be protectable. Originality also depends on the author's creating a work independently and without access to any other work that closely resembles it. Nearly identical creations produced by different people without access to each other's work could thus both gain copyright protection. Unlike applicants for patents and trademarks, copyright seekers need not search records for similar, previously copyrighted materials; indeed, they may be better off if they haven't done so. If a work has been published and widely distributed before a similar one appears, however, the courts will assume that the author had access to the first work unless the author can prove otherwise.

Works that are adapted from an original work, either by the original author or by someone else, are termed *derivative works* and include translations, condensations, and screenplays made from novels, as well as novelizations made from screenplays. Persons other than the original author who wish to create a derivative work must receive authorization from the copyright owner unless the original work is in the public domain.

As noted earlier, copyright protection is available to many kinds of works. Writers and editors should be aware of the following variations.

Plots and Characters

Because there is nothing new under the sun and a finite number of basic plots underlie most literature, writing or compiling something entirely original is nearly impossible. Plots and characters are essential aspects of a novelist's creation, but their protection under copyright law is a gray area.

Generally speaking, the more unusual a plot's twists and turns or the more distinctive a character is, the more they will be protected. And since copyright applies to graphic and audiovisual works, cartoon and television characters can also be protected by copyright. In addition, some characters, such as Mickey Mouse, may also be protected as trademarks.

Joint Works

A work created by two or more authors who intend to generate one unified product is called a *joint work,* and the authors share the copyright. Shares are assumed to be equal in the absence of a written agreement to the contrary. Unless barred from doing so by contract, any joint copyright holder can authorize the use of the work without the consent of any other, although the authorizing copyright holder must hold and pay over on demand the other copyright holders' shares of the proceeds. The expression *joint copyright holder* is used here because each joint author can sell, give away, or will his or her share of the copyright.

Compilations and Collective Works

A compilation is distinguished in U.S. copyright law from a collective work. The latter is an assembly of individual pieces that are separate and independent; an example would be a magazine or an anthology. Generally, each contributor owns the rights to his or her contribution to the collection, although there can also be a copyright in the collective work as a whole, which is separate and distinct from the copyrights in the individual works. If no specific transfer of rights is included in the author's contract with the publisher of a collective work, the publisher holds only the rights to include the contribution in that collective work, in any revision of that collective work, and in any later collective work in the same series.

A compilation is a work "formed by the collection and assembling of preexisting materials or data" and includes collective works but is broader. Any collecting and assembling of materials that passes the threshold test for originality is a compilation and will be protected by copyright. Compilations can include photo albums and computer databases as well as anthologies and encyclopedias.

Graphic Elements

Photographs, illustrations, and other graphic depictions—even road maps—are also afforded copyright protection. Writers and editors must obtain permission from the copyright owners to reuse these materials just as they do for literary rights. Exceptions are clip art books and software, which are produced and sold specifically for reproduction purposes, and works that have fallen into the public domain, either because of their age or because of some defect in notice or registration. However, use of works in the public domain without source attribution may result in charges of plagiarism, an area of law separate and distinct from copyright.

The use of optical scanners to create electronic forms of photographs and illustrations has made it easier to copy and use others' materials, but production editors should be aware that doing so without permission infringes the copyright, even if the material is further edited and manipulated. Indeed, such editing and manipulation, which in essence creates an unauthorized derivative work, may violate the "moral right" of the artist or photographer in the integrity of the work.

Musical Works

Music, including accompanying lyrics, is another category of protected work. Quoting a line or lines of a song in text may require permission of the copyright owner; see "Fair Use and Permissions" later in this chapter.

WHAT COPYRIGHT DOES NOT PROTECT

Works in the Public Domain

Works in the public domain are afforded no copyright protection and thus may be copied, distributed, performed, displayed, and adapted at will. However, because a work does not have to include a copyright notice to be protected under the law, it has become increasingly difficult to determine whether a work has entered the public domain. The safest course is to assume a work is protected unless you know for certain that it is not.

In general, two categories of works always fall into the public domain: publications of the federal government (but not of state or local governments) and works whose copyrights have expired. The latter includes most works first published in the United States more than 75 years ago and those first published before 1966 whose copyrights were not renewed.

Works first published before 1978 that did not contain a proper copyright notice also generally fell into the public domain; the law then allowed for works first published without a valid copyright notice after 1978 and before March 1, 1989, to make up for a defective or omitted notice in a variety of ways, including registration with the Copyright Office within 5 years of publication. No copyright notice is required to gain copyright protection on works distributed publicly after March 1, 1989.

Facts and Ideas

Facts, procedures, concepts, and ideas cannot be protected by copyright. Only the way in which they are written or expressed is covered under this area of the law. For example, the facts given in a newspaper story may be used in another work, but the way in which those facts are expressed may not. However, protection for facts, ideas, or procedures may exist under other areas of law, such as patent, trademark, or contract law.

Although facts are not protected under copyright law, their unique arrangement or compilation can warrant protection if the compiler's efforts in assembling and verifying the data demonstrate a level of originality that crosses the threshold of copyrightability. Determining this copyrightability is a technical judgment that may warrant consulting an expert on the law.

When certain expressions of fact—such as historic, biographical, and scientific information—can be recorded in only one or a few ways, such writing generally receives limited or no copyright protection. In addition, scenes or devices common to a genre of writing—for example, cowboys wearing ten-gallon hats or detectives wearing trenchcoats—are also generally unprotectable under copyright law.

Names, Titles, Slogans, and Formats

Copyright law does not protect titles of publications nor their layout, format, logo, slogans, or typography; these items may be protectable under trademark law, however. Sometimes a trademark can be obtained for a publication's title (normally possible only for a periodical or series, not for a single volume). Editors should be aware that trademark is a very complex area of law, subject to both federal and state authority. General questions about federal trademarks and information on applications can be addressed to the U.S. Patent and Trademark Office, Washington, DC 20231, but attorneys specializing in the field should be consulted regarding specific concerns.

Trade Secrets

Copyright is sometimes mistakenly suggested for materials that contain trade secrets—business plans, marketing strategies, and other guarded information. Such material may be protected by copyright from reproduction and distribution; when the package as a whole is distributed in confidence, however, a copyright notice will not protect the ideas and facts it contains, only their expression. Written agreements are often used to protect the content of written documents; such confidentiality agreements are a trap for the unwary, so attorneys with expertise in this area of law should be consulted if such an agreement is considered.

COPYRIGHT NOTICE: WHEN, WHERE, AND HOW TO PLACE IT

Is Notice Necessary?

Here are two correct ways to display a copyright notice:

© 1994, The Stonesong Press, Inc.
© 1994 by The Stonesong Press, Inc.

For works publicly distributed on or after March 1, 1989, placing a copyright notice on a publication is optional. But writers and editors should continue to use the notice both to deter infringement and because doing so may strengthen the copyright owner's position in court should an infringement occur. Adding notice costs nothing and can prevent problems later. In addition, works exported to or published in countries that are not members of the Berne Convention may not receive copyright protection if notice is omitted.

Placement and Wording

The Copyright Office accepts any "reasonable" location for placement of the copyright notice. In books, the most common place is on the page backing the title page; in magazines, newsletters, and newspapers, it typically appears near the masthead or on the front of the issue near the issue number, date, and title. In the case of individually copyrighted articles used within another copyrighted publication—for example, in a newspaper or an anthology—the notice on a collective work as a whole will protect all works in the work. However, an individual notice may also appear, usually next to the byline or credit line, at the end of the piece, or on the back of the title page in a book. On printed illustrations and photographs, the notice can run along the bottom or along one of the sides, usually in smaller type than the caption.

A copyright notice includes three elements, all of which must be present to constitute a valid notice.

1. *The word* Copyright *or the abbreviation* Copr. *or the symbol* ©. The symbol must be the letter *C* in a circle, not *C* in parentheses or any other enclosure. The symbol © is preferred because it is honored in foreign countries that do not recognize *Copyright* or *Copr.* It is not wrong to include both the copyright symbol and the word *Copyright* together on the notice, but the practice is unnecessarily redundant. A small *p* in a circle (℗) is used to protect a performance copyright in an audio work.

2. *The year of first publication of the work.* If the manuscript is a draft being submitted for review, the year that the draft was completed may be used; if the work is subsequently published, however, the year of first publication should appear in the notice on the published work. The year may generally be omitted from greeting cards, jewelry, toys, and other useful articles; when a compilation incorporates previously published materials, only the publication date of the compilation is necessary. The year should appear in arabic numerals, not roman numerals, not only because roman numerals are harder to decipher, but also because some countries may not accept dates written in that form.

3. *The name of the author or other owner of the copyright.* This can be the original author or authors, the party commissioning a work for hire, or anyone to whom the author has transferred the copyright. The word *by* before the owner's name is optional.

If a publication will be distributed in Bolivia or Honduras, the notice should be followed by the phrase "All Rights Reserved." These countries do not recognize *Copyright,Copr.,* or © as proper notice of ownership.

Although materials prepared by the U.S. government are generally not subject to copyright protection, if an author has interspersed federal contributions with commentary or explanations, the parts that are protected by the author's copyright and the parts that are in the public domain as excerpts from government publications should be clearly distinguished. One way this can be done is by stating, after the copyright notice, that "Chapters 5, 6, and 10 are government documents in the public domain, and their reproduction is not restricted by copyright."

New editions or major revisions of a book may warrant a new registration and hence a new date in the copyright notice. A simple reprinting, however, even if minor changes have been made, should retain the copyright date of the original printing. Some publishers include a printing history on the page with the copyright notice to give readers an idea of the currency of their copy, but this should not be part of the copyright notice. Instead, a separate line is usually added; it could read, "First printing January 1991; second printing February 1992."

If a substantial amount of the original material is changed, the work may be called a second edition, and the work should receive a new copyright date. When reregistering the new edition, the Copyright Office will require that you identify the new material, and only *that* material will be protected under this later registration. For such cases, the notice might read

First edition © 1990, John Smith
Second edition © 1994, John Smith and Mary Jones

A collective work or other compilation need carry only a single copyright notice to afford protection to all of the works in it (except for advertisements). However, listing any owners of individual copyrights contained in the work may help deter future infringement of their contributions.

Finally, it is not necessary to place a copyright notice on unpublished manuscripts, although, again, doing so may deter others from the unauthorized use of an author's work.

WHO OWNS THE COPYRIGHT?

In most cases, creators initially own all rights to their work, although they may grant publishers certain limited rights. But this is not always the case. A copyright can belong to whoever commissions the work if the stringent legal conditions for a "work made for hire" are met.

The Copyright Act of 1976 defines the circumstances under which certain works can be classified as "made for hire." When a work is created by an employee within the scope of his or her employment, the employer is legally the "author" of the work, and the copyright in it is the employer's property. Employees can negotiate in advance, however, for certain rights or for transfer of specific parts of the copyright to them from their employer.

Writing done under commission or contract can also be considered work for hire if three conditions are met: the work must have been specially ordered and commissioned, there must be a written agreement signed by both parties specifying that the work is "made for hire," and the work must fall into one of nine specific categories—contributions to collective works, contributions to audiovisual works, translations, supplementary pieces to a main work, compilations, instructional texts, tests, test answer material, and atlases.

Works made for hire differ from those to which all rights or the copyright has been assigned in two important ways:

- First, they differ in duration, because a work-for-hire copyright endures for 100 years from creation or 75 years from first publication, whichever is shorter, rather than for the life of the author plus 50 years.
- Second, because the "author" is the commissioning party, the person who actually did the creative work cannot terminate the grant of rights as he or she could do in the case of a copyright or all-rights assignment.

TYPES OF PUBLISHING RIGHTS

Writers who sell their work to publishers of books, magazines, and newspapers should become familiar with the various types of rights the publisher hopes to acquire in connection with a manuscript. These are three of the most common grants of rights:

- *Assignment of copyright or all-rights transfer.* The author transfers all rights in the work to another person or entity. To be valid, such a transfer must be in writing and signed by the owner of the rights conveyed or by the owner's agent.
- *First serial rights.* The author grants the first right to publish the work in a serial publication such as a magazine or newspaper. If the rights are further narrowed to "first North American serial rights," this right of first publication in a periodical is limited to the United States, Canada, or (technically but not traditionally) Mexico. All other rights, including book rights, derivative rights, and even European serial rights, remain with the author.
- *One-time rights.* The author gives another person or company a one-time right to use all or a part of a work; there is no exclusivity involved, and the author may grant the same or similar permission to any other publisher either sequentially or simultaneously; hence, this is sometimes called a *simultaneous* or *nonexclusive license.*

Under U.S. law, a transfer of copyright or of any of the exclusive rights that make up the copyright must be in writing and signed by the grantor or the grantor's agent. Documents of transfer can be recorded with the Copyright Office; although recording is not required for a transfer to be valid, it can provide extra protection for the grantee in the event of conflicting transfers.

FAIR USE AND PERMISSIONS

The fair use provisions of copyright law allow writers and editors to use the copyrighted works of others, under certain limited conditions, without asking permission of the copyright owner.

When Is Permission Required?

The 1976 law states that using copyrighted work for purposes such as criticism, comment, news reporting, teaching, scholarship, or research without the consent of the copyright holder does not necessarily constitute infringement. The law sets out four test factors, which are listed below, for judging fair use; they are intentionally general to allow for judicial discretion in striking a balance between creators' rights and the spread of knowledge from which further creative work may spring.

As discussed earlier, permission is not required to quote from works in the public domain—that is, works whose copyright term has expired and works of the federal government—or to use facts and ideas.

In addition, case law (as it has developed) allows parodies and satires of original works, as long as they are clearly intended to be humorous and only as much of the original is taken as is necessary to conjure it up in the minds of those reading or watching the satire.

How Is Fair Use Determined?

Copyright law requires that all of the following factors be considered when determining whether use of a work falls under the fair use provisions. Note, however, that there have been many lawsuits based on disputes over fair use; a user who has any doubts at all should check with a qualified attorney before proceeding.

1. *The purpose and character of the use, including whether it is of a commercial nature or for nonprofit educational purposes.* Scholarly and scientific research papers published in journals are normally permitted more latitude, providing that quoting is done with attribution. Quoting small portions of works in book reviews, literary criticisms, and newspaper stories is also normally considered fair use. In addition, one may generally make photocopies for personal use; distribution of such copies to students may, however, run afoul of the law, depending on how frequently it is done.

2. *The nature of the copyrighted work.* Information of a factual nature falls under fair use provisions more readily than do literary works. An article on a scientific breakthrough that provides important source information or helps

the author illustrate a point may be excerpted more readily than dialogue and description from a novel.

3. *The size and substantiality of the portion used in relation to the copyrighted work as a whole.* No set rule applies here, even though many publishers and writers believe that 300 to 500 words may be used without permission. Obviously, even fewer words than that would constitute a relatively large portion of a short work—for example, a line from a song or poem; permission to quote from a poem or song is almost always needed. And if a quotation, however small, contains the essence of the original work, however large, its use cannot be considered "fair."

4. *The effect of the use on the potential market for, or value of, the copyrighted work.* Making and sending copies of a newsletter that is available only by subscription to a number of nonsubscribers cuts into the newsletter's potential profits. So does reproducing a chapter out of a textbook—or an article—for distribution to students so they won't have to purchase the original.

Recent cases have held that because using unpublished material might diminish the future market value of the work to the original owner of such material and because the author should have the right to control not only *when,* but *whether,* a work is published, the fair use provisions will be interpreted more narrowly for unpublished works. Because even the paraphrasing of such copyrighted materials has been limited by some courts, the safest course is for authors always to obtain permission before quoting or closely paraphrasing published or unpublished material. This area is highly controversial and has been the subject of a number of lawsuits and of attempted legislative clarifications.

Moderation is the watchword in using copyrighted quotations, even among scholars and critics. If any doubt exists after reviewing the four factors listed above, quoters should err on the side of caution and request permission from the owner. The requesting writer should be aware that the copyright owner might refuse permission or ask for unreasonable compensation. For these reasons, permission requests should be mailed several months before the final manuscript goes to the publisher.

Securing Permission

Requests for permission should be addressed to the permissions department of the book or periodical publisher, which may forward the request to the copyright owner. Many publishers offer guidelines or supply a form to be used when requesting permission to quote from their publications. The sidebar that follows gives a list of suggested items for inclusion in permission letters.

GETTING PERMISSION

Authors are traditionally responsible by contract for securing permission to use copyrighted materials in their works. Permissions should always be obtained in writing. Normally, a letter will suffice. Anyone requesting permission to quote from, reproduce and distribute, perform, or adapt a work can expedite the response by including the following information with the request:

- A complete description of the copyrighted material from which permission to quote is being requested, including author, title, year of publication, and page number and paragraph; and date or volume number if the source is a periodical
- Title, author, projected publishing date, and publisher of the work in which the requested material will be used
- Type of work and intended audience (textbook, scholarly journal, novel, magazine article) for the work in which the material will be used
- Manner of distribution (handout at conference, hardback trade book, paperback, for-profit seminar manual) of the work in which the material will be used
- Length or number of pages in the work in which the material will be used, cover price (if known), and approximate size of first printing (or circulation if a periodical)
- Rights being requested (nonexclusive world rights will let you use the material worldwide in all languages and in any future revisions)

It may expedite matters to append a photocopy of the manuscript pages in which the quote will appear so that the context is evident.

Obtaining permission can be further expedited by appending a sentence at the end of the request that says "The permission requested above is hereby granted" and enclosing a duplicate copy of the form or letter (for the copyright owner's records) and a self-addressed, stamped envelope. It is also helpful to leave a line on which the copyright holder can state the wording of the credit.

This, of course, does not preclude negotiations that may result in restrictions on the grant or a request for payment. However, it will move things along in the event that the copyright owner has no objections to the grant as made.

Commercial services are available to obtain permissions for writers; *Literary Market Place* provides a listing.

Sometimes finding the owner of a copyright poses problems, since which rights belong to the author or the author's heirs and which belong to the publisher can often be determined only by reading the publishing contract. When an author is dead, heirship may be unclear, or the publisher may no longer be in business.

Several options are possible. One is to personally research the records at the Copyright Office in Washington, D.C. For an hourly fee, this office will conduct a search for an author; for more information, call (202) 707-6850. Copyright search firms are also available to provide this service. Since registrations are voluntary and transfers need not be recorded, however, such a search may prove fruitless. A biographical source such as *Who Was Who* may yield an author's last residence, and probate records in that jurisdiction may contain the names of heirs.

If all attempts to locate the copyright holder fail, the best course is probably not to use the material. Under current copyright law, stating that a good faith effort has been made to reach the copyright holder and obtain permission will *not* provide protection against an infringement suit down the road.

Permissions are usually acknowledged somewhere in the work that incorporates the quoted material. For a book, this is usually the front or back. (See Chapter 22, Parts of a Book, for details.)

The Difference Between Copyright Infringement and Plagiarism

The question of plagiarism sometimes arises in connection with discussions of copyright infringement, but the two are not synonymous. Plagiarism is an ethical issue, as well as a legal one. It involves attempting to pass off as one's own the words of another. If such theft involves the use of copyrighted materials, infringement prohibitions apply as well. Publishing an obscure work of Thomas Hardy as one's own, on the other hand, constitutes plagiarism but not copyright infringement because the work is in the public domain.

Writers should be aware that charges of plagiarism and copyright infringement can be made, under certain circumstances, against paraphrased material as well as material copied verbatim. Citing original sources is the best defense against a charge of plagiarism. Obtaining permission is the best defense against a charge of copyright infringement.

COPYRIGHT PROCEDURES

Copyright protection begins automatically at the moment an original work is fixed in any tangible medium. Registration with the Copyright Office is not required to protect a work with copyright. Although the choice to register is voluntary, registration can be important for many reasons. It establishes a public record of the copyright claim; it is one of the means for salvaging the copyright in a new work published before March 1, 1989, with insufficient notice; and it is a prerequisite for bringing a suit for infringement of a U.S. work. If made before or within 5 years of publication, registration will establish prima facie evidence in court of the validity of the copyright and of the facts stated to certify it. And registration before an infringement occurs (or within a 3-month grace period after publication) allows alternative remedies and reimbursement of legal fees if an infringement occurs.

Getting Information from the Copyright Office

The copyright office is the agency of the federal government that processes copyright registrations and serves as a repository for copyright records. This agency provides application forms and guidance on filling them out.

The Copyright Office is located in the Madison Building of the Library of Congress, in Washington, D.C. The mailing address is Copyright Office, Library of Congress, Washington, DC 20559. General information is available by calling (202) 707-3000 during normal business hours. The office also maintains a forms request line at (202) 707-9100; callers who know what forms they need may leave a message requesting those materials.

Copyright Registration

Registering a copyright with the Copyright Office is an optional act that is not required to secure copyright protection but may be necessary before one can enforce that protection. Generally, only one registration is permitted for a work; if a work is registered before publication, however, it may be reregistered after. It may also be reregistered if it is substantially revised or expanded. In book publishing, the publishing contract generally obligates the publisher to register the copyright; authors should check their contracts to verify who is responsible.

Form TX is used to register most written works. Serial publications, such as newspapers, magazines, newsletters, journals, annuals, and other periodicals, use form SE; works intended for performance, such as plays, scripts, lyrics, and music, use form PA. Form CA is used to correct or amplify previously registered information. Adjunct form GR/CP, to be filed with form TX or form PA, can be used to register all works by a single author that are published in periodicals within a 12-month period.

Forms are issued by the Copyright Office and usually come with line-by-line instructions on how to complete them. The office also provides information kits on copyright on books, contributions to collective works, drama, poetry, pseudonymous works, fair use, and other topics of interest. The Copyright Office can provide general help and clarification, but its staff cannot offer legal advice. Writers and editors should consult an attorney specializing in publishing issues for answers to questions that may affect their livelihood.

The three elements essential to copyright registration are a properly completed application form, a nonrefundable filing fee for each application, and nonreturnable copies of the work being registered—the number varies with the type of work and its publication status. All of these pieces should be sent in the same envelope. Copyright Office guidelines concerning the number and form of these deposit copies are available upon request.

Even though registration is not mandatory, the Copyright Act requires that copies of works published in the United States with notice of copyright be deposited for the use of the Library of Congress. Fines and other penalties can be levied for failure to comply. Copies submitted with registrations satisfy the deposit requirement; however, additional copies must be submitted when registering after a deposit has been made.

Generally, the deposit requirement is two complete copies of the "best edition," which is defined in copyright law as the one "that the Library of Congress determines to be most suitable for its purposes." The best edition is fully described in a circular available from the Copyright Office.

Copyright Renewal

To avoid being consigned to the public domain after their first term of copyright, works published before 1978 had to be renewed in their 28th year. A 1992 amendment to the U.S. copyright law now provides automatic renewal for works first published or copyrighted between 1964 and the end of 1977. However, incentives for formally renewing include more control over copyright ownership for the 47-year renewal term and more authority over the continued exploitation of derivative works licensed during the first term. Renewals use form RE; no deposit copies are required.

Copyright Transfer

The U.S. copyright law states that transfers of copyright or of the exclusive rights contained in a copyright are valid only when documented in writing. However, many, if not most, periodicals purchase publication rights without using contracts. The 1976 copyright law provides that in such cases, the collective work obtains the right to publish the work "as part of that particular collective work, any revision of that collective work, and any later collective work in the same series." Where there *is* a publishing contract, the potential value of all the rights that make up the copyright may merit review by a knowledgeable publishing attorney before the contract is signed.

U.S. law provides that grants of rights made since January 1, 1978, can be terminated by the author if living or, if the author is deceased, by certain of his or her heirs 35 to 40 years after the grant was made. Documents transferring all or part of a copyright can be recorded in the Copyright Office. Notices of termination of transfer *must* be filed there; check with the Copyright Office for regulations detailing the appropriate procedure.

Copyrights can also be transferred by will and by state rules of intestate succession, although renewal rights and termination rights can be inherited only as provided in the copyright law. And since copyrights are property, they are subject to the same rules of distribution as are any other assets in bankruptcy proceedings.

INTERNATIONAL COPYRIGHT PROTECTION

Copyright is a matter of national law, but treaties can be, and are, used to extend copyright protection beyond national boundaries. Countries that have signed two major multinational treaties that protect copyrights worldwide—the Berne Convention and the Universal Copyright Convention—agree to extend the protection of their laws to works that originate in other member nations. However, the protections their laws extend may not be the same as those enjoyed in the country of origin. Almost every country in the world now belongs to one of the two conventions, and many belong to both. Bilateral treaties may protect U.S. works in other countries. However, enforcement may be difficult even in countries that have signed these treaties. The Copyright Office advises authors to investigate the extent of protection afforded to foreign works in any countries targeted for distribution, preferably before the work is published anywhere because protection may depend on circumstances at the time of first publication. A list of countries that maintain copyright relations with the United States is available from the Copyright Office, but international copyright is such a complex area of law that no one should venture into these troubled waters without a lifeline to a competent counsel.

24

EDITING

EDITING

If, as Olin Miller has said, "writing is the hardest way of earning a living, with the possible exception of wrestling alligators," editing is surely a close second. Too often, writers regard editors as the enemy—people who obsess over commas or, worse, miss the point entirely and change the meaning. For most people, writing engenders a feeling of ownership and an involvement of the self. People who write for a living learn to accept editorial changes to their work as a necessary evil, with equanimity or resignation, as the case might be. But it is easy to forget that good editing leaves the author's voice and style intact and improves the piece. Bad editing, like bad writing, jars the ear and sometimes the soul and leaves the reader behind.

Writing and editing share the same goal: to communicate. Good writing and good editing are based on the same principles—clarity, precision, balance, euphony, appropriateness for the intended audience, and adherence to the rules of grammar and style. Writing and editing are simply two sides of the same coin; often they are done by the same person, although a person who writes and rewrites as he or she goes along might be hard-pressed to distinguish one from the other. Many writers find it difficult to edit their own writing, primarily because they know exactly what they want to say and assume that they have said it and also because they are not in the habit of reading their own work critically. Writers then turn to another pair of eyes to evaluate what they've written. Together, writers and editors try to produce the perfect sentence, the perfect paragraph, or the perfect book.

ROLE OF THE EDITOR

With this goal in mind, writers and editors strive above all for clarity. The audience and the purpose of the piece determine the tone and the style, and they in turn influence syntax—the way words are put together to form phrases, clauses, and sentences. A person's style can be as distinctive as a signature; whereas Picasso could and did paint in different styles, writers usually have a *voice,* a distinctive mode of expression that encompasses diction, rhythm, inflection, and so on. While striving for clarity, editors must be very careful to leave a writer's voice intact.

HEMINGWAY AND MAILER: A CONTRAST IN STYLES

These first paragraphs from two novels—one by Ernest Hemingway and one by Norman Mailer—illustrate differences in writing style.

> In the late summer of that year we lived in a house in a village that looked across the river and the plain to the mountains. In the bed of the river there were pebbles and boulders, dry and white in the sun, and the water was clear and swiftly moving and blue in the channels. Troops went by the house and down the road and the dust they raised powdered the leaves of the trees. The trunks of the trees too were dusty and the leaves fell early that year and we saw the troops marching along the road and the dust rising and leaves, stirred by the breeze, falling and the soldiers marching and afterward the road bare and white except for the leaves. (Ernest Hemingway, *A Farewell to Arms*)

> At dawn, if it was low tide on the flats, I would awaken to the chatter of gulls. On a bad morning, I used to feel as if I had died and the birds were feeding on my heart. Later, after I had dozed for a while, the tide would come up over the sand as swiftly as a shadow descends on the hills when the sun lowers behind the ridge, and before long the first swells would pound on the bulkhead of the deck below my bedroom window, the shock rising in one fine fragment of time from the sea wall to the innermost passages of my flesh. *Boom*! the waves would go against the wall, and I could have been alone on a freighter on a dark sea. (Norman Mailer, *Tough Guys Don't Dance*)

As an aside, another novelist made this interesting observation about how writers strive to achieve a certain style of writing:

> I have no time for a mystery writer who wants to be Norman Mailer when he grows up. As a matter of fact, I have no time for Norman Mailer, who after all wants to be Ernest Hemingway when he grows up. And I even get impatient with Hemingway, 'cause he obviously wanted to be Joseph Conrad when *he* grew up. (Max Allan Collins, *Kill Your Darlings*)

What then do editors do, and how do they proceed? Editors serve as the reader's advocate and the author's challenger: Is the author stating what she or he has to say as clearly as possible? In the editorial process of give and take, the editor probes the author's work, polishing it to facilitate communication. Editors also serve as objective reviewers. Writers are often too involved emotionally or professionally to be objective. Editors are more detached, and distance brings with it a certain amount of objectivity.

With the audience in mind, editors check content insofar as possible and review logic and organization. They check tone; they look for transitions to make sure that the reader will be able to follow the author's lead. Relying on up-to-date reference books and dictionaries for validation, they look for spelling, grammar, usage, and punctuation errors. Most important, they promote good, careful writing.

Successful editors have developed a discerning ear; they strike a balance between retaining the author's voice and revising the words to improve flow and readability. Good editors have a reason for every change they make or suggest; they do not stifle the writer's voice by imposing their particular preferences or favorite turns of phrase. Good writing has a point, which the editor helps elucidate. Good writing draws the reader in. Good writing is smooth and sounds natural. Good writing uses good syntax to reinforce the points it is making. The editor helps the writer achieve these goals.

SUBSTANTIVE EDITING

Editing subsumes many tasks, and the particular order in which they are performed depends on the individual editor. Editing means making a manuscript say all that the writer intended it to say by revising and reorganizing the text to improve readability and precision and by correcting spelling, grammar, punctuation, and style.

There are different levels of editing. Substantive or line editing deals mainly with content, organization, and tone, whereas copyediting focuses on stylistic consistency and spelling, grammar, and punctuation. Editing is not proofreading, which involves marking for typographical and spelling errors (and perhaps querying factual, grammatical, and style points) and deviations from typesetting or word processing specifications.

There is certainly a gray area between copyediting and substantive editing: They can be thought of as a continuum, with overlap in the middle. Both are concerned with redundancy and felicity, for example. Outside of book publishing, substantive editors are often expected to attend to copyediting problems as they go along unless the manuscript will be so extensively revised that another whole review will be necessary. Some works receive only copyediting, either because there is no time or because no reorganization or rewriting needs to be done. But copyediting is not the editor's main focus. Substantive editors are looking at larger issues.

Substantive editors, then, look at the manuscript on a deeper level than copyeditors. They ask, Is the tone right for the audience? Is the presentation balanced? If not, is it intended to be? Is all the material here? One of the hardest jobs an editor faces is determining whether any important information has been omitted. Is all the material accurate and up to date? Are the transitions in place? Can the reader follow the logic and the presentation? Is the organization right for the material? Do the conclusions follow from the facts or are they forced? Sometimes editors are subject matter experts, and such experience is certainly helpful. But most editors are not. They simply bring a critical eye, an objective viewpoint, and a sense of what to change and what to leave alone.

Editors need to guard against bias, overt or not, in any form—racial, sexist, ethnic, and intellectual. As the consciousness of the reading public has been raised, editors have begun to look carefully at the words writers use to describe people or nationalities. Language and social change are inextricably linked; the past few decades have seen sweeping social change, and as particular groups have become more active politically, they have imposed their linguistic preferences on the language. African Americans, American Indians, and the elderly are cases in point. The idea of political correctness is a logical extension of the relationship between language and social change. (See Chapter 1, Usage, for a discussion.)

There is another kind of bias, however, that is more subtle: intellectual bias. Editors must be alert to any shade of condescension, whether in tone or terminology. Nothing will kill a reader's interest faster than being talked down to.

Editors must also realize that not all writing is intended to fairly reflect all points of view or sides to an argument. Some pieces are intended to be polemics, and the ordinary rules of fairness may not apply. Once more, the purpose and the audience determine the tone, the language, and the logic.

Checking Logic

When checking logic, the editor asks, Is the purpose clear? Are all the terms defined? Are all the assumptions stated? Are the facts organized and analyzed or merely presented? Is the organization clear and easy to follow? If the editor cannot follow the organization, it often helps to outline the section. Outlining is useful for checking logic, following an argument, and pointing out missing information. Outlining is also a way to clarify thinking, to force organization where none existed before. Organization can be continuous—that is, an argument proceeds in a straight line from the beginning to the end—or circular—that is, the piece begins and ends at the same point.

The circular method announces its conclusion at the start; there are no surprises here. Continuous organization, however, moves the reader logically from point to point. Neither form is intrinsically better than the other (although some writers would disagree), and the same writer might use different organization at different times for different reasons.

Editors take a close look at the organization within sections and throughout the whole. Are there sections, paragraphs, or sentences out of place? When sections are moved, new transitions are often required, and, unless they are extensive or require research, the editor is expected to provide them. Editors should remember that transitions—*nevertheless, further, in addition, in contrast,* to cite some simple ones—point the way for the reader. Not only do they smooth the text and help the flow, but they serve as roadside signs and let the reader know where the writer is heading. Whole paragraphs serve the same purpose as phrases; they sum up the arguments or the facts presented. They tell readers how the writer interprets what has been presented thus far. If there are no transitions, the work appears choppy and disorganized.

Further, the editor must be alert to sloppy thinking or ambiguity. If the writer has generalized on the basis of insufficient information or introduced a conclusion that the facts do not support, the editor must explain where the problem lies. After all, the material is perfectly clear to the writer, who may have access to information the editor or reader lacks. Sometimes the writer simply forgets to add the necessary details that support the conclusion or tie in what seems to be a non sequitur.

The Words Themselves

Once the editor has attended to all these points, it is time to focus on the words. How are they strung together? Is the rhythm of the sentences and paragraphs natural? Has the writer varied the sentence structure, or has he or she written "with ink of opium on pages of lead"? Every language has a rhythm; those who write well use this rhythm to underscore their points, and editors must be alert to the cadence and euphony of the words.

Because emphasis often falls on the last word of the sentence, editors sometimes turn sentences around so that the most important word is last. Editors also try to put words where they sound the most natural to the ear of a native speaker; for that reason, editors will sometimes "break" those inflexible rules we learned in high school—"Never split an infinitive with an adverb; never start a sentence with *and* or *but.*" Not splitting the infinitive leads to constructions like *to go boldly where no man has gone before,* instead of *to boldly go.* Which sounds more natural? Today, only the most rigid grammarians do not allow split infinitives at least once in a while. And sentences can begin with *and* when it helps the flow.

QUERYING THE AUTHOR

In the course of their work, editors must often pose questions to the author. These questions are called queries. What sorts of things does an editor query? (1) Unclear constructions or antecedents that can confuse readers; (2) unintentional repetition that gets tedious and weakens the organization of the manuscript; (3) illogical organization that makes it hard for the reader to follow the writer's lead, and (4) discrepancies between names or descriptions of events or, in scholarly works, between in-text citations and reference lists that make the reader mistrust the writer's authority or grasp of the facts. Grammatical errors and style points are usually changed rather than queried, although pervasive stylistic changes should be discussed with the writer.

Too often, writers and editors have an adversarial relationship. Some writers don't want to see a word of their prose changed, and some editors make thoughtless changes that distort the meaning (an unforgivable sin to a writer) or make tactless and even snide remarks in the margins. The tone of the queries is especially important; the question should be concise and explain the problem clearly. Saying that a sentence is "unclear" or "confusing" doesn't give the writer enough information to make an intelligent change—after all, the sentence was perfectly clear to the writer.

How does an editor query? If the manuscript is being edited online, the queries are normally embedded in the text in boldface or brackets, but some software lets editors use a hidden text option, in which queries can be viewed at the user's discretion and which do not print. If editing is done on paper, the queries can be written directly in the margins, written on flags attached to the pages, or typed together on a separate page that lists queries by page and paragraph. Queries placed on self-stick flags are easily pulled off when the query is resolved; this method, as well as embedding queries in the electronic file, results in a neater page for the typesetter and proofreader but leaves open the possibility that the same query may be raised again later in the production process, at a cost of lost time.

Good editors also look for balance and symmetry. Parallel construction has long been a rhetorical device used by the best writers and public speakers from Shakespeare ("Double, double/ Toil and trouble/ Fire burn and cauldron bubble") to John F. Kennedy ("Ask not what your country can do for you; ask what you can do for your country").

Paragraphs as well as sentences can be balanced, although this is much harder to do. As Winston Churchill said,

> We shall go on to the end. We shall fight in France, we shall fight on the seas and oceans, we shall fight with growing strength and growing confidence in the air, we shall defend our island whatever the cost may be; we shall fight on the beaches, we shall fight on the landing grounds, we shall fight in the fields and in the streets, we shall fight in the hills; we shall never surrender.

Editors should look at the effect the writer is striving for and make the sentence work toward it. For example, in ordinary prose, having all sentences the same length leads to monotony. The editor must decide whether that is the effect the writer wants—creating an oppressive mood by using the same construction over and over to reinforce a point.

Normally, however, sentence structure should be varied. Modifiers should be kept close to the words they modify or ambiguity can result. This sometimes entails putting phrases first—"Fighting to stay awake, the sentry shifted uneasily," instead of "The sentry shifted uneasily, fighting to stay awake." If sentences are long, they must be constructed and punctuated so that the reader can grasp them; the relationship among the parts must be clear. Here, transitions, prepositions, and conjunctions are essential. These allow readers to keep track of the internal connections. A useful trick for untangling complex sentences is to read them aloud. Somehow hearing them makes them easier to fix.

PARALLEL CONSTRUCTION

Writers often rely on symmetry or parallel construction to structure their sentences. Parts of a sentence that are parallel in meaning should be parallel in structure. Writers and editors should balance a word with a word, a phrase with a phrase, a clause with a clause, and a sentence with a sentence.

> I can govern the United States or I can govern my daughter Alice, but I can't do both. (Theodore Roosevelt)

> The one important thing I have learned over the years is the difference between taking one's work seriously and taking one's self seriously. The first is imperative and the second is disastrous. (Margot Fonteyn)

> In an undeveloped country, don't drink the water; in a developed country, don't breathe the air. (*Changing Times*)

Editors also note whether the writing has been couched positively or negatively. All else being equal, it is better to use the affirmative, especially when analyzing or giving instructions. This is not to say that qualifiers like *most of the time* or *tend to* should always be eliminated. Nuances are important and should stay.

Recasting in the Active Voice

The active voice, where someone or something does the action, is stronger than the passive voice, where someone or something receives the action. Preferring the active voice does not mean that the writer or editor should ruthlessly excise every instance of passive voice. The passive voice has a bad reputation because it allows statements to be made without attribution: "Problems were defined and a consensus was reached." Who defined the problems and who reached the consensus? Excessive use of the passive has a way of burying responsibility; it is impersonal: "The decision was made to pull the plug on the life-support machine."

Sometimes there is a compelling reason to use the passive voice—sometimes the thing done is more important than the doer of the action. In this case, the passive should be used, of course. Otherwise, the active voice is to be preferred.

Plain English Versus Jargon, Clichés, and Redundancies

Some writers fear that if they use simple words ("plain English"), they will be thought to have simple ideas—always the kiss of death for a serious writer—so they make their words and sentences unnecessarily long and complicated. Editors should determine whether the intended audience would be better served by simpler language and, if so, propose it.

The word *jargon* originally meant a "confused, unintelligible language"; however, it has now come to mean the "technical terminology or characteristic idiom of a special activity or group." When writing for a specialized audience—one familiar with the topic or field—a writer must use jargon; it is the common idiom. When writing for a lay audience or the general public, a writer should use jargon only when necessary and define it carefully. Where plain English serves equally well, it should be used instead.

Gobbledygook is defined as wordy and generally unintelligible jargon. Sometimes its use is accidental or incidental—the writer simply doesn't know any better—but sometimes it is deliberate. In this case, like jargon, gobbledygook can fall into the category of *doublespeak*.

> Doublespeak is language that pretends to communicate but really doesn't. It makes the bad seem good, the negative appear positive, the unpleasant appear attractive or at least tolerable. Doublespeak is language that avoids

or shifts responsibility, language that is at variance with its real or purported meaning. (William Lutz, *Doublespeak*)

This is not to say that all euphemisms are bad. Doublespeak, however, subverts communication; it uses words like *negative patient care outcome* to mean that the patient died or *students deficient at a grading period* to mean that the students failed. It is human nature to put things in the best possible light, but writers and editors must be alert to doublespeak.

Noun strings—nouns strung together as modifiers, some as nouns and some as adjectives—are often the basis of jargon and gobbledygook: *student loan program office facilitator, multimillion dollar data management peripheral equipment leasing industry.* Such strings tend to confuse readers because the relationship between the words in the string is not clear. There are no articles or prepositions and no punctuation to clarify the meaning. Some noun strings like *sample selection bias* and *health maintenance organization* have passed into the language; others like *utilization board review* and *human resource management models* are part of the common idiom of a profession. But many others simply make it hard for the average reader to understand, and the writer or editor should look at each noun string individually to decide which of them are necessary and which should be recast. The best way to deal with noun strings is to work backward through the string to convert nouns to verbs where possible and to insert prepositions and articles: *the multimillion-dollar industry that leases peripheral equipment for data management.*

In the same vein, writers and editors should be alert to smothered verbs—verbs that have been turned into nouns. Verbs are the action words that carry the force of the language. Turning them into nouns dilutes them and weakens prose. *To investigate* is much clearer than *to conduct an investigation of,* just as *to help* is easier to understand than *to give some assistance to.* Smothered verbs are simply padding, and clear, powerful prose requires that every word carry its own weight.

Clichés—trite phrases or expressions—should be avoided in formal writing. It is difficult to do so because they are often the expressions that come most immediately to mind: *cool as a cucumber, bag and baggage, happy pair, beneath contempt, walk on water, skeleton in the closet, bottom line, ground zero, crazy as a loon, sick as a dog, lazy as the day is long, old as the hills, off the top of my head, never see the light of day, pushing the envelope, drawing a blank.*

Also to be avoided are *redundancies* that are fast becoming clichés: *serious crisis, new initiatives, consensus of opinion, end result.* A crisis is by definition serious, and a consensus is a shared opinion. Finally, if there are preliminary results, there can be an end result. If not, *result* alone suffices.

The ancient Greeks said that the only constant is change, and that is particularly true of language. New words are being created with astonishing rapidity; words that began as colloquial expressions or slang (for example, *blizzard, goodbye, jeans, gangster, movie,* and *phone*) pass into more common use and become accepted if they fill a gap and help people communicate. Or words that began as nouns (*function* and *archive,* for example) are now being used as verbs. Living languages are in continual flux, and authorities often do not agree on usage or definitions. In such cases, a writer's or editor's first priority is the audience. Will readers understand this language, and is it appropriate for the subject?

Editing is part science, part art. The science is based on rules of grammar and accepted terminology; the art is based on cadence, euphony, and felicity:

> The art of editing has most to do with felicity—with making just the right improvement to create light, joy, song, aptness, grace, beauty, or excitement where it wasn't quite happening. (Arthur Plotnik, *The Elements of Editing*)

No editor expects to complete all the editorial tasks discussed so far in one reading. Careful editors may read a piece several times and focus on a different task each time. Every manuscript is different, and editors often adjust their approach depending on the time available and the difficulty of the material. Some editors prefer to do substantive tasks like checking the logic last, and others do them first and save the more mechanical copyediting tasks for last.

COPYEDITING

Copyediting means checking a piece for internal inconsistencies and for errors in spelling, grammar, punctuation, format, and style, as well as verifying references, text citations, and callouts. Changes that an editor makes here are often easier for a writer to understand and for an editor to explain. A grammar book, a dictionary, and a style manual are a copyeditor's constant companions. (See Chapter 32, The Production Process, for a list of standard editing marks and a sample editing checklist.)

Verifying Spelling, Grammar, and Punctuation

As more projects are being copyedited directly on computers, some editors have come to depend on spelling and grammar checking software. Both of these tools are useful, but neither can substitute for an editor's judgment. A word can be spelled correctly and still be the wrong word in a particular context. A grammar checker will flag every single instance of the use of passive voice in a scientific research paper where the thing done is more important than the person doing it. Even after editing, much of what is said will remain in the passive, and rightly so. Search and replace functions can make global changes, but if the computer is left to do these automatically, absurdities can result. (For example, a global change from *lawyer* to *attorney* will also change *Lawyer Road* to *Attorney Road*.) See Chapter 29, Computers in the Editorial and Production Process, for more about the hazards of automated editing.

Reviewing for Consistency, Format, and Style

These sorts of changes are fairly straightforward, but instead of being dictated by grammar or a dictionary they are required by internal structure or style. *Style* in the largest sense means those issues about which a writer has a choice. Should *federal* be capitalized or lowercased when it refers to the government? Should figures or words be used to express numbers? Should headings be italic or boldface? Inconsistencies in style, format, or capitalization are distracting to the reader, and so editors try to eliminate them. Sometimes these decisions are imposed by a style guide (see Part III, Style), but often the editor simply establishes a style on the basis of internal consistency and produces an individual style sheet for a particular publication. Consistency also refers to internal information. Is the information in the text the same as the data in the accompanying table? Does the birth date given at the opening of the article gibe with the dates given for later events in the subject's life?

Format as well as word or style choice should be consistent: All chapter titles should be similarly styled; all paragraph indents should be the same. There should be an established style for displayed lists, tables, and subheads. Editors also standardize and verify cross-references and text citations and style bibliographies.

Verifying Cross-References, Text Citations, and Callouts

Writers often refer the reader to another section of the work. ("For a more extensive discussion of this study, see Chapter 4, Population Trends.") When works are extensively revised, this sort of cross-reference is often overlooked. The editor will verify that chapter 4 does indeed deal with population trends.

Text citations refer to other works mentioned in the body of the manuscript—for example, *(Evans 1991)*. Convention dictates that works referred to in text be included in a reference list or in notes. All works in the list must be mentioned in text and vice versa. Works that are not mentioned in the text but are nevertheless important are usually put in a bibliography or in a section called "Selected Readings."

In any case, references must be complete—that is, contain all the necessary publication information so that a reader can find them—and they must be styled consistently. If abbreviations are used for medical journal titles (per *Index Medicus,* for example), they must be the correct ones. Capitalization of titles must be consistent, and so on.

Callouts are text references to figures, tables, or notes—for example, "see figure 1." Callouts must be sequential—that is, the first reference to table 2 must precede the first reference to table 3. Again, verifying the order of all things numerical is a fairly mechanical but essential task. Many editors find it helpful to highlight all citations, callouts, and cross-references with a colored marker so they can be checked separately.

SUMMARY

What then do editors do? They serve as a bridge between the writer and the audience; they also act as the reader's advocate. Whatever changes an editor makes should be defensible, not arbitrary, and should improve the piece—make it more coherent, more tightly organized, easier to understand and assimilate, and more pleasing to the ear.

In making all these changes, the editor should not lose sight of the fact that he or she is a facilitator, that the work belongs to the writer, that there are often no hard and fast rules to fall back on. To edit well, a person must read often and cultivate a discerning ear and a love for words.

As one editor put it,

> In truth, there is nothing editors care so much about as the endless possibilities for combination and recombination in language, and finding the right set of combinations for a particular manuscript. This passion is usually put in terms of the editor's responsibility to the author; what we really must care about is creating that arrangement of the author's words that best expresses the author's intention. What we seek is a kind of harmony, a crystallization in which message and medium merge. (Bruce O. Boston, *The Editorial Eye,* June 1985)

25

TABLES

TABLES

A well-prepared table is often the most effective way to convey large amounts of specific information. If presented in text, the same information might take hundreds of words, making it difficult for the reader to make comparisons or locate particular facts; if summarized in chart or graph form, key details may be lost.

When deciding how to best present a mass of facts and figures, writers and editors should ask a few basic questions: Will the reader find a certain level of detail to be helpful? Can the information in the table stand alone, reducing or eliminating the need for lengthy text discussion? Is the amount of data small enough to be easily digestible in tabular form? Tables that are too long or too complex should probably be broken out into several smaller tables, or—if precise figures are not important—made into charts.

A table is usually made up of statistical information relating two or more variables arranged in columns and rows. Increasingly, however, writers and editors are using word or text tables to summarize information or reduce the amount of text. And matrixes, such as those familiar to readers who study the car repair records in *Consumer Reports,* provide a visual image in table form that allows the reader to make almost instant comparisons among features or products.

Easy-to-use table-generating software has eliminated the two traditional drawbacks to tables: cost and time. Publishers can often take existing tables, created in word processing or spreadsheet and database software, and move them into desktop publishing programs for final production. An added benefit is that because rekeying and reproofreading are kept to a minimum, accuracy is improved.

This chapter offers general guidelines on table formatting, terminology, and editing. Most aspects of table editing are style issues, which means that

PREPARING ELECTRONIC TABLES

Capturing tabular material electronically has always been a problem for typesetters. In the past, it was often easier and faster to rekey the material than to do the cleanup work needed to salvage the information. Today, depending on the software used, tables created in word processing programs can be "imported" or transferred to desktop publishing programs, but only if special table-generating features are *not* used. Here's how:

- Keep tables in separate files or on separate disks.
- Type the table the old-fashioned way—with tabs (never spaces) and as few rules as possible. Later, when moving the data into the publishing program, the typesetter can use the tab settings as "hooks" to transfer the column data without rekeying it. The typesetter will also delete the rules in the word processing file and use the publishing software to set up the table's rules, indentions, alignment, and so on.

Tables created in many popular spreadsheet programs can be imported into most of the well-known word processing programs and then, with some minor cleanup and preparation, moved into publishing software.

Recent advances in publishing software are also allowing information in databases to be easily used and manipulated. In short, capabilities are improving at a rapid pace, and editors should always investigate the possibility of importing any existing electronic data before having it rekeyed. The time spent rekeying and reproofreading and the likelihood that new errors will result are powerful arguments for using existing electronic files.

consistency within and among tables in a publication should be the editor's goal.

KINDS OF TABLES

Formal tables usually feature horizontal rules to set off titles, notes, and headings. They have titles and may be numbered, and the information can stand on its own; although a table may support the text, no further text explanation is required. These tables should be placed as close as possible to their first mention in the text, whether they are numbered or not.

Informal or in-text tables, on the other hand, do not need titles or numbers because they are really part of the text and depend on the text to explain their meaning. They are short, with just a few rows and columns; rules, except perhaps beneath column headings, are usually unnecessary. For example, the Library of Congress reported the number of copyright registrations in 1991 as follows:

Monographs	193,800
Musical works	191,200
Serials	109,200
Visual art works	79,200
Sound recordings	36,800
Semiconductor chip products	1,200
Renewals	52,300

In word tables, either fragments or sentences are acceptable, and the editorial style for the accompanying text is usually followed in the table. The extensive use of abbreviations common in numerical tables is often not acceptable in word tables, however.

A matrix is a form of word table in which short words (e.g., *yes, no*), numbers, or symbols (bullets, circles, check marks, and so on) denote a relationship between items in columns and rows.

Crosswalk of Strategies from Strategic Plan with 6 Major Goals Addressed in COPE Report Card

COPE's 6 Major Goals	Washington, DC, 2000 Goals							
	1	2	3	4	5	6	7	8
(1) Improved student performance	●		●	●		●	●	●
(2) Higher graduation rates		●	●		●	●		●
(3) Higher attendance rates		●	●			●		●
(4) Improved facilities	●			●	●	●	●	●
(5) Stronger teaching workforce	●		●	●				●
(6) More efficient central administration			●			●		●

Source: *Building Learning Communities.* The District of Columbia Public Schools, June 1992.

PARTS OF A TABLE

The table *title* should be brief and descriptive—it's not necessary to draw conclusions or explain the significance of the data in the title. If the manuscript contains several tables and these tables are referred to (or "called out") in the text, they should be numbered consecutively, either throughout the manuscript (table 1, table 2, and so on) or within each section or chapter (e.g., table 2–1 would be the first table in chapter 2). Appendix tables are usually numbered as table A–1, B–1, and so on to reflect the appendix lettering scheme. Typographic treatment is determined by the designer.

The *headnote,* usually located somewhere near the table title, explains how the table is set up; for example, if the final three digits have been dropped from all numbers in the table, the headnote will read "in thousands." Other examples of headnotes are "in 1980 dollars" and "in millions of dollars." Not all tables need headnotes.

Columns run vertically; *rows* run horizontally. The traditional name for row headings is the *stub,* and the headings that top the columns form the *boxhead.*

The *stub* is the left column, and stub headings are usually set flush left, with runover lines indented. To save space, all words except the first should be lowercased. Abbreviations are acceptable as long as the reader can decipher them and they are consistent. Different levels of subordination

Table 1. Per Capita Consumption of Selected Beverages, by Type: 1970 to 1990 (in gallons)

Beverage	*1970*	*1975*	*1980*	*1985*	*1990*
Nonalcoholic*	95.8	95.8	101.7	102.1	105.8
Milk	31.2	29.5	27.6	26.7	25.7
Whole	25.4	21.0	17.0	14.3	10.5
Lowfat	4.5	7.1	9.2	10.9	12.6
Skim	1.3	1.3	1.3	1.5	2.7
Tea	6.8	7.5	7.3	7.1	6.9
Coffee	33.4	31.4	26.7	27.4	26.7
Soft drinks	20.8	22.2	35.0	35.7	42.5
Citrus juice	3.6	5.2	5.1	5.2	4.0
Alcoholic	35.7	39.7	42.8	40.5	39.5
Beer	30.6	33.9	36.6	34.4	34.4
Wine	2.2	2.7	3.2	3.5	2.9
Distilled spirits	3.0	3.1	3.0	2.5	2.2

*Excludes vegetable juices, noncitrus fruit juices and drinks, canned concentrated citrus juices, and chilled fresh juices produced for local sale.

Source: U.S. Department of Agriculture, Economic Research Service, *Food Consumption, Prices, and Expenditures,* annual; and unpublished data.

can be shown by indenting subentries or setting main headings in boldface type.

Headings in the boxhead can be stacked in *decks;* the heads in these decks are called *spanner* heads. To save space, abbreviations and symbols are often used—% instead of percent, for example. The words and symbols used in headings should not be repeated in the body of the table. If a table carries over to two or more pages, boxhead information should be repeated on each page for ease of reference; the table number, if any, and title are usually repeated as well, followed by the word *continued.*

The *body* or *field* of the table is made up of *cells.* The type of alignment may vary, sometimes even within a table. Word tables are usually aligned flush left for ease of reading, whereas columns of numbers are set so that commas and decimals align. When words and numbers are mixed or when units of measure are mixed, it may be best to center all entries in a column. The key is to pick the treatment that works best and treat all tables having similar data consistently throughout a publication.

To assure the reader that nothing has been dropped, no cell should be left blank (except in matrix tables); dashes, zeros, or abbreviations such as NA (for "not available" or "not applicable") should be used instead and defined in a note. These notations are usually centered even if the column numbers are aligned on the decimal.

For the past several years, the trend has been to eliminate most rules, especially vertical rules, in formal tables. There are many other ways to improve the readability of long or dense tables, including typographic treatments such as dot leaders, shading of alternate rows, or varied spacing between rows or groups of rows.

Following the table body are *notes, footnotes,* and *source* information. Again, style choices dictate the order of this information, so consistency among tables in a document is more important than the format chosen. General information about the table is usually presented as a *note* or *notes.* Following the general notes are *footnotes* for specific items within the table. There are several options for denoting footnotes, and the choice depends on the extent and nature of the footnotes; these options should not be mixed within a manuscript. Symbols may be used, in this traditional order: asterisk (*), dagger (†), double dagger (‡), and section sign (§). If only one or two footnotes appear, single and double asterisks are often preferred. If the table has numerous footnotes, superscript letters or numbers are best. To prevent confusion, it's a good practice to use symbols or superscript letters with tables of numbers and to use superscript numbers with tables of letters and words. The numbers or letters of the footnote itself do not have to be set as superscripts; they may be set normal size, on the line, followed by a period.

The *source* should be cited if the table or the information in it was derived from a work other than the author's. Writers and editors should keep

Table 2. Civilian Employment in the Fastest Growing and Fastest Declining Occupations: 1990 and 2005

	Employment (in thousands)				*Percent Change 1990–2005*		
		2005[1]					
Occupation	*1990*	*Low*	*Moderate*	*High*	*Low*	*Moderate*	*High*
Fastest Growing							
Home health aides	287	512	550	582	78	92	103
Systems analysts	463	769	829	864	66	79	87
Medical assistants	165	268	287	306	62	74	85
Human services workers	145	231	249	264	59	71	82
Radiologic technologists and technicians	149	234	252	268	58	70	80
Medical secretaries	232	363	390	415	57	68	79
Psychologists	125	193	204	214	55	64	72
Travel agents	132	199	214	224	51	62	70
Corrections officers	230	342	372	400	49	61	74
Flight attendants	101	146	159	168	45	59	67
Computer programmers	565	811	882	923	44	56	63
Fastest Declining							
Electrical and electronic assemblers	232	112	128	131	−52	−45	−44
Child care workers, private household	314	176	190	200	−44	−40	−36
Cleaners and servants, private household	411	287	310	326	−30	−25	−21
Machine forming operators and tenders[2]	174	119	131	137	−32	−25	−21
Farmers	1074	822	850	876	−23	−21	−18
Sewing machine operators, garment	585	368	469	478	−37	−20	−18

[1] Based on low, moderate, or high trend assumptions.
[2] Metal and plastic.

Source: U.S. Bureau of Labor Statistics, *Monthly Labor Review*, November 1991.

in mind that tables are covered by the same copyright laws that apply to text, and permission must be obtained before tables or parts of tables are reproduced from a copyrighted source (see Chapter 23, Copyright).

Notes, footnotes, and source information are placed at the end of the table, which may mean the last page of a multipage table. To save the reader from having to search for footnote information, it may make sense to repeat this information on each page. For tables that run for several pages, a phrase such as "See footnotes at end" is often placed at the bottom of all pages but the last.

EDITING TABLES

A few basic guidelines apply to editing tables. Of course, ensuring consistency—in both style and format—within and among tables in a manuscript is the first rule. Except for more liberal use of abbreviations, symbols, and figures, the style for capitalization, punctuation, and hyphenation should follow the style used for the text. Headings should be grammatically parallel. Repetitious terms and symbols should be eliminated; for example, if the dollar sign or "in dollars" appears in the headnote or column heading, the dollar sign is unnecessary in the table body. Format—column alignment, use of bold and italic typefaces, indention levels, and rules—should be the same across tables.

Further, the writer or editor should take a critical look at the way the table is set up. Numbers that are meant to be compared should usually run down, not across; if it is difficult for the reader to draw comparisons or conclusions, it may be necessary to reverse the positions of the stub and column heads.

The size of a table, which depends on the page size of the final product, can pose production problems. Editors may need to take creative approaches to make a table fit on the page, for example, by shortening headings and entry lines, reducing the space between columns, dropping the type size by a point or two, adding hyphenation, or breaking a large table into two or more smaller tables.

Table width can be decreased by using a condensed typeface or by adding a headnote (e.g., "in thousands") that allows long strings of numbers in the table body to be shortened. Reducing the entire table photographically or electronically is also a possibility but should be done only when all else fails; readability is usually at stake.

Whenever possible, tables should be oriented vertically (referred to as *portrait* in desktop publishing jargon) on the page; tables placed sideways on the page (known as *broadside, turn,* or *landscape* tables) force the reader to rotate the document, making quick references between text and table cumbersome. If the table must run broadside, the editor should make sure the layout artist places the bottom edge of the table so that it faces the righthand margin of the page. Also to be avoided are column headings set sideways or at an angle; again, ease of readability is a factor.

If the manuscript contains many tables or if the tables supplement rather than support the text, the editor should consider moving them to an appendix so that the flow of text is not interrupted.

Table 3. Employed Writers, Artists, Entertainers, and Athletes, 1983 and 1991

	1983				*1991*			
		Percent of Total				*Percent of Total*		
Occupation [1]	*Total (000s)*	*Female*	*Black*	*Hispanic*	*Total (000s)*	*Female*	*Black*	*Hispanic*
Authors	62	42.7	2.1	0.9	91	53.2	1.4	1.0
Technical writers	(2)	(2)	(2)	(2)	62	50.0	5.3	1.8
Designers	393	52.7	3.1	2.7	527	53.4	2.9	4.3
Musicians and composers	155	28.0	7.9	4.4	156	31.1	7.6	6.2
Actors and directors	60	30.8	6.6	3.4	87	33.2	10.5	4.8
Painters, sculptors, craft artists, and artist printmakers	186	47.4	2.1	2.3	208	55.3	2.7	3.2
Photographers	113	20.7	4.0	3.4	136	23.0	7.7	4.4
Editors and reporters	204	48.4	2.9	2.1	279	51.1	4.5	2.8
Public relations specialists	157	50.1	6.2	1.9	173	56.2	8.3	3.1
Announcers	NA	NA	NA	NA	60	21.3	6.2	5.2
Athletes	58	17.6	9.4	1.7	77	24.7	7.5	4.2

Notes: NA = not available. Figures represent civilian noninstitutional population 16 years old and over. Annual average of monthly figures. Based on "Current Population Survey"; see text, section 1, and appendix III. Persons of Hispanic origin may be of any race.

1. Includes other occupations, not shown separately.
2. Level of total employment below 50,000.

Source: U.S. Bureau of Labor Statistics, *Employment and Earnings*, monthly, January issues.

Table placement should be indicated for the typesetter or layout artist by making notes in the manuscript margin (e.g., "table 3 goes here" or "place all tables in appendix B"). In the text itself, simply placing the table callout in parentheses—(see table 1)—after its text discussion is usually sufficient; a sentence that starts "Table 1 reveals" often sounds forced.

Finally, the writer or editor should check to be sure that all references to table data in the text or any conclusions drawn from tables are accurate and match those in the table. The table title should be edited so that it is clear, concise, and complete. Any mathematical totals should be checked with a calculator for accuracy unless the author has indicated full responsibility for this task. On a last pass through the manuscript, the editor should check that all tables are present and numbered consecutively; a table may have been deleted in earlier revisions and the remaining table numbers may not have been adjusted.

Although editing tables can be tedious and time consuming, completing all of these steps is an important part of the editing process and is essential to the overall integrity of the manuscript.

26

CHARTS, GRAPHS, AND MAPS

CHARTS, GRAPHS, AND MAPS

There may have been a time in the history of communication when words alone, thoughtfully grouped, were sufficient to convey information. If so, it wasn't in the Stone Age, when early humans carved pictograms into cave walls. And it isn't today, the Information Age, when experts routinely design computer systems capable of handling terabytes—that's 1,000,000,000,000 bytes—of data transmitted from such instrumentation as the Hubble Space Telescope. To be analyzed, data this dense must take a form that can be "read" far more swiftly than words. That form often turns out to be charts and graphs.

This chapter explains the basics of information graphics for editors who, possibly for the first time, are being asked to create or edit the charts, graphs, and maps that are a natural by-product of the Information Age. Implicit in these suggestions is a warning: View charts and graphs with a critical eye. Because graphics communicate relationships and concepts so well and so quickly and because people tend to believe what they see, the danger of conveying misinformation or a wrong impression is far greater with graphics than with words alone.

Writers as well as editors must also guard against the temptation to use charts and graphs as ornaments, with little thought given to their purpose other than to fill up space, break up text, or generate visual interest. Needless to say, the ready availability of computer-generated graphics has also led to increasing numbers of poorly conceived and executed charts and graphs. More than ever, then, part of the writer's and editor's job is to evaluate graphics for accuracy, relevance, and clarity and to suggest revisions and refinements. To perform these tasks, writers and editors should understand some basics of placement and typography as well as the general principles—and pitfalls—of chartmaking and mapmaking.

The concepts explained in this chapter reflect the views of contempo-

CHARTJUNK VERSUS CHART ART

There is no dispute that the use of data graphics in every form of communication is on the rise. Yale statistics professor Edward Tufte estimates, for instance, that between 900 billion and 2 trillion statistical graphics are printed each year worldwide.

One ongoing dispute, however, involves how that data should be presented and is neatly exemplified by the stylistic tendencies of two contemporary information design experts: Tufte himself and *Time* magazine graphics director Nigel Holmes.

Tufte, a prophet of information design, embraces simplicity in underlying design and complexity in information displayed. According to Tufte, needlessly decorating a graphic generates a lot of ink that tells the viewer nothing new. The purpose of decoration varies, but it is all what Tufte calls *non-data ink, redundant-data ink,* or *chartjunk.* Such decoration, which prospers in technical publications and in commercial and media graphics, he writes, comes cheaper than the hard work required to produce intriguing numbers and secure evidence. Most chartjunk does not involve art. It is conventional graphic paraphernalia routinely added to everyday display: over-busy grid lines, excess ticks, and redundant representations of simple data.

Stylistically, no one is farther from Tufte than Nigel Holmes, the father of contemporary "infographics." Holmes' signature charts and graphs combine a picture or drawing of a subject with information about the subject. This style, he says, tells readers what the subject is, gives them the information, and tells them what the information means.

In contrast to Tufte, who packs as much information as possible into a graphic, Holmes believes in paring, or editing, the information down to the subject's bare bones. He also thinks that color is overrated and urges restraint, especially in information graphics. Holmes suggests designing the chart or graph in black and white, then adding color for emphasis, not for decoration. As long as an artist understands that the primary function is to convey and respect statistics, Holmes says, fun can be had with the form statistics take.

rary experts, whose books should be referred to for more detailed information. They include Yale University political science and statistics professor Edward Tufte, *Time* magazine graphics director Nigel Holmes, graphics expert Jan White, and Syracuse University geography professor Mark Monmonier.

EDITING CHARTS AND GRAPHS

Editing and revising are as important to sound graphic design as they are to writing. Serving as the reader's advocate, editors must approach graphics critically, with three basic questions in mind:

- Does the graphic serve to enhance the text, or is its purpose decorative, doubtful, or unclear?
- Is the information complete, correct, and consistent with the text, and does it clearly support the author's points?
- Does each graphic portray a single thought or conclusion, so that the reader will understand and immediately grasp its meaning, helped by clear and appropriate labels, headings, captions, and overall design?

The following sections offer specific advice on typographical as well as content considerations.

Editing for Appearance and Clarity

The look of a finished graph or chart is almost as important as its accuracy. Obscure symbols and abbreviations, missing elements, cluttered backgrounds, and hard-to-read labels are just a few examples of ways a graphic can fail to inform. Certain principles of typography and layout apply to all kinds of charts and graphs, from a technical report to the pages of *Time* and *USA Today*.

All graphs in a document should look as if they belong together. Elements that should be standardized are type sizes and faces and placement of the title, caption, label, source line, and footnotes. Similar graphs should be of similar size and not enlarged or reduced just to fill a hole on the page.

Charts and graphs should be kept as uncluttered and simple as possible; squeezing several different messages into one graph to save space defeats the purpose of clear communication.

Placement in Text. All graphics should be placed as near their text mention as possible. If figure numbers are used (usually necessary if there are more than a few graphics), the figure number, or *callout,* should also be mentioned in the text. Any symbols, abbreviations, and terminology used in the graphic should be used consistently in the figure caption, other figures, and the text.

Typeface and Type Size. The typeface used for labels, captions, and notes should be clear and simple. The most readable form is caps and lowercase (known as *clc*), not all caps; over the years, studies continue to show that speed and comprehension are reduced when all uppercase letters are used. The type size can be somewhat smaller than text type—6- to 8-point type is an ideal size—since these lines are usually short and surrounded by white space.

Titles and Captions. Most charts and graphs need titles; short titles are preferred, but not so short that they confuse or fail to convey the meaning. Titles often are best supplemented by captions, written in complete sentence form, that summarize the conclusions to be drawn from the graph's information. Often, titles go at the top and captions at the bottom of graphs and charts, but there are no hard-and-fast rules. If used, figure numbers should be consecutive either throughout the document—figure 1, figure 2, figure 3—or, in larger documents, throughout the chapter or section—figure 1–2, figure 3–1.

Notes, Footnotes, and Source Information. Notes are traditionally placed first, at the bottom left of the chart, followed by footnotes and source information. Traditional symbols such as asterisks, double asterisks, daggers, and double daggers can be used if footnote numbers or letters could be easily confused with numbers or letters in the chart. Editors should keep in mind that some readers may look at a chart without reading the footnotes. For example, in figure 26–1a, a small asterisk notes that figures in the third column are for 6 months, compared with 12 months for the others. But many readers may overlook that important piece of information. It is safer to project the next 6 months with a dotted line (figure 26–1b) and omit the footnote.

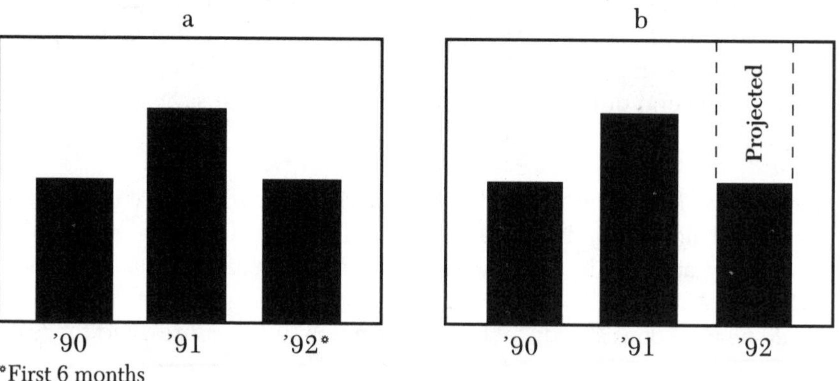

Figure 26–1. All important information should appear in the body of the chart whenever possible, as in b; *the reader may overlook information or disclaimers placed in footnotes, as in* a.

Lines and Shading. Various kinds of line widths and treatments (dashed, dotted, and so on) and shading are often used to distinguish variables. In general, lines that represent data should be heavier than background grid lines or axis lines. Keep in mind that within a chart, if one line of data is heavier than another, the message to the reader may be that the heavier line is more significant. The same holds true for variations in shading in bar graphs and pie charts, with the darker portions taking on more visual importance (figure 26–2).

The scale used in a graph or chart should be carefully checked to make sure that accurate comparisons can be made both within and among similar charts. For example, a chart that uses 10-year intervals for a few points and then switches to 5-year intervals will present a distorted picture of a trend over time (figure 26–3).

The units of measurement used to establish a scale can also affect how the data are perceived; small differences in the data can be enhanced by using a small scale, and large differences can be minimized by using a large scale. The scale used can also affect the shape of the chart or graph, which in turn affects the relative flatness or steepness of the data lines—and thus the impression conveyed to the reader. (See Edward Tufte's *Visual Display of Quantitative Information* for examples and explanations of distortion resulting from faulty use of scale.)

Labels, Tick Marks, and Other Details. Finally, the editor should make sure that all labels, legends, and other details are correctly placed and readable. Spacing between tick marks—the short lines on the left and bottom sides of

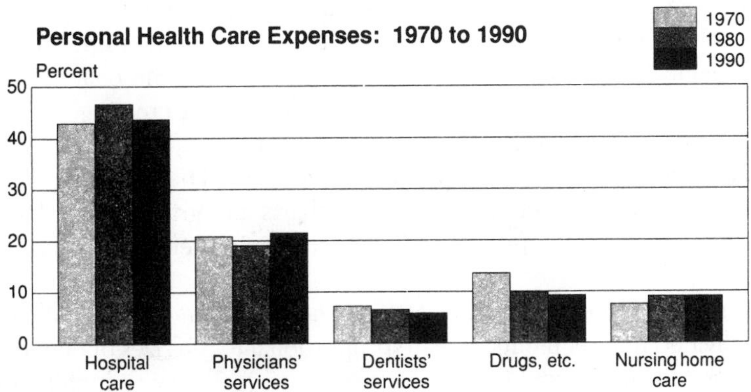

Figure 26–2. Darker shading generally indicates more important data; in this case, the most current information is represented by the darkest bars.

Note: The source for figures 26–2, 26–4, 26–6, 26–7, 26–9, 26–10, and 26–11 is *Statistical Abstract of the United States: 1992,* U.S. Bureau of the Census.

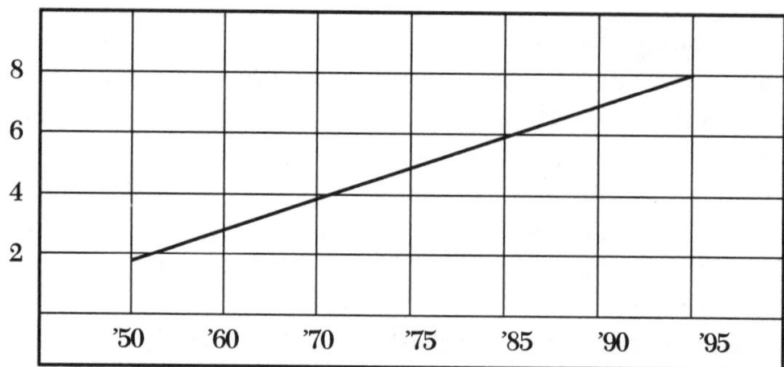

Figure 26–3. The scale used should be consistent; this chart mixes 10-year and 5-year intervals, distorting the overall picture.

a chart that indicate units of measurement—should be checked. Any excessive or unnecessary scale markers or background grid lines should be removed, and hard-to-distinguish data lines, shading variations, or fill patterns should be replaced.

Editing for Content and Accuracy

A chart or graph is only as good as its data. Writers and editors should be alert to possible distortion caused by missing or irrelevant information. Very simple graphics or those that show drastic results should be questioned; important data could be missing. Information can be taken out of context as easily in pictures as in words.

The next thing to note about charts and graphs in general is that each type of chart and graph best serves a particular purpose. Computer programs that let the user flow data into a pie chart, bar chart, or line chart may be to blame for encouraging the belief that selecting the chart type is a matter of personal preference, not logic. The person creating a chart or graph should first determine the purpose of the information to be shown and let that purpose dictate the type of graphic used. The following sections explain the three most common types of charts and graphs—pie, bar, and line—and point out the pitfalls and problems associated with each.

To Show the Proportion of Parts to the Whole: Pie Charts. A pie chart is a circle divided into segments that are proportional to the sizes of elements to be illustrated (figure 26–4). The pie chart is a good way to highlight data when percentages tell the story. Some experts say it is best not to show more than 6 segments, and others say 8 or 10 should be the maximum; it may be possible to group several small segments under more general headings, including "Other," and explain as necessary in the text or caption. Different colors or shades of gray can help to separate and classify segments of the pie.

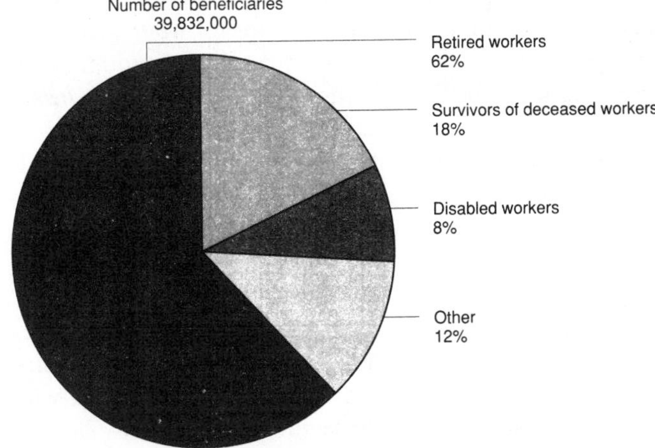

Figure 26–4. Pie charts are an effective way to show percentages; pies with more than 8 or 10 "slices" are hard to read and make comparison among the categories difficult.

Editors should check that the percentages shown accurately reflect the segment sizes and that the total of the slices equals 100 percent.

The best place for labels is inside the pie, but if there's not enough room, labels can be placed on the outside, with arrows pointing to respective segments. Whatever the approach, it should be used consistently throughout a document.

Placing the pie chart at an angle may make the chart look more interesting, but this use of perspective may distort the relative sizes of the segments; in addition, the elements that are closer to the reader will seem more important (figure 26–5).

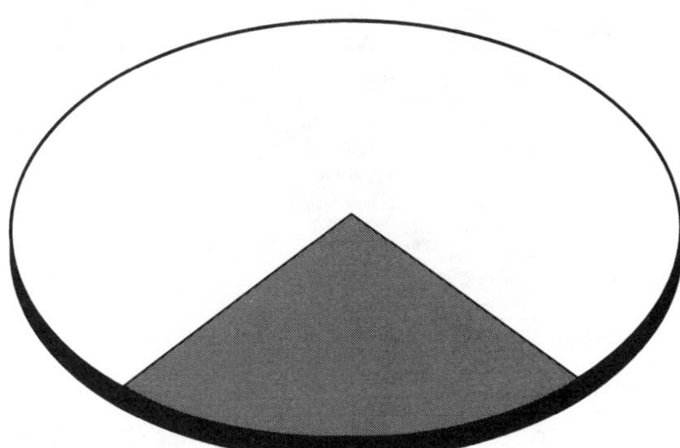

Figure 26–5. Placing graphics at an angle can result in a distorted view of the parts of a chart or graph.

To Compare Amounts: Column and Bar Charts. Column and bar charts are good for comparing specific amounts and for showing trends, unless the quantities don't vary significantly. Although the term *bar chart* is often used to refer to both types, technically a chart with vertical or upright bars is called a *column chart.* If all the bars touch, the chart is called a *histogram.*

Bars or columns are usually solid lines, but they may take the form of symbolic representations of the item being measured, such as piles of coins or barrels of oil. They can be single or multiple, flat or three-dimensional. In general, the bars or columns should be wider than the spaces between them (figure 26–6).

Bars or columns must be placed on a grid or scale to show the quantity being measured. Color or shading can be used to emphasize trends or data features. If the columns are divided to show different items, the largest element is usually placed at the foot of each column or bar, with different shading or colors distinguishing the segments (figure 26–7).

It is important to check bar and column charts for several possible areas of distortion. Variations in thickness can make a bar look larger or more important, and bars that are drawn with perspective or three-dimensional effects can be difficult to read accurately and may even mislead the reader (figure 26–8).

When there are too many numbers, the columns become so thin and close together that the individual bars lose their effectiveness. If the information cannot be grouped into larger categories, presenting the data in table form may be the best solution.

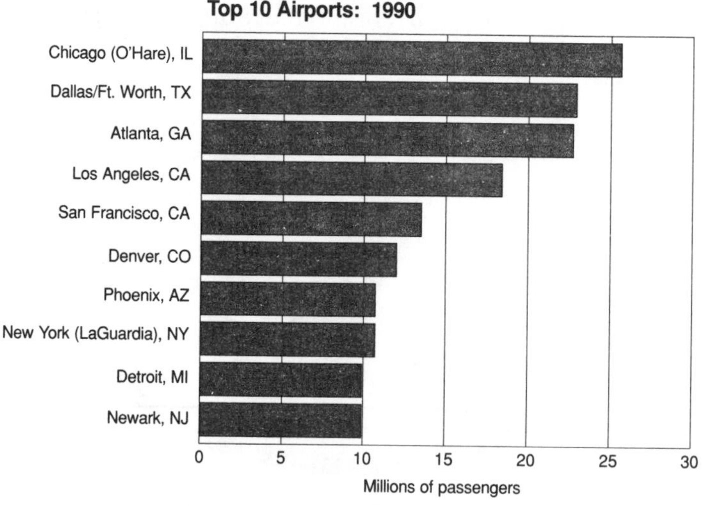

Figure 26–6. Bar charts are best used to compare amounts or show trends.

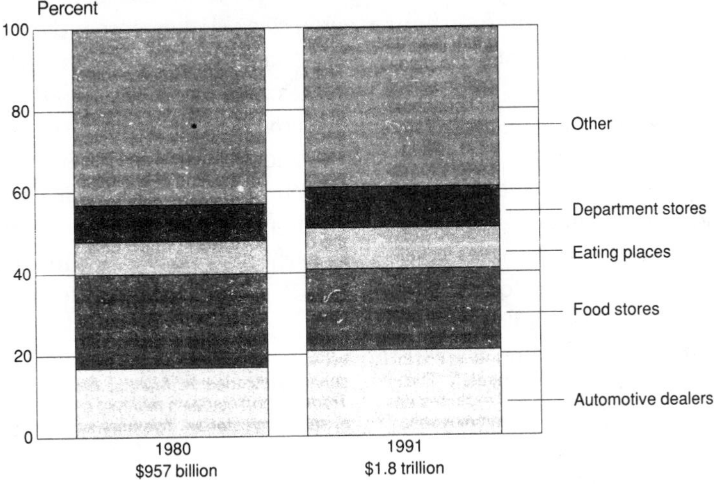

Figure 26–7. In column charts, the largest single category is usually placed at the bottom of each column.

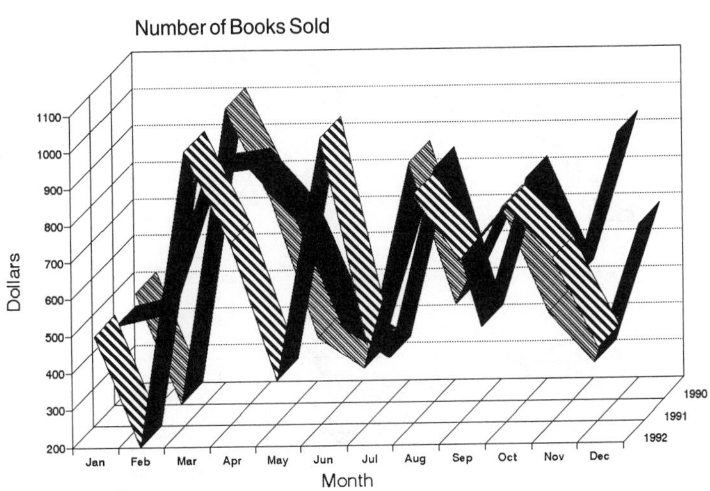

Figure 26–8. Graphics software offers many special effects, but some of these options—like the three-dimensional effect here—may make the chart impossible to read.

To Show Change over Time: Line Graphs. Line graphs—also called *curve charts* or *fever charts*—join plotted points with a line or several lines to pinpoint change over time. A line's steepness or shallowness indicates the rate of change, with a steep line meaning fast development. The line is formed by joining points plotted on two axes. Time is plotted on the x axis across the bottom, and quantity is plotted on the y axis up the left side. A grid is formed by extending lines vertically or horizontally from the x and y measurements. Plot points mark the intersection of time and quantity on the grid and form the line's skeleton. Clear labels are needed to denote amounts and time and show units of measure. Dollars should be expressed in the form of a constant, adjusted for inflation (figure 26–9). Color or pattern can be used to differentiate multiple lines.

A variation on the line graph is the *surface chart,* in which each data line becomes the top of a shaded area (figure 26–10). Surface charts illustrate the results of cumulative change over time and are good for showing gradual change.

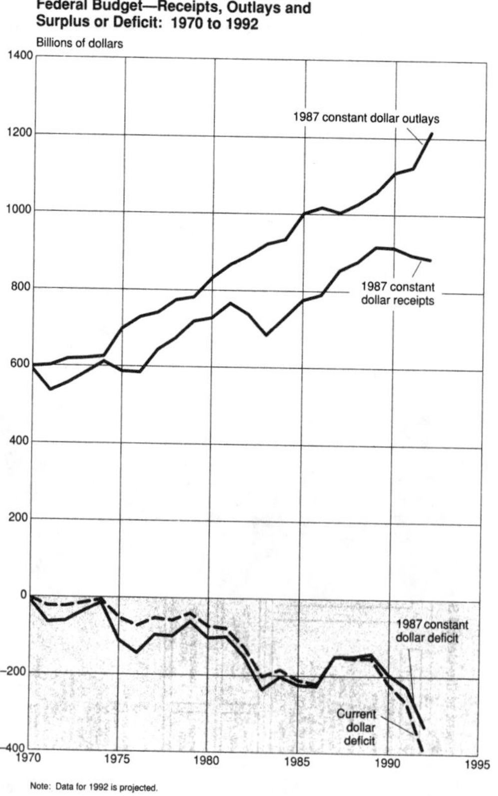

Figure 26–9. Line graphs, also called fever charts, are used to show change over time.

❧

THE FLY: A GRAPHIC TALE

One day in France during the early 1600s, a young soldier lay on his bed, watching a fly hover in the air. Someone else might have swatted at the fly and gone back to sleep, but this young man was René Descartes, the philosopher and mathematician.

As the fly buzzed lazily above him, Descartes realized that the fly's position at each moment could be described by three planes, at right angles (perpendicular) to each other, that intersected at the fly's position. On a flat surface, each point could be located by two perpendicular lines intersecting at the fly's position.

Though this was not an original concept, Descartes also saw that these *coordinates* could represent every point in a plane through an ordered two-number system in which (2,4) represented two units east, four units north from the starting point and (–3,–6) meant three units west, six units south (points in space need a three-number system, the third representing units up or down). This concept combined algebra and geometry. Since a synonym for algebra was *analysis,* Descartes' system of fusing the two branches of mathematics came to be called *analytic geometry.* Descartes' approach to geometry, which gave mathematicians a new way to look at equations, is the heart of plotting statistics used in charts and graphs.

Line graphs can be hard to follow if there is too much information, if the scale jumps from a tiny amount to a huge one, or if quantities vary only slightly. Editors should watch out for problems of exaggerated scale, inconsistent units of measurement (especially units of time), and too many or too few underlying grid lines, as discussed earlier in this chapter.

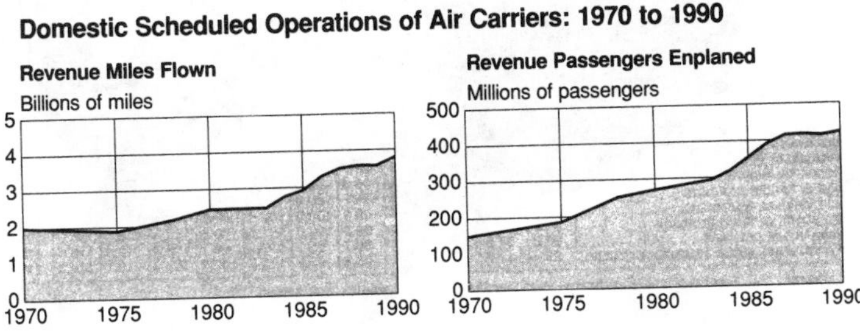

Figure 26–10. Surface charts, in which the area below the plotted line is shaded, are useful for showing gradual change over time.

EDITING MAPS

Since the time of the Greek mathematician Anaximander—about 540 B.C.—maps have been a popular, if not always an exact, way to present information. Today, computers and increasingly available mapping software have made it easier to produce new maps *and* have made it easier to perpetuate error and distortion.

Maps can take many forms. Reference maps, made by astronomers and cartographers, are surface representations of regions of the earth or sky. They tell the reader where things are in relation to each other. Pictorial maps use pictures or symbols to convey a specific message—where in the United States certain kinds of industries have concentrated, for example, or how many doctors practice in each U.S. county (figure 26–11).

Writers and editors who work with maps should understand a few underlying principles and be aware of the kinds of mistakes and blunders that can be generated by human mapmakers as well as by computer software. By their very nature, maps distort reality to some degree. No flat map can precisely match a globe's three-dimensional geographic areas, angles, shapes, distances, and directions.

Editors should be skeptical of maps generated using off-the-shelf graphics software, since many programs still have a fair number of problems. Checking these maps against a current atlas or other source can pay off. Common mistakes include misspelled place names, dropped features, and mis-

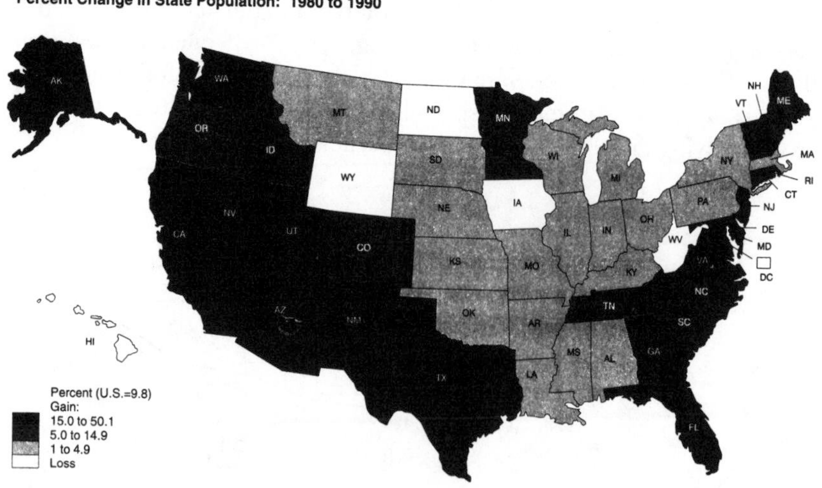

Figure 26–11. Various degrees of shading show groupings of percentage change, with the darker areas representing the largest gains.

❧

FROM MERCATOR TO ROBINSON

No one has ever been able to wrestle the image of a sphere onto a flat surface without distorting it, but many have tried. Starting with Flemish geographer Gerardus Mercator in 1568, more than 100 world map projections have been invented for drawing a spherical network of coordinates and points on flat paper. The projections have been shaped like rectangles, circles, ellipses, and stars; they have enlarged continents or shrunk them, and even altered the shapes of oceans.

Until the early 1900s, the National Geographic Society grudgingly used the Mercator, which distorted the relative sizes and shapes of land masses. Then, in 1922, the society's chief cartographer created a new map based on a projection patented in 1904 by Alphons van der Grinten. In 1988, the society began using another projection for its map of the world, this one named for its creator, cartographer Arthur H. Robinson of the University of Wisconsin.

For its world maps the society prefers an uninterrupted projection that shows earth's features and their relationships as accurately as possible. Robinson's projection, devised in 1963, seemed the best compromise. In shape and area the Robinson is more realistic than the Van der Grinten, and it shows the former Soviet Union and Canada at 1.5 times their relative size versus twice their relative size for the Van der Grinten.

---

placed boundaries. Errors are most common in maps compiled from other maps, a bad practice because most maps are copyrighted; permission from the copyright holder is necessary for any kind of borrowing or adaptation.

Unnecessary details should be edited out, simplifying the map to illustrate the point it is making. The map's legend and scale should be checked for accuracy and appropriateness. The editor should check that all important features are labeled and that the map is oriented to the north.

Shading, texture, and color are often used to emphasize certain map features. Inexperienced users of mapping software may be tempted to use colors to show differences in quantity, but varying shades of gray usually work just as well and reduce printing costs dramatically. Most readers can distinguish five or six gray tones, ranging evenly from light gray to black. Darker tones traditionally indicate larger quantities.

The printing process can change a map's appearance; it is important to be aware that gray tones and fine dot screens are especially vulnerable to over- or under-inking.

MAP PROJECTIONS: THE PITFALLS

Cartographer Richard Furno has spent most of his career at two publications—the *Washington Post* and *National Geographic*—creating maps and, more recently, computer-aided design and mapping software. The traps are many for those who create and edit maps, and Furno lays out some of the most common.

"The most difficult things to comprehend and use correctly are map projections," he says. "Map projections have basic properties, and writers or editors who use maps must ask themselves what they want to achieve. Two basic map types are *equal area* and *conformal* projections. You don't want to use one when you meant to use the other."

Equal area projections preserve areal relationships and allow map angles to be measured accurately. If one country is three times larger than another on the globe, it will also be three times larger on an equal area projection. In such maps, all areas are in true proportion to each other and to the globe. This is important when showing statistical information such as distribution of resources or populations.

Conformal projections preserve local angles, allowing map angles to be measured accurately. On such a projection, the angle between any two intersecting lines is the same on a globe and a flat map. This property of keeping angles true creates true geographical shape in localized areas. The virtue of conformal maps for navigators, for example, is that true bearings can be taken from such maps.

"One of the easiest traps is to show a distribution on a conformal map," Furno says. "Even cartographers make this mistake. For editors and people who produce books, this is one of the most important points: show distribution on an equal-area projection." Another trap is true scale. Most maps present a scale by indicating that 1 inch equals a certain number of road miles on the map.

"Map readers tend to think that if they take that scale and measure along a portion of map, they will get true distance," Furno says, "but the scales generally only give an approximation. Conformal maps [which are hardest to make scales for] often use multiple scales. No map has true scale throughout."

27

PHOTOGRAPHS AND ILLUSTRATIONS

PHOTOGRAPHS AND ILLUSTRATIONS

Words and pictures go together, each telling a story in its own particular language. Photographs and illustrations can range in purpose from technical and representational to ornamental and evocative, with many variations in between. A photograph in an advertising brochure is meant to attract the reader and stimulate an emotional response, while an illustration in a technical article provides detailed information and clarifies the meaning of the text. Writers and editors who work with illustrated publications should cultivate a familiarity with these different styles and tones.

Using photographs and illustrations is not simply a matter of dropping them into the layout as an afterthought or a way to break up text. When images are selected and presented with as much care as words, they can substantially enrich communication. A well-illustrated publication fully involves its readers on both a verbal and a visual level.

A good editor does more than just write or edit captions and keep track of the art in a manuscript. The images themselves should be carefully examined and edited:

- Do they support, enhance, and clarify the text or provide additional information?
- Do they reflect the text in terms of mood, tone, and content?
- Are they well executed and of good reproduction quality?

Superfluous images, like needless words, should be excised from the manuscript. By the same token, the editor should be alert to—and suggest to the author—ways in which additional illustrations could improve the manuscript as a whole. Could a lengthy narrative description, for example, be replaced by a simple diagram? Ideally, an editor should work closely with the author and the designer in selecting and developing illustrations and photo-

❧

BEWARE THE EMPTY PHOTO

We've all seen them—the smiling congressmen shaking hands, the executive at her desk, the researcher perched at his microscope. What they have in common is a nearly complete lack of content. These types of ostensibly *candid* photos—and their more formal counterpart, the *mug shot* head-and-shoulders portrait—have become standard fare in many publications. The shaking hands version even has its own name—the *grip and grin.*

Writers and editors who wish to generate more reader interest need to think beyond these hackneyed images and look for photos that reflect the story: Can the photo somehow show where the congressmen are shaking hands—and why they're smiling? Could the background of the picture give the reader a better idea of what this executive has done to warrant a photograph? And wouldn't a photo that shows the benefits of a big research breakthrough be more compelling to the reader than the back of the head of the fellow who made it? Context and environment give meaning to a photo—but details must tell a story or they amount to clutter.

If directing the photography is not an option, working creatively with the images in the layout can enhance visual interest. Here are a few possibilities: a full or partial silhouette of the image that creates an irregular shape, an image that bleeds off the page, mug shots cropped tightly to show only the face, or a row of postage-stamp-size images that creates a border along the edge of the page. With a little imagination, less-than-inspiring photos can be brought to life.

---

graphs and should stay involved to ensure that the purpose and meaning are not altered or obscured during the production process.

In terms of production requirements, images in publications are usually classified as either *line* art or *tone* art. Line art contains no shades of gray—a black-and-white ink drawing is an example—and can be reproduced directly from mechanical artwork. Tone art includes any photo or illustration that contains shading; for reproduction, this type of image must be converted into a *halftone,* which replicates the various shades of gray by means of a pattern of black dots. (See Chapter 33, Printing, for more about line and tone art.)

BUYING, FINDING, AND CREATING IMAGES

Photographs and illustrations may be supplied by the author, obtained through clip art or stock photo services, or commissioned specifically for the manuscript. Once in hand, illustrations and photographs can be mechanically or electronically altered to suit the needs of the publication. The responsibilities of a writer or editor in this area are twofold—knowing how to take advantage of the vast array of illustration sources and options and staying up to date on copyright law and other legal implications of those options.

Images Made to Order

If the author has not provided appropriate artwork with the manuscript, the most direct route to locating a photograph or an illustration is to assign the work to a photographer or an illustrator. The advantage of this approach is the ability to direct the work to get exactly the image required; the disadvantage is the time and expense involved, particularly for publications that do not have photographers or illustrators on staff.

Photographers and illustrators all have different styles and approaches to their work; given the same assignment, each will create a different picture. Editors should therefore carefully review portfolios to select an artist with a style appropriate to the manuscript. There is a significant distinction between photographs and illustrations at the literal, representational end of the scale—for reference, instructional, and technical publications—and conceptual, creative advertising and editorial work. The latter will generally entail higher fees, and the artist will want to retain more control over rights to the work.

Figure 27–1. The image on the left is an example of line art; the image on the right is tone art.

Before starting an assignment, the photographer or illustrator should clearly understand the design and purpose of the project as a whole. It helps to have dummy layouts or sketches completed at this point so the artist will also know, for instance, if vertical or horizontal images are needed, as well as such basics as whether to work in black and white or color.

Writers and editors should become familiar with how copyright law relates to the work of photographers and illustrators (see Chapter 23, Copyright), especially the concept of *works made for hire,* whereby the publisher assumes copyright ownership of works created for a fee. Today, artists and photographers are more likely to consider their fee as remuneration for work performed and for reproduction rights in connection with a specific publication or product. For example, if a publisher hires a photographer to take pictures for an annual report, those photos may not be used in another publication unless the photographer has specifically agreed to additional uses. Agreements and contracts with commercial artists and photographers should clearly spell out the allowed uses of the work and the period of time during which the reproduction rights are in effect. The length of this period, the nature of the use (advertising, promotional, editorial), and the degree of exclusivity of the rights are the usual criteria for setting fees.

Working with a Photographer. Depending on the requirements of the job, photographs are shot either on location or in a studio. If the services of other professionals, such as models or stylists, are required, the photographer can usually arrange for them for an additional fee. For more complex, creative assignments, a photographer will often ask the client, designer, or art director to be present during the shoot.

For shots that require a staged setup of models or products, a photographer will take preliminary Polaroid photos to check such aspects as composition, lighting, and camera angle. It is not uncommon for a photographer to shoot an entire roll of film to get a good range of choices, even when just one photo is needed; the cost of film and processing is small compared to the expense of setting up another photo shoot.

Photographing an event as it happens is another matter entirely. If the photographer is given freedom to "shoot at will," some fine, serendipitous shots can result. But in most cases, a certain amount of guidance from the client is usually necessary—to point out important individuals and significant moments, for example.

For black-and-white work, the photographer will submit *contact sheets,* which show all the shots taken, printed directly from the negative strips. These are best viewed with a magnifying glass, since the individual photos are the same size as the negatives. The client selects shots by circling them with a grease pencil or china marker or by specifying the negative number; the photographer then makes prints of only the selected shots.

Color work is usually shot using transparency film, so the photographer delivers the work in the form of slides. A light box or projector is necessary for viewing and selecting slides. Photos that will be reproduced in a large size—on a poster, for example—should be shot using large-format film so that the integrity of the image is not lost in the enlargement.

Working with an Illustrator. An illustrator needs to know whether the work is planned as line or tone art in order to select an appropriate medium. Also, the illustrator should be told at the outset the form in which the illustration is to be submitted—electronic file, black-and-white camera-ready copy, or scannable full-color art.

Editors should ask to review and approve preliminary sketches, especially in the case of complicated, full-color illustrations. These sketches can save everyone time and expense by giving the artist feedback before the final illustration is executed.

Many illustrations today, particularly technical illustrations, are created faster and more accurately on computers. Although it is relatively easy to revise electronic files, editors should be aware that revisions cannot always be made instantly. Often the same level of skill and time required for revising traditional art is required for electronic "drawing."

"Off-the-Rack" Images: Clip Art and Stock Photos

Thousands of existing photographs and illustrations are available for use in print. In many cases, using these ready-made images can save both money and time.

MODEL RELEASES

Even though they may not be pulling down astronomical fees—or any fees at all—people who appear in a photograph are, at least in one sense, considered to be models. Before publishing a photo, an editor should be sure that any identifiable individual in it has signed a *model release.*

Some releases are long legal documents with clauses and contingencies; others are quite simple and straightforward. In essence, though, a model release simply conveys permission for an image to be reproduced. The person or organization to whom permission is given is thus protected to a certain degree from claims for compensation or damages. Such protections, however, are not ironclad; models can still pursue claims if the photo is used in an obviously exploitive or libelous manner.

FREE (OR NEARLY FREE) IMAGES

Not everyone has the budget to hire a photographer or illustrator or to use stock photography. A little research, however, can often unearth a wealth of photos and illustrations that can be used for free or for the cost of making a print or photostat. The Library of Congress' Prints and Photographs Department, for instance, has extensive files of photos and prints in the public domain. The telephone number is (202) 707-6394, but the service is not for those in a hurry—researching and filling a request can take many weeks. Here are some other places to look:

- Historical societies and museums
- Print and photo collections in public and private libraries
- Local, state, and federal government agencies
- Embassies
- Corporate communications departments of manufacturers and other businesses
- Estates of famous people

Stock Photos. When one or two shots of a general nature are needed, stock photography can often fit the bill. Stock photo agencies maintain vast libraries of images to fit nearly any requirement. Some houses may specialize in a specific subject, such as industry, medicine, or technology, while others may concentrate on a geographic region. Photos of past events and certain historical figures may be available only through a stock agency.

Stock agencies charge a fee for the use of an image; this fee entitles the client to *very specific* reproduction rights, as spelled out in an agreement. By no means does the client purchase the photograph for unlimited use unless a (usually very expensive) contract to that effect is executed. Most often the fee is for one-time use; an additional fee may be charged even to use the photo again in an additional print run.

Fees are based on such factors as the type of publication, the size of the print run, the purpose of the publication (educational, advertising, informational), whether the publication will be sold or distributed free of charge, whether the photo will be run in black and white or color, placement in the publication (on the cover or on inside pages), and the anticipated size of the printed photo.

In response to a research request, the stock agency searches its files for photos that meet the client's criteria and sends as many shots (usually slides) as possible for review. Most agencies respond quickly to requests and will express ship photos to out-of-town clients.

The client is expected to review the group quickly and return the obvious rejects as soon as possible, return others as they are eliminated, and return the selected photo as soon as possible after printing, keeping track of photos received and returned. Stock agencies generally reserve the right to charge a holding fee for the late return of photos and often require that photos be returned by messenger, certified mail, or some other reliable, traceable means.

Clip Art. In the realm of illustration, editors and writers have at their disposal volumes of noncopyrighted images known as clip art. Books of camera-ready images can be purchased from graphic arts suppliers; some clip art publishers operate on a subscription basis. Clip art is also widely available in various electronic formats.

Because clip art is often clumsily handled—that is, not appropriately selected and edited, not well integrated with the style and content of the manuscript and the layout, or not sized in correct proportion—it is sometimes regarded as amateurish and not worthy of a serious publication. But some of these images can be effective if they are used selectively and judiciously.

Manipulation of Images

With a certain amount of skill, an artist can alter a clip art image to suit the project. The customizing of "packaged" electronic images is becoming a legitimate, time-saving way to create new illustrations.

Photographs, too, need not be simply printed as they were shot. Creative photographic effects can be produced with specialty conversions—instead of the conventional dot halftone screen, the printer or an independent photographic service can apply different screens to a photo to create pattern effects such as circles, lines, squares, fabric, etching, or mezzotint. The range of tones in a photo can also be manipulated to produce subtle or dramatic effects. One example is a high-contrast line conversion, in which all shades of gray below a certain density are converted to white and all shades above that density are converted to black—creating black-and-white line art from a continuous tone photo.

The actual content and composition of a photograph can also be altered by various means. Airbrushing is widely used to disguise or obliterate unwanted or unnecessary portions of an image. Traditionally done by hand, airbrushing is one of several sophisticated electronic retouching and composition features of desktop photo manipulation programs, which can also produce specialty conversion effects. Widely available desktop scanners, too, have made it possible to convert any image to an easily manipulated, printable electronic format. A caveat, however: Editors and artists must remem-

Figure 27–2. This photograph was shot as line art to produce a special effect of stark black and white.

ber that many photographs and illustrations are copyrighted works and, as such, may not legally be reproduced or altered without permission.

PHOTOGRAPHS AND ILLUSTRATIONS IN THE LAYOUT

Selecting or creating the perfect image is half the battle of producing a well-illustrated publication. Just as important is the task that remains—to orchestrate words and pictures into a visually pleasing and communicative whole.

Developing the final layout involves reconciling various priorities among the text, the illustrations, and the overall design of the publication. Illustrations are intended to clarify and accentuate text and so in some ways may be thought of as subordinate; however, if an illustration is not presented to its best advantage, the overall effectiveness of the publication may be diminished.

Placement

The ground rules for placing illustrations and photographs in the layout are set by the overall design, which in turn is dictated by the nature of the text.

The layout of a medical journal is structured and fixed to reflect its purpose of efficiently conveying information, whereas the layout of a fashion magazine is creative and freeform to influence and entertain its readers.

In technical and instructional publications, photos and illustrations are usually specifically referred to in the text. Their position in the layout, therefore, must be as close as possible to the corresponding discussion in the text. In works of more general interest, the placement of illustrations in relation to text is not as critical; here, the goal is to create a pleasing, inviting graphic arrangement.

In any case, text and artwork should be arranged on the page so that the reader can move easily and naturally through the pages. A rough rule of thumb is to place illustrations at the top or bottom of a column. Although an illustration can be very effective in the middle of text, care must be taken not to isolate islands of type between illustrations, interrupting the flow of the text. The lower right-hand corner is traditionally considered a strong position in the layout because most readers normally "size up" a new page by scanning it diagonally from the top left.

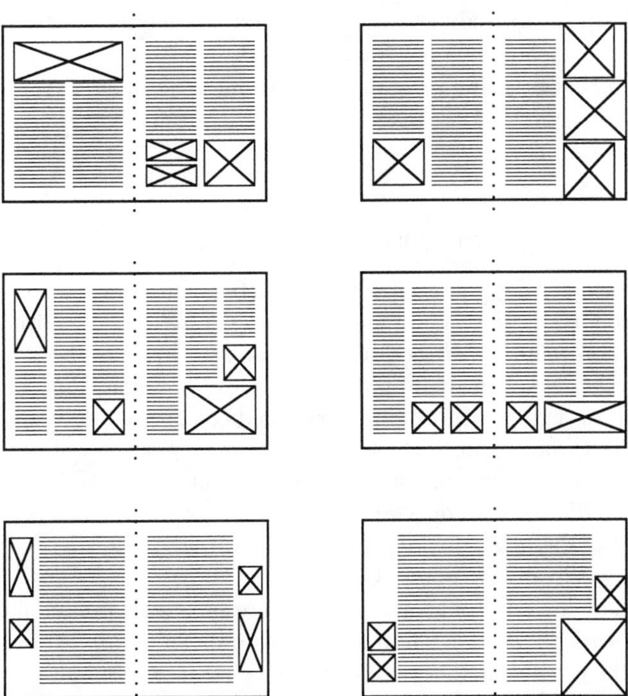

Figure 27–3. Using a grid system for page layout allows varied yet orderly placement of photographs and illustrations.

Many designers base their page design on a grid that allows the placement of various sizes and shapes of illustrations. The purpose of the page grid is to provide regularity and structure to the page layouts. The grid also provides a context for the occasional injection of variety into the normal rhythm and order—interrupting the regularity of the page layout, for instance, with a photo that extends off the edge of the page.

Practical considerations, too, can play a role in the placement of illustrations and photographs in text. For example, if a photo with very warm tones is placed next to a photo with very cool tones, the printer may be forced to compromise on the ink levels on press to achieve an appearance that is acceptable for both, but not necessarily optimum for either. In the case of a publication heavily illustrated in full color, therefore, the designer will often work closely with the production manager and the printer in planning the layout of each signature (see Chapter 33, Printing) to avoid such *in-line* problems.

Scaling and Cropping

Images are custom fitted to the pages by *cropping,* which means defining their final shape and content by editing out unneeded portions, and by *scaling,* which means defining their final size.

The process of sizing or scaling determines the final, or reproduction,

---

SEPARATE SIGNATURES

The process of designing a book is often a tug of war between esthetics and economics. Illustrations and photographs are most effective when printed on coated stock, yet uncoated book stock is most economical.

In the case of an art or photography book, there is little question of the appropriateness of printing the entire book on the more expensive stock. But what about the text-heavy book with just a few illustrations that must appear in full color? Here a compromise is often made to print the full-color art on a separate signature of a different stock from the rest of the book; the loss of continuity with the text is made up for by the quality of the reproduction.

There are different ways to bind these separately printed illustrations. A single page or a four-page signature can be *tipped,* or glued along the edge of another page; a signature can also be simply gathered and bound in between other signatures. If the color signature is placed within another signature before binding, it is called an *insert;* if the color signature is placed around another signature, it is a *wrap.*

Figure 27–4. Cropping can be shown by mounting the photo on a larger sheet and marking the areas of the image to be used (left), by tracing the desired portion of the image on a tissue overlay (right), or by cutting a mask of amberlith or rubylith acetate film.

size of the photo or illustration. The desired reproduction—or *repro*—size is expressed as a percentage of the original size; the percentage is obtained by dividing the repro size by the original size. For example, if the image to be reproduced is 20 picas wide and it must fit a 15-pica column width, the image would be reproduced at 75 percent (15 divided by 20 equals 0.75). Because the image will be reproduced to scale, the repro height will be 75 percent of the original height of the cropped image. The repro percentage can also be determined with the help of a *reproduction* or *proportion wheel,* an easy-to-use graphic arts tool that displays a repro percentage when the user lines up the original and repro values on the edge of the wheel.

Generally the layout artist begins work with an ideal crop and size for the image. The desired position of the image is usually indicated by an in-text callout or a note from the editor ("photo 7 goes about here"). As the pages take shape, there is a certain degree of give-and-take between the best way to crop and scale the art and the best position within the text. Often a photocopy of the image, cropped and shot to reproduction size, is used first to check that the printed image will be effective and later to show its position on the camera-ready mechanical.

Creating Captions

Traditionally, a title of an illustration is referred to as a *caption,* while a descriptive phrase or sentence is called a *legend,* although in current usage the two terms have become interchangeable, with *caption* the more commonly used. A caption is also sometimes referred to as a *cutline* (in journalistic jargon, a *cut* is a photo or illustration).

An effective caption not only clearly describes the content of the image but also indicates the significance of the image to the text. In the case of scientific and technical works, the caption should be straightforward and concise:

> The Arctic daisy (*Chrysanthemum arcticum*). Dark green, leathery spatulate leaves are pinnately divided into three to five shallow lobes.

In works of more general interest, a certain degree of creative license is desirable:

> The many varieties of chrysanthemum bring a rich, long-lasting palette of brilliant color to the autumn garden.

Regardless of the type of publication, the caption should serve a descriptive purpose and add to the text rather than restate the obvious. The caption and the illustration together should make up a discrete unit that tells its own story; in other words, readers should not have to read the supporting text to understand the photograph or illustration. Captions may be written as either phrases or complete sentences, but editors should maintain consistency throughout the publication.

When organizing the manuscript for production, editors conventionally group all captions together on separate sheets and in a separate electronic file, since the exact placement of captions on the page is not made final until the page layouts are completed.

Traditionally, captions are placed below their illustrations, although in certain formats they may be set above, to the left, or to the right. At least 6 points of space should be left between the photograph or illustration and its caption.

Captions are usually set in type different from the main text of the publication—usually a smaller point size and often italic or boldface. Figure number designations, if used, are often set off in boldface or small caps and followed by a period. Titles are generally followed by a period if they are run in on the same line with a descriptive caption:

> **Otter Cliffs, Mount Desert Island.** Millions of visitors a year enjoy the spectacular views from the Park Loop Road, which meanders through Acadia National Park.

CAPTIVATING CAPTIONS

- A caption should not simply label, it should describe the significance of what is happening in the photo and serve to connect the photo with the text content. For example, the caption "A dalmatian on a fire engine" does nothing but state the obvious; a better caption would be, "Since the days of horse-drawn fire engines, the dalmatian has been the traditional mascot of fire departments throughout the country."
- Conventional introductory phrases such as "In this photo" or "This illustration depicts" generally add little to the content of the caption and make it less concise.
- Titles of persons appearing in a photo should be repeated in the caption, even if they are fully identified in the main text.
- Technical works often require that captions include a figure number because the text is closely cross-referenced to the content of the photo or illustration. Depending on the size of the publication and production considerations, the numbering of photos and illustrations may be done consecutively from the beginning to the end or chapter by chapter.
- Credits, when appropriate, are usually placed at the end of the caption in parentheses ("Photograph by Ansel Adams"), and a copyright line may be placed in small type beside the photo or illustration. A reprint permission statement may be included as part of a caption, or a summary of reprint permissions may be listed in the front matter (see Chapter 22, Parts of a Book); the source of noncopyrighted materials may also be credited ("Courtesy of the Library of Congress").

28

INDEXING

INDEXING

An index makes the content of a book quickly accessible to its readers. By presenting a detailed guide to the ideas, persons, places, and things discussed, the index serves as a road map to specific information in the book and in addition gives an overview of the work as a whole. Thus the index contributes to the value of the book as a reference source.

A successful index reflects the way the book will be used, so understanding the needs of the intended audience is crucial. The true test of an index is whether the degree of detail—both in subject selection and in identification of the relationships among the subjects—matches the needs of the reader.

This chapter is directed at authors who must index their own books, publishers who are evaluating indexes, and professional indexers. It covers the terminology of indexing, the choices that must be made by an indexer both at the beginning of a project and as the work progresses, the principles of indexing and the process of creating an index, specific style points to be considered, and design and typography. It deals primarily with the preparation of subject or subject/name/title indexes.

A FEW GENERAL NOTES

Types of Indexes

The nature of the publication and of the subject matter determines the type of index to be created. Most book indexes are arranged in dictionary style and list subjects, authors, and titles in a single alphabetical sequence. The user looks in that list, regardless of the category of information sought. In some works it is appropriate to break out certain elements into separate special-purpose indexes—for example, a title or name index.

THE BEST PART OF EVERY BOOK

The chief purpose of an index is distillation, and in performing that task it can manage to suggest a life's incongruities with a concision that the most powerful biographical stylist will have trouble matching. The index to *My Turn,* the story of Nancy Reagan's life, is full of juxtapositions that, as they say, Say It All. "Screen Actors Guild" immediately precedes "SDI (Strategic Defense Initiative)"; "Jimmy Stewart" is one line above "Potter Stewart"; the comedian Danny Thomas comes just before the Washington reporter Helen Thomas. . . .

As for the author's own pleasures, there are few keener than seeing the index to his book. . . . It hardly matters how fleeting are the appearances of some of the indexed items in the text of the book he's written. How learned the author feels just seeing those hundreds of alphabetized subjects and names, and how organized, as if someone had finally gone into his brain and—all for the gentle reader's sake—put those heaps of clutter into a gleaming row of file cabinets.—Thomas Mallon, "The Best Part of Every Book Comes Last," *New York Times Book Review* (March 10, 1991)

Subject. A subject index provides an analysis of the concepts covered in the work and gives cross-references leading from one topic to another. Compilation of a subject index is a complex task that requires judgment in selecting appropriate entries and omitting peripheral material.

Name. The simplest type of index is a straight alphabetical arrangement of authors, persons, or places. This is a routine task, often simplified by using a computer for sorting. A separate index to the names of authors is useful in a scientific survey or literary review. A geographic index is essential in atlases, gazetteers, maps, and travel books.

Title. A separate index of titles is often found in anthologies or works of literary criticism. An index of first lines or names of art works serves a similar function in anthologies of poetry, books of quotations, or art histories. A table of cases in a legal book is similar in concept to a title index.

Keyword-in-Context. A keyword-in-context (KWIC) index is generated by computer. It is most useful in providing a "quick and dirty" index to a large number of titles of scientific or technical reports or to headings and subheadings in a set of regulations. Each word in the title is displayed on a single line, surrounded by the words preceding it and following it. A KWIC index points out the locations where a certain word occurs but does not indicate whether the coverage of the topic is significant. Figure 28–1 shows a variation known as KWOC (keyword out of context) that gives the word in the left-hand column and the regulation title containing it in the right-hand column.

ACCOUNT	Preparation of ACCOUNT Adjustment Voucher, Form 2424, 6810-(11)22.3
ACCOUNTING	ACCOUNTING Period Change Application Form, use, 6810-(15)25
ADJUSTMENT	Preparation of Account ADJUSTMENT Voucher, Form 2424, 6810-(11)22.3
ADJUSTMENT	Form 3870, Request for ADJUSTMENT, preparation, 6810-(11) 22.1
ADVANCE	ADVANCE Earned Income Credit, Notice 523, 6558
ADVICE	ADVICE of Credit, Form 2284, use, 6810-648
ALCOHOL	ALCOHOL, Tobacco and Firearms Return, Form 154, 6810-(10)12.1
AMENDED	Form 1040-X, AMENDED Individual Income Tax Return, 6810-(11)27
APPLICATION	Accounting Period Change APPLICATION Form, use, 6810-(15)25
CHANGE	Accounting Period CHANGE Application Form, use, 6810-(15)25
CREDIT	Advance Earned Income CREDIT, Notice 523, 6558
CREDIT	Advice of CREDIT, Form 2284, use, 6810-648

Figure 28–1. Part of a keyword-out-of-context (KWOC) index to regulations.

Indexing Terminology

Standard terms for the elements that make up an index are defined below as used in this chapter. Figure 28–2 shows a sample index with these elements labeled.

Entry. A complete index entry consists of a main heading together with all of its subheadings, locators, and cross-references. A subentry consists of a subheading and its locators.

Main Heading. A main heading is a concise term that sums up a topic.

Subheading. A subheading is a word or phrase subordinate to a main heading that describes a single aspect of the broader topic.

Cross-reference. A cross-reference leads the user from one main heading in the index to another main heading where information or additional related information can be found. The two types of cross-references are known as *See* and *See also* references.

Locator. A locator is an indicator following a main heading or subheading that tells the user where to find information. It is usually a page number or a range of page numbers. It may also be a section, paragraph, item, or figure number.

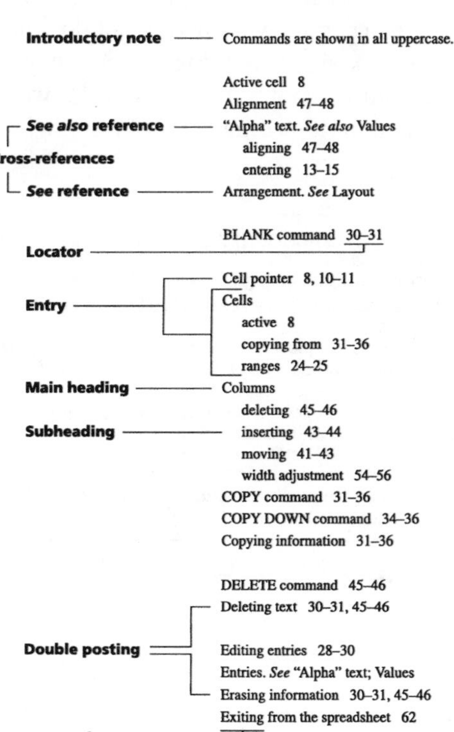

Figure 28–2. This sample index to a computer manual shows the terms used for the elements of an index.

Introductory Note. An introductory note is a brief explanation of any coverage limitations, abbreviations, or typographical conventions used in the index.

Double Posting. Entering locators under two synonymous headings instead of using a *See* reference from one to the other is called double posting.

Keyword. A keyword is the most significant word in a heading or subheading—the word under which the user is most likely to search for the information.

Who Should Prepare the Index?

Who will prepare the index? Most trade publishers expect the author to prepare it or to pay for its preparation. Indexing is an acquired art, however, and not all authors have the knack or the patience. Writing a book and indexing it require two different sets of skills. Authors tend to be too close to the subject and to get bogged down in endless detail rather than thinking,

ARE YOU A PUZZLE SOLVER?

Indexers share certain traits: a logical, analytical mind; a retentive memory; an insatiable appetite for new information; good judgment; and a fascination with solving puzzles.

Good indexers needn't be subject-matter experts, although familiarity with the content is certainly helpful. It is more important that indexers be analytical, organized, detail oriented, and objective. They should approach the work from the readers' perspective and be able to anticipate differing needs. Being able to grasp the key concept and place that word first in the index entry is vital. Knowing what to leave out is equally important.

One corporate indexing manager always asks job applicants, "Do you like puzzles?" Her crackerjack group of technical indexers includes a dog lover who tackles computer problems with relish, a world traveler with a degree in art history, an attorney, a naturalist, and an aerobic dance instructor. The dance instructor claims that creating an index uses exactly the same skills as choreographing a new dance routine. Whether it's *New York Times* Sunday crosswords, cryptograms, mathematical puzzles, tracking down obscure literary references, or placing fast-moving bodies in attractive patterns, a true indexer has the urge to fit everything into its proper place in the universe to produce a graceful whole.

"What are the three or four most important topics covered on this page?" A good indexer, like a good editor, serves as the reader's advocate, making the author's work accessible and comprehensible.

DECISIONS TO MAKE BEFORE STARTING AN INDEX

Parts of the Book to Cover

The first step in preparing an index is to decide which parts of the book should be covered by the index.

Main Text. The body of the book is the main source of index entries. These pages are always included in the index coverage.

Front Matter. Acknowledgments should not be indexed. A preface or foreword may be indexed if it contains additional information on the subject. An introduction can be indexed, but ideas mentioned there are usually covered in greater depth in the main body of the text.

Back Matter. Appendixes are included in the index but are not usually analyzed in the same detail as is the body of the text. Each appendix may be represented by one or two entries covering the unit as a whole. Glossaries are sometimes indexed, especially where the terms defined in the glossary are also used as index entries for the body of the text. In this case the subheading "definition" leads to the appropriate page of the glossary. Bibliographies are not usually included in the index.

Figures, Tables, and Illustrations. Figures, tables, or illustrations should be indexed on the same basis as the text—that is, if they are substantive. A different typeface can be used in the index to denote such references. This is particularly helpful in scientific works or art books. If locators for such tables and graphic elements are not to be distinguished by typeface, the content is usually covered by a reference to the text page that gives the callout for the figure.

Substantive Notes. Footnotes or endnotes that amplify information in the text are indexed. The locator is the page number followed by "n." If the text reference to the subject is on the same page as the footnote, the page number is given only once.

182, 184n *But not:* 182, 182n

If more than one note appears on a page, the number of the note must be added (234n.2, 334n.4). Simple reference notes should not be indexed.

What Not to Index

Sometimes the decision on what to omit is as important as that on what to include. The two categories of headings that most often present problems to inexperienced indexers are opposite in nature—minor passing mentions of a topic within a book and the major topic of the book as a whole.

Passing Mentions. Each entry in the index should lead to useful information about that topic. Do not index peripheral mentions of a subject. This is where human judgment is essential; computers cannot make the distinction between meaningful and meaningless mentions. It is the book's treatment of the topic rather than the topic's own importance that should be evaluated. The index to Peter Schickele's *Definitive Biography of P.D.Q. Bach* includes these wonderful examples of extraneous entries.

acute, 16
facts, few scattered, 11
skin, thick, 4
straw
  drinking, 74
  final, 12

Main Topic of Book. The overall subject of a book should not be used as an index heading. If it were used, multiple subheadings covering almost every page number would have to be included under that heading. Specific aspects of the topic should instead become main headings in their own right. In a book on plumbing procedures, "Plumbing" is useless as an index entry. The reader will need instead "Pipe selection," "Elbow connections," and other specific topics.

Level of Detail

Before making the first entry, the indexer must make a policy decision on the depth of indexing—that is, how exhaustive and specific the index should be. Indexes can be classified as light (an average of 1 to 2 references per text page), average (3 to 5), scholarly or detailed (6 to 9), or exhaustive or encyclopedic (10 to 15). Some pages of a work will, of course, require more entries than others. The indexer must use good judgment.

A light index to a book on working with stained glass would reflect a broad approach to the topic.

Copper foil as a material 157–158
Copper foil method 159–161
Lampshades 160–161
Suncatchers 160

A detailed index to the same pages would reflect a more analytical approach to the subject, in which each aspect of a topic was given a separate subheading and additional main headings were selected.

Copper foil as a material
  design considerations 157
  lampshade use 160
  price 158
  thicknesses available 157
  width choices 157–158
Copper foil method
  steps to follow 160–161
  versus leading 159–160

Design considerations
  copper foil versus leading 159–160
Lampshades
  copper foil in 160
  Tiffany style 161
Leading
  versus copper foil method 159–160
Suncatchers 160
Tiffany, Louis Comfort 161

Three factors are involved in determining the level of detail used in an index—the intended audience, the time available for completion, and the space allotted for the index by the publisher.

Audience. Is the book directed at a specialized audience or a more general one? A good indexer perceives the level of background knowledge of the intended audience. The indexer uses that insight to judge the level of detail in the index, the phrasing of subject headings and subheadings, and the cross-references that will be needed to guide readers to the information they need. Determining the appropriate level of detail offers a challenge to the indexer's creativity and judgment.

Time and Cost. The traditional elements of the unattainable triad in publishing are time, cost, and quality. In indexing the triad is time, cost, and detail. There is no point at all in doing an index of less than top quality. Ideally, 2 weeks would be allowed to create the index to a 400-page scientific book. If the book absolutely must be published by a certain date and delays in receipt of the page proofs leave only 4 days for indexing, the index can still be done on time but in considerably less detail than would be considered optimum for an audience of specialists. Cost is, of course, proportional to the amount of time spent on the work.

Length. One rule of thumb for judging the length of an index is 1 page of index (double-column, usually containing about 100 lines) to 20 to 50 pages of text. This would make the index 2 percent to 5 percent of the text pages. The percentage will vary depending on the nature of the material covered and the sizes of type used. Indexes presented in run-in format take fewer pages than those in indented format (see "Style Choices," later in this chapter).

Hans Wellisch's *Indexing from A to Z,* a reference book for specialists, has 39 pages of index to cover 408 pages of text (index length is 10 percent of text). Wellisch gives these estimates as appropriate index lengths for different types of material:

Number of Index Pages as a Percentage of Text Pages

Nature of the Text	*Percentage*
Popular expositions of factual topics, elementary textbooks, children's books	1–3
History, biography, high school and undergraduate textbooks	5–8
Reference books	10–15
Scientific and technical monographs	15 or more

For a serious reference work or an important report, the indexer does not usually work to a predetermined length. For a typical trade book, however, the space allotted to the index is sometimes determined by the number of blank pages left in a signature after the text has been set in type. (See the sidebar on casting off on page 681.)

THE PRINCIPLES AND PROCESS OF INDEXING

Computers or Index Cards?

The author faced with creating an index thinks, "How can I produce this index on a computer?" Authors should beware of software advertised as having the capability to create an index automatically from an electronic text file. Two types of rather limited "index" products can be produced this way. One is a concordance, an index to all of the words on the page with the exception of specified common words that are ignored; a keyword-in-context index is an example of this type. The other possible product is a list of all pages where a word or term from a list predetermined by the author appears. Both products are indexes to words on the page, not to the ideas discussed.

Professional indexers use specially developed indexing software to manage the clerical aspects of preparing an index—arranging entries in alphabetical order, combining like entries, sorting locators in the correct sequence, formatting the index, printing drafts, and checking cross-references. But these are mechanical tasks; the job of indexing is more intellectual than clerical. Only a human being can select indexable topics and discriminate between casual mentions of a subject and sentences or paragraphs that discuss important ideas.

Two basic types of software are available for indexing—stand-alone programs (called *dedicated software*) and indexing modules included in word processing and desktop publishing programs. See the sidebar on the next page for an explanation of the differences.

❧

SOFTWARE FOR INDEXING

Most professional indexers use dedicated indexing software. These programs allow the indexer working from the book pages to input selected headings, subheadings, locators, and cross-references; the software takes care of the mechanical chores.

Using the best of these programs, the indexer can display or print the index in final format at any time, manipulate various elements of the index at will, control the filing order of unusual headings, verify cross-references, and make global substitutions. Indexes produced using such software can be automatically converted to word processing or text files or to files specially coded for typesetting or desktop publishing programs.

The indexing features available in many word processing and desktop publishing programs work quite differently; they generate an index directly from the tagged electronic file of a document. This feature, ranging from basic to fairly sophisticated, allows the indexer to mark index headings by tagging words and phrases throughout the electronic file. Most programs also permit the indexer to create an entry with words that are not part of the text by inserting a special embedded tag. The program then generates an index by reading these tags and picking up the page numbers on which they appear.

The advantage of generating an index with an embedded program is that if the flow of text is changed because material is inserted, deleted, or edited, the indexing feature will automatically pick up the revised page numbers.

The drawbacks are many. Even an experienced indexer using such a system will have serious problems. Headings must be tagged separately on each page where the subject is mentioned. Very few programs allow the insertion of a range of pages for a topic. The indexer cannot see the work in progress and may inadvertently pick up inconsistent terminology when tagging the text. To edit the index, the indexer must go back and revise the tags on each page to make the final product concise and consistent, instead of being able to make global substitutions. Choice of final format is limited.

In short, embedded indexing modules are useful only for a very simple index to a document that is expected to be revised frequently. And even though it is possible to produce a good index with this kind of software, the process is agonizingly time consuming.

Indexes can also be prepared by writing entries on 3- by 5-inch cards, sorting them manually, typing a first draft, editing, and then rekeying to produce the final manuscript, but this is a slow process.

The principles described in the remainder of this section apply regardless of the method used to produce the index.

Analyzing the Content

To ensure a balanced viewpoint in the selection of indexable material, indexers begin by reading the table of contents, the preface, and the introduction. They then skim the entire text to get a sense of the structure and depth of the work. In this pass they determine the scope of coverage, the intended audience, and the author's approach. In a second pass they read for content, identifying and highlighting indexable topics and noting the range of pages on which a subject is covered. Next they select headings that will best represent those concepts.

Each index entry is keyed into a computer or typed on an index card. Both a heading and a subheading for each subject should be included at this stage. It is easier to eliminate unneeded subheadings in the final editing than to go back to each of many page references to see what aspect of the topic was treated there. An indexer working from the page shown in figure 28–3 might select these index entries:

Americans with Disabilities Act of 1990
  passage 25
Americans with Disabilities Act of 1990
  coverage 25
Disabled persons
  definition 25
Discrimination
  in the workplace 25
AIDS
  as a disability 25
HIV infection
  as a disability 25

Main Headings

A main heading should lead to all pertinent information in the book on that topic. Avoid unnecessary headings such as peripheral mentions and the subject of the book itself.

What is the ADA?

DETAILED: The ADA, or Americans with Disabilities Act of 1990, is a discrimination law that protects people with disabilities. It was passed by Congress in July 1990 and provides the most far-reaching protection to date on behalf of disabled people. Starting in July 1992, the ADA applies to all employers with 25 or more employees. After July 1994, it will apply to all employers with 15 or more employees. (definition)

Under the ADA, a disabled person is someone who—

- Has a physical or mental impairment that substantially limits one or more major life activities.
- Has a record of such an impairment.
- Is regarded as having such an impairment.

The ADA protects disabled workers from discrimination (in the workplace) *because* of their disabling conditions. People who are HIV-positive are considered disabled under this new law and are protected in the same way as workers with any other type of disability. Some employers will not be covered by the ADA, however, because they have fewer than 15 employees.

The Americans with Disabilities Act—

- Prohibits discrimination against "qualified individuals with a disability."
- Includes AIDS and HIV infection as definitions of (as disabilities)
- Requires employers to "reasonably accommodate" qualified disabled employees.

Figure 28–3. Sample page marked by indexer.

Selection. There are two questions the indexer should consider in selecting a main heading. Will readers look for this subject in this book? If so, will they find enough information on this page about the subject to make it worth their time to look it up?

Choosing the best entry terms for a subject is a matter of judgment. Headings should be concise and limited to one subject. They must be specific enough for ready access, yet comprehensive enough to prevent scattering of information. The important question to consider is, "Where will the reader look for this subject?"

Nouns. Most main headings are nouns or noun phrases; an adjective alone is never used as a heading. Usually the plural form of a noun works well as an index heading. This choice also erases the temptation to use the noun as an adjective.

In a book about trees, an entry might look like this:

Maples
  bigleaf
  Japanese
  red
  striped

In a book about Vermont, however, the adjective *maple* might be combined with the noun *trees* to form a noun phrase as a main heading:

Maple furniture manufacturing Maple sugar Maple trees	*Not:* Maple furniture sugar trees

Verbs. The gerund forms of verbs can also be used as main headings, especially in a procedures manual—for example, *Cleaning, Printing.*

Keyword Position. The most significant word should come first when phrasing a heading. It should come from the text wherever possible.

Format settings
  customizing 45
  default 43–45

Not:

Changing default format settings 45

Homographs. Main headings that are spelled alike but have different meanings should be identified by a descriptor in parentheses.

Bearing (machine part)
Bearing (direction)

Acronyms. The usual practice is to use the full term as the main heading. Make a cross-reference from the acronym to the full term.

American Standards Association 123–126, 198, 250
ASA. *See* American Standards Association

If, however, the acronym is in general use and is much better known than the full term, choose the acronym as the main heading.

Acquired immunodeficiency syndrome. *See* AIDS
AIDS 389–396, 407–410

In subheadings, the use of acronyms saves space and minimizes the need for runover lines.

Mortgages
  adjustable-rate
  FHA
  Ginnie Mae
  insurance on
  points
  VA

Government Units. A careless indexer might scatter information about a single government unit in many places by following the varied wording of the text.

Department of Labor 64–69
Labor Department 57, 93
U.S. Department of Labor 101–107

All these references must be grouped under a single heading. There is no absolutely right or wrong choice. The third heading is technically the most correct, but one of the other choices may be more appropriate in certain cases. The determining factor is always "Where will the reader look?" The indexer must be consistent and make *See* references as needed. Here are two ways of handling the above information.

Department of . . . *See* U.S. Department of . . .
Labor Department. *See* U.S. Department of Labor
U.S. Department of Labor 57, 64–69, 93, 101–107

Or

Department of . . . *See first distinctive word in name of department*
Labor Department 57, 64–69, 93, 101–107
U.S. Department of . . . *See first distinctive word in name of department*

Dictionaries, thesauruses, glossaries, and reference works covering specialized fields provide guidance on standard usage and the relationship of terms. Here are examples covering medicine, banking, government, and geography, respectively.

Stedman's Medical Dictionary, 25th ed. illustrated. Baltimore: Williams and Wilkins, 1990.
Banking Terminology, 2nd ed. Washington, D.C.: American Bankers Association, 1985.
The United States Government Manual. Washington, D.C.: Superintendent of Documents. Updated annually.
Webster's New Geographical Dictionary. Springfield, Mass.: Merriam-Webster, 1984.

Subheadings

Subheadings are used to modify a main heading; they lead the reader directly to a single aspect of a broader topic. Any entry that includes more than five or six locators should be divided into subentries. No one wants to look up a long string of page references to find specific information on a topic.

Conciseness. The index is not intended to tell a story but to lead to the place in the text where the topic is discussed. The keyword in a subheading should be placed first and unnecessary prepositions and conjunctions should be omitted unless absolutely necessary to convey the meaning.

Poor Wording	*Better*
Computer rooms	Computer rooms
air circulation in	construction
design of wiring layout	electrical layout
how to construct	floors
use of raised floors	ventilation

Relationship to the Main Heading. The relationship of subheadings to main headings must be logical. One common fault is to use a heading both as a noun and as an adjective:

Acid
  acetic
  -free paper
  hydrogen ions
  neutralization
  rain
  solutions
  sulfuric

A better solution is to organize the headings this way:

Acetic acid
Acid-free paper
Acid rain
Acids. *See also* Acetic acid; Sulfuric acid
  hydrogen ions
  neutralization
  solutions
Sulfuric acid

Wrong	*Right*
Light	Light
bulbs 51–52, 57, 78–85	color effects 95–98
color effects 95–98	intensity 7–11
-emitting diode 157	sources 51–57
intensity 7–11	Light bulbs 51–52, 57, 78–85
sources 51–57	Light-emitting diode 157

Prepositions. Whether an index is crisp and useful or long and rambling will depend on the choice of words in the headings and subheadings. Prepositions and conjunctions such as *of, and,* or *with* should be avoided in subheadings where possible, along with all superfluous words. Consider the following:

Physicians' offices
  full-time personnel needed for operation 75–78, 88
  scheduling of appointments in 90–95
  use of microcomputers in 42–47, 104

A thoughtful indexer would achieve more clarity and conciseness by using tightly worded subheadings, with the keyword placed first.

Physicians' offices
  appointment scheduling 90–95
  computer use 42–47, 104
  personnel needs 75–78, 88

Sometimes a preposition is needed in a subheading to make the meaning clear:

Students
  as security employees 127–128
  security of 114–118

Arrangement. See "Alphabetization" below for a full discussion of alphabetical arrangement. Two styles are in common use. The first places subheadings in strict alphabetical order. This makes it easy for the eye to skim down the column:

Quotations
  correction of errors
  direct and indirect
  from speakers
  in speech
  in titles
  of phrases
  on citizenship
  versus paraphrases

The second style ignores any prepositions and conjunctions at the beginning of a subheading, alphabetizing according to the first important word. The theory here is that the eye will seek the keyword. In the indented format, however, the eye is forced to jump back and forth to find the topic of interest:

Quotations
  on citizenship
  correction of errors
  direct and indirect
  versus paraphrases

of phrases
from speakers
in speech
in titles

This style is clearer in the run-in format:

Quotations: on citizenship, 23; correction of errors, 35; direct and indirect, 90; versus paraphrases, 56; of phrases, 57; from speakers, 56; in speech, 42; in titles, 85

A third style, useful in histories and biographies, is to arrange subheadings in chronological order. This choice is often combined with the run-in format.

Anastasia, Grand Duchess of Russia: birth, 20; childhood, 32–36; education, 26; marriages, 68–69, 323–325, 355–357; guardianship of, 364; death and burial, 371–375

Once again, usefulness to the reader is the most important factor; any system that is not obvious to the reader should not be used.

Sub-subheadings. This third level of index heading should be avoided where possible, although it is sometimes a useful way to arrange technical information. An index is not a classification scheme or an outline. Every indexable topic should have its own heading, providing additional ways for the user to find the information. Often a multilevel index entry in the first draft can be converted to two or more main entries in the final index.

Not:	*But:*
Air bases 20–45	Air bases 20–45
Maryland	Andrews AFB, Maryland 39
Andrews 39	

Cross-references

Cross-references are an index's transportation system. They refer from a term not used in the index to the wording that has been selected as an index heading *(See)* or from a valid term to other related headings *(See also).* Different types of materials require different thinking when setting up the structure of an index. Accurate, logical, and useful cross-references are a mark of a good index.

To illustrate how an indexer chooses headings and cross-references, suppose that the author of a book on automobile safety has used these terms at various points in the text:

seat belts
safety belts
restraint systems
automatic seat belts
mandatory seat belt use laws
passive restraints
air bags
automatic restraints
head restraints

The indexer must decide which of these are distinct concepts, what the relationship among them is, and what users are likely to look up. One solution might be

Air bags
Passive restraints. *See* Restraint systems
Restraint systems. *See also* Air bags; Seat belts
  automatic
  head
  passive
Safety belts. *See* Seat belts
Seat belts. *See also* Restraint systems
  automatic
  mandatory use laws

Indexers insert such cross-references when they choose the corresponding main headings. They may modify them as the work progresses.

"See" References. A *See* reference leads from an alternate term under which a user might search to the term used in the index to cover that topic. Here are some of the instances where a *See* reference is used.

- From an acronym to the full term

  BLS. *See* U.S. Bureau of Labor Statistics

- From a full term to a more commonly used acronym

  Deoxyribonucleic acid. *See* DNA

- From a synonym

  Congenital malformations. *See* Birth defects

- From an older usage to the current form of a name

  Byelorussia. *See* Belarus

- From an inverted form of a multiword term

Circuits, electric. *See* Electric circuits

- From the second part of a compound heading

Colleges. *See* Universities and colleges

- From a common name to a scientific name

Tulip tree. See *Liriodendron tulipifera*

- A *See* reference may also lead from a broad concept that has no index entry to specific aspects of the concept that appear in the index.

Allergies. *See* Allergic contact dermatitis; Asthma; Atopic conjunctivitis; Chemical sensitivities; Hypersensitivity pneumonitis
Associations. *See* Trade associations

Double Posting as an Alternative to a "See" Reference. If there are only a few references under a heading, it is simpler to include the locators in two places than to use a *See* reference and force users to move from their first point of entry to another point in the index.

Mail service 59–67
Postal service 59–67

If the subject has multiple locators or includes subheadings, however, a cross-reference to the valid term is preferable.

Mail service. *See* Postal service
Postal service
  delivery routes 60–62
  hours of operation 59, 75
  policies 65–67, 142–148
  staffing 63–64

The danger in double posting is that the indexer will end up with some locators under one form of the heading and others under a second form.

Mail service 59–67
Postal service 75, 142–148

That is a disservice to the reader. It can happen all too easily if the book uses varied terminology for the same concept and the indexer does not pick up this relationship. Users should expect to be able to locate all information on a topic from a single index entry.

"See also" References. A *See also* reference leads to related information that appears under more specific or parallel headings. Sometimes the second

heading could have been subordinate to the first, but because of its size or significance the indexer has chosen to pull it out to become a separate main heading.

Decision-making skills 68–80

Leadership attributes. *See also* Decision-making skills
  enthusiasm 95
  integrity 71, 75–78, 90
  risk-taking 91, 96–99

A common use of the *See also* reference is to refer the reader from a generic term to specific aspects of the term that are covered elsewhere in the book.

Dogs. *See also* Golden retrievers; Pembroke Welsh corgies; Yorkshire terriers

These examples are from a book on accessibility for handicapped persons.

Building entrances
  200-foot separation 15
  number of 11–12
  pedestrian 13
  vehicular 13

(There is no cross-reference to "Entrances" because the references there have no further information on the main entrance to a building.)

Doors. *See also* Entrances
  clearances 29–30
  construction specifications 31–34
  revolving 30
  thresholds 28, 34

("Door" is used in the text to refer to the door itself. "Entrance" is a broader concept taking in the whole approach area.)

Entrances. *See also* Building entrances; Doors
  dining hall 83
  health care facilities 86
  libraries 83
  restroom 95

(Users searching under "Entrances" might want the more specific information given under "Building entrances" and "Doors.")

At times it is also useful to refer from a specific term to a more general heading.

Furniture. *See also* Decorative arts

See also references must lead to additional information cited under a related or more specific topic, not just to the same page numbers repeated under another main heading.

Animals 57–63. *See also names of specific animals*
Bears 58, 65–66
Elephants 60, 64, 77–79

The second heading is cited in full exactly as it appears in the index. A general cross-reference such as

Arctic. *See also* Polar

is not acceptable. The cross-reference must lead to specific index headings and might read

Arctic region. *See also* Polar exploration; Polar front

In linking parallel terms, two-way *See also* references are used.

Cornet 34–38. *See also* Trumpet
Trumpet 42–51. *See also* Cornet

Blind and Circular Cross-references. In the course of constructing and revising an index, it is easy to end up with references to main headings that no longer exist. An indexer might create an entry for *Washington Cathedral* with a cross-reference reading like this.

Cathedral Church of St. Peter and St. Paul. *See* Washington Cathedral

Later on he or she decides that the correct name for the structure is *National Cathedral* and changes the original entry for *Washington Cathedral* to *National Cathedral.* Unless it is changed also, the entry under *Cathedral Church of St. Peter and St. Paul* has become a blind cross-reference.

A circular cross-reference leads the reader from one term to another and back again without ever finding real information.

Diskettes. *See* Disks
Disks. *See* Floppy disks; Hard disks
Floppy disks. *See* Diskettes

Extra care must be taken at the editing stage to catch these types of errors. They are marks of a sloppy index.

Locators

A locator is usually a page number or a range of pages, but it can also be a paragraph, section, item, or figure number.

Page Numbers. These are the most common locators used in indexing. Punctuation indicates whether a topic is covered continuously on a range of pages or is mentioned sporadically on a series of pages.

Franklin, Benjamin 153–157
Franklin, Benjamin 153, 154, 155, 157

See "Style Choices" below for methods of abbreviating inclusive page numbers.

Section Numbers. These can be used instead of page numbers as the locators for a technical manual. This practice theoretically enables the index to be prepared at an earlier stage in the production process and makes it easier to update the index in a later edition.

Work-to-rule 3-1-4.2
Payroll processing I:36.238
Rollovers IV (c) 34
Printing F602-F603, P591

Item Numbers. These are used to index a book that is arranged as a series of numbered items, such as a volume of abstracts or a reference work on chemical compounds.

Mercury
  engineering and cost data OFR 84–35
  recovery from concentrates RI 9140
Saccharin 8170

Introductory Notes

An introductory note should always be used to note typographical conventions used in the index, indicate coverage of a category of information, or explain complex locators. Here are some examples:

Page numbers in italics refer to illustrations.
References are to paragraph numbers. Specific codes are not included in this index; for a complete list of codes see appendix A.

The not quite traditional index to Schickele's *Definitive Biography of P.D.Q. Bach* includes this amusing introductory note, an example of a system so complex as to be useless:

Important references are given in boldface. Italicized numbers indicate fleeting references, whereas numbers in parentheses refer to mere implications or unwarranted extrapolations. Asterisks are used to identify particularly distasteful passages.

A look at the index to this "biography" will reveal no boldface numbers.

Editing the Index

Once the initial selection of index entries has been completed, the polishing begins. This editing and review may take one-third to one-half of the total time spent on indexing. The same steps are followed whether the indexer has used a computer-assisted method or has done the work on 3- by 5-inch cards.

Alphabetize. Sort all entries in correct alphabetical order, following the principles covered under "Alphabetization" later in this chapter. A well-designed computer program with built-in options for special cases will take care of this step automatically and display the index in final order as the work progresses. Some indexers using manual methods prefer to keep the cards in alphabetical order as they work, and others sort them all at this stage.

Print Draft 1. Print the draft by computer or type it from the cards. A double-spaced draft allows room for editing notations. Indexers working on cards may wish to skip this step and edit directly on the cards to avoid laborious retyping, but it is hard to visualize the finished product without a printed version.

Revise. An initial list of main entry selections requires considerable review and revision before it becomes a cohesive index. At this stage, inconsistent entries are spotted and corrected, superfluous headings are deleted, subheadings are added or combined into meaningful groups, entry terms are changed for consistency and clarity, and additional cross-references are inserted. This is the point at which a superior index is created. Figure 28–4 shows examples of edited index entries.

Print Draft 2. The final draft is typed from the edited index cards or printed from the computer. The manuscript should be double spaced, single column, with 1½-inch margins. Each page should be numbered.

Proofread. If the index is so detailed that proofreading of each entry against the original page of text is required, this must be done while the entries are still in page number order. This step would be necessary for the index to an encyclopedia or an index with many personal or corporate names or scientific terms.

In proofreading a completed index, it is not practical to trace each page reference back to the original page of the printed text. The proofreaders should read the index for typographical errors, for format, and for obvious errors in page numbers. They should also check the alphabetical order, the order of page references, and the accuracy of cross-references.

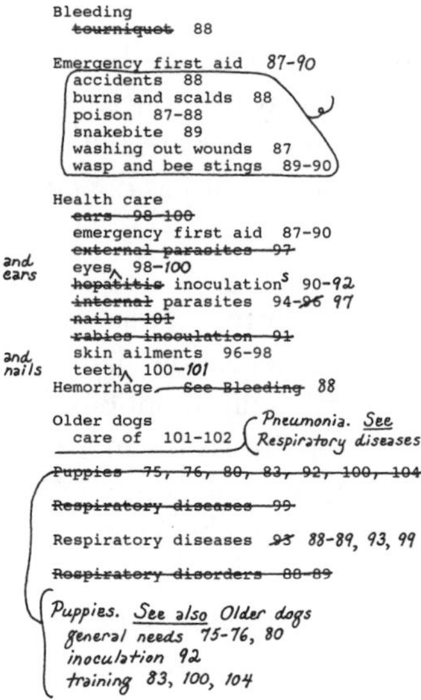

Bleeding
  ~~tourniquet~~ 88

Emergency first aid 87-90
  accidents 88
  burns and scalds 88
  poison 87-88
  snakebite 89
  washing out wounds 87
  wasp and bee stings 89-90

Health care
  ~~ears 98-100~~
  emergency first aid 87-90
  ~~external parasites 97~~
  eyes and ears 98-100
  ~~hepatitis~~ inoculations 90-92
  ~~internal~~ parasites 94-~~96~~ 97
  ~~nails 101~~
  ~~rabies inoculation 91~~
  skin ailments 96-98
  teeth and nails 100-101
Hemorrhage ~~See Bleeding~~ 88

Older dogs
  care of 101-102

Pneumonia. *See* Respiratory diseases

~~Puppies 75, 76, 80, 83, 92, 100, 104~~

~~Respiratory diseases 99~~

Respiratory diseases ~~95~~ 88-89, 93, 99

~~Respiratory disorders 88-89~~

Puppies. *See also* Older dogs
  general needs 75-76, 80
  inoculation 92
  training 83, 100, 104

Figure 28–4. Sample edited draft.

Review. A review of a completed index by a second indexer or an editor includes these steps:

- Read the main headings for coverage and wording.
- Check the table of contents and the introduction to see that all principal topics discussed there are covered in the index.
- Determine whether the subheadings under each topic are logical and pertinent. Watch for confusing or unnecessary articles, prepositions, and conjunctions.
- Confirm all cross-references. Nothing is more maddening to the user than a cross-reference loop that leads the reader on a winding path. No index should tell a reader who looks up "Firearms" to "*See* Arms" if "Arms" says "*See* Weapons." A *See also* reference must lead to additional information, not to the same locators repeated under a different heading.
- Check the alphabetization. If a computer program has been used, watch for such common problems as misfiling caused by quotation marks, parentheses, and other punctuation marks; symbols; numbers; and other special characters such as accented letters. All of these may sort according to their ASCII number value when they should be ignored or forced to sort in a meaningful arrangement.
- Spot-check page references against the text.

STYLE CHOICES

In an index all style choices should be governed by ease of use and immediate clarity to the eye. Choose the simplest style that will serve the purpose of quick access to information.

Indented Format Versus Run-in Format

In the indented format (also called *line-by-line style*), each heading and subheading is on a separate line. In the run-in format (also called *run-on style*), all subheadings follow the main heading in hanging paragraph form. See figure 28–5 for an example of the difference. The indented format is clearer and is always used in reference books. The run-in format saves space. It is commonly used in histories and biographies.

Indented format

Trucking deregulation. *See also* Interstate Commerce Commission; Trucking industry
  commission actions 75, 81–83
  congressional actions 6, 97–98, 100–101, 104–5, 108, 113–16, 118–36, 171–74
  effects of 1, 3, 5
  history 6
  presidential actions 106, 111–12, 130–31
  pressures for 66–68, 71, 73–74
  small-community service issue 125–30

Run-in format

Trucking deregulation: commission actions, 75, 81–83; congressional actions, 6, 97–98, 100–101, 104–5, 108, 113–16, 118–36, 171–74; effects of, 1, 3, 5; history, 6; presidential actions, 106, 111–12, 130–31; pressures for, 66–68, 71, 73–74; small-community service issue, 125–30. *See also* Interstate Commerce Commission; Trucking industry

Figure 28–5. Indented format versus run-in format; page numbers are elided in this example.

Cross-references

Usually cross-references follow immediately after the main heading. However, some house styles place *See also* references as the final subheading. Most indexers think that placing *See also* references immediately after the main heading lets the user know immediately what other entries are listed. Others believe that the users need to be made aware of additional possibilities only after they have read the subheadings given under the first main heading.

A distinctive typeface, usually italic, is used for the words *See* or *See also*. These words can be set off by a period and an initial capital or follow immediately after the main heading in all lowercase.

Lepidoptera. *See* Butterflies
Schooners *see* Sailing vessels

If the heading in the cross-reference is in italic type, the *See* is set in roman type to provide a contrast.

Apple. See *Malus*

Multiple cross-references are arranged in alphabetical order and separated by semicolons.

Government. *See* Federal government; Local government; State government

Capitalization

Index entries follow text for spelling, capitalization, and hyphenation. However, the indexer chooses the method of distinguishing main headings from subheadings. Many choices are possible, but usage must be consistent.

Capitals for the first letter of a main heading with lowercase for subheadings is a clear and straightforward standard style.

Fact sheets
Federal National Mortgage Association
Fee-splitting
Fixed-rate mortgages
  comparison with ARMs
  graduated payment
  growing equity

Making all headings lowercase except for proper nouns is useful where it is important for the proper nouns to stand out.

subject-verb agreement
typography
  design
  spacing
  typefaces
WordPerfect 5.1
writing
  legal aspects
  readability indexes

The use of initial capitals for both headings and subheadings takes away a visual clue that gives the user an instant read on the level of the heading.

Canada
  Geography
  History
  Tourist information
Costa Rica
  Exploration
  Industries

The use of all uppercase for main headings is effective when relatively few main headings are followed by multiple subentries.

BUTTERFLIES
  monarch
  swallowtail
TREES
  ash
  birch
  maple
  oak
  pine

Punctuation

Punctuation in an index should be used as sparingly as possible. Simplification contributes to ease of use.

Between Heading and First Locator. A comma is often used here, but two spaces (1 em) serve the same purpose and avoid visual clutter. Most examples in this chapter use no punctuation between index headings and locators.

Africa 57–63   *or*   Africa, 57–63

Between Locators. A comma usually separates multiple locators. If the locators have a complex format that includes a comma, a semicolon is used instead.

Africa 52, 55, 57–63, 80–82
Agricultural regulations I–5,7; II–7; IV–10,12

Before Cross-references. Either a period or no punctuation at all is used before a *See* or *See also* reference. A comma is not a good choice here.

New Scotland. *See* Nova Scotia

or

Company names *see* Corporate names

Between Cross-references. A semicolon is used to separate multiple cross-references.

Lenders. *See also* Loans; Mortgages
Taxes. *See* Estate taxes; Excise taxes; Income taxes; Sales taxes; Taxation policy

Ranges of Numbers

Locators that indicate a range of pages or sections are separated by an en dash. The indexer must choose between full numbers for both the first and last pages of a range and the use of shortened numbers for the second element. Full numbers are preferable because there is no possibility of confusion.

4–9, 10–11, 103–107, 245–253, 400–412, 1234–1239

The second number is sometimes shortened to save space. Styles of elision vary.

Chicago style:	4–9, 10–11, 103–7, 245–53, 400–412, 1234–39
Other variations:	4–9, 10–11, 103–7, 245–53, 400–12, 1234–9
	4–9, 10–11, 103–07, 245–53, 400–12, 1234–39

ALPHABETIZATION

Alphabetization is a simple process for a short index using only subject headings in the English language, but it can become a complex issue when the index entries include symbols, numerals, abbreviations, foreign language characters, and personal names preceded by particles. The treatment of initial articles can also be open to choice.

National standards that cover arrangement of entries in large indexes are called *filing rules* rather than *alphabetization rules* because they deal with numerals, symbols, and spaces as well as letters of the alphabet.

These codes provide filing rules:

ALA Filing Rules. Chicago: American Library Association, 1980.
Library of Congress Filing Rules. Washington, D.C.: Library of Congress, 1980.
Proposed American National Standard Guidelines for Indexes and Related Information Retrieval Devices. (Draft 4.1, September 1993) American National Standards Institute/National Information Standards Organization. Work in progress.

The American Library Association (ALA) rules and the Library of Congress (LC) rules differ. LC rules are scholarly and call for the classification of entries according to whether they represent a person, place, thing, or title; thus they are better suited to the arrangement of bibliographic records for a large library collection than to the arrangement of book index entries. ALA rules are more straightforward. Entries are filed strictly by the letters, characters, and spaces included in the heading. The user does not need to know the filing rules, and the filing can be done by computer. The American National Standard Guidelines are based on ALA rules with some adjustments for use in indexes instead of library catalogs.

Two major systems of alphabetization are in common use, word by word and letter by letter.

Word-by-Word Style

In the word-by-word style, entries are alphabetized by the first word of the heading. If more than one entry begins with the same word, they are then alphabetized by the second word of the heading and so on. The basic concept of this style is "nothing before something"; thus a space precedes any letter or character. A hyphenated word is considered two separate words, and a hyphen or slash is equivalent to a space. This is the style used in most encyclopedias, library catalogs, and the American National Standard Guidelines. It is the natural order for most nontechnical indexes.

Cost accounting
Cost basis
Cost-of-living index
Cost-plus pricing
Cost-volume-profit relationship
Costa del Sol
Costa Rica
Costa, Victor
Costilla County, Colorado
Costume design

Letter-by-Letter Style

In the letter-by-letter style, all spaces, hyphens, and apostrophes are ignored; the index heading is treated as a single stream of letters up to the first punctuation mark preceding a modifying element or an inversion, then alphabetized by the stream of letters following the punctuation mark. This is the common dictionary arrangement. It is especially well suited to technical material with acronyms, symbols, and specialized vocabulary.

Costa, Victor
Cost accounting
Costa del Sol
Costa Rica
Cost basis
Costilla County, Colorado
Cost-of-living index
Cost-plus pricing
Costume design
Cost-volume-profit relationship

Either style is acceptable, but style within a single index must be consistent. Some publishers have a house style for indexes. In the average short index the difference between the two styles is not significant, but in a long technical index it will be quite apparent.

Word-by-Word	*Letter-by-Letter*
tank cars	tank cars
tank cleaning	tank cleaning
tank trucks	*Tankerman Manual*
Tanker Owners Agreement	Tanker Owners Agreement
Tanker Safety Conference	tankers
Tankerman Manual	Tanker Safety Conference
tankers	tank trucks

This book's index uses the word-by-word style.

Numbers

Numbers expressed as numerals precede words consisting of letters and are arranged according to their numerical value. Numbers expressed as words are filed alphabetically.

Numerals. In all modern alphabetization systems, such as the *ALA Filing Rules,* numbers written in numerals are sorted before letters of the alphabet, not as if they were spelled out. House styles may differ.

Numerals Before Letters	*Numbers as if Spelled Out*
1812 Overture	Boeing passenger aircraft
Boeing passenger aircraft	747
727	767
737	737
747	727
767	Edwardian era
Edwardian era	1812 Overture
Elgar, Sir Edward	Elgar, Sir Edward

Subscripts and Superscripts. Subscript and superscript numerals are filed as if they were "on-the-line" numerals preceded by a space.

C^3 Corporation
C Is for Cat
CCM Company

Prefixes in Chemical Names. Numbers used as prefixes in the names of chemical compounds are ignored in alphabetization.

Human immunodeficiency virus
5-Hydroxyindoleacetic acid
Hypertension

Non-Arabic Notation. Roman numerals should be filed in numerical order according to their arabic equivalents.

George II
George V
George VI

Numerals in non-arabic notation are listed with their arabic equivalents.

Louis XII
Louis XIV
Louis 14th furniture
Louis XVI
Louis Quatorze
Louis the fifteenth

Dates. Dates or other numbers that form a time series are arranged chronologically.

1979 annual report
1991 annual report
1992 financial results
  first quarter
  second quarter
  third quarter
1993 budget forecasts

Subentries such as those above can be simplified by the use of numerals instead of words for ordinal numbers.

1992 financial results
  1st Q
  2nd Q
  3rd Q

B.C. dates precede A.D. dates in chronological order.

Roman history
  500 B.C. to 31 B.C.
  30 B.C. to A.D. 284
  A.D. 284 to A.D. 476

Symbols

Indexes to computer manuals and some scientific documents present the problem of how to arrange entries that begin with special symbols that are neither letters nor numerals.

One solution is to group all symbols at the beginning of the index, before any entries that begin with a numeral. Symbols are presented in the following order, determined by the value of their ASCII codes in the standard computer character set.

! ″ # $ % & ′ ( ) * + , – . / : ; < = > ? @ [\ ] ^ _ ` { | } ~

Any symbols occurring in the middle of a heading are ignored in both word-by-word and letter-by-letter alphabetization.

Hyphens

Hyphens are ignored in alphabetical arrangement. In word-by-word alphabetization a hyphenated word is considered two separate words.

Word-by-Word	*Letter-by-Letter*
Broker-consultants	Brokerage firms
Brokerage firms	Broker-consultants
Brokers	Brokers

Apostrophes

Apostrophes are ignored in alphabetization.

Abbreviations and Acronyms

Abbreviations and acronyms are alphabetized as written, not as if spelled out, according to all indexing codes published since 1980. This simplifies computer sorting and is more straightforward than the old practice of listing as if spelled out.

Mac, Mc, St., Ste. Following the above rule for abbreviations, names beginning with *Mac, Mc, Saint, St.* or *Ste.* are alphabetized exactly as written.

MacDonald, John
Macdonald, John A.
Machinery
Mackenzie, Alexander
MacKenzie, Allan
Macleod, John J.
Macromolecules
Magic shows
McCarthy, Joseph R.
McDonald, Ian
McKenna, Siobhan
McLeod, David
Saint John (apostle)
Saint John (New Brunswick, Canada)
St. John's (Newfoundland, Canada)
Ste.-Adèle
Ste.-Marie

Initial Articles

Initial articles in titles and names are often a source of confusion. Should they be omitted, inverted, or ignored? How do the rules apply to foreign languages? The answer is, "It depends." Initial articles should not be inverted or omitted, but in some cases they are ignored for alphabetization purposes.

In Place Names and Personal Names. Place names and personal names that include initial articles as an integral part of the name are alphabetized under the article.

El Greco
La Fontaine, Jean de
Los Angeles
The Dalles
The Hague

In Titles and Corporate Names. The initial articles *The, A,* and *An* as part of a title or a corporate name that does not begin with a personal name or place name are ignored in alphabetization.

Daylilies
Fragrant plants
An Introduction to Navigation
The Kamber Group
Lilacs

A Manual of Sailing
The New York Times Book of House Plants
Sailmaking

Appendix 2 of the *ALA Filing Rules* lists initial articles in 39 foreign languages that should also be disregarded in titles and corporate names. When a book is written for an audience that is not expected to know a variety of foreign languages, however, it may be more helpful to alphabetize under the foreign language article. Thus *Das Kapital* could be filed under D in some cases. Always provide a cross-reference if it would be helpful to the reader.

Prepositions and Conjunctions

Of the two alphabetization styles mentioned in the discussion on page 667 on arrangement of subheadings, the most common approach is to ignore any initial prepositions or conjunctions. The more straightforward style of alphabetizing under the first word of the subheading is gaining favor, however.

NAMES

For most Western-style personal names, corporate names, and place names, the choice of index heading form is straightforward. The names are taken from the text, with personal names inverted to place the surname first.

Complications can arise when text usage varies, when surnames are preceded by particles (definite and indefinite articles, prepositions, or conjunctions), when it is not clear which element of the name is the surname, when place names have initial articles or use abbreviations, and when corporate names include personal names. For scholarly indexes with many name entries, indexers can refer to standard codes that cover both the correct form of headings for names (library cataloging rules) and the correct filing order for these headings (filing codes). (Standard filing codes are discussed above in "Alphabetization.") Rules for form of name headings are given in *Anglo-American Cataloging Rules,* second edition (AACR2), published by the American Library Association. This is the standard code used for cataloging in American, Canadian, and British libraries.

AACR2 rules are used in library catalogs, ongoing databases, and cumulative indexes to periodicals to provide consistency in headings over time. They need not be followed slavishly in an index to a single book, but they are useful in resolving difficult questions.

Personal Names

For Western-style personal names with a single-word surname, the surname is placed first, followed by a comma and the given names or initials as used in the text.

Leonard, Jennifer
Nickerson, T.B.
Patrick, David C.

Fullness of Name. Choose the fullest form of the name in common use. When more than one form of the name is in use, make a cross-reference from one to the other.

Eisenhower, Dwight D.
Eisenhower, Ike. *See* Eisenhower, Dwight D.

Ruth, Babe
Ruth, George Herman. *See* Ruth, Babe

The cross-references shown above would not be necessary in a book index with only one or two entries for *Eisenhower* or *Ruth.* Academic rules should be modified to suit the text being indexed. President Clinton might be indexed as *Clinton, Bill* in a popular book that used only that form of his name. In a scholarly history of the United States covering the 1990s or in a periodical index, the entry should read *Clinton, William Jefferson.*

If only a surname is given in the text, the indexer should try to supply a given name by querying the author or consulting standard reference sources. If no given name is available, a modifier should be added after the name for identification. A surname alone is not an acceptable index entry.

Simpkins (storekeeper)

Compound and Multiple Surnames. Compound and multiple surnames, whether hyphenated or not, should be entered under the first part of the name, except where usage favors another practice. The preference of the individual must be followed where known. This is especially important in the case of compound Spanish surnames (see below). Cross-references should be added where necessary to link all possible forms of entry.

George, David Lloyd. *See* Lloyd George, David
Lloyd George, David 23, 48–56, 67–69

Hyphenated surnames are entered under the first element of the surname.

Boutros-Ghali, Boutros
Pemberton-Smith, Nancy

Prefixes. Names that include prefixes made up of particles such as *d', de, den, der, des, du, van, von, ul,* or *y* can be a source of confusion. It is necessary to know the nationality of the individual and alphabetization conventions in that country before determining the correct form of entry for the name. Consult AACR2 for definitive answers and *Indexing A to Z* for guidance covering selected countries. A few examples follow.

In English-speaking countries the particles are always considered to be part of the surname. This rule also applies to persons who lived or worked most of their lives in an English-speaking country.

d'Arcy, Philip
de la Mare, Walter
de Laura, John
De Shields, Kim
De Valera, Eamon
l'Enfant, Pierre
Van Allen, Nancy

Prefixes that have been fused with the main part of the name to become a single word are entered under the (former) prefix in all languages. Internal capitalization may vary according to personal preference.

Delacroix
DeLaura
Descartes
DeShields
Vandenburg

In Germany, the Netherlands, and Portugal, names with prefixes are entered under the main part of the name and the prefix follows the inverted part.

Beethoven, Ludwig van
Braun, Wernher von
Gama, Vasco da
Goethe, Johann Wolfgang von
Gogh, Vincent van

Since the Dutch artist is widely known in English as Van Gogh, a cross-reference should be made from that form.

Van Gogh, Vincent. *See* Gogh, Vincent van

In France, names beginning with the preposition *de* as a prefix are entered under the main part of the name, with *de* following the inverted part. Surnames beginning with the articles *la, le, les,* or their contractions with *de, des,* and *du,* are entered under the prefix, but *de la* is split into *La* before and *de* after the name.

Des Prés, Jacqueline
Du Barry, Marie Jeanne
Gaulle, Charles de
La Fontaine, Jeanne de
La Pérouse, Compte de

Spanish Names. In Spanish-speaking countries most people use a compound surname consisting of the family names of the father and the mother (her father's surname), usually in that order, sometimes joined by *y*. Such names are alphabetized under the father's surname.

Ortega y Gasset, José
Pérez de Cuéllar, Javier

Cross-references should be made from other variations that the reader might try.

Cuéllar, Javier Pérez de. *See* Pérez de Cuéllar, Javier
De Cuéllar, Javier Pérez. *See* Pérez de Cuéllar, Javier
Gasset, José Ortega y. *See* Ortega y Gasset, José

Because of particles that may be included in one or more parts of the compound surname and variations in custom, it is sometimes difficult for the indexer to identify the surname preferred by the individual. For example, Ramon Miguel Guilas de la Paz is a native of the Philippines. Assuming that his name followed usual Spanish format, an indexer might enter it as

Guilas de la Paz, Ramon Miguel

But in Ramon's case the customary order of names is reversed—his mother's maiden name is Guilas and his father's surname is de la Paz. The correct index entry as a Spanish name would be

Paz, Ramon Miguel Guilas de la

Since Ramon has lived and worked in the United States for many years, however, he has adopted the style of English-speaking countries on the use of particles. The name should be entered as

De la Paz, Ramon Miguel Guilas

Patronymics as Part of the Surname. Patronymics and other relational terms used as prefixes occur in many languages. Examples include *Ab, Abd-al, Abdul, Abu, Ap, Bar, Ben, Bin, Fitz, Ibn,* and *Umm.* All such names are entered under the prefix.

Ben Gurion, David

Russian Names. Russian names include a given name, a patronymic, and a surname. Patronymics for men usually end in *-ovich* or *-evich* and those for women in *-ovna* or *-evna.* In addition, surnames ending in *-ov* are modified to reflect gender by adding an *-a* for women. Helena, the daughter of Leonid Potapov, would be known as Helena Leonidovna Potapova. She might be called Helena Leonidovna in text. Leonid's son Alexander would be known as Alexander Leonidovich Potapov. It is important for indexers to avoid confusion between the patronymic and the family name. The correct entries are

Potapov, Alexander Leonidovich
Potapova, Helena Leonidovna

Non-Western Names. Consult reference sources for the structure of African and Asian names. The order of name elements may be quite different from that of Western names, or a personal name may be used without a family name.

Chinese names are written with the family name first, followed by a two-syllable given name. In the Wade-Giles system of romanization, the given name is hyphenated; in pinyin it is closed up (see Chapter 21, Foreign Languages). Follow the form used in the text. Do not invert the name and do not use a comma.

Deng Xiaoping
Mao Tse-tung

Japanese names were traditionally written with the family name first, but in recent years many Japanese have adopted the Western style of placing the family name last. The indexer should attempt to determine individual preference and practice.

Titles of Office. Titles of office and military rank are not included in index headings for personal names unless they are needed as a qualifier to distinguish between two persons with the same name.

Titles of Honor or Nobility. Persons normally identified only by a title of honor or nobility should be entered under that title, expanded if necessary by their family name.

Dalai Lama
Marlborough, John Churchill, first Duke

Terms of Honor or Address. In entries beginning with a surname, terms of honor and address (e.g., *Dame, Lady, Lord, Sir, Mrs.*) are included in the name but are disregarded in alphabetizing.

Fonteyn, Judith
Fonteyn, Dame Margot
Olivier, Sir Lawrence
Olivier, Malcolm D.

Forenames Without Surnames. Persons identified only by a given name or forename should be entered under that name, qualified by a title or office or other distinguishing epithet. The order of the title or other qualifier determines the arrangement of identical given names.

Charles, Prince of Wales
Dorothy (mother)
Elizabeth II, Queen of England
Ethelred the Unready
John XXIII, Pope
John, King of England
John of Gaunt
John, Saint
Leonardo da Vinci

Homographs. When two or more persons have the same name, their names are homographs and should be distinguished with qualifiers such as a fuller form of name, nickname, dates, occupation, title, or nationality.

Phillips, John (carpenter)
Phillips, John (teacher)
Beattie, Elnora (Doris Elnora Elizabeth)
Beattie, Elnora (Elnora Jane)

In the case of members of the same family, suffixes such as Jr., II, and III can be used, but it should be remembered that these designations can change over time. Nicknames, dates, or other distinguishing qualifiers are preferred.

Rockefeller, John D.
Rockefeller, John D., III
Rockefeller, John D., IV
Rockefeller, John D., Jr.

Note that numerals precede letters, so *III* and *IV* come before *Jr.*

Changes of Name. If a person has been known by more than one name at different times and both are significant in the work being indexed, use both forms and make reciprocal cross-references. In a history that deals with Hillary Rodham Clinton's chairmanship of a panel on health care and also mentions legal opinions written under her maiden name, use

Clinton, Hillary Rodham. *See also* Rodham, Hillary
Rodham, Hillary. *See also* Clinton, Hillary Rodham

In a book that mentions Mrs. Clinton only after she took her husband's name, use *Clinton* as the surname with a cross-reference from other possible forms.

Clinton, Hillary Rodham
Rodham Clinton, Hillary. *See* Clinton, Hillary Rodham

Corporate Names

Names of corporate bodies present two challenges in indexing—they change over time, and they are sometimes confused in format with personal names.

Corporate bodies should be entered in the form most commonly used. Use an acronym or abbreviation if that is the most common form. If more than one form is common, use the fuller form. Do not transpose or omit initial articles that are part of the commonly used name. Do not invert a personal name that is part of a corporate name to place a surname first.

DuPont Company
James Madison University
J.C. Penney Company
John Greenan and Sons
UNICEF

Make cross-references from other forms of the name to the one chosen as an index entry.

E.I. Du Pont de Nemours and Company Inc. *See* DuPont Company
Greenan (John) and Sons. *See* John Greenan and Sons
Penney's. *See* J.C. Penney Company
United Nations International Children's Emergency Fund. *See* UNICEF

Identical names for different bodies are homographs and should be distinguished with qualifiers.

Metropolitan Museum of Art (Chicago)
Metropolitan Museum of Art (New York)

Place Names

Indexers should follow the text usage wherever possible in the selection of main headings. If the book uses *Viet Nam,* for example, the indexer should follow that style and not arbitrarily change it to *Vietnam* for the index entry.

In texts where geographic names play a significant role and many forms of names for the same place may be encountered, a standard reference source is needed. The U.S. Board on Geographic Names is the official standard-setting body.

Prefer the English form if there is one. Otherwise use the form in the official language of the country.

Buenos Aires
Florence (Italy)
Florence (SC)

Names Beginning with Geographic Terms. For names beginning with *Bay, Lake, Mount, Cape, Gulf,* etc., an index entry is made under the full name as written.

Cape Fear
Lake Champlain
Lake Memphremagog
Mirror Lake
Mount Mansfield
Mount Washington

In gazetteers and similar works containing many place names, however, such a name should be indexed under the distinctive word followed by the geographic term in parentheses. The name of an incorporated town or city, however, should not be inverted.

Mansfield (Mount)	*But:*	Lake Forest, Ill.
Memphremagog (Lake)		Mount Desert Island, Maine
Washington, D.C.		Mount Holly, N.J.
Washington (Mount)		
Washington (State)		

Homographs. Identical place names are differentiated by a descriptor in parentheses.

Mount Vernon (city, New York)
Mount Vernon (George Washington's home, Virginia)
New York (City)
New York (State)

The name of a city is followed by the name of the state if necessary to distinguish it from another city of the same name.

Springfield (Ohio)
Springfield (Vermont)
Springfield (Virginia)

Standard U.S. Postal Service abbreviations may be used.

Middletown (CT)
Middletown (OH)
Middletown (Powys, Wales)

Initial Articles. An article or preposition should be retained in a geographic name of which it forms an integral part.

Des Moines
Las Vegas
Los Angeles
The Dalles
The Hague

Changes of Name. In an index spanning a period of years over which a country has changed its name, use the most recent name with a cross-reference from the former name.

Dutch East Indies. *See* Indonesia
Indonesia 104–115
Southern Rhodesia. *See* Zimbabwe
Zimbabwe 54–58

A country that has split will require multiple entries.

East Germany. *See* German Democratic Republic
Federal Republic of Germany. *See also* Germany for events before 1949 and after 1990
German Democratic Republic. *See also* Germany for events before 1949 and after 1990
Germany. *See also* Federal Republic of Germany; German Democratic Republic
West Germany. *See* Federal Republic of Germany

Titles of Publications and Works of Art

Initial Articles. Do not invert initial articles in titles. According to the *ALA Filing Rules,* initial articles in titles are ignored in the alphabetization of indexes.

Manual of Accounting Procedures
The Merck Index
"Mountain Greenery"

In a scholarly work initial articles in foreign languages as well as those in English should be ignored. The *ALA Filing Rules* includes a list of initial

CASTING OFF

To a knitter the term *casting off* means finishing off the stitches so they won't unravel and to a sailor it means beginning a voyage, but to an editor or designer the term has yet another meaning—determining how long manuscript copy will be when set in type.

In casting off an index, the page designer must consider the size of the type, the number of lines on a page, the number of columns, the width of margins, the width of a column line, and the number of runover lines caused by narrow columns.

When an index must be cut at the last minute to fit the number of pages available, there are several possible approaches. Here are some steps that can be taken by the typesetter:

- Reduce the size of the type.
- Use more columns.
- Eliminate key letters at start of alphabetical sections.
- Use a run-in instead of indented format. This will involve changes in phrasing and punctuation as well as mechanical changes in layout and should be reviewed by the indexer. Extra time must be allowed for the conversion.

Steps to cut out lines require judgment by the indexer:

- Shorten headings that have runover lines so that they will fit on a single line.
- Eliminate double postings.
- Combine or eliminate subentries.
- Delete the least important entries.

Making an index shorter by eliminating entries is a difficult and time-consuming process that should be attempted only as a last resort. It is very important to consider the potential effect on cross-references when deleting entries after an index has been completed.

articles in 39 languages. In works for nonspecialists where only a few titles occur, however, titles in foreign languages are often filed under the initial article.

Style of Type. Follow the text style for usage of italics and quotation marks to distinguish titles of books, articles, songs, films, chapters, works of art, etc.

DESIGN AND TYPOGRAPHY

The basic principles of typography are covered in Chapter 31, Typography. In this section we look at the special factors to be considered in designing the printed page for an index.

Ease of Scanning

An index is not read in sequence. The user is looking for specific information. The design should make it easy for the eye to find that information. For this reason any introductory note that explains typeface conventions should be repeated on every page.

The distinction between indented and run-in formats has been discussed above. The indented format is much easier to use. The only advantage of the run-in format is a saving in space.

Margins

A ragged right margin in an index column is preferable to a justified margin because the lines are short. The use of leader dots before the page numbers is unnecessary and should be avoided.

Indentions

In the indented format each succeeding level of subheading is indented 1 em from the previous level. Runover lines should always be indented more than the lowest level of subheading, as shown in figure 28–6, so that they cannot be confused with a subheading as the eye runs down the page.

In the run-in format, shown in figure 28–7, all lines after the main heading are runover lines. They can be indented 1 em or more.

Correct indentions are critical to an index. The distinction between runover lines and indentions for levels of subheadings should be carefully checked by the typesetter and watched for in proofreading. In desktop publishing indention errors may occur when the text of an index is imported from a word processing program. Importing the index text as a standard ASCII file with a very long line length and a code for each level of indention results in fewer errors.

Figure 28–6. Example of index page using indented format and full page numbers.

Figure 28–7. Example of index page using run-in format and elided page numbers.

Page and Column Breaks

Page and column breaks should be carefully controlled so that they do not sever the logic of the index. At least two subheadings should follow a main heading at the bottom of a column, and a single subheading should not appear alone at the top of a column.

Continuation Lines

Repeating a main heading at the top of a new page or column where subheadings are continued makes it much easier for the user to locate information.

. . .	Retail trade *(continued)*
. . .	establishments
. . .	finances
Retail trade	franchises
collective bargaining	inventories
earnings	. . .
employees	. . .

Italics and Boldface

The use of special typefaces has two roles in the index—to distinguish one element from another and to make the index easier to use. Italic type is often used for locators indicating figures or illustrations. Boldface can indicate a volume number in a locator or can be used to indicate the principal coverage of a topic. Any such special usage should be explained in an introductory note.

Boldface is also effective for main headings where relatively few main headings are followed by many subheadings.

PART FIVE

PRODUCTION AND PRINTING

29

COMPUTERS IN THE EDITORIAL AND PRODUCTION PROCESS

COMPUTERS IN THE EDITORIAL AND PRODUCTION PROCESS

Computers are rapidly replacing the traditional tools of writers, editors, and designers, bringing about the biggest change in publishing since the printing press revolutionized communications in the late 1400s. Style manuals, thesauruses, and dictionaries are now stored on the computer as well as on the bookshelf; the designer's grid boards, rub-on letters, and waxers have gone the way of carbon paper, stencils, and mimeo machines. Much of the editorial and design work that was once done with a pencil can be done faster using a keyboard or a mouse.

Technology has shuffled the steps in the production process and changed the roles of writers and editors. In some offices, particularly in corporate settings, writers and editors also serve as keyboarders, designers, graphic artists, typesetters, proofreaders, and production coordinators. To do these jobs well, editors must understand the capabilities and limitations of the software and hardware they work with. This knowledge will let them plan ahead, avert problems, and offer suggestions. Even writers and editors who aren't directly involved in production should have a basic knowledge of computers.

It is not possible, nor is it necessary, to be an expert on every aspect of computer technology. The goal of today's publishing professionals should be to understand the steps in the process, know what is possible and what is not, and stay informed about new products and technologies. This chapter gives a broad overview of computers and their capabilities. Because of the ever-changing developments in the computer industry, the discussion here focuses only on general products and capabilities; readers should use it as a springboard to understand and discover the specific ways in which technology can make their jobs easier.

COMPUTERS: AN OVERVIEW

The widespread use of personal computers has affected every aspect of the publishing process; the benefits are saved time, reduced costs, and room for increased creativity. Writers and graphic designers can try and reject ideas quickly without excessive rekeying or redrawing. Manuscripts can be transferred long-distance rapidly. Text for books and periodicals can go from the author's computer to camera-ready composition without the costly and time-consuming step of rekeying for typesetting.

Today, it is likely that a computer is used at some stage of the production process of virtually every publication. Laptops and notebook-size computers offer portability to reporters and writers on the go. Computers can be connected, or networked, either locally (within an office) or long-distance (over phone lines) and shared by hundreds of users at a time. Many publications today are produced from beginning to end by teams of people who are linked electronically yet never meet face to face. To help writers and editors understand more about this rapidly changing process, the rest of this chapter explains some of the software programs used to create, edit, and produce publications.

Computer Hardware: Bigger Is Better

Whether you are talking bytes, baud, RAM, megahertz, or dots per inch, a bigger number is almost always better to computer users. Big numbers signify more storage space, higher speed, or finer resolution. They also usually mean more dollars when making a purchase.

Processing. The speed of the computer is determined by the size of the microprocessor, which is an integrated circuit contained on a small chip; it is the part of the computer that does the actual "thinking." Microprocessor speed is measured in megahertz; the faster the microprocessor, the more sophisticated programs the computer will be able to run. Although speed may not be as important to writers and editors who do only word processing, it is important to those who use more complex software such as desktop publishing or graphics programs.

Memory is required by the microprocessor to carry out its functions. The more memory the computer has, the better equipped it is to run large, memory-hogging programs. There are two basic types of memory:

- *Random access memory,* also called read-write memory and commonly referred to as *RAM.* RAM is the computer's short-term memory—it clears when the computer is turned off. RAM provides the temporary work space for the data that the user is currently working on. Because software programs vary greatly in size, it is important to know the RAM requirements of the programs you want to run. For example, a full-featured desktop publishing program requires much more RAM than does a basic word processing program.

- *Read-only memory,* commonly referred to as *ROM*. ROM contains the computer's basic instructions. It is called read-only because the computer cannot delete information stored in ROM or write new information over it. Information stored in ROM does not go away when the computer is turned off.

The Monitor. A monitor's resolution is determined by the size of the dots (known as *pixels*) that the monitor uses to form characters and images. Resolution is referred to in terms of the number of horizontal and vertical pixels that make up the screen. The more dots there are, the higher the resolution; the higher the resolution, the clearer the image. For example, VGA monitors offer resolution of 640 pixels horizontally by 480 vertically. Super-VGA monitors offer even higher resolution—1,024 pixels horizontally by 768 vertically. Although high resolution is not necessary for people who use the computer only for word processing, it is critical for those who work with sophisticated graphics and layout programs.

The "bigger is better" rule applies to the size of the monitor itself as well as the number that indicates its resolution. Monitor size is indicated by diagonal measurement, as with televisions. Many monitors show only part of a page at a time; the user must "scroll" (move the cursor up or down) to see the rest of the page. Some applications, such as desktop publishing programs, are best used on a full-page monitor, which shows an entire page at a time. Better still is a dual-page monitor, which shows two pages side by side—a particularly useful feature for designing magazine and newsletter page layouts. Needless to say, the price of monitors increases as the size increases.

Printing. Resolution is an important consideration for output as well as for the monitor. Printers, both laser and dot matrix, offer varying levels of resolution. Resolution in this sense is the clarity of the print—it is measured in terms of dots per inch (dpi). The higher the resolution of the printer, the more dots that make up each character. As with monitors, more dots mean better resolution. The more dots there are, the less visible the individual dots are; therefore, characters printed at a high resolution (such as 1,000 dpi) look smoother than those printed at a lower resolution (such as 300 dpi).

Telecommunicating. A modem is a device that transfers information from one computer to another over telephone lines. The speed at which the modem transfers data is known as its *baud rate* and is measured in bits per second. The higher the baud rate, the faster the computer can send and receive information (most modems run at 300, 1,200, 2,400, or 9,600 baud). Users who frequently send data long-distance will want to invest in a high-speed modem to save on long-distance charges. Faster modems can be set to work with slower modems, but they can send only as fast as the slower modem can receive.

Data Storage. With regard to storage devices, bigger is most definitely better. Data can be saved to a computer's hard disk, a floppy disk, or a secondary storage medium such as magnetic tape or optical disk. Stored information is measured in bytes, kilobytes, megabytes, and gigabytes. One byte equals one character (spaces made with the space bar count as characters).

The amount of data to be stored determines which mode of storage is best. File sizes differ because of a variety of factors in addition to the number of words in the file (special characters and codes, for example, take up additional space). As a rough guideline, a single-spaced page of word-processed text takes up about 4,600 bytes. The text of one page from a 6- by 9-inch book, in 9-point type, would take up about 3,400 bytes on disk (before any formatting codes are inserted).

Floppy disks come in two sizes: 5¼ inch and 3½ inch. This is the one exception to the "bigger is better" rule; the 3½-inch disks hold more data than the 5¼-inch. The 3½-inch disks come in a hard plastic casing and are not actually "floppy." Because of this casing, they are less susceptible to damage than the 5¼-inch disks. Both sizes come in one of two formats: double density or high density (also known as quad density). High-density disks look like double-density disks but have a greater storage capacity.

Floppy disks are useful for storing relatively small amounts of data. Compared with hard disks, however, floppy disks are slow, can be damaged easily, and do not hold very much data (a double-density 5¼-inch disk holds about 130 double-spaced pages of text). A hard disk serves the same function as a floppy disk but has a much greater capacity and remains in the computer. (Removable hard disks can be used when security is a concern or when portability is important.) Hard disks can read and write data 10 to 20 times faster than a floppy and come in different sizes. The smallest holds 20 megabytes, which is the equivalent of about sixty double-density 5¼-inch floppies or about twenty-five 3½-inch double-density disks. Most users need at least 40 megabytes, and those who use large programs such as desktop publishing and graphics programs should have at least 80 megabytes.

SOFTWARE IN THE PRODUCTION PROCESS

Virtually every task in writing, designing, producing, or managing a publication can be streamlined by using the appropriate software. The challenge lies in sorting out the useful, well-developed software from the poorly conceived or poorly developed programs. Some tasks, such as complex page layout, require specialized software; simpler tasks can be accomplished with a package that combines several programs. These bundled programs usually cost less than buying each type of software individually, but the components are not as full-featured as the single-application programs. To make a good choice, first determine exactly what needs to be done and then match a software program or programs to those needs. Buying a package and trying to make it perform the needed tasks only wastes time and money. Extra features can be tempting, but if they're not really needed, they only add to the cost and take up valuable disk space.

Problems can arise when there are misconceptions about a program's capabilities. For example, many word processing programs are advertised as having desktop publishing capabilities. Be aware, however, that although it is possible to achieve some desktop formats with a word processing program, it may take many more steps than with a desktop program. Desktop programs are more flexible; formats can be set up more easily, and last-minute changes can be made more quickly. Knowing the strengths and weaknesses of each kind of software can help writers, editors, and production specialists use these tools to their fullest capabilities.

The following discussion of computer software covers the programs most commonly used in the publication process: word processing software, grammar and style checkers, reference software, desktop publishing and graphics software, database publishing software, and a few miscellaneous programs referred to collectively as utilities, which can be added to increase efficiency and prevent problems.

Word Processing Software

Some word processing programs offer little more than the basic functions of an electronic typewriter; others approach desktop publishing capabilities. The ideal word processing program should be simple enough for such basic needs as manuscripts and correspondence, with advanced features readily available, and its files should easily convert to other software formats. Compatibility is important; even though it is easier than ever to convert word-processed files from one brand of software to another, some older or lesser-known brands cannot be converted easily.

Most word processing programs offer the following helpful features to writers and editors:

- *Block commands,* or "cut and paste," can copy, move, or delete whole sections of text at once. Editors no longer have to mark inserts on paper with "kite strings." They can try out possible changes on the screen and go back to the original easily with the "undo" command.
- *Search and replace* lets the user go backward and forward through the document to find all instances of particular words or phrases and change or delete them quickly. Copyeditors who must make a manuscript conform to a particular style can make good use of this feature; they can backtrack through a document when they make a style decision that affects previously edited text and quickly find every instance of the word or expression.
- *Macros* allow the user to combine a series of commonly used words or commands into a single keystroke. Writers who use the same name or phrase over and over can save themselves the trouble of keying it every time by setting up a macro. For example, a writer who refers to *The New York Public Library Writer's Guide to Style and Usage* can turn this 11-word title into a two-keystroke command by choosing the combination of the alternate (ALT) key and the letter *n* (ALT-n) to represent the entire title. Pressing ALT-n will "key" the title automatically. Macros can also be written to insert formatting commands such as headers and

---

SEARCH AND REPLACE: TO CONFIRM OR NOT TO CONFIRM?

The search-and-replace feature of your word processor gives you a choice: "Do you want me to ask you before I make each change, or should I just rip right through the document and make the changes without stopping?" Although there are some instances when you may choose to search and replace "without confirming," you should do so with care.

Suppose you are writing a software manual for a new program called "Go." You learn from the marketing department that the official name of the program will be set in all caps. No problem—you can use your search-and-replace feature to change Go to GO in every instance. But be sure to type a space before the G and after the O when setting up the search-and-replace command, or else the letters G and O will be capped wherever they appear together, even in the middle of other words. You may end up with a sentence like this: "If you accidentally overwrite the data in this cateGOry, the GOod file will be GOne from the disk."

❧

SPELLING CHECKERS: NO SUBSTITUTE FOR CAREFUL PROOFREADING

When spelling checkers first became available, many people viewed them as the most valuable part of their word processing programs. However, most of us have learned the hard way not to become too dependent on the spelling checker for catching errors. An acceptable word used in the wrong context can be just as embarrassing as an outright typo if it slips through unnoticed. Although the spelling checker saves time by catching *some* errors, it is still necessary to proofread text before considering it final. It is also important to remember to run the spelling checker every time changes are made to a document.

The author of the following letter to a computer magazine ran the spelling checker on it; no errors were flagged.

> I thought ewe mite bee interested in a revue of a currant hot software product witch is used fore finding spelling errors in word processing text.
>
> I halve bin using won four quite a wile and found it to bee invaluable. I have bin trying two improve my spelling for sum time now since my secretaire always commented that it isn't to grate.
>
> The spelling checker I'm using is such a good program it has maid me interested in the vendors' grammar checker, witch I will bee testing next. I will send ewe a revue of that program two.

footers or to remove unwanted format codes before a document is taken into a desktop publishing program.

- *Spelling checkers* find spelling and typographical errors. Some check for other types of errors as well, such as double words. However, spelling checkers have several limitations, including the inability to catch typographical errors that form acceptable words, such as *in* instead of *is* or *of* instead of *on.* Also, the spelling checker must be run every time new text is added or existing text is changed.
- *The preview feature* displays the document on the screen exactly as it will look when printed. This feature is helpful when using special formatting, because not all word processors are WYSIWYG (what you see is what you get). If, for example, a writer included a table in his text and positioned the columns by using spaces rather than tabs, the information might appear to be aligned on the screen. However, if the font he chose was proportional rather than monospaced, the columns would be misaligned when printed out. The preview feature can reveal these kinds of errors so that they can be corrected before the material is printed.

- *Format templates* can be used to quickly reproduce frequently used formats. Some programs supply ready-made templates; others let users create their own. A writer who regularly produces the same kinds of documents can set up a template for each type. This way, he does not have to enter formatting specifications for each new document. He might set up one template for correspondence, with a letterhead; another for newsletters, with a logo, banner, and three-column format; and another for technical reports, with a scholar's margin.
- *Graphics integration* is a desktop feature that brings in files created in graphics programs. With this feature, the user doesn't have to paste the graphics into every draft. The graphics become part of the file and can be resized and repositioned as necessary.
- *Automatic generation of table of contents and indexes* and *automatic cross-referencing* let the user insert codes that will create a table of contents, an index, or both. Some programs will also automatically update in-text references to the document's page, figure, or table numbers if changes are made to any one number during the writing or editing cycle. For example, if the writer or editor deletes figure 1, the program will correctly renumber the remaining figures and update any text references to them.
- *Automatic alphabetization and sorting functions* order such information as references and bibliographies with a single command. Editors can insert a code command and no longer have to alphabetize by hand.
- *Mathematical functions* can calculate data and link numbers in the text to tables created in a spreadsheet program (the data in the document change when a change is made to a number in the spreadsheet). If, for example, a writer includes a table of data and also discusses the information in the narrative, she could link the data to the text so that if a number changed, she would have to make the change in only one place rather than two.
- *Revision tracking and document comment* show revisions to a document and allow users to insert comments that do not print. Editors who work online but still need a way of showing authors their changes can use this feature to create marked-up drafts. Once the edits are approved, the "markup" can be removed automatically. This feature is also useful for writers who must submit their work to several people for review. Each reviewer can make changes or insert comments (such as "need more information here") directly into an electronic file. The files can then be merged into one draft, with each change highlighted. The comments can be inserted so that they can be seen on the screen but will not print out with the text.

Word processing software often includes many more features than those discussed here, some of which may be valuable to one person but never used by another. For example, many programs include conversion capabilities that enable the user to bring in files that were created in other software programs. Some include an equation creator, which allows those who work with mathematical and scientific material to key equations exactly as they should appear in final format. Most programs have a table-formatting function, which arranges tabular material into cells that adjust spacing automatically as the user enters information. Word processing programs are constantly being expanded and improved, and editors and writers should keep up with new developments.

Grammar Checkers

Most writers and editors who have used grammar checkers agree that these programs are no substitute for human editors. However, they can help people with weak writing skills to identify certain grammatical errors. These programs use artificial intelligence techniques to break the sentences into the various parts of speech *(parsing)* and analyze the parts. Grammar checkers are rule-based expert systems, meaning that they analyze the text by applying a series of IF . . . THEN rules and make or suggest changes based on the results. They cannot analyze intended meaning, so they offer a success rate of only about 50 percent.

Most grammar checkers must be purchased separately and work in conjunction with specified word processing programs, although some word processing programs include a grammar-checking feature. Some programs check documents interactively, meaning that the user responds to every suggested change as it is found; others run through the entire document and make changes without stopping. The program then produces an electronically marked-up version. Some programs provide a detailed explanation of each problem in addition to on-screen queries. Most programs finish with statistics on overall readability.

Typical errors found by these programs include incorrect verb forms; improper usage of infinitives, articles, and possessive forms; incorrect homonyms; incomplete sentences; and double negatives. They also catch mechanical errors such as incorrect capitalization and punctuation, inconsistent number style, and doubled words. Most programs can be customized; the user can turn off certain options and add others. In this way, grammar checkers can help copyeditors do style edits.

Some programs go beyond basic grammar checking and are better classified as writing aids. In addition to finding the errors that grammar checkers catch, these programs also attempt to show a writer how to improve clarity, readability, and rhythm. The software asks the user to specify the general style desired (business, technical, fiction, and so on). The program then checks the text for problems such as archaic expres-

SUBMITTING A MANUSCRIPT ON DISK: THE DO'S AND DON'TS

Because there are so many different software programs used in publishing, most publishers have their own guidelines for authors who submit their work on disk. However, some precautions are common to all:

- Make sure your software is one the publisher can use. If your material has been converted from one format to another, indicate which program was used originally and how the files were converted.
- Send a paper copy of everything that is on the disk, and include a list of all files on the disk and what they contain.
- Save each chapter of the manuscript as a separate file. Files should not contain more than about 40 pages of text; break long chapters into two or more files and label them accordingly. Name files in a way that will make sense to everyone who will use the disk. If you have named the files in some cryptic code that makes sense only to you, be sure to rename them before sending the disk.
- Don't include any extraneous material—especially early drafts—on the disk.
- Label the disk with enough information so that it can be identified if it gets separated from the manuscript (your name, address, and phone number; the name of the project; the name of your contact in the publisher's office). The label should also contain the name and version number of the software program that was used to create the material (for example, WordPerfect 5.1).
- Ask if the publisher has any formatting requirements. Do not insert any generic codes unless you know they can be used; conversion programs have become available for more and more word processing and desktop publishing software, and coding may not be necessary. If the publisher asks for coded text but does not supply a list of codes to insert, choose a consistent method of identifying the different formatting elements, such as chapter openings, block quotations, footnotes, and special characters. For example, you can identify paragraph breaks by inserting a <p> at the beginning of each paragraph and a <p> at the end of each paragraph. *The Chicago Guide to Preparing Electronic Manuscripts* provides a coding system that is used by many publishers.
- When preparing the disk, turn off any special features that your word processor has that involve formatting, such as justification and automatic hyphenation. Check with the publisher before using features such as automatic footnoting or indexing; these features may not translate from one application to another.

SUBMITTING A MANUSCRIPT ON DISK:
THE DO'S AND DONT'S (*continued*)

- Do not put two spaces after periods. Only one space should be used when the final copy will be printed in a proportionally spaced typeface or will be converted to desktop publishing (which always uses proportional spacing).
- Use the correct keys when typing numbers and symbols. For example, do not use the same key for the letter *l* and the number *1*. This habit developed because many typewriters didn't have a 1 key. With word-processed or desktop-published text, these characters are different, so it is important to choose the correct symbol on the keyboard. The number *0* and the letter *O* are also often miskeyed.
- Do not put a return at the end of every line. Use the word processing program's word-wrap capability, and use RETURN (or ENTER) only at the ends of paragraphs.
- Always keep complete backup disks of anything you send.

sions, clichés and jargon, redundancy, sexist language, wordy phrases, and passive voice.

Other programs claim that they can help writers conform to a particular writing style. These style-replicating programs either provide sample documents that can be used as models or allow writers to provide other documents to use as models. These programs use statistical models to analyze each document by counting word and sentence lengths. Although there are some uses for these programs, most professional writers find that their approach to style is oversimplified.

The most common problem cited by users of grammar-checking programs is the frequency with which these programs point out allowable phrases as errors. Telling the program to bypass incorrectly flagged items takes time, and these programs tend to run slowly. In addition, the programs often fail to flag actual errors. Often the mistakes outweigh the useful recommendations, which causes all but the most desperate users to give up. With advances in artificial intelligence research, future versions of grammar checkers are bound to improve in these areas.

Document Comparison

Document comparison software can be used to track changes made when editors work on computers (rather than on paper) and to manage the production of large documents that have multiple authors and reviewers. Most document comparison programs can do the following:

- Compare two word processing files and highlight the differences, both on the screen and on a printout.
- Merge the changes from several different drafts into one document, highlight conflicting changes, and indicate which changes came from which reviewer.
- Allow reviewers to insert comments that do not print with the text (a feature also found in some word processing programs).
- Preserve changes from old drafts of evolving documents and indicate when each change was made.

Most document comparison programs offer several choices for highlighting changes on a printout (text can be underlined, displayed in bold, shown with strike-through, or shown in italics). Users can also select how the screen looks (text can be in certain colors, brightened, or reversed out).

Writers and editors who work directly on a computer with no hard copy can run the original against the edited files and produce a copy that shows the author what was changed. For regulations and users manuals, or any other type of document that is updated regularly, new text can be permanently highlighted to emphasize changes. Typesetters sometimes use this kind of software to replace human proofreading. Two different operators key the same text, and the software compares the two versions electronically. An operator then reconciles the differences and corrects the errors. This approach to quality control is based on the theory that the odds are against two people keying exactly the same mistake.

This software has a few limitations. For example, most programs will not catch changes in automatically generated elements such as headers and footers, and they will not catch format changes such as bold text that was changed to italics.

Online Information Services

Online information services connect users to large networks consisting of hundreds of information databases. Research that once took hours and required a trip to the library can now be accomplished in minutes without leaving the office. By dialing in through their modems, writers and editors can obtain information from medical journals, legal documents, government reports, and many other categories of publications. Some services charge subscribers a monthly fee; others charge an hourly rate for connection time.

Reference Software

Writers and editors can save trips to their bookcases by using electronic reference materials directly on their computers. Many encyclopedias and dictionaries have electronic counterparts that can be "called up" when a user is in a word processing program. Some reference software programs are sold separately; the best ones are available only on CD-ROM discs, which require a CD-ROM drive. Less complete programs come with some word processing software. The electronic encyclopedias and dictionaries are usually abridged, however, and they take up a large chunk of disk space.

Electronic dictionaries provide definitions when the user highlights a word and presses a "hot key" (a key programmed to activate the software). The user can also look up spellings by using "wildcard" symbols (such as an asterisk) to stand for unknown letters. Many electronic dictionaries give pronunciations, syllable breaks, and etymology. Not all recognize hyphenated terms, however, and some are thrown off by capitalization and plural forms.

Specialized spelling checkers are available for foreign languages and certain subject areas (for example, electronic versions of *Stedman's Medical Dictionary* and *Black's Law Dictionary* are available). Some packages combine a dictionary and thesaurus and give access to words, meanings, and synonyms.

Electronic encyclopedias consist of preprogrammed string searches that link conceptually related words. For example, the user can look up a particular historical figure and get a list of related topics and historic events. These programs are sometimes criticized for their lack of depth but are usually praised for their good retrieval capability. Electronic atlases operate in a similar manner and usually include colorful graphics and special effects.

Online thesauruses work with word processing programs and are often provided with these programs as an added feature. (Most high-end word processing packages contain both a dictionary and a thesaurus.) Thesaurus programs vary in terms of the quantity and quality of words generated as synonyms. Good programs display a range of suitable alternatives; poorly designed programs offer too many choices that don't apply.

Pop-up style guides are programs that give grammar and style options on the screen while the user is working in word processing software. The better programs contain extensive cross-referencing and thorough explanations with each rule.

HYPERTEXT: ELECTRONIC BOOKS

A hypertext document can be thought of as an electronic book. Instead of turning pages, the reader views the information on a computer screen and moves quickly from one related topic to another in a document via electronic links. One developer of this kind of software refers to this new way of presenting information as "the joy of jumping."

You may have already used a hypertext product without realizing it. If you've ever seen a computerized museum exhibit that allowed you to see more information about a particular subject by just hitting a certain key or touching the computer screen, it was probably hypertext based. Even the HELP function of your word processing program may be hypertext based if it allows you to highlight items on a list of functions and press a key to get more information about each one.

Hypertext software—dozens of programs are available—applies database functions to text and graphics files. Hypertext documents can contain both words and graphics. The term *hypermedia* is used to refer to systems that combine text, graphics, photographs, sound, or animation.

The creator of a hypertext document uses hypertext authoring software to connect related pieces of information, or *nodes,* by using associational phrases, or *links.* Just as headings and subheadings in a printed document guide readers through the text, the links in a hypertext system guide users along various paths within basic units of information (the nodes). Links are cross-references that tie common subjects together even though they may not appear together consecutively in the narrative. These links are displayed on the screen, usually as highlighted words or phrases. The reader then moves the cursor to this highlighted phrase and presses a key to advance to a further explanation or discussion.

Hypertext documents can be useful training tools. The software can be used to create computerized instructional materials, museum and trade show exhibits, and reference works. Another example might be an electronic repair manual. A technician, using a computer, can view a troubleshooting checklist, highlight the name of a specific component, and be shown a detailed drawing along with repair instructions.

Strategies used in designing hypertext documents are similar to those used in creating book indexes. The links must be useful and intuitive—the author must anticipate the users' needs and assign the links accordingly.

Graphics Software

The main advantage of computer graphics software programs is that the user need not be highly skilled in pen-and-ink techniques to create high-quality graphics. Most graphics software programs fall into one of two categories—*paint programs* and *draw programs*. Writers and editors who work with computer-generated graphics should understand how these programs work, even if they never use them, just so they can understand their limitations and capabilities.

Paint programs let the user create picture-type images made up of hundreds of tiny dots called *pixels*. An artist can create fine images and shading by adding or removing individual pixels. In the jargon of computers, these kinds of images are known as *bit-mapped* or *raster* graphics. Photos and drawings can be scanned into an electronic file and retouched in much the same way that airbrushing is used to retouch a photograph. However, when a graphic created with a paint program is enlarged, distortion can occur—as the image grows, the pixels also grow and can become visible.

Draw programs are used to produce line art (known as *vector graphics* in computer lingo). Icons on the screen represent "tools" that can be used to produce different shapes and shading. For example, one tool may be used to draw lines and curves, another draws rectangles and squares, another draws ellipses and circles, and yet another creates text. The software stores all the component shapes of line drawings (circles, lines, curves, etc.) as mathematical formulas (rather than as the dots of paint programs). The artist selects a shape and then, using a keyboard, a mouse, or a light pen, tells the software where to start and end each line. Shading and cross-hatching can also be specified. These graphics can be easily resized and scaled without distortion. Draw programs vary in their ability to provide precision and control.

Draw programs allow the user to create original art or manipulate and enhance art created in other programs. Most graphics programs are designed so that they can be "pulled into" page layout programs, which combine text and graphics to create books, magazines, and newspapers.

Most computer graphics can be stored in a variety of file formats, many of which are compatible with a full range of software programs. For formats that cannot be used directly with another program, special software is available that lets the user convert from one format to another. However, some programs have their own proprietary formats, which means that their files cannot be read by other programs.

Computer graphics programs vary in ease of use. A wide range is available, including sophisticated drawing programs for technical illustration, cartography, and architectural drawing. Most programs include these basic capabilities:

- Images can be moved, stretched, condensed, rotated, mirrored, and skewed. Text can be wrapped around curves.
- Objects can be stacked on top of one another or grouped with other objects to form one graphic; objects can also be ungrouped so that individual parts can be edited. Different portions of a graphic can be automatically aligned.
- Objects can be filled in with specified shading and patterns. The thickness of the outline of a shape can be altered automatically.
- Most graphics programs let the artist specify colors for the final output, either in terms of process color or a PMS (Pantone Matching System) number. Specifying exact colors is important because even the best computer monitors may not give an accurate representation of what the final printed colors will look like.
- Typefaces and electronic clip art can be modified to create special effects.
- Objects can be sized to any magnification.

Writers and editors who serve as their own art directors can purchase electronic clip art to illustrate their publications. This ready-made art is stored on disk and can be brought into desktop publishing programs and computer graphics programs. Electronic clip art can be purchased by theme—such as business, industry, travel, and holiday—in a wide range of drawing styles and subject matter. The art is in the public domain, which means that it can be used without obtaining permission. Most clip art can be modified in computer graphics programs. Clip art choices are not limited to line art—photos can also be purchased from stock photo houses in this manner. The same rules apply for electronic stock photography as for the traditional kind—charges are determined based on how the photos are used in the publication and how many copies of the publication are printed.

Existing graphics and photos can be scanned and brought into graphics software programs for further manipulation. For example, if an artist wanted to use a picture of an eagle but didn't quite like the way it was positioned in the illustration, he could scan the picture and then make changes. He could resize the eagle, add or remove detail, or rotate the picture to a different angle. If the picture was a photograph, the artist could also make changes to it; he could change the background color, add more scenery, or add shading to give depth to the picture.

Some scanners scan only graphics; others can scan graphics and text. Some can be set to scan a page and pick up only the text or only the graphics. Text is converted to an electronic file with optical character recognition (OCR) software. OCR software is often criticized for being unreliable, and many programs give a fairly high error rate. Although some vendors claim

❧

TEXT SCANNING: DOES IT ALWAYS SAVE TIME?

People who think that scanning is a quick and accurate way to bring text from paper to an electronic medium may be disappointed. The technology for optical character recognition (OCR) scanning has been around since the early 1980s, but improvement has been slow. To date, no scanner can provide 100 percent accuracy.

High-end scanners have software that can be "trained" to recognize virtually any typeface. The user produces a "training set" by scanning in a sampling of characters. The system sees these characters as shapes and guesses what character each shape is supposed to be. The user chooses the correct guess for each character. In this way, the alphabet is established for the typeface being scanned, and previously unrecognizable text can be scanned with some measure of success.

The actual scanning process is relatively quick, about 15 to 20 seconds per page, but processing the training set and translating the scanned images can take an additional 30 seconds to a minute and a half per page. Then the scanned data must be "cleaned up" with the help of spell-checking and verification software—*and* the human eye, because errors still slip through. To scan a typical document, using high-end equipment and software, the user spends about 70 percent of the time on the actual scanning and about 30 percent of the time on cleanup.

No matter how advanced the scanning equipment, there are some factors that can make scanning virtually impossible:

- Heavily formatted text, with many levels of indention, lists, or tables.
- Third-generation photocopies or any other faded or light print.
- Text printed on a dot matrix printer.
- Faxes that were sent at standard, not high, resolution.

Even though scanners are improving with each new generation of hardware and software, it is still sometimes more efficient to rekey material than to scan it.

---

accuracy rates of 90 percent and higher, these claims are often based on clean text with few variables (one typeface throughout, no symbols or special characters, no special formatting). Users should test the software with their own material before purchasing it.

Desktop Publishing Software

Desktop publishing software is widely used today to produce everything from newspapers and magazines to books and brochures. These programs were once the only programs that could combine text and graphics, but many word processing programs can now produce some of the same text layouts as desktop publishing programs. The problem is that with a word processing program the user often has to work harder to achieve the same results. In general, word processing programs are better at text handling, and desktop publishing programs are better at page layout.

Desktop publishing programs can be categorized as either low-end or high-end. High-end programs are more expensive, have more sophisticated features, take more time to learn, and require more computer memory. Low-end programs are less expensive, offer fewer capabilities, but have a shorter learning curve. Low-end programs usually have some limitations, but they may provide just the right amount of control for users who prefer not to wade through seldom-used options.

Certain basic features are common to almost all desktop publishing programs, including the ability to

- Merge text and graphics from other programs into one document.
- Insert, delete, copy, and move text.
- Manipulate typographical elements such as typeface, size, and spacing and control the spacing around text.
- Create simple graphics and graphical elements such as bullets, rules, and shading.
- Design custom layouts or use prebuilt page layouts that come with the program.
- Create templates (also called style sheets) that specify a document's typeface, point size, type style, indentation, and justification. These templates save time and ensure consistency of appearance for documents that share a standard format. The word processing file can be coded with *tags* that correspond to the elements of the style sheet before being brought into the desktop publishing program.
- Create *frames* that hold text and graphics. Frames act as space-holders and can either be "tied" to stay with certain paragraphs or made to stay in one location on the page, allowing the text to flow around them.

Conversion Software

The challenge of merging the writing of several authors—all of whom use a different word processing program—is becoming less of a problem than it used to be, thanks to the advent of software made for this purpose. In

❧

THE NEW YORKER GOES ELECTRONIC

When *The New Yorker* magazine moved from traditional production methods to electronic publishing in 1991, the editors faced many of the same challenges that other publications have encountered—and then added a few of their own.

The first problem was introducing computers into a typewriter environment. *The New Yorker* staff was more tweedy than high-tech. Management took a go-slow approach, installing Macintosh computers in two groups at first, word processing and "Goings on About Town," according to an article in *Publish* magazine (November 1991). Plans for future expansion include having editors edit directly on screen.

The next problem was selecting a system that was both flexible in terms of software choices and easy to learn. Months of comparisons and investigation preceded the decision.

But one of *The New Yorker*'s challenges was unique. Editor Robert Gottlieb believed it was critical that the look of the magazine's typography—the essence of the magazine's design—be preserved. Electronic versions of the Caslon body type were available, but they were slightly different from the version being used. The editors decided to hire a custom typeface designer to generate digital replications of Caslon and the hand-drawn Irvin display type so that they could preserve the somewhat quirky character of *The New Yorker*'s long-time look.

The staff then tested the typefaces on two page-layout programs, QuarkXPress and PageMaker. Quark did a fine job of evenly spacing the letters and words—the last thing they wanted. PageMaker, however, provided the irregular spacing the editor desired, a look that closely matched the old *New Yorker.*

The New Yorker's switch paid off early, saving $1 million in production costs in its first year alone.

---

addition, many desktop publishing and word processing programs offer conversion capabilities.

Time and cost are important factors to consider when deciding whether to purchase special software or use an outside service for conversion. If the need for conversion arises infrequently or if the conversion is particularly complex or involves a large amount of data, a better choice may be to send the disks to a service bureau or conversion house. Most services base their charges on number of characters converted.

Just because a conversion is technically possible does not mean that it is always the best way to produce an electronic file. Conversion has several pitfalls, the most important of which is its lack of reliability. Converted documents sometimes contain stray symbols or characters that did not convert properly. And some conversions leave the document full of unwanted codes that must be deleted. For short documents, it is sometimes more efficient to rekey the material than to spend time converting it and then cleaning up the converted file.

Indexing Software

The process of compiling an index can be accomplished either by a human being or by a computer or by a combination of the two. Most word processing programs and some desktop publishing programs have an indexing feature that allows the user to insert tags next to the terms in the text that will be used as index entries. The program then creates the index by reading these tags. The computer, however, cannot discriminate between casual mentions of a subject and sentences that represent important ideas, and the result is often an incomplete index or one that has many useless entries. The main advantage of this kind of index is that it can be quickly regenerated if page numbers change. (See Chapter 28, Indexing, for a further explanation.)

Most professional indexers avoid the indexing feature described above and instead use indexing software that is designed especially for indexers to help eliminate the tedious aspects of their jobs. Most indexing software of this kind works by allowing the indexer to key each entry into a record—an electronic version of the index card. The indexer can edit, search and replace, and create macros to recall frequently used subheadings without having to rekey them each time.

Some programs sort instantly as the indexer makes each entry. These programs can use standard alphabetization conventions, but indexers can set their own preferences. Formatting functions can be automated; for example, all cross-references can be italicized. Redundant subheadings are eliminated automatically, and desktop publishing codes can be inserted as the index is being created. Indexers can work on several types of indexes simultaneously (for example, an author index and a subject index can be created at the same time). Most software allows the indexer to see the work in progress as it will appear in the final format.

Database Publishing

Corporations and government agencies have used databases for years to manage massive amounts of information. Recently, publishers have been exploring how database software can automate the production of large or time-sensitive documents.

A database program stores related information about a subject in a way that will allow the user to add to, delete, retrieve, and sort the information. A database can be thought of as a file cabinet—each drawer of the cabinet contains a category of information, and each folder within the drawer contains a subcategory. In a database, information is divided into records, and each record contains a group of fields. A file is a collection of records, and a database can be one file or a collection of files that work together.

Information in a database can be turned into a publishable form through the use of database publishing software. Database publishing software is particularly useful for directories, catalogs, phone lists, price lists, timetables, or any other publication that must capture timely data from another source and present the data accurately.

This type of software serves as a link between database software and desktop publishing software. It converts the information in a database into a format selected by the user and then adds the formatting instructions needed to produce camera-ready pages in a desktop publishing program, where it is automatically formatted. The user can produce customized documents by selecting all or only some fields within the database. Each unique combination of choices can be saved as a "recipe" and reused whenever a particular document is to be updated.

Database publishing can be best understood with an example: The editor of a newsletter wants to produce a directory of subscribers. She has a database that contains detailed information about each subscriber: name, job title, work address, phone number and fax number, renewal status, form of payment used, and length of time as a subscriber. She wants the directory to list only each person's name, job title, and address, and she wants the names grouped by state and alphabetized within each group. With database publishing software, she can specify which information she wants to extract, instruct the program to sort it as required, and automatically add the codes that will tell her desktop publishing software the specifications for the page layout (type size, column width, page size, and so forth). She then imports this coded file into the desktop publishing program and, after performing only a few more steps, prints out camera-ready pages. When the directory is updated the following year, she can reuse this same set of instructions to pull in current information.

General Utilities

In addition to the many software programs that are used in the publishing process, most writers and editors also own an arsenal of utilities—a variety of software programs that work with existing hardware and software to help the computer run efficiently, to prevent problems, or to facilitate other functions.

TOOLS FOR MANAGING THE EDITORIAL AND PRODUCTION PROCESS

Because so many editors and writers also have project management responsibilities, a review of publishing software would not be complete without a mention of some of the tools that can be used to track costs and monitor schedules.

Spreadsheet software can be especially useful to writers, editors, and production managers who have budget responsibilities. The user can create formulas that perform calculations automatically and can be linked so that when one number is changed, all other numbers are recalculated. For example, a production manager may use a spreadsheet package to control the budget on a book project. The spreadsheet can list the functions involved, the estimated number of hours for each step, and the hourly rates for each function. The software can then calculate the total cost for each function and the grand total. To see the cost implications of a proposed change to the production process, such as using desktop publishing instead of traditional typesetting, the production manager can change a few numbers and get the new cost instantly; the program does the calculating.

Scheduling and planning software can be a useful tool for managers who have to track resources across multiple projects. These programs can be used to monitor deadlines, track productivity, and estimate costs and completion dates. Most programs offer choices for displaying project data that include PERT chart and Gantt chart formats. Some programs allow the user to choose a bar chart format that shows planned versus actual schedules. Schedules can be collapsed or expanded to show the necessary amount of detail—time can be shown in months, days, or hours. With high-end programs, the graphic displays can be set up for presentation-quality output. Sophisticated scheduling and planning programs can be used as aids to decision making and long-range planning. Such programs can be essential tools for writers and editors who must juggle a variety of different projects with different deadlines and requirements.

Software may not be the answer for every situation. Some people are more comfortable with a pencil and a piece of graph paper, but project management software programs are definitely worth a look.

Backup Programs. Most writers and editors who work on computers have learned the hard way about the importance of backing up their files. Backup programs provide an automated way to copy data and programs from one mode of storage to another (for example, from a computer's hard disk to an optical disk or a tape) to protect against loss. The user can choose to back up only selected files (data files but not program files, for example) or to back up only the files that have been created, copied, or changed since the last backup. Most backup software also detects damaged files while backing up and can create a log of files included in each backup. Some programs can be set up to run backups when the computer is not in use or has been idle for a specified period.

Screen-Saver Programs. Screen-saver programs make the computer screen go blank after a specified period to prevent an image from being burned into the monitor. Some programs provide a moving image to show that the computer is still on. Some offer password protection—once the screen goes blank, the user has to type a password to get back into the computer.

Virus Protection (Vaccine) Programs. Writers and editors who exchange disks with other computer users must be constantly aware of the threat that viruses pose to their data. Viruses are computer programs that are designed to damage or destroy data. Some originate as games or pranks, but most can cause severe damage. Viruses can display a graphic or message on the screen (HA HA HA—YOU HAVE A VIRUS), play music, or send across the screen a bouncing character that removes data as it goes. Some viruses are programmed to lie dormant until a specified date. They duplicate themselves and spread, and when a virus lodges in a computer, it "infects" every disk that is used in that computer.

Virus protection software detects the presence of a computer virus by tracking the size of the files and recording sudden changes. These programs can be set up to provide continuous monitoring by scanning files, directories, and disks. Although files may not always be recoverable once they have been attacked by a virus, some virus protection programs can repair files. Most programs provide a report of what was checked, found, and removed. The software can be set up to detect and remove viruses in one pass or simply to detect them.

Virus software must be updated regularly—as new strains of viruses emerge, the software must be modified to combat them.

Font Software. Font software allows the user to add new typefaces to those that come with the printer. Font software comes in two forms: *scalable* and *bit-mapped.* With scalable fonts, the outline of each character is stored as a mathematical formula that defines the character's exact shape. Scalable fonts are more versatile and efficient than bit-mapped fonts because only one outline of each character is needed, whereas bit-mapped fonts require a separate file for every size of every typeface. Although scalable fonts take a little longer to print because they are being created as needed, they take up much less memory. Scalable fonts are often cleaner looking than bit-mapped fonts, which sometimes look jagged. Font software groups different families of typefaces together into one package. Prices vary according to the brand name, the number of fonts in the package, and the number of printers that will recognize the fonts. Bit-mapped fonts tend to be less expensive than scalable fonts.

Data Protection Programs. No computer system is complete without a data protection program. This valuable utility can

- Restore data that was accidentally deleted.
- Find lost files by searching through all of the computer's drives and directories in one pass. Most programs allow users to use wildcard characters (usually an asterisk) when they do not know the full names of files.
- Restore deleted material by moving it to an unused portion of the disk as it is deleted so that it will not be immediately overwritten.
- Reconstruct directories and files after a disk is accidentally reformatted.
- Repair corrupted files.
- Give system information, such as reports on hardware status and memory usage.

Most data protection programs also offer security features. The software can secure files by setting up password protection, lock the keyboard when the computer is not in use, or "wipe" the system to make data completely unrecoverable.

30

DESIGN

DESIGN

A well-designed house seems to invite the passerby inside, suggesting that here is a pleasant place to live. The major difference between the little New England saltbox house and the huge faux Victorian in the subdivision down the street lies in design. The design of the smaller structure is understated and functional, almost subconscious; the design of the larger house relies on external devices and ornamentation copied from another era that seem to be pasted on for the sake of decoration. The saltbox will endure as an attractive house; the faux Victorian may soon look faded and dated.

Successful graphic design, too, reflects a considered plan rather than a compilation of special effects. Like a well-designed building, a well-designed book or brochure is an invitation, and just as living space should be sensibly and functionally organized, so the "traffic pattern" of any printed piece should easily guide the reader through the pages.

The simple presence of type or illustrations on a piece of paper will influence readers in one way or another; in this sense, there is no such thing as the absence of design. Even the most content-oriented writer or editor will benefit from an understanding of how graphic presentation supports and reinforces the written word. This understanding will not only allow a more productive working relationship with a graphic designer, but also—since so many writers and editors now have computers and are becoming designers by default—provide a framework for making everyday design decisions.

THE PRINCIPLES OF DESIGN

Graphic design decisions are subjective; in a broad sense, there is no right or wrong, only more or less appropriate or effective, design. But even determining the appropriateness or effectiveness of a design is a subjective judgment. So where does one go to learn the rules of this game?

There are many schools that train designers over a long period of instruction and apprenticeship. To assume that this process can be boiled down to a list of rules is presumptuous at best. Before any list of rules about external *form*—or design—can be drawn up, a would-be designer must understand the specific, desired *function* of the piece to be designed. Then it is important to keep in mind some basic goals of communication: coherence, direction, and consistency.

Inside Out: Conveying a Message

Graphic design is a vehicle of communication. The starting point for any design should be its intention or message, expressed and implied. In a book, good design can reinforce the author's words and clarify meaning; in a logo or corporate identity, it can convey a company's image and philosophy. The message of the piece should always be thought of in terms of the intended audience; all design should be directed *outward* to that audience and not *inward* to some corporate or personal sense of identity or importance. Everything about the final design should work coherently to reinforce the message and intention of the piece.

Design Should Be Invisible

The job of the designer is to create the mood, the atmosphere that facilitates the communication of a message, and to structure the text and graphic elements to deliver that message effectively. A good design, then, provides a sort of invisible roadmap to the audience; it conveys not only a feeling but a structure that allows readers to easily absorb the message or information. Readers should never be more conscious of the design than of the content. When readers become conscious of design effects in their own right, the design is misdirecting readers instead of doing its job of underscoring the message of the piece.

Total Design

Successful graphic design must also take into account the various elements of the entire piece, bringing consistency to the whole so that the message and information can be unambiguously understood.

A brochure, for example, may have various physical divisions—an introduction, a body of text, illustrations, pull-out information, a reply coupon. It also most likely has a variety of purposes—to convey specific information to the readers, to motivate them to act, and to provide a vehicle by which they can act. A successful design communicates these purposes and intentions through a well-integrated, consistent presentation of the various physical parts of the piece.

Graphic Design as Blueprint

The design of a publication amounts to a plan that reflects its goals and intentions through the use of various graphic effects and techniques. With this plan the designer lays a groundwork that reinforces the coherence, direction, and consistency of the publication's message.

Before a designer develops a plan, he or she must know the length of the publication and the various elements it contains. In books, for example, this means an estimate of character or word count (called *castoff* and usually easily available from the word processing software used to prepare the manuscript) and a description of the various parts—number of footnotes, endnotes, appendixes, front matter, and so on. This knowledge helps determine type size and typefaces and the approximate length of the finished book.

Underlying all is the page format, which establishes the margins and columns, if any. The page format guides the eye and speeds comprehension. In magazines, newsletters, and heavily illustrated books, a predetermined *grid* dividing the page into sections horizontally and vertically is often used to guide the placement of text and illustrations. Many publications are designed in *spreads*—the design is not considered one page at a time but in terms of facing pages because that is how the reader will digest the material.

The typographic plan, too, plays an important part in the blueprint of the entire piece, whether it's a display ad, a brochure, or a book. (See

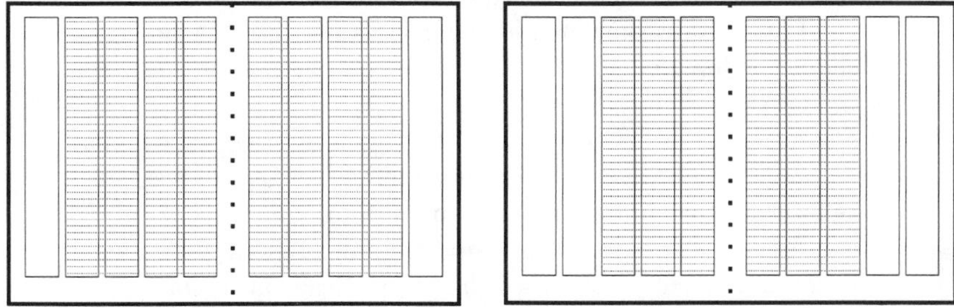

Figure 30–1. The number of columns in a design grid does not necessarily indicate the number of columns of text on a page; rather, the grids provide a useful, consistent tool for dividing the image area into units that can be used in different combinations depending on the requirements of text and illustration.

CLARITY BY DESIGN

A good page design should avoid anything that creates an obstacle for the reader. Here are some common problems:

- *Inappropriate selection of type styles.* It is easy to be tempted by the availability of so many sizes and styles of type, but a typeface shouldn't be chosen just because it's different; type should reflect and reinforce the content, tone, and style of the text. Highly stylized or oversized display type calls far too much attention to itself at the expense of the text as a whole.
- *Insufficient white space.* In an effort to cram as much information as possible on a page, perhaps to save money, designers will sometimes slash the size of the margins and intercolumn gutters. This creates a tight, cramped, uninviting page; tightly spaced columns can also hinder readability, since the eye will tend to wander straight across the page without a stronger division.
- *Lack of clear distinction between head levels.* Readers should intuitively understand the hierarchy of head levels within the text. Type and placement should make clear which head is primary, which is secondary, and so on.
- *Poorly planned running heads and folios.* Like heads, running heads and folios—page numbers—are guides for the reader. Their position and content should be determined by how a book will be used—will it be read from cover to cover or thumbed through for specific information?
- *Inconsistent sink.* All columns of text should start at the same point on the page, as should all chapter and part titles.
- *Poor spacing around heads.* Spacing visually connects the head with the text that follows it. Equal space above and below sets the head off as a disconnected element in its own right. More space should be inserted above the head, to end one section and begin the next.
- *Desktop disease.* Symptoms include putting rules above and below—and boxes around—everything; creating irregularly shaped and angled blocks of text; underscoring instead of italicizing; leaving two spaces after ending punctuation; and using a different typeface, size, or weight on practically every line.

Chapter 31, Typography, for more information.) Type treatments organize information for readers, allowing them to identify the order of importance of each element and to move easily through the text. In books, this includes running heads and folios, which serve as signposts to orient the reader to the work as a whole. (See Chapter 22, Parts of a Book, for a discussion of many of the elements that designers must consider.)

Together, the page format and the typographic plan should help readers feel at home, as if nothing is standing between them and the information being conveyed. This blueprint provides a context for the effective introduction of a bit of "spice" to stimulate interest—the illustration that breaks the grid, for example, or the contrasting bold sidebar or pullout quote. Without a consistent context, irregular effects serve more to confuse than to intrigue readers.

THE INGREDIENTS OF DESIGN

No design is universally appealing; a successful design depends, again, on a clear understanding of the audience. Different ages, cultures, and professions respond to different colors, typefaces, and imagery. The designer's toolbox contains a variety of graphic elements and effects that should be applied deliberately to convey and reinforce the tone of each piece; each element in the piece has a voice of its own, either straightforward or subliminal.

Paper and Ink

Paper provides the physical form and shape of the printed piece; most often, it is the only tactile element in a design. Sometimes it is appropriate for the paper itself to take a strong role in the design—this is often the case in specialty pieces and annual reports—and at other times paper is called upon to play a supporting role—as a neutral background to text and illustration in a book, for instance.

The designer evaluates the physical attributes of various papers to select the most appropriate stock. A high-gloss coated stock might be chosen for a flashy advertising brochure; a dull coated stock may be more appropriate for an annual report. An opulent and formal laid text may be chosen for invitations to a fundraising benefit, while the choice for a mass membership drive might be an unassuming plain white recycled offset. Color, too, is a factor, and very often the choice is among varying shades of white, from cool, crisp, bright white coated stock to warm, soft, natural white book paper.

Color in a printed piece also comes from the ink that is used to print it. Color can enhance the mood of the piece; a well-thought-out publication design can also feature color—in rules, headlines, or solid blocks, for instance—as an organizing device. The use of color should be integral to the piece, not just something tacked on.

There are a number of color conventions—red is an attention-getter, blue and green are soothing, yellow is motivating—but the use of color also follows trends; people respond to different colors at different times—consider the psychedelic colors of the 1960s and the muted mauves and pinks of the 1980s. And different color palettes suggest different tones, from the playful, childlike feeling of the primary colors to the sedate and restrained moods of charcoal, maroon, or forest green.

Perception of color is also subjective and emotional; the mere idea of purple may make an executive uneasy, but a 10-year-old will embrace it happily. Black, too, should be thought of as a color; when a second color would be too expensive, black can be printed solid and also screened to shades of gray to create an effective monochrome design. Using black or another colored ink on colored paper can also provide the look of a more expensive piece.

COLOR BASICS

Two types of color are used in printing—*spot* and *process*. For spot color, every different color is created with a separate ink; for four-color process work, all colors come from overlaying separated screens of only four colors—cyan, yellow, magenta, and black (see Chapter 33, Printing, for more information on process and spot color printing).

Color is always seen in combination with what surrounds it. Blue printed next to red will not look the same as blue printed next to green.

The *color wheel* was devised to help organize discussion of color. The 12 basic *hues*, or colors, are arranged in a circle, according to the order of the spectrum. The farther one color is from another, the greater the contrast; colors spaced three steps apart on the wheel are often considered to provide optimum contrast in design. Colors directly across from one another on the wheel are called *complementary*—the combination of two complementary colors like red and green creates a visually disturbing contrast.

Besides the basic color (or hue), the qualities of color are also discussed in terms of *saturation*—purity and intensity—and *brightness*—lightness or darkness. Colors of different hues combine most successfully if they are of similar saturation and brightness.

Aachen

Halls of Academe Vlad the Impaler

Avant Garde

Halls of Academe Vlad the Impaler

Benguiat

Halls of Academe Vlad the Impaler

Caslon

Halls of Academe Vlad the Impaler

Dom Casual

Halls of Academe Vlad the Impaler

Eras

Halls of Academe Vlad the Impaler

Hobo

Halls of Academe Vlad the Impaler

Kauffman

Halls of Academe Vlad the Impaler

Machine

HALLS OF ACADEME VLAD THE IMPALER

Peignot

Halls of Academe Vlad the Impaler

Figure 30–2. The choice of a typeface should enhance and reinforce the text.

❧

SOME CLASSIC FACES

Here is a brief and by no means exhaustive list of a few classic typefaces often used in book design:

Baskerville	Granjon
Bodoni	Janson
Caledonia	Palatino
Electra	

These faces are often used for text because they are distinctive enough to be interesting but not so fussy as to become tiresome after many pages. The text for this book is set in Caledonia; the heads are set in Baskerville.

Type

Type is the graphic translation of the written word and as such is a critical element in any design. (See Chapter 31, Typography, for a full discussion.) Typefaces have distinct voices and moods; they can be casual or formal, serious or lighthearted, traditional or contemporary. A good selection of type accurately reflects the subject matter, writing style, and tone of the piece.

Another graphic property of type is referred to as *type color*—the darkness of the type as it appears as blocks on the page. Type color is determined by the amount of spacing between words and letters and between lines, the incidence of capital letters, and the darkness of the ink itself. Masses of type can create visual gray areas that in themselves become an intrinsic part of the overall design of the piece. A strong, heavy type color may be appropriate for a book about the industrial revolution but not for a history of the romantic movement.

Illustrations and Photographs

The addition of images brings much to the design of a brochure, book, or advertisement. Images can convey information, literally illustrate a point, or suggest an idea or a mood. (See also Chapter 27, Photographs and Illustrations.)

Photographs are most often very literal, depicting a specific person, place, or thing. Photographic or printing techniques such as light diffusion or

Avant Garde

The next time you read a book, make a point to notice the overall color created by blocks of type. Different elements contribute to type color: among them are the size and weight of the type, the x-height, and the amount of leading. A book designer uses type color as a design tool that reinforces the tone and content of the book and contributes to the impact of the overall design.

Palatino

The next time you read a book, make a point to notice the overall color created by blocks of type. Different elements contribute to type color: among them are the size and weight of the type, the x-height, and the amount of leading. A book designer uses type color as a design tool that reinforces the tone and content of the book and contributes to the impact of the overall design.

Times

The next time you read a book, make a point to notice the overall color created by blocks of type. Different elements contribute to type color: among them are the size and weight of the type, the x-height, and the amount of leading. A book designer uses type color as a design tool that reinforces the tone and content of the book and contributes to the impact of the overall design.

Optima

The next time you read a book, make a point to notice the overall color created by blocks of type. Different elements contribute to type color: among them are the size and weight of the type, the x-height, and the amount of leading. A book designer uses type color as a design tool that reinforces the tone and content of the book and contributes to the impact of the overall design.

Helvetica Condensed

The next time you read a book, make a point to notice the overall color created by blocks of type. Different elements contribute to type color: among them are the size and weight of the type, the x-height, and the amount of leading. A book designer uses type color as a design tool that reinforces the tone and content of the book and contributes to the impact of the overall design.

Figure 30–3. The color of type refers to the overall design effect of masses of gray blocks of text on a page.

special effect screens, however, can create a less literal, more suggestive tone. Illustration, too, can range from the informational—a machine diagram, for instance, or a chart reflecting the national debt—to the evocative.

An effective design uses images in a manner appropriate to the audience and to the piece as a whole. Care should be taken not to "mix metaphors"; shifting between the literal and the symbolic and evocative—for example, using realistic, representational photography in a work of fiction—can create confusion if not handled skillfully.

Other Design Elements and Effects

Designers can also call on a variety of graphic devices, such as borders, rules, and dingbats, to complete their designs. These items can add interest and ornamentation to the page; used consistently, they can lend a feeling of unity to a publication. An intercolumn rule, for example, can provide a visual framework for columns of unjustified text.

Such devices, too, can also be used in the overall design to help organize material and guide the reader through the text. For instance, a specially selected *dingbat,* or icon, can be used as a signpost to alert readers to important points.

Other design effects include *screens,* or tints of a solid color, which can add tone and variety when the use of color is limited to one or two inks. Combinations of tints of different colors can create multicolor effects in a two- or three-color piece.

A block of color or a photo that runs off the edge of the page is called a *bleed.* This is a way of adding interest by breaking out of the image area imposed by the regular margins; it brings a sense of dynamism and movement to the page.

Attention is drawn to the solid block of color or black that contains text in white. Known as a *reverse,* this device is very effective when used for small blocks of text like pull quotes and heads.

A special piece sometimes will call for a special effect to make it stand out. Foil stamping and embossing are often used, sometimes together, to impart a feeling of elegance and luxury; die cutting allows a piece to be cut in irregular shapes, adding another dimension to the piece's physical channel of communication. (See Chapter 33, Printing, for more about these special finishing touches.)

THE DESIGN PROCESS

Design should start with a clear objective, which in turn guides the selection of the right designer for the job, the development of the design concepts, and the evaluation of the final concept. It is vital to select a designer whose strengths are in the area of the project. It is also important to keep sight of the objective of the project and evaluate the designer against the original instructions.

Selecting a Designer

Before hiring a designer, arrange to see his or her portfolio. It is best to allow the designer to present the work in the portfolio because he or she can explain the context for the work; it is difficult to judge whether a piece represents an appropriate design solution without an understanding of the purpose and special considerations of the piece.

It is important to remember that a designer presents his or her best work in the portfolio, in the style he or she likes best and is proudest of. Beyond screening for quality, the portfolio review is also the time to evaluate whether a particular designer's style is appropriate for the project at hand.

The portfolio review is also an opportunity to get an idea of how the designer might be to work with. A verbal and analytical person will often have difficulty communicating effectively with an intuitive, less verbal type.

Design Development

After gaining an understanding of the project, a designer generally goes through a process of developing and refining ideas for possible approaches. In the case of a book design, the editor, being most familiar with the content, tone, and special aspects of the manuscript, prepares a design memo that covers the various elements and particular problems in the manuscript for which the designer will need to develop design solutions and typographic treatments.

Very often, the designer will first submit rough, quickly produced sketches (usually called *thumbnails*) for review before investing a great deal of time in pursuing an approach that may turn out to be unacceptable. Once the alternative approaches are narrowed down, the designer will produce *comps*—comprehensive layouts—that accurately depict what the final printed piece will look like. A book designer will submit sample pages that reflect how an overall design will work in the various parts of the book—text, front matter, title page, and so on. These samples will illustrate and provide specifications for proposed type treatments for special manuscript elements such as extracts, play dialogue, poetry, recipes, equations, or formulas.

In the past, comps were often produced only as a way of refining the final design concept before actual production. This phase followed an interim process of developing and submitting tighter sketches on the way to the final design selection. But now that most design is done with computers and desktop color printers, it has become practical to submit fairly polished

COMMUNICATING WITH DESIGNERS

If design revisions are needed, it is helpful to be clear and specific in communicating the required changes. Just as important is expressing the logic behind the revisions being requested. The designer may be able to suggest a more effective solution to the problem if, instead of being instructed to change the A-level heads to 48-point bold italic type, he or she is told that that particular head needs more emphasis.

By explaining the reasons for revisions, you can often solicit the designer's help in solving a problem, especially when it is difficult to pinpoint just what the problem is.

design alternatives earlier in the development process. It is not unusual for the designer to provide fully rendered presentations of two or three design approaches, leaving less to the imagination.

Evaluating Design

You don't have to be a designer to evaluate design; after all, in most cases the ultimate audience for a book or a brochure doesn't consist of designers, either. It is important, though, to bring to the evaluation a certain understanding of and openness to design.

The first step, then, is to approach the design comps or sample pages from the same point of view and perspective as the ultimate reader of the piece. If the design works on this level, it is probably acceptable.

It is a little more difficult to take a closer look at the specifics and evaluate them individually. Especially important is how each element in the design contributes to the overall tone and objectives of the piece and how it relates to the other elements.

The evaluation of the design should focus on the key points of coherence, direction, and consistency. Does the piece make sense? Will the reader understand it? Does the design have a logical structure and plan?

Many writers and editors feel uncomfortable with graphic designers; often it seems as if the two come from different worlds. But in a successful publication, the skills of each are brought together to achieve the ultimate goal of publishing: clear communication.

31

TYPOGRAPHY

TYPOGRAPHY

The letters of an alphabet are remarkable workhorses. Combined with a sprinkling of punctuation and a few numbers, they let us communicate thoughts and ideas across the physical boundaries of distance and time. It's little wonder that from calligraphy to the computer screen, so much attention and energy have been focused on the art and craft of the letterforms that are the foundation of written language.

Typography is a complex subject, but an understanding of the basics of type, how type is used, and the mechanics of typesetting can be an important part of a writer's or editor's education.

TYPE BASICS

Terminology and Measurement

The *point,* 0.01383 inch, is the basic unit of type measurement. Type is commonly described by its point size. There are 12 points in a pica, and 6 picas equal roughly an inch.

X-height is literally the height of the lowercase *x* in a given face because that letter defines the height of the body of all other letters, minus their ascenders or descenders. The height of the capital letters is referred to, simply enough, as the *cap height; small caps* are capital letters that are x-height, or the size of lowercase letters in that face.

An *em* is a unit of measure equal to the point size of the type in question. Originally based on the widest letter in the alphabet, the uppercase *M,* the length of an em is the same as the point size: in 10-point type, an em is 10 points, for example. An *en* space is half of an em space. Ems and ens are the basis for linear measures such as indents and dashes (*em dashes* and *en dashes*).

Type that is 14 points and larger is referred to as *display type* since it is most frequently used for heads; smaller type—8 to 12 points—is called *text type* or *body type.*

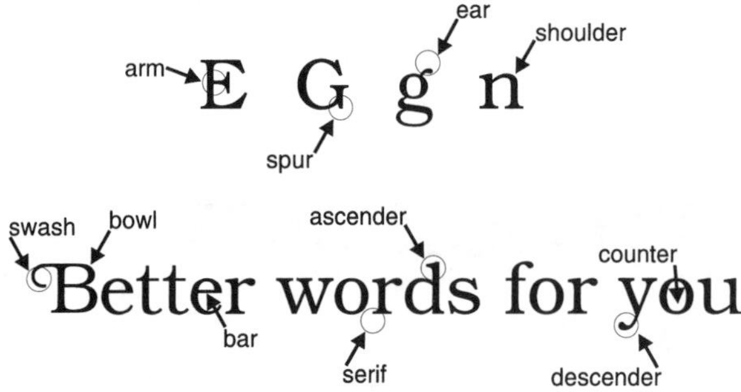

Figure 31–1. The anatomy of letterforms.

WHEN IS 72 POINTS NOT 72 POINTS?

"How can this be 72-point type? This capital *E* is barely more than 50 points high."

"That can't be 10-point Helvetica. *This* is 10-point Goudy, and it's nowhere near the same size."

Type cannot be measured by the individual letter, and type sizes are not consistent from typeface to typeface. These facts are easier to understand with a knowledge of the anatomy of metal type, the basis for typographic measurement.

Each piece of type in a complete 10-point metal font is 10 points high. That 10 points must accommodate all the ascenders, descenders, and capital letters of the font, keeping the baseline in the same position for each letter. Ten points, then, is the measurement from the bottom of the descenders to the top of the capitals and ascenders, depending on the face. Faces with long ascenders and descenders will, obviously, have to have a smaller x-height—thus the visual size difference between 11-point Bodoni and 11-point Century. That is, a 12-point capital letter in one typeface could be a different size than the same letter in the same size in a different typeface, and neither would measure 12 points high.

Figure 31–2. Baseline, cap height, and x-height.

Styles and Families

A particular style of type—Times Roman, Frutiger, Palatino—is called a *face.* Traditionally, the complete collection of all the letters, symbols, and figures in a typeface *in a particular size* was called a *font,* but today font (or more loosely, *family*) generally refers to a typeface's entire collection of sizes, weights, special characters, and any variations, such as book, italic, bold, or condensed. The word *family* is also used to describe groupings of typefaces of similar styles.

The different typefaces can be broadly classified into three divisions. *Serif* faces are characterized by finishing strokes on letterforms. Faces lacking these finishing strokes are called *sans serif* (*sans* is French for "without"). The third major category, known by the descriptive label *miscellaneous* or the somewhat more helpful *decorative,* comprises novelty typefaces as well as formal and informal *scripts* or *cursives* and faces that emulate old English and German calligraphic lettering. The faces in this last category are reserved for special effects in advertising, book jackets, posters, and so on.

❧

SERIF OR SANS SERIF

There are many opinions about the choice between the two major groups of typefaces—serif and sans serif—and much of the discussion focuses on readability. A time-honored rule dictates the use of serif type for body text, especially in longer works, because in certain studies subjects have found serif type easier to read than sans serif.

A theory behind that rule is that the horizontal *stress*—contrast between thick and thin strokes, which draws the eye in a certain direction—created by a line of serif type contributes to superior readability. On the other hand, it has been found that people find most readable the typestyles they're most used to seeing. In other words, children who grow up on Helvetica will find sans serif type easy to read.

Custom, too, plays a role in decisions about typefaces. People may feel comfortable with a geometry textbook set in sans serif type, but they wouldn't want to read a novel in the same face. A general rule is that serif faces are perceived as more formal and traditional than sans serif. Sans serif body text is found more frequently in scientific or technical works; serif, in the humanities and works of fiction.

FACE

Garamond

FONT

ABCDEFGHIJKLMNOPQRSTUVWXYZ abcdefghijklmnopqrstuvwxyz ABCDEFGHIJKLMNOPQRSTUVWXYZ 1234567890$(&?.,:;"-""!)ﬀﬁﬂﬃﬄ

FAMILY

ABCDEFGHIJKLMNOPQRSTUVWXYZ

italic

ABCDEFGHIJKLMNOPQRSTUVWXYZ

condensed

ABCDEFGHIJKLMNOPQRSTUVWXYZ

book

ABCDEFGHIJKLMNOPQRSTUVWXYZ

bold

Figure 31–3. Face, font, and family. Here is a sample of the varieties of a face that would be included in a type family. Not every face has the same varieties, and some have more than others.

❧

A CASE FOR METAL TYPE

When your third-grade teacher admonished you to "mind your *p*'s and *q*'s," probably neither of you knew that the phrase's origin dates back to the early days of typesetting. After metal type was set and printed, the individual characters had to be taken from the forms and sorted into their proper drawers in the type case—the capital letters in the upper case, the rest in the lower case, the origin of our terms *uppercase* and *lowercase*—ready to be used again. Because *p* and *q* each have a round shape and a descender and because metal type reads backward, special care was needed to make sure the *p*'s and *q*'s ended up in the right type box.

HOW TYPE IS USED

The Typographic Plan

The basis of any graphic design is the typographic plan, which provides a translation of the text into type. To prepare the typographic plan, the designer takes into account the *head schedule*—the hierarchical organization of parts, chapters, heads, subheads—and all of the special text treatments—lists, extracts, footnotes—that are required by the manuscript and organizes them into a coherent design.

The editor should provide the designer with a written description of the publication's purpose, audience, tone, structure, trim size (the size of the final printed pages, including all margins), and other unique elements, along with any particular preferences or prohibitions. A designer who is given this information, however, should not consider it a substitute for a personal reading and understanding of the text.

The head levels and special type treatments should be designed in relation to the text type, which is the graphic foundation of the typographic plan. Text type is selected to complement and underscore the overall tone and purpose of the text and to achieve the length required. The other type treatments should support this with variety and contrast—different enough to be distinctive, but not so different as to send a conflicting or confusing message. The typographic plan should make clear to the reader what is most important.

Although the selection of an appropriate typeface and point size is an extremely important aspect of design, just as critical are decisions about vertical and horizontal spacing and justification of lines. For centuries type was made of metal and composed line by line. The typesetter inserted lead strips of varying thicknesses between the lines for vertical spacing; today the spacing between lines is still referred to as *leading* (pronounced "led-ding"). The most common formula specifies spacing between lines to be 120 percent of the point size of the type; in the most commonly used text type sizes, this comes to about 2 extra points of leading between lines—for example, 10-point type with 2 points of leading, referred to as 10 on 12 or 10/12. The amount of leading is also determined by the characteristics of the typeface selected. Lines of text in a typeface with a large x-height will appear closer together than equally spaced lines of text with a smaller x-height.

In computerized horizontal spacing, the programmed setting of space between individual characters and words is known as *tracking;* this governs the overall "tightness" or "looseness" of the line. Manipulating the horizontal spacing of a line to a pleasing arrangement is referred to as *letterspacing.* For visual harmony, certain pairs of letters have traditionally been more closely fitted together—*kerned*—so that they appear properly spaced in a line of text. Most film typefaces and desktop publishing and typesetting programs include *kerning pairs,* or certain combinations of letters, numbers, and punctuation that are automatically spaced more tightly, with one character extending into the space of its partner. In hot metal typesetting, certain pairs were coupled on one mold, called a *ligature;* examples include *fi, fl,* and *ff.* Ligatures are less commonly seen today—often available only in special versions of electronic typefaces—but they remain a mark of high-quality typography.

Justification refers to the margins of the type page. Left-justified or *flush left* type aligns at the left margin; *flush right* type is the mirror image of flush left. *Justified* type, the most common arrangement of type on a page, aligns at both the right and left margins. An irregular margin is called *ragged*—ragged right or ragged left, depending on which side is irregular. This arrangement is commonly used in brochures, children's books, and informal pieces. In justified text, the spaces between words must be stretched and shrunk as necessary to align on the right margin. Word spacing is constant in unjustified text, however, and many designers believe that this uniform spacing means improved readability. End-of-line hyphenation, a necessity and sometimes a cause of problems in justified text, is often avoided in ragged right settings.

The width of the text area from the left to right margin is known as the *measure* and is expressed in picas. Instructions for justified type set on a measure of 20 picas would read "flush left and right on 20 picas." For left-justified text, a designer will sometimes give a range of acceptable line lengths to avoid excessive raggedness.

P. T. Y.

PA TA WA

Ta Te To Tr Tu Tw Ty Wa We Wo Ya Yo

yo we

ff fi fl ffi ffl

Figure 31–4. Some common kerning pairs (top lines) and ligatures (bottom line).

Typesetting Principles

Effective use of space is basic to good typography. The arrangement of type should invite the reader into the page and make the words easy to read and follow. Proper spacing—between letters, words, lines, paragraphs, and other elements of text—is a basic part of effective typographic design.

Spacing should enhance clarity. Excessively tight or loose letterspacing and word spacing inhibits readability because the shapes of individual words become distorted; recognition of those shapes speeds the deciphering of combinations of letters. For the same reason, blocks of type in all caps are more difficult to read than caps and lowercase; use of all caps should be kept to a minimum. A similar warning applies to extensive use of italics.

Leading, or the space between lines, should be sufficient to give each line breathing room. Excessively spaced lines, however, lose their relation to one another, causing the reader's eye to wander between the end of one line and the beginning of the next.

Length of the line is also crucial to readability, and it should always be considered in relation to the size of the type being used. For this reason, ideal line length is usually thought of in terms of number of characters per line (including spaces and punctuation marks) rather than the absolute length; optimum line length is generally 40 to 50 characters for multiple-column text and 45 to 75 characters for single-column pages. Fewer than 30 characters per line creates too many line breaks and often too much hyphenation for comfortable reading; lines of 80 or more characters cause difficulty in reading smoothly from one line to the next. In terms of picas, the line length is usually about 30 times the point size of the type, so that a good line length for 12-point type might be around 30 picas (12 times 30 equals 360 points, divided by 12—the number of points in a pica—equals 30 picas).

Breaks between paragraphs should be indicated by one of two—but not both—styles: either extra line spacing (usually 3 points) or a paragraph indent (usually 1 or 2 ems). It is common practice not to indent the first paragraph after a head when using the indent style.

TYPESETTING PITFALLS

Avoiding a few common typesetting pitfalls will produce more effective results in most publications.

- *Don't hyphenate headlines.* Breaking up words in large type slows comprehension by creating ugly, nonsensical word fragments. If there is a frequent need to hyphenate heads, the type is probably too large for the material.
- *Don't justify headlines even if the rest of the text is justified.* There usually aren't enough words on a line to justify, so justifying introduces great gaps of space.
- *Put more space above heads than below them.* A head that is equidistant from the text that precedes and follows it doesn't visually "belong" to either. The head should be clearly tied to the text it introduces.
- *Break headlines logically and evenly.* When possible, break at connecting words rather than in the middle of a phrase. And don't leave one word of a head stranded on one line of a two-line head; lines of roughly equal length are easier to read and more pleasing to the eye. In most cases breaking a head so that the longer line is on the bottom provides a more balanced and stable feel to the layout.
- *Don't justify text type on a short measure.* Justification of short lines of type causes large gaps that, in a column of text, can create visual "pools" and "rivers" of white space.
- *Don't underscore in text.* Underlining is a typewriter convention that translates to italic type in typesetting. It has been traditionally used on typewriters simply because italics aren't available.
- *Keep text hyphenation under control.* More than two successive end-of-line hyphens will derail a reader's smooth absorption of the text. Some purists will balk at two; some styles will allow three. Editors of promotional copy often decide on no hyphenation at all, although this format may require some copyediting after typesetting to take care of extremely short lines.

TYPESETTING MECHANICS

The steps in typesetting vary somewhat according to the technology being used and the type of piece being produced, but in principle the process remains the same—setting the designer's typographic plan in stages; anticipating and resolving problems at each stage; and finishing with a complete, accurate, and readable publication.

In traditional or hot metal typesetting, the first stage was to set the manuscript in *galleys,* which were long frames that held many lines of text. Thus the first typesetting proofs are sometimes still called *galley proofs* or simply *galleys;* they contain the type set as marked but in the form of running text, not formatted as pages. It is increasingly common, however, to see *first-pass pages* as the first proofs; here the type is set in pages, perhaps even with running heads in place, but it is understood that these proofs are not the final pages and that text may still shift from page to page in subsequent versions.

In shorter pieces, typesetting will usually go directly from manuscript to galleys or first-pass pages. The economics of book production, however, usually requires a preliminary calculation to determine the number of pages in the book before the type is actually set. Known as a *castoff,* this process involves determining the number of characters in the manuscript and, using *characters per pica (cpp)* for the specified typeface, the width of line, the number of lines per page, and other design information, calculating the number of pages in the book. In other areas of design, such as advertising, where the exact placement of lines and even specific words is critical, a similar exercise—known as *copyfitting*—is sometimes performed to anticipate the final layout. Designers today, however, are more likely to experiment with their layout on a computer screen.

In desktop publishing applications, page layout information—margins, columns, page break rules, and so on—is included in the electronic style specifications that are set when the design is created. Therefore, the first pass at setting the manuscript more closely resembles finished pages than traditional galley proofs. Nevertheless, these first-pass pages must be treated like galleys—thoroughly proofread, revised, and fine-tuned through subsequent passes before they can be considered final.

Type Specification

Whether the manuscript is sent out to a typesetter for composition or set in house using a desktop publishing system, it must carry with it complete type specifications, summarized in a *specification sheet.* This sheet includes the estimated number of final pages, the size of the type page (trim size), typeface, point size, leading, line length, indention, justification, and extra space above and below certain elements, such as heads, *for every type*

REVISED SPECIFICATIONS JOB NO. 2985(FP)
THE NEW YORK PUBLIC LIBRARY
WRITER'S GUIDE TO STYLE AND USAGE
Harper Reference

Trim Size: 6⅛″ x 9¼″
Page Size: 27 x 47 picas, including 2.3 picas for running head
Margins: 7/16″ Head; 7/8″ Gutter
Text Type: 10½/12½ Caledonia x 27 picas
Number of lines per page: 43
Number of lines on Chapter Opening: 28
Part Titles: Will begin new pages right
Part Number: 14 pt. Baskerville Bold caps, (spell out number) ltr. spaced 2 pts., 2½ pica sink, centered, with ½ pt rule x 6 picas, centered, 1 pica visual space below
Part Title: 36 on 36 Baskerville caps, ctr., 7 pica sink
Part Introduction: backs PT/Head: set as (CT) for regular text
First Line of all Intros: Initial Cap only, Flush left. 28 lines as on Chapter Opening pages
Chapters will begin on new right pages with chapter titles and chapter contents. Actual chapter text opens following the contents, new right with CT repeated. 2 picas space below to COQ; 1st text line sinks 19 picas from top to base.
(CN) Chapter Numbers: Sink 2-1/2 picas to 14 pt. Baskerville Bold Arabic lining figs. 2 pts ltr. spaced, ½ pt rule x 6 picas, centered, 1 pica visual space below
(CT) Chapter Titles: Sink 7 picas from top to CT, 24/24 Baskerville caps, centered
(CCNT) Chapter Contents: 10½/12½ as marked. First line of chapter contents sinks as first chapter line (19 picas from top of rh to base of 1st line)
(CA) Head: (in contents): 10½ point Caledonia Bold caps & lc, flush left; 1 line space above
(CB) Head: 10/12½ point Caledonia small caps, flush left
(CC) Head: 10/12½ point Caledonia italic, upper/lower case, indents 18 points; turns indent an additional 18 pts
CCNT folios: 10½ point italic Modern non-lining figs, preceded by 18 points (folio sets in bf italic after CA heads). No page folio on first page of CCNT
Note: Some chapter openings contents pages are short, some will run 2–3 pages
Chapter Opening Quote: 10/12 Caledonia Italic, upper/lower case x 24 picas, indent 1½ picas left and right. 7 pica sink, quotes hang
Sources: names set in 9 pt. small caps, with roman upper/lower case as marked on m.s.
Chapter Opening Initial: opening initial 10½ pt. Cal cap flush left

Figure 31–5. The first three pages of the type specification sheet developed for this book.

Drop Folio: Caledonia 9 pt. at foot, 2 picas base to base, flush outside
Poetry: 10/12 Caledonia italic set line for line align left, indent 18 points from left, ½ line space above and below
HEADS:
(A) 9/12½ point Caledonia Bold caps, 1 point letterspaced, 2 lines space above, 1 line space below (when followed by B Head, 8 pts. space below). Text following begins flush left (turnovers ctr. on measure)
(B) 10½/12½ point Caledonia bold italic caps and lc, 18 pt space above, 7 pts. space below, flush left; text following begins flush left (turnovers flush left)
(C) 10½ point Caledonia italic, upper/lower case, flush left, with 1 line space above. ½ line space below when not run-in. Text begins flush left
(E) Text Example: 10/12 Caledonia x 27 picas, indent 18 pts left, with turns indented an additional 18 pts. 1/2 line space above and below.
(EXT) Text Extract: 10/12 x 27 picas, indent 18 pts on left, ½ line space above and below
UNL in text: 10/12 Cal. Indent 18 pts from left. Turns indent additional 18 pts
NL in Text: 10½/12½ Caledonia x 27 picas, indent 18 pts at left to number, followed by word space, turnovers indent 18 pts, 1 line space above and below, 2 em space between columns
BL in Text; 10½/12½ x 27 picas, indent 18 pts at left and hang 3 pt. bullets. Align t.o.'s with first lines. Word space between bullet and text. 1 line space above and below BL
NL in Examples: 10/12 x 27, indent a total of 3 picas from left. Turnovers indent an additional 18 pts. Word Space between number and text.
BL in examples: 10/12 x 27, indent turns 3 picas flush left and hang 3 pt. bullets. Turns align with first line above. Word space between bullet and text
(CH) UNL Column Heads: 10/12 Caledonia italic, C&lc, 4 pts space below, align left on column
Sidebars: By 24 picas, centered on 27 picas
(ST) Sidebar Title: Caledonia esc, 9 on 12 point centered, 12 points space above to 12 pt leaf ornament, 6 points above ornament to hairline rule x 24 picas
(STXT) Sidebar Text: 10/12 x 24 with 1/2 line below to extract/example
(SEXT) Sidebar Extract: 9½/11 indented 18 pts on left, with 1/2 line space above and below
(SE) Sidebar Example: indent 18 pts on left, turns indent additional 18 pts. Hairline rule x 24 picas 6 pts above and below to text.
Position sidebars at top or bottom of pages, but avoid breaking over pages. Do not position 2 sidebars on the same page. 2 lines space above or below sidebar to text.
(SNL) Sidebar Numbered Lists. 10/12 x 24 picas; indent text 18 pts from flush left. Word space between numbers and text, turns indent 18 pts

Figure 31–5. The first three pages of the type specification sheet developed for this book (continued).

SBL: Sidebar Bulleted Lists: 10/12 x 24 picas. Indent 18 pts at left and hang 3 pt. bullets. Turns align with first line above. Word space between bullet and text

SB: B-Head. 10/12 italic C&lc, 8 pts space above, 4 pts space below. Flush left. Text following sets flush left

SUNL: Sidebar Unnumbered Lists: 9½/11 x 24. Indent 18 pts from flush left. Turns indent additional 18 points

(EQ) Equations: 10½ x 12½ Caledonia with math symbols as in manuscript, 1 line space above and below; indent 18 pts from left

Chapter 21: Confusables: sets in double column: 10/12 x 12.75 picas per column, with 18 points space between columns. Alphabetical breaks are 11 point Caledonia initials, indent 18 points on left; in 2 lines space, with 1/2 line space below

Text charts: x 24 picas

Chart Head: 9 point Caledonia Bold caps, 1 point letterspaced, centered, 6 points space above to ½-point rule x 24 picas

Compounding Chart: has varied heads and rules, please follow marking on manuscript.

(CTXT) Chart Text: 10/12

Boxes: x 24 picas

Box Title: 9 point Caledonia Bold caps, 1 point letterspaced, centered

Box subtitle (BST): 9/12 italic C&lc. ctr on line below title

Box Text: 10/12 x 24 picas

Box Heads: 10/12 Caledonia Bold italic c&lc, flush left. No additional space below

Box Examples: 9½/11 x 24 picas, indent 18 pts left. No additional space between entries. Turns indent 18 pts additional

Rules at top of box: hairline rule x 24 picas, center on 27 picas, Box title centers, 6 points space to first line of box text, 12 points space to end of box, which will have a rule when box text is completed.

Captions: 9½/11 Caledonia italic x 27 picas, flush left, 1 line space above

Tables:

(TN) Table Number (TT) Table Title: Run-in 9/11, center x 27 picas

(TCH) Table Column Head: Body size italic with 4 pts below

(TB) Table Body: Size on Table 3 with 1 pt less leading

(TFN&TS) Table Footnote & Table Source: 8/10 Caledonia x 27, block style, turnovers align on first word above with 4 pts additional space between TFN and TS

Running Heads: Left: chapter title; 9 point Caledonia small caps, 1 point letterspaced, centered

Right: A head: 9 point Caledonia italic, upper/lower case, centered

Folios: 9 point Caledonia lining Bold figures, flush outside in head. 6 pts space below to hairline rule x 27, 1 line space below rule to text

Paragraph Indent: 18 points

Prepared by
Pagesetters Inc., Brattleboro, VT
Revised 5MAY1994

Figure 31–5. The first three pages of the type specification sheet developed for this book (continued).

❧

THE FACE IS FAMILIAR . . .

Although typeface names can be trademarked, the letterforms themselves are not protected by law; thus, it is possible for software companies and type foundries to market their own version of a particular face using different names. Is the type you want Swiss or Helvetica? Times Roman or Dutch? The answer in both cases is "yes." And just as photocomposition renditions look slightly different from their hot metal precursors, there will be variations, usually most noticeable in spacing and weight, in the same typeface set in different vendors' versions of it.

element in the manuscript. Additional specifications may be required for special treatments like rules, tables, or equations.

In so-called traditional *mark-up* the typesetter receives a hard copy of the manuscript with the type specifications (or *specs,* pronounced "specks") written in by hand or typed up and accompanied by layout sheets.

Because today's electronic files are readily transferable, it is no longer necessary to rekey the manuscript into the typesetting system, as was regularly done well into the 1970s. Instead, the operator generally translates the manual mark-up into codes accepted by the system and keys those into the text file submitted by the customer.

Writers and editors for publications with formats that vary little from issue to issue often code the disk themselves before giving it to the typesetter. In this case, the typesetter acts as a service bureau and simply provides type from the output device for a fee without making any changes to the customer's electronic file.

Desktop publishing programs provide the same functions but make it easier to achieve the desired typesetting effects. These programs immediately translate commands into a WYSIWYG (what you see is what you get, pronounced "whizzy wig") display that clearly represents the actual page, allowing for easy revision and correction before a hard copy of the type is printed out.

Photocomposition Versus Laser Type

Desktop publishing applications, with the use of high-resolution laser printers, have brought "typesetting" capabilities to many production and publishing offices. Although type from laser printers is sometimes used as camera-ready copy because it is fast and relatively inexpensive to produce, its graphic quality is lower than that of type produced by photocomposition. (See Chapter 33, Printing, for further discussion.)

Desktop users who need a higher level of type resolution can use the laser printer through the production process to generate page proofs. When the text and layouts are absolutely final, they can then send their files to a service bureau to be output by a high-resolution typesetting machine that generates complete camera-ready pages, crop marks and all.

The tools of the typographer's craft are increasingly available with today's sophisticated desktop publishing programs, but the ability to produce attractive, professional-looking typeset materials doesn't come so easily. An understanding of the principles of design and typography should be a continuing pursuit for anyone who works with words, as technology brings writers and editors closer than ever to the process of putting those words into print.

❧

SPECIAL CHARACTERS

Complete type fonts include a number of special characters—Greek letters and symbols used in math and science work, for example, and accented characters used in foreign language texts—beyond those found on the standard typewriter or computer keyboard. When type is set traditionally, the insertion of such characters must be specified by the editor.

In desktop publishing software, these characters are produced by inserting special codes into the file. The manuals that come with these programs usually include code tables and instructions for inserting special characters. When preparing texts that include extensive use of mathematical expressions or foreign languages, it is best to use software created especially for those applications.

32

THE PRODUCTION PROCESS

THE PRODUCTION PROCESS

To those outside, the production of publications often seems a mysterious process. Somehow a manuscript, that basic vehicle for words and ideas, becomes an object—a tangible *thing* of dimension, weight, and color. To many, it seems that turning manuscript into finished publication takes an inconceivably long time, usually because they lack knowledge of the many steps involved in bringing about the transformation.

PLANNING, SCHEDULING, AND ESTIMATING

Planning, scheduling, and estimating are the very essence of production. Before a copyeditor picks up a pencil, before a designer makes a sketch, their work should be directed by a clearly thought-out plan. This plan guides the entire project, ensuring that each individual's time and effort are effectively and efficiently applied.

Planning is not a one-time task; the staggering number of details and variables involved in production makes it impossible to simply set a project in motion and expect it to run like clockwork. The individual responsible for production management must constantly keep one eye on the plan, re-evaluating assumptions and making interim adjustments as needed.

Assessing the Project

Most production departments have standard procedures for completing their work. An effective production plan, though, makes no assumptions and takes into consideration the particular demands of each project. The more information gathered at the outset, the more realistic the production plan will be.

The first step is to gather the vital information about the manuscript:

- *Physical properties*—Number of pages; number of photographs and illustrations, if any; form of the manuscript (disk or hard copy only); whether it contains text only or text plus technical and tabular copy. This information will help in assessing the type of editing required and the amount of time the editing will take.
- *Other uses*—Whether the publication will be indexed, abridged, or made available for electronic retrieval or as an online or CD/ROM edition. These are issues that can have an impact on the way electronic files are prepared for publication.
- *Publication data*—Number of copies being produced, printing method, and desired publication date. This information will be used to select vendors and determine staff requirements.
- *Budget requirements*—The prescribed maximum length for a book, dictated by the printing budget, affects both the editor's task in keeping the manuscript to a certain length and the designer's in developing type specifications that will allow the book to be laid out within those parameters.

This information supplies the basic framework needed to determine requirements for staff, equipment, and outside services. A comprehensive production plan, however, goes beyond specific tasks and includes the organizational and strategic details of the project; this information further refines the goals of the project, better defines time frames, and provides the production manager with a clearer context within which to make decisions. Such planning is extremely important; problems with the finished publication that seem on the surface to be technical mistakes can often be traced to poorly communicated project requirements.

Besides knowing the proposed publication date, a production manager should also understand the significance of that date. In the case of a book, is the publication date tied to an event that will boost sales significantly? Does the book have only seasonal appeal? Knowing whether a publication date is crucial, flexible by a few days, or simply a broad target makes it possible to gauge whether there is any flexibility in the schedule.

Also important is an understanding of production priorities: Which is most important—low cost, high editorial quality, production speed, or all three? In other words, what is the person or company funding the project willing to pay for in terms of overall quality, appearance, and publication date?

A final critical issue in planning and scheduling is clarifying approval procedures and authority. Lack of information in this area, probably more than any other, can wreak havoc with the production schedule and the level of effort expended. For instance, if a person with veto authority is not included in the review and approval of rough layouts, finished artwork may have to be redone when that person sees the art and wants to make changes.

Knowing who has to see what when—and to what degree that person is authorized to make changes—can make the difference between a workable, realistic production schedule and one that keeps breaking down.

Estimating Time and Costs

The information gathered in the early stages of planning makes it possible to break the project down into individual tasks and to establish the order in which those tasks should be performed. Once this step is accomplished, the production manager can determine the amount of time that will be needed to complete these tasks in house, as well as the costs and time associated with any tasks to be performed by outside suppliers.

Tasks to Be Performed in House. Estimating in-house time is an often-neglected area of production planning. In some companies, there is a tendency to think of in-house time as free or infinitely flexible; besides contributing to poor staff morale, this notion often results in wasted time, an absence of priorities, and chaotic planning.

PRODUCTIVITY STANDARDS

Productivity standards for in-house work, which can be based initially on experience and refined over time, can be an effective tool for planning and scheduling. Used intelligently—in other words, flexibly, not as a management club—such standards can provide a framework for managing workflow, distributing the workload, and clarifying expectations and goals.

Some middle-of-the-road industry standards follow, although particular jobs may require adjustments up or down, depending on the length of average documents, the level of technical difficulty, and whether the staff members involved work exclusively on a specific task or have other responsibilities. Pages here are defined as double-spaced typewritten manuscript containing about 250 words.

Word processing input—8 pages/hour
Computer graphic/medium complexity—1.5 hours
Electronic page layout—10 pages/hour
Electronic coding—25 pages/hour
Copyediting—5 pages/hour
Proofreading—10 pages/hour
Pasteup—10 typeset pages/hour (with color breaks, 7 pages/hour; page layouts from galleys, 5 pages/hour)
Sizing and cropping art and photos—4 pieces/hour

Tasks to Be Contracted to Outside Vendors. The key to accurate cost estimates for such services as typesetting, printing, and photography is providing the vendor with the most complete information possible. It is important to go back to the vendor for a revised estimate if the original specifications of the job change significantly during the production process. A good practice is to document the assumptions made in preparing the quote; these provide a baseline for comparison as the job progresses. It is important, too, to clarify such matters as whether there is an additional charge for proofs, how many sets are included in the standard charge, whether delivery charges (of drafts or proofs, as well as the final product) are included in the estimated costs, and what constitutes—as well as what charges will be made for—alterations.

Estimates from vendors should cover time as well as costs. It is also important to know whether the supplier can provide rush service and, if so, the supplier's definition of a rush and any extra charges involved. The added flexibility of being able to request rush service can often be well worth a surcharge; a well-prepared production manager will try to become aware of as many such service vendors as possible because they are the key to performing flexibly in a tight schedule.

Setting the Production Schedule

The framework of any production schedule consists of major *milestones,* points that measure the progress of the job from start to finish. The most obvious and important milestone is the final deadline; very often the other milestones in the schedule are points at which drafts or proofs are submitted for review and approval. For every one of these submittal deadlines, there must also be a deadline for the reviewers to respond, or the rest of the schedule becomes meaningless.

There are two ways to approach a production schedule: forward or backward. The first is the easier of the two, for it simply starts with today and assigns completion dates to each milestone based on the time estimates gathered during planning. The second is the more common, usually because of an immovable final deadline; the trick then becomes finding a way to compress 30 days of work into 10, by dividing tasks and overlapping operations where possible.

THE PRODUCTION CYCLE

Prepress production is a term that describes the numerous tasks and processes needed to bring the publication or other printed piece to fruition in a form that a printer can use for reproduction.

Traditional prepress production procedures are roughly similar to the

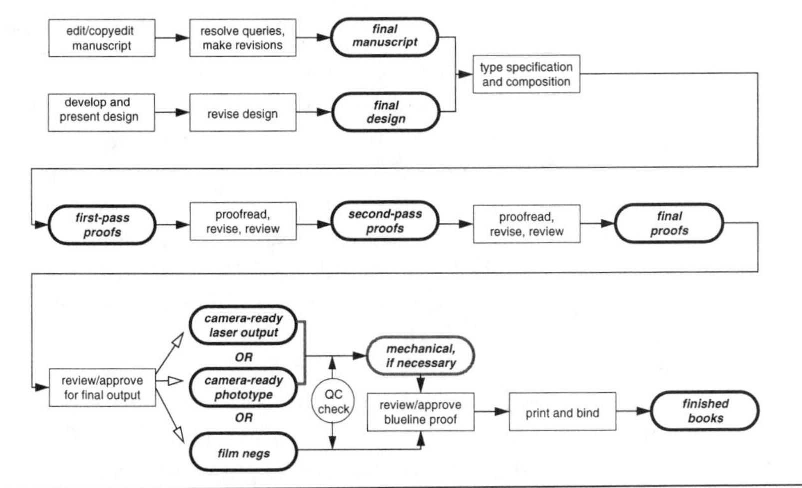

Figure 32–1. The basic steps in the production process.

steps in electronic production, even though the end products of each traditional step may be different from those in the electronic operation. In both cases, the process can be seen as steps on a linear flow chart. What the chart does not capture, however, is that each step is highly dependent upon the step that precedes it.

THE RIGHT TIME AND PLACE

The guiding principle of efficient production is to find the best point to do any given task—that is, the time at which there is the least possibility that that task will have to be substantially revised or even completely redone. It doesn't make sense to typeset a book before the copyediting is done because the text may be significantly edited or revised and much of it would have to be set again. If page layouts are completed before the typesetting is proofed and checked, there is a good possibility that corrections will make it necessary to redo much of that work. In some production departments, especially those that have recently converted to desktop publishing, a great deal of effort is often expended in laying out draft manuscript in complicated page formats, an unnecessary initial investment of time that in turn makes editing, proofreading, and final formatting more complicated and time consuming—and thus more expensive.

Copyediting

On the road from draft manuscript to camera-ready mechanicals, copyediting is the critical first step. The copyeditor corrects grammatical, punctuation, spelling, and style errors and may tighten, reword, or rework sentences, all of which make the text easier for the reader to understand. The copyeditor also checks formatting and marks up the manuscript for the word processor, desktop publishing operator, or typesetter (for reasons of convenience, the term *typesetter* will be used throughout this chapter to mean the person making changes to the electronic file). Note that on hard copy all of the copyeditor's marks are made in the text, between the lines of the double-spaced manuscript.

Because the copyeditor is usually and ideally a person unfamiliar with the manuscript, copyediting will sometimes unearth underlying flaws and inconsistencies in logic, organization, or content; the copyeditor should query these points. In some instances, especially in book publishing, another editor—known variously as the content editor, substantive editor, acquisitions editor, or line editor—will have worked on the manuscript before it went to the copyeditor. This editor looks at larger issues such as content, logic, organization, tone, and completeness, often working directly with the author and reworking and reorganizing as necessary.

During editing, the copyeditor should compile a style sheet that notes the style and spelling decisions made; this sheet should follow the manuscript through production, serving as a reference for proofreaders and others involved in production. Also during editing such items as cross-references that will need to be verified or completed later in the process should be flagged in the manuscript. A consistent identification system makes last-minute insertions of final page numbers and other cross-reference numbers easy to manage. Inserting characters that wouldn't normally occur in text—$$$, ???, or XXX, for example—is often a good way to flag text cross-references, since they will stand out visually to an editor or proofreader and can also serve as a search string for finding cross-references electronically, using the search-and-replace feature in word processing and desktop publishing software. Some desktop publishing programs allow the insertion of "live links" between cross-references and their sources, making last-minute updating a less tedious process. The copyedited manuscript, with all queries resolved, is now the master manuscript, or manuscript of reference. This is the copy that the typesetter or desktop publishing operator will work from and the proofreader will read against.

As the manuscript proceeds through production, editors may participate in decisions about graphic presentation and layout to ensure that the manuscript's original intent and content remain intact. A balance must be

Background on Copyright

The first legislation on copyright was an Act of Parliament passed in Britain in 1907, aimed at preventing scrupulous book-sellers from publishing works without the consgent of the authors. It provided that the author of a book had the soul right of publication for a term of twenty-one years, and the penalty for infringement was a penny a sheet. The British Copyright Law was amended and changed in 1801 (the fine went up to three-pence a sheet), and again in 1842. In 1887 a group of Nations, which was not including the US ratified the Berne Union copyright convention, which required members of said group to have minimum standards of copyright protection and applying them equally to all citizens of all the nations that are all represented.

In the U.S.A., copyright found its protection in the constitution (Article One, section 1, Clause eight), ratified in 1879. In 1790, seperate legislation on copyright was enacted. The copyright Law was revised and altered again in 1831, 1870, 1909, 1976 and 1978, and the 1978 Law was amended in 1890.

Figure 32–2. A sample edited page.

Editor's Checklist

A. General Procedures Required on All Jobs

- Write neatly and legibly using a dark black pencil.
- Use standard editing marks.
- Show additions and changes above the lines, not below.
- Make alphabetical list of all words in ms. about which you have made a choice of treatment re: consistency in hyphens, caps, abbreviations, etc.
- Number all pages sequentially. Indicate added pages by adding a, b, c, etc., to the preceding page number.

B. Minimal Copyediting Tasks on All Jobs

1. ______Review and correct spelling, grammar, and punctuation.
2. ______Correct inconsistencies in capitalization, compounding, number style, abbreviations, use of italics or underscores, and sequence of anything alphabetical or numerical.
3. ______Point out, but do *not* rewrite, awkward, turgid, confusing sections.
4. ______Point out, but do not fix, major organizational problems.

C. Additional Copyediting Tasks Specified for This Job

5. ______Check heads in text and tables against table of contents; make the same or query.
6. ______Make table of contents. ______Make list of tables.
7. ______Format. ______Renumber footnotes. ______Renumber pages. ______Mark heads (A,B,C; 1,2,3; etc.) ______Add typesetter instructions. Other: ________
8. ______Mark end-of-line hyphens to be deleted or retained.
9. ______Put into a specific style. ________
10. ______Put all tables in consistent, proper form; ensure parallelism.
11. ______Check parallelism throughout text; rewrite to make parallel.
12. ______Check pronouns; check for clear antecedents; replace with nouns or rewrite.
13. ______Check passive constructions; when appropriate, replace with active voice.
14. ______Eliminate smothered verbs. ______Rewrite to break up noun strings.
15. ______Remove first person throughout. ______Remove except for preface/foreword.
16. ______Eliminate sexist language.
17. ______Explain unfamiliar abbreviations at first mention.
18. ______Substitute one word for many; short words for long.
19. ______Make sure all referenced matter (tables, charts, etc.) follows its first callout.
20. ______Check cross references for accuracy and consistency.
21. ______Put bibliography and footnotes in consistent format.

D. Heavier, More Substantive Editing, Rewriting, and Related Tasks

22. ______Check math, numbers, problems, answers to questions in exercises.
23. ______Check text descriptions of tables against information in tables.
24. ______Review whole manuscript for sentences and paragraphs that can be eliminated.
25. ______Add or delete heads and subheads as necessary.
26. ______Check organization and reorganize if necessary.
27. ______Rewrite awkward, turgid, confusing sections.
28. ______Review logic of arguments; look for weak points.
29. ______Write transitions.
30. ______Write summaries (______for chapters/sections; ______for entire document).
31. ______Check accuracy of content (editor is expected to be familiar with subject).

Figure 32–3. An editor's checklist defines specific editing tasks, organizes work for the editor, and provides documentation for the project.

Instructions	**Editing Marks** (in text only)	**Proofmarks** (in text and margin)	
Operations			
Delete	to err is yhuman	to err is yhuman	
	to err is ~~not~~ human	to err is ~~not~~ human	
Delete & close up	to err is humyan	to err is humyan	
Insert	to err human (is)	to err human	is
		(for a long out)	out, see copy, p.x
Insert & close up	to er is uman (cr hc)	to er is uman	cr/hc
Replace	to err it human (s)	to err it human	s
	to ~~hum~~ is human (err)	to ~~hum~~ is human	err
Transpose	to err human is	to err human is	tr
	to err is uhman	to err is uhman	tr
	(or)	(or)	
	to err is uhman (hu)	to err is uhman	h/u
Special Marks			
Message ring: Don't set ringed explanation in type	(Same as proofmark)	Ring around message for example: $5	$ set dollar sign
Let it stand (ignore marked correction)	To ~~err~~ is human (stet)	To ~~err~~ is human	stet
Query to author	(Same as proofmark)	To roar is human	err (?)
		(or)	
		To roar is human	err?
Counting slashes	(Not applicable)	Example: Mke sme correction consecutively as many times as slashes	a//
Spell out	2nd Ave.	2nd Ave.	sp
Abbreviate or use symbol	Second Avenue	~~Second Avenue~~	2nd Ave.
End of document	*end* (or) *30* (or) #	(Same as editing mark)	
Retain hyphen at end of line	...twenty- six letters	(Same as editing mark)	
Delete line-end hyphen & close up word	...mis- takes do happen	...mis- takes do happen	

Figure 32–4. Editing and proofreading marks compared. Editing marks are placed directly in the text and are the most practical method of marking when there is room for them, as in double-spaced manuscript. Proofreading marks are used in single-spaced and typeset copy; a mark is made in text to show the location of the correction, and the instruction for the correction is made in the margin.

Source: *Mark My Words: Instruction and Practice in Proofreading,* 2nd ed., by Peggy Smith (EEI, 1993).

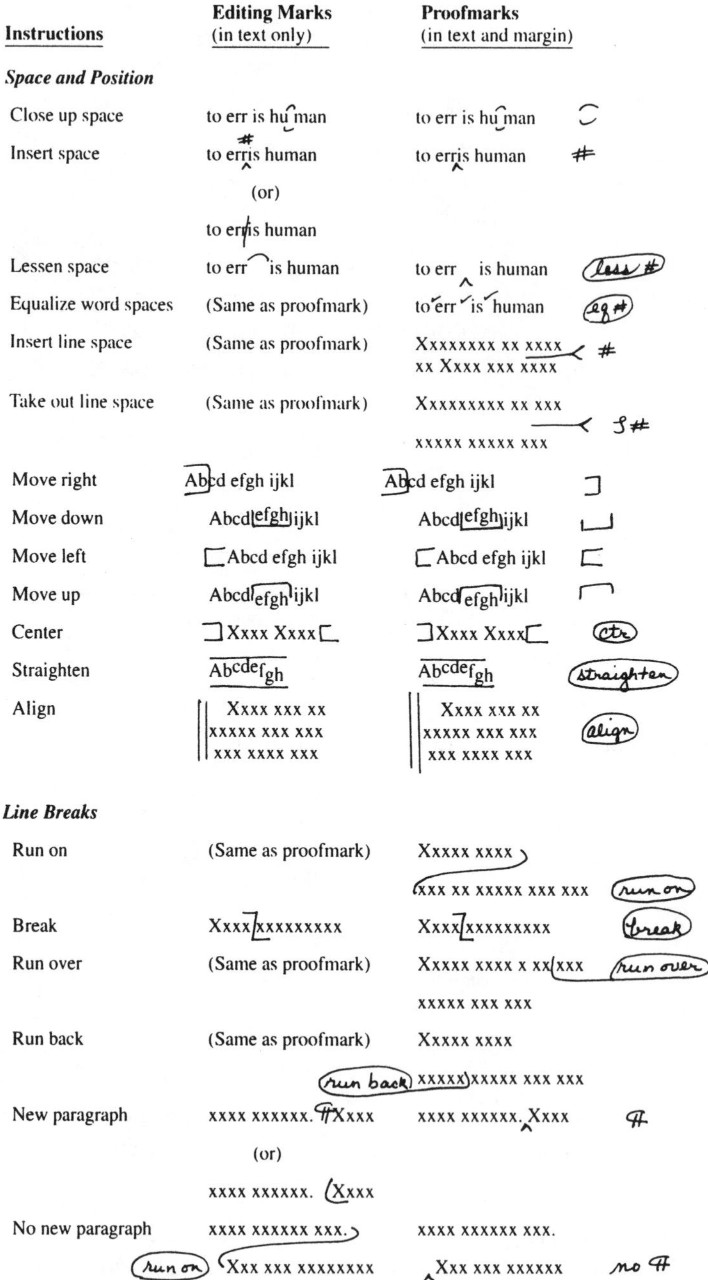

Instructions	Editing Marks (in text only)	Proofmarks (in text and margin)	
Space and Position			
Close up space	to err is hu man	to err is hu man	⁀
Insert space	to erris human (#) (or) to err/is human	to erris human	#
Lessen space	to err is human	to err is human	less #
Equalize word spaces	(Same as proofmark)	to err is human	eq #
Insert line space	(Same as proofmark)	Xxxxxxxx xx xxxx xx Xxxx xxx xxxx	#
Take out line space	(Same as proofmark)	Xxxxxxxxx xx xxx xxxxx xxxxx xxx	ℐ#
Move right	Abcd efgh ijkl	Abcd efgh ijkl	]
Move down	Abcd efgh ijkl	Abcd efgh ijkl	⊔
Move left	Abcd efgh ijkl	Abcd efgh ijkl	[
Move up	Abcd efgh ijkl	Abcd efgh ijkl	⊓
Center	] Xxxx Xxxx [	] Xxxx Xxxx [	ctr
Straighten	Abcdefgh	Abcdefgh	straighten
Align	Xxxx xxx xx xxxxx xxx xxx xxx xxxx xxx	Xxxx xxx xx xxxxx xxx xxx xxx xxxx xxx	align
Line Breaks			
Run on	(Same as proofmark)	Xxxxx xxxx xxx xx xxxxx xxx xxx	run on
Break	Xxxx xxxxxxxxx	Xxxx xxxxxxxxx	break
Run over	(Same as proofmark)	Xxxxx xxxx x xx xxx xxxxx xxx xxx	run over
Run back	(Same as proofmark)	Xxxxx xxxx (run back) xxxxx xxxxx xxx xxx	
New paragraph	xxxx xxxxxx. ¶Xxxx (or) xxxx xxxxxx. Xxxx	xxxx xxxxxx. Xxxx	¶
No new paragraph	xxxx xxxxxx xxx. (run on) Xxx xxx xxxxxxxx	xxxx xxxxxx xxx. Xxx xxx xxxxxx	no ¶

Figure 32–4. Editing and proofreading marks compared (continued).

Instructions	Editing Marks (in text only)	Proofmarks (in text and margin)
Insert 1-em space	(Same as proofmark)	□ Xxxx xxx xxx xxx
Insert 2-em space	(Same as proofmark)	□□ Xxxx xxx xxx xxx
Insert 3-em space	(Same as proofmark)	[3] Xxxx xxx xxx xxx
Correct word division	Perfection is inh- uman	Perfection is inh- uman
	Perfection is inhum- an	Perfection is inhum- an
		(or)
		Perfection is ~~inh-~~ ~~uman~~ in-hu-man
Type Style		
Italic	Abcdef	Abcdef ital
Small caps	abcdef	abcdef sc
Full caps	abcdef	abcdef caps
Boldface	Abcdef	Abcdef bf
Caps & small caps	Abcdef	Abcdef c & sc
Lowercase letter	AbCdef	AbCdef lc
Lowercase word	ABCDEF	ABCDEF lc
Capital letter	ABCdEF	ABCdEF D
Caps and lowercase	abcdef	abcdef clc
Caps and lowercase	ABCDEF	ABCDEF clc
Wrong font	(Same as proofmark)	abcdefghijkl wf
Subscript	H20	H20 2
Superscript	33=27	33=27 3
Ligature	(Same as proofmark)	fly off lig
Kern	(Same as proofmark)	Valued Work kerns
Punctuation		
Apostrophe	abcs	abcs
Colon	Hamlet To be or not to be...	Hamlet To be or not to be... :
Comma	To err, I say is human.	To err, I say is human.

Figure 32–4. Editing and proofreading marks compared (continued).

Instructions	Editing Marks (in text only)	Proofmarks (in text and margin)
Dashes, typeset		
en (short) dash	pages 10 20	pages 10 20 1/N
em (long) dash	To err well, it's only human.	To err well, it's only human. 1/M
3-em (extra-long) dash	Shakespeare, *Comedies* 3/M *Tragedies*	Shakespeare, *Comedies* *Tragedies* 3/M
Dashes, typewritten		
short dash (same as hyphen)	pages 10 20	pages 10 20 =/
long dash (2 hyphens)	To err well, it's only human.	To err well, it's only human. --/
extra-long dash	Shakespeare, *Comedies* (6x) *Tragedies*	Shakespeare, *Comedies* *Tragedies* =(6x)
Exclamation point	Wow!	Wow (set) !
Hyphen	Nobody is error free.	Nobody is error free. =/
Parenthesis, opening	To err is lamentably) human.	To err is lamentably) human. (
Parenthesis, closing	To err is (lamentably human.	To err is (lamentably human.)
Period	Proofreaders live by error⊙	Proofreaders live by error ⊙
Question mark	Why?	Why (set) ?
Quote marks, single*		
opening	BATMAN' SIGHTED	BATMAN' SIGHTED
closing	'BATMAN SIGHTED	'BATMAN SIGHTED
Quote marks, double		
opening	Who said, To err is human" ?	Who said, To err is human" ?
closing	Who said, "To err is human ?	Who said, "To err is human ?
Semicolon	Chicago, Ill. St. Louis, Mo.	Chicago, Ill. St. Louis, Mo. ;
Virgule (slash, shill)	$20/bushel (slash)	$20bushel /(slash)

Figure 32–4. Editing and proofreading marks compared (continued).

achieved between pleasing layouts and page arrangements that are logical, unambiguous, and easy to read.

Editing may take longer than planned because it is difficult to anticipate the problems that may arise. Although this sometimes necessitates an adjustment to the production schedule, the extra time is almost always worth it. This is because the production steps that follow depend on the editorial integrity of the manuscript, time is more easily absorbed this early in the schedule, and problems at the manuscript stage are less complicated to fix than the same problems in page proofs or mechanicals.

Proofreading

More than an individual step, proofreading is a vital link in controlling accuracy and quality at each step of the many transformations in the production process. For each revision or format change, there is a corresponding proofreading check to ensure that the typesetter has followed all instructions on the marked copy. The time and effort spent at each step depends on the extent of changes made at the previous step and the number of new elements introduced.

First-Pass Proofs. The first major transformation in the production process is the move from raw manuscript to typeset columns or pages. The proof step for this process is the galley or first-pass proof. The term *galley proof,* which dates to the early days of printing, refers to a proof taken from the narrow metal trays that held columns of type. In desktop publishing, the first proofs usually take the form of roughly made-up pages, but functionally they serve the same purpose as galleys. The objective of proofreading at the galley stage is to ensure that all text has been set correctly before pages are fully made up.

At the first-pass stage comes the most thorough proofreading, since this is the point of most dramatic transformation of the text. The proofreader's job here is twofold: to ensure that typesetting and formatting instructions have been followed and to proofread the text word for word against the master manuscript to see that every letter, word, and mark has made it through the typesetting process correctly. The proofreader is aided by the spec sheet, style sheet, and any other information provided by the editor; these sheets can prevent mistakes and unnecessary querying throughout the production cycle by informing everyone in the process with details about style and format decisions.

In its most technical sense, proofreading means comparing the current version of the text, called the *live copy,* to the previous version, the *dead copy,* which is marked with revisions, corrections, and often formatting instructions. The proofreader is expected to mark any variation between live

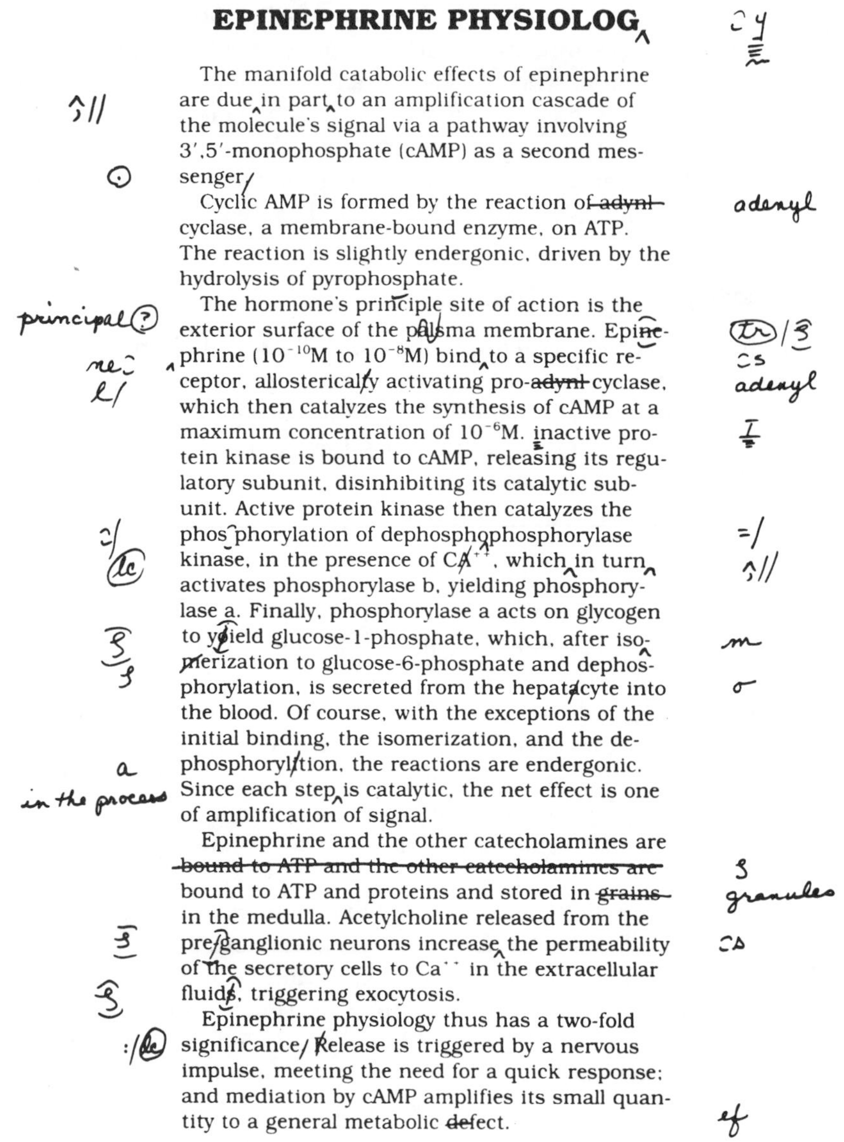

EPINEPHRINE PHYSIOLOG

The manifold catabolic effects of epinephrine are due in part to an amplification cascade of the molecule's signal via a pathway involving 3',5'-monophosphate (cAMP) as a second messenger

Cyclic AMP is formed by the reaction of adynl cyclase, a membrane-bound enzyme, on ATP. The reaction is slightly endergonic, driven by the hydrolysis of pyrophosphate.

The hormone's principle site of action is the exterior surface of the palsma membrane. Epine-phrine (10^{-10}M to 10^{-8}M) bind to a specific receptor, allosterically activating pro-adynl cyclase, which then catalyzes the synthesis of cAMP at a maximum concentration of 10^{-6}M. inactive protein kinase is bound to cAMP, releasing its regulatory subunit, disinhibiting its catalytic subunit. Active protein kinase then catalyzes the phos phorylation of dephosphophosphorylase kinase, in the presence of CA^{++}, which in turn activates phosphorylase b, yielding phosphorylase a. Finally, phosphorylase a acts on glycogen to yeield glucose-1-phosphate, which, after isoerization to glucose-6-phosphate and dephosphorylation, is secreted from the hepatacyte into the blood. Of course, with the exceptions of the initial binding, the isomerization, and the dephosphoryltion, the reactions are endergonic. Since each step is catalytic, the net effect is one of amplification of signal.

Epinephrine and the other catecholamines are bound to ATP and the other catecholamines are bound to ATP and proteins and stored in grains in the medulla. Acetylcholine released from the pre ganglionic neurons increase the permeability of the secretory cells to Ca^{++} in the extracellular fluids, triggering exocytosis.

Epinephrine physiology thus has a two-fold significance Release is triggered by a nervous impulse, meeting the need for a quick response; and mediation by cAMP amplifies its small quantity to a general metabolic defect.

Figure 32–5. A sample proofread galley.

IS THIS PROOF NECESSARY?

When production operations first started setting manuscripts directly from disk rather than rekeying the text into a typesetting system, many people thought that one of the time savings in this new electronic process would be less proofreading. After all, they reasoned, the manuscript should come out the same way it went in. It should, but it doesn't; the simple reason is that the task of typesetting and formatting is not an airtight process.

To introduce the commands and codes that allow the typesetting equipment or desktop publishing software to do its work, the operator must manipulate the data on the word processing file to make it "speak" in typesetting language. This procedure opens the possibility of introducing errors, of accidentally deleting or adding characters, or losing or duplicating lines of text. There is also the chance that unseen electromagnetic gremlins may take it upon themselves to garble a paragraph because of a power surge or a flaw in a disk. For this reason, many in the electronic publishing business have gone back to a complete word-for-word proofreading after typesetting, just to make sure.

---

and dead copy. Corrections necessitated by typesetter's errors are known as *PEs,* or *printer's errors,* and are flagged by a circled *PE* in the margin. These are reset at no additional cost to the publisher. Corrections of errors not introduced by the typesetter are called *author's alterations,* or *AAs,* and will be charged to the publisher or to the author if he or she has made substantial changes. Corrections that should not be charged to the author because of editorial error or the necessity of updating, for example, are flagged as *editor's alterations,* or *EAs.*

Any seeming error that is not indicated as such on the dead copy should be marked by the proofreader as a query, which in turn will be passed back to an editor for resolution. Many editorial operations, however, allow the proofreader a certain amount of latitude in correcting, for example, obvious spelling and grammar errors; in this case the proofreader is often asked to mark such corrections differently—often in blue pencil rather than the usual red to show a variance between live and dead copy. The proofreader customarily makes two marks for each correction—one mark in the margin that shows the typesetter the change to be made and a corresponding mark in the text that shows where the correction should be made.

In many publication processes a duplicate set of proofs is sent to the author to read for errors, sense, and any last-minute changes and updating. The proofreader then incorporates these alterations, often consulting with the editor, into the master set of proofs. In this most traditional of proofreading procedures, the master set then goes back to the typesetter for correction.

Second-Pass Proofs. Once galleys or first-pass proofs are proofread and corrected, layouts, dummies, or—in the electronic example—revised pages are created. In a publication with many illustrations or a complex design, these pages bring together type and any illustrations into page formats according to the layout created by the designer. The realities of the text sometimes create layout problems for which there is no clear resolution; when this happens, the editor may be brought in to review the work, suggest revisions, and approve solutions. In a publication that is almost purely text, second-pass proofs may also serve as final page proofs, which show what the page will look like in the finished publication.

In the traditional production process, dummy page layouts are created by cutting and pasting photocopies of illustrations into the typeset text. Once these pages are approved, they serve as models for pasteup artists to create the next stage, the camera-ready mechanical, or the master from which the publication will be printed. These mechanicals are photocopied to produce page proofs; any revisions or corrections found during their review are retypeset and then "patched" directly onto the finished mechanicals.

In the electronic process, no scissors or glue is needed—the pages are returned to the computer for revisions until the final page is achieved. The final product of in-house electronic publishing may be a laser-printed original, high-resolution output from a digital imagesetter, or film, the negatives used to create the printing plates.

Second-pass proofs are proofread against the master first-pass proofs, not the manuscript. Even though this step consists of checking only the revisions and not a complete proofreading, the proofreader should also check the text above and below the revision to see that no new errors have been introduced. The proofreader should also *slug* the text—that is, check the beginnings and ends of all lines against the dead copy to make sure nothing has been dropped, a not uncommon problem with electronic files. Neglecting this final step *at each revision stage* is a common production mistake.

Several passes may be needed to create the final pages, and the proofreader should check corrections at each stage. When the final page proof stage is reached, the proofreader carefully checks elements such as *folios* (page numbers), running heads, notes or footnotes, cross-references, illustrations, and tables, including proper wording and placement of titles and captions. Pages should also be checked for correct hyphenation (electronic hyphenation is not foolproof), the number of successive end-of-line hyphens (some publications allow only two end-of-line hyphens in a row), and such page layout concerns as *widows* and *orphans* (the "stranded" single lines at the bottom or top of a page or column).

There is no later stage of proof amenable to corrections after this step; the next set of proofs is known as *bluelines* or *blueprints,* which are made from the photographic film used to make the printing plates.

The best way to check a blueline proof is systematically, planning for at least two or three passes to check for different concerns. Anything that seems the slightest bit wrong or ambiguous on the blueline should be noted or questioned. Just as there is no stupid question but the one that goes unasked, it's better to mark something that turns out not to be a problem than to assume that something that looks odd is all right. *After the blueline proof is approved, any remaining mistakes are assumed to be the customer's responsibility, even though they may have originally been the result of a printer's error.*

The printer will return the original camera-ready art with the blueline; it should serve as a guide for the first pass, to check that the art was shot as intended, in the right size and place; that every element—folios, captions, charts—is in its proper position; and that color break instructions were followed. Particular attention should be paid to photographs that were separately supplied for the printer to strip in; an important person may have

WHERE ERRORS LURK

Professional proofreaders all know their individual weaknesses, the points they always need to go back to and double-check for errors. There are also some general rules about the types of copy that are often fraught with proofreading perils:

- Heads and subheads
- Typeface changes within a document
- The first few paragraphs after a head
- Front matter
- Strings of small words ("if it is in the best . . .")
- Pages that have only a small amount of type
- Proper names
- Numbers (transposed figures are a common error)
- Corrections made in a hurry late in the process
- Dropped lines, especially at bottoms of columns and pages and before or after graphics
- Words that are repeated from the end of one line to the beginning of the next

disappeared thanks to a cropping mistake, or the team's star southpaw may be right-handed if a photo has been *flopped* (stripped in backwards).

Color will not appear on the blueline; a second color may appear as a lighter shade of blue. The printer should indicate what elements are to be printed in color and write in percentages for screens. If this information is not already on the blueline, the customer should write it in. A double-check of color breaks should be made against the original mechanical to make sure that each element appears—a common stripping error is to omit a line of type that is to print in a second color.

The trimming and folding of the blueline should be checked against the original art; the images and text should be straight, and the front and back of the piece should be in proper relative position. In publications with many pages, a separate pass should be made just to check the pagination and consistency of margins.

Even though the text should have been thoroughly proofread and reproofread before it went to the printer, it's often a good idea to reread the copy—particularly in small promotional pieces—for easily missed errors in headlines, for instance, or in names, addresses, and phone numbers.

Yet another pass should be made to look for such problems as dust spots, smudges, errant registration or crop marks, and broken or missing type. A check should be made of the edges of images and the ends of lines of type to assure that they were properly stripped.

The printer will usually attach an approval slip to the blueline, noting the quantity to be printed and the paper stock to be used; the buyer should verify this information. The approval slip should indicate whether the blueline is approved as is or is approved with changes (meaning that the job may proceed after the indicated changes have been made, without a second blueline) or that a second blueline should be submitted after the changes have been made. Any changes that are not corrections of printer's errors will be charged to the customer, as will, most likely, a second blueline. If the blueline is not returned to the printer by the date requested on the approval slip, the customer can expect delivery delays.

MANAGING THE PRODUCTION PROCESS

Clarifying Tasks and Objectives

The most important part of the production manager's job is to effectively direct the numerous individual efforts that go into a successful project. The production manager breaks down the overall tasks into assignments, allowing all players in the process—often a combination of in-house staff and outside vendors—to concentrate on their specific functions.

Between the macro milestones in the overall production schedule, the production manager sets the interim, micro milestones that will go into achieving those goals. For instance, between galleys and page proofs there is proofreading, correcting, finalizing figures and illustrations, cropping photographs, laying out pages, sizing art, and so on. The production manager decides who performs each task, at what time, and in what order. A checklist or a workflow tracking sheet can be a useful tool for making sure that steps aren't missed and that the project stays on schedule.

Setting Deadlines

Each task in the production process must also be assigned a completion date or deadline. Though these interim deadlines are used only within the production team, they should be treated no less seriously than the overall schedule milestones.

The more specific the deadlines are, the less likely it is that any one function of the process can get hopelessly behind without the production manager's knowledge. Miscalculations of the tasks at hand, equipment problems, and any number of other complications can cause schedule delays; specific interim deadlines, though, provide a system of "yellow alerts" that make it possible to avoid the "red alert" of a missed milestone.

Tracking Workflow

Armed with a specific, detailed schedule, the production manager has an easier job of monitoring the performance of production tasks, especially with the help of a tracking system. A tracking system can take many forms, depending upon the environment—the type and number of projects to be completed, the percentage of work done in house or by outside vendors, the turnaround time, and the responsibilities for reporting to those outside the production operation. The tracking system may be sophisticated project management software or a bulletin board or notebook filled with handwritten notes; the key is finding a method that works effectively to monitor workflow and allows the production manager to react quickly to changes in the original plan. Maintaining and updating schedules and status reports should not become a full-time job in itself.

Depending upon the pace of the operation, a manager may update the status of projects weekly, daily, or even hourly. Very often meetings of key staff are helpful in keeping up with the progress of projects, but meetings should always be short and productive so as not to take people away from their work.

A useful format for status updates and production meetings consists of three topics:

- The tasks to have been accomplished since the last update
- The tasks actually accomplished since the last update
- The tasks to be accomplished before the next update

From this perspective, the project manager can evaluate progress and determine necessary adjustments.

The job of production management requires analytical and problem-solving skills as well as the ability to direct the efforts of a team and make decisions and adjustments on the fly. Those responsible for production must keep track of the details without losing sight of the big picture. To do that while maintaining a semblance of sanity, the key is control—control of schedules, budgets, and quality throughout the process.

33

PRINTING

PRINTING

There has always been an air of romance about printing, from black-and-white movies where reporters shout "Stop the presses!" to stories of legendary pressmen who could hear a single errant click above the cacophony of the presses and then fix the problem with a hairpin.

Although today there are more whirs and hums than clicks and clacks in a printing plant, it's still thrilling to see the process at work. And as copy preparation has become electronically telescoped into print production, the writers and editors who start the process of producing the printed word—and picture—are now connected more closely than ever with the mechanics of bringing ideas to print. The purpose of this chapter is to explain that process so that writers and editors can better understand the problems and possibilities that are part of creating a printed product.

Printing, at its most basic, is the process of putting an image on paper. It can be as simple as black type on a single sheet of white paper or as sophisticated as a full-color art book. For most buyers of printing, however, the objective is to produce multiple copies of one original. Although most printers can work with nearly any form of original to achieve this objective, the key to efficient and economical printing is supplying the best original material. Knowledgeable customers who understand all aspects of the printing process are better equipped to predict quality, schedules, and budgets.

Some aspects of printing are extremely specialized and technical, and the process itself is changing every day. It is certainly not possible for the average customer to attain a printer's level of knowledge, but technical knowledge isn't required to understand why making editorial changes to blueline proofs will cost more and take longer than making the same changes before negatives are made or why a print run of 1,000 brochures is going to cost more per copy than a run of 10,000.

This chapter focuses on offset lithography because it is the most widely

BEYOND THE CAMERA

Camera-ready mechanicals are going the way of hot metal type as new technology makes the most of desktop publishing files. Negatives that traditionally have been created by camera are now being produced with high-end imagesetters directly from computer files. Photographs can be digitized and cropped, sized, and placed on the page electronically, making it unnecessary to strip them in manually.

Some printers can also go directly from computer files to printing plates, avoiding negatives and the accompanying mess of chemical processing. The advantages are faster turnaround and lower cost; the disadvantage, for editors and production managers, is the lack of blueline proofs, which are made from negatives.

Although these developments place more control over prepress in the hands of those who generate the copy, these people often don't have the specialized knowledge needed to prepare negatives for the printer. It's expensive to generate negatives and find out that the printer can't use them or has to do so much manual work that the job ends up costing more anyway. Most printers are becoming proficient in using desktop systems, and production managers should let their printers help them through the process.

used method of printing; the annotated bibliography offers suggestions for further study. The discussion of prepress work concentrates on the traditional process of photographically shooting negatives from positive artwork because it provides a framework for understanding the prepress phase, even with today's computer-driven technology.

The printing process is usually broken down into three phases—prepress, on press, and postpress or finishing. *Prepress* is the transition from editorial and design to manufacturing. This phase is primarily a photographic process. Most often, the printer creates negatives from the positive black-and-white images supplied by the customer and then assembles and proofs them before making plates, one for each ink color. Next, the plates are fitted to the press and inked to transfer a repeating image to paper—the *on-press* phase.

After printing, the *postpress* phase, the piece is finished and assembled. A brochure may require only trimming and folding; a catalog will need a simple binding; a book will require collation and binding into a paper or hard cover; and a special promotional piece might be die cut or embossed.

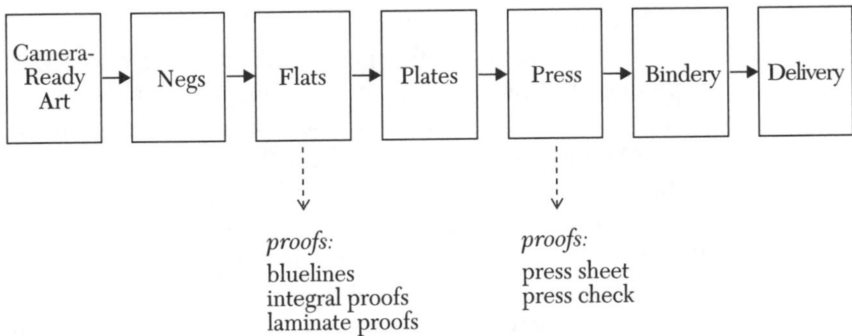

Figure 33–1. These are the basic steps in the traditional offset production process; direct-to-plate printing uses electronic files to create printing plates, bypassing the initial steps.

PREPRESS

Preparing Camera-Ready Copy for the Printer

Although the term *prepress* generally refers to preparing negatives and printing plates, this discussion begins with the phase of the printing process over which the person supplying camera-ready copy has the most control—the preparation of that copy. Well-prepared originals are the key to printing quality. Although adjustments can be made throughout the process to compensate for less-than-perfect originals, the costs of doing so can often escalate enormously as production proceeds.

Text or text with graphics may be pasted up manually on illustration board, or the page may be generated all in one piece from desktop publishing or graphics software. Camera-ready copy, also called *repros* or *mechanicals,* provides the printer with both a reproducible image and the instructions needed to print it.

The Graphic Quality of Type. Most printed pieces consist primarily of text. The graphic quality of type can vary a great deal, however, and it does affect printing quality.

Resolution is the term most often used when discussing the quality of type; it refers to the fact that, in digital typesetting, the letterform is made up of numerous dots. The smaller and closer together the dots, the higher the resolution; the higher the resolution, the clearer and sharper the final image. Resolution is measured in *dpi* (dots per inch).

Laser printers have made "typesetting" available to anyone with a computer, but the graphic quality of laser type, which consists of toner deposited on electrostatically charged paper, is coarser than that of type generated photographically on RC (resin-coated) paper by a digital *imagesetter.* Most laser printers produce type at 300 dpi, though 400-, 600-, and 1,200-dpi printers are in use. By comparison, standard digital imagesetting machines, such as Linotronic, produce type at 1,270 and 2,540 dpi.

Checking the consistency of type density is important when evaluating the quality of laser type. Problems arise when density varies from one side of the page to the other or from one page to another. These problems most often occur when the toner cartridge of the laser printer is nearly empty. Problems can also arise when pages are printed at different times or from different machines; this is also true with type generated by an imagesetter.

Illustrations and Photographs. Besides type, illustrations and photographs are the other major elements provided to the printer. The easiest, most efficient, and least expensive way to ensure a satisfactory printed piece is to supply the printer with high-quality originals with all instructions clearly and

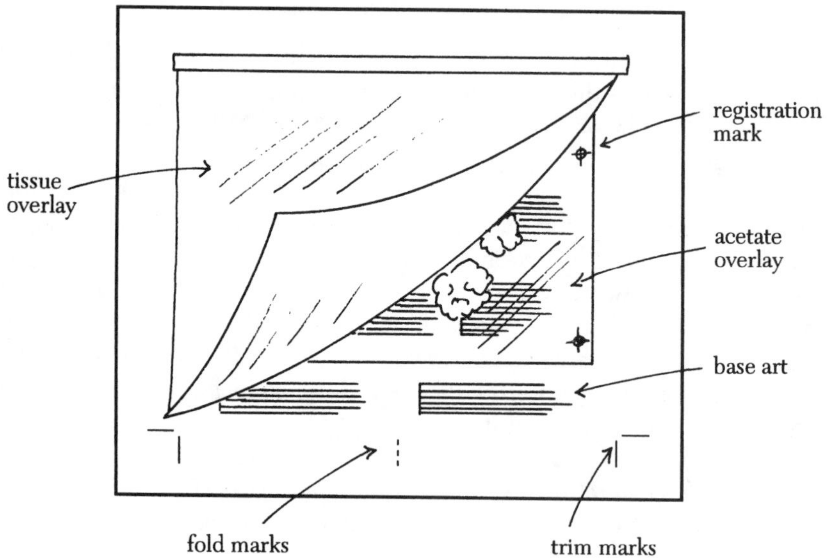

Figure 33–2. The mechanical gives the printer the information needed to complete the printing job. The board shows where trims and folds should be made; separated art is prepared on an overlay registered to the base art. The tissue overlay carries color break information and any special instructions. A non-repro *light-blue pen or pencil, invisible to the camera, is usually used for writing on the mechanical. Red masks and keylines are used on mechanicals to mark the position of photos and other art because the camera reads the color red as black.*

Figure 33–3. The enlarged portion of this photograph shows how dots of ink or toner are arranged to create halftones for use in printing.

fully marked. The art should be clean and free of flaws. Photographs should be properly exposed and in sharp focus; detail in both shadow and highlight areas should be clear. Any imperfections in the original will be magnified if the image is enlarged in printing. *Line art,* black-and-white illustrations with no shades of gray, is *shot*—photographed—directly from the mechanical, just as the type is. Photographs or illustrations with tonal qualities, however, must first be *screened,* a process that involves breaking up the image into dots whose size and placement emulate shades of gray or color.

Artwork that must be sent to the printer separately should be clearly keyed to the mechanical and the text. For a publication of many pages that includes numerous photographs, an alphanumeric code might be assigned to each photo based on the number of the page on which it appears; for instance, the four photos on page 6 would be coded 6A, 6B, 6C, and 6D.

In most cases, illustrations and photographs will appear in the printed piece in different sizes and shapes than the originals, so the size and position of each photo or illustration should be clearly and accurately indicated on the mechanical with a red *keyline,* which is an ink or pencil line drawn to describe the shape of the photo or illustration, or an opaque *mask* or *window* applied to the board. *Sizing* or *scaling*, indicated as a percentage of the original size, should be marked on each piece of art.

Cropping instructions indicate what part of the image is to appear in print. If the image is to be cropped as a rectangle, marks defining the edges of the rectangle—called *crop marks*—can be used. If an irregularly shaped portion of the image is to be used (such as when one element in a photograph is to be isolated), it can be traced onto an overlay taped over the image. A more precise method is to make a mask of the portion of the art to be printed, using *amberlith* or *rubylith*. Those unsure of their graphic skills should simply give the printer instructions and pay a bit extra to have the mask professionally prepared. (See Chapter 27, Photographs and Illustrations, for more on cropping and scaling.)

The code number or letter for the appropriate art should also be indicated; for further clarity, a photocopy of the art can be used—always, though, with the letters *FPO* ("for position only") written across it so that the photocopy is not mistaken for camera-ready art.

Preseparated Art. A black-and-white mechanical is also used to print preseparated, or flat, color. Instructions called *color breaks* tell the printer what portions of the artwork are to be used to create plates for each ink color. For example, if an element to be printed in one color—say, a headline or a line illustration—does not touch any element that is to be printed in another color, only one mechanical is necessary, and the color can be indicated simply with a marker on tracing paper taped over the mechanical. If, on the other hand, different ink colors will touch or overlap, each color must be indicated on a separate *overlay*, generally of clear acetate. Usually art that is to be printed in black is prepared on the main board—called *base art*—and the color elements are positioned on the overlay. *Registration marks,* which resemble cross-hair sights or bull's-eyes, are placed on the base art and each overlay to ensure that each color will be properly aligned when printed.

If a lighter tone of color is desired, the mechanical should specify a *screen*. A screen is a mechanical means by which color is broken into dots to create a darker or lighter color. Screens are indicated as percentages of color; the higher the percentage, the darker the tone.

If the design of the piece requires the ink to extend all the way to the edge of the paper, the artwork must be prepared to allow for a *bleed*. This means that rather than stopping exactly at the edge of the page, the color will actually print beyond the edge. The piece will be printed on larger paper to accommodate the bleed and then trimmed to size.

Full-Color Originals. The use of separate, specific ink colors, as discussed above, is known as *spot color;* the reproduction of full-color photography or illustration is accomplished through *four-color process* printing, which is explained later in this chapter. Art for color process printing is provided separately to the printer as full-color originals, cropped, sized, and keyed to the main mechanical in the same way as any other separately supplied photo or illustration. Color photographs should go to the printer as transparencies or slides; cropping and sizing can be done on a print, with instructions to the printer to shoot from the transparency. Full-color illustrations should be created on *strippable* illustration board, the top layer of which can be separated from its backing and wrapped around the cylindrical drum of the laser scanner the printer uses to make separations.

In full-color printing, the quality of the originals is especially critical; retouching four-color negatives is extremely expensive and time consuming. To ensure quality, a magnifying glass or light box should be used to inspect originals. The light box should conform to the 5,000 degrees Kelvin lighting standard. (*Kelvin,* abbreviated K, is a measurement of light output. The standard of 5,000K has been adopted because it approximates the most common daylight/incandescent lighting.) Most printers have a light box.

As with black-and-white photography, the color original should be free of flaws, scratches, or dirt and have good exposure and contrast. Photographs shot with low-ASA film are preferable, since the grain of slow film is finer and less likely to become visible as the image is enlarged. Sharpness of detail is extremely important to successful reproduction.

What the Printer Does with Camera-Ready Copy

Negatives. In the printing plant, the mechanicals first go to the camera department to be converted to negatives and then to plates. Any color specified on the mechanicals will have its own negative, which is shot from the art using large-format cameras.

Special photographic techniques are used to create certain printing effects. If type is to appear in white against a color background, it is *reversed*—the type is shot as a negative image to leave letter-shaped "holes" in the positive color background. If that type is intended to print in another color, a *knock-out and trap* is required—the second ink color is "trapped" within the reversed area. In this case and in the case of any two ink colors meeting, the art is prepared with the separate colors butting exactly, but on press that kind of precision isn't possible. Everyone has seen the telltale rim of white at the edge of a poorly executed trap; to prevent this, the camera operator creates the negatives so that one color slightly overlaps the other, leaving a little margin for error. In a *spread,* a foreground object is shot to slightly overlap its background; in a *choke,* the background overlaps the object.

Halftones and Duotones. Halftones are created from *continuous tone* black-and-white photographs by *screening,* or breaking up the image into black dots of varying sizes that can be reproduced on the printing press. The density of the screen—expressed as *lines per inch*—controls the sharpness and detail of the final printed photograph. Newspapers often use a coarse—65-line—screen; a 133-line screen is standard for most printing. Special-effect screens like mezzotints are sometimes used to make photographs look more like illustrations. A *double-dot halftone* creates a richer reproduction. Screens to produce tints of color are created in the same way, except that the dots, instead of varying in size, are of a consistent size and density.

In a *duotone,* the same halftone in two different colors is combined to create a photograph that has a color tint. A *duotone effect* (or, less charitably, a *fake duotone*) can be less expensively created by printing a tint of color over the black-only halftone, but because the dot pattern of the color tint is consistent across the photo, the effect is flat compared to the variation of tone achieved by using the second halftone negative.

Color Separations. In full-color printing, four negatives—one for each of the four process colors—are created by *color separation.* This process isolates the four component colors that make up practically every color visible to the human eye—cyan (blue), magenta, yellow, and black, abbreviated in printing terminology as *CMYK.* The separations are created as halftone negatives, which are oriented at different angles to prevent the *moiré* effect caused by laying one screen on top of another. Separations are created to the size specified in the artwork; if the same photo is to be used in a different size, a different separation must be made. (This is also true for halftones.)

Most color separations are now made on scanners, which use lasers to isolate the four color components of the full-color originals. This technology has brought down considerably the cost of quality color separations. Large-format separations and separations of rigid artwork that cannot be wrapped around the scanning drum call for either shooting an interim, scannable transparency or using an older technology in which a camera shoots four successive shots through filters that isolate each of the component colors.

How the Pieces Fit Together

Stripping and Platemaking. The various negatives must be assembled before they can be used to make plates. This process is known as *stripping.* The negatives for each color plate are attached to *flats,* usually orange or yellow plastic sheets that can be cut away—stripped—to expose the desired portion of the negatives. Strippers work on light tables to properly align negatives and cut halftones and screens into position. The registration marks that

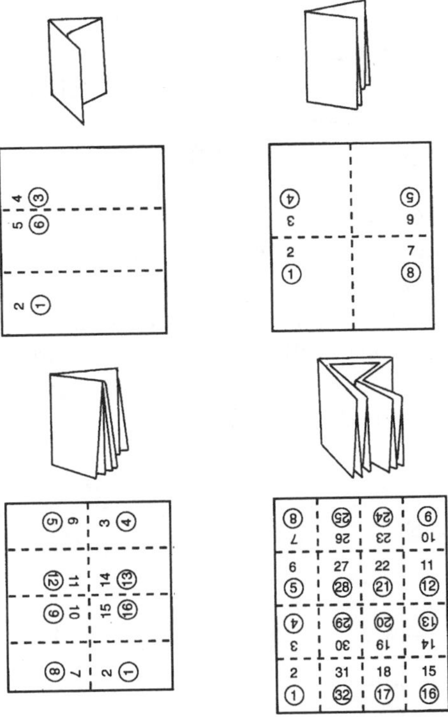

Figure 33–4. Various signature configurations for different sizes of publications are shown; page numbers in circles indicate pages on the reverse side of the sheet.

were placed on the base art and overlays when the mechanical was created are aligned to check color registration.

Imposition. Only simple and low-quantity printing is done on paper that is the exact size of the desired product; in most printing multiple pages are printed at once on one sheet and then folded and cut to size. The placement of these multiple pages on one flat is called *imposition* and is based on the size and type of the printing press and the paper to be used. The objective is to print the job as efficiently and with as little paper waste as possible.

Presses are designed to run with one of a few standard sizes of paper. The sizes of the finished publication most often seen–8½ by 11, 6 by 9, 5 by 8, and so on—reflect the most efficient use of those standard sheets. Odd sizes can, of course, be created, but to do so usually requires trimming off and wasting portions of the sheet, bringing up the cost per unit. A compelling financial or esthetic reason can sometimes justify the cost, however.

When printing publications with many pages, imposition is extremely important. The pages of books and magazines, for example, are printed on large sheets of paper, called *signatures,* which are folded, trimmed, and bound so that the pages read sequentially. Signatures are always created in multiples of four, and planning for layouts should always take this fact into account—if the copy in a booklet fills 13 pages, a booklet of 16 pages must be created. Smaller pieces may be printed in 4-page signatures; book printing is often done on 32-page signatures.

Because it is less expensive to print color on only one side of a signature, books and magazines are often planned this way. Knowing the configuration of the signature is vital. In figure 33–5, pages 1, 4, 5, 8, 9, 12, 13, and 16 will have color; the remaining pages in the signature—the circled page numbers representing the pages on the other side of the signature—will be printed in black only. Note that a color spread across two pages is possible only on pages 4 and 5, 8 and 9, and 12 and 13.

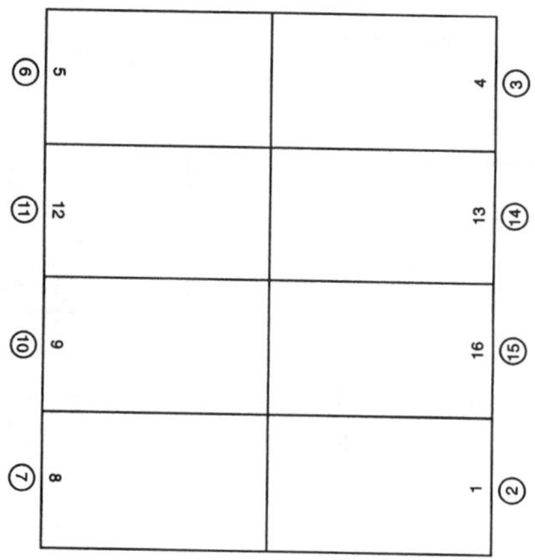

Figure 33–5. The costs of color printing can be reduced by restricting its use to certain signatures and sides of signatures.

Prepress Proofs: One Last Check. Before plates are made, the prepress work up to this point must be checked or *proofed.* The most common proof is the *blueline,* which is a facsimile of the final printed piece made on special light-sensitive paper. The negative flats are used to expose the paper, and the image to be printed appears in blue. Different colors are usually exposed for slightly less time so that they appear as lighter shades of blue. The blueline is generally cut and folded just as the final piece will be, so the blueline also serves as a proofing step for the printer's finishing process. Other processes used at this stage to produce proofs are known as *blueprints, whiteprints, silverprints, brownlines, ozalids,* and *vandykes.*

The blueline is a technical proof—the chance to make sure that instructions have been followed and to check the prepress work for quality. Ideally, the only corrections that should be made at this point are corrections in those areas. This step is not intended as an opportunity for one last chance at editing or proofreading the text or revising the art. It is important to remember the exponential increase in costs incurred during prepress; changing the originals at this point means reincurring those costs and also may mean added costs for overtime to meet the original schedule. (Chapter 32, The Production Process, describes how to check bluelines.)

Obviously, if the blueline check reveals that the name of the company president is misspelled in a marketing brochure, the correction will be made regardless of the complications. Needless to say, however, it is much better to allow time for one last proofreading step *before* the camera-ready copy goes to the printer.

More complex color work often calls for *overlay color proofs,* in which transparent acetate overlays indicate the various colors. ColorKey and NAPS are the most common brands of overlay proofs. This proofing process allows the checking of color breaks, screens, registration, and alignment. However, the overlay proof cannot be trimmed and folded and shows only one side, so a blueline is also needed. Overlay proof sets are manufactured in a limited number of colors that only approximate those used in the actual printed piece. These proofs are used to evaluate only color breaks and registration, not color quality.

Various proofing systems are used for evaluating four-color separations. Generically referred to as *laminate* or *integral* proofs, they are usually known by trade names—most often, Cromalin and Matchprint. These proofs reproduce each of the process colors on a separate clear acetate sheet; the sheets are laminated together to give an approximation of four-color printing. This creates a very high quality proof; in fact, color in the laminate proof will sometimes be more intense than that of the final publication. It is important to work closely with the printer when color accuracy from proof to press is critical. Because of their high cost, laminate proofs are often only created to proof a specific four-color element of a piece—in the case, for example, of a single color photograph appearing on a full page of black type. This is called a *random color* or *show-color proof.* If full color is critical in the piece as a whole, the composite artwork can be created in laminate proof. Like overlay proofs, though, laminate proofs can show only one side of the piece at a time and cannot be folded or trimmed.

Plates. Once negatives are proofed and approved, they are used to make the plates that will go on the press. This is also a photographic process, whereby a thin metal plate coated with a light-sensitive chemical is exposed through the negatives, often called *burning.* In the case of lithographic plates, the exposed area attracts ink and the unexposed area repels it. In direct-to-plate printing, electronic pages are sent through a raster image processor (RIP),

CHECKING COLOR QUALITY

Many new buyers of four-color printing are disappointed with color quality. What they should keep in mind, however, is that a color transparency will appear about 20 times brighter than the separated and printed version; they should also remember that in most cases no one will know what the original art or transparency looked like. From the start, it is important to be clear about the level of color duplication required. *Pleasing color* is the first level, when an acceptable color image is required but matching the original colors is not critical. *Match transparency* and *match product* are the second and third levels of color quality, requested when the colors of the transparency or the actual object pictured must be absolutely accurate, as in reproducing paintings. Achieving the second and third levels will obviously cost more; it doesn't make sense to pay for such accuracy when pleasing color is appropriate. Here are some pointers for reviewing full-color proofs:

- The reviewer should examine prepress color proofs under 5,000K lighting to be sure of using the same point of reference as the printer or color separator.
- The physical quality of the negatives should be good; broken screens, spots, scratches, pinholes, and other stray marks will mar the quality of the final printed piece.
- The registration of the four-color negatives should be exact and accurate; problems here will show up as blurring of fine details.
- Neutral areas of the image—gray and white areas—should be free of any "off" cast of color—a faint tint of green or pink, for instance—which would indicate that one of the colors is out of balance and may be causing problems in other areas of the image.
- Perception of color is subjective, so the reviewer should try to communicate color corrections clearly. "The background needs more red" or "Adjust color of tree—see original" are less ambiguous and therefore more useful than "Brighten the mood."

which drives a device that produces electric charges that burn the image onto the plate.

So-called quick printers create plates directly from the camera-ready originals without the intermediate step of creating negatives, keeping cost and time involved relatively low. These direct plates are often made of lightweight plastic or paper and can produce acceptable results for short runs of lower-quality black-only or simple two-color work.

ON PRESS

When a printing project finally gets on press, it enters a new realm; press operators control a multitude of details in a complex interplay of machinery, ink, water, and paper to manufacture the finished publication. A visit to the printing plant will dispel any notion of an automatic pushbutton process and make clear that the successful practice of the craft of printing depends heavily on skillfully executed prepress work.

Offset Lithography

Putting ink on paper by lithography depends on a basic physical principle: oil and water don't mix. Although the root of the word—*litho*—means "stone," there is no stone involved in offset lithography. The process takes its name from the fine art technique of lithography, which does indeed create an image on the surface of a stone slab; the principle of chemically attracting and repelling ink on a flat surface is the only resemblance between the two.

In offset lithography a thin metal plate is fitted around a press cylinder. Water—actually a *dampening solution* that contains alcohol and other ingredients—and ink are applied to the surface of the plate. The areas that were exposed when the plate was burned now chemically repel water and attract ink. The unexposed areas repel ink and attract water.

The plate applies ink to a flat rubber blanket that is fitted to another press cylinder. This blanket then rolls over the surface of the paper, creating the printed image. This intermediate transfer of ink is called *offsetting*. Printing from the rubber blanket produces a sharp, crisp image; printing directly from the plate would result in smearing.

Additional plates for multicolor printing are fitted to additional printing units—one for each color. Sophisticated presses may have six or more; smaller printers may need only a one- or two-color press. Although multiple colors can be printed on a press with fewer ink stations, better color registration can be achieved on presses that can print all colors in one pass.

The plates used in direct plate-to-paper methods must read backward to transfer a *right-reading* image to the paper. Anyone who has tried to read a letter upside down or read a sign in a mirror will know how difficult it is to visualize an image from wrong-reading copy. Because of the offsetting step, lithographic plates are right reading of necessity, a characteristic that makes them easier for in-plant staff to check and work with.

Printing presses are built to accept paper either in sheets *(sheet-fed)* or on rolls *(web)*. Sheet-fed presses feed sheets one at a time through the press; a web press uses a large roll of paper that is cut into *press sheets* at the end of the line. Generally, the size of the *print run* determines when to use one press or the other; web presses can print large quantities economically. Some special and premium papers, too, are available only in sheets, making it necessary to use a sheet-fed press. Most printers specialize in either sheet-fed or web printing, though a web printer may have a sheet-fed press as a backup and to do smaller pieces.

Web and some sheet-fed presses are *perfecting* presses—able to print on both sides of the sheet. *Multicolor perfectors* can print multiple colors on both sides.

The Raw Materials: Paper and Ink

One of the very first things a printing customer learns is that two completely different papers can have the same weight. Paper can be a very confusing topic.

Understanding ink is somewhat simpler—the printer deals with the technical problems involved in selecting and working with the correct ink; the customer simply specifies the color. Even so, there are many variables.

Paper. Generically, paper is often referred to in the printing industry as *stock.* When speaking of a specific paper, a printer may call it a *sheet,* as in "an uncoated sheet," "a premium sheet," or even "a really nice sheet."

The first broad classification of papers is that of *grade;* this groups papers into seven categories on the basis of how they are used. *Bond* or *writing* papers are used for hand writing and photocopying rather than printing. They can be very fine writing papers or paper for the copier or laser printer. *Book* and *coated book*—also called *offset* and *coated offset*—make up the most widely used group of papers for general printing. *Text* papers are manufactured in a variety of textures and colors for use in "prestige" projects

---

BOOKS MADE TO ORDER

Although printing is traditionally an ink-on-paper technique, a new technology—called *on-demand printing*—is being used in more and more "printing" applications. In this type of printing, desktop publishing files are used by a system that features a high-speed, high-quality laser printer that can print both sides of a page. Books produced this way can be bound like traditionally printed books. This technology is economical for small runs, normally fewer than 1,000 copies, and for publications that must be frequently updated, such as catalogs and directories. Because copies can be printed as needed, the expense of maintaining large inventories is eliminated.

---

like annual reports and promotional brochures. *Cover* stock is heavier than book papers and is used for the covers of paperback books, business cards, and so on. *Board* is stiffer and stronger than cover stock and also often comes in colors. The *specialty* category comprises papers manufactured for specific applications and includes newsprint and brown kraft paper, as well as carbonless form paper (NCR is a common brand name), gummed and pressure-sensitive paper, and synthetic paper.

Beyond these categories, papers are also classified in terms of quality. The very best (and most expensive) papers are *premium* and *#1 sheets;* a range of lower qualities appropriate for various uses is available.

The customer is expected to specify the *basis weight* of the paper for the project. Weights of paper may seem arbitrary at first glance, since a 20-pound bond is roughly the same weight as a 60-pound offset paper, and 60-pound cover stock is obviously heavier than 60-pound text. But the weight measurements are not absolute; basis weight is the weight of a *ream* (500 sheets) of a given paper, *cut to the basic size for its grade.* The basic size for bond papers is 17 by 22 inches, so a ream of bond weighs less than a ream of offset, for which the basic size is 25 by 38 inches. And since the basic size of cover stock is 20 by 26, it makes sense that 500 sheets of a heavier stock could weigh the same as the same number of lighter-weight sheets cut to a bigger size. (Basic sizes are not the only available sizes within a grade; paper of all grades comes in a range of sheet sizes, and some comes in rolls for web presses.) To distinguish between the two weight systems for book and cover stock, the paper is specified as "60# cover," for example, or "60# text." Some cover stocks are specified by their thickness, measured in thousandths of an inch, rather than by weight. A cover stock that is .008-inch thick and coated on one side is specified as "8-point (or pt.) C1S."

The surface qualities of the sheet are a key aspect to consider in selecting paper for a particular project because ink behaves differently on different surfaces. The major division in book paper finishes is between *coated* and *uncoated* papers. The coating is a thin layer of clay applied to the surface of the paper during the manufacturing process. It prevents ink from being absorbed quickly by the paper fibers; instead, the ink "sits up" on the surface and dries there. This is called *ink holdout,* and it is the reason colored inks appear brighter, making photographs and illustrations sharper, on coated stock. Uncoated stocks are usually used when illustrations and photograph reproductions are not critical and for text-only books, since the nonreflective surface of uncoated stock is easier on the eyes.

Other major paper characteristics are a bit more technical, but they can be critical in planning a printing project. Rating scales have been developed to measure brightness, bulk, and opacity, making it easier to compare one paper to another.

PAGE TALK

When expressing the number of pages in, say, a catalog that will use the same stock for the covers as for the text, a buyer will specify "16 pages self-cover." A publication that will use different stocks for cover and text will be referred to as "16 pages plus cover." The front, inside front, inside back, and back covers are referred to, respectively, as *C-1, C-2, C-3,* and *C-4,* rather than being included in the pagination of the rest of the book.

Brightness is an indication of the amount of light reflected by the surface of the paper. Most papers rank between 60 and 90 percent on the brightness scale. A very bright sheet provides a pure background for what is printed on it; on the other hand, brightness can turn to glare in page after page of dense text.

Bulk is the thickness of paper, measured in thousandths of an inch. Bulk is of particular importance in book manufacturing; book paper manufacturers provide a pages per inch (ppi) rating to aid publishers in planning the bulk of the book and the width of the spine.

Opacity is the degree to which printing on one side of the paper shows through to the other side. This is obviously a concern in pieces that have heavy ink coverage or illustrations. Opacity is measured on a scale of 100—the higher the number, the more opaque the paper. Papers with a rating in the 90s will be opaque enough for most uses.

Availability is also often an issue in the cost and practicality of using a particular paper. If the stock must be special-ordered and take weeks to be delivered, it's not the right choice for a piece that must be delivered in 2 weeks or a book that may have to be reprinted quickly. And if the number of copies to be printed is not enough to make up a minimum order of the special stock, a different choice will probably have to be made.

Printers often have *house stocks* on hand, depending on the types of paper they are most often called upon to supply. Customers should check with the printer to see whether appropriate house stock is available.

Paper suppliers and printers can provide samples of most available paper stocks. They can also make up dummy books with the proposed cover and text stocks, so the customer can see how a finished book will look.

Ink. Ink consists of tiny particles of pigment suspended in a (usually) petroleum-based vehicle. Additives to this mixture aid setting and drying of the ink. Printers keep a supply of the inks they use most often; first on the

PERPETUAL AND RECYCLED PAPERS

The purchaser of paper may have special considerations in selecting a stock. In book manufacturing, for instance, most publishers now use *acid-free* paper. Like fine art papers, this paper is pH neutral and therefore will resist discoloration and deterioration over many years. Since the promulgation in 1984 of the ANSI standard for permanence of book papers, most paper manufacturers have made acid-free or "permanent" paper readily available. Books manufactured with this paper may carry the trademarked infinity symbol (∞) and a statement of conformance to the ANSI standard.

Recycled papers are available in a range of grades and finishes. They are classified in terms of percentage of *preconsumer* and *postconsumer* waste content—respectively, waste paper from mills and manufacturers and paper that has been printed, recovered, and deinked for remanufacture. Two symbols are used: The recycling symbol, shown on left, below, means that recycled paper was used. The words "Printed on recycled paper" may accompany the symbol. The recyclable symbol, shown on right, below, can be used on paper products that can reasonably be expected to be recycled.

A concern raised by the recycling of paper is that waste products created by the deinking process are often toxic, creating one waste problem while solving another. And because reused paper fibers are not as strong as virgin fibers, paper manufacturers are also working on formulations to improve the tensile strength of recycled paper, particularly for use on web presses.

list, of course, is black. Rounding out the supply are the basic colors used in *ink matching systems.*

The graphic arts industry uses standardized systems to specify ink colors. The Pantone Matching System, or PMS, is nearly generic, but there are other systems, such as Toyo; designers should specify the matching system they used.

Ink matching systems consist of specific formulas for mixing basic inks to create hundreds of colors; a numbering system provides a simple shorthand for communicating with the printer. To specify an ink color, the designer lists

GETTING A COLOR PREVIEW

One way to see in advance how a particular ink will print on paper is to request a *draw-down* or *roll-out*, a sample of specified ink printed on a sample of specified stock. A printer will often provide a draw-down for little or no charge. Although not always appropriate or necessary, this advance check can provide peace of mind on an important project.

the matching system, color number, and general color group to which the specified color belongs—for example, "PMS 548 Blue." Stating the color provides a double check because it is easy to transpose numbers when writing or reading.

Swatch books with all available ink colors in a particular matching system can be purchased from graphic arts suppliers and are sometimes available through printers and ink manufacturers. The swatch book should show inks on both uncoated and coated stock. Books that show ink colors in a range of screen percentages are also available.

Other ink matching systems are designed for use in four-color process printing. Using the four process colors, these systems build "solid" colors that can approximate the range of spot ink colors available through the other systems. TruMatch and Pantone are two such systems. Note, however, that the brilliance of many spot colors cannot be achieved in four-color process. Many blues and purples that can be created by mixing pigments are especially difficult to approximate in four-color printing.

Printing inks are basically transparent; although a higher degree of opacity can sometimes be achieved by double printing, a special order of opaque ink may be worth the added expense in some cases. Other specialty inks include metallics and fluorescents. The printer may need some extra lead time to order specialty inks.

Laser ink, which contains an additive that prevents it from melting and smearing from the heat generated by laser printers and photocopying machines, is another special ink now being used for items such as letterhead.

Environmental concerns have prompted ink manufacturers to develop alternatives to traditional petroleum-based inks. Soybean oil is being used to produce a more environmentally friendly ink. Its use is becoming more widespread as its quality improves.

Because they require a dedicated printing unit on the press, varnishes are considered a separate ink color. Both matte and gloss varnishes are available, and they may be clear or specially tinted. Varnish provides a protective coating, often useful for pieces with heavy ink coverage, and can also be used as a design element—a spot gloss varnish, for example, can add impact to a photograph on a matte paper. Book jackets frequently feature spot varnishing.

On-Press Proofs: One Last Check

In most cases, once prepress proofs have been examined and approved, the customer leaves it to the printer to ensure that the project is completed satisfactorily. The next thing the customer sees is the finished publication. Any problems that occur on press are usually considered the printer's responsibility; when there is doubt, some mutually agreed-upon resolution is usually worked out after the fact.

There are ways, though, to check on the actual printing of the job. One way is the *press proof;* in essence, this is a very limited run of the actual printing job, using the same press, plates, inks, and paper that will be used for the rest of the run. The customer receives a *press sheet,* an untrimmed copy of the piece, to review and approve. When the press sheet is initialed and returned to the plant, the job is set up again for the full run, with the approved sheet as a quality standard.

Sometimes an art director or production manager will be present at the plant to approve the job as it is running; this is known as a *press check.* The first press sheets are reviewed as they come off the press in order to set the standard for the rest of the run; in some cases, the customer remains on site for the entire run, reviewing samples pulled from the run at specified intervals to assure adherence to the standard. Press checks and press proofs will tie up equipment and incur extra costs, so the customer should inform the printer at the beginning of the project if on-press proofing will be required.

In light of the costs involved and as a matter of professional courtesy, the customer should use judgment in determining the need for an on-press proof. On-press proofing is most common in the printing of color magazines, advertising, and high-quality books. Here obtaining the very best print quality the first time is often crucial because of tight schedules, long print runs, or expensive specialty papers and inks.

Often, too, the customer is not as qualified as plant staff to evaluate the quality of printing. It may be enough to request a press proof or press check to ensure that a difficult printing job is, for example, registering properly, leaving the other areas of quality checking to the in-plant experts. While the job is running, the press operators also routinely do press checks to make sure the job is set up correctly and to ensure consistency and quality throughout the run.

POSTPRESS

A variety of machines and processes transform press sheets into the finished product. These postpress processes are called *bindery and finishing operations* and range from simple trimming and folding to binding and special operations such as die cutting and embossing.

Trimming and Folding

A few types of printed pieces—most stationery, for example—are printed directly on finished size stock. Most printing, though, is done on larger press sheets that need to be cut down to finished size, or *trimmed.* This is perhaps the simplest bindery operation. Using a paper cutter with a fearsome guillotine blade, the operator follows the trim marks and a *rule-up*—a printed press sheet marked by the stripping department with cut and fold lines—as a guide to slice through stacks of press sheets.

Slightly more complicated pieces, like brochures, may require folding. Most standard folds can be done by machine, avoiding costly hand folding. It is often wise to consult a printer about any planned fold that seems out of the ordinary; the printer may be able to either devise a way to accomplish it by machine or suggest an alternative fold. Even if the fold ultimately must be done by hand, it's better to plan for it from the outset rather than learn about it later, when a machine operation has been budgeted and scheduled.

When planning the printing of a folded piece, the printer takes into consideration the *grain* of the paper—the orientation of the paper fibers. Folds are easier and smoother with the grain; folds across the grain break fibers, making the fold appear rough and weakening the paper. Sometimes a piece is *scored,* or crimped, to allow a smoother fold.

Binding

Binding brings together the numerous pages of a publication. Generally, publications are bound along one edge, allowing pages to fan open. In-house reports, proposals, and similar documents reproduced in limited quantities and on short schedules are often bound using plastic binding methods, with trade names such as GBC, a type of comb binding, and Velobind, which uses plastic strips. Here we will discuss the various methods of binding signatures into magazines, catalogs, and books.

In books and other publications of many pages, signatures are folded and then collated for binding. The method of collating and the imposition of the pages on the signatures depend on the planned method of binding.

Saddle-stitching or *wiring* is a fast, inexpensive method of binding, used for such projects as booklets, magazines, and catalogs. A rule of thumb states that a maximum of 96 pages can be saddle-stitched effectively; above that number, the stitch may not hold securely and the bulk of the pages may make the booklet flop open rather than fold flat. This maximum may vary up or down if the paper is either very light or very heavy.

Saddle-stitched pieces, when finished, look as if they've been stapled in the fold. Actually they've been passed through a stitcher that runs wire "thread" through the pages as the signatures go through the machine, draped over a saddle. A saddle-stitched piece is collated so that one signature rests inside another, known as *inserted signatures.* Booklets up to 32 pages long may consist of only one stitched signature. A stitcher can also be used to bind pages from front to back along the edge of the pages. This is known as *side stitching.*

For books, the signatures are *folded and gathered,* or stacked one on top of the other, for binding; at this stage the signatures are known as *folded and gathered sheets,* or *f and g's.* In *perfect binding,* the backs of the signatures are trimmed off, and glue is applied to the tightly gathered pages. A paper

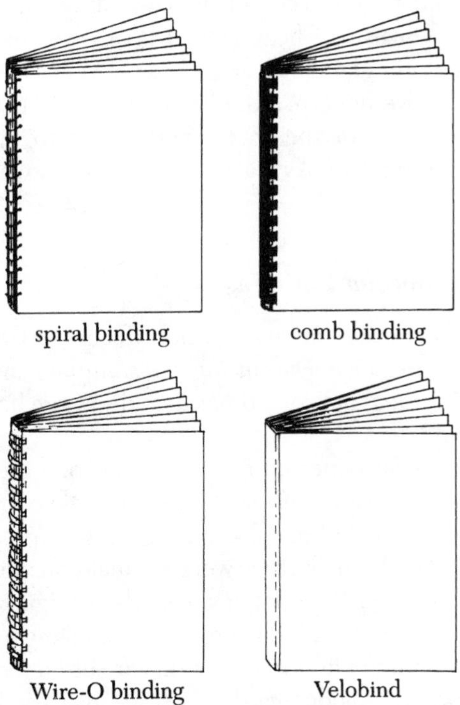

Figure 33–6. These mechanical binding methods are useful for binding limited quantities or for binding publications that need to lie flat when opened.

cover is then applied to the glued surface. This method is most often used for paperback books.

A variation of perfect binding known by the trade name Otabind allows the book to lie flat when opened; this is a helpful feature for computer documentation, cookbooks, and travel guides.

Two variations used for both paperback and hardcover books are *notch* and *burst binding*. In both instances the signatures remain intact but are either notched or perforated at regular intervals along the back edges. Glue is then squirted into the spine, giving greater adhesion than with perfect binding. The cover or case is then fitted on.

In *case binding,* also known as *edition binding,* the bound signatures are enclosed in hard covers. Many textbooks, library editions, and trade books are sewn together by a technique known as *Smyth sewing* or *side sewing* before insertion into the case. In a Smyth-sewn book the signature is sewn through the fold and the sewn signatures are then joined; in side sewing the thread passes from front to back of all signatures. Smyth-sewn books have the advantage of opening flat. After sewing, *end papers,* which are heavier stock than the book pages and are sometimes colored or printed, are glued to the bound book and to the inside of the case, attaching the pages to the binding. The case consists of heavyweight board covered in fabric, vinyl, paper, or another material.

Because of improvements in durability, notch and burst binding are now sometimes used instead of the traditional sewing to bind signatures in hardcover books, although books that will receive heavy wear are usually still sewn.

Custom Touches: Special Finishing

The bindery can also be the source of special effects—extra touches that add interest, sparkle, or elegance. *Die cutting, foil stamping,* and *embossing* cost more than basic finishing, but sometimes the effects can be worth the added expense.

Dies are used to cut paper into any shape beyond the basic rectangles that can be achieved on paper-cutting equipment. Dies work something like cookie cutters; they consist of metal knives set up on a press to cut paper to the desired shape. Traditionally, they were manually shaped, and the cost of creating the die reflected the complexity of the design. Computer-driven laser technology is now being used to create dies, making more complex cuts easier to achieve. Common uses of die cutting are often seen in promotional pieces like preprinted Rolodex cards; dies are also used to manufacture envelopes and pocket folders. Because standard dies are used for this type of item, the costs are generally moderate. The costs for custom die cutting will of course be higher because they will include the cost of creating the die.

❧

TRADITIONAL BOOKMAKING

The manufacture of hardcover or *case bound* books involves a number of features not encountered in other kinds of publications; many of these features have origins in the early days of bookmaking. First, most hardcover books have two covers—the attached cover of the book and the dust jacket. An advertising concept developed during the early 20th century, the dust jacket, a formerly plain and utilitarian component of book packaging, became a vehicle to promote sales. With the explosion of graphic design and printing technology, the jacket has become a crucial part of the marketing of a book. In fact, today jacket design is considered almost completely separate from the interior design of the book. Jackets are generally printed on heavyweight stock; 80-pound stock is standard, although heavier weights may be specified for books that will receive heavier wear. Often jacket papers are varnished or even coated with plastic for improved appearance and durability.

Early books were sold with the signatures untrimmed; the customer would separate the pages by slitting the signatures at the folds. Today pages with rough or *deckled* edges are considered a sign of book quality because they recall this early era of bookmaking.

Before books were mass produced, they would be bound to order after they were sold. The simple purpose of the *half title* page—the page containing the title only that appears before the full title page—was as a sort of cover sheet, to protect and identify the contents of the book before it was bound. The half title serves no real purpose today, but trade books would seem incomplete without it.

The purpose of *top stain,* the coating of the top edges of pages with a dye or stain, is to protect the pages of the book from dust. It is a less expensive evolution of the earlier practice of coating the edges of the pages with gold leaf. Today it is largely decorative.

Headbands are fabric strips glued to the top and bottom edge of the book's spine; they serve as a reinforcement against the usual practice of pulling a book off the shelf by its spine.

End papers, the means by which the bound pages are attached to the case binding, can be as simple as plain white text paper or as sophisticated as handmade or handpainted papers. They are often used to carry design elements from the cover inside the book.

Another type of die is used for foil stamping, the process by which a film of colored pigment is applied to paper or cloth. Foil is most often thought of as metallic, but foil stamping is done in a wide range of matte and glossy colors as well as metallics. In fact, foil is often used instead of ink when a high degree of opacity is required—to print white type, for example, on a dark stock. It is also commonly used to imprint the cases and spines of hardcover books.

Each area to be stamped requires a die; these are made of metal and are created from the same type of black-and-white mechanical used for printing. The stamped area is called a *hit.* A book cover that is to be stamped only on the spine will take one hit of foil; stamping the front cover as well as the spine makes two hits.

In embossing, paper is pressed between matched pairs of dies called *male* and *female dies,* creating a dimensional image. *Embossing* raises the image from the surface; *debossing* creates an image lower than the surface of the paper. The technique can be used to accentuate images printed in ink or foil stamped, or it can be used alone as *blind embossing.*

Single-level dies are the least expensive to create. Depending on the complexity of the image, a multilevel die will be etched chemically or crafted by hand; these dies will obviously be more expensive.

Die cutting, foil stamping, and embossing are sometimes done in a printer's own shop, but often this type of finishing work is subcontracted to a specialist. Generally, this subcontractor works on flat, untrimmed printed sheets and then returns the work to the printer for final folding and trimming. It is wise to allow more time for these processes than for printing alone.

WORKING SUCCESSFULLY WITH A PRINTER

Choosing the Right Printer

Selecting a printer can be a daunting task, for any mistakes are sure to be obvious—missed deliveries, poor printing, or higher than expected costs. To gain some control over this process, it is helpful to understand printers' specialties.

Most printers have a specialty—an area where they can perform best and most economically. The easiest printing company to work with is the one that clearly states its specialty: for example, "We specialize in premium quality four-color work." The most difficult to evaluate are "all things to all people" printers: "We can do anything!" The customer should try to find out as much as possible about a printer's strongest areas, in terms of both products printed and level of quality.

❧

CHECKING PRINT QUALITY

There are many variables in the process of printing and at least that many things can go wrong, even if every aspect of the job is perfect until it goes on press. Here are some symptoms of on-press problems:

- The surface of the paper being pulled off during the printing process is called *picking* if caused by excessive tackiness in the ink, *pickout* if caused by improper manufacture of the paper.
- Tiny specks of paper dust or other contaminants in the press room can interfere with the contact between the paper and the blanket, creating tiny white circles known as *hickies* or *fisheyes*.
- Several problems have to do with the flow of ink to the printing stations and the transfer of the ink to the paper. Customers should examine printed pieces for consistent ink density from one side of the sheet to the other and from one page to another. *Dot gain* is the increase in size of the halftone or screen dots, which causes an obscuring of detail in photographs or a generally dark, muddy appearance. When the paper makes a second contact with the blanket as it runs through the press, *doubling*, or a second unwanted shadow of the image, occurs. If the paper should slip across the blanket, a smear called *slurring* results. A shadow of an image that appears near the intended image is known as *ghosting;* this is associated with the placement of heavy solids in the layout and can often be avoided if the printer is consulted before the layout is finished.
- *Offsetting* occurs when the ink is not quite dry as sheets come off the press. One press sheet transfers ink to the sheet that is stacked on top of it.

Customers should use common sense in determining whether flaws should be corrected, depending on the job. Not every job need be perfect; a few fisheyes in a weekly newsletter will not ruin any reputations, whereas the same problem in a showcase art book or expensive advertising piece could be disastrous.

Printers in large cities may be able to support themselves with a very narrow specialty, but more often the divisions among printers lie along the lines of two-color versus four-color work, or brochures and similar small pieces versus books and other long publications. Requesting samples is a good way to get an idea of the type of work a printer does most often.

Many levels of printing quality are available, and one of the first things to learn is that the highest quality is not always the best for every job. The key is analyzing the level required and selecting the appropriate level for the project at hand.

Being a regular customer of a printer means that many routine projects will run more smoothly; a printer familiar with a customer's needs and preferences will require less supervision. Sometimes, too, volume discounts can be negotiated for recurring jobs like journals or newsletters. And a regular customer often will receive priority when tight schedules are an issue. A customer can play a part in this relationship—and get better service and prices—by not always requiring competitive bidding on routine jobs and by not putting every job on a crisis schedule.

Predicting and Controlling Costs

Printing cost estimates are based on assumptions, which are based on an accurate understanding of all aspects of the project. From the customer's specifications, the estimator calculates the costs for labor that will be required throughout the prepress, on-press, and postpress operations: the costs of the materials required—not only paper and ink, but film, negatives, proofing materials, and plates; the costs of setting up *(makeready)* and running the presses and other equipment; and costs for subcontractors, deliveries, and any other special requirements.

To obtain accurate cost estimates, the customer must provide the printer with complete and accurate specifications. And if competitive bids are to be obtained, the same specifications should go to each potential supplier. It is good practice to assemble specifications in writing to document the printing estimates, to evaluate the eventual billing, and to keep track of changes in the job that may affect the final cost.

Complete specifications should include the following information:

General description of the project—a brochure, a book, a catalog, etc.

Quantity—if there is some question about the quantity desired, the customer should request quotes at two or three different quantities (say, 1,000, 2,500, and 5,000); there is often a price break, or unit cost reduction, at the higher quantities.

Size—if the piece is to be a single, flat sheet, the trim size should be indicated; for a folded piece like a brochure, the flat and folded size should be given; both the overall trim size and the number of pages should be given for a multipage project.

Paper—any specified paper stock or generic stock; paper color, weight, and grade should be included.

Ink—all ink colors to be used and whether all inks will print on both sides of the sheet (if, for instance, the job is to be printed using three ink colors on only one side of the sheet, the printer will call it a *three over zero* job;

three inks on one side and one ink on the other would be *three over one*).

Special camera considerations—the number of halftones, pieces of separately supplied art, color separations, bleeds, screens, reverses, and traps; this information should also include whether tight registration or heavy ink coverage will be required.

Bindery requirements—type of binding; any custom finishing like embossing, die cutting, or foil stamping.

Proofs—blueline, overlay proofs, integral proofs, press sheets, press check; number of sets needed.

Schedule and delivery—this information should include when the camera-ready art will be *let*, or released to the printer to begin work, and when and where final delivery is expected; how the material is to be packed; and special delivery requirements such as split, partial, or drop shipments.

The customer should obtain written estimates on most jobs that are competitively bid to make sure that all bidders used the same assumptions. An extremely low bid may mean one of two things: The printer has made an error in interpreting specifications or is *low-balling*, deliberately taking a loss on a job to develop new business. A print buyer may want to take advantage of such an opportunity but should be aware that future bids from the same printer may not be as low.

A preliminary estimate is frequently necessary to prepare a budget. Often, quite general assumptions are used; some aspects may simply be made up to provide a "ballpark quote." For an accurate quote the job should be reestimated when it becomes a reality.

The customer should keep a record of the assumptions used in formulating the estimate. If an assumption changes later, it is a good idea to ask the printer to reevaluate the estimate. For instance, the difference between printing 1,000 and 100,000 copies of a brochure is more than just the difference in the amount of paper and ink consumed; that change could mean a change of press, which might mean that the plates will be prepared differently; it might even mean that the printer originally selected to do the job may no longer be the best choice. Other seemingly minor changes—adding four pages to the text or color in one spot or extra halftones—may have as dramatic an effect.

The Fine Print: Trade Customs

The backs of printer's invoices and estimate forms often carry a list of *Printing Trade Customs;* customers should be aware that in the absence of other agreements, these customs represent the standard of the industry and are the basis for resolving disputes between the printer and the customer.

There is nothing terribly obscure or arcane about trade customs; indeed, by their very nature they reflect the most commonly found understandings and trade relationships in the printing industry. Most often misunderstood, however, are the issues involved in sections 4 ("Creative Work"), 6 ("Preparatory Materials"), 11 ("Over-runs and Under-runs"). It is a good idea to become familiar with trade customs and reread them periodically.

IF SOMETHING CAN GO WRONG. . . .

Many slips can occur in the course of producing a publication. Some are foreseeable, some are not, and some look pretty silly to anyone who hasn't been involved in getting something printed. There is, quite simply, a certain quota of embarrassment that every publisher has coming.

It helps to remember that these things happen to the big guys, too; the *Washington Post* (Jan. 9, 1992) reported that Little, Brown had shipped 1,500 copies of a classic children's book to booksellers before it was discovered that the copies began with pages from a book of gay erotica. Enough such nightmares happen, in fact, that the *Post* noted that certain companies, such as Dunn & Co. of Clinton, Mass., specialize in repairing botched books.

ANNOTATED BIBLIOGRAPHY

Most of the books listed here were in print at the time of this writing; a few are out of print but can generally be found in libraries. A mail-order source for a wide range of books on writing, editing, production, and design is Tools of the Trade, 3148-B Duke Street, Alexandria, VA 22314, phone (800) 827-8665.

HISTORY OF THE ENGLISH LANGUAGE

The English Language. Robert Burchfield. Oxford University Press, 1985. 194 pages. This short history of English explains how the language has been recorded in dictionaries and grammar books; other topics include pronunciation, slang, dialects, and the formation of words.

The Mother Tongue: English and How It Got That Way. Bill Bryson. Avon Books, 1990. 270 pages. This book presents an anecdotal tour through the history of how a language spoken by peasants grew into an international tongue.

Our Marvelous Native Tongue. Robert Claiborne. Times Books, 1983. 339 pages. This story of English begins with the Indo-Europeans of the Danube Valley and ends with a look at the future of the language.

The Oxford Companion to the English Language. Tom McArthur, ed. Oxford University Press, 1992. 1,184 pages. More than a history, this is the most inclusive and wide-ranging single volume on the English language. More than 35,000 entries cover every topic imaginable, including literary terms, linguistics and rhetoric, grammar, style, and sexist language.

The Story of English. Rev. ed. Robert McCrum, William Cran, and Robert MacNeil. Penguin Books, 1993. 394 pages. This book, based on the television series of the same name, offers a comprehensive and entertaining look at the history of English from Anglo-Saxon Britain to its use worldwide today.

Unlocking the English Language. Robert Burchfield. Hill and Wang, 1989. 202 pages. The author, who was editor of the Supplement to the *Oxford English Dictionary,* provides an informative look at how lexicographers make dictionaries.

USAGE

American Usage and Style: The Consensus. Roy H. Copperud. Van Nostrand Reinhold, 1980. 435 pages. The author offers a consensus of style and usage by comparing the judgments of leading authorities, as well as drawing on the definitions in seven dictionaries.

The Careful Writer: A Modern Guide to English Usage. Theodore M. Bernstein. Macmillan, 1977. 490 pages. With more than 1,500 entries, this is one of the most consistently useful books on usage; it is sensible, authoritative, and genial. *Dos, Don'ts, and Maybes of English Usage* is another popular Bernstein title.

The Columbia Guide to Standard English. Kenneth G. Wilson. Columbia University Press, 1993. 482 pages. The most up-to-date general reference on usage and confusable words, this book offers practical advice on what is appropriate in speech as well as in writing.

Coming to Terms. William Safire. Doubleday, 1991. 398 pages. This collection of Safire's "On Language" columns from the *New York Times* is both entertaining and useful. Taking a more permissive approach than other authorities on some issues, Safire tackles current issues and offers sensible advice. His other books on language include *Fumblerules, Language Maven Strikes Again, You Can Look It Up,* and *Take My Word for It.*

The Dictionary of Bias-Free Usage: A Guide to Nondiscriminatory Language. Oryx Press, 1991. 293 pages. More than 15,000 alternatives for 5,000 terms and phrases are included and are preceded by an essay that discusses the rationales for the decisions made.

The Dictionary of Confusable Words. Laurence Urdang. Facts On File, 1988. 391 pages. This book explains the differences between commonly confused words by emphasizing the differences in their meanings rather than using strict definitions.

Elements of Nonsexist Usage: A Guide to Inclusive Spoken and Written English. Val Dumond. Prentice-Hall Press, 1990. 90 pages. This concise handbook offers alternatives to offensive language, advice on how to recognize it, and a glossary of alternative nonsexist terms.

The Handbook of Nonsexist Writing: For Writers, Editors and Speakers. 2nd ed. Casey Miller and Kate Swift. HarperCollins, 1988. 160 pages. This classic, helpful guide provides techniques for avoiding sexism in writing, editing, and speaking.

Harper Dictionary of Contemporary Usage. 2nd ed. William and Mary Morris. Harper & Row, 1985. 641 pages. Although this work is out of print, it can usually be found in libraries and is a useful reference for confusable words and other aspects of usage.

Modern American Usage: A Guide. Wilson Follett and Jacques Barzun, eds. Avenel, 1980. 436 pages. This reference offers detailed guidelines and ideas about usage and grammar.

Webster's Dictionary of English Usage. Merriam-Webster, 1989. 978 pages. This is the most definitive guide to word usage available; it takes into account all major writings on usage in the past 50 years and contains more than 20,000 illustrative quotations.

GRAMMAR AND PUNCTUATION

The Deluxe Transitive Vampire: A Handbook of Grammar for the Innocent, the Eager, and the Doomed. Karen Elizabeth Gordon. Pantheon, 1993. 180 pages. While entertaining the reader with the unexpected, Gordon explains every grammatical rule with clarity and precision and makes the most intricate and impossible usages clear; a certain level of grammatical knowledge is helpful, however. Also by the same author is *The Well-Tempered Sentence: A Punctuation Handbook for the Innocent, the Eager, and the Doomed.*

The Elements of Grammar. Margaret Shertzer. Macmillan, 1986. 224 pages. Shertzer presents a concise, comprehensive course in the basic rules of grammar and usage, along with invaluable tips on how to implement these rules in everyday writing and speaking.

Grammar for Grownups. Val Dumond. HarperCollins, 1993. 250 pages. This book provides guidelines to enable you to make your own decisions, as well as handy tips for remembering those guidelines.

The Gregg Reference Manual. 7th ed. William A. Sabin. Macmillan/McGraw-Hill, 1992. 502 pages. This grammar and style book is aimed at users in the business and academic worlds and takes pains to note the differences in guidelines and requirements. It presents sample formats for many types of business documents and discusses tables, references, and footnotes.

The Handbook of Good English: Revised and Updated. Edward D. Johnson. Facts On File, 1991. 440 pages. Not a book for the novice, this comprehensive book covers syntax, punctuation, style, organization, and tone. The author does more than dictate the rules—he gives examples, exceptions, and clear, easily understood explanations of why grammar has the rules it does. The lack of a detailed index limits its usefulness, however.

Working with Words: A Concise Handbook for Media Writers. 2nd ed. Brian S. Brooks. St. Martin's Press, 1993. 260 pages. This practical handbook offers solid guidance on grammar and usage for writers and editors at all levels of experience. Included is a chapter on avoiding sexist and racist language and a quick-reference appendix of common mistakes in grammar.

STYLE MANUALS

The ACS Style Guide: A Manual for Authors and Editors. Janet S. Dodd, ed. American Chemical Society, 1986. 264 pages. Meant primarily for ACS authors and editors, this book provides guidelines for preparing scientific text and includes chapters on grammar, style, and copyright.

American Medical Association Manual of Style. 8th ed. Cheryl Iverson et al., eds. Williams & Wilkins, 1989. 377 pages. This guide focuses on medical writing and editing, where lack of precision and clarity can have far-reaching consequences. The sections on medical terminology (abbreviations and nomenclature) and measurement and quantitation (units of measure and statistics) are particularly useful. The guide is thoughtfully laid out and well indexed.

Associated Press Style and Libel Manual. The Associated Press, 1993. 345 pages. The journalist's bible, this handbook is a guide to the AP's rules on grammar, spelling, punctuation, and usage. It includes a discussion of libel with sections on defenses and privileges; public officials, figures, and issues; and the right of privacy. Entries are arranged alphabetically.

The Chicago Manual of Style. 14th ed. University of Chicago Press, 1993. 936 pages. This classic reference for writers and editors, with emphasis on scholarly and formal writing, is used by many publishers; this new edition adopts a more flexible approach and includes more examples.

Mathematics into Type. Ellen Swanson. American Mathematical Society, 1987. 90 pages. This small book includes complete instructions on preparing a manuscript in the field of mathematics and provides detailed instructions for editors.

The MLA Style Manual. Walter S. Achtert and Joseph Gibaldi. Modern Language Association, 1985. 272 pages. This manual offers the comprehensive guidance essential to scholarly writers interested in publishing in the humanities.

The New York Times Manual of Style and Usage. Times Books, 1976. 231 pages. This stylebook is used by the writers and editors of the *New York Times* and is used by many publishers, newsletters, and trade papers.

Publication Manual of the American Psychological Association. 3rd ed. American Psychological Association, 1984. 208 pages. Used by many publishers in the social sciences, this guide has useful sections on dealing with illustrations, tables, and reference citations. A revised edition is scheduled for publication in 1994.

Scientific Style and Format: The CBE Manual for Authors and Editors. Council of Biology Editors, 1994. This manual of style is followed by many journals and publications in the scientific disciplines, including biology, medicine, chemistry, earth sciences, physical sciences, and social sciences.

U.S. Government Printing Office Style Manual. Government Printing Office, 1984. 488 pages. This book is the style guide for U.S. government publications and contains detailed sections on capitalization, spelling, compound words, abbreviations, and numbers, as well as a complete section on setting type in foreign languages. A revised edition is scheduled for publication in 1995.

Words Into Type. Marjorie Skillin. Prentice-Hall, 1974. 585 pages. A favorite resource of many editors, this sensible guide covers points of grammar as well as style.

DICTIONARIES AND THESAURUSES

The American Heritage Dictionary of the English Language. 3rd ed. Houghton Mifflin, 1992. 2,140 pages. This new and expanded edition gives definitions in order of frequency of use; several hundred entries contain word histories and synonym paragraphs. Unique to this dictionary are notes on regional American English and some 500 usage notes based on the comments of 173 educators, writers, and public figures. More than 4,000 photos and illustrations lend added interest.

The Cambridge Dictionary of Science and Technology. Peter M.B. Walker, ed. Cambridge University Press, 1988. 1,008 pages. This is a good general reference containing 45,000 entries covering 100 scientific and technical fields, from architecture to zoology; spellings are British, however.

Merriam-Webster's New Collegiate Dictionary. 10th ed. Merriam-Webster, 1993. 1,559 pages. The latest edition of this classic descriptive dictionary features up-to-date listings of geographical and biographical names.

The New Shorter Oxford English Dictionary. Lesley Brown, ed. Oxford University Press, 1993. 3,801 pages. More than an abbreviated version of the 20-volume Oxford English Dictionary (which is now available on CD-ROM), this 2-volume set is considered to be more up to date in terms of usage and new words. It contains 500,000 definitions, 97,000 headwords, and 87,400 quotations showing the use of the defined word in published material.

The Oxford Thesaurus: American Edition. Laurence Urdang. Oxford University Press, 1992. 1,005 pages. This volume combines the two styles of thesaurus organization for thorough cross-referencing: Roget's style of grouping words according to concepts and the dictionary style of alphabetical headword listings. A synonym index lists an additional 250,000 words.

Random House Webster's College Dictionary. Random House, 1991. This descriptive, not prescriptive, dictionary contains 180,000 entries, listing the most current meaning first. Some 230 usage notes provide information for readers to make their own decisions.

Roget's International Thesaurus. 5th ed. Robert L. Chapman. 1,141 pages. HarperCollins, 1992. This classic has been revised to reflect contemporary usage and includes more than 325,000 words and phrases in 1,073 categories, of which 31 are new to this edition.

Stedman's Medical Dictionary. 25th ed. Williams & Wilkins, 1990. 1,784 pages. This leading medical dictionary is available on disk for use with most word processing programs. The main entry-subentry format is easy to use and the dictionary is extensively illustrated and cross-referenced.

Webster's Third New International Dictionary. Merriam-Webster, 1986. 2,662 pages. This unabridged dictionary has more than 470,000 entries, 200,000 usage examples, and 3,000 illustrations. This revised edition contains a 55-page listing of 12,000 new words and meanings.

WRITING AND EDITING

Copy-Editing. Judith Butcher. Cambridge University Press, 1992. 471 pages. This is a comprehensive guide for editors, authors, and publishers in the technical and academic fields; some of the style, usage, and grammar points reflect the author's British point of view.

Copyediting: A Practical Guide. Karen Judd. Crisp Publications, 1990. 320 pages. This book is a useful introduction to manuscript copyediting practices and procedures.

Doublespeak. William Lutz. HarperCollins, 1989. 290 pages. Lutz provides examples showing how writers in business, government, and the military use the four kinds of doublespeak—euphemism, jargon, gobbledygook, and inflated language—to mislead readers or avoid responsibility while appearing to communicate.

Editing Your Newsletter. Mark Beach. Writer's Digest Books, 1988. 168 pages. This basic reference book for editors of small newsletters has been completely updated for the computer age, but traditional methods of newsletter production are still fully covered.

The Editorial Eye. Linda Jorgensen, ed. EEI. Focusing on publications standards and practices since 1978, this national 12-page monthly newsletter contains articles and information on a wide range of topics of interest to writers, editors, and production managers.

Editors on Editing. 3rd ed. Gerald Gross, ed. Grove Press, 1993. 377 pages. This is a collection of essays by working editors of all kinds, compiled, as the preface says, "as much to help the editor understand how to work with a writer as for the writer to understand how to work with an editor."

The Elements of Editing. Arthur Plotnik. Macmillan, 1986. 156 pages. This book details editorial responsibilities and describes the relationship between author and editor. It includes an inside look at book editing, a rating system for manuscripts, and a summary of copyright and libel laws.

The Expert Editor. Ann R. Molpus, ed. EEI, 1990. 101 pages. This is a collection of guidelines, suggestions, and inspirations for working editors from articles originally published in *The Editorial Eye* newsletter. It offers advice and solutions for editors trying to balance all facets of the "unattainable triad" of high quality, speed, and cost-effective production.

Good Style: Writing for Science and Technology. John Kirkman. Chapman & Hall, 1992. 221 pages. This book explains the techniques that can be used to write technical material in a coherent, readable style. It is helpful for those who have an excellent command of their subject but have difficulty expressing their knowledge in simple, accurate English.

Handbook of Writing for the Mathematical Sciences. Nicholas J. Higham. Society for Industrial and Applied Mathematics, 1993. 241 pages. This book covers virtually every issue authors face when writing a technical paper, from choosing the right journal to handling references.

Help Yourself: A Guide to Writing and Rewriting. Marylu Mattson, Sophia Leshing, and Elaine Levi. Charles E. Merrill Publishing Co., 1983. 378 pages. This popular and useful book provides exercises for improving writing skills.

Line by Line: How to Improve Your Own Writing. Claire Kehrwals Cook. Houghton Mifflin, 1985. 219 pages. This book focuses on getting rid of five major stylistic faults, many of which involve grammar and punctuation, that prevent readers from getting the point. It also addresses wordiness, unbalanced sentence elements, and faulty sentence structure, with more than 700 examples of faulty sentences and techniques for repairing them.

Mark My Words: Instruction and Practice in Proofreading. 2nd ed. Peggy Smith. EEI, 1993. 482 pages. This self-study book, used by many colleges and publishers to train proofreaders, is a detailed explanation of professional proofreading, with more than 100 pages of exercises and answer keys.

The Modern Researcher. 5th ed. Jacques Barzun and Henry F. Graff. Houghton Mifflin, 1992. 430 pages. This book tells how to turn research into readable, well-organized writing.

On Writing, Editing, and Publishing: Essays Explicative and Hortatory. Jacques Barzun. University of Chicago Press, 1986. 160 pages. In this collection of essays, one of today's outstanding masters of English prose gives his ideas of what good writing is and how it can be achieved. He also addresses some of the problems of the related fields of editing and publishing.

On Writing Well. 5th ed. William Zinsser. HarperCollins, 1994. 304 pages. Zinsser teaches the principles of good writing in a wide variety of forms (the interview, travel, science, sports, humor, etc.) and also deals with tone, individuality, confidence, and self-esteem.

Rewrite Right! How to Revise Your Way to Better Writing. Jan Venolia. Ten Speed Press, 1987. 197 pages. This is a handy guide to the process of reviewing and rewriting your work; the author encourages writers to revise their work in stages that divide the editing tasks.

Self-Editing for Fiction Writers. Renni Browne and Dave King. HarperCollins, 1993. 230 pages. This book has chapters on dialogue, exposition, interior monologue, and other techniques that take the reader through the same process an expert fiction editor would use.

Stet! Tricks of the Trade for Writers and Editors. Bruce O. Boston, ed. EEI, 1986. 310 pages. This book, a collection of articles and tips from *The Editorial Eye* newsletter, covers writing, editing, publications management, abstracting, and proofreading.

Style: Toward Clarity and Grace. Joseph M. Williams. University of Chicago Press, 1990. 240 pages. This is a master teacher's tested program for turning rough drafts and clumsy prose into clear, powerful, and effective writing.

Substance and Style: Instruction and Practice in Copyediting. Mary Stoughton. EEI, 1989. 360 pages. This practical self-teaching guide discusses issues of grammar, usage, punctuation, and style and provides exercises to help the reader develop professional copyediting skills.

Technical Editing: The Practical Guide for Editors and Writers. Judith A. Tarutz. Addison-Wesley, 1992. 460 pages. This lively, practical book deals with the real-world problems that face technical editors and writers, such as editing bulleted lists, references, and computer manuals, and when to bend the rules to avoid technical ambiguity. It also gives pointers on how to edit under tight deadlines and constantly changing product specs; one list describes the top 10 things to check if you have only one hour to "edit" a book.

Writing Past Dark: Envy, Fear, Distraction, and Other Dilemmas in the Writer's Life. Bonnie Friedman. HarperCollins, 1993. 128 pages. The author discusses the mental pitfalls that writers must face and conquer—envy, distraction, guilt, and writer's block—as well as the difficulty of finding the courage to write from intuition.

Writing That Means Business. Ellen Roddick. Macmillan, 1986. 136 pages. This simply written book quickly gets across the basics of writing effective business memos, letters, and reports; the author stresses how good writing can confer a competitive edge in the business world.

Writing with Precision: How to Write So That You Cannot Possibly Be Misunderstood. 6th ed. Jefferson Bates. Acropolis, 1993. 253 pages. In this new edition of a classic, the author addresses the communication problems of the 1990s with new sections on organization, file management, word processing, and computerized writing aids.

Zen in the Art of Writing: Essays on Creativity. Ray Bradbury. Capra Press, 1990. 154 pages. This book is not a how-to guide but rather a celebration of writing as a creative endeavor.

INDEXING

ALA Filing Rules. American Library Association, 1980. 50 pages. These rules, following the word-by-word system, were developed for the arrangement of bibliographic records, not index entries, but they provide answers for many problematic cases. The appendix contains a list of definite and indefinite articles in 39 languages.

Anglo-American Cataloging Rules. 2nd ed. (AACR2). American Library Association, 1988. 677 pages. This library cataloging manual is too complex to use for most indexes, but its rules on form of entry for proper and corporate names are useful as a guide in difficult situations.

A Guide to Indexing Software. 4th ed. American Society of Indexers, 1992. 39 pages. This pamphlet evaluates nine stand-alone indexing programs for the IBM PC and compatible computers and a preview of one program for the Macintosh.

Indexing and Abstracting in Theory and Practice. F.W. Lancaster. University of Illinois, 1991. 330 pages. Designed as a classroom text as well as a reference tool, this book covers indexing principles and practice, consistency and quality of indexing, types and functions of abstracts, and more.

Indexing Books. Nancy Mulvany. University of Chicago Press, 1994. 352 pages. The author provides a thorough guide, including how to determine what is and what is not indexable, how to select terms to create clear and succinct entries, how to choose headings and subentries, and how to lay out and edit an index.

Indexing from A to Z. Hans H. Wellisch. H.W. Wilson, 1991. 465 pages. This is the most complete reference book available to the indexer. It covers both back-of-the-book and periodical indexing, giving the scholarly background as well as the modern approach to many situations. Arranged alphabetically, this book covers all aspects of indexing, including alphabetical, chronological, and classified order of entries.

COPYRIGHT

The Copyright Book: A Practical Guide. 4th ed. William S. Strong. MIT Press, 1992. 264 pages. Written by an attorney specializing in copyright issues, this book covers all aspects of this sometimes thorny topic.

The Copyright Handbook: How to Protect and Use Written Works. Stephen Fishman. Nolo Press, 1992. 280 pages. This comprehensive large-format paperback book has an easy-to-follow format and illustrative examples. The appendixes provide 12 Copyright Office forms for photocopying, along with examples of properly completed forms.

Every Writer's Guide to Copyright and Publishing Law. Ellen M. Kozak. Henry Holt, 1990. Helpful and reader-friendly, this handbook guides writers through the issues of copyright, publishing contracts, and even bankruptcy and wills.

The Writer's Lawyer. Ronald L. Goldfarb and Gail E. Ross. Times Books, 1989. 274 pages. In addition to copyright, this book covers libel, confidentiality issues, publishing contracts, and other aspects of law related to writing and publishing.

DESIGN, GRAPHICS, AND PRODUCTION

Basic Desktop Design and Layout. David Collier and Bob Cotton. North Light Books, 1989. 160 pages. This book presents fundamental design principles as well as an outline of the design process and ways to develop ideas. It includes nearly 60 pages of sample layouts and discussions.

Book Design & Production for the Small Publisher. Malcolm E. Barker. Londonborn Publications, 1990. 233 pages. This book should be required reading for anyone who purchases a desktop publishing system with the intention of producing a book. Sections on the mechanics of book design and production guidelines offer basic advice; the accompanying illustrations make the book invaluable for beginners.

Bookmaking: The Illustrated Guide to Design/Production/Editing. 2nd ed. Marshall Lee. R.R. Bowker, 1980. 490 pages. This classic volume, although certainly out of date regarding computer technology, should be on the shelf of every person producing books. It covers the profession, basic knowledge, and procedures for both the editing/design and production phases of book production.

Color in the 21st Century: A Practical Guide for Graphic Designers, Photographers, Printers, and Anyone Involved in Color Printing. Helene W. Eckstein. Watson-Guptill, 1991. 144 pages. In addition to a wealth of information on color printing, this practical, working textbook contains all the handy checklists, order forms, bid request forms, inventory sheets, and other forms hassled production departments need.

Designer's Guide to Creating Charts & Diagrams. Nigel Holmes. Watson-Guptill, 1991. 196 pages. This book gives pointers to the artist for combining suitable visual elements with statistical information.

Designing with Two Colors. Betty Binns. Watson-Guptill, 1991. 128 pages. This is a guide to designing effectively using black plus one ink color. It classifies color characteristics and their effects in printing and is illustrated with numerous examples of printing techniques and color combinations.

The Design of Books. Adrian Wilson. Chronicle Books, 1993. 160 pages. A classic on the subject, this book's topics include the art of layout; typography; printing methods; paper; anatomy of the book; design approaches; binding; jackets and paperback covers; trade book design; and textbooks, references, and manuals.

Diagram Graphics. Fumihiko Nishioka. Books Nippon, 1992. 225 pages. The author presents examples of hundreds of unique and lucid diagrams in categories including tables and graphs, charts, maps, architectural drawings and plans, and scientific illustrations.

Editing by Design: A Guide to Effective Word-and-Picture Communication for Writers and Editors. Jan V. White. R.R. Bowker, 1982. 248 pages. This classic work shows how to use color, create a personality for a publication, use limited resources to attain powerful effects, and simplify design so it clearly communicates a message.

The Elements of Graph Design. Stephen M. Kosslyn. W.H. Freeman, 1993. 304 pages. The author explains step by step how to create effective displays of quantitative data, with guidelines based on current understanding of how the brain processes information. It demonstrates clearly why certain graph formats and elements work better than others in specific situations.

Envisioning Information. Edward R. Tufte. Graphics Press, 1990. 126 pages. This book provides practical advice about how to explain complex material by visual means and uses extraordinary examples to illustrate the fundamental principles of information display. It contains 400 illustrations, many of them in color.

Everyone's Guide to Successful Publications. Elizabeth W. Adler. Peachpit Press, 1993. 425 pages. Written mainly for those producing business, promotional, and direct mail pieces, this book covers everything a writer or editor needs to know to produce an excellent printed piece, from planning through writing, designing, understanding type, using desktop technology, and getting it printed and distributed. Previously published as *Print That Works.*

47 Printing Headaches (And How to Avoid Them). Linda S. Sanders. North Light Books, 1991. 136 pages. This is a primer on printing designed to help graphic artists work effectively with printers and new printing technology.

Getting It Printed. Rev. ed. Mark Beach. North Light Books, 1993. 208 pages. This easy-to-use guide to preparing artwork for printing shows how to cut production time, inspect mechanicals, review proofs, do press checks, write specs, select the right printer, and work effectively with service bureaus and designers.

Graphic Design for the Electronic Age. Jan V. White. Watson-Guptill, 1988. 212 pages. This comprehensive design manual offers advice on how to choose type, select column width, decide on headlines and subheads, handle pictures and captions, and set up tables—in short, directions for constructing a publication from front to back.

Graphic Idea Notebook. Jan V. White. Rockport Publishers, 1991. 206 pages. Among the many visual ideas in this book are 270 ways to indicate motion and direction; 31 ways to show change in time; 103 ways to use boxes; 201 kinds of charts and graphs; 116 ways to break up text with subheads, initials, indents, and so on; and 118 ways to present alphabets and numbering.

The Gray Book: Designing in Black & White on Your Computer. 2nd ed. Michael Gosney, John Odam, and Jim Schmal. Ventana Press, 1993. 315 pages. This unique "idea gallery" offers a lavish variety of the most interesting black, white, and gray graphic effects from laser printers, scanners, and high-resolution output devices.

How to Check and Correct Color Proofs. David Bann and John Gargan. North Light Books, 1990. 144 pages. An essential book if you do color printing and need to know how to make sure what you see is what you get.

How to Draw Charts and Diagrams. Bruce Robertson. North Light Books, 1988. 192 pages. The author shows step by step how to evaluate raw data, then select the chart or diagram style that best communicates the information. Emphasis is on bar charts, graphics, and maps, and the author explains what works, what doesn't, and why.

How to Lie with Maps. Mark Monmonier. University of Chicago Press, 1991. 176 pages. This lively, cleverly illustrated book on the use and abuse of maps teaches how to evaluate maps critically and promotes a healthy skepticism about these easy-to-manipulate models of reality.

Illustrating for Science. George V. Kelvin. Watson-Guptill, 1992. 192 pages. Included in this book are chapters devoted to problem-solving approaches to the challenges presented by specific scientific subject areas, such as biology and medicine, astronomy and space technology, geology and geography, and architecture and structures.

Looking Good in Print: A Guide to Basic Design for Desktop Publishing. 3rd ed. Roger C. Parker. Ventana Press, 1993. 423 pages. The standard reference for desktop publishing design, this book features hundreds of illustrations and includes makeovers and design tips on creating persuasive presentations and information graphics.

The Makeover Book. Roger C. Parker. Ventana Press, 1989. 278 pages. The author offers before and after examples of how to put basic design tools to work to make documents more attractive and persuasive.

Making a Good Layout. Lori Siebert and Lisa Ballard. North Light Books, 1992. 128 pages. The authors offer a practical, hands-on approach for non-designers, beginning designers, and desktop publishers to the basic elements and principles of good design and layout.

Papers for Printing. 2nd ed. Mark Beach and Kathleen Ryan. North Light Books, 1991. 168 pages. This book tells how to get the most for your money on paper purchases, which can represent 25 to 40 percent of the cost of a typical printed piece. Paper samples are included.

Photography for Graphic Designers. Joseph Meehan. Watson-Guptill, 1993. 128 pages. This book focuses on three central concerns: improving communications between graphic designers and photographers; giving designers an understanding of photographic materials to help them judge quality more accurately; and explaining fundamental photographic principles so that designers can produce simple yet high-quality photographs.

Pictorial Maps: History, Design, Ideas, Sources. Nigel Holmes. Watson-Guptill, 1991. 192 pages. Beginning the book with an illustrated history of pictorial maps through the ages, the author then follows the use of pictorial maps in America, in the world, in war and its news coverage, and in weather reporting.

Picture Editing and Layout: A Guide to Better Visual Communication. Angus McDougall. VISCOM Press, 1990. 300 pages. This book explains various aspects of picture editing, including the photo's message, the psychology of visual perception, photo techniques for nonphotographer editors, cropping, captions, and editorial illustration. Written for newspaper editors, this guide will help anyone who uses photos.

Pocket Pal: A Graphic Arts Production Handbook. 15th ed. Michael H. Bruno. International Paper Co., 1992. 233 pages. This is the authoritative introduction to the graphic arts for artists, designers, publishers, advertisers, students, and buyers of printing. This edition covers the almost complete conversion of prepress functions to computerized technologies.

Production for the Graphic Designer 2. Rev. ed. James Craig. Watson-Guptill, 1990. 208 pages. This book distills an enormous amount of production detail into a single volume that not only explains but graphically illustrates what everyone needs to know about production.

Publication Design. 5th ed. Roy Paul Nelson. William C. Brown, 1991. 325 pages. This book deals with a continuing concern in journalism—how to coordinate art and typography with content. Through text and illustration, it suggests ways to make pages and spreads in magazines, newspapers, books, and other publications attractive and easy to read.

Roger Parker's One-Minute Designer. Roger C. Parker. Que Books, 1993. 256 pages. This book presents more than 200 ideas that can be read and implemented in less than a minute. Each idea is introduced by a short headline, accompanied by two or three paragraphs of text, supported by two before and after illustrations.

Using Charts and Graphs. Jan V. White. R.R. Bowker, 1984. 202 pages. This is a how-to guide and idea file for anyone who needs to use charts and graphs imaginatively, showing the reader how to combine them into informative, eye-catching hybrids.

The Visual Display of Quantitative Information. Edward R. Tufte. Graphics Press, 1983. 197 pages. This book, a classic on statistical graphics, is devoted to the theory and practice in the design of graphs, charts, maps, and tables, covering scientific, mass media, business, and medical disciplines.

Visual Literacy: A Conceptual Approach to Graphic Problem Solving. Richard Wilde and Judith Wilde. Watson-Guptill, 1991. 191 pages. This book documents the learning process by which principles and techniques needed for effective visual communication can be acquired. Presented are 19 challenging visual assignments and more than 1,000 pieces of solution art executed by students.

Working with Words & Pictures. Lori Siebert and Mary Cropper. North Light Books, 1993. 128 pages. This book shows how to make type an attractive, effective communication tool and how to use visuals and graphics to beautify and communicate.

TYPOGRAPHY

Designer's Mix & Match Type. Ian Pape. McGraw Hill, 1992. This book illustrates more than 166 million potential typeface combinations, which gives the designer a unique visual opportunity to view a range of typographic possibilities.

Designing with Type: A Basic Course in Typography. 3rd ed. James Craig. Watson-Guptill, 1992. 176 pages. This unique combination of student textbook and professional reference presents an overview of the field of typography from origins to contemporary methods. All fundamentals, whether they apply to traditional methods or desktop technology, are discussed.

The Elements of Typographic Style. Robert Bringhurst. Hartley & Marks, 1992. 254 pages. This is a beautifully written book full of lore, advice, and commentary on the art and science of typography.

The Form of the Book: Essays on the Morality of Good Design. Jan Tschichold. Hartley & Marks, 1991. 180 pages. This book summarizes the author's lifetime devotion to the art of typography and good design.

Stop Stealing Sheep & Find Out How Type Works. Erik Spiekermann and E.M. Ginger. Prentice Hall, 1993. 176 pages. The authors shepherd their decades of typographic experience into a unique and lively guidebook that shows that type is easy to use, easy to understand, and, in the hands of a savvy user, a powerful communications tool. They show that type—good type—reaches across all boundaries, computer platforms, and professional distinctions.

Type: Design, Color, Character & Use. Michael Beaumont. North Light Books, 1991. 145 pages. This book gives the typographer/designer an idea of the infinite possibilities for using type creatively with color. It explains terminology; shows how to determine type weight, leading, and line spacing; and discusses the suitability of colors and typefaces for a range of designs.

Type in Use: Effective Typography for Electronic Publishing. Alex White. McGraw-Hill/Design Press, 1992. 192 pages. The author explores the issues designers face every day. Elements covered include text, headlines, breakouts, captions, department headings, covers, contents, bylines and bios, folios and footlines, and the history of type in use.

Type Recipes: Quick Solutions to Designing with Type. Gregory Wolfe. North Light Books, 1991. 138 pages. This book is organized around 10 popular and flexible type styles classified in terms of the mood they convey. An easy-to-use reference for designers and desktop publishers, it gives 121 time- and money-saving tips.

Index

Boldface numbers indicate principal coverage of a topic.

D

Q